Revolutionary Iran

Revolutionary Iran

A History of the Islamic Republic

MICHAEL AXWORTHY

OXFORD
UNIVERSITY PRESS

OXFORD
UNIVERSITY PRESS

Oxford University Press is a department of the University of Oxford.
It furthers the University's objective of excellence in research,
scholarship, and education by publishing worldwide.

Oxford   New York
Auckland   Cape Town   Dar es Salaam   Hong Kong   Karachi
Kuala Lumpur   Madrid   Melbourne   Mexico City   Nairobi
New Delhi   Shanghai   Taipei   Toronto

With offices in
Argentina   Austria   Brazil   Chile   Czech Republic   France   Greece
Guatemala   Hungary   Italy   Japan   Poland   Portugal   Singapore
South Korea   Switzerland   Thailand   Turkey   Ukraine   Vietnam

Oxford is a registered trade mark of Oxford University Press
in the UK and certain other countries.

Published in the United States of America by
Oxford University Press
198 Madison Avenue, New York, NY 10016

Library of Congress Cataloging-in-Publication Data
Axworthy, Michael.
Revolutionary Iran : a history of the Islamic republic / Michael Axworthy.
pages   cm
Summary: "A tour through recent Iranian history from the 1979 Islamic revolution through
the summer of 2009, when Iranians poured into the streets of Tehran by the hundreds of thousands,
demanding free, democratic government. Axworthy argues that the Iranian revolution was centrally
important in modern history because it provided the world with a clear model of development that
was not rooted in Western ideologies."—Provided by publisher.
ISBN 978-0-19-932226-8 (hardback)
1. Iran—History—Pahlavi dynasty, 1925–1979. 2. Iran—History—Revolution, 1979.
3. Iran—History—1979–1997. 4. Iran—History—1997– 5. Iran—Politics and government—1941–1979.
6. Iran—Politics and government—1979–1997. 7. Iran—Politics and government—1997– I. Title.
DS318.A88   2013
955.05'4–dc23   2013015836

1 3 5 7 9 8 6 4 2

Printed in the United States of America
on acid-free paper

In memory of Isabelle Borg (1959–2010)
and Chris Rundle (1938–2012)

Question: You have been accused of cynicism, but a more recent suggestion is that you take the view that, in the face of the transcendence of God, no moral or political system has any authority.

Answer: I think one needs to put into that sentence 'No absolute authority', because I obviously don't believe it to be the case that no moral or political system can have authority. One has, I think, to be very mindful of the limits and ignorance of even legitimate government.

Maurice Cowling, answering a question from Naim Attalah in 1990

Contents

List of Illustrations

List of Maps

Acknowledgements

Many people helped me to write this book. Prime among them were Baqer Moin and the late Chris Rundle, who both read the whole text and commented extensively. Chris's death in March 2012 was a shock and a great sadness to all who knew him – he was a kind, modest and generous man, and a deeply knowledgeable, wise and sympathetic authority on all matters Iranian. I also profited by extensive comments and help from Mahnaz Zahirinejad, Ali Mossadegh and Siavush Ranjbar-Daemi; and (on specific points or more limited sections of the book) from Ali Ansari, Mahdi Dasht-Bozorgi, Sadegh Zibakalam, Luciano Zaccara, Farhad Taheri, Mark Gasiorowski, Esmail Khoie, Wayne White, Hamid Naficy, Walter Posch, Hashem Ahmadzadeh, Farhang Jahanpour, Dominic Brook-shaw, Ahmad Salamatian, Shirin Ebadi, Christopher Andrew, Lord Owen and Haideh Sahim. For part of the period of writing I was living in New Delhi, where I benefited from the debates at the School of International Studies at Jawaharlal Nehru University; and through the kindness of Professors A. K. Pasha, Gulshan Dietl and P. R. Kumaraswamy, I was made a visiting scholar there. I also had the good fortune to meet Dr Seyyed Yunus Jaffery, to benefit from his advice and several long conversations, and to visit the *havelis* of Old Delhi, and the roof of the Sunehri mosque. I am grateful to everyone at Penguin Books for their help towards publication especially Simon Winder, Marina Kemp, Richard Duguid, David Watson and Penelope Vogler, who for me have confirmed that Penguin is, as ever, the Rolls – Royce of international publishing. I also have to thank my colleagues at the Institute of Arab and Islamic Studies at the University of Exeter for their help and support – especially Gareth Stansfield, Rob Gleave, Sajjad Rizvi, Lenny Lewisohn and Tim Niblock; my students, for their liveliness and their patience; my children, for theirs; my agent, Georgina Capel, for her sound advice and unfailing cheerfulness; and as ever, my wife Sally.

Note on Transliteration

In my books I have sought to transliterate Persian words in a way that will sound familiar rather than alien to Iranians, and I have tried (and occasionally failed) to be consistent. Beyond that, in my view, there is room for dispute, but little for any claim to absolute correctness.

Introduction:
The Hidden Continent of Iran

In the summer of 2009 the world was watching Iran. Not because of the unresolved question of Iran's nuclear programme, nor Iran's troubled relationship with the United States, nor (at least not primarily) because of human rights abuses. The world and its media-wife were watching Iran because, thirty years after the Islamic revolution of 1979 (and a hundred years after the Constitutional revolution of 1906–11), Iranians were again on the streets of Tehran in hundreds of thousands, demanding free, democratic government and an end to tyranny. Iranians sometimes have an exaggerated sense of their country's importance in the world. But for once it appeared justified. Would the Islamic republic fall? Or might it shift to a more open, freer version of itself that permitted elections to run their course – in contrast to the manipulated process enforced by repression many believed they had suffered after 12 June 2009? If there is a spirit of movement and change in world events, which moves from place to place over time according to crises in human affairs, then that spirit was alive in Tehran in the summer of 2009.

As it turned out, repression seemed to succeed that time. The spirit moved on, after a pause, to other places in the region, to Tunisia, Egypt and Libya, where it was more successful; and to Bahrain and Syria. In Iran, repression has deepened. But the story is not yet over. Iran appeared central then and continues to be of central importance.

This book is about the history of Iran since the beginning of the Islamic revolution of 1978–9. But, as with any historical subject, the roots of events go back long before the events themselves. This is, if possible, all the more so with Iran; a country with a long, complex history that is for the most part unknown to ordinary citizens of Western countries – something that often frustrates and irritates Iranians, who are proud of their history and their contribution to world civilization. The apparent strangeness of Iranian politics and Iranian behaviour in the last thirty or forty years is only explicable through an understanding of the history of the country. So, although this book is focused on the revolution of 1978–9 and the three decades since then, it is necessary to go back further into the history of the twentieth century, and even beyond (for the history of Shi'ism for example) to explain recent events.

Iran is less a country than a continent, more a civilization than a nation. In the past, countries like the USA, China, Russia and India have supported enough diversity and cultural self-confidence for at least some of their citizens to be able to feel that they were worlds unto themselves – self-sufficient, sometimes arrogant and superior. That they could do without the rest of humanity. As the process of globalization advances, such notions become less tenable, even for those large, imperial-scale countries. But they retain their attitudes to a certain extent. China and India have in addition a sense of ancient depth, of history, that strengthens their sense of self still further.

Iran has this too – albeit often infused with nostalgia, and a sense of loss and decline – but the Iranians tend to measure themselves not against China or India (still less against their Middle Eastern neighbours), but against Europe and North America. Iranians, like the Chinese, have been able to feel that theirs was the original, the oldest civilization. Many Iranians have believed – and deep down, may still believe in some way – that they have the best poetry, the best music, the best philosophy, the best food – or at any rate the best rice – and of course the best religion. However untenable, such notions could not even be thought of without there being at least an element of justification to them. It *is* great poetry, great music, wonderful food and great rice.

Within Iran, there is, as ever, still a remarkable, continental diversity of ethnicity, language, climate, geography, flora and fauna. And, thanks partly to the lonely path trodden by Iran in its revolutionary, anti-Western politics, Iran maintains that variety and is still less globalized than many other countries. The bazaars, their merchants and their traditions were close to the revolution of 1979, have been among the revolution's prime beneficiaries and are still close to the centre of the country's economic and political life. Iran's bazaars still sell more home-produced goods than are on the market elsewhere and sustain more artisans producing traditional craft items (metalwork, ceramics, printed textiles, rugs and other items), of higher quality than you find elsewhere.

If you go to hotels on the southern shore of the Persian Gulf, in Dubai or Qatar for example, you may find that the better-quality souvenirs on sale in the gift shops (with the price marked up enormously), presented as local, were actually made in Iran. The apparent economic self-sufficiency of Iran's bazaars (perhaps something of an illusion) still reinforces the country's sense of cultural self-sufficiency.

Since the second millennium BC and the very beginnings of mankind's recorded past, Iranian history can be seen as a microcosm of human history as a whole: empires, revolutions, invasions, art, architecture, warriors, conquerors, great thinkers, great writers and poets, holy men and lawgivers, charismatic leaders and the blackest villains. A visiting Martian wanting to see the full range of human activity, good and bad, to understand mankind, could well look at Iran as a kind of introductory course.[1] Within this, the history of the last fifty years in Iran is particularly dramatic, eventful and characteristic.

A further reason to look at Iran is that since the time of the Iranian revolution, European and Western attitudes to the rest of the world have been forced to change. Previously we tended still to think in terms of linear development in the Middle East and elsewhere towards a Western economic and social model, a Western idea of modernity, away from the traditional patterns of life of those countries, which were perceived as backward and outdated. Now, we cannot afford to think in that simple way any more. There is for example, a realization that countries like China and India are following their own developmental path and that their economic weight in the globalized world is going to demand respect, if not predominate. The Western model is no longer the only option. This does not mean we should be shy about values like liberalism and representative government – it may mean we have to argue for them with greater urgency, clarity and consistency. The Iranian revolution of 1979 and the Islamic revival in the wider world that followed (triggered by the revolution if not directly led or inspired by it) changed assumptions about the direction of development. The history and culture of the Middle East, and of Iran within that, has taken on a greater importance because we have to accept that it is going to be a formative part of the future of that part of the world, and all parts of the world are closer to us and more intimately involved with us than formerly. After 1979 we can no longer work on the assumption that the history and culture of the Middle East are irrelevant.

There are other good reasons to study Iran, beyond the old reason, the best reason, for studying other countries and cultures – to understand humanity, and therefore ourselves, better. In a world of intellectual uncertainty, doubt, complexity and ambiguity, where for many in the West the old certainties and the old gods of the past have fallen from their plinths, Iranian intellectual culture has a lot to say. Iranian thinkers have been at home with complexity, paradox, ambiguity and irony for a long time – at least since the era of the great Persian poets, between the eleventh and the fourteenth centuries, who explored those categories as fully as anyone since.

Some Misconceptions

In the West, we think we know about Iran, but what we think we know is often misleading or simply false. Many people, even otherwise well-educated people, think of the Iranians as Arabs, but they are not. They speak Persian, an ancient language of Indo-European origin, like Latin, modern German and English. It has an elegantly simple grammatical structure much more like that of German or English than that of Arabic. Unlike in many other territories conquered by Islam in the seventh century AD, Arabic did not simply replace the previous speech in Iran, and in many ways Iranians have traditionally defined themselves against the Arab identity of much of the rest of the Middle East region. We are encouraged to think of the Iranians as fanatical Muslims, world-leaders in Islamic fundamentalism. But the fact is that the experience of Islamic government in Iran since 1979 has turned many Iranians against political Islam, and the political attitudes of those Iranians have secularized.

The Iranian Islam of the Islamic republic, rather than being fundamentalist (in the sense of a deliberate return to the style of Islam of earliest times, as advocated for example by the Wahhabism of Saudi Arabia), incorporates radical modern innovations that many Shi'a Muslims, let alone Sunnis, regard as dubious. If the term fundamentalist has any solid meaning beyond its use as a boo-word then it is incorrect to label the Iranian revolution and regime as fundamentalist.[2] And the Iranians are Shi'as, which means that any kind of leadership they could offer the rest of the Islamic world would be questionable at best, given the Sunni/Shi'a schism, the strong antipathy many Sunnis feel toward Shi'as and the fact that the majority of the world's Muslims are Sunni.

We think of images of demonstrations and chanting crowds and assume (encouraged by our news media) that Iranian Shi'ism is a dangerous, uncontrollable, fanatical force. But in truth the religious hierarchy that Iranian Shi'ism has developed means that religious Iranians are more controlled, more subject to religious discipline and the guidance of senior clerics (most of whom are pragmatic and moderate, and many of whom are out of sympathy with the Islamic regime) than Sunni Muslims, who since the dissolution of the Caliphate in the 1920s have lacked that kind of structure. Some experts have pointed to that lack as a factor in the rise of radical, theologically incoherent groups like Al-Qaeda.[3] Iran has been historically central to humane and reflective strands of Islamic thought, including the hugely influential Sufi tradition, which inspired some of the most profound and beautiful Persian poetry. An important strand of Iranian Shi'ism is a traditional, quietist principle that commends decent, honest conduct and the patient endurance of adversity.

Iran is often depicted as an aggressive power, but it has not waged serious aggressive war since the time of Nader Shah, in the mid-eighteenth century, and its defence spending today is moderate to low for a state that size, not faintly comparable with that of militaristic states like the Soviet Union during the Cold War, for example. Since the eighteenth century Iran has fought wars, but normally defensive ones – notably the long, devastating Iran–Iraq War of the 1980s. In that war the US and other Western powers supported Saddam Hussein in Iraq against Iran, in the belief that it was necessary to contain Iranian religious extremism. For similar reasons, the US later funded the Taliban and Al-Qaeda in Afghanistan, to prevent pro-Iranian groups taking control after the Russians left. In both Iraq and Afghanistan the US eventually had to intervene against the monsters that their policy of containment had helped to create. The Iranians helped the coalition powers to set up new democratic structures in both countries, though this has often gone unacknowledged. Instead, Iran has perversely been blamed for the fact that the removal of these enemies in Iraq and Afghanistan has enhanced Iran's regional influence.

None of this should permit a whitewash of the current regime ruling Iran. It is a repressive, autocratic regime run in the interests of a narrow clique that systematically denies political freedoms and natural rights to the Iranian people. The defects of the regime have only become more apparent since the crisis that followed the presidential elections of June 2009. The regime continues to be responsible for systematic, serious abuses of human rights. But because of its (largely self-imposed) isolation and its opposition to the West, and the inflammatory rhetoric of figures like Ahmadinejad, more opprobrium has been heaped on Iran more indiscriminately than is justified by the facts, and (even after the Arab spring-cleaning, unfortunately) there are other regimes in the region that in many respects are as bad, or worse. If we are to find solutions to the problems of the Middle East it is essential to see Iran and the region as they really are, in their true form.

It is normal in Western countries for people not to have very much reliable information about Iran, and yet for certain aspects of Iran to be familiar. There are things about Iran that are striking and memorable; useful for news media programming because they make an immediate, strong visual impression. This often means a mullah, with a beard, in a turban and robes, talking into a microphone, and an agitated crowd chanting something. Then perhaps a graph showing the latest movement in the price of oil, which affects everybody. But how did a cleric get into a position of such authority? Why has Iran, under the Islamic republic, followed such a different path? This book tries, by describing the events of recent Iranian history, to answer some of those questions.

In doing so, I have written a book that is necessarily history in summary and overview rather than one that attempts to evaluate every item within the huge quantity of available source material on every event or episode. In addition, while explaining events as they unfolded, I have tended to focus on moments and episodes that have been turning-points, which have been important in determining the shape of what followed, rather than try to chronicle every month and year as of equal weight. This is why, for example, the book devotes attention to the origins of the revolution of 1979, and a long chapter to the Iran–Iraq War, which left such a deep mark on contemporary Iran. To illuminate the narrative it also presents the words of ordinary Iranians and other observers, giving an immediate sense of events, opinions and motivations.

Again and again, the usual kind of reporting and comment in the West stresses how strange, how alien, how irrational and how disturbing Iran and Iranian politics are. One of my tasks in this book is to show that Iranian concerns, values, problems, actions and reactions are wholly explicable and rational when seen in their own proper context, in the round; quite open to sympathy, and even familiar.

Prologue: 'Ten Days of Dawn' (*Daheh-ye Fajr*)

On 1 February 1979, just after 9.30 a.m., an Air France 747 airliner landed at Mehrabad airport on the western outskirts of Tehran, and a member of the crew, with others in attendance, helped an elderly, bearded man down the steps to the ground. This was no ordinary flight. As the aircraft had entered Iranian airspace, many on board had feared it might be shot down. As it landed, several million Iranians were waiting on the streets to welcome the bearded man in clerical robes, and every move he made was shadowed by crowds of minders, reporters, photographers and hangers-on of all kinds. The special passenger for whom the aircraft had been chartered was Ayatollah Ruhollah Khomeini, returning from exile, and the photographs and film of his descent from the aircraft became some of the defining images of the Iranian revolution.

Khomeini had been away from the country since the autumn of 1964; initially in Turkey and Iraq, later (briefly) in Paris. The Shah, whose government had exiled Khomeini, had left Iran from the same airport fourteen days before, on 16 January, after a year-long crescendo of mass protest against his rule. Newspapers that had carried the headline 'Shah raft' ('The Shah Is Gone') now printed 'Emam amad' ('The Emam Has Come').

Many people had waited up all night to witness Khomeini's arrival. The crowds cried 'Allahu Akbar!' and 'Khomeini, O Emam!' In the airport building he made a short speech thanking the students, clergy and bazaar merchants for their sacrifices in the demonstrations over the previous year and exhorted them to remain united to defeat the remnants of the Shah's regime. At one point the hubbub was such that he had to be carried outside.[1] There was some tension between the clerics welcoming Khomeini and those who had accompanied him from Paris.

As Khomeini arrived, the Shah's last prime minister, Shapur Bakhtiar, was still attempting to hold his government together. He seems to have

I

contacted Khomeini in Paris after the Shah's departure and offered to resign, but Khomeini ignored the message.[2] Bakhtiar was next to powerless before the mass movement of Iranians that had united itself behind Khomeini. The behaviour of the armed forces was crucial; two days earlier troops had killed thirty demonstrators on the streets near the university and injured hundreds more. Bakhtiar had been forced to give the troops his backing, saying that they had acted in self-defence; but the incident discredited him further, linking him in the minds of the pro-Khomeini populace with the actions of the Shah's regime against demonstrators in previous months.

From the airport Khomeini was driven through the packed streets towards the Behesht-e Zahra cemetery on the south side of the city. Mohsen Rafiqdust drove the car – no simple task, because more than once it was mobbed and almost overwhelmed by the crowd. Rafiqdust later said that he nearly lost control several times. Several of Khomeini's followers rode on the outside of the vehicle (a white four-wheel-drive) to fend off the people, and Rafiqdust drove bumper-to-bumper behind a Mercedes bus some of the way so that the bus could force a way through (and to prevent people jumping on the front of the car or going under the wheels).[3] Khomeini's son Ahmad accompanied him – as they went along, Ahmad had to explain to his father where they were, because building over the previous fifteen years had transformed this part of the city. Eventually the crowds in the streets became so thick that a helicopter had to take him the last part of the way.[4]

At Behesht-e Zahra Khomeini spoke again, denouncing Mohammad Reza Shah and the remnants of his government under Bakhtiar:

[The Shah] destroyed our country and filled our cemeteries. He ruined our country's economy. Even the projects he carried out in the name of progress pushed the country towards decadence. He suppressed our culture, annihilated people and destroyed all our manpower resources. We are saying this man, his government, his Majlis are all illegal. If they were to continue to stay in power, we would treat them as criminals and would try them as criminals. I shall appoint my own government. I shall slap this government in the mouth.[5]

He urged the armed forces to join the people, to realize their independence, and to throw off the influence of foreign advisers. (The most senior US military adviser, General Huyser, left on 3 February;[6] there was a mass departure of Americans and other foreigners in these weeks.) He also said that from now on the people would take charge of their own destiny.

Some time in early November 1978 an initially secret Council of the Islamic Revolution had been formed at Khomeini's behest to coordinate action against the Shah's government.[7] Now Khomeini and the Council set up their base at the Refah school, near the parliament building in the centre of the city. The school had been founded in 1968 to educate girls according to Islamic principles; several personalities associated with the school were significant in the revolutionary movement. Khomeini gave a press conference there on 3 February, again urging the military not to use their weapons against the people.[8] The Council had already made contact with some of the leaders of the armed forces, and with the US ambassador, William H. Sullivan, but their first priority was to set up a provisional government to supplant that of Shapur Bakhtiar.

On 5 February Khomeini announced the appointment of Mehdi Bazargan as prime minister of the provisional government. Bazargan agreed to this only after a day or more of reflection, and after warning Khomeini of his continuing commitment to democratic, moderate principles.

There were some striking similarities in the political backgrounds of Bakhtiar and Bazargan – also in the political predicaments in which they found themselves. Both had a lifelong commitment to liberal, democratic, nationalist principles – the principles of the revolution of 1905–11 and the constitution of 1906. Both had been educated in France at the end of the 1930s, and while there both had volunteered to fight with the French against the Nazis. Bakhtiar had served in the nationalist government of Mohammad Mossadeq in the early 1950s as deputy minister of labour; Bazargan had been the first head of the nationalized oil company (the National Iranian Oil Company) at the same time. There were differences; Bakhtiar came from a privileged position as a member of one of the leading families of the Bakhtiari tribe, had studied politics in Paris and had a more secular outlook, reflecting also the influence of Mossadeq and his membership of Mossadeq's National Front. Bazargan came from a more traditional Islamic family background, had trained as an engineer and was a member of the Freedom

Movement – which had nonetheless normally been closely aligned to the National Front. Both were wooed into accepting the post of prime minister; neither was wholly in sympathy with those who had chosen them. It was a tribute to the strength of the constitutionalist, democratic tradition in Iran that both the Shah and Khomeini had felt the need for such men at this time of crisis – but also a sign of its weakness, that such men were not able to take power in their own right.

So, on his return, as he sought to consolidate his position, avoid repression from the military and move toward the establishment of an Islamic republic, Khomeini's first act was to form an alliance not with the leftist Tudeh Party, nor the more radical paramilitary leftist groups, but with the liberal constitutionalists. And this surely reflected the aspirations and expectations of most of the Iranians who had been demonstrating over the previous year. They had been protesting both against the autocracy of the Shah and political repression and for a return to representative government. There were economic grievances also; there had been nationalist, radical leftist, anti-American and anti-British elements in the mix. The whole had been given form by the appeal to Islam as the underlying, authentic focus of the people's identity, and by Khomeini's own simple, direct, charismatic leadership. None of this was strange or entirely new, at least not to Iranians – in 1906 senior clerical figures had led a revolution in Iran that had combined similar ingredients. The history of that revolution was well known, and according to that template many middle-class liberals and leftists, more or less secular-minded, expected this time also to take over the popular movement, and for Khomeini and the clergy to recede into the background. But Khomeini knew the history too. It is unlikely that he had at the outset any precise blueprint for the eventual outcome, but he was not going to let religious authority be sidelined.

When Khomeini announced Bazargan as prime minister on 5 February he presented himself before the press and other news media with his close adviser and companion Hashemi Rafsanjani, as well as Bazargan. Rafsanjani spoke first, setting out a programme for the establishment of a new revolutionary state. There would be a referendum to establish popular support for an Islamic republic. Then a Constituent Assembly would be set up to agree a new constitution. That being done, elections would be held and a new Majles (parliament) would be elected.

After Rafsanjani, Bazargan spoke self-deprecatingly of his suitability for the responsibilities now thrust upon him, but Khomeini, speaking last, had a message that was firm, sombre and austere:

through the guardianship that I have from the holy lawgiver [i.e. the Prophet Mohammad] I hereby pronounce Bazargan as the Ruler, and since I have appointed him, he must be obeyed. The nation must obey him. This is not an ordinary government. It is a government based on the shari'a. Opposing this government means opposing the shari'a of Islam and revolting against the shari'a, and revolt against the government of the shari'a has its punishment in our law ... it is a heavy punishment in Islamic jurisprudence. Revolt against God's government is a revolt against God. Revolt against God is blasphemy.[9]

That press conference, within four days of Khomeini's return to Iran, combined in this way the two cardinal elements of the revolution and of Iran's constitution ever since – Islam and democracy. But the two elements were in tension from the start. Khomeini's speech showed that his vision was of a government blessed and legitimated by God, first and above all. But the programme of the provisional government, endorsed by him and presented as a decree from him, though read at the press conference by Rafsanjani, showed an almost equally strong, indeed almost pedantic, attachment to an idea of popular sovereignty – of government according to the will of the people. The tension between these two principles could be, and was, glossed over in revolutionary rhetoric; and much of the time they might genuinely work in parallel. Khomeini no doubt believed that they would harmonize, reflecting his understanding of the nature of God and of divine agency in the world. Rousseau once wrote that the voice of the people was the voice of God; seldom can that idea have been given more precise expression than by the crowds that welcomed Khomeini in February 1979 and later voted in a referendum overwhelmingly for an Islamic republic. Khomeini may also have expected that his involvement in government could be relatively light. Once the Islamic system was set up, politicians like Bazargan could run things from day to day. But politics, and especially revolutions, tend be messier than that.

Two obstacles remained between the revolutionary movement and the achievement of complete dominance – Bakhtiar's government and the armed forces. But neither was as impressive as it seemed. After a year of conflict with the demonstrators the armed forces were uncertain and divided – both the rank and file and the leadership. Many officers and some units, notably the Imperial Guard, which had been specially favoured with pay, prestige and promotion by the previous regime,[10] were still devoted to the Shah. But recruitment to the armed forces was based on conscription, and many ordinary servicemen were as enthusiastic about the revolutionary movement and the return of Khomeini as other, ordinary citizens. The Shah himself had put rival officers and even mutual enemies into senior positions in the armed forces, in order to reduce the chance of their combining against him and plotting a coup.[11] But this meant that when the Shah had gone – 'with no forwarding address'[12] – those senior officers found themselves at odds with each other and unable to agree upon concerted action. Even when the Shah had still been in place, there had been much disagreement about how best to deal with the demonstrations, with the Shah himself exerting a restraining influence, and some officers favouring much harsher measures.

Disaffection among the military increased after the Shah's departure, and, although there has been disagreement over estimates of the level of desertions,[13] it seems plain that these increased to perhaps 1,200 per day by the second week of February. The revolutionaries encouraged the disaffection, not just by propaganda and planting flowers in the muzzles of carbines during demonstrations, but also by setting up centres to provide deserters with civilian clothes and expenses to cover their journey home by bus.[14] Many officers had resigned after 16 January, and several senior figures defected after Khomeini's return. And many, retired or otherwise, were offering their services to Bazargan or his colleagues (or to anyone who would listen) after 5 February.

Significantly for what was to follow, 800 air force technicians from the aircraft servicing organization known as the Homafaran had defected together to the revolutionary movement in the second half of January. Attempts to discipline them were lost in the general chaos, and they became an important militant element in the revolutionary movement, comparable with the Kronstadt sailors in the February and October revolutions of 1917 in Russia. Most of them were non-commissioned officers, specialists with a grievance because, although technically qualified, they felt their promotion within the service was blocked by a structure that favoured socially and politically privileged officers trained in cadet college – in its way a situation that echoed the wider disposition of socially insecure petit-bourgeois classes toward the revolutionary movement.[15] But a number of air force officers and cadets joined them too.

After 5 February, with two rival governments in the country, the leaders of the armed forces were in an awkward position. Many of the senior officers knew that some of their number were negotiating with Bazargan and/or clerics close to Khomeini, like Ayatollah Beheshti; as were the Americans, through their embassy. General Huyser, who had wanted to keep open the option of a military coup, had left the country. It seems that, although the account of this episode in his own memoirs is quite vague,[16] General Hosein Fardust, head of the supervisory Special Intelligence Bureau under the Shah, may have been instrumental between 5 and 9 February in steering other generals away from action against Bazargan's nascent government. Having been a childhood friend of the Shah, Fardust seems to have sided with the Islamic regime in 1979 and controversially, afterwards helped the new SAVAMA, later renamed the Ministry of Intelligence and Security (VEVAK), the ugly phoenix that rose out of the remnants of the Shah's infamous secret police, SAVAK.

On 8 February a large number of air force cadets, Homafaran technicians and others went to the Refah school in uniform and declared their loyalty to Khomeini and the new provisional government. A photograph of them doing so was published in the newspaper *Kayhan* the following day. The following evening (Friday), possibly fired up by the screening on state television of footage of Khomeini's return eight days before, the radicalized air force personnel at Doshan Tappeh air base formed up as a body to salute the Emam. Provoked by this, a detachment of Imperial Guard troops (200-strong or less) stationed at the base attacked them, and serious fighting ensued, continuing on the morning of 10 February. Both sides called for help, but whereas the air force commander authorized distribution of weapons to his men, the Imperial Guard commander went over to the revolutionaries on 10 February and did his best to prevent reinforcements being sent to his former comrades. Armed radicals of the Fedayan-e Khalq and Mojahedin-e Khalq organizations (the latter known as the MKO) moved in to support the cadets and Homafaran, and large crowds of revolutionary demonstrators formed across the whole area, leading to what turned out to be the decisive confrontation.

Two columns of tanks were sent to Doshan Tappeh by hardline military commanders. The BBC reporter John Simpson, who had arrived on the same flight with Khomeini on 1 February, saw twenty-six Chieftain tanks pass by the InterContinental Hotel, breaking through an improvised barricade there:

> The lead tank, finding only an upturned Buick and some skips filled with rubble in its path, scarcely checked its speed at all. It struck the Buick's roof with a grinding sound and flipped it aside as if it were made of tinfoil. The Buick crumpled up and lay in the middle of the road, twitching now and then as another Chieftain struck it in passing.[17]

But the tanks eventually faltered amid the crowds and roadblocks. Some were captured, others were set alight by Molotov cocktails, and some of their crews defected with their vehicles to the revolutionaries. Other commanders recalled troops to their bases, and the fighting spread. Armed revolutionaries and crowds broke into police stations and other places where weapons could be found. With the situation rapidly running away from him, Bakhtiar ordered a dusk-to-dawn curfew for the night of 10/11 February and urged the army and police commanders to enforce the curfew strictly, but Khomeini told his followers to ignore the order, and cars with loudspeakers drove through the streets announcing his instruction, calling forth further large crowds. Bazargan was with Khomeini at the Refah school:[18]

> Most of our time we were in Refah school and that particular night, we stayed in the same place. Since we could hear the sound of much shooting, and there was news on the possibility of an attack on the school, we went to a house nearby and spent the rest of the night there. When we got up the next morning, we realized that the whole situation had been turned on its head and the nation had achieved victory, praise be to God.

The following morning, 11 February, twenty-seven generals and other senior military commanders met at 10.20 a.m. to discuss whether they could continue to support Bakhtiar. Even those most loyal to the Shah were by now despondent. Field Marshal Qarabaghi did his best to get an overview of the situation by collating the views of those present and presenting himself further reports that he had received by telephone:

> We ordered them all together that morning to attend a meeting . . . Lieutenant General Sanei had telephoned earlier from ground forces headquarters to say: 'General . . . you can no longer count on the ground forces . . .' I told him: 'I do not understand. If I am not going to count on the ground forces, what am I going to count on?' He replied: 'This is it. There is nothing we can do.' I said: 'This is highly regrettable.' . . . I proposed . . . to summon . . . a council of commanders and find out what is happening. During that meeting, each commander described the situation of his own units. The ground force commander said that there was nothing he could do. The air force commander said the same thing . . . I presented the reports, which I had received, to the council. We had a lengthy discussion. Some of the commanders were in favour of declaring solidarity [with the revolution], whereas others were in favour of neutrality.

Qarabaghi reminded the commanders that the Shah had ordered them to keep the army intact, in order to safeguard the country's independence. He urged them that they had to make a unanimous decision: 'The discussion continued and eventually the minority, who were in favour of declaring solidarity, agreed that we should declare neutrality.'

It was agreed that Qarabaghi would inform Bakhtiar of the decision, and that it would be announced on Tehran Radio. Bakhtiar had been expecting to see Qarabaghi at his office at 8.30 a.m.:

> I was in my office at eight-thirty the next morning, but he [Qarabaghi] did not turn up. I waited until nine o'clock, but there was still no sign of him . . . I became suspicious as to why he had not turned up. I telephoned his office several times, and each time I was told that he was in a very important meeting. I went to the balcony, where I could hear the sound of sporadic machine-gun fire.

Finally, Qarabaghi telephoned.

> I asked him: 'General, what happened? Where were you?' He replied: 'Your Excellency, Prime Minister, the army has just now declared its neutrality.' As soon as I heard that, I went to a different world. I told him: 'Neutrality between who and who? Is it neutrality between law and anarchy? Is it

neutrality between Iran and Iran's enemies? . . . Thank you, General. Thank you very much.' I then put the phone down.

Tehran Radio broadcast the commanders' announcement at 1.15 p.m.:

In view of the recent developments in the country, the Supreme Council of the armed forces met at ten-twenty hours this morning, 22 Bahman 1357. It unanimously decided that, in order to prevent further chaos and bloodshed, it declares its neutrality, and military units have been ordered to return to barracks.

Bazargan and the other revolutionaries welcomed the announcement, which was what they had been working towards in previous contacts with army commanders. Bazargan believed the US embassy had been exerting itself to the same end:

Yes, we were in favour of the army's neutrality. This was achieved by the arrangements and promises secured through General Moqaddam. The other side of the coin was that the Americans wanted the army not to become involved in the affairs. I am not fully aware of the details, but they wanted the Iranian revolution to take place without bloodshed and without catastrophe. Well, we also wanted the same thing.

Bakhtiar was left powerless to affect events:

I waited until one-thirty in the afternoon, before deciding that there was no alternative left to me. I could see that when the people realized that the military men had decided to withdraw, no other force could stop the others. I ordered a helicopter to land in the grounds of the cadet training college. The helicopter arrived at about two o'clock in the afternoon. I picked up a few of my personal belongings and went downstairs . . . As I came through the doorway, there was one captain, two NCOs and four soldiers . . . One of them said: 'We are almost totally surrounded now.' . . . I got into the helicopter, and it took off. I said: 'How amazing! We want to give these people freedom and democracy, and they do not want it.' What could we possibly do? I do not know, but, despite the sadness, I experienced relief. Believe me, it seemed as if a huge burden, as heavy as Damavand Mountain, had been lifted from my shoulders. I felt as if I were flying with my own wings.

It had been arranged previously that Bakhtiar, Bazargan, Qarabaghi and others would meet that afternoon at Kazem Jafrudi's house in

North Tehran. Jafrudi had been a member of the Majles under the Shah and was a friend of both Bakhtiar and Bazargan. But as the time of the meeting drew closer Jafrudi advised Bakhtiar by telephone that he should not come after all:

The prime minister had arranged to come straight from his office with Dr Abbasqoli Bakhtiar. After taking off in the helicopter from the cadet training college, he had landed at Aqdassiyeh. From there, he went in a Peykan car to a previously arranged hiding place. Before going, he telephoned me from Aqdassiyeh, and I informed him that my house was crowded with people and it was impossible for him to come there and also quite dangerous. As a result, these gentlemen proceeded to their hiding place.

Jafrudi then telephoned General Qarabaghi and advised him not to wear uniform to the meeting:

at about five minutes past four, he [Jafrudi] telephoned me again to say that the gentlemen had arrived and were waiting for me. He also asked me not to go there in my uniform. I asked: 'What has uniform got to do with the meeting?' He said that he would explain later, but insisted that for my own safety I should go in civilian clothes. I was very distressed and hung up. Lieutenant General Hatam, who was sitting next to me, asked me what had happened, and when I told him I was supposed to attend the meeting in civilian clothes, he said: 'Well, General, does it matter so much?' I said that I had no civilian clothes with me. He said: 'Then send someone to fetch your civilian clothes.' After one hour they arrived with my civilian clothes, and I went to a room and changed. My civilian clothes saved my life. I left for Mr Jafrudi's house. He opened the gates himself and let me in. He led me to a room first and said: 'General, I wanted to make a request before taking you into the meeting room.' ... He told me that Prime Minister Bakhtiar had submitted his resignation. I was astonished and added that I had not gone there to submit mine. I asked whether the prime minister was there, and he told me that he was not at the house but was somewhere in the vicinity and had not been brought to the house for reasons of security. I said: 'But you did not tell me that the prime minister was not going to be here.' His reply was: 'The prime minister is not far away and he is in touch with us. The other gentlemen are waiting for us next door so that we can reach an agreement.' I asked who the other gentlemen were. At this point he asked me to follow him to another room.

When I entered, I saw seven or eight people were sitting there, who were introduced as Messrs. Dr Siassi, [Mehdi] Bazargan, Dr Sahabi, [Abbas] Amir-Entezam, Engineer Khalili and someone else . . . After I sat down, one of them began praising the army for its decision and said that the army and the nation belonged to each other and they asked me to help them to establish security. I said: 'Security would be maintained if you were to issue a statement to this effect. You [addressing Bazargan] have been appointed prime minister by Khomeini, therefore either you or Khomeini should issue a statement ordering the people not to attack army barracks and to respect its dignity and honour. If you were to issue such a statement, security would automatically be established.' He said: 'Fine. I shall order such a statement to be issued immediately.'

In fact, two statements were made on Tehran Radio, one from Khomeini himself, read out by Ayatollah Musavi-Ardebili:

Now that the armed forces have stepped back, have declared their neutrality in the face of political affairs and have expressed support for the nation, the dear and courageous nation is expected to maintain law and order when the troops return to barracks. You should stop saboteurs, who may try to create catastrophe and instruct them of their religious and humanitarian obligations. Do not allow anyone to attack foreign embassies. If, God forbid, the army were to enter the arena again, you must defend yourselves with all your might. I hereby inform senior army officers that if they were to stop the army's aggression, and instruct them to join the nation and its legal Islamic government, we would regard the army as part of the nation and vice versa.

In addition, Tehran Radio contacted Jafrudi while Bazargan was still in his house, spoke to Bazargan and got him to make a statement:

We were all sitting in my house, when a friend of mine, who was in charge of the radio, telephoned and asked to interview Mr Bazargan. He asked whether they should come to my house or Mr Bazargan should go to the radio station. I passed the message to . . . Bazargan, who volunteered to go to the radio station and there he broadcast the following speech: 'I am delighted to offer my congratulations to the combative Muslim nation of Iran, who today has survived a torturous and anxious journey to achieve victory for its revolution. I deem it necessary to express my gratitude to army officers and soldiers. I would like to recommend that in accordance with Emam Khomeini's assertion, the army is part of the nation and you must treat army officers and soldiers as your brothers. Our dear compatriots must demonstrate patience and must give this government a chance to employ far-sightedness and justice to direct the country along the right path. It is obvious that chaos, anarchy and confusion will not only prevent us from achieving something positive, but it will, God forbid, make matters much worse and more catastrophic than ever before.

By the end of 11 February revolutionary crowds had broken into Evin prison, releasing all the prisoners, including the politicals; and had ransacked the former headquarters of SAVAK. Elsewhere in the country, in Shiraz, in Rasht, and in other places, the revolutionaries, often led by air force personnel, took over police and SAVAK buildings and established locally the same outcome as in the capital.[19] Bakhtiar went into hiding.

On the afternoon of 11 February, US Ambassador Sullivan was attempting to organize the safe evacuation of some US military personnel who were trapped in a building that was under attack, when he received a series of telephone calls from the White House. In one of these, David Newsom asked him on behalf of Zbigniew Brzezinski what were the chances of a successful military coup: 'The total absurdity of such an inquiry in the circumstances then existing in Tehran provoked me to a scurrilous suggestion for Brzezinski that seemed to shock mild-mannered Under-Secretary Newsom.' Back in the US, General Huyser was asked the same day, as part of the same deliberations, whether and under what conditions he would return to Iran to 'conduct a military takeover'. His response was more polite, but no more encouraging than Sullivan's.[20]

The fighting that finally toppled Bakhtiar's government had been spontaneous; instigated by the enthusiasm of the revolutionaries themselves, by the Homafaran, and by the Fedayan and the MKO rather than by Khomeini, who was more concerned to avoid the revolution descending into complete anarchy. But the outcome left him dominant. Since 1979 the Islamic regime has regarded 11 February as the date of the final victory of the Islamic revolution – and has celebrated the ten days between Khomeini's return and 11 February as the *Daheh-ye Fajr* – 'ten days of dawn'. Others since have cynically called the festival *Daheh-ye Zajr* – 'ten days of torment'.[21]

Within a short time Khomeini approved summary trials for killings and other acts of oppression by members of the regime over the previous months and years, and appointed Sadegh Khalkhali, who was to become infamous, to carry them out. One of the first to be arrested was General Rahimi, who had been responsible for enforcing martial law in Tehran. Rahimi's captors allowed Western journalists to put questions to him on the evening of 11 February. He was unrepentant, confirmed his continuing loyalty to the Shah and said it had been necessary to send in forces to restore order. He was asked:

'Do you believe your life is in danger from the decision of the court which, we understand, will try you?'

General Rahimi smiled slightly, looked up and lifted his hands a little, as though all these questions were an irrelevance.

'I came into this world once, and once I will leave it'[22]

Rahimi and three other generals (including the former head of SAVAK, General Nasiri, who had been badly injured after his capture) were shot on 14 February on the roof of the Refah school.[23]

I

The Background: *Ma Chegoneh Ma Shodim?*[1] ('How Did We Become What We Are?')

Revolutions

The Iranian revolution of 1979 is sometimes spoken of as the third great revolution of modern times, after the French and the Russian.[2] The interpretation of all three of these revolutions will always be controversial, but many people still broadly think of the first two in terms set out by Karl Marx in the nineteenth century. According to that analysis, the French revolution was a bourgeois revolution, in which the perennially rising middle class pushed aside the old forms of feudalism and asserted its growing economic power in political terms, setting up the forms of representative government and establishing the bourgeois class and capitalist economics as dominant for the period that followed. The Russian revolution, following on from the French, was the proletarian revolution predicted by Marx, bringing in an era of socialist government in the interest of the working class, at least according to the theory.

These crude characterizations conceal many contradictions. Even a cursory reading of the events of the French revolution shows the way that populists exploiting the militant influence of the urban poor of Paris (and the threat of war from France's enemies) diverted the revolution away from the principles of bourgeois liberalism toward terror, political murder and repression. One of its prime outcomes was a redistribution of land to peasant farmers that in the long run had profoundly conservative and anti-capitalistic consequences. The Bolshevik revolution of October 1917 took place in one of the European states in which the proletariat was least developed and least numerous as a proportion of the population as a whole, directly contradicting Marx's own predictions. It had less of the character of a mass movement, and more of the character of a *coup d'état*. Nonetheless, the labels still stick.

The Iranian revolution was an Islamic revolution – that much is clear.[3] But beyond that label, despite some family resemblances to those earlier revolutions, it remains an enigma, and many non-specialists in the West (and not just in the West), despite so much writing and comment on the subject since, have no conceptual moorings for it – no clear sense of why it happened or what it signified. We are still living through the consequences of the Iranian revolution of 1979, and the longer-term outcomes remain hard to assess.

The bare facts of the Iranian revolution of 1979 can be quite briefly told. It began in a period of economic uncertainty, after the oil-fuelled boom of the early 1970s had begun to falter, with rising inflation and unemployment. In 1977 the Shah's government relaxed some of its previous repressive measures, permitting the reappearance of some expressions of dissent from the liberal left. But an attack in a government-backed newspaper on the exiled Ayatollah Khomeini in January 1978 led to a demonstration by religious students in the shrine city of Qom in which a number of demonstrators were shot and killed by police. Fuelled by condemnations from Khomeini outside Iran and from other clerics within, a cycle of further demonstrations and shootings followed, after intervals of forty days' mourning each time. The demonstrations (mainly involving young students and people from the bazaars) got larger and more violent, and the number of dead increased. Over the summer and early autumn workers frustrated at low pay joined demonstrations and went on strike – the strikes in the oil industry being especially damaging. On 8 September (afterwards known as Black Friday) martial law was declared, and a large number of demonstrators were killed in Tehran. After this the Shah lost whatever credibility he had left, and the general wish (aligning with Khomeini's longstanding demand) was for him to go. Strikes and demonstrations continued and increased in intensity, especially in the religious season of Ashura in December. Troops began to desert, and on 16 January 1979 the Shah flew out of the country. Khomeini returned on 1 February, troops loyal to the Shah's government gave up the struggle ten days later (the *Daheh-ye Fajr*), and at the end of March a nationwide referendum gave 97 per cent support for an Islamic republic.

But these bare facts may leave the uninitiated little the wiser. Why did the Shah lose control? Why did leadership of the revolution fall to the Shi'a clergy? What were the people's grievances and how did they come to be expressed so forcefully? And why did the Shah's regime fail to accommodate them? Why were the revolutionaries so hostile to the West? Was it primarily a religious, or a democratic, or a social revolution? Or a nationalist revolution? To begin to answer these questions it is necessary to reach further back into the history of Iran, of the Islamic religion, and of Shi'ism.

Islam and the Shi'a

When Mohammad first began to preach the revelation of Islam in Mecca in AD 613, he soon encountered opposition from the leading families that controlled the city. Prime among these were the Quraish, to a junior branch of which Mohammad's own family belonged. Those families drew their prosperity partly from their trusteeship of the pagan shrines in Mecca, which Mohammad was attacking, and they felt threatened also by his emphasis on fair dealing in business and generosity to the poor. Most of what Mohammad preached either stated or implied a criticism of the status quo, of which the Quraish were the prime proprietors and beneficiaries. The Quraish retaliated against the growing number of Mohammad's followers with ridicule, and later with violence. So on the one hand, in the form it has come down to us, we have a picture of wealthy, corrupt, impious, unjust rulers; and on the other, virtuous, poor, oppressed Muslims, bravely speaking out against them. This image of arrogant power and virtuous resistance (initially not unlike the position of Jesus and his disciples vis-à-vis the ruling Pharisees and Sadducees in the New Testament) repeats itself again and again in the history of Islam, and especially in the history of Shi'a Islam, reinforced each time by new exemplars, right down to modern times and the 1979 revolution.

Eventually Mohammad and his followers were forced to leave Mecca, to set up a new Muslim community in Medina. War followed between the Quraish of Mecca and the Muslims of Medina (the migration from Mecca to Medina in AD 622, the *Hijra*, became the date for the beginning of the Muslim calendar, representing as it did the proper founding of the Muslim *umma*, the community of Muslim believers). Most of the rulings in the Koran, and in Islam more widely, regulating the conduct of war (conditions for just war, restrictions on the waging of war, the treatment of captives, etc.) derive from positions taken on this conflict.

Eventually (in AD 630) the Medinans triumphed, occupied Mecca, converted the Meccans (including the Quraish) to the new religion, removed pagan idols from the Ka'ba in Mecca and made it the central shrine of Islam that it has been ever since. Islam became the dominant religion of the Arabian peninsula.

But in AD 632 the Prophet Mohammad died, and the new religion faced a crisis over who should succeed him as the leader of the *umma*. The way it was resolved was fateful for the future of Islam. One of Mohammad's closest companions, Abu Bakr, was selected as *khalifa* (caliph – successor). But some Muslims felt that the wrong choice had been made, and that another of the companions should have been chosen – Ali, the Prophet's cousin and son-in-law. They believed the Prophet himself had chosen Ali to succeed.

Despite continuing argument and strife, the caliphs Omar and Othman succeeded Abu Bakr, and eventually Ali himself became the fourth caliph. But there was conflict between those who supported Ali, and those who had supported his predecessor (who had been murdered). There were tensions also over the spoils yielded by the enormous conquests made by the Muslims at this time, which had taken rich swathes of territory from the Roman and Persian empires (the latter conquered after Persian defeats at the battles of Qadesiyya and Nahavand in 637 and 641 respectively). The followers of Ali tended to be those who wanted to uphold the austere principles of Islam against what they saw as the corrupting influence of wealth and government in the expanding Arab Empire. After Ali's death in 661, these tensions continued, and the caliphs of the Umayyad line that followed him (relatives of the murdered Othman) were regarded as increasingly worldly. Those who had followed Ali held to the view that the real leaders of Islam should be the children of Ali (who by virtue of his marriage to the Prophet's daughter Fatima were also the descendants of Mohammad himself).

So by now the Muslim followers of Ali saw themselves in much the same position as that in which the original followers of Mohammad had perceived themselves in opposition to the pagans of Mecca; virtuous austerity resisting worldly authority, oppression, immorality and corruption. It was in this spirit that Ali's son, Hosein, led a small group of followers in revolt in AD 680. He tried to link up with sympathizers in Kufa, south of present-day Baghdad, but was confronted by the forces of the Caliph Yazid at Karbala. The Kufans failed to turn out in his support, and Hosein refused to make terms. The caliph's troops loosed arrows into Hosein's camp, killing Hosein's infant son among others. Outnumbered, his followers tried to fight back but were overwhelmed and massacred, and Hosein was cut down also.

For the Muslim sect that later called themselves the Shi'a Ali (meaning the partisans or followers of Ali) or simply the Shi'a, the desperate battle of Karbala was the defining moment. Ever since that time the Shi'a have mourned the event as the essence of injustice; as the victory of the oppressors over the righteous, of the strong over the weak, of the corrupt over the pious. The Caliph Yazid became the archetype for all worldly wickedness, and Hosein the model for heroic self-sacrifice. Karbala became one of the central shrine cities for Shi'a Muslims, along with Najaf (the tomb of Ali). Initially Shi'ism was more a tendency than a sect, drawing to it people who especially revered the memory of Ali and Hosein, and who believed that the leadership of Islam should have descended in their line. Their descendants were known as the Shi'a Emams, who in each generation were rivals or at least potential rivals to the caliphs. There was a further schism after the death of the seventh Emam, Jafar al-Sadiq, in AD 765, with the supporters of his elder son splitting away to form the Ismaili sect (despite the fact that he predeceased his father), while the majority of the Shi'as followed his younger son, Musa al-Kazim. The succession followed Musa's descendants until the twelfth Emam, who was believed to have disappeared at the time of the eleventh Emam's death in AD 874. Iranian Shi'as believe that the twelfth Emam (the Hidden Emam, to whom rightful leadership on earth should fall in principle) never died, but will reappear at the day of judgement. They are known as twelver Shi'as (because they recognize twelve Emams) to distinguish them from the Ismailis and some other minority Shi'a sects.[4] In time, Shi'ism developed a separate body of traditions and religious-legal rulings of its own, in parallel to the main Muslim tradition of Sunnism.

Shi'ism, the Ulema and the Revolution of 1979

Shi'a Islam became the religion of Iran after it was imposed by Shah Esmail I and his descendants, the Safavid dynasty, from 1501. Prior to that, Iran's Muslims were predominantly Sunni, with scarcely more

Sh'ia Muslims than other parts of the Islamic world. The centres of Shi'ism were the shrine cities of what is now Iraq – Najaf, Karbala, Samarra. After that date, those shrines remained important centres of Shi'a religious learning and pilgrimage (as they have to this day), but Iranian Shi'ism took on a much greater significance. The Safavids enforced adherence to Shi'ism as a matter of state policy. Learned men of religion – *ulema* – drew close to the Safavid rulers, in a relationship of mutual support, especially towards the close of the Safavid period of rule in the years around 1700. Religious endowments (tax-free grants of wealth and land to institutions like mosques, schools and shrines) proliferated and channelled wealth to the *ulema*. Shi'ism became deeply entrenched in the cultural, intellectual and political life of Iran.

Did Iran turn Shi'a simply because the Safavids imposed Shi'ism? Or was Iranian Shi'ism also an expression of the Iranians' distinctive, separate consciousness of themselves within the Islamic world? The complex nature of Iran's national identity and Iranian nationalism is discussed in a later chapter. But Iranian Shi'ism had a series of essential, interrelated effects on the development of modern Iran, and the revolution of 1979. Most fundamental was the development of the independent social and political authority of the *ulema*.

In 1722 the Safavid regime, ruling from its splendid capital in Isfahan, succumbed to a revolt by militant, plundering Afghans. Most of the next seventy years were marred by foreign invasions, civil war, internal revolts, military adventures, punitive taxation, expropriation, general chaos and unpleasantness. The *ulema* fell from their previous position of privilege and wealth, many of their endowments were confiscated or plundered, and some criticized them for their perceived complicity in the failure of Safavid rule.[5] Many of them emigrated, along with many other refugee Iranians, to southern Iraq or to India or elsewhere (it is possible, for example, that Khomeini's ancestors emigrated to India at this time). This emigration had a lasting impact in parts of India, in the shrine cities of Iraq and in some of the territories along the southern shore of the Persian Gulf.

In these circumstances, new patterns of thought emerged among the Shi'a *ulema*, partly in response to this trauma (though the thinking closely mirrored debates that had rolled back and forth in the early centuries of Islam, and its beginnings had emerged already in the Safavid period). One school – the Akhbari – argued for a theological position that each individual Muslim had in the Koran and in the *hadith* (the written traditions of the sayings and actions of the Prophet and, in Shi'ism, the Emams) all he needed for his guidance, and that there was only a limited place, if any, for the interpretation of religious law based on reason (*ijtihad*). The Akhbari position was close to the traditional line of Sunni Islam on these points. The other school – the Usuli – argued, on the contrary, that *ijtihad* was necessary to reinterpret religious law afresh in each generation, in the light of new circumstances and new understanding, and that only trained, learned *ulema* could be trusted to do this. By the end of the eighteenth century, as a greater degree of order was restored by the first Qajar Shahs, the Usulis were winning the argument, and a new arrangement emerged, according to which ordinary Muslims gave their allegiance – and often, a portion of their material earnings – to a class of specially qualified *ulema* called *mojtahed* (those qualified to perform *ijtihad*). In each generation, among the whole body of *mojtahed*, one or two clerics emerged to serve as a supreme guide to other *ulema* and to ordinary Muslims in religious matters. Such a cleric was called a *marja-e taqlid* (source of emulation) or *marja*.

In this way the Shi'a clergy developed a religious hierarchy, analogous to that of other religions – to that of the Catholic church, for example – but quite unlike the looser arrangements of Sunni Islam. As time went on, and more ambitious young men strove to qualify as *mojtahed*, new, more elevated levels of dignity were added to distinguish between the clerics – *hojjatoleslam* ('proof of Islam'), and *ayatollah* ('sign of God'). This system helped the *ulema* to reassert their social authority and to restore their wealth, as a class; this time quite independently of secular rulers, at a time (the nineteenth century) when the monarchy continued to be relatively weak.

Religious law has a much wider significance in Islam than in Christianity and other religions. In principle, it is meant to govern every aspect of a Muslim's life. This gave clerics a role much more important than that of mere prayer-leaders in the mosque. They were arbitrators in family or business or other legal disputes and acted as judges in criminal cases. They served as notaries for official documents. Often they were the only authority figures in smaller towns or villages and acted effectively as governors, in association with elders or village headmen. In the larger towns and cities the *ulema* tended to have specially close connections with the merchants and craftsmen of the bazaars, who often demonstrated their piety by giving money for religious purposes – for example to repair the roof of a mosque or to help set up a religious school (*madreseh*). *Bazaari* and *ulema* families often intermarried. Between them, the *ulema* and the *bazaaris* tended to be the dominant urban classes, and their close relationship came to be of central importance in politics from the end of the nineteenth century onwards. Through the religious hierarchy, the contacts established during their long training, and family connections, the *ulema* had access to a network of clergy and ordinary Muslims across the whole country, and beyond.

The strong position of the *ulema* in Iranian society meant that when secular authority failed or was challenged, almost always the *ulema* (or at least some of them) emerged as leaders of political dissent. This happened in 1890–92 (when the government attempted to grant a tobacco monopoly to a British contractor, Major Talbot, but had to reverse the policy in the face of a determined boycott organized by clerics and *bazaaris*), in 1905–6, in 1953, in 1963 and, of course, in 1978–9. They were able to communicate and coordinate action with other *ulema*, and to disseminate propaganda, often using the most up-to-date communications technology (in 1892, the telegraph system; in 1978, cassette-tapes, telephone and Xerox copiers). Their religious authority gave them a unique advantage by comparison with other potential leaders of mass movements; it meant independence and a degree of immunity from repression, as a class. Secular rulers found it difficult, and often counterproductive, to act even against individual mullahs. And in addition, the most senior *marjas* were often out of reach of the Iranian government altogether, living in Najaf or one of the other shrine cities of Ottoman Iraq (the three provinces of Ottoman Iraq – Mosul, Baghdad and Basra – were ruled under a British mandate from 1920 and became the independent Kingdom of Iraq in 1932).

Popular Shi'ism

Another important element in Iranian Shi'ism, often viewed with mixed feelings by the orthodox *ulema*, were the public, popular manifestations associated with the death of Hosein, and the other traditions of the early history of the followers of Ali. Each year, Shi'a Muslims take part in processions that are in effect commemorative funeral processions, to mark the anniversary of the martyrdom of the Emam Hosein at Karbala.[6] The participants weep and beat their chests. They carry heavy funerary symbols, including replicas of the Emam's coffin, and huge multi-pronged objects that represent Hosein's banner. Strongmen train specially to compete for the honour of carrying these symbols. They also may beat themselves with chains and in the past some cut themselves on the head with swords to show their devotion and their fellowship with the martyrs of Karbala. The grandest processions would take place in the bazaars of great cities, but smaller versions would go ahead each year even in otherwise quiet villages. These rituals of collective grief may seem strange, even threatening, to outsiders (and images often appear to this effect on Western TV screens), but there are close parallels, both in the way the processions take place and in the spirit in which they are enacted, with practices in traditional Good Friday processions in many Catholic countries.

This parallel is echoed again in the *ta'zieh* – a form of traditional street theatre in which the events of Karbala and other incidents in the lives of the Emams are acted out, to the accompaniment of traditional verses – very like the mystery plays of medieval Europe. The *ta'zieh* may also be performed at other times of the year, but the usual time is at Ashura, the anniversary of Karbala, like the processions. In former times itinerant preachers called *rowzeh-khans* would visit villages and urban households to deliver the same verses telling the same stories from memory.

Many of the *zur-khaneh* ('houses of strength') in the towns also incorporated a religious element, venerating the Shi'a martyrs in their practices (though the *zur-khaneh* tradition is of obscure origin, and some argue that it includes significant pre-Islamic features). The *zur-khaneh* is a distinctively Iranian institution, in which men train for wrestling and for public performances of bare-chested brawniness, including the impressive juggling of large, heavy wooden clubs, performances of drumming and poetry recitations.[7]

These traditional, popular manifestations repeat and stress the wickedness of Yazid and the other oppressors of the Shi'a, and the virtue of Hosein and the other Emams. They are alien and often abhorrent to Sunni Muslims, elsewhere in the Islamic world, who regard them as idolatrous and as innovations not justified by religious texts. In 1979 they were familiar to all Iranians; even to socialists, secular nationalists, atheists or modernizers, soldiers or rich playboys who had turned away from Iran's religious tradition. The Ashura processions in particular made a template for the public expression of collective solidarity and moral feeling that was significant in the revolution – as well as reinforcing the common understanding among all classes of Shi'a beliefs about the Emams. The processions reconfirmed and reinforced ideas about the arrogance and corruption of power and wealth, and the virtue of modesty and poverty, that run deep in Shi'ism and in Islam more generally.

Two Revolutions

The revolution of 1979 was the second revolution of the twentieth century in Iran. The first happened in the years 1905–11, and is a convenient starting-point for considering the origins of the second.

Like many previous monarchies in Iran, going back to the time of the Achaemenids, the Qajar dynasty that ruled from 1796 until the 1920s did so with a relatively light touch. Turning their back on the example of eighteenth-century military monarchs like Nader Shah and the founder of the Qajar dynasty, Agha Mohammad Shah, the later Qajars employed only a small standing army. They relied instead on regional governors, who were often the leaders of local tribes, to maintain their authority in the further-flung parts of the country. Their rule had more the character of a system of alliances than that of the centralized government of a modern state.[8]

But this relatively weak state showed its disadvantages as the nineteenth century progressed and foreign powers began to take an increasing interest in Iran. Russia and Britain watched each other's involvement in Iran jealously – the Russians expanding their influence southwards; the British seeking to protect their possessions in India. With little coercive power within the borders of the country, and therefore little ability to raise taxes, the Qajar monarchs became increasingly dependent on loans from Russia and Britain, and they made economic concessions to them in return (the tobacco monopoly was just one example). This was unpopular with ordinary Persians, and especially with the *bazaaris*, who would be among the first to feel the economic damage from the foreigners' activities (some of them would also have benefited, but they tended to keep quiet). The economy, still predominantly agricultural, had also adjusted to outside pressures (cheap imports of food commodities and textiles in particular), changing from a simple subsistence structure with only small surpluses towards the production of cash crops for export. But this meant domestic production of food staples could no longer support an expanded population in times of famine or economic disruption.

In the later nineteenth century Naser od-Din Shah, who had ruled since 1848, had gone from an initially liberal position at his accession to a much more conservative stance, distrustful of reform. The early part of his reign had been marred by his removal and murder of the reforming prime minister Amir Kabir, and by government persecution of the Babi religious movement. The Babis were largely destroyed and driven into exile, where the movement evolved into an independent religion, the Bahai faith. Since that time, with just a few periods of respite, Bahais have been persecuted in Iran, sometimes viciously. By the 1890s Naser od-Din's finances were in a mess, the most efficient armed force in the country was officered by Russians (the Cossack brigade – only around 400–600 soldiers) and the national bank, the Imperial Bank of Persia, was run under the ownership of the British-based Baron Paul de Reuter (the founder of Reuters news agency).

When Naser od-Din Shah died in 1896, he was replaced on the throne by his more liberal-minded (but sickly) son, Mozaffar od-Din Shah, who removed censorship and constraints on political associations. The result was an upsurge in press and political activity, with new newspapers appearing, and the formation of political societies (*anjoman*). Many of these new newspapers and groups were critical of the government: the latest grievance was that the Shah's ministers had given control of customs to a Belgian, Joseph Naus. They were also saying, drawing upon Western models, that the country needed a proper constitution, that the arbitrary rule of the Shah had to be limited, and the rule of law regularized. Iranians (some of them at least) have been struggling for those things ever since, down to the present day.

In 1905 these various developments came to a head under the direct influence of a price crisis caused by a disruption of trade with Russia, following the abortive revolution and general turmoil in Russia that year. In the northern part of the country the price of sugar went up by a third and the price of wheat by 90 per cent. The government responded by accusing bazaar merchants of profiteering, but the slump in imports also brought a collapse in customs receipts and state revenues, which meant there was not enough money for the Shah to make his usual payments to some of the *ulema*, or to the small number of troops at his disposal.

After some demonstrations and unrest in June, in December 1905 two sugar merchants from the Tehran bazaar were given beatings on the feet (the bastinado or *falak*) at the orders of the governor of Tehran for charging too much for sugar. One of them was a respected elder figure who had paid to repair both the buildings of the bazaar itself, and three mosques. The bazaar merchants closed their shops, and several thousand *bazaaris*, religious students, *ulema* and others went to the shrine of Shah Abd ol-Azim to the south of the city, led by two senior clerics, Ayatollahs Behbehani and Tabatabai. From the sanctuary of the shrine (taking sanctuary in this way was called *bast*) they demanded the removal of the governor who had ordered the beatings, enforcement of shari'a law, dismissal of the Belgian, Naus, and the establishment of an *adalatkhaneh* (House of Justice – a representative assembly). After a month of stalemate the Shah gave in and accepted the protestors' demands.

But (as with earlier promises) the Shah made no attempt to convene the House of Justice, and in July 1906 there were further street protests by theological students when the government tried to take action against some radical preachers. One of the students, a *seyyed* (someone believed to be descended from the Prophet Mohammad), was shot dead by the police, which caused an uproar and more demonstrations, in which a further twenty-two were killed.[9] In the streets the Shah's government was denounced as the rule of Yazid, recalling Hosein and Karbala. Behbehani, Tabatabai, 2,000 *ulema* and their students left Tehran for Qom (then as now the main centre for theological study in the country), and a larger group of merchants, mullahs and others (eventually several thousand) took *bast* in the extensive grounds of the summer residence of the British legation at Qolhak, to the north of Tehran. The *ulema* and the *bazaaris* were effectively on strike, bringing the capital to a standstill. The Qolhak compound became an impromptu academy of political discussion and speculation, with liberal and nationalist intellectuals joining in and addressing the assembled crowds. Many of them spoke of the need to limit the powers of the Shah by establishing a constitution (*mashruteh*), and the demand for a House of Justice became more specific, shifting to a call for a properly representative national assembly (Majles). Coordinated by the *ulema*, like-minded groups from the provinces sent telegrams in support to the Shah.

One might think that the protection given to the constitutionalist opposition by the British legation in the summer of 1906 would have created goodwill toward the British among progressive-minded Iranians at least. But this did not happen, at least not in any lasting way. British hospitality toward the revolutionary opposition had more to do with weakening Russian influence at the Qajar court than any deep commitment to the fostering of representative institutions in Persia. For nearly a century Britain and Russia had been rivals in the country, but their rivalry had been aimed more at spoiling the position of the other in the short term than about winning Iranian affections or creating a partnership with Iran in the longer term. Russian expansionist motives were fairly plain; British motives (primarily, until the discovery of oil in Iran in 1908, concerned with the security of British India) had often been disguised under a mask of friendship and an ostensible commitment to development and liberal institutions. Britain had made alliances with Persia at the beginning of the nineteenth century, at the time of the Napoleonic wars, only to renege on them or slither out of their provisions when they became inconvenient. This had contributed to the humiliating loss of Persian territory in the Caucasus to Russia in 1813 and 1828. In the middle of the century Britain had intervened to prevent Persia from retaking Herat (part of Afghanistan today but a Persian territory before 1747). Eventually British policy turned against the constitutionalists and through the rest of the twentieth century was primarily interested in Iranian oil. For many Iranians Britain was the most dangerous of Iran's enemies, and (notwithstanding friendliness toward individuals) that reputation still lingers: the British have been thought to be devious, untrustworthy and always looking for new ways to damage Iran.[10]

On 5 August, threatened by a potential mutiny among the Cossack brigade, whom he had been unable to pay, Mozaffar od-Din Shah gave in again and signed an order for the convening of a national assembly. By this time the Shah was seriously ill. The Majles met for the first time in October 1906, and rapidly set about drafting a constitution, which was ratified by the Shah on 30 December (one story says that members of the *ulema* advised him, in the light of his many sins, to do one great good last thing before he died).[11] The revolutionaries had won their constitution. Mozaffar od-Din Shah died only five days later.

The Majles was elected on the basis of partial, not full, suffrage, on a two-stage system, and represented primarily the middle and upper classes (as was the case in most other countries with elected assemblies at the time). In each region electors voted for delegates to regional assemblies, and those delegates nominated 156 members for the Majles (except in Tehran, where they were elected directly). Outside the Majles, both in the capital and in the regional centres, the political changes and the elections stimulated the creation of more new political societies, some of which quickly grew powerful and influenced the deliberations of the Majles itself. Some represented occupations, others regions like Azerbaijan, others ethnic or religious groups. There were *anjoman* for women for the first time. There was another new wave of political activity and debate across the country, manifested also in the expansion in the number of newspapers; from just six before the revolution began to over 100.[12] This burgeoning of political consciousness was disturbing in itself to the more traditional-minded; especially to the more conservative members of the *ulema*.

The constitution stated explicitly that the Shah's sovereignty derived from the people, as a power given to him in trust; not as a right bestowed directly by God. But the power of the *ulema* and of Shi'ism as the dominant faith of the country was also confirmed in the constitution.[13] Shi'ism was declared to be the state religion, shari'a law was recognized, clerical courts were given a significant role, and there was to be a five-man committee of senior *ulema* to scrutinize legislation passed by the Majles, to confirm its spiritual legitimacy; until the Hidden Emam – whose proper responsibility this was – should reappear. But the civil rights of non-Shi'a minorities were also protected, reflecting the involvement of many Jews, Babis, Armenians and others in the constitutional project. Jews and Armenians had their own, protected seats for their representatives in the Majles. Many of these features reappeared in the post-1979 constitution.

Mozaffar od-Din Shah's successor, his son Mohammad Ali Shah, had more autocratic instincts than his father. He resolved from the start, although he took an oath of loyalty to the constitution, to overturn it and restore the previous form of untrammelled monarchy, with Russian help. Opposition to constitutionalism began also to harden from the religious side. Through 1907 and the first half of 1908 the Majles passed measures for the reform of taxation and finance, education and judicial matters. The last were particularly disturbing to the *ulema*, because they saw their traditional role encroached upon.

Sheikh Fazlollah Nuri was prominent among the *ulema* who changed their minds at this time. He had supported the protests of 1905–6 (which in most respects were quite conservative in motivation), but by 1907 he was saying that the Majles and its plans were leading away from the initial aims of the movement and that the constitutionalists were importing 'the customs and practices of the abode of disbelief' (i.e. the West). Eventually he shifted further, to express open support for the monarchy against the Majles, which he denounced as illegitimate. He also railed against Jews, Bahais and Zoroastrians, exaggerating their part in the constitutionalist movement. Other *mojtaheds*, like Tabatabai, were more willing to accept Western ideas into the framework of political structures that were necessary to govern human affairs in the absence of the Hidden Emam. But it is fair to say that Nuri understood better than many of the *ulema* the direction that constitutionalism was leading, and (from his perspective) the dangers of it. The general ferment of ideas had affected the *ulema* too, and the *ulema* had never been a united bloc of opinion (no more than any group of intellectuals ever is). The initial success of the revolution had opened up divisions within the revolutionary movement, as has happened with similar movements in other times and places (something similar happened in several countries in Europe in the revolutionary year of 1848–9). The shift of part of the *ulema* into opposition to the constitutional movement was ultimately fatal for the revolution.

In June 1908 the Shah decided that he had enough support to act and sent the Cossack brigade to attack the Majles. The troops fired shells at the building until the delegates gave in, and the assembly was closed. Many leading members were arrested and executed, while others escaped overseas. The Shah's coup was successful in Tehran, but not in all the provinces. Many of the most dedicated and enthusiastic constitutionalists came from Azerbaijan, which had long been one of the more agriculturally productive, densely populated and prosperous parts of the country, as well as socially and educationally more advanced. In the years around 1900 some of the inhabitants had travelled over the border into Russia for work, bringing back radical political ideas with them. Now, in Tabriz, the regional capital, delegates from the constitutionalist regional assembly and their supporters (notably the charismatic ex-brigand Sattar Khan) successfully held the city against the royal governor and his forces for a time. In doing so they had the help of a young teacher, Howard Baskerville, an idealistic American from Nebraska, only recently arrived in the city to work as a teacher. Baskerville fought alongside the constitutionalists and was eventually killed leading an attack on the besieging forces in April 1909.

In 1907, newly allied to each other and France, and concerned at Germany's burgeoning overseas presence, Britain and Russia had finally set aside their mutual suspicions and reached a treaty over their interests in Persia. The treaty showed no respect for the new conditions of popular sovereignty in the country (and proved inter alia that the apparent British protection of the revolutionaries in their legation in 1906 had little real significance). It divided Persia into three zones: a zone of Russian influence in the north (including Tabriz, Tehran, Mashhad and Isfahan – most of the major cities), a British zone in the south-east, adjacent to the border with British India, and a neutral zone in the middle.

One consequence of the treaty was that the Russians, following the Shah's coup of June 1908, intolerant as ever of any form of popular movement, were emboldened to send in troops to restore Qajar rule in Tabriz. But the nature of the electoral process for the Majles had helped to create a depth of resilience in the revolutionary movement. The regional assemblies set up in cities like Tabriz and Isfahan by the first stage of the process served as refuges and as centres of resistance for the constitutionalists, which meant that defeat in Tehran was not the end of the story. Even when the Russians took Tabriz some of the revolutionaries were able to escape to Gilan and continue their resistance with other locals there. In July 1909 they made a move on Tehran, coordinated with a move from the south, where revolutionaries in Isfahan had allied themselves with the local Bakhtiari tribe. As the revolutionaries moved back into the capital Mohammad Ali Shah fled to the Russian legation. He was deposed, went into exile in Russia, and was replaced by his young son, Ahmad (though Ahmad was not crowned until July 1914).

The constitutionalists were back in control, but the revolution had turned more dangerous. The divisions between radicals and conservatives had deepened, and the violence that had first destroyed and then reinstated the Majles also had its effect; many of the armed groups that had retaken the capital stayed on. Several prominent Bakhtiaris took office in the government. The *ulema* were divided, and many sided with the royalists, effectively rejecting the whole project of constitutionalism. But within a few days the leader of the conservative *ulema*, Nuri, was arrested, tried and hanged for his alleged connections with the coup of June 1908. Both wings of political opinion carried out a series of assassinations – Behbehani was killed, and later Sattar Khan. The radicals (the Democratic Party in the Majles) found themselves denounced by bazaar crowds as heretics and traitors and some of them were forced into exile. There was disorder in many provinces, it became impossible to collect taxes, tribal leaders took over in some areas, and brigandage became commonplace. To try to restore order, to counter the influence of the Russian-officered Cossack brigade, and above all to establish a body that could enforce tax collection, the Majles set up a gendarmerie trained by Swedish officers.

The constitutionalist government also appointed a young American, Morgan Schuster, as financial adviser. Schuster presented clear-sighted, wide-ranging proposals that addressed law and order and the government's control of the provinces as well as more narrowly financial matters; and began to put them into effect. But the Russians disliked Schuster and objected to his appointment of a British officer to head up the Swedish gendarmerie, on the basis that the appointment should not have been made within their sphere of influence without their consent. The British acquiesced. Schuster assessed, probably correctly, that the deeper Russian motive was to keep the Persian government's affairs in a state of chaotic bankruptcy, and thus in a position of relative weakness. If the Russians could keep the Persian government as a supplicant for Russian loans then they would be better able to manipulate it. Any determined effort to put the government of Persia on a sound financial footing, as Schuster's reforms threatened to do, was a threat to Russian interests. The Russians presented an ultimatum: Schuster had to go. A body of women surged into the Majles to demand that the ultimatum be rejected, and the Majles agreed, insisting that the American should stay. But the Russians sent troops to Tehran and as they drew near, the Bakhtiaris and conservatives in the cabinet carried through what was effectively another coup, and dismissed both Schuster and the Majles in December 1911.[14] That date is the one normally taken for the end, and the failure, of the Constitutional Revolution.

Like a love affair, a revolution can turn the familiar world upside down. It is easy for the participants to be so overwhelmed with delight at their initial success that they make mistakes later because they fail to grasp that the revolution will continue to revolve. While new possibilities may excite some, others may be afraid. New, previously concealed forces may be released. And however poignant the memory of the early days of unity and excitement, later developments and mistakes, however much regretted, make their loss irretrievable. In a revolution, new leaders emerge from unexpected directions, surprising those who were too quick to think themselves the masters, or proprietors. This happened in the French and in the Russian revolutions; also in the Iranian revolution of 1906–11. And also in 1979.

Schuster later wrote a book about his time in Iran called *The Strangling of Persia*, in which he expressed his admiration for the moral courage and determination of the people he worked with in Iran. The book explained much about the revolution, and about Iran at the time, but also about Schuster's attitudes to the country, and something of the reasons why he and by extension the US were so highly regarded by Iranians. Earnest, idealistic Americans like Schuster and Baskerville made a strong impression on Iranians at this time, as did wider US principles of anti-colonialism and self-determination, later promoted by Woodrow Wilson. The United States in this phase and later looked like the partner Iran had long hoped to find in the West; anti-colonial, liberal, progressive; modern, but not imperialist; a benevolent foreign power that would, for once, treat Iran with respect, as an agent in her own right, not as an instrument. That sentiment toward the US persisted, despite disappointments.

The efforts of well-meaning individuals like Schuster and Baskerville could do little enough to swing the balance in favour of the constitutionalists in 1906–11. The revolution fell victim to violent factionalism among the Iranians themselves, and also to the machinations of the Russians and the British. But the Constitutional Revolution was an important event, not just for Iran but for the region and arguably the world as a whole; and it was far from a complete failure. Apart from an abortive move in Ottoman Turkey in the 1870s, it was the first attempt in the Middle East by a people of the region to set up a liberal, representative government by its own efforts. The experience of representative government had a powerful, unifying effect in confirming and energizing Iranian nationalism. The spirit and the goals of constitutionalism stayed alive and vigorous, and were a major factor in Iranian political life for the rest of the century. Subsequent regimes repeatedly bypassed or flouted it, but the constitution of 1906 remained in force until the revolution of 1979. The Majles continued to be elected and to meet, and in 1919 was instrumental in preventing a post-war attempt to establish a British protectorate in Iran.

A young British officer in Persia at the time, Arnold Wilson, wrote sceptically and rather patronizingly after a long conversation with two optimistic Majles deputies on the road from Shiraz to Isfahan in 1907:

> The majlis will not work: it has no roots in the soil and no tradition: either the Qajars or some other dynasty will eventually destroy it ... but Persian nationalism will get stronger for it has roots and a tradition as old as Persia itself.[15]

Morgan Schuster blamed the Russians and the British for the failure of the revolution (and perhaps, by extension, the attitudes of some like Wilson). He wrote of the Majles:

> It was loyally supported by the great mass of the Persians, and that alone was sufficient justification for its existence.[16]

Ahmad Kasravi, who was a supporter of constitutionalism and also lived through the period of the revolution, blamed the split between the constitutionalists and the conservative clergy:

> So the people were of two minds. Bit by bit, a division appeared between the two ways of thinking, and when the mullahs did not see it in their interests to cooperate with the constitution and had to part, a big faction went with them. But the faction that stood fast did not find the way forward to struggle and remained confused. This faction of modernists could not show the people the way forward, either.[17]

All three views have some truth to them. Many of the alliances and interests that played out in 1906–11 made their appearance again in 1979. But the events of the Constitutional Revolution were also present in the minds of Iranians in the 1970s as a warning. In particular, the more politically minded among the clergy had learned the lesson that the *ulema* should not allow political leadership to slide out of their hands as they had in 1906.

Although the Qajar government, with Russian support, ostensibly regained its position in December 1911, it never really restored its authority in the country as a whole. In many parts of Iran local tribal leaders were the only authority, and in the north, in Gilan, an insurrection that came to be known as the Jangali movement (named after the dense forests of the region, which favoured guerrilla fighting), descended from the constitutionalist groupings of 1907–9, continued to fight the Russians and the monarchists for years under its charismatic leader, Kuchek Khan ('Little Khan').

Oil and War

Another story that begins in the time of the Constitutional Revolution is that of Iran and oil. One month before Mohammad Ali Shah ordered the Cossacks to fire on the Majles building in the summer of 1908, a British exploratory venture struck oil at Masjed-e Soleiman in Khuzestan in the south-west (on 26 May). This was the first major discovery of commercially viable oil in the Middle East, and the Anglo-Persian Oil Company (later the Anglo-Iranian Oil Company, eventually to become BP) was set up to exploit it. From this time onwards, the British government's prime interest in Persia was no longer directed at securing the borders of British India (as had been the case for a hundred years), but ensuring the continued supply of cheap Iranian oil. The importance of Iranian oil was led by the fact that the British fleet changed over from coal to oil to fuel its battleships at this time. Competition to build battleships was a focal point of the escalating tension between Britain and Germany – accelerating after the launch of HMS *Dreadnought* in 1906 – that helped to bring about the First World War. Iranian oil became a vital strategic asset for the security of the British Empire.

The contractual basis of the oil strike was a concession granted by the Persian government to the British commercial adventurer William Knox D'Arcy in 1901. Like other concessions granted to foreigners in those years, the terms were poor for the hosts: in the event of oil being discovered, they would only get 16 per cent of the profits. Successive governments were not able to break free from the D'Arcy concession until the 1950s, and over that period Iran got a bad return for such an important national asset.

The First World War deepened further the chaos that followed the end of the Constitutional Revolution. Iran was never a major theatre of war – was barely even a minor one – but at various times Ottoman,

Imperial Russian, British, Kurdish, Jangali, Bolshevik and all sorts of tribal forces were fighting in one part of the country or other. At one point in 1915 the Ottomans, with help from allied German officers, were in control of parts of the west and briefly hosted a Committee of National Resistance in Kermanshah, drawn from members of the Majles of 1914.[18] In and around Shiraz a talented German, Wilhelm Wassmuss, organized attacks against British interests in cooperation with local Qashqai tribesmen. The British countered by building alliances with other tribes in the south-west and by establishing a British-officered force recruited locally, the South Persia Rifles, to protect the oilfields. The Ottomans and Germans had some successes early on, but were pushed onto the defensive from 1917 onwards. Russian interest in Persia collapsed with the revolution of 1917 (although the Bolsheviks were active in northern Persia in 1919–20, working with the Jangalis) and with the collapse of the German and Ottoman war effort in 1918 the British were left dominant in Iran.

The British were dominant in the sense that the other external contenders had faded from the scene, but they were not in control. Iran came low on a long list of priorities, and Britain could not spare enough troops fully to impose order in the country. Britain was globally overstretched at the end of the First World War and heavily in debt. The British foreign secretary, Lord Curzon, had a particular interest in Iran: he had spent some time travelling through the country in 1889–90 and had written a weighty book afterwards – *Persia and the Persian Question*. But he seems to have dismissed the significance of the Constitutional Revolution, and his approach to the country was more redolent of the 1890s. His plan was for Iran to become a kind of British protectorate (similar to the arrangements being set up by the British in Egypt, Palestine and Iraq at the same time), with Iranian institutions functioning under British control, a British-officered army and Britain controlling the country's foreign policy. In return Iran would get help with economic development – railway construction, road building and so on.

Ahmad Shah's government, encouraged with bribes, accepted Curzon's plan (framed as the Anglo-Persian Agreement), but when its terms became more widely known there was a strong nationalist reaction against it across the country, and the Majles rejected it, which meant it could not legally enter into force. There followed a year or more of grim limbo. The country was in a desperate state. Law and order had broken down completely across wide areas; trade and economic activity generally had been disrupted and had slumped; fighting continued sporadically in parts; nomadic tribesmen raided towns and villages; and bandits made the roads unsafe for travellers. The north-west in particular had suffered widespread destruction in the fighting between the Russians and the Ottomans. There had been extensive famine in 1917–18, and more deaths had been caused among the weakened population by the influenza pandemic of 1918. In London Curzon still hoped to force through implementation of his plan, but in Iran British soldiers could see that the situation was hopeless: they did not have enough troops to hold their existing commitments safely, let alone pacify and police the whole country, which was turning increasingly hostile.

General Ironside, the senior British officer in the country at the end of 1920, without troubling to consult London over his intentions, found a solution that would enable him to withdraw British troops safely. The Cossacks, expanded to weak division strength during the war, still had Russian officers (marooned in Iran after the revolution of 1917). Ironside removed them and appointed Iranians from the ranks in their place. He then selected one of them, Reza Khan, as the de facto commander and gave him to understand that, if he were to march on Tehran and set up a military government, British forces would not stand in his way.

In February 1921, Reza Khan did just that, and set up a new government in association with a mixed group of nationalists and former constitutionalists. British troops withdrew, maintaining only a presence in the south-west to protect the oil. Less than five years later, having defeated the Jangalis and some tribal resistance in the provinces, Reza Khan had himself crowned as the first Shah of a new dynasty, the Pahlavi dynasty. The name Pahlavi derived from the name given to the pre-Islamic language of Iran (otherwise known as Middle Persian), but the term drew colour also from the fact that the heroes of the *Shahnameh* had been called *Pahlavan*; the latter word was also used for the contemporary strongmen of the *zur-khaneh*.

The Pahlavi Dynasty

From the beginning the Pahlavi monarchy was a strange creation. When Reza Shah was crowned in 1926 he had been prime minister for three years under the authority of Ahmad, the last Qajar Shah, and he had attempted unsuccessfully to make the country a republic in 1924 (just after Mustapha Kemal had deposed the Ottoman Sultan and made himself president of the new Republic of Turkey, in October 1923). Reza Shah's family origins were obscure – no hint of any royal or even aristocratic forebears. The monarchy was a parvenu regime that resembled other nationalist military dictatorships of the 1920s and 30s elsewhere, with the difference that it came later to be seen in the eyes of many Iranians (somewhat unfairly) as tainted from the outset by the hand of the British in its establishment.

A revolution, a military coup and a military dictator who makes himself a monarch: a familiar pattern. Like Napoleon, Reza Shah inherited many of his initial supporters and much of his programme from the revolution that preceded his time. Many constitutionalists supported him as a strong leader who would restore order and bring in reforms that would develop the country (so far they were right) – realizing too late just how autocratic and illiberal his instincts were. But Reza Shah was not Napoleon. He lacked Napoleon's triumphal prestige and his freedom of action. Similarly, he fell short of the model closer to him in time and place – Mustapha Kemal (Atatürk) in Turkey.

At the start, Reza Shah had a lot of support, including from many of the *ulema*. Notable constitutionalists like Abdolhosein Teymurtash and Hasan Taqizadeh joined his government as ministers. Others who had opposed Reza Shah, like Seyyed Hasan Modarres (probably the most prominent surviving pro-constitutionalist among the clergy, who had been instrumental in the rejection of the Anglo-Persian Agreement), tried to negotiate a settlement that left room for liberal government – but failed.

Ordinary people wanted predictability, order and stability to return to their lives, and the chance for economic recovery. Reza Shah delivered that. His priority from the first was to build a modern army, and in the 1920s 40 per cent of state expenditure was devoted to it. Already in 1922 he had brought forward a plan for an army of 50,000 men. By the later 1930s the army was 100,000 strong, and because it was based on conscription, there were a larger number of reservists who could be called upon in time of war. The army was used to pacify the country,[19] and especially the more troublesome nomadic tribes – who still made up perhaps a quarter of the population at this time. The tribes disliked conscription, and enforcement of conscription served as an additional pacifying measure. The policy was implemented brutally, but the majority of the population would have approved of strong measures – for most Iranians of the towns and villages the previous independence of the tribes carried no romantic connotations. It signified disorder, danger, brigandage, unpredictability and weak central control. The income that Reza Shah's new government derived from oil was spent almost entirely on military equipment, including artillery, tanks and aircraft.

But the army could not exist in isolation, and its efficiency demanded wider changes in the country – many of which echoed earlier, failed reform programmes. Financial administration and taxation were reformed. Ambitious plans for road and rail construction were brought forward and implemented. New industries were set up (notably in areas like textiles and foodstuffs), aimed at stemming imports and keeping capital within the country by supplying demand domestically. Some were fostered as state monopolies. Perhaps most importantly for the future, education was greatly expanded. By 1938 school attendance was over 450,000 by comparison with 55,000 in 1922 (out of a total population of around 12 million). Secondary school attendance went up proportionally; the Shah established the country's first full university in Tehran (including a theology faculty, and with it the opportunity for religion to be taught in Iran as a phenomenon, rather than simply as the Truth); and the government gave scholarships to talented students to study in universities abroad.[20] The education provided was somewhat narrow and technocratic, aimed at producing efficient officers and administrators rather than encouraging independent thought, but it is seldom possible for the state fully to manipulate the uses to which individuals may put the education they have been given. Most of the new schools were in towns and cities – the illiteracy of the majority of Iranians, who still lived in the villages and in the countryside, was almost untouched.

Like those of Atatürk in Turkey, Reza Shah's policies followed a nationalist, secularizing pattern that sought to modernize the country on a Western model. They reasserted the position of Iran against foreign interference, but also sought to push the *ulema* aside. The educational reforms aimed at giving a Western-style education rather than the traditional Koran-based education of the *madreseh*. The Shah brought in a wholesale reconstruction of the legal system, with courts supervised by secular judges and civil and penal legal codes designed along European lines. For a time this went in parallel with the traditional shari'a legal framework; then in 1936 the religious courts were abolished. But a Westernizing programme did not mean subservience to Western powers. Reza Shah also, in 1927–8, abolished the treaties (aptly named Capitulations) by which foreigners had enjoyed exceptional legal status in the country. He avoided using British or Russian technical advisers for his development projects (from the countries with the worst record of interference in Iran), preferring to use Germans, Frenchmen or Italians. He renationalized the administration of customs in 1927, and the central bank in 1930 as Bank Melli – the 'National Bank'. In 1935 the Shah directed foreign embassies to stop using the name Persia in diplomatic correspondence, telling them instead to use the name Iran. This reform was in one way simply an assertion of self-determination – the term Iran had been the word used by Iranians for their country since the time of the Sassanids, at least. But Reza Shah probably intended it also to distance his regime from that of the Qajars, who had acquiesced, in this as in other ways, in letting foreigners determine too much of what went on in the country (the name Persia had been used since classical times in the West, deriving ultimately from the fact that the Achaemenid dynasty of Cyrus and Darius I, with which the Greeks had fought lengthy wars, had originated in the province of Persis – Pars (modern Fars).

Reza Shah did not, like Atatürk in Turkey, attempt to replace Arabic script with Roman. But he did copy Atatürk's reform of Turkish by trying to impose a reform of Persian to exclude words of Arabic or non-Iranian origin. Most controversially, he ordered that Iranians wear Western dress, banning traditional robes and headgear, and most radically of all, banning the veil for women. Many women simply ceased to go out of doors, and the new rules provoked strong opposition. A protest in Mashhad in 1935 culminated in the Shah's troops opening fire on demonstrators in the precincts of the shrine of the Emam Reza, which caused greater resentment.

There was a wider mood of secularizing nationalism among intellectuals at this time. Tending to blame reactionary mullahs for the failure of the constitutional revolution, such nationalists went further, to blame the *ulema* and Islam as a whole for Iran's backwardness. Nationalists looked back to the pre-Islamic past, to what they thought of as a purer

Iran, before the Arab conquest. The mood fitted with some of the attitudes of the Shah and his regime, but was not simply a function of regime
self-projection – as time wore on some of the writers became critical of
the Pahlavi regime too.

Three Writers

Ahmad Kasravi was a central figure among the nationalist thinkers
and writers of this time. He wrote extensively on Iranian history and politics; including the most important history of the Constitutional
Revolution. Kasravi came from Azerbaijan, from a family of Turkic origin, and spoke Azeri Turkish as his mother tongue – a good example of
the way that Iranian culture and even Iranian nationalism have transcended narrow ethnic categories. He was born in Tabriz in 1890, to a
clerical family, was given training in a seminary (though he also attended
the American Memorial School in which Baskerville had taught) and was
involved in the dramatic events of the Constitutional Revolution in
Azerbaijan. In his early days as a student Kasravi turned away from his
religious training (according to one story, this happened when he discovered that Western scientists had predicted the reappearance of Halley's
comet in 1910) and became a wickedly intelligent critic of the *ulema* – but
also a critic of many other aspects of contemporary Iranian society. One of
his pamphlets, entitled *What Is the Religion of the Hajjis with Ware-
houses?*, poured scorn on bazaar traders who were keen to present
themselves as pious Muslims, but whose commercial and general behaviour was amoral, grasping and hypocritical. Another, entitled *Hasan Is
Burning His Book of Hafez*, attacked the disposition, as he saw it, of
many Iranians to substitute quotation from the classic Persian poets for
genuine thought – illustrating (albeit negatively) the centrality of that
great poetic tradition in Iranian cultural life.[21] Like many of his generation Kasravi was a committed believer in the principles of constitutionalism
and secular government. He was a nationalist, and attacked the linguistic
and other divisions that had created suspicion between Iranians and, in
his opinion, had made them weak. He worked for many years in the Ministry of Education and as a journalist and writer. In 1946 he was
assassinated by a group called the Fedayan-e Eslam, followers of a man

who had chosen to call himself Navvab Safavi (thereby associating him-self with the dynasty that had imposed Shi'ism on Iran).[22] The Fedayan-e Eslam dedicated themselves to eliminating those they identified as the enemies of Islam.

Kasravi was significant for a number of different reasons. He stood for a strand of thinking in Iran, typical of the Pahlavi period, which became important again in the 1960s and 70s, and which rejected the backward-ness of Shi'ism as it was practised, blaming it for many of the weaknesses and failures of the country (though his anticlericalism was less extreme than that of some others). His thinking was a key influence on a genera-tion of educated, middle-class Iranians who benefited from the opportunities that arose under the Pahlavis; and on the generation of intellectuals and writers that followed him.

Sadegh Hedayat was a more radical writer in a variety of ways: more troubled, and more of a loner. Born into an a quasi-aristocratic family of courtiers and scribes in Tehran in 1903, he travelled to France on one of Reza Shah's first scholarships and studied a series of different sub-jects including architecture and dentistry there in the later 1920s, but never took a degree. As a young man he became an enthusiast for a romantic, sometimes chauvinistic Iranian nationalism that laid much of the blame for Iran's problems on the Arab conquest of the seventh cen-tury. His short stories and novellas like *Talab-e Amorzesh* (*Seeking Absolution*), *Sag-e Velgard* (*Stray Dog*) and his best-known, *Buf-e Kur* (*The Blind Owl*) combined the everyday, the fantastic and the satirical, rejecting religion, superstition and Arabic influence, but in an innova-tive, modernist style combined with a relentlessly honest observation of everyday life. He translated works by Kafka, Chekhov and Sartre into Persian (he knew Sartre in Paris). His writing reflected contemporary European existentialism and the influence of those writers; but he was also an enthusiast for the poetry of Omar Khayyam, and translated texts from the pre-Islamic Sassanid period into modern Persian. In his last years, after a period of renewed vitality after the fall of Reza Shah, his writing grew more bitter and pessimistic again. His story *Tup-e Morvarid* (*The Pearl Cannon* – published in 1947) included diatribes against the government of Reza Shah, as well as the writing of history, colonialism, Islam and the clergy (the passages on religion include some of the most forthright condemnations of Islam written in any language).

He never joined the Tudeh Party, but like many others at the time was sympathetic to it.[23] Hedayat committed suicide in Paris in 1951 by gassing himself. He was buried in Père Lachaise cemetery.

Unlike Kasravi, Hedayat received little attention in his own lifetime and was regarded by his family as a failure who could not hold down a job. Financial and family problems contributed to his suicide. He only acquired his reputation as the prime modernist prose writer of twentieth-century Iran after his death, partly because other writers like Jalal Al-e Ahmad and Mohammad Ali Jamalzadeh drew public attention to his work.

Mohammad Ali Jamalzadeh was a little older than Hedayat – he was born in Esfahan in 1892, the son of a well-known constitutionalist cleric, Seyyed Jamal al-Din Esfahani, who was murdered in prison in 1908 at the orders of Mohammad Ali Shah. Jamalzadeh himself was a committed constitutionalist and joined a group of like-minded exiles led by Hasan Taqizadeh in Berlin during the First World War. While there he contributed to the political magazine *Kaveh*, which had been established by Taqizadeh and others. It was a political journal, anti-British and anti-Russian, but also included historical and literary material. At the end of the war it became less partisan, but continued to favour the principles behind constitutionalism. Jamalzadeh published several articles and other pieces in *Kaveh*; most notably 'Farsi shekar ast' in 1921 (literally, 'Persian Is Sugar' – usually translated as 'Persian Is Sweet'). This was a short story, written in a realist style and using simple, colloquial Persian to satirize both the language of the mullahs, often overburdened by vocabulary and constructions taken from Arabic, and that of the Western-educated, full of loan words from French and other European languages. Later the same year it was republished with five other stories in a collection with the title *Yeki bud, yeki nabud* (literally, *There Was One, There Wasn't One*: the phrase used to introduce children's stories in Persian – the equivalent of 'Once upon a time'). It created a furore – attacked by some of the clergy, but welcomed by many other writers and intellectuals as a breath of fresh air. Many later writers of short stories in Iran followed Jamalzadeh's lead (including Hedayat). Jamalzadeh wanted Iranian literature to avoid over-complicated language that aped the usage of other countries. Politically, he was against foreign interference in Iran and against the dead hand of intolerant, traditionalist clergy within Iran. From 1931 until his retirement in 1956 he worked at the International Labour Organization in Geneva, but continued to write and publish in Iran, especially after 1941, when censorship was lifted. He held true to his constitutionalist principles, and the principles of the European Enlightenment. Jamalzadeh visited Iran but continued to live in Geneva, and died there in 1997.[24]

Writers like Kasravi, Hedayat and Jamalzadeh, building on the sacred tradition of Persian poetical literature, created a new prose literature in Persian and carved out an important new role for writers in the life of Iran – not just in literature but also in politics; as standard-bearers for political and cultural values – as cultural heroes. Plenty more followed in their path in later decades.

Reza Shah's policies brought the country many benefits, but by the later 1930s the shine had come off his rule. Most of the constitutionalist politicians he had appointed as ministers had been removed. Some went into exile – others were murdered in prison. The constitutionalist cleric Modarres was killed in prison too (in 1938). The Shah was suspicious, and his treatment of political dissent, or failure, was harsh. His court minister, Teymurtash, was imprisoned after he failed to get better terms for the exploitation of Iran's oil from the British, and he died in prison in 1933. The cause of death was given officially as heart failure; but he was generally believed to have been murdered on the Shah's orders (as with other political prisoners in those years, the story was that he was one of the victims of Dr Ahmad Ahmadi, whose favourite technique was allegedly to inject air into a vein, which caused cardiac arrest when the air bubble found its way back to the heart).

The Shah later secured a marginal improvement in the revenue he got for Iran's oil; an increase in the share of the profits from 16 to 20 per cent; but the failure to get a properly fair division of the benefits and the continuing presence of the British AIOC in the country was a persistent humiliation, especially as other countries, with whom oil companies made deals later in the century as oil exploration uncovered new reserves, made deals yielding a better return to the host country. It is instructive to compare Reza Shah's Iran with Atatürk's Turkey. Atatürk was able to remove all the concessions his Ottoman predecessors had made, and to eliminate every vestige of foreign interference in Turkey – no external power controlled any asset to compare with Iranian oil. And Atatürk never lapsed into dictatorial paranoia. He maintained his commitment to representative government – albeit a trammelled version of it – and ended his life in his own bed, in his own country, still revered by his fellow countrymen (and for long after his death). The Pahlavis never properly learned the value of politics as a lightning-rod to make safe the dangers of political dissent. Perhaps Reza Shah never shook off the contempt for popular politics that he learned from the Tsarist Russian officers of the Cossack brigade.

By the later 1930s the Shah had alienated many Iranians, and a similar dangerous combination of opposition forces to that which had caused the revolution of 1906–11 had begun to form. Most hostile were the *ulema*, who saw traditional values abused and alien Western principles followed in their stead. They had been pushed out of their roles in education and law. Their close confederates in the bazaar were uneasy at the Shah's reforms of the economy and were aggrieved at the way state monopolies took profits out of their hands. But most of the liberal intellectuals were hostile too. Some of their number had been killed in prison, others had gone into exile, and it was not safe for any that remained to express criticism of the Shah. In 1937 he turned on a new generation of intellectuals: some politically minded young students returned from study in Europe, including both fascist sympathizers and Marxists, were arrested and imprisoned. His rule had become repressive and brutal. Incidents like the shooting in Mashhad roused the deep-seated Shi'a distrust of secular power, and the abuse of it.

Another aspect to the Shah's nationalism was an element of pro-German Aryanism. The emphasis on linguistic purity and on pre-Islamic Iran led some further, to an idea of an Aryan/Indo-European identity that made some kind of racial commonality between, for example, Aryan Germans and Aryan Iranians (there is, of course, a common linguistic root[25] – but since the 1930s it has become clearer that race, culture and language can be very different things; and genetic research makes race as a concept increasingly problematic). In the 1930s some Germans advised the Shah's government on his linguistic policy, and there were German technicians in the country helping with engineering and other projects. But a large part of the Shah's apparent pro-German inclination was based on the simple fact that the Germans were not British. The Shah was keen above all to maintain the limited degree of independence he had achieved.

With the outbreak of war in 1939 that independence became more problematic. In 1941 the strategic situation in the Middle East was dangerously fluid, and the supply of oil from Iran was as vital as ever. Iran had again declared neutrality, but the British government demanded that the Shah should expel German nationals from the country. The Shah refused, the British and Russians invaded, and the Iranian army was mobilized, but proved no match for the invaders; within a few weeks, in September 1941, Allied troops entered Tehran.

War and Occupation

Reza Shah abdicated in favour of his son, Mohammad Reza, and went into exile. He died in South Africa in 1944. Some have suggested that the British moved into Iran not because Reza Shah was too pro-German, but because they feared a pro-German coup against him (as had just happened in Iraq).[26] But the outcome was the same – another occupation, and rule by the Allies (with the US joining in later) until 1945.

There was no popular outcry at Reza Shah's removal. Many Iranians felt relief, and the tribes in particular were able to return to their traditional ways of life. An American, Arthur Millspaugh, returned to the country to administer state finances (he had served a similar function in Reza Shah's earlier years, but had fallen out with the Shah over military spending). Another American, H. Norman Schwarzkopf (father of the military commander who led Operation Desert Storm in Iraq in 1991) also played a significant part in the years of occupation. Having been gassed during the First World War, after which he joined the New Jersey State Police, he had made a name for himself through his involvement in the Lindbergh kidnapping case and publicizing colourful exploits against gangsters.[27] In Iran he headed a US military mission and supervised an Imperial gendarmerie that restored order when trouble broke out in different parts of the country. Americans were more acceptable to Iranians in these roles than other foreigners.

The period of occupation was another episode of political and intellectual ferment, similar to that of the early years of the century. Reza Shah's censorship regime was lifted, political prisoners were released, new political parties and labour organizations formed, and there was another outpouring of journalistic activity. It was also the time when radio and radio broadcasts began to reach a large proportion of the population – another novelty that helped Iranians to feel part of a nation, that national politics belonged to and involved them.

But, impelled by this new freedom (of a kind), the intellectual mood was shifting. In the 1940s many writers moved toward a leftist position, aligning themselves with the Tudeh Party, which formed in 1941 almost as soon as Reza Shah had gone; founded by some of the leftist students he had imprisoned in 1937. Notable among the founders was Khalil Maleki, who also persuaded the young Jalal Al-e Ahmad to join.

Tudeh (the name means 'The Masses') was set up initially as a social democratic party, but quickly moved to a communist position, aligning itself with Moscow for the most part.[28] Tudeh drew support from large numbers of workers in the new state-sponsored industries. It was well organized and consolidated that support in the later 1940s by successfully pushing through social legislation, including a minimum wage. But the educated middle class had also grown, and with it support for the liberal democratic tradition that still espoused the values of the Constitutional Revolution.

Tudeh's pro-Soviet alignment was exposed at the end of the war, when the Soviet Union backed separatist republics in Iranian Azerbaijan and Kurdestan (the latter probably represented the political aspirations of the local population rather more than the former). The Soviet Union also claimed an oil concession in the north-west, which made its actions resemble Tsarist policy, and Tudeh had to support the concession. The US and Britain demanded that the Soviets withdraw their troops from Iran, as had been agreed previously, but the Russians refused, and for a time there was a stalemate. Internationally, the confrontation was the first of its kind in what was to become the Cold War, but it also roused further the spirit of Iranian nationalism that had already been stimulated by the foreign occupation and the relaxation of previous political restrictions. The Soviets eventually withdrew; the army regained some of the credit with Persian-speaking nationalists that it had lost in 1941 by moving in to crush the pro-Soviet republics, and Tudeh lost much of its credibility. Hundreds of Azeris and Kurds who tried to defend their separatist republics were killed, and thousands fled over the border into the Soviet Union, including perhaps 10,000 Kurds.[29] With the last Allied troops withdrawn from Iran, political attention turned to another unresolved nationalist grievance – the oil question.

Mossadeq, Oil Nationalization and Ayatollah Kashani

By the 1950s world oil production had spread and diversified to many new countries, and oil companies were exploiting reserves in Iraq, Saudi Arabia, Venezuela and Mexico. In each of these places European and/or American companies had made deals with the host governments to exploit the oil, but all the more recent contracts of this kind had been on much better terms for the hosts (after some of them had found effective ways to exert pressure for change) than the terms of the Iranian contract with the AIOC. A 50/50 split of profits between host country and oil company had become the standard arrangement. But the AIOC (with the backing of the British government, long a majority shareholder) were obstinately reluctant to renegotiate. Britain was even more desperate economically after the Second World War than after the first, with a critical balance of payments deficit, and could not contemplate losing its supply of cheap oil.

A significant figure in opposition to the Allied occupation and against British exploitation of Iranian oil was Ayatollah Abol-Qasem Kashani. He was not one of the most senior *ulema* (Ayatollah Borujerdi was the senior *marja* at the time and supported the monarchy), but his forthright position on political matters gave him special prominence. Unlike some other *ulema*, after the experience of the 1930s he regarded the constitution as a potential protection against the dictatorial power of a secularizing monarch.[30] Kashani was imprisoned during the war by the Allies (his father, also a cleric, had died fighting the British during the revolt of 1921 in Iraq).[31] He served in the Majles as speaker. He had a following in the Majles and among the *bazaaris*, but also had connections with Nav-vab Safavi and the Fedayan-e Eslam, the extremist Islamic group who had assassinated Kasravi.

The years following the Second World War were important for the development of Iranian politics. The monarchy was still relatively weak under the young Shah, and once the occupying foreign powers had left the country the interlude of political freedom was sustained. The central figure to emerge out of this new ferment was Mohammad Mossadeq, who formed a coalition of parties – the National Front – around the nationalist, liberal principles of the Constitutional Revolution. Mossadeq was descended from the Qajar royal family. He had been educated in Switzerland and had first entered politics before the First World War. He had opposed Reza Shah in the 1920s and 30s and had withdrawn from politics, to emerge again after Reza Shah's abdication. His populist speechmaking (his voice had a distinctive sing-song quality)[32] and his use of new media have since prompted a comparison between him and other anti-colonialist politicians active in the 1950s, like Nasser in Egypt and Sukarno in Indonesia. He had an emotional and passionate nature that lent itself to this role. He saw the monarchy as the main enemy of liberal democracy in Iran – but he was no great friend of the *ulema* either. At one point in the crisis that followed, according to one story, some of Mossadeq's supporters put a pair of spectacles on a dog and named it 'Ayatollah'. They showed it in the Majles and then took it through the streets. Years later Khomeini commented how at the time he had said Mossadeq should be slapped – 'and it was not long before he was slapped; had he survived, he would have slapped Islam.'[33]

Mossadeq became prime minister in April 1951, having led the Majles in a vote to nationalize Iranian oil the previous month. His oil policy was hugely popular – and Ayatollah Kashani's commitment to that cause meant that he supported Mossadeq too, bringing with him an important slice of traditional, conservative, clerical and *bazaari* opinion. But he also needed the support of the Tudeh Party. Tudeh had been banned officially in 1949, in the aftermath of a failed attempt on the Shah's life, but regrouped and continued on an underground basis; as time went on the party came forward again, and the ban, though technically still in force, was passed over more and more.[34] Mossadeq also intended to limit the power of the Shah and establish the country on a permanent basis as a modern, constitutional monarchy. He thought the US would help, as in the time of Schuster, Baskerville and Millspaugh.

The British government set about mobilizing international support against oil nationalization and against Mossadeq. AIOC technicians left the country, and Britain imposed an oil blockade. The oil industry suddenly became a burden on the economy and the state, as the government had to pay maintenance costs and workers' wages, with no revenue coming in. Inflation began to rise, and unemployment too. Having grown strongly since 1945, the economy slumped.[35] Tudeh remained steadfast in their support for Mossadeq, but support from others began to waver. Mossadeq pressed on boldly, including with divisive measures like land reform. But as the fiscal and economic strain intensified, and uncertainty about the direction of his programme spread, he leaned more heavily on Tudeh, and doubts within and without the country about communist influence also strengthened.

The standard view of the events that toppled Mossadeq says that he was removed by a coup orchestrated by the CIA and the British Secret Intelligence Service. But the reality was more complex. In particular, the role of the clergy in the fall of Mossadeq has sometimes been neglected. Many senior clergy had opposed Mossadeq and supported the monarchy from the outset.

By the summer of 1953 the US and the British were ready to act in Iran to remove Mossadeq. It might seem strange that the US fell in with the British government in this resolve, but this was a strange time in US politics. It was the era of Senator Joe McCarthy and the House Committee on Un-American Activities, of the Dulles brothers heading the State Department and the CIA. Mossadeq's populism, his attacks on the Shah, whom the US regarded as their prime ally in the country, the anti-Westernism and anti-capitalism of some among Mossadeq's supporters and above all his ambiguous but apparently close relationship with Tudeh made him suspect for the policy-makers of the Eisenhower administration. This was perhaps combined with a certain lack of confidence in Middle East affairs that led the US to listen too readily to British arguments. The communist threat was the prime danger, and other actors and forces were seen as useful or otherwise only in relation to the struggle against communism. In those terms, Mossadeq just wasn't anti-communist enough.

In reality Mossadeq was more pro-US than many other politicians in the region – Nasser in Egypt, for example (to whom the US effectively gave their support, against the British interest, in the Suez crisis three years later). Mossadeq's doomed efforts to secure American help showed poignant faith in fundamental American values. With US backing Mossadeq could have governed effectively and popularly in Iran and kept Tudeh in their place. Or (more likely) he might have failed later, under the weight of his own errors, as democratic politicians generally do. But he did not get the chance.

In 1952 Mossadeq's position was confirmed by a new election, and by a crisis in July (known afterwards as the *Si-ye Tir*) between him and the Shah, over who had the right to appoint the minister for war. Mossadeq briefly resigned, but the Shah had to reappoint him when public feeling expressed itself in widespread demonstrations and riots. Mossadeq had faced down the Shah, and he was able to face down opposition to his land reform plans from the conservative landowners, but only by taking emergency powers that neutralized their grip on the upper house of parliament, the senate. Gaining confidence, he appointed secular-minded and anticlerical ministers, and his government brought forward policies for further nationalization, which appeared to threaten *bazaari* interests.[36] Kashani and his followers, having supported Mossadeq in July, began to express doubts about the government's actions against the constitution. They also protested against plans to extend the vote to women, and to rescind a ban on the sale of alcohol. When Mossadeq asked for an extension of his emergency powers, clerical members of the Majles who supported Kashani left the National Front coalition and set up their own Islamic fraction.

So although a referendum in July 1953 again showed huge support for Mossadeq, there were doubts about the fairness of the poll, and important leaders of the traditional middle class – the clergy and the *bazaaris* – had gone over to the conservative, monarchist side (as had also happened in 1906–7, of course). There were demonstrations against Mossadeq, and CIA-sponsored newspaper articles agitated against him. This was the background against which Kermit Roosevelt Jr – grandson of Theodore 'Teddy' Roosevelt – coordinated a CIA operation in Tehran with a group of Iranian army officers (the Americans called it Operation Ajax; the British, who first put forward the idea, gave it the more prosaic codename 'Boot'). The plan was for a coup that would appoint one of the Iranian officers, General Fazlollah Zahedi, as prime minister in place of Mossadeq. In July–August 1953 they put their plan into effect. The Shah's twin sister, the formidable Princess Ashraf, came back to Tehran from the Riviera to persuade the Shah, who was fearful and hesitating, to sign the documents necessary for Mossadeq to be removed. At first Mohammad Reza refused even to see her, but eventually they had a stormy interview on 29 July. Schwarzkopf also returned, and did his best (they met on 1 August), but the Shah did not actually sign until 12 August.[37]

The Shah

Mohammad Reza Shah was thirty-three years old in the summer of 1953. He had been educated in Switzerland, and his youth had been dominated by his father; always a severe, daunting man, who as time had gone on had become ever more domineering and distrustful of ordinary Iranians. These experiences and traits all left their mark on his son, who grew up to be diffident, rather remote, lacking in confidence and without any kind of easy or natural connection with the people he was to govern – but with a firm sense of duty and a compulsion to continue his father's work. His first decade as Shah had been traumatic. His father's deposition and death had been followed by the failure of his first marriage to the strikingly beautiful but spoiled Princess Fawzia, daughter of the King of Egypt, who abandoned and divorced him in 1945: after her racy, Westernized lifestyle in Alexandria, she had found the court in Tehran backward, dour and claustrophobic. His divorce of her according to Iranian law, after the humiliating failure of attempts at reconciliation, followed only in 1948.

In February 1949, as the Shah entered Tehran University to award diplomas, a man walked up to him and fired five shots at point-blank range. Three went through Mohammad Reza's hat, then one through his cheek. In a bizarre moment of black comedy, the Shah tried to confuse the assassin and dodge the bullets – 'I suddenly started shadow-dancing or feinting.' The man fired again, and another bullet hit Mohammad Reza in the shoulder. The pistol jammed with the sixth round,[38] after which the would-be assassin was gunned down by the Shah's bodyguards, who had by then remembered their job. 'I had the queer and not unpleasant sensation of knowing that I was still alive,' the Shah said later. The man was found to have been a member of Tudeh, and this was the incident that caused the party to be banned. The attack shook the Shah (there was another attempt in 1965) and led him to adopt tighter security – security that went to even greater lengths in later years and contributed significantly to his distancing from ordinary Iranians. In the early 1950s the young Shah was confident of neither his own abilities, nor his judgement, nor his standing with his people.

Mohammad Reza remarried in 1951, to another beautiful woman, the half-German Soraya Esfandiari Bakhtiari; unlike his first, this marriage was a happy one, but was again to end in divorce seven years later, after it became apparent that Soraya could not give him children. After the divorce, Soraya wrote a memoir that gave some insights into the character of the young Shah. He liked fast cars and was a keen pilot, having learned to fly in the 1940s. But he had a near-fatal crash in 1944,[39] and those who had to fly with him were not always so cheerful about it:

On another occasion we were flying to Isfahan. I was seated in the cockpit, next to the Shah . . . Suddenly I saw that the engine had cut out and that we were losing altitude with terrifying speed . . . Then the Shah noticed that the fuel tanks were as good as empty. At the last moment, when we had almost crashed into the mountains, we began to pump petrol furiously from the reserve tank and thus gained just enough altitude to clear their peaks.

After this incident I was somewhat dubious about the return flight that same evening. This time I sat in the cabin, next to General Zahedi, and we reached Tehran without trouble. As we were circling the airfield . . . Zahedi said:

'There's nothing more for your Majesty to worry about. We're here.'

'Keep your fingers crossed,' I replied. 'We haven't put down yet.'

Mohammad Reza came lower, the wheels touched the runway, but we did not come to a standstill. Just before we reached the end of the runway the Shah gave his engine gas and the plane's nose went up. It almost scraped the roofs of a couple of houses.

'God God!' I shouted. 'Didn't the undercarriage come down properly?'

'It's nothing,' said the Shah. 'There was a man standing at the end of the runway, and it made me nervous.'

After ten minutes he tried again, but . . . exactly the same thing happened. It was simply his nerves. The Shah said:

'I'll manage it next time.'

The officer in the control tower, however, alerted the fire-engines and the ambulance. When the Shah's third attempt to land was equally unsuccessful, that officer suggested, in polite tones:

'If your Majesty has enough fuel, it would be better to circle for a quarter of an hour or so, until you are feeling more yourself.'

Thereupon Zahedi and the other passengers took out their copies of the Koran and began to say their prayers. They murmured these softly, so as not to make the Shah more nervous than he already was. But Allah must have heard them all the same, for eventually we landed on the runway, though with such a lurching and bumping that my hat ended up three hundred yards from where we did.

One result of this day was that I felt a growing dislike of flying . . .[40]

Coups That Fail, and Coups That Succeed

On the night of 15/16 August 1953 Colonel Nasiri of the Imperial Guard led an armoured column to Mossadeq's residence in Tehran to deliver the *ferman* (royal decree) removing him from office. But the plotters had taken too long to put their plan into effect, and news of it had leaked. Nasiri was intercepted on Mossadeq's doorstep by officers loyal to the elected government, commanded by General Riahi, the chief of staff. They arrested Nasiri and put him behind bars. In the morning Tehran Radio announced that a coup attempt had been foiled.[41] Mossadeq himself came on air and named the Shah and unspecified foreigners as the instigators. Within minutes of the broadcast, taking only Soraya, the pilot and one other companion with him, the Shah flew out of the country in a light aircraft, to Baghdad. From there he flew on to Rome. Because they had left so rapidly, the couple had to go shopping, buying a new grey suit for the Shah and a white polka-dot dress for Soraya. Because he was anxious not to displease Mossadeq, the Iranian ambassador in Rome made himself diplomatically absent – he went swimming in Ostia. He also refused Queen Soraya the key to a car she had left in Rome two years previously – but another embassy official found it for her. The couple were worried about money. Soraya later wrote that the Shah told her: 'We shall have to economise, Soraya, for I am sorry to say that I haven't much money. Enough perhaps to buy us a farm somewhere or other.'[42]

Back in Tehran, crowds went onto the streets to demonstrate for Mossadeq, and Kermit Roosevelt sent a telegram to Washington to break the bad news that his coup attempt had failed.

Quite what happened next is not easy to tease out, nor who was in control or determined events.[43] No one in those days can have felt in control – all of them were groping in the dark, trying to find a way through to what they wanted, rather desperately, without much confidence.

The demonstrations against the coup attempt grew and turned more militant. Crowds toppled statues of the Shah and his father, and it became clear that Tudeh were using the situation to press for abolition of the monarchy. On Monday 17 August Mossadeq ordered that the Shah's name be removed from prayers in military barracks,[44] a highly symbolic act in an Islamic country (the inclusion of a ruler's name in Friday prayers was traditionally as important as a mark of sovereignty as its appearance on the coinage). But Mossadeq soon realized that there was a danger of the situation escaping his grip, and this was reinforced by a meeting he had with the US ambassador on 17 August, in which the ambassador noted that the influence of the communists seemed to be growing and urged that order be restored.

There was time over these days for others also to become concerned at the situation and to reconsider their own position. Plenty of moderate Mossadeq supporters would have been taken aback that the monarchy as an institution was now under threat. If the monarchy were to go, would there be enough security left in the system to prevent Tudeh taking over? The clergy in particular were alarmed at that prospect – alarmed at the possibility of an atheistic communist regime and (among other concerns) the loss of their endowed property (*waqf*) that would presumably follow.

Many if not most of the officers that Roosevelt had been dealing with had been arrested at Mossadeq's orders, Zahedi himself was in hiding, and the CIA's ability to influence events must have been damaged, to say the least. The Imperial Guard had been disarmed (in the pre-coup planning the CIA assessment had been that most police and army units in the capital were loyal to Mossadeq in any case). Once again, Tudeh networks within the armed forces helped Mossadeq to do this effectively. There is evidence that most of the US actors in Tehran had given up the game; in Washington, Eisenhower's advisers were telling him that the CIA had failed, and it would now be necessary to 'snuggle up' to Mossadeq if the US were to retrieve anything from the situation.[45]

But the situation, and some loyalties, were shifting. On the afternoon of Monday 17 August, deciding that enough was enough, Mossadeq told Tudeh to back down and authorized the police and army to use force to break up the Tudeh-led demonstrations if necessary. This they did the next day – leaving the field open for anti-Mossadeq and pro-Shah demonstrations, which followed on 19 August. After their experience on the Tuesday, Tudeh kept their people at home, and a confrontation developed outside Mossadeq's residence, in which a number of brawny members of bazaar *zur-khaneh* seem to have participated. This turned to violence as some troops arrived, including six Sherman tanks. There was an exchange of fire between these tanks and the soldiers guarding the house. The shooting continued for two hours, with many casualties, and three tanks that had been in position to defend the house were destroyed.[46] Meanwhile, pro-Shah demonstrators took over the radio station and began broadcasting from there. Eventually, with General Riahi telling him the situation was hopeless, Mossadeq gave up, announced at about 5 p.m. that the building would no longer be defended and left by a ladder over a back wall.[47] He was arrested the following day. Zahedi came out of hiding to take control as the new prime minister, and the Shah flew back to Tehran on 22 August. At the airport a military honour guard turned out to welcome him, but was kept at a distance in case one of the soldiers made an assassination attempt.[48]

So three days after Roosevelt had announced the failure of his coup attempt to Washington, Mossadeq had fallen from office. Statements made at the time, both by the US ambassador in Tehran and by the administration in the US when the news reached them, show that they were dumbfounded by this reversal of fortune.[49]

What had happened? Roosevelt and the CIA did their best to take the credit later, claiming the coup as one of their greatest successes against the Soviets in the Cold War. Among other things, they claimed that they passed $10,000 to Ayatollah Kashani, to pay mobs to turn out on the streets on 19 August. But Kashani and other senior clergy did not need money to persuade them to act against Mossadeq, and their influence and connections were quite enough to bring crowds on to the streets without American cash. In fact, Kashani himself had created the conditions for the coup by turning against Mossadeq earlier in the year.

The CIA operation had set a number of personalities and groups in motion. Some, but not all of these had been neutralized on Monday 17 August, after the initial attempt failed. Some were presumably still running. But more important was the jolt given to moderate opinion by the disappearance of the Shah, the breakdown in law and order and the triumphalism of Tudeh on 17–18 August. Against the background of the withdrawal of clerical support for Mossadeq and suspicions about his high-handed treatment of the constitution, these factors were enough to convince enough Iranians in Tehran on Wednesday 19th (Tudeh having removed themselves from the scene) that the Shah was a better guarantor of their security and that Mossadeq had to go. The clergy (as at other times in the twentieth century) were more effective at mobilizing action on the streets than the CIA could ever have been. Their move to oppose Mossadeq was the decisive factor in his downfall – but it may not be entirely correct to regard it as a betrayal. Kashani's decision was openly made and was made in response to Mossadeq's own actions – it was a development that Mossadeq should have foreseen. He could have made a greater effort to keep Kashani and his supporters on his side; or to outmanoeuvre them.

It should go without saying that none of this should be taken as an exculpation of US or British policy. Both governments deliberately connived at the removal of a democratically elected prime minister, and the long-term damage to the interests of Britain and the US in Iran was enormous. The events of the summer of 1953 are still much debated. For some Iranians, it reinforced their view of Iran as a victim, and the belief that most events, whatever their outward appearance, were in fact manipulated by foreigners. When the Shah returned it was not so much as the victor as the inglorious beneficiary of a victory that others had won for him, in dubious circumstances. Many Iranians quickly perceived the hand of the US in his reinstatement and in Mossadeq's removal, and for them the coup discredited both the Shah and the US as a friend to Iran. Whatever the realities of 1953, this perception was important in the attitudes that led to the revolution of 1979. The CIA themselves, their critics on the left of US politics and many Iranians, whether nationalist, leftist or anti-Western clerics, have all tended to stress the CIA role, for their own reasons. Other factors in the drama, such as Mossadeq's own mistakes and the role of the clergy, have tended to be forgotten.[50]

For Tudeh, 1953 was the zenith of their political fortunes, and a major lost opportunity. They never reached the same position of power and influence again. They had been well organized and well connected (especially within the armed forces), providing Mossadeq himself with timely and accurate information at a number of points. But their demonstrations against the monarchy proved ill-judged, and they had arguably been too timid in standing down their street activists after 18 August.[51] They had suffered from a number of contingent problems, aside from the usual handicaps of their stultifying ideology[52] and factional strife. Stalin's death in March had crippled Soviet policy-making and turned Moscow in on its own concerns, leaving the Iranian party without the guidance to which it had become accustomed. In addition, many of the leading personalities of Tudeh had been in the Soviet Union at the time for one reason or another. Once again, the left in Iran was the bridesmaid, not the bride. But perhaps their greatest error was their failure to grab the bouquet. How realistic was it to think that they could use Mossadeq to smooth their path to power? Why did they never bring forward a leader of their own to capture the public imagination in a comparable way? Were they really too weak to make their own coup attempt on 18 or 19 August? Or just not prepared or flexible or bold enough? The historian and authority on the Tudeh Party Ervand Abrahamian has pointed to Tudeh's failure to mobilize support among the rural population (still the majority of the population at that time) as the party's crucial error:

> As the Tudeh leaders admitted in analyzing the defeat of August 1953, the royalist officers could not have carried out their coup d'état if their peasant rank and file had mutinied or the rural masses had risen up in revolt.[53]

But was that really so? The French and Russian revolutions were largely made in cities. The Bolsheviks in Russia had been predominantly an urban party, like Tudeh, and the Russian peasantry's support for them in the period 1917–21 had been less than wholehearted. When the Iranian revolution came in 1978–9, it was not led or dominated by a rural uprising or revolt as such. Tudeh's real failure was a failure of leadership – a failure to plan realistically for the long term, and a failure to take their fate and the fate of the country into their own hands, rather than trying to work through proxies.

However, as the reaction against them after 16 August showed, it is probably correct that Tudeh were opposed by forces too powerful, with too much to lose, for them ever to have succeeded in 1953. In the aftermath, Tudeh suffered from political repression more severely than any other group. Many of the leadership as well as the rank and file were taken and imprisoned (some, notably the charismatic Khosrow Roozbeh, were executed) and by the end of the decade Tudeh had almost ceased to function as a movement.[54]

In London, Churchill was jubilant at Mossadeq's fall – it was a bright point in his failing premiership (he had just suffered a stroke). Churchill had been involved in the story of Iranian oil since the beginning, when he had directed British naval policy before the First World War. When Kermit Roosevelt met him in London later in August 1953 Churchill said the AIOC had 'fouled things up' but congratulated Roosevelt:

> The Prime Minister seemed to be in bad shape physically. He had great difficulty in hearing; occasional difficulty in articulating; and apparently difficulty in seeing to his left.
>
> In spite of this he could not have been more kind personally nor more enthusiastic about the operation. He was good enough to express envy of Roosevelt's role and a wish that he had been 'some years' younger and might have served under his command.[55]

British celebration over Mossadeq's fall did not last long. Diplomatic relations with Britain, broken off by Mossadeq at the end of 1952, were restored in 1954, but from 1953 onwards the US became by far the most influential foreign power in Iran. The US government mediated a new agreement with the Shah whereby the profits from Iranian oil were shared 50/50 between the Iranian government and an international consortium of oil companies. Within this consortium US oil companies took a 40 per cent share; the AIOC (soon to be renamed BP) also got 40 per cent – 20 per cent of the total. If the British had compromised with Mossadeq early enough they could have got a much better deal than that. Following in his father's traditions, the Shah spent much of the increased revenue from oil on military equipment.

Autocracy

With US backing and with opposition to him crushed, the Shah was firmly in control, and as time went on he gained confidence. The period of democratic politics that began under Allied occupation during the Second World War ended with Mossadeq. Pro-Mossadeq newspapers were closed, and over 2,000 people were arrested by the end of the year, mainly Tudeh and National Front activists and sympathizers. Government ministries and the army were purged, and the Majles elections of 1954 were rigged, setting the pattern for subsequent elections up to the revolution of 1979.[56] Two bogus parties, the National Party and the People's Party (Melliyun and Mardom) were set up in the Majles, competing only in their enthusiasm for the Shah's policies (they were satirized as the 'Yes' party and the 'Yes sir' party).[57] Melliyun was replaced by Iran Novin ('New Iran') in 1963. From 1953 onwards the post of prime minister was in the Shah's pocket – Mossadeq's successors were appointed and removed as the Shah pleased. All this was done with US government and CIA support.

Even if the vexed question of responsibility for the coup is set aside, the CIA's role in suppressing democracy in Iran *after* the coup, working with Zahedi, is undisputed. Most notable was its part in forming the Shah's secret police, which later became notorious as SAVAK (Sazeman-e Ettela'at va Amniyat-e Keshvar – National Intelligence and Security Organization). The manipulation of constitutional and democratic institutions, combined with SAVAK's sustained and effective attacks on underground opposition, succeeded in crippling politics in Iran for the next quarter of a century; permitting the continued autocratic rule of the Shah, but also facilitating the eventual re-emergence of the only opposition group with any kind of independence or immunity from persecution – the clergy.

For the second time, this time under Kashani's leadership, a section of the clergy had attempted an alliance with the idea of constitutional, representative government – with a form of liberal democracy. But eventually, as some had done in 1908, they had pulled back and sided with the monarchy instead. For the next few years, under the leadership of Borujerdi, Behbehani and Kashani, the clergy supported the monarchy. The Shah's government massaged their goodwill; most notoriously, in 1955, by turning a blind eye[58] to attacks on the Bahais, who were hated as apostates and heretics by the *ulema*. Ultimately though, the Shah's political instincts were no more favourable to the clergy than his father's had been. His vision of a modern, Westernized, technocratic Iran had little place for the *ulema*. This vision emerged gradually through the following years.

Gharbzadegi

As a writer and political thinker, Jalal Al-e Ahmad's life was strongly affected by Mossadeq's fall. He and his thinking can be seen as a connecting link between the era of Sadegh Hedayat and the era of Ali

Shariati. Al-e Ahmad was born into a religious family in 1923, but under the intellectual influence of the time and of writers like Kasravi and others turned away from religion toward Marxism. In the 1940s he was close to the leftist thinker and politician Khalil Maleki, but like Maleki he disliked the subservience of Tudeh to Soviet interests. Having been a strong supporter of Mossadeq, he renounced politics after his fall, but remained strongly political in much of his work while withholding support from any particular party or group. Like many of his generation, he favoured a lean, colloquial way of writing over the more ornate style of earlier decades and centuries. His most famous work was first published in 1962 – *Gharbzadegi*, which can be translated as 'Sick from the West', 'Sick of the West', 'Westoxication' or 'West-strickenness'. Neither the idea nor the term was wholly new, but Al-e Ahmad developed it further than before. In the opening lines of the book he compared *gharbzadegi* to a disease that destroyed an ear of grain from the inside, eating it away but leaving the husk so that from the outside it appeared quite healthy. *Gharbzadegi* was an influential concept and after the revolution became one of the standard terms of revolutionary politics. Al-e Ahmad's intention with it was not to attack the West or Western ideas as such, at least not directly (his grasp of the culture and politics of the West was in fact probably rather inferior to Hedayat's), but rather the uncritical way in which Western ideas had been accepted and advocated and taught in schools (often without being properly understood); producing people and a culture that were neither genuinely Iranian nor properly Western. Following a story by Molana Rumi, he compared it to a crow who saw one day the elegant way that a partridge walked. The crow tried to imitate the partridge and failed, but kept trying, with the result that he forgot how to walk like a crow, but never succeeded in walking like a partridge.[59]

More strongly than anything, Al-e Ahmad wanted Iranian culture and Iranian life to be *genuine*, not bogus or emptily imitative or imported. In this, like Hedayat, he showed the preoccupations of the 1940s and 50s, and the influence of existentialists like Sartre and Camus. But as time went on, he gave up the anticlericalism of Kasravi and Hedayat and turned back to Iranian Shi'ism as the central, authentic identity of Iran, while remaining critical of the old-fashioned, superstitious form of Shi'ism they had rejected. In later years, he drew attention to the way that oil wealth was spent on imported absurdities that earlier generations of Iranians could never have imagined they could want, and to the false historical heritage presented by Mohammad Reza Shah as the backdrop to the Pahlavi monarchy. He supported Khomeini's attacks on the Shah in the early 1960s. For many he was a charismatic hero; the archetype of the politically committed intellectual. After his death in 1969 his widow, Simin Daneshvar, went on to make a literary reputation in her own right, and her descriptions of their troubled married life diminished his reputation only slightly.[60]

As elsewhere, in many parts of the world, the second half of the 1950s was a period of growth in Iran. Between 1954 and 1969, albeit with some blips, the economy grew (adjusted for inflation) by an average of around 7 per cent per year, but fluctuated between 3 and 14 per cent.[61] The Shah's government did not invest only in the armed forces – the new stream of oil money went also into roads, railways, education and medical services. Improvements in living conditions and medical care led to rapid population growth – from 19.3 million in 1950 to 27.3 million in 1968.[62] Tehran and other cities began to grow as new industries drew in surplus population from rural areas.

But at the beginning of the 1960s a series of new developments came together to create a new atmosphere of uncertainty and crisis, anticipating in several ways the crisis of 1978–9. After a sustained boom came a recession,[63] encouraged by government policies of retrenchment after a period of overspending and over-borrowing. The cost of living had risen, and with it the number of strikes. The Shah's proposals for land reform, prompted by the Kennedy administration in the US, encountered opposition, including from Ayatollah Borujerdi (previously the Shah's close ally). Land reform was tricky for the clergy, who collectively owned a significant proportion of the country's best agricultural land. The proposed reforms drove a wedge between them and ordinary peasants, with whom it was understandably popular. The clergy also disliked proposed changes to the law for the election of local councils – including provisions for councillors to take an oath on religious books other than the Koran, and allowing women to vote for the first time.[64] Taken together, these measures broke the rapprochement between the monarchy and the clergy that had held since 1953 and reminded the *ulema* of their worst moments in Reza Shah's time. The new US administration was also encouraging political liberalization – in response the Shah lifted the ban on the National Front, which led to further strikes and demonstrations. Then two deaths among the top *ulema* left a sudden vacuum of religious authority. Borujerdi died at the end of March 1961, and Kashani just under a year later.

Among the *ulema*, Seyyed Ruhollah Khomeini had a degree of prominence as a thinker and pious scholar before this time, but he had avoided speaking out on controversial subjects and was not well known among the population generally. He was sixty years old in 1962. The deaths of Borujerdi and Kashani allowed him to emerge as a religious leader and also, within a short time, as a major figure in national politics. It has been suggested that other clerics made Khomeini a *marja* to protect his life when he was arrested at a later stage, but it seems in fact that his elevation to this status occurred in the normal way after Borujerdi's death. Clerics talked among themselves in Qom over a period of days or weeks and visited each other's houses. Khomeini's followers acclaimed him, and his new status was gradually accepted by his most senior peers.[65]

The government's initial proposals for land reform stalled, so in 1962 the Shah brought forward a new Land Reform Act, which he then (in January 1963) presented for a national referendum as part of a six-point plan he called the 'White Revolution'. The other five points were privatization of state factories, nationalization of forests, female suffrage, profit-sharing for workers and a literacy corps of young educated people who were to go into rural areas to teach reading and writing at primary level (many rural areas were still without schools). The referendum, according to the results announced by the government, gave the plan massive support; but the National Front had boycotted it, on the grounds that the proposals should have been drawn up by a constitutionally elected government. After a series of critical telegrams to the government, and coordinating his actions with other senior clerics, Khomeini had begun to speak out against the Shah's regime.[66] A loose association called the Coalition of Islamic Societies, formed largely of *bazaaris* with clerical leadership, came together to support Khomeini. In March troops and SAVAK agents attacked the *madreseh* in Qom where he was preaching, killed some of the students and arrested Khomeini himself. He was released a few days later but continued his attacks on the government, denouncing corruption, the rigging of elections and other constitutional abuses, neglect of the poor and the sale of oil to Israel. He avoided the subject of land reform (and, for the most part, female suffrage), instead targeting issues with mass appeal on which the government was vulnerable. According to one story that circulated at the time (which shows the sort of things that were being said, even if the exchange never actually happened), the Shah sent Khomeini a message threatening to put on his father's boots and come to Qom to sort Khomeini out. In response Khomeini is supposed to have replied, 'Your father's boots are too big for your feet.'[67]

In that year Ashura came at the beginning of June, and that was when the tension reached its climax. Khomeini gave his strongest speech yet on 3 June, the day of Ashura itself. Khomeini addressed the Shah directly and referred to the events of 1941:

> I don't want you to become like your father. When America, the Soviet Union and England attacked us people were happy that Pahlavi [i.e. Reza Shah] went . . . Isn't it time for you to think and reflect a little, to ponder about where this is leading you, to learn a lesson from the experience of your father?[68]

There were demonstrations in Tehran and several other major cities in the days that followed, which drew added force from the intense atmosphere of Moharram. The government, directed by Asadollah Alam (prime minister from July 1962 to March 1964), acted decisively, imposed martial law and put troops on the streets, and hundreds of demonstrators were killed before the protests ended, after three days. The Shah later thanked Alam for his firm handling of the crisis.[69] The deaths, especially because they took place at Ashura, invited comparison with the martyrs of Karbala on the one hand, and the tyrant Yazid on the other.

Khomeini was released in August but despite SAVAK announcements that he had agreed to keep quiet, he continued to speak out, and was rearrested. Finally, he was deported and exiled in 1964 after a harsh speech attacking a new law that gave the equivalent of diplomatic immunity to US military personnel in Iran:

> They have reduced the Iranian people to a level lower than that of an American dog. If someone runs over a dog belonging to an American, he will be prosecuted. Even if the Shah himself were to run over a dog belonging to an American, he would be prosecuted. But if an American cook runs over the Shah, the head of state, no one will have the right to interfere with him.[70]

Shortly after this new law was passed in the Majles a new US loan of $200 million for military equipment was agreed – a conjunction all too reminiscent of the capitulations conceded in the time of the Qajars and abolished by Reza Shah.

Khomeini went into exile first to Turkey, then to Iraq and finally (after the Shah put pressure on the Iraqi government to remove him from the Shi'a shrine city of Najaf) to Paris in 1978. In Iran, the Shah had a range of his opponents arrested, including the leadership of the National Front. Protest faded, aside from occasional manifestations at Tehran University and from members of the *ulema*. But underlying resentment remained, and despite his exile Khomeini continued to be regarded by religious Iranians as the leading cleric of the time.

For the Shah, the lesson from 1963 seemed to be that autocracy worked: he could govern with a firm hand and overcome short-term dissent with repression (one might add that the Shah's autocracy worked when there was a firm, loyal minister to apply the policy for him – Asadollah Alam in this case). In the longer term, his policies for development – his White Revolution – would bring material benefits to ordinary people, overcome any temporary unpopularity and secure his rule. The term White Revolution was revealing in itself and showed the Shah's preoccupations. It wasn't a Red, or communist, revolution, but a White, monarchist revolution (reflecting the terminology of the civil war that followed the Russian revolution of 1917, and of the French revolution before that): a progressive social and economic transformation of the country, but launched by the Shah rather than a political movement from the left. The juxtaposition showed also the Cold War parameters of the Shah's thinking. To him, the prime danger was Red revolution. Marxism declared that material inequalities between classes would eventually produce revolution, so the way to avoid revolution was to undercut it, by stimulating economic development and providing material improvements for society as a whole, reducing class tensions (but also by resisting Soviet influence and infiltration, and crushing leftist political activity). After the defeat of clerical opposition in 1963 the clergy appeared irrelevant to this programme of ideas. The Shi'a clergy belonged to the past: a new, economically developed Iran would naturally turn in a secular direction, as had the Western societies Iran was emulating (and neighbouring countries like Turkey and Egypt also). This programme was congruent with the expectations of the US and other Western governments too: Iran and other Middle Eastern countries had been somewhat backward, but they would embrace material development, reject elements of their traditional culture that had been holding them back (notably, Islam) and, if they could avoid the seductions of Soviet communism, become normal countries just like those of Europe and North America.

And for fifteen years this model appeared to work. There was little sign of overt political dissent, but there was a queasy, widespread awareness of discontent that manifested itself in a variety of ways. One was the growing popularity among young people and students of the writings of Ali Shariati.

Shariati was born in 1933, in the small village of Kahak, near Mashhad in Khorasan.[71] His father had studied as a religious scholar but became a teacher, and Ali grew up largely with his mother while his father was away. Intelligent, but often absent-minded and lazy, with a tendency to melancholy in private despite his good humour in company, he developed a witty and independent way of thinking that often got him into trouble with his teachers. His thinking was influenced by his father, who was an advocate of progressive political Islam in his own right, by Sufism, by Kasravi (absorbing his criticism of contemporary Shi'a Islam without accepting his rejection of it) but also by Western thinkers like Maeterlinck, Schopenhauer and Kafka. He had a particular attachment to various forms of mysticism – especially to the poetry of the great Molana (Rumi) – but the events of 1953 also made a strong impression on him. He had been and remained a fervent supporter of Mossadeq; but, in addition to strengthening his criticism of the traditionalist clergy, Mossadeq's fall persuaded Shariati that democratic institutions were too weak for the stresses involved in lifting a country like Iran out of tyranny.[72]

As a student Shariati went to Mashhad University, and then to Paris, where he attended lectures by Marxist professors (but also the Islamic scholar Massignon), read Guevara and Sartre, communicated with the theorist and revolutionary activist Frantz Fanon and took a doctorate from the Sorbonne (in 1964). His political activities also attracted the attention of SAVAK. Returning to Iran in 1965, from 1967 he lectured to students in the university of Mashhad, attracting large numbers, and wrote a series of essays, books and speeches. His criticism of the traditional forms of Shi'a Islam in Iran, combined with his burgeoning popularity, soon led to increasing criticism from some members of the clergy, especially after the publication of a book based on his lectures (*Eslamshenasi – The Study of Islam*) in 1969. Some clergy tried to get Khomeini to condemn Shariati's views from his exile in Iraq, but Khomeini declined to do so, saying that they were not un-Islamic.[73] Khomeini gave no direct approval of Shariati's opinions either, but recognized his popularity and the harmony of their aims. In time Khomeini's own anti-imperialist rhetoric came to reflect the ideas popularized in Iran by Shariati, and Al-e Ahmad.

In the same year that *Eslamshenasi* was published Shariati met Jalal Al-e Ahmad in Mashhad several times, and on one occasion (on which Al-e Ahmad argued for the importance of cooperation between the clergy and the non-clerical intellectuals) future supreme leader Ali Khamenei was also present, as a young religious student.[74] When his teaching post was withdrawn in 1971, Shariati went to Tehran and lectured at the recently established Hoseiniyeh Ershad instead (he had given occasional lectures there since October 1968).[75] The Hoseiniyeh Ershad had been set up as a charitable institution for the exchange of ideas and for the application of Islamic principles to contemporary issues. Mehdi Bazargan and Morteza Motahhari were among the figures, later to become prominent in politics, who were instrumental in founding it.

Shariati's general message at the Hoseiniyeh Ershad and in Mashhad was that Shi'ism had its own ideology of social justice and resistance to oppression. This had been masked by a false Shi'ism of superstition and deference to monarchy, which he called Black Shi'ism or Safavid Shi'ism, but the essential truths of the religion were timeless, centring on the revolt and martyrdom of Hosein and his companions. Shariati was not a Marxist, but could be said to have recast Shi'a Islam in a revolutionary mould, comparable to the Marxist model, urging not quietism and immersion in the details of religious observance, but earnest involvement in the vital political and moral questions of the day – 'Every month of the year is Moharram, every day of the year is Ashura and every piece of land is Karbala.'[76] It was a powerful and influential message, but (as with other revolutionary ideologues) his critique of the present showed more intellectual depth than his prescriptions for the future. He was incensed when some clergy so far missed the point of his message that they criticized his lectures at the Ershad for the presence of girls in mini-skirts. Even though he seldom attacked the Shah's rule directly, the

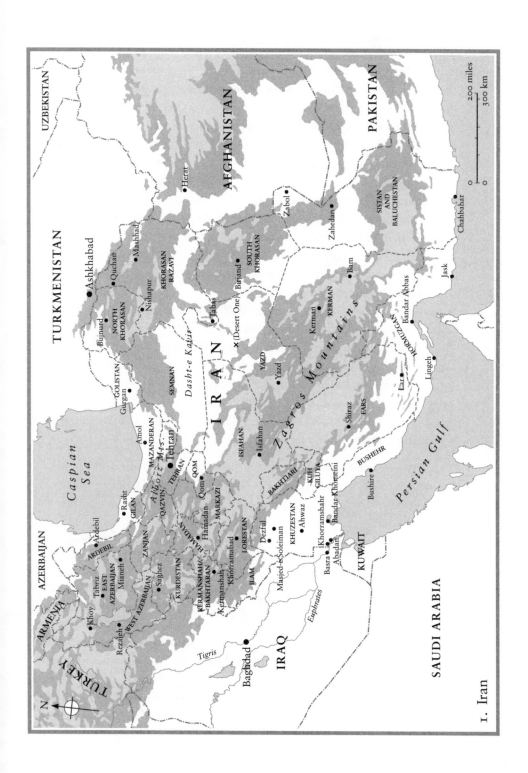

1. Iran

subversive message of his thinking was plain enough to the regime, which closed the Hoseiniyeh Ershad in 1972. Shariati was imprisoned in 1972, released in 1975 and kept under house arrest thereafter. He continued his writing and his support for his version of radical Islam. He managed to escape to England in 1977, but was stricken by his failure to take all his family with him. He died in Southampton, apparently of a heart attack, in June the same year[77] (many Iranians believe he was murdered by SAVAK, but it is hard to see, from the circumstances, how this could have been carried out). In an echo of the *bast* of 1905 and 1906, there was a demonstration later in the year at the shrine of Shah Abd ol-Azim to the south of Tehran to commemorate Shariati's death[78] – prefiguring the larger and more momentous demonstrations of the following year. Iranians in exile marked his passing with other events and demonstrations.

Khomeini would never endorse Shariati's thinking directly, but was careful not to condemn it either. Shariati's radical Islamism, both fully Iranian and fully modern, was a strong influence on the generation of students that grew to adulthood in the 1970s;[79] slogans drawn from his writings were everywhere on the streets in 1979, and his face still appears on fresh graffiti in Tehran thirty years later.

One young high-school student, Massoumeh Ebtekar, attended Shariati's lectures at the Hoseiniyeh Ershad:

> It was impossible for me, as a young person, to understand everything he said, but I could feel that a change in direction was coming. Islam, he taught, could be a viable alternative to the ideologies of fatality and despair that emanated from the West.
>
> I was certainly not alone. Many young people found in Dr Shariati's message a new meaning and direction in life. I met him shortly before he left for London, where he was to die under suspicious circumstances. We spoke about my views, and he encouraged me to do further reading. That meeting was one of the decisive moments in my life.[80]

Massoumeh Ebtekar was later one of the students who occupied the US embassy in November 1979 and, later still, became vice-president under President Khatami.

Shariati's story illustrates some important points about Iran in the 1960s and 70s – particularly about the limits of the Shah's control, and

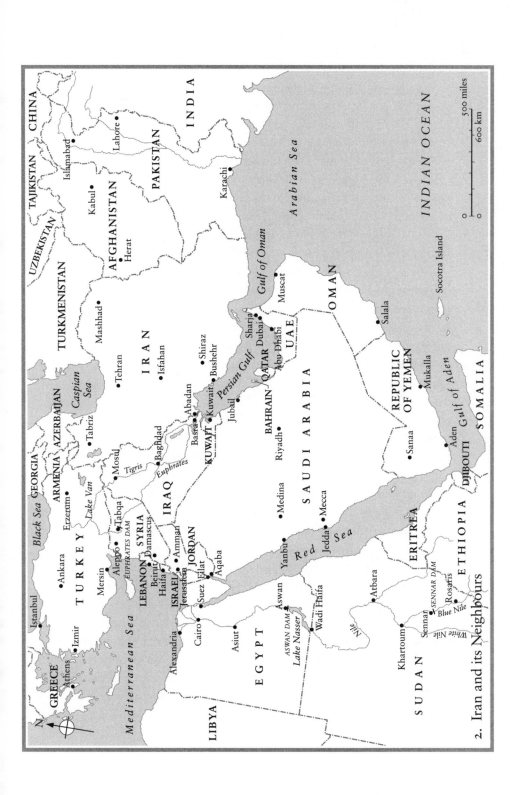

2. Iran and its Neighbours

changes in the intellectual climate. One lesson of 1953 was the failure of secular leftism; many intellectuals (like Jalal Al-e Ahmad) and many young people especially, turned toward political Islam instead in this period. The broad umbrella of Islam gave at least a degree of immunity from repression; not least because the Shi'a centres of Najaf (where Khomeini spent most of his exile) and Karbala in Iraq were beyond the Shah's control. Large numbers of Iranians were studying abroad during this period (many of them, like Shariati, on state scholarships). The Shah could control education within Iran to some extent, but he could have little control over the political influences young Iranians absorbed while studying in foreign countries.

This was a period of political radicalism in universities in Europe and the US, where the Shah's regime and its poor human rights record were special targets for criticism. Young Iranians studying in the West were exhilarated by the fashionable enthusiasm for Marxism and Maoism, for revolution and against the Vietnam War. A further illustration of the interlinked nature of international and national politics at this time is the shooting of Benno Ohnesorg in Berlin in June 1967. Ohnesorg, although unarmed, was shot by a policeman and killed on the fringe of a demonstration against the Shah's presence in the city (the Shah was going with Queen Farah to see a performance of Mozart's *Magic Flute* at the Deutsche Oper). The temperature of the confrontation between protestors and police had risen after some provocative actions by the Shah's own SAVAK security men. The shooting was an important event in the radicalization of the left in Germany, leading to the greater unrest of the following year and the formation of the Baader-Meinhof terrorist group. Ironically, although some on the German left justified turning to political violence on the basis that the shooting showed the latent fascism of the state, the killer turned out much later to have been an agent of the East German Stasi (though his motives for the killing seem to have had more to do with the fact that he was a thug).[81]

Through the later 1960s the Shah was able to keep a grip on politics within Iran, gaining confidence as time went on. But he still distrusted his ministers and other subordinates, and avoided allowing any to get too powerful by permitting and indeed encouraging a degree of rivalry. This helped to produce a poisonous atmosphere at court and in the upper reaches of government,[82] as is illustrated by the case of Ahmad Nafisi, who was mayor of Tehran in the early 1960s. Having been something of a favourite with the Shah, Nafisi was suddenly arrested and imprisoned in December 1963 on vague charges of fiscal abuse, accompanied by even vaguer allegations from SAVAK of consorting with the clerical opposition. Months in prison dragged into years with little sign of proper legal proceedings. Nafisi rebutted the accusations against him at every opportunity (though he never was properly charged), and it emerged that the real problem was probably the jealousy of the prime minister of the time, Hasan Ali Mansur.[83] After Mansur was assassinated in January 1965 pressure on the government to release Nafisi increased, but in a twist reminiscent of Kafka he was told that for this to happen he would have to write a letter to the Shah expressing contrition for his alleged crimes – thereby exonerating the Shah for his unjust imprisonment. Nafisi wrote a letter, but it obstinately denied any wrongdoing. He was eventually released in August 1966, after his friends had paid a huge sum in bail.[84]

After Mansur died, he was replaced as prime minister by Amir Abbas Hoveida, who continued in that office for twelve years, until 1977. Hoveida was born in 1919 to an aristocratic family in Tehran. His mother was descended from a sister of Naser od-Din Shah. His father, who had been a Bahai but who moved away from that religion, was a diplomat, and so Amir Abbas had a rather disjointed childhood as his father moved his family from posting to posting (the Bahai connection was used against him by some at the time of the revolution). His education was predominantly in French; although he did also spend some time studying in England, like many of his contemporaries he always preferred French culture and French literature. Back in Iran after 1942, he served briefly in the army and then took up a diplomatic career, like his father. He was a cultured, intellectual man, and a friend of Sadegh Hedayat, with a louche, bohemian side. Some hated him, thinking him devious and unprincipled – Al-e Ahmad believed his interest in writers and thinkers was merely a screen for self-advancement. It seems he became more cynical over his years as prime minister. Others admired his integrity.[85]

For thirteen years after 1963 Iran's economic development, guided by the Shah's government, seemed only to accelerate. Under the new arrangements with the international syndicate, oil revenue grew to $555 million in 1963–4 and to $1.2 billion in 1970–71. But after that, boosted by the Shah's successful takeover of control of oil production and by the quadrupling of oil prices achieved by the OPEC oil cartel from 1973 (in which the Shah played a significant role), revenue ballooned even more extravagantly, to $5 billion in 1973–4 and $20 billion in 1975–6.[86] Large sums were spent on Western military equipment, as before, but most of the revenue was put back into economic development; both through direct state investment into infrastructure, industry and education, and through state loans to private entrepreneurs. Initially, the government focused on infrastructure and agricultural development; later, on industry, education and health services. The railway from the Caspian to the Persian Gulf was finally completed, and other railways were built, including from Tehran to Tabriz and Mashhad. Large dams were built for the generation of electricity. Thirteen thousand miles of new roads were constructed. Education and health services expanded too – the number of children in primary schools went from 1.6 million in 1963 to over 4 million in 1977; new universities and colleges were set up, and enrolment expanded from 24,885 to 154,215. The number of students at foreign universities grew from under 18,000 to over 80,000. The number of hospital beds went from 24,126 to 48,000. Improved living conditions, sanitation and health services all contributed to a big drop in the infant mortality rate and a spurt in population growth that continued until the 1990s; in the mid-1970s half the population were under sixteen, and two-thirds under thirty.[87]

Some have contrasted the economic growth achieved in the two decades before the revolution with the growth in the 1930s, judging that, whereas under Reza Shah growth was a by-product of the policies he followed in constructing a modern state, under his son government pursued economic development as a primary goal.[88] No doubt there were errors and inefficiencies in the way the investment was carried out, but the results were impressive. Growth rates between 1963 and 1976 averaged around 8 per cent; the non-oil sector grew even more than the overall economy, averaging 8.6 per cent.[89] Industrial production expanded hugely between 1965 and 1975, and thousands of new factories were set up. Coal production jumped from 285,000 tons to over 900,000 tons; iron ore from 2,000 tons to just under 900,000. Over the same period production of motor vehicles of all kinds went from 7,000 to 109,000. Other manufactured items showed similar dramatic increases. The middling class of managers and professionals expanded with the industrial economy – an educated class of entrepreneurs, factory managers, retail and wholesale managers, teachers, doctors, engineers and so on.

This was the period in which Iran made the transition from an agricultural economy to an industry- and services-based structure. But, as in other countries that had made this transition, the other half of the process was the transformation going on in the countryside, in the agricultural sector. The question of whether the Shah's land reform was a success depends to some extent on what one believes it was intended to achieve.

The declared aims of the programme were to break the death-grip of absentee landlords, to make agriculture more efficient and to achieve a fairer distribution of land among those who actually worked it.[90] The reform drew credibility for its modernizing, anti-feudal character, and perhaps from the fact that Mossadeq had championed it. In acting against the traditional landowning class (previously some of the staunchest supporters of the monarchy), the Shah appeared to be sacrificing his own political interests for the sake of the country. But the results were mixed. About two million peasant householders became landowners in their own right for the first time, and some were able to prosper in their new circumstances. For many more, the holdings they were given were too small to be economically viable – 65 per cent of peasant landowners in 1972 owned less than 5 hectares[91] (though some were able to pool their resources in state-run farms, which in the Soviet Union would have been called collectives) – and large numbers of agricultural labourers were left out of the redistribution altogether, because they had not had cultivation rights as sharecroppers before the reform. It has been estimated that 1.1 million families fell into this category of landless rural labourers and nomads.[92] The landlords who were expropriated (in return for compensation) were only allowed to keep one village each, but some were able to evade the provisions, for example by giving their property to relatives or by creating mechanized farms, which were exempt. Because the reform was accompanied by a general push for the mechanization of agriculture (the government subsidized land reclamation, irrigation projects and the cost of tractors, fertilizers and pesticides) there was less work for the poorer peasants and labourers anyway. Some agricultural production became more efficient. But the low prices for staple foods imposed by the government, and the inflow of cheap imports, eroded incentives for farmers and tended to depress agricultural production overall. Disruption to traditional landholding arrangements and to traditional methods of land management also reduced production.[93] Combined with the long-term countrywide trend of rapid population growth, the net result was rural unemployment and an accelerating movement of people from the villages to the cities, especially Tehran, in search of work. It has been suggested that the rate of internal migration reached 8 per cent per year in 1972–3; and that by 1978 the urban population was 46 per cent of the total.[94] By 1976 Tehran had grown to become a city of 4.5 million people. In general, the Shah's policies bene-fited the cities more than the countryside. For example, the efforts of the literacy corps in the villages were largely unavailing. Despite some successes by some of the *sepahis* (corps members), most of them failed to establish a cooperative relationship with the villagers. There was a gap of understand-ing between the peasants, who were suspicious and felt patronized by the whole initiative, and the young urban middle-class *sepahis*, too conscious of their own superiority and often resentful at being forced to do the work. (There were corps also for health and for development of agricultural tech-niques.) Serious spending on education was mainly directed at those living in towns and cities, and there was little real impact on rural illiteracy:

> The *sepahi* doesn't come here any longer. We had two before. The first boy was good. He built the school. I sent my son there for three years. And I went to the adult class, too. The other *sepahi* was a bad example [for the children] and we were happy to see him go. Now we have a teacher from town. He comes every day. He always curses at the children and calls them stupid [*khar* – donkey]. And we have to pay for this teacher. But I can't. I know my son must learn if he is not to be a poor peasant like me. But where do I get the money? My family must have bread. So my son doesn't go to school any longer.[95]

In many countries an industrial revolution has been accompanied by an agricultural revolution. In England, particularly in the slump after the Napoleonic wars, the enclosure acts drove peasants off the land and into the cities, where they worked for long hours for low wages in new industries because the alternative was even more miserable rural unemployment. In the Soviet Union in the early 1930s Stalin's collectiviz-ation policy achieved something similar, more quickly, by more brutal methods and with much greater loss of life. The process in Iran in the 1960s and 70s was rather gentler than that, but nonetheless traumatic for those involved. Whether the mass movement to the cities was a cen-tral part of the plan remains obscure (though, as under Stalin, government control of agricultural prices systematically worked to give the urban population cheap food while making survival even more difficult for small farmers).[96] But the rapid expansion of new industry could not have happened without it. The Shah once apparently said to US Ambassador William Sullivan:

> Mr Ambassador, don't you understand? I don't want those villages to survive.
> I want them to disappear. We can buy the food cheaper than they can produce
> it. I need the people from those villages in our industrial labour force. They
> must come into the cities and work in industry. Then we can send all those
> Afghans, Pakistanis and Koreans back home.[97]

The Shah seems to have envisaged the creation of a new rural class of prosperous peasants, who would be loyal to the Pahlavis, and the extension of state control, his control, over the countryside. But as well as alienating the landless, the interference of the state in the villages alienated even the peasants who profited from land reform.[98] The Shah may have thought he could cleverly split the peasants from their traditional attachment to the clergy with his land reform measures, but that link remained too strong.

In Tehran the newcomers from the countryside settled on the southern edge of the city, in collections of makeshift dwellings with poor or nonexistent services that were little better than shanty-towns. People from the same village or area tended to seek each other out and settle down together, and often they would know a mullah from the same locality also, who enjoyed added authority in these new circumstances of dislocation and uncertainty.[99]

2

The 1970s and the Slide
to Revolution

(THE VOICE OF IOKANAAN) *He shall be seated on his throne. He shall be clothed in scarlet and purple. In his hand he shall bear a golden cup full of his blasphemies. And the angel of the Lord shall smite him. He shall be eaten of worms.*

Oscar Wilde, *Salome*[1]

The 1970s were an uncertain decade of seedy flamboyance, bad taste, soft furnishings in brown and orange and (in Europe at least) ideological radicalism on the turn, when a realization began to dawn on some that the zeal for the new of the 1960s had sometimes destroyed things of value and replaced them with meretricious mediocrity. In the Middle East old assumptions about development and Westernization still dominated, but were coming more and more into question.

Despite the successful, rapid development, or perhaps at least in part because of it, the contradictions and the unease were in no place more concentrated than in Iran – and few events of that decade were more extravagant and contradictory than the celebrations held in 1971 at the historic sites of Persepolis and Pasargadae for 2,500 years of monarchy in Iran. In the 1950s the Shah had proposed a similar celebration for 1959; he had set aside the idea for lack of support, but it had continued to bubble away.[2] The occasion was anomalous in a variety of ways. It had to be 2,500 years 'of monarchy in Iran' rather than 'of Iranian monarchy' because there was an awkward period between the seventh century AD and the sixteenth (at least) when most of the monarchs were not Iranian. It seemed the 2,500 years could be celebrated as readily in 1971 as in 1959. To take the 2,500 years literally (from 1971) would be to go back to 529 BC; one year before the usually accepted date for the death of Cyrus the Great, who established the Achaemenid Empire. Why pick 529 BC? Cyrus had been a king for perhaps thirty years already by then, and there had been many Iranian kings (notably, the Medes) before him. But the date was not meant to be taken too precisely, and the point was that the Shah wanted to connect himself and his monarchy with Cyrus, as the founder of the first great Persian empire.[3] He wanted to assert the strength and enduring character of Iranian kingship, at a time when monarchy as an institution was menaced by republicanism and communism internationally, and when some in Iran were asserting Islam rather than monarchy as the true centre of Iranian identity. Perhaps, too, he felt the provisional, parvenu nature of the Pahlavi claim to royal status. To counter accusations of extravagance and waste, the occasion was accompanied by the building of thousands of new schools, a new Pahlavi Library to foster all aspects of Iranian studies and a variety of infrastructure projects in the Shiraz region and around the country.

Over the two days of the celebration (15–16 October 1971), the event went smoothly. Television images of an impressively grand Parade of History at Persepolis with thousands of participants dressed up as the soldiers of the ancient Medes and Persians were broadcast around the world by satellite. Heads of state of many of the most important countries of the world, along with senior representatives of many others, were lavishly wined and dined. The catering was laid on by Maxim's of Paris in three huge air-conditioned tents and fifty-nine smaller ones, and 25,000 bottles of wine were imported for the event. Rumours of the overall cost ranged from $100 million to $300 million.[4] The Shah made a speech at the tomb of Cyrus at Pasargadae claiming a rebirth of ancient Iranian greatness: 'Sleep easily, Cyrus, for we are awake.'[5] As an event for the world to mark both the ancient heritage of Iran and the country's new-found wealth and power, it was a success.

But the festivities left most ordinary Iranians nonplussed. The spectacle of distinguished foreigners drinking wine and eating foreign food meant little to them. Along with the international TV broadcasts, the event indeed seemed primarily designed for foreigners.[6] For them, the emphasis on Cyrus and the ancient past might have the appeal of a Hollywood epic, but for most Iranians it ignored the Shi'a Islamic heritage that was central to their identity.[7] To many, the celebrations seemed bogus and artificial, and served only to distance the monarchy further from the people. Like the prophet in the wilderness, Khomeini denounced what he called the decadent debaucheries of the event from his exile in Najaf in Iraq, thundering that Islam was fundamentally opposed to monarchy in principle, that the crimes of Iranian kings had blackened the pages of history, and that even the ones remembered as good had in fact been 'vile and cruel'.[8] Shariati criticized the event, in passing, as part of a series of fiery lectures at the Hoseiniyeh Ershad in the following weeks that contributed to the closure of the institute shortly afterwards. By contrast with the Shah's eulogizing of 2,500 years of monarchy, he spoke of 5,000 years of 'deprivation, injustice, class discrimination and repression'.[9]

As the decade proceeded, the decade in which 2,500 years of Iranian monarchy were to come to an end, the impression given by the celebrations was confirmed, of a Shah remote from his people and their thinking in a range of important ways.

Montazh and Gharbzadegi

Tehran in the 1970s was a strange place. The city was already largely a city of concrete, with only a core of a few older palaces and government buildings. But despite the American cars, the traffic and the ugliness, the older Iran was still there in the *chadors* on the streets, in the smell of mutton kebab grilling on charcoal and fresh *barbari* bread being carried away from local bakeries, in the mountain water running swiftly down the *jubs* at the sides of the road in the dappled shade of the plane trees, and the call to prayer floating over the city at dusk. The West, and the US especially, were constant presences, from the Coca-Cola and Pepsi on sale everywhere to the American advertising and American Forces Radio playing Abba and Blue Oyster Cult – but constant also (beside a continuing admiration for America and an associated desire for economic development) was a tension and a distaste for that presence.

The juxtaposition of old and new, Iranian and foreign, rich and poor, produced odd contrasts common to many developing countries, but odder for the rapidity of the development, the tensions below the surface and the large sums of money being spent in all directions. Wealthy people, many wealthy to a degree most Europeans could only dream of, lived hard by poor people poorer than could be seen anywhere in western Europe. At the end of December 1969 Asadollah Alam, the Shah's court minister, was held up by a traffic accident as he drove in the early morning ('in my sleek Chrysler Imperial') through Farahabad, on the eastern side of the city:

> I waited, and meanwhile I got a glimpse of the life that goes on in that squalid district of Tehran. The street running off from the highway was filthy, not an ounce of asphalt since there's no risk of an inspection by HIM (His Imperial Majesty – i.e. the Shah). It was still early, the traffic police had not come on duty, but a single policeman strutted around, dragging on his cigarette, puffed up like the monarch of all he surveyed. A few men, women wearing the veil, on their way home from the communal bath house . . . a gaggle of children, the girls all veiled. The upper classes would never be up so early in the morning, nor would the girls wear veils. They converged haggling on a merchant selling hot beetroot. Pariah dogs and a few unwashed babies pawing over a heap of rubbish at the street corner . . . shaven-headed servicemen wearing badly cut trousers, ill-fitting boots, strolling along clearly enjoying their Friday morning off. It was both droll and desperately depressing; a scene from a top-heavy society. The Shah struggles day and night, confident that within a decade we shall have surpassed much of the developed world; change can never come quickly enough for him. Yet no manner of wishful thinking can alter life in these streets.[10]

There were a lot of Americans in Tehran in the 1970s, employed as advisers and technicians, and in many other roles. The number of US residents (leaving aside visitors and tourists) in Iran increased from less than 8,000 in 1970 to nearly 50,000 in 1979. There were foreigners from many other countries too, of course, attracted likewise by the money to be earned in activities related to Iran's economic, military and infrastructure development – but benefiting from the special favour of the Shah's regime, the US was much the most important foreign influence. Most of the foreigners lived in Tehran (though many were also to be found in Isfahan, where large numbers of Americans worked in new defence-related industries around the city outskirts). The Americans tended to live entirely separate lives, shopping in the US commissary (the biggest of its kind in the world at the time) and often living on American-only compounds. Many British and other expatriates lived in a similar way. The American school admitted only children with US passports (unusually by comparison with American schools in other countries), and occasional suggestions that the children be taught something about Iran generally failed – a school board member said in 1970 that the policy had been 'Keep Iran Out'. Other Americans, notably those working for the Peace Corps, worked with ordinary Iranians and were much appreciated. But the majority (some of them moving on from the debacle in Vietnam) were in Iran for the money and the lavish lifestyle, which they could not have afforded at home. The American observer James A. Bill commented:

> As the gold rush began and the contracts increased, the American presence expanded. The very best and the very worst of America were on display in the cities of Iran. As time passed and the numbers grew, an increasingly high proportion of fortune hunters, financial scavengers, and the jobless and disillusioned recently returned from Southeast Asia found their way to Iran. Companies with billion-dollar contracts needed manpower and, under time pressure, recruited blindly and carelessly. In Isfahan, hatred, racism and ignorance combined as American employees responded negatively and aggressively to Iranian society.[11]

Within Iranian society there were other tensions. South Tehran was full of young men, newly arrived from conservative-minded villages, either with no jobs or with only poorly paid jobs. For many of them, that meant little prospect of being able to afford to marry or support a family for some years – perhaps indefinitely. But if they paid a small fare for a shared taxi to the richer central and northern parts of the city, for nothing they could see pretty young women parading up and down the streets, dressed in revealing Western fashions, unaccompanied or with girlfriends, flaunting their freedom, money, beauty and, from a certain point of view, immorality and disregard for religion. To those used to life in more traditional parts of the country (where many women spent most of their time in the family home), there just seemed to be *more* women around in Tehran:

> Parviz told him that he was lucky (or unfortunate, depending on how you looked at it) to miss Tehran in the miniskirt craze of the sixties, for one hour on a principal shopping street would have provided him with enough thoughts to repent for a month.

On hoardings, garish posters of half-dressed women advertised the latest films: 'The threatening forwardness of the posters was increased by the large number of tough and sullen-looking young men hanging around.'[12]

Status, and the lack of it, is not just about money – it is also about sex and desire. For those that had moved there from the country, Tehran was a place of aspiration, but in the late 1970s it became a place of resentment, frustrated desire and frustrated aspirations for many.[13]

Aspiration is also about *direction*. The US presence in Iran in the 1970s was small in relative, statistical terms. But in Tehran it dominated advertising, TV and print media – even when the medium was Persian-language. The Iranian upper classes were those most obviously Westernized. So for the rest of society, the models presented to them to aspire to were predominantly Western – and American. They were new and exciting. American advertising and the image of American culture it presented was not shy and retiring. It was self-confident and brash. Even other foreigners in Iran found it so. The response of Iran and Iranians was contradictory and troubled. Many Iranians admired the US and many hoped for the sort of economic development the US stood for. But Iranians had (and have) a great pride in Iran, its history and culture also. Seeing that history and culture shouldered aside in their own country was not easy for them.[14]

One Iranian woman, later a radical student, has written of that time:

> Most of the Americans who lived in Iran behaved in a way that revealed their sense of self-importance and superiority. They had come to expect extra respect, even deference from all Iranians, from shoe-shine boy to shah ... in our country, American lifestyles had come to be imposed as an ideal, the ultimate goal. Americanism was the model. American popular culture – books, magazines, film – had swept over our country like a flood. This cultural aggression challenged the self-identity of people like us. This was the idol which had taken shape within Iranian society. We found ourselves wondering, 'Is there any room for our own culture?'[15]

In his great book *The Mantle of the Prophet* Roy Mottahedeh described this time in Tehran as the time of *montazh* (from the French word *montage* – a setting-up or assembly of parts), when imported things were being assembled and put together in the city, often rather less than satisfactorily, and never quite completed – a time when everything in Tehran seemed to be 'intimately connected with the airport', when 'in joking, Tehranis called all sorts of jerry-built Iranian versions of foreign ideas true examples of Iranian montazh'.[16]

The most obvious examples of *montazh* were the Paykan cars assembled in great numbers just outside Tehran from imported parts (to the design of the British Hillman Hunter) – becoming by far the most common vehicle on Iranian roads. But the same principle could be seen or imagined at work elsewhere too – in the mutual incompatibility of ideas brought home by enthusiastic graduates from American, French and German universities; in corrupt property deals, in big buildings put up without enough cement and left half-finished, in the chaotic traffic, and in the new statues of the Shah that appeared everywhere.

The idea of *montazh* also applied to the huge Shahyad monument, inaugurated just after the celebrations for 2,500 years of monarchy in 1971 to commemorate the reign of the Shah himself; supposedly an amalgam of architectural styles from all periods of Iranian history – and erected just where all visiting foreigners would see it, on the way to the centre of Tehran, just outside Mehrabad airport. *Montazh* recalls Al-e Ahmad's concept of *gharbzadegi* – an intoxication with the West that prompted abandonment of all other principles in pursuit of an alien ideal that could not be properly understood, applied, absorbed or assembled.

Another example was a little pamphlet published in Tehran in 1978 called *Iran Scene*, designed for foreign visitors. The second (April) issue contained articles on Noruz, the province of Fars and the city of Yazd; and a factual section ('Iran at a Glance') including the sentence 'The new single party system known as Rastakhiz (national resurgence) was begun in 1975.' The advertisements contained enough information to enable a foreigner to live almost as he or she might have done in a large Western city – shops, hotels, restaurants (including French, Italian, Greek, Chinese, Indian, Japanese, US-style steak and fried chicken, Mexican, as well as Persian and the Polynesian restaurant Tiare in the InterContinental Hotel); nightclubs and cabarets (including 'La Boheme – Old Shemiran Road, *International show. Expensive*'). There was also a 'Meat Service' offering imported meat, including pork, and all kinds of shellfish; range shooting and skating at the Ice Palace, bowling, and cinema – American, French, German and English films – (including '*Far from the Maddling* [*sic*]*Crowd* with Julie Christie'). And then, amid this international junk, a page entitled 'Literary Scene', and, like a splash of cold water, the poem 'Window' ('Panjareh') by Forugh Farrokhzad, from which the following is a short extract (translated by Ardavan Davaran):[17]

I feel that the time has passed
 I feel that the moment of my portion is of the pages of history ╲
I feel that the table is a false distance between my hair and the
      hands of this sad stranger.
                        Speak a word to me
The person that bestows upon you the kindness of a
      living body
Would want from you what else but the perception of the
      sense of existence?
                        Speak a word to me
I, in the shelter of my window,
Have communication with the sun.

The poetry of Forugh Farrokhzad reflected the wider period in which she lived (she died in a car accident in 1967 when she was only thirty-two years old), but it was also vividly personal, alluding to erotic encounters and traumatic affairs, and their bleak aftermath. The personal nature of the verses and the reaction to it is itself a reflection of the time – such poetry was only barely possible. Its frankness created a furore of shock, and prurient interest in her private life, that threatened to overwhelm Farrokhzad; she said in a radio interview in 1964: 'I really think talking about it is tiring and pointless.'[18] She had married young, giving birth to a son, but separated from her husband in 1955, divorced and was denied access to her son, after which she had a mental breakdown and later attempted suicide.[19] In 1962 she made a hard-to-watch but moving film with the title *The House Is Black* (*Khaneh siah ast*) in an institution for lepers. Her work, insistent above all on the diamond-hard validity of her own voice, fused the edge of European modernism with a strongly Iranian anger about politics, veering between despair and crazy hope. In particular, the poem 'Someone Who Is Like No Other' ('Kasi ke mesl-e hich-kas nist'), mingling millenarian Shi'a religious and Marxist imagery, had an urgent visionary quality:

        I've dreamed that someone is coming.
        I've dreamed of a red star

        . . .

        Someone who is like no one. Not like father,
            not like Ensi, not like

Yahya, not like mother,
And is like the person who he ought to be.

. . .

And his name is just as mother says
at the beginning and the end of her prayer,
the judge of all judges,
the need of all needs,
Someone is coming.
Someone is coming.
Someone who's in heart with us.
In his breathing is with us.
Someone whose coming can't be stopped, and
      handcuffed and thrown in jail.[20]

Aryamehr – 'Light of the Aryans'

Most of the symptoms of strangeness were the outcome of the huge sums of money rolling into the country. Investment rose dizzyingly as Iran continued to benefit from a windfall bonanza of oil income – especially after the oil price doubled in 1973 following the Yom Kippur War, and doubled again at the end of the year, when the Shah led the other OPEC countries to demand higher prices on the claim that oil had not kept pace with the price of other internationally traded commodities. Between 1971 and 1973 the Shah, with the help of his chief adviser and negotiator on oil matters Jamshid Amuzegar, achieved secure control over domestic oil production, a strong position in the OPEC cartel to protect Iranian interests and beyond that, through his leading role in OPEC itself, much higher returns on oil sales for Iran and the other OPEC producers (notably Saudi Arabia and Iraq, but also Kuwait and Venezuela).[21] It was a major achievement, in which the Shah took justifiable pride. Yet more money was pumped into the Iranian economy, though a large amount went back to the West – especially to the US and the UK – in return for quantities of new military equipment. The Shah bought more Chieftain tanks from the UK than the British army itself owned, and by the end of the decade his forces were equipped with some of the very latest military technology, including British Rapier/Blindfire anti-aircraft missile systems and American F-14 fighter aircraft (both of which caused the originators anxiety after 1979, lest the technology fall into the hands of the Russians).[22] The government was awash with money, and a proportion of it flowed, through corrupt commissions and bribes, into private hands; often removed to bank accounts in other countries.

Personally, the Shah was more confident by the 1970s than he had been in the 1950s. He was older and more experienced. His second divorce in 1958 had been traumatic, but he had remarried in 1959, and his new wife, Queen Farah, had given him a son the following year and more children later. He gained confidence from the success, as he perceived it, of the October 1971 celebrations as a breakthrough for him on the international stage; but more seriously from his success in negotiating secure control of Iran's oil production and, through that, influence over OPEC and oil prices. His new confidence emerged in a number of ways. He took a greater interest in foreign policy in the 1970s than he had earlier, and Iran became a more assertive regional actor. The Shah faced down Iraq and secured a favourable settlement of the dispute over the Shatt-al-Arab waterway in the Algiers Accords of 1975. Earlier, he moved into the vacuum left by the departing British imperial presence and occupied the small islands of Abu Musa and the Tunbs (creating a minor dispute with the United Arab Emirates over possession of the islands that continues to this day). Some called him the Policeman of the Persian Gulf. He was lauded by Western leaders and by US presidents in particular as a bulwark against Soviet encroachment in the region, and this role was again reflected in the level of arms sales. The rise in oil prices altered the power balance between the Shah and the West; he had been the partial architect of the rise, and it had damaged Western economies, but the West still needed him. To benefit from Iran's wealth, Western politicians, including those from countries like Britain that had hurt Iran and the Shah's family in the past, fell over themselves to secure contracts.[23] The Shah would not have been human if he had not derived some satisfaction from this.[24]

But the Shah was still scarred by experiences earlier in his reign. In particular, he was wary of further assassination attempts and had himself surrounded by heavy security arrangements. He went from place to place by helicopter and usually viewed parades and other events (carefully staged to give the best impression for the TV cameras) from inside a special bullet-proof glass box.[25] These measures cut him off still more from the people.

The scars showed also in other ways. In 1976 a hugely popular television comedy, *Dear Uncle Napoleon (Dai jan Napoleon*, based on the book of the same title by Iraj Pezeshkzad,[26] one of the funniest comic novels in any language) satirized, among other things, the widespread tendency at the time to blame a concealed British plot – *kar kar-e Ingliseh*, the work of the British – for almost everything, however trivial. From some accounts the Shah himself seems to have been not so far removed from the paranoia of the comedy's main character. Talking to Asadollah Alam in 1970, recalling the attempt to kill him at Tehran university in 1949, the Shah apparently mentioned that his assailant's girlfriend had been the daughter of the head gardener at the British embassy. Alam respectfully doubted that the British would have 'hatched such a stupid plot'. After a pause, the Shah said (alluding to the further attempt on his life in 1965): 'You realize, of course, that British communists made another attempt on my life four years ago?' Alam again demurred.[27] It is hard to accept that the Shah seriously believed that British intelligence were behind both assassination attempts, *and* the communists in Iran, *and* the clerical opposition. But this ingrained suspicion was the legacy of persistent British meddling in the events of the first half of the twentieth century in Iran and in the early part of the Shah's reign. It is borne out by the rueful account of Sir Anthony Parsons, who was British ambassador in Tehran from 1974 to 1979 (the Shah's book that Parsons refers to was published in exile, after his fall):

> In his book, 'Answer to History', the Shah has implied that he did not believe in the sincerity of my advice and that he could not clear his mind of his obsessive suspicion that I was the front-line instrument of some devious British plot to rob him of his throne. But I can only repeat that the advice I gave him was genuinely personal and based on my best judgement of events in a country in which I had served continuously for nearly five years. Indeed, I can still hear my own voice telling the Shah on numerous occasions that I would not tell him what I thought unless he assured me that he would accept what I had to say as the disinterested advice of a genuine well-wisher, untainted by any ulterior motive. He invariably gave me such assurances, although I now know, as I suspected at the time, that he was intellectually and emotionally incapable – who can blame him in the light of his own history? – of accepting my views at their face value.[28]

Despite his successes, the Shah had a persistent sense of insecurity, and his thinking about the forces opposed to him was unrealistic. He was still fundamentally a shy man – 'a rather awkward, withdrawn person, at his best with technocrats, Westerners or cronies, at his worst with people en masse'.[29] A further consequence of the Shah's insecurity was his encouragement of factions and division in his government and court. As in the army high command,[30] his aim was to prevent any one personality from becoming powerful enough to become a danger to him. As under other tyrants, spheres of responsibility overlapped in such a way as to create disputes. Alam and Hoveida were particular enemies.[31]

The atmosphere of rancour and intrigue at court was encouraged, and complicated, by the Shah's extramarital amusements. The Shah had affairs and briefer liaisons with many women; both in Iran and on his trips to other countries. Alam, who was similarly promiscuous, and with whom the Shah compared exploits,[32] recorded that 'even when he finds a companion, however attractive she may be, he sooner or later tires of her'. There were many rumours and much gossip, and anxiety lest the rumours should reach the ears of Queen Farah.[33] Various courtiers acted as procurers for the Shah, but the main man was Amir Hushang Davallu (an offshoot of the old Qajar royal family):

> a man of great shrewdness who by intelligence and sycophancy has risen high in HIM's favour. At court we know him by the accurate enough nickname 'Prince Pimp'. Every year he accompanies HIM to St Moritz, to carry out his rather sordid functions and to indulge his [Davallu's] taste for opium.[34]

Remarkably enough, Davallu appears to have rendered similar services for Nazi generals in Paris during the German occupation of France in the 1940s.[35]

Two further salient features of the court were sycophancy and corruption. The Shah was not stupid, but he was susceptible to flattery, and this contributed to the dangerous unreality of the atmosphere around him.[36] Alam criticized this tendency, but was aware that he too was guilty of contributing to it:

> Submitted the *Daily Telegraph*'s review of HIM's latest book. I told him it struck me as being favourable. 'What on earth's "favourable" about it?' he snapped back, as soon as he'd read it. I told him to look again at the

final paragraph. 'What do you suppose this word "megalomania" means?' he said. 'Greatness,' I replied. 'Greatness be damned,' he exclaimed. 'Greatness to the point of madness.' I was thoroughly ashamed of myself. I should have read it more carefully, but by then it was too late.[37]

On another occasion, the urbane Alam was perhaps playing with a rather gullible interlocutor when he said (replying to her question as to whether the Shah had a flaw):

'I cannot say that he is faultless,' Mr Alam at last replied. 'Everyone, as you say, has faults. But I may say something that – he might not like it, and perhaps it's bad for me to say it, or it might be interpreted as flattery, but what I can say (perhaps you will laugh at me too), his fault to my mind is that he is really too great for his people – his ideas are too great for we people to realize it [sic].'[38]

The effect of the sycophancy (even if tinged, in Alam's case, with a knowing irony) was strengthened by the fact that courtiers and ministers kept information from the Shah, avoiding telling him anything he might not want to hear; concentrating instead on good news and the recycling of propaganda.[39]

Corruption was endemic. Sometimes the Shah accepted it with weary resignation; at other times (when he uncovered a new scandal) it made him furious.[40] It has long been believed that corruption was widespread among the Shah's family.[41] But newly released documents from British diplomatic records indicate that, although the Shah himself has usually been given the benefit of the doubt, he too had been taking sweeteners on defence contracts. After the fall of the Shah, David Owen, foreign secretary at the time, commissioned Nicholas Browne, then seconded to the Cabinet Office, to carry out a post mortem on the conduct of British policy toward Iran. Sir Anthony Parsons (whose valedictory despatch had prompted the exercise) was consulted carefully as the review went forward. Browne wrote to Parsons on 9 October 1979:

The Randel papers strongly suggest that, in accordance with this general behaviour, the Shah personally had been taking money from the British, indirectly through Sir S. Reporter[42] and the Pahlavi Foundation, in return for defence contracts ... I wonder whether we took this into sufficient account in our assessments of the Shah's character, and political standing ... If you think I am prying too much please tell me to shut up ...[43]

From the files so far released, it appears that Browne never had a proper reply, and this angle was passed over when the post mortem was completed. Within the papers so far released that bear upon these matters, some sections have been withheld, several of which appear to relate to the activities of defence attachés.

Pumped-up Autocracy

On several occasions during his time as court minister, according to his own account, Alam urged the Shah to reintroduce a real degree of democracy in the country, in order to close up the dangerous gap between the people and the government.[44] Instead, in the mid-1970s the Shah turned in the direction of reinforcing autocracy. In March 1975 the two parties in the Majles (Mardom and Iran Novin) were abolished and replaced by the Rastakhiz (Resurgence) party. The Shah dismissed criticism that only a decade before he himself had stressed the importance of a two-party system for preparing the way toward democracy; notably in his book *Mission for My Country*, in which he had written:

> If I were a dictator rather than a constitutional monarch, then I might be
> tempted to sponsor a single dominant party such as Hitler organized or such
> as you find today in Communist countries. But as constitutional monarch I
> can afford to encourage large-scale party activity free from the strait-jacket
> of one-party rule or the one-party state.[45]

Now, his statements and those of his ministers were rather less enthusiastic about democracy, echoing the line taken by Hoveida in a speech to the Iran Novin Party's Central Committee in 1970 (confirming the regime's faith that economic development had to precede political development):

> As the Shah has said, social democracy cannot exist without economic
> democracy. In my view most of those who talk about democracy are still
> limited in their concept to the schools of thought advocated by Plato [*sic*],
> Montesquieu and others. We do not believe democracy means anyone should
> be free to act against national interests and moral values and traditions.
> From our standpoint democracy means respecting human rights and indi-
> viduals. The interesting question is whether such democracy exists in those
> countries which are preaching to us on democracy.[46]

By the mid-1970s many of the democratic countries of western Europe and North America were suffering from recession and inflation, unemployment, political unrest, strikes and (in some cases) home-grown anti-democratic terrorism. They (especially the UK) looked weak. Those countries struggled as Iran boomed and prospered, and the Shah was less inclined than previously to defer to them as a model. Democracy also appeared to be in trouble in some of the states that were Iran's neighbours or near neighbours – notably in Pakistan, and in India, where Indira Ghandi declared a state of emergency in June 1975.

Rastakhiz was intended as the apparatus of a one-party state (although it did retain something of the previous fiction of pluralism, in having two wings that were supposed to represent different shades of opinion). Some of its inspiration seems, following the logic of the Shah's White Revolution, to have derived from Leninist theory of a political avant-garde (some of those involved in the early stages had formerly been members of Tudeh).[47] Within a few months Rastakhiz activists set up bodies for farmers, women and industrial workers, and a youth movement; and the party had extended its influence into all sectors of the state bureaucracy. The purpose was to ensure that all elements of Iranian life fell into line with the political opinions, aims and objectives of the party and the Shah – something like Hitler's *Gleichschaltung* ('co-ordination').[48] In introducing the party the Shah gave Iranians a stark choice. He said that anyone who did not join Rastakhiz or support its principles was to be regarded either as a member of Tudeh, in which case he belonged in jail, or as a traitor, in which case he was no longer an Iranian and should leave the country for good.[49]

Before long the effects began to be felt. Under the strictures of Rastakhiz vetting, the number of books published per year fell from 4,200 to 1,300. Writers were imprisoned, some suffered torture, and one was forced to make a televised confession (a tactic now associated more with the Islamic republic) – to the effect that he had not given enough credit in his writing to the successes of the White Revolution. SAVAK men went into libraries and bookshops to remove copies of the Shah's own book *Mission for My Country*, because its statements about freedom and democracy were now out of date. Twenty-two writers, poets, academics and other well-known intellectuals were in prison by the end of 1975.[50] The disillusionment of the intelligentsia was deepened and reconfirmed. Regime propaganda and adulation of the Shah reached new levels. He had taken the title *Aryamehr* ('Light of the Aryans') in 1965 – now he was being called by the ominous title *Farmandeh* ('Commander'). The regime came in for more criticism from human rights organizations (notably Amnesty International),[51] and in June 1977 the Red Cross reported privately to the Shah that 900 out of 3,000 political prisoners in Iranian jails bore signs of torture.[52]

Particular targets for Rastakhiz were the bazaar and the *ulema*. Both had traditionally been centres of potential opposition; both were now subjected to infiltration and coercion. Bazaar guilds were reformed and placed under the direction of state governors. Rastakhiz activists set up offices in the bazaars and forced donations from the merchants and artisans. Employment legislation on minimum wages and health insurance was enforced rigorously on traders who had become accustomed to ignoring it. This pressure added to the economic pressure the *bazaaris* were already feeling. They were seeing their products and businesses edged aside by imports, new factories, suburban stores and supermarkets; and by the introduction of state corporations to import and carry out the wholesale distribution of basic foodstuffs.[53] Newspapers carried articles about the outmoded character of bazaar trading, demolition plans and new boulevards being driven through the bazaar quarters.

The Shah's attack on the *ulema* (building on measures taken by his father to control religious endowments and to influence the training of mullahs) was an attempt to replace the existing Shi'a hierarchy with a new structure whose defining characteristic would be loyalty to the Shah's regime – a *din-e dowlat* (state religion). Rastakhiz intensified the measures taken to achieve this since 1963, which included action to monitor and regulate the operation of religious endowments, and a religious corps (like the literacy corps) to disseminate the official line on Islam in the countryside. The *ulema* also regarded the Family Protection Law of 1967 as an unacceptable attack on important traditions. The new law discarded shari'a practice to allow women to petition for divorce and to have custody of children after divorce if the secular court so decided. It stipulated that a man could only take a second wife if his first wife gave written consent (a largely theoretical provision; polygamous marriage had become, and remains, uncommon in Iran). The government selected and supported pro-regime mullahs to conduct Friday prayer in major mosques.[54] It made a further symbolic change in 1976 to replace the traditional solar calendar that took the year of

Mohammad's flight from Mecca as year 1 with a new calendar taking year 1 as the date of the accession of Cyrus the Great. So instead of 1355, the year was now 2535. The symbolism of dumping Islam as the point of reference in favour of a monarchical date was significant.[55] But also, in terms of the Western date (1976), Iran had jumped from the medieval period to the era of the far future. It was *montazh* again – time itself had been reassembled. In some strange numerological sense, Iran was now ahead.

Khomeini blasted the foundation of Rastakhiz from his exile, claiming that it both violated constitutional norms and was aimed at the destruction of Islam. The regime responded swiftly. Within a short time many of Khomeini's most prominent supporters were arrested, including Ayatollahs Montazeri, Beheshti and Rabbani Shirazi, and more junior clerics who would later take greater roles, including Ali Khamenei.

The aggressive actions of Rastakhiz intensified the political debate within Iran, without creating a genuine link between state and society as the Shah had intended. It appeared that quiet dissent was no longer an option: the regime was intent on erasing all dissent. It was not just Tudeh and extremists that were threatened – large sections of Iranian society became anxious that their interests were in danger.

The 1970s were also the period in which new forms of political extremism appeared, and faded. The two most important groups were the Sazeman-e Cherikha-ye Fedayan-e Khalq-e Iran (usually called the Marxist Fedayan or just the Fedayan) and the Sazeman-e Mojahedin-e Khalq (known as the MKO or the MEK – though since 1979 this organization in exile has disguised itself with a plethora of front organizations, cover names and acronyms – PMOI, NCRI, NLA, etc.). Both groups rejected peaceful politics and the previous political parties on the basis that these had failed to bring about change in Iran – for them the events of 1953 and 1963 amply demonstrated this. They believed the Shah's regime could only be removed by armed struggle, along the lines of what political guerrillas had achieved in Cuba and Algeria. Some of the MKO trained with the PLO in Lebanon. The Fedayan and the MKO were recruited predominantly from educated backgrounds – most of their leaders had been students, and their leftist and anti-US attitudes again reflected the international student activism of the late 1960s and early 70s.

The Fedayan, initially the larger group, were Marxist; the MKO's ideology fused Marxism and Islam (they claimed Shariati as their ideologue but their ideas developed independently and Shariati appears to have kept them at arm's length). On 8 February 1971 guerrillas later associated with the Fedayan attacked a gendarmerie post at Siahkal in Gilan, in an attempt to rescue one of their companions who had been arrested. SAVAK and the authorities responded quickly, and harshly, and within three weeks all thirteen of the attackers were found and executed. Under continuous pressure and having failed to light up the people's revolution as they had anticipated, the Fedayan split in 1975, with one faction favouring continued armed struggle, while the other, at least as a temporary measure, sought instead to work through infiltration of labour organizations and more conventional (if still radical) political activity.

Where the Fedayan grew out of circles associated with Tudeh, the original members of the MKO had connections rather with the Freedom Movement and the Hoseiniyeh Ershad. The MKO attempted to disrupt the Shah's celebrations for 2,500 years of monarchy in October 1971 with a bomb attack and an attempt to hijack an airliner. Like the Fedayan, many of the MKO's people were arrested in 1971 and although they continued to recruit through the 1970s and continued attacks, including assassinations of six Americans in Iran between 1973 and 1976,[56] recruitment was unable to keep pace with the arrests. By 1976–7 SAVAK had effectively repressed both organizations (more than 300 MKO and Fedayan, plus fighters and supporters from similar, smaller groups, were killed in these years) but when the revolution began and some political prisoners were released both guerrilla movements were reinvigorated.[57]

Achievements

The Shah's regime had achieved a lot by the mid-1970s. Unlike many other national leaders in many countries (including some democratic politicians) the Shah deserved credit not just for governing to secure himself, his dynasty or his interest group in power, but for a genuine effort to move his country forward in its development, which achieved real gains. Gross National Product per capita had jumped to $2,000 from $200 (in 1963). Much of this was down to the oil boom – but the Shah was himself partly responsible for the big rise in oil income, and the income was being reinvested. The country had reoriented away from agriculture toward more developed economic activities that would yield greater benefits to the people, in industry and services. The movement of population to the cities, however traumatic and marked by deprivation it was in the short term, could be regarded as a necessary step towards a more sophisticated, developed, modern society. Investment had greatly improved infrastructure and the standard of education and health services.[58] Women and minorities had benefited from his reforms. Iran was respected internationally and had taken on a more confident regional role, as evidenced by her influence both within OPEC and within the regional security organization CENTO. The Shah's relationship with the US had also matured since the 1950s; he was less of a stooge and more of a partner.

But it was a mixed picture. There was also waste and corruption, and huge inequality.[59] The surge of investment for growth created a problem of what the planners called 'absorptive capacity' – the scale of investment was such that the existing administrative, transport and other infrastructure could not cope with the expansion. Vital industrial supplies waited for weeks and months at Iran's borders because customs officials could not process the paperwork quickly enough, or because the ports did not have the capacity to unload them from ships quickly enough, or because there were not enough lorries to carry them away once unloaded. When extra lorries were imported, there was a shortage of drivers. This situation was of course a dream for corrupt officials, who took bribes from those who could pay to jump the queue.[60] Because the population was expanding rapidly (from about 15 million in 1939–40 to just under 19 million in 1956, 25.3 million in 1966 and 33.7 million in 1976),[61] improvements in health and education provision, for example, did not have the impact that had been hoped. Infant mortality dropped, but was still high; 68 per cent of adults were still illiterate and fewer than 40 per cent of children completed primary school. Illiteracy was particularly marked in the countryside, reflecting again the Shah's inclination to sacrifice traditional, rural Iran for the development of urban Iran.[62] Standards of housing in the poorer parts of the cities were desperately inadequate. Not all the effects of the oil boom were beneficial. Some of the elements of what has been called the rentier economy began to emerge: an overgrown, inefficient (and often corrupt) bureaucracy, real-estate speculation, damage to import-substitution industries by rising costs of domestic production and erosion of non-oil exports by a high currency exchange rate.[63]

The most important failures were primarily political. The state was not totalitarian, but it was not free either, and the dynamic was heading in the wrong direction. As the Shah had grown more confident, his rule had grown more autocratic, and his previously declared aspirations to democracy had faded. By 1975 he had no programme for restoring representative government, and his only solution for dissent was propaganda and repression. If he had succeeded in making the monarchy truly popular, perhaps he could have sustained that for a time, but instead the monarchy had become ever more remote and disconnected from the attitudes and concerns of the people. Rastakhiz had succeeded only in destabilizing assumptions and stirring up resentment, rather than thickening the attachment between the Shah and ordinary Iranians, as Alam had advocated it should. Partly as a result of combating real and imaginary Marxists for so long, the Shah made the mistake of himself taking an overly materialist, Marxist analysis (as we have seen, his thinking showed a Marxism-through-the-Looking-Glass tendency in a number of areas). He believed that material prosperity would yield political stability, and that his faith in the ancient bond between people and monarch would be justified by economic success and renewed gratitude. But few economies deliver continuous sustained growth indefinitely, and politics is often an ungrateful business.

Iraq – and Khomeini

Another manifestation of the Shah's stronger position and greater confidence in the mid-1970s was the successful resolution of outstanding disputes with Iraq. For the most part the position of the long border between the two countries was uncontroversial and had been stable since the Zohab treaty agreed between the Safavids and the Ottomans in 1639 (given more exact delineation by a multi-nation border commission in 1914). But for many years there had been uncertainty and disagreement over the precise position of the border at its southernmost point, where the waters of the Tigris and Euphrates flowed into the Persian Gulf along the waterway known as the Shatt al-Arab (Arvand Rud in Persian). The uncertainty was important because of the proximity of both countries' oilfields, and because both used the waterway for the passage of oil tankers carrying oil away for export. As vice-president of Iraq, Saddam Hussein had claimed the whole waterway up to the Iranian shore.

Tension rose in 1974–5 as the Kurdish leader Mostafa Barzani led a successful insurgency against the Iraqi regime further north, supported by the Shah with weapons and other supplies.[64] As this progressed, the Shah went further, allowing artillery fire across the border in support of the Kurds and finally, sending two units of the Iranian army into Iraqi territory. With the Kurds increasingly successful and the threat of war with Iran looming, Saddam sought a settlement through Algerian mediation. An agreement was signed in Algiers in March 1975 which, as set out in more detailed treaties signed later, agreed to the Iranian position that the Shatt al-Arab border should be in the deepest part of the river, where the flow was most rapid (the *Thalweg* – this solution was potentially still problematic because the pattern of flow of the river changed over time, and the waterway had to be dredged regularly to remove silt). In return, Iran agreed to end its support for the Iraqi Kurds. The result for the Kurds was that their insurgency collapsed within days, Barzani had to take refuge in Iran, and large numbers of Kurds surrendered to Iraqi troops. Iraq resented the concessions over the Shatt al-Arab, and the dispute surfaced again in 1980 as one of the causes of the Iran–Iraq War.

Another consequence of the Algiers agreement was that Shi'a pilgrims were again free to visit the shrines at Karbala, Najaf and elsewhere in Iraq. This new freedom of movement made it easier for pilgrims to bring propaganda material back with them when they returned to Iran, notably Khomeini's speeches recorded on cassette tapes. After a time the Shah began to put pressure on the Iraqi government to expel Khomeini, who had been living in Najaf (the city of seminaries that contains the shrine of the Emam Ali) since he left Turkey in 1965. While in Najaf Khomeini had developed further his network of contacts within Iran, and a theory of Islamic government, but he was opposed in Najaf by the powerful Ayatollah Abol-Qasem Khoei, who took a more traditional, more quietist position like that of Borujerdi in the 1950s; resistant to involvement in politics. His followers came to be known as the Najafi school, opposed to the school of Khomeini, and since Khoei's death in

1992 these positions have been maintained and taken forward by Ayatollah Ali Sistani. Khoei and Sistani were both Iranian-born. Although both spent most of their lives in Iraq, and despite the Iranian revolution, large numbers of ordinary Iranians have followed their example as their *marja-e taqlid* (source of emulation).

Khomeini's theory was not accepted by the Shi'a *ulema* as a whole; indeed initially, it was not accepted by very many at all. In 1906–11 the *ulema* had controlled a hierarchy and a national network of supporters that allowed them to be an actor in politics, while remaining reluctant to take the responsibilities of government upon themselves. Then and later (notably in 1951–3) their beliefs limited them to encouraging and supporting secular political actors with whom they thought they were in sympathy – with mixed results, as we have seen. But now Khomeini's new ideas (prompted and radicalized by his experience in 1963–4) meant that the clergy, or at least a section of them, might try to take power in their own right.[65] Khomeini stayed in Iraq until October 1978, when the Iraqis finally ejected him. Having failed to get into Kuwait, he went (briefly, as it turned out) to Paris.

The Economy Falters; Carter Arrives

By mid-1976 the economy was overheating, there was too much money chasing too few goods, imports could not keep pace, there were bottlenecks and shortages, and inflation rose sharply – especially on items like foodstuffs and housing rent, and especially in Tehran, where rents rose by 300 per cent in five years in some areas. Then growth began to subside, as inflation ramped up.[66] The Shah blamed profiteering for the price rises, arrested some well-known entrepreneurs, and then turned on small traders, sending gangs (backed by SAVAK) into the bazaars to make arrests. Shops were closed down, 250,000 fines were issued, and 8,000 shopkeepers were given prison sentences – none of which altered the underlying economic realities one jot. The arrests and fines joined the list of grievances felt by *bazaari* artisans and merchants, fuelling their anxiety that the regime intended to eradicate them altogether.[67]

The government realized in the early part of 1977 that there was serious trouble ahead.[68] Iran's developing economy had run out of control, and the period of heroic spending was coming to an end because there was going to be a slump in oil revenues (against the Shah's wishes, Saudi Arabia had negotiated a cut in production within OPEC). In mid-1977 the worrying economic picture prompted the Shah to change his prime minister. After twelve years in that job Hoveida moved over to become court minister (taking over from Asadollah Alam, who had been forced to retire by ill-health; leukaemia killed him the following year). Jamshid Amuzegar took over as prime minister, and introduced a new, deflationary economic policy, designed to moderate government spending, bring inflation under control and restore some stability. But the result, as growth declined further, was a jump in unemployment. Inflation and the sudden faltering of the economy particularly affected the poor, but to some extent everyone; rents were high for the middle- class engineers, managers and professionals in Tehran just as for the slum dwellers, and those with a stake in new businesses and loans to service felt the impact of deflation acutely. The sense of economic crisis added to the political uncertainty that had been created by Rastakhiz, and those who had forgiven the regime's other shortcomings for their competence in economic development felt their faith slipping away.

In January 1977 Jimmy Carter took over from Gerald Ford as president of the United States. The Shah had always been more at ease with Republican presidents than with Democrats. From this point on, he came to feel greater pressure on his regime's human rights record. Carter and his advisers were less tolerant of repressive allies than their predecessors had been, and the Shah began to relax some of the instruments of repression.[69] In February some political prisoners were released. Later on court rules were changed to allow prisoners proper legal representation, and access to civilian rather than just military courts. The Shah met representatives from Amnesty International and agreed to improve prison conditions. In May a group of lawyers sent a letter to the Shah, protesting at government interference in court cases. Politicians and activists who had kept out of trouble for years began to wonder whether they might now cautiously re-emerge. In June three National Front activists, Karim Sanjabi, Shapur Bakhtiar and Dariush Foruhar, sent a bold letter to the Shah criticizing autocratic rule and demanding a restoration of constitutional government. Later that month the Writers' Association, suppressed since 1964, resurrected itself and pressed for the same goals, and for the removal of censorship (many of the leading members were Tudeh sympathizers or broadly leftist). When the Shah replaced Hoveida with the more moderate Amuzegar in July, the change was interpreted as part of a movement towards a more liberal position. In the autumn more political associations reconstituted themselves; notably the National Front, under the leadership of Sanjabi, Bakhtiar and Foruhar; and the Freedom Movement, closely associated with the National Front, under Mehdi Bazargan and Yadollah Sahabi.[70] At this stage, all these groups, representing mainly the educated middle classes, were calling for a constitutional monarchy and the full restoration of the constitution of 1906.

The Freedom Movement (Nehzat-e Azadi-ye Iran – sometimes translated as the Liberation Movement) had been founded in 1961 by Mehdi Bazargan and Ayatollah Mahmud Taleqani, among others. Both were important figures in the history of political Islam in Iran. Ali Shariati was also active in the Movement in its early years, but the line taken by Bazargan and Taleqani was less radical than Shariati's in the main – aimed at a liberal, democratic politics that was compatible with Islam, while keeping a distance from the anticlericalism of some in Mossadeq's circle (Taleqani had been one of the few clerics to continue supporting Mossadeq after his split with Kashani in the run-up to the crisis of August 1953). The Freedom Movement was significant in the events of 1963–4, supporting the demonstrations against the Shah and suffering with other opposition groups in the aftermath. Like Khomeini, Taleqani was arrested in 1963 – and again in the early 1970s amid the fuss that led to the closure of the Hoseiniyeh Ershad (which he and Bazargan had helped to establish). The Freedom Movement kept up a stream of propaganda against the Shah's regime in its publications outside Iran, coordinated by Ebrahim Yazdi, often stressing its ideas' line of descent from those of the Constitutional Revolution, and the need for an alliance between the *ulema* and the secular intelligentsia if free, democratic government were ever to be established in Iran.

In the later 1960s and 70s the Freedom Movement continued activity at a low level within Iran, but also among students and others in the US and in France (where its leaders were Ebrahim Yazdi and Sadegh Qotbzadeh – Abol Hassan Bani-Sadr was associated with the Freedom Movement but had connections with the National Front also, and generally kept a somewhat semi-detached position). Bazargan, Taleqani, Sahabi and their movement were influential in their advocacy of political Islam, but also because, from their activity in 1963 and their pro-Islamic position, they were trusted by Khomeini and were able to keep contact with him in exile.[71] In 1978–9 this put them in a crucial position as a hinge between Khomeini and the rest of the non-clerical opposition to the Shah. All these members of the Freedom Movement became important figures in the first two years of the revolution.

Khomeini and his supporters among the clergy were also alert to the rise in tension and the relaxation of regime repression in 1976–7, and set up a group to coordinate their work against the regime. It was called the Jame-ye Ruhaniyat-e Mobarez (the Combatant Clergy Association) and was effectively a tighter reconfiguration of the Coalition of Islamic Societies that had backed Khomeini in 1963–4 – where the Coalition had included secular *bazaari* members, the new group positioned the clergy firmly to the fore. Founder members were Morteza Motahhari (the first leader of the association), Mohammad Beheshti, Ali Khamenei, Akbar Hashemi Rafsanjani, Mohammad Javad Bahonar, Mohammad Reza Mahdavi-Kani and Mohammad Mofatteh. The association and its leading members were central to the development of the pro-Khomeini revolutionary movement and its establishment of control over the countrywide network of mosques, *madresehs* and religious societies in 1978. Most of them took important positions in the new Islamic republic in 1979.

On 10 October 1977 the Goethe Institut in Tehran hosted an evening of poetry readings organized by the newly revived Writers' Association. It was the first of a series of ten such evenings, which from the beginning had a political character, demonstrating again the close association between politics and literature in Iranian cultural life. The German director, coming under pressure from the authorities, became more and more anxious that SAVAK would close the institute down, and watched the proceedings from a distance with a bottle of whisky that gradually emptied as each night went on. Many of the speeches made in between the readings were strongly critical of the Shah's regime, pushing against the boundaries of what was becoming permissible again. Many, if not most, of the speakers were Tudeh sympathizers; most of the audience were young students. On the fifth evening one speaker asked for a minute of silence for those writers of the previous half century who had suffered under censorship and repression and had died prematurely – among them the poet Nima Yushij, Sadegh Hedayat, Samad Behrangi,[72]

Jalal Al-e Ahmad, and Ali Shariati, who had died only four months earlier.[73] By this time (despite the fact that there was virtually no reporting of them in the state-controlled media) the evenings were attracting crowds of several thousands, some of them from distant parts of the country, to huddle in the garden of the institute. Audio and video tapes were recorded, reproduced outside the country, reimported and distributed. The poet and playwright Saïd Soltanpur, a prominent member of the Association, agreed to moderate his readings in order to avoid trouble, but when he came to the microphone found himself unable to hold back, reading some of his most radical poems against the Shah, some of them written when he had been in prison. The bolder and more anti-regime the poems became, the more popular they were with the audience. By the end of the series the organizers had managed to avoid serious trouble, but a further series of evenings held at the Aryamehr University ran into greater difficulties.[74] On 22 November a rally of National Front supporters just outside Tehran, aimed at forming a new anti-regime coalition, was violently broken up by SAVAK before it could really start.[75]

Another event that raised the tension that autumn was the suspicious death of Khomeini's son, Mostafa. A respected cleric in his own right, Mostafa had been living in exile in Najaf in Iraq like his father. One evening in October he was visited there by two unidentified Iranians and the next morning he was found dead, apparently from a heart attack.[76] The news reached Qom quickly, and memorial gatherings took place there (organized by Morteza Motahhari and others), in Tehran, and also in Yazd, Shiraz and Tabriz. At first Khomeini himself responded to the news calmly and non-committally, but at the memorial events there were calls for Khomeini to return to Iran, anti-Shah slogans, and accusations that SAVAK had murdered Mostafa. Over the next few weeks, word spread in Qom that there would be further substantial demonstrations at the beginning of December, on the traditional fortieth day (arba'in, or in more common usage chelom) after Mostafa's death. The forty-day period of mourning was to take on greater significance the following year. Khomeini's supporters used the network of contacts and the hierarchy of relationships among the clergy and religious students to organize speeches and demonstrations on the day. In Qom large numbers attended the speeches, which had been coordinated and made relatively moderate demands: for Khomeini's return, the release of prisoners like Ayatollahs Taleqani and Montazeri (Khomeini's close ally), freedom of speech, and the restoration of the Islamic calendar. But the mood was turning more radical. After the speeches religious students went on to the streets, chanting 'Marg bar Shah' ('Death to the Shah') outside the Faiziyeh seminary, which had been closed down by the authorities after disturbances in 1975. Police broke up the demonstrations, beat people up, and arrested some. There were further disturbances in the bazaar district of Tehran around Ashura on 21 December, including marches with banners, and there were more arrests. Mostafa's death had brought Khomeini's name back on to people's lips. SAVAK bosses noted the upsurge in religious dissent.[77]

The Shah himself was in Washington in November, where he had talks with President Carter at the White House on 15 and 16 November.[78] Much of the visit was taken up with discussions on the supply of military equipment and the regional politics of the Middle East. Some at least of Carter's officials found the Shah an impressive interlocutor – Hamilton Jordan, who was Carter's chief of staff, commented later rather fulsomely that the Shah had been one of the most astute international statesmen that Carter met around that time. But the Shah's response to Carter's tentative probing on the human rights situation was defensive in a way that was becoming characteristic – according to him the critics of his rule were all communists, and his response was dictated by the law, leaving him little room for manoeuvre. For his part, privately, he judged that Carter was naive about the communist threat. The Shah continued to misunderstand the domestic opposition and perversely to pretend that his regime's response was out of his hands.

While in Washington, the Shah was given an official welcome by the president in front of the White House. But there were demonstrations against the Shah by a large mixed group of Iranian and American protestors, who appeared mainly to be young students. The US ambassador to Iran, William Sullivan, who was in Washington to accompany the Shah, noted with surprise that some of them carried placards with Khomeini's face on them. Queen Farah was surprised too – she could not understand why students with a progressive political agenda would take as their hero someone she regarded as a reactionary traditionalist.[79] At one point the police, in danger of losing control, used tear gas on the demonstrators. Unfortunately the wind was in the wrong direction, and the gas drifted toward the VIP group. The Shah had to bring out his handkerchief to wipe his eyes, in full view of the TV cameras. The Shah's loss of face made an impression in Iran, where some (unable to accept that it was an accident) assumed the US government had deliberately humiliated him to show that their support for him was waning.

Another incident on this trip showed the Shah's shyness, and lack of a common touch. Knowing the Shah's liking for jazz, Carter had arranged a private performance by Dizzy Gillespie and Sarah Vaughan. Another even more legendary figure, Earl 'Fatha' Hines, was present in the audience as a guest, and at the end Carter persuaded him to join Gillespie for a final impromptu session together. 'As the applause was swelling,' Carter went on stage with the First Lady to congratulate and thank the performers. Empress Farah tried to nudge the Shah to do the same, but he sat stiffly in his place until she was forced virtually to shove him up on to the stage, where he shook hands 'in evident discomfort'.[80]

Whatever the rumours and suspicions in Iran, Carter was keen to display his backing for the Shah's regime. He accepted an invitation for a quick return visit only a few weeks later. He was in Tehran on New Year's Eve and made a speech that became notorious, declaring the Shah's Iran to be an 'island of stability' in the region, saying that 'There is no other head of state with whom I feel on friendlier terms and to whom I feel more gratitude.'[81] In his first year, and having had a more domestic perspective previously than some presidents, Carter was still finding his feet in international politics. He had a clear sense of Iran's importance to US policy. But his praise was already more perhaps a sign of unease than an indicator of his true feelings, and the enthusiasm of his speech was misleading.

At around the same time the British ambassador, Anthony Parsons, sent his usual annual review despatch back to London. He used it to draw attention to the awakening of political dissent and the economic difficulties of the regime, though he assessed 'no threat to basic stability'. The response of his colleagues in London was mixed. The formal reply to his despatch airily asked whether the character of Iranians had really changed from their stereotype ('the epitome of idleness, deceitfulness, corruption, charm and conceit'), and suggested that other regional leaders (Sadat in Egypt for example) 'would be glad to exchange their problems for the Shah's'.[82]

Four Times Forty Days

On 7 January 1978, presumably in response to the earlier protests over the death of Mostafa Khomeini, a politically motivated article attacking the clergy and Khomeini appeared in the paper *Ettela'at*. The article had been written by someone trusted by the regime (under the pseudonym Ahmad Rashidi Motlaq) and according to one account had been passed to the editor of *Ettela'at* via the court minister, Hoveida, and the information minister, Dariush Homayun. Alarmed by its content, the editor queried the instruction to publish, but was given to understand that the Shah himself had given his approval.[83] Published under the title 'Black and Red Imperialism', the article alleged that Khomeini was plotting with communists and British interests against the Shah's government, and that other senior clerics did not support his opposition to the monarchy. It also said that he was a foreigner (from his grandfather's birth in India) and a poet (the last was true, and was intended to detract from his clerical seriousness: most *ulema*, with some backing from the Koran, disapproved of poetry), and even suggested that he was a homosexual.

Many of the religious class were outraged. Within a few hours of its arrival in Qom, religious students were going from house to house en masse, pressing religious leaders to sanction protests against the article, which they regarded as a deliberate insult. In the streets they clashed with the police, abused the 'Yazid government' and demanded an apology, a constitution, and the return of Khomeini. But on the first day (8 January) there were no serious casualties. The senior clerics recognized the indignation of the students, but were worried that the authorities would use demonstrations as an excuse to take further action against religious institutions. Some prevaricated (Haeri, Shariatmadari); others cautiously supported peaceful protest (Golpaygani). There was a student strike on 8 and 9 January, and the bazaar closed in support. On 9 January the leaders of the demonstrations called for calm and silence rather than the chanting of the previous day, but there were further confrontations with the police, stone-throwing and broken windows. The crowds were now thousands strong. The police fired in the air initially and the demonstrators scattered, but when they regrouped some police fired directly at them. Several were killed – early reports suggested twenty or thirty, but the real number was perhaps as low as five.[84] When news of the deaths spread, there were protest demonstrations in cities across the country. The next day Khomeini praised the courage of the students and called for more demonstrations. Shariatmadari and others in Qom condemned the shootings (several at least of those killed had been religious students from Iranian Azerbaijan; Shariatmadari's followers), supported the call for a return to constitutional government, and urged people to observe the traditional commemoration (*chelom*) after forty days.

In the intervening period many of the clergy spoke out to urge restraint, and the demonstrations in twelve cities on 18 February, after the forty days, were mainly peaceful. Bazaars and universities closed. But in Tabriz (where the demonstrations were large, reflecting the origin of the victims shot in Qom) the police locked the main mosque of the city, next to the bazaar and attempted to bar entry. The demonstrators overwhelmed them and turned to attacking and occupying buildings that were symbols for disapproval – police stations, Rastakhiz Party buildings, banks, cinemas and shops that sold alcohol. Again the police fired on the crowd, causing more deaths, and within a few hours army units, including armoured vehicles, were brought in to restore state control. Again the number of deaths was exaggerated in reports – research after the revolution has suggested the real number killed was thirteen,[85] but there would have been a larger number of wounded. The forty-day rhythm continued, breathing in indignation, breathing out more demonstrations and intensified radicalism like a great revolutionary lung. With each cycle moderate clerics like Ayatollahs Shariatmadari and Marashi-Najafi in Qom, Khademi in Isfahan and Abdollah Shirazi in Mashhad came under greater pressure from radicals and supporters of Khomeini, who exhorted them to condemn the regime as well as the killings, and in some cases camped in the clerics' houses. As in previous crises in Iran, the informal network of contacts and associations between mosques, seminaries, bazaar guilds, *marjas*, mullahs and their followers came into play to organize and coordinate the protests. The moderates began to take a harder line, and support among religious students shifted to favour more radical clerics.[86] The demonstrations grew larger and more vocal.

On 29 March there were large commemorations for the dead of Tabriz in fifty-five cities and towns, most of which were peaceful, but violence broke out in several places, including Tehran, Isfahan and

Yazd. The rioters targeted similar buildings to those that had been assaulted in Tabriz, but some statues of the Shah and his father were also attacked, as in 1953. This time the violence was worst in Yazd, where Ayatollah Mohammad Saduqi, a follower of Khomeini, became the centre of protest. As protestors came out of his mosque, heading for the main police station, they were fired on, and many were killed – the official figure given was twenty-seven, but the opposition claimed more than 100.[87] On 10 May, after another forty days, there were large demonstrations again across the country, and the Shah cancelled an overseas trip to stay close to developments in Tehran, where the bazaar district was sealed off with troops and the authorities used tear gas to disrupt a gathering outside the Friday Mosque (in fact the protests ran from 6 to 11 May). In Qom the city was rocked by demonstrations and riots for ten hours, more died in shootings, and at one point agents of the regime pursued activists into Shariatmadari's house and shot two dead.[88]

But although mourning was called for again on 17 June, the cycle of demonstrations was broken at this point, and there was a pause. One reason for this was that Shariatmadari, supported by Golpaygani and Marashi-Najafi in Qom, urged that mourners should stay at home on the day in order to avoid further deaths. There was a perception that the regime's stance was hardening and that the response on 17 June might be particularly harsh. But Khomeini called for the street demonstrations to continue. Why did Khomeini's followers, notably Beheshti and the others coordinating the radical effort in Tehran, acquiesce to Shariatmadari's policy of restraint? They might have felt that they had temporarily reached the limit of the support they could mobilize by this tactic, and that to continue with it would only make themselves more vulnerable. Initially the forty-day rhythm had worked in favour of the protests, by providing dates for demonstrators to rally to. But now, with the cycle established, the dates might begin to work for the regime, by enabling them to prepare for repression (this was perhaps the lesson of what happened in Tehran on 10 May); and the protestors might begin to lose out if their numbers, intimidated by the violence of the authorities, started to fall off. Perhaps they just felt the need for a breathing-space or wanted to avoid a division between the followers of Khomeini and the more moderate clergy.[89] Perhaps it was a combination of these factors. Whether the pause was tactical or not, approved by the radicals or not, there was no particular sign of a disagreement among the clergy over the issue, and 17 June passed off peacefully. But feeling was still running high.

Over the previous months the Shah's government had followed a tough policy of arresting and intimidating leading opposition figures. By mid-summer about seventy of Khomeini's clerical supporters had been arrested, including important members of the Combatant Clergy Association like Ali Khamenei and Akbar Hashemi Rafsanjani.[90] SAVAK also targeted members of the secular opposition – the Writers' Association, the Freedom Movement and the National Front. Human rights activists and others received threatening letters, some were beaten up and the offices of Karim Sanjabi, Mehdi Bazargan and Dariush Foruhar among others were bombed. Meetings were attacked by thugs in the pay of the regime and were broken up.[91]

At the same time as it attacked opposition groups, over the summer the government tried to placate popular feeling by making concessions. The regime promised truly free elections for the following year (the Shah made a speech to this effect on 5 August),[92] and to reopen the Faiziyeh seminary in Qom – it ended the harassing measures against small *bazaari* traders, apologized to Shariatmadari for the attack on his home and replaced the chief of SAVAK, General Nasiri. The Shah also tried to address accusations of corruption against his own court by directing that members of his family should end their business activities.[93] Some secular liberals were encouraged by the concessions, but Khomeini and his followers were implacable.

The Shah was reluctant to permit all-out violent suppression of the demonstrations, but despite his extensive security apparatus, he was largely baffled by the protests against his rule. Members of that apparatus seemed scarcely better aware. Part of the problem was that what was happening did not fit with their expectations of the threat – primarily, as they had thought, from Marxism – or their rhetoric against it. Others in the regime fell back on the suspicion that foreign powers were involved – usually code for the British or the US. Prime Minister Amuzegar seems to have genuinely believed, such was the level of malicious backbiting at court, that the protests were engineered by Hoveida and others to get rid of him personally.[94] Amuzegar was wrong – but right too in a sense; on 27 August the Shah removed him and appointed Jafar Sharif-Emami, who came from a clerical family and had connections with the *ulema*. There was a further tentative relaxation of some regime controls: some press restrictions were lifted, the Shah's Imperial calendar was abolished and the old calendar was restored. In addition, in another attempt to appease religious opinion, the government banned casinos.

Mashhad, Ramadan, Isfahan, Abadan

Despite 17 June passing off quietly, other incidents in June and July showed that tension was still high and opposition to the government still strong. On 15 July some protestors were shot in Rafsanjan, but more serious demonstrations in several cities followed the death in a car crash of Sheikh Ahmad Kafi, a popular preacher, on 20 July. In Mashhad several mourners were shot and killed. Ramadan began on 6 August. The month of daytime fasting was always an unusual time, sometimes tense, of heightened religious feeling. It was normal for there to be daily gatherings at mosques at dusk, and in August 1978 these became regular occasions for political debate and the intensification of feeling against the government. There were renewed demonstrations in several cities, more or less spontaneous, but in Isfahan feeling was stronger because of the recent arrest of Seyyed Jalaloddin Taheri, one of the most prominent and popular clerics in the city. There were nightly demonstrations until 10 August, when the authorities lashed back with force, and a number of participants were killed. They then imposed martial law and a curfew, with troops and tanks on the streets. There were demonstrations and killings on 10 August in Shiraz also, and protest demonstrations against the killings followed in other cities in subsequent days.

On 19 August a terrible incident raised indignation against the government to a new pitch. A fire broke out in the Rex Cinema in Abadan and killed about 370 people – emergency doors were locked from the outside. Government and opposition both accused each other, but events, trials and investigations in later years indicate that a radical Islamic group with connections to *ulema* figures was responsible.[95] Despite the fact that clerical disapproval of cinemas was well known, and that cinemas had been attacked by demonstrators earlier in the year, the mood was such that most believed SAVAK had started the fire in order to blame religious radicals. The fire was important in turning many ordinary Iranians definitively against the Shah's rule. Many had reached that point at which they not only did not believe what their government told them – such was their distrust that they assumed that the opposite of what they were being told must be true. There were new demonstrations in cities across the country, and many jumped in size from around 10,000 to double that number or more. By the end of the month ten more cities were under martial law.[96]

Eid-e Fetr is the holiday at the end of Ramadan that ends the month of fasting. In 1977 prayers had been held in the open air at Qeytarieh in north Tehran on the day, and in 1978 the authorities gave permission for the event to be repeated, on the understanding that it would be peaceful and limited to the designated site (this may have been one aspect of the gentler line taken by the new prime minister, Sharif-Emami). The prime organizers were two *bazaaris* with National Front connections, but the cleric chosen to lead the prayers was Ayatollah Mohammad Mofatteh, who was aligned with Khomeini. There is some uncertainty about just what was intended by whom, but some of those present had brought banners and placards with pictures of Khomeini, and as the planned event came to an end, large additional numbers appeared. Mofatteh announced that the programme was over and (perhaps disingenuously) asked the crowd to follow marshals to the exits, but instead an impromptu march began, heading off almost the length of the city, downhill towards the bazaar district. As it went the demonstration grew in size; later estimates ranged between 200,000 and 500,000. The hum of the crowd and their chanting could be heard far over the city, even in normally quiet, affluent parts of north Tehran like Shemiran and the Elahieh ridge, where butterflies floated among the tall trees and swimming pools. Participants, impressed by the size of the demonstration, felt as though the whole country was marching. Troops encountered along the route stood aside and asked the marchers to avoid violence, because they did not want to shoot. Members of the crowd threw flowers at them and chanted 'Soldier, Brother, why do you kill your brothers?' It was much the biggest demonstration up to that time and marked a shift up to a genuinely popular movement; no longer just one or two radicalized sections of society. And it was peaceful.[97]

The Shah had flown over the demonstrations in a helicopter, and afterwards listened to recordings of some of the chanting. He was shocked by what he heard – it seems it was in these days that the seriousness of what was happening in the country finally broke through. But he still could not grasp the *nature* of the force that was growing against him. Perhaps it was not the communists who were behind it, but the US and the British? A revolution was growing on the streets, but in the Shah's thinking no revolution dawned.[98] In his book *Shah of Shahs* Ryszard Kapuscinski wrote:

> The Shah was reproached for being irresolute. Politicians, they say, ought to be resolute. But resolute about what? The Shah was resolute about retaining his throne, and to this end he explored every possibility. He tried shooting and he tried democratizing, he locked people up and he released them, he fired some and promoted others, he threatened and then he commended. All in vain.[99]

The Shah's Illness

Some have suggested that a major reason for the Shah's inability to deal with the protests, and therefore a major reason for his eventual fall, was that he was ill.[100] He had been diagnosed with a form of leukaemia in May 1974, having himself noticed a swelling in his abdomen the previous autumn, which turned out to be an enlarged spleen. There followed one of those odd chains of events that sometimes take place in royal courts, which demonstrate that, bizarrely, even an autocratic court circle may work against the personal interests of the monarch it is supposed to serve. When the Shah was diagnosed, the French doctors who made the diagnosis gave it not to him, but to the Shah's doctor, General Ayadi, who passed on the news to the Shah himself, to Professor Safavian (chancellor of Tehran University and a trained physician – he had arranged the contact with the French doctors) and to Asadollah Alam, but to no one else beyond that restricted group. But even to them, Ayadi seems not to have passed on the full seriousness of the diagnosis – he did not want to upset the Shah. Concern that the news should not get out was paramount; at several points the need for secrecy interfered with and prevented treatment. Queen Farah was not told at all (she only found out in the spring of 1977). There was no further investigation or treatment for four months, until September 1974, when the French doctors were asked to return (to their surprise – they had expected that American doctors would be called in). As time went on, it became clear that the Shah's condition was worsening, but the same casual attitude to treatment continued. The Shah was not told the disease was cancer, but was given vague terms like 'lymphoma' (he probably worked it out for himself, nevertheless). Only when Queen Farah was told did the treatment become more intensive, and by then it was probably too late. It may be that from the beginning nothing could have been done anyway, but the situation within the Shah's court certainly did not help.[101]

The main effect the illness had on the Shah's thinking seems to have been to add a sense of urgency that the country should be brought on in its development, and that things should be ready for a transition of power so that, when he died, his son Reza could take power smoothly. The disease may have affected the Shah's judgement in the crucial months in the middle of 1978, but it is far from clear that it was a decisive factor. The French doctors noted that the Shah was tense and tired during the visits they made in 1978, but they seem to have attributed this to the increasing strain of political matters, rather than the effect of the illness. One would have to ask, how might the Shah have behaved differently, in such a way as to shape events differently, if he had not been ill? If he had been fully fit, is it more likely that he would have ordered a brutal crackdown at a point when it might have worked – perhaps in the spring of 1978? There seems no good reason to think so – his illness did not affect the reasons that held him back. If he had not been ill, might he have been better able to identify the real nature of the movement against him, and the way it was developing, such that he would have been better able to act against it? Perhaps that is more plausible, but again, we have seen there were major obstacles to the Shah perceiving those realities, which were in any case difficult for anyone to perceive (virtually no one else did). The operation of the court and the intelligence services seems to have worked *against* the Shah getting the analysis he would have needed; his erroneous assumptions and prejudices about the nature of the opposition were deep-seated and tenaciously held.

His illness was a factor in the Shah's behaviour, undoubtedly. It is possible, perhaps even likely, that it made a difference to the way events fell out in some chance way. But it is far from obvious that it acted in such a way that we can say that his illness was a significant *determining factor* in bringing about his fall, or in making the Islamic revolution successful.

Black Friday

Clerics participating in the march on 4 September told the crowd that there would be another on 7 September, starting from the same place. There was some unease among the organizers in the intervening hours, because there were rumours of a military crackdown. On the day, the 7 September march was even bigger, and violence was limited to vain attempts early on by the security forces to disperse the demonstrators with tear gas. But the mood was more subdued and militant, ending in the square around the Shahyad monument with the chanting of a new slogan – calling for an Islamic republic.[102]

That evening, the Shah appointed General Gholam-Ali Oveissi as military governor of Tehran. Oveissi had a reputation for ruthlessness from his involvement in the suppression of demonstrations in 1963. Early the following morning (Friday 8 September), the government declared martial law in Tehran and eleven other cities. The announcement may have come too late for some of those who had planned to take part in further demonstrations that day, but perhaps they would have demonstrated anyway. By 8 a.m. a crowd thousands strong had formed in Jaleh Square, where they were confronted by troops. Tear gas forced the demonstrators to pull away, but they came back. The second time, the troops fired in the air as well as using the tear gas. Again the crowd retreated, then re-formed, following the example of three who walked back to stand just a few metres away from the soldiers. Then the soldiers fired straight into the crowd with their automatic weapons. Hundreds fell, some taking cover behind the bodies of the dead, dying and wounded. The rest fled. There were further clashes across the rest of the city over the rest of the day.

In the following days estimates of the dead ranged from hundreds to thousands (in fact, the number that died was probably around eighty, with a larger number wounded). Rumours spread that crowds had been machine-gunned from helicopters, and that the regime had used Israeli troops against the demonstrators. No one credited reports playing down the numbers killed; everyone believed a wholesale massacre had occurred. In the space of four days Tehran had gone from peace and love to blood and fury. The mood shifted again, from shock to anger and general rejection of the Shah.[103] From this point onwards street confrontations in Tehran became more bitter and violent. The events of the beginning of September were a turning point. After 3 and 4 September (and even more so by the end of October) participation in the opposition and in demonstrations became normal; more the thing to do than to stay at home or avoid trouble. People participating in acts against the government had the feeling from this point on of safety in numbers.[104] In addition, after 8 September, notwithstanding the fact that he had been pressing upon his security chiefs the need for restraint, the Shah lost the remainder of what in medieval Iran had been called *farr* – the aura of rightful kingship, associated with just rule and military success. People rejected him. They did not want to hear new suggestions or ideas from him, they just wanted him to go.

There is evidence that the shooting at Jaleh Square was a shock to the Shah also. When he spoke to President Carter on the telephone on 10 September he sounded 'stunned and spoke almost by rote, as if going through the motions'.[105] It seems that this was the week in which the Shah realized, too late, the full gravity of the opposition to him, and his predicament.

Strikes

As summer turned to autumn, profiting from Sharif-Emami's liberalization to combine and organize again, the number of workers going on strike grew. Some accepted settlements that improved pay and working conditions, but others increased the scope of their demands. Khomeini called for a general strike, but a more powerful inducement was the deflationary policy of the regime, which had brought wages down, slashed government spending and government-funded projects, and boosted unemployment. At the same time, rents and food prices in particular were still high after the preceding period of inflation. The discontent over living conditions, pay cuts and the threat of unemployment fused with the general disillusionment and anger with the regime – after all, the Shah's government had laid great emphasis on, and made great claims for, their economic planning and economic management. It seemed legitimate to blame him rather than industry managers or business owners. And when the workers were on strike, it was natural enough that they would take part in the demonstrations. Through the five years before 1978, one authority recorded an average of around twenty-three strikes per year, but in October 1978 alone there were thirty-six. By the beginning of November most of the country was on strike, including railways, airports, banks, some newspapers, and most crucially, the oil workers, some of whom went on strike within days of the Jaleh Square massacre. The oil workers' demands were both industrial and political, including an end to martial law, the release of political prisoners and the dissolution of SAVAK. It has been estimated that by the end of October oil production had fallen to just 28 per cent of normal. The economy began to grind to a halt.[106]

The strikes were important in bringing down the regime. The Shah could conceivably have continued to face down the demonstrations, if the rest of the structure of his regime had remained solid. The strikes undermined that solidity, and the instruments of repression (army and police) could not, ultimately, break mass strikes if they persisted. But one should be wary of assuming that from the summer of 1978 onwards a growing flood of industrial workers and other poor Iranians joined the movement against the Shah and made his overthrow inevitable. The majority of Iran's population still lived in the countryside in 1978, and there was little sign of the rural poor taking more than a minor part in demonstrations even by December. The revolution was predominantly urban. Even among the poor of south Tehran, there is evidence that many were more preoccupied with the day-to-day business of survival, and had little interest in the demonstrations.[107] Iranians from humbler backgrounds were involved in the protests, and more of them joined in from the summer of 1978 onwards, but the social home of the revolution lay with the *bazaaris*, the religious students, lower-middle-class clerical, business and public-sector workers who found their aspirations frustrated by corruption, cronyism and rising living costs, and the secular intellectuals and their followers among the educated middle class.[108]

For a period after Black Friday, concerned to avoid more massacres, Khomeini and his followers encouraged strikes as a weapon against the regime rather than calling for more demonstrations. Nonetheless, demonstrations continued in regional towns like Qazvin, Amol and Sanandaj. Some of these were in response to the activities of groups of thugs hired by SAVAK and local police chiefs. On 16 October, one such regime-aligned mob attacked a mosque in Kerman and then moved on to make mayhem in the bazaar district, while police and the city authorities did nothing. Similar actions were reported around the country. Pro-regime mobs attacked students, teachers, bazaar shops and mosques in places like Khoy, Kermanshah and Hamadan.[109] The intention of these actions was presumably to intimidate regime opponents into silence. The result was rather to discredit the regime still further, and to emphasize the lawlessness in the country and the Shah's loss of control. Rather than intimidating the opposition, in many cases it stimulated communal self-protection (notably in Amol, where on 31 October the opposition took matters into their own hands, arresting SAVAK agents and organizing patrols on the streets to identify troublemakers) and a new wave of anti-regime violence. In the latter part of October, after an abortive and seemingly half-hearted attempt by the government to negotiate with representatives of the *bazaaris*, SAVAK paid hoodlums to attack, loot and burn shops in the bazaars of some towns. As a result, many merchants cleared their shops of goods, making a strike or shut-down of the bazaar superfluous. In the last week of October, in Hamadan, police officers were accused of raping three girls, one of whom, Mahin Ardekani, later committed suicide. Within a few days the city descended into chaos, with protests on the streets, fires lit and barricades erected. Eventually troops moved in and many were killed.[110]

On 4 November, demonstrations resumed in Tehran, especially in the central area around the university, where students were shot at. The next day, they pulled down a statue of the Shah. Crowds sacked a number of buildings in the same area, and broke into the British embassy compound.[111] Merope Coulson had recently married another member of embassy staff; she was working on the first floor:

> The atmosphere throughout the day was very tense. Fires were raging across the city and I could see spirals of smoke from my office window. By mid-afternoon I could hear shouting and chanting 'death to the Shah' in the distance, getting louder and louder. From my window I could see a huge demonstration marching up Ferdowsi [Avenue], armed with bricks and stones. I watched as the demonstrators pulled the grille off the bank on the opposite side of the street, smashing the windows and setting it on fire.

Turning their attention to the British embassy, the mob started hurling great bricks over the wall, smashing all our windows in a mad frenzy. They then broke down the iron gate to the compound and surrounded the building. I can hear the shouting and the smashing of glass to this day. A young embassy Third Secretary took charge and urged all embassy staff to go up to the third floor of the building, to the 'safe' area, where a grille came down. Together in the central corridor of the building, away from the windows, we thought we would be protected from the mob by the iron grille. By this time the mob had broken into the foyer of the building, setting it on fire. They had also thrown a firebomb from the street into my office which I had only recently vacated. Rubber tyres had been set alight in the emergency exit. With this area and the main entrance hall on fire we had no means of escape. I thought 'this is a good start to married life'. And where was my new husband? I couldn't see him.

My colleagues and I, filled with fear, huddled together in the corridor, listening to the angry mob shouting as they advanced up the wooden staircase. By some miracle, the Third Secretary who had taken charge and spoke fluent Farsi, learned that the crowd did not in fact realize we were all working in the building at the time of the attack, that they didn't want to hurt us. He negotiated with them to let us out of the burning building. By this time the fire had spread across the entire first floor.

The staircase to the foyer was smouldering and some of the steps were now missing, but the young revolutionaries held out their hands to help us climb down. It took tremendous faith and courage to take their hands, enemies one minute, saviours the next. There was glass everywhere, shouting in my ears and the constant smell of burning. The Iranians were trying to communicate with us amidst the confusion and the chaos but I couldn't understand what they were saying. Eventually we escaped and ran towards the rear of the compound, where we congregated in a colleague's house. And then I saw my husband: he had been outside the building all along and now he was busy fighting the fire with other embassy members. Eventually the army moved in and the crowd dispersed.[112]

Many other buildings in Tehran burned on 5 November, including banks, expensive hotels and airline offices. It was the worst damage to property that the capital had yet seen, and of course it attracted more attention in the international media than regional demonstrations had. It seemed that this time the security forces had lost control. The Shah responded the next day by removing Sharif-Emami and appointing a military government, with General Gholam-Reza Azhari as the new prime minister. Six other generals became ministers; one of them, Oveissi, became minister of labour and immediately imposed martial law in Khuzestan in order to suppress the strikes in the oilfields.

The Shah Speaks

On the same day, the Shah made a broadcast on TV and radio. He addressed the broadcast to the 'Dear Iranian Nation', approved what he called their revolution, and the way that they had stood up to oppression and corruption, but said that some had taken advantage of the situation to engage in 'riots, anarchy and revolts'. He said he was aware of the risk that in preventing these, mistakes like the 'mistakes of the past' might be made. But he promised that these mistakes would not be repeated, and that after order had been restored a national government would establish basic freedoms and free elections, and the Constitution of 1906. He repeated that he had heard 'the message of your revolution, nation of Iran'.[113]

Perhaps he had. Others at the time had been impressed by the determination, the discipline and the restraint of the crowds. But for the Shah it was too late now. The bizarre speech gave an impression of weakness; that he was following, not leading. How could the Shah praise the people for standing up to the oppression of his own government? Why should they trust him to enforce now the constitution whose principles he had flouted and ignored for thirty years? For many Iranians, ironically, his mention of 'their revolution' crystallized for the first time the idea that this was, or could be, a revolution. But the crucial change that the revolution sought, that Khomeini had demanded with brutal clarity all along, inexorably gathering support, was the removal of the Shah.

Was the Shah vacillating?[114] He did not really hesitate as such – he was reacting quickly to events. He just did not know what to do – partly because he did not understand what was happening, and many of his assumptions about what lay behind what was happening were incorrect. He continued to try a combination of harshness against demonstrators and activists and conciliatory measures toward ordinary Iranians (a policy which, if it had been more successful, might later have been praised as wise, firm statesmanship). He did not want to use full brutal force, despite the urgings of some of his generals.[115] His father would have, at an early stage. It was not the illness – the Shah was just not his father. It was partly that he did not want to lose the backing of the Carter administration; it was also his own personality and inclinations. But the son's methods did not work. By this point, people no longer wanted to give him another chance.

In foreign capitals, too, there was uncertainty. Having regarded the Shah's regime as more or less stable until the summer, the Carter administration were suddenly pitchforked into a predicament in which they had to consider the possibility, becoming a probability as autumn moved into winter, that the Shah would fall. If they continued to support him now, might that prejudice their relationship with whatever regime might replace him? Or was it time to encourage the Shah to repress the opposition with an all-out military crackdown? In Washington, Carter's national security adviser, Zbigniew Brzezinski, was arguing for the military option, while Cyrus Vance in the State Department, backed by Ambassador Sullivan in Tehran, was arguing against.[116] In a move that did little more than lose time, Carter appointed George Ball as an outside adviser; he presented a report to Carter in mid-December, but the report did not resolve the argument.[117]

In London the prime minister and the foreign secretary both agreed that events should take their course in Tehran without any overt British interference. On one aspect they disagreed – David Owen was reluctant to cancel the Queen's visit to Iran – planned as part of a regional tour of the Middle East for February 1979 – preferring to give the Shah more time to suggest himself that it be postponed (in the end the Iran leg of the trip was of course dropped, and David Owen recognized the new government in Iran while accompanying the Queen on the tour; he did so on the advice of the embassy in Tehran before the Foreign Office in London, because of the time difference, had woken up).[118]

Ambassador Parsons in Tehran was more cautious, and more prepared to keep giving the Shah a chance than some of his Foreign Office colleagues, but he had acquired a sincere respect for the revolutionary movement. In fact, the situation in Iran by this stage was moving beyond the ability of outside powers to influence events significantly, no matter how agonized their deliberations. Gary Sick, who was then on the NSC staff in Washington, told a British diplomat on 26 December 1978 that 'the situation in Iran was beyond the US's ability to understand, still less to control or influence'.[119]

As the revolutionary wave swelled, the attitude of Westerners and Western governments to Khomeini himself moved from bafflement to incredulity. How could this man, a cleric whose experience of life revolved around theological colleges, who plainly had no idea how to run a modern country, offer Islamic government as an alternative to the government of the Shah? Roger Cooper (who was later imprisoned under the Islamic Republic as a spy) interviewed Khomeini in Paris for the BBC and *The Financial Times* in January 1979, but also reported his findings to an official at the Foreign and Commonwealth Office. Frustrated by requirements to submit questions in writing in advance, Cooper managed nonetheless to ask a few supplementary questions in person. He asked Khomeini how it would be possible to reconcile the Islamic prohibition on usury with the banking system in Iran. 'Khomeini replied that it would be necessary to invent a different system. Other answers showed a similar naivety and lack of realism'.[120]

Of course, as events were to prove, it was Cooper's vision and the vision of others like him that was limited – they were still unable to grasp the full magnitude and the real shape of what was happening; nor the charisma of Khomeini's utter self-confidence. But Khomeini saw the essentials. Power was the essential thing – the rest was trivial and would follow; banking system, whatever; willy-nilly.

Descent into Collapse

For a short time Oveissi's hard line in Khuzestan had some success, and the authorities were able to achieve a greater level of oil production again. At different points this was achieved by forcing the strikers back to work, or, less efficiently, by bringing in personnel (including troops) from outside. But in December the oil workers walked out again, and many of them resigned.[121] The opposition agreed to allow some oil production for domestic purposes, but supplies ran out in many places, and many Iranians had a cold winter for want of heating oil. There was a similar pattern in other industries and sectors, though few were regarded as so vital or came under such direct and heavy regime pressure as the oil industry. Workers struck for a few days or weeks, returned to work and then went on strike again. Often, even when they were at work, little productive activity could go on because of the general dislocation and the knock-on effect of strikes elsewhere.

Another development at the beginning of November was that Sanjabi and Bazargan, representing the National Front and the Freedom movement respectively, both met Khomeini in Paris. If they had given serious consideration to the Shah's reform proposals over the summer, Black Friday and the events that followed had turned them, like most of their supporters, definitively against the regime. After meeting Khomeini, both made statements showing that they aligned themselves and their followers unequivocally with Khomeini and against the Shah. Bazargan's statement said that the demonstrations had shown the support of the people for Khomeini and that they wanted an Islamic government to replace the monarchy.[122] When Sanjabi returned to Tehran he was arrested – in protest the bazaar closed and there were renewed strikes.

Across the country there were sporadic protests through the rest of November and December, and where these were met with armed force from the authorities the protestors now on occasion responded with violence themselves. After the imposition of military rule in Ahwaz, a six-year-old girl was shot and killed by police at a demonstration. Two of the police who had opened fire were killed in response. Similarly, two police were killed in Nishapur on 19 November, after two demonstrators were killed. There were assassinations and bomb attacks on police, SAVAK and army personnel over the same period, carried out by the Fedayan, the Mojahedin-e Khalq and other militant groups. When crowds were able to identify SAVAK agents, their response was often harsh. On 21 December, demonstrators in Tehran spotted one such on top of a building – some of them swarmed in and up the stairs and threw the SAVAK man down to his death.[123]

The mourning month of Moharram began that year on 2 December, and there were renewed protests on the streets of Tehran as young men went on to the streets at night, defying the curfew and in some cases wearing white shrouds to advertise their indifference to danger. Many were killed. Others showed their support by going onto rooftops and shouting 'Allahu Akbar' ('God is Great'). The opposition organized huge demonstrations for Tasu'a and Ashura, the commemoration of the death of Emam Hosein, on 10 and 11 December. In an attempt to limit the violence, to reassure the people and draw larger crowds, the organizers successfully negotiated permission for the demonstrations with the military government by stipulating prearranged routes, peaceful, orderly behaviour, no arson or other violence, and no chanting of 'Death to the Shah'. They also arranged for marshals to supervise the marchers along the route. Similar arrangements were made in other cities. Karim Sanjabi and Ayatollah Taleqani led the marches in Tehran,[124] symbolizing the opposition's alliance of secular and religious intellectuals, and perhaps the heritage of the similar alliance that had led the Constitutional Revolution in 1906.

The result was demonstrations of unprecedented size. Estimates for the size of these demonstrations in Tehran have ranged between 500,000 and 4 million, but it is difficult to know what the true figures were. Somewhere between 500,000 and 1 million for 10 December and upward of 1 million for 11 December seems moderate (the fact that the marches on 10 December passed off peacefully seems to have encouraged even larger numbers to participate on the 11th). Huge marches, in proportion, took place in most of the other major cities and towns of Iran on the same days, such that it has been estimated that altogether between 6 and 9 million Iranians took part.[125]

On both days, the marches were almost wholly peaceful, although on 11 December the marshals failed to prevent anti-Shah slogans and the waving of banners and placards that broke the agreed rules (Fedayan and MKO followers were particularly keen to push beyond the limits). With or without the slogans and banners, the message of the marches was clear enough, transcending the religious significance of Ashura. The people wanted the Shah to go. Notwithstanding the greater level of violence on both sides in December, the peaceful, dignified conduct of the marches on 10 and 11 December (like those of 4 and 7 September at an earlier stage) impressed many observers at the time.[126] Former diplomat Desmond Harney, now in Tehran as a representative for Morgan Grenfell, recorded in his diary for 10 December:

> The day seems to have been a triumph of trust and discipline. As Goudarzi [Harney's gardener] said with shining eyes, 'I told you so. If they do not provoke us and shoot us, we are not men of killing and burning. Let us express ourselves as we want, and there cannot be any trouble.[127]

As the regime lost control and lost credibility, the opposition gained moral authority and self-confidence.

In general, over the autumn and into December, the revolutionary crowd had shown restraint, despite the shouting and slogans. When violent, most of the violence of the crowds was directed at property, not at people. There were individual acts of killing – usually provoked – but no massacres. This was another reflection of the fact that the people saw themselves as united against the Shah and his government, not against a class or any other group – except perhaps SAVAK.

At the end point of the march on 11 December, in the huge square around the Shahyad monument, a manifesto was read out on behalf of all the opposition parties and acclaimed by the crowd. It declared that Khomeini was their leader and must be obeyed; that the monarchy must be removed, an Islamic government established; that exiles must return; that the army must combine with the people; that minorities must be protected, agriculture revived and the poor given social justice.[128]

The exceptions to the peaceful conduct of the demonstrations on 10 and 11 December were in Isfahan and Shiraz, where there were outbreaks of violence. In Isfahan leftists attacked the offices of SAVAK, the crowd were shot at from the building, and ten people were killed. The protestors then turned to arson, burning cinemas, shops and banks until troops moved in.[129]

Nonetheless, there were some dissenting voices among ordinary Iranians:

> on the day of Ashura, there was a march from Emam Hosein Square to Azadi Square, led by Grand Ayatollah Taleqani. A lot of people participated in this gathering. Although there was a probability of violence against this crowd, people unwaveringly prepared to sacrifice themselves regardless, even if some would lose their lives. Nobody was able to stop this crowd. On our return, in Kush Street an old lady stood and told the demonstrators – who were mainly young people, 'Why did you make this demonstration?' Many youngsters stood there, and the old lady encouraged them not to participate and to stop being anti-monarchist, and these youngsters stated their point of view. The old lady said, 'Up to now, the Shah and his family have taken enough wealth and they are full up and now they give the money to the people, but these mullahs, their pockets are too big and deep: by the time they were full up, nothing would be left for us, and we would

be miserable.' Why didn't we listen to what the older generation, like this old lady, was saying?[130]

And:

At the time of the demonstrations I had a neighbour who was absolutely unreligious. The husband was a known drunkard, and none of his daughters conformed to Islamic attire. One of the girls was in the navy and another was in the army – at that time it was unusual to see a female in the forces, and such women had a bad reputation. But these girls broke all of these cultural customs. One day, after I had been at the demonstrations, I came towards my house and in the alleyway, as usual, I saw the women – opposite these girls' house, standing and chatting with each other. At that time, during the evening, women came out and sat somewhere to chat together. I approached these ladies – my mother was among them – and they noticed that I had just come back from the demonstrations. My neighbour's mother asked me, 'Do you know what this revolution is all about?' and I said Islam and God, and she responded, 'No, it means in the winter you have to use a Korsi [an old-fashioned foot warmer run on charcoal] and all of you will have to use it since you won't have a heater. Under the Korsi your feet will heat each other!' What she meant was, this revolution is a step back. But these sorts of comments did not change our minds. We thought we would go to the demonstrations and would eventually go to heaven and these people would go to hell, and at the time I felt sorry for them.[131]

After Tasu'a and Ashura, the Shah cast around for a way to stabilize the situation and keep himself in power. It seems that he tried to negotiate with Sanjabi, to get him to head up a government of national reconciliation that would enable the Shah to stay as head of state. But Sanjabi refused, allegedly because the Shah would not give up his position as commander-in-chief of the armed forces, or because such a plan was impossible without Khomeini's acquiescence, which Khomeini would not give unless the Shah abdicated. Discussions with another politician who had been a minister under Mossadeq, Dr Gholam-Hosein Sadighi, also broke down eventually.[132] The strikes continued and intensified; there were more demonstrations and protests across the country, under the black flags that had led the revolt of Abu Muslim over 1,200 years before. People began to speculate about the loyalty of the army. Khomeini's portrait was everywhere on the streets; many had already taken down their pictures of the Shah. US citizens and other foreigners were leaving the country – numbers dropped from 58,000 Americans in the country to 12,000 by early January. The movement was accelerated by attacks against foreigners, notably the assassination of an American oil executive in Ahwaz on 23 December. Some wealthy Iranians were leaving too. Others took advantage of the early snow in the mountains to try to forget their troubles by going skiing – Desmond Harney recorded in his diary that thousands were skiing at the most popular resort, Dizin, on 23 December.[133]

Finally, on 31 December, it was announced that Shapur Bakhtiar would form a government. At the same time it was given out that the Shah would leave the country for rest and medical attention, but there were conflicting rumours about this over the days that followed. On 6 January Bakhtiar announced his cabinet, and the Shah made a statement saying he needed a rest and that this *might* take place outside Iran. Bakhtiar made a flurry of liberalizing announcements as he took office, promising free elections, to close down SAVAK and to lift martial law, and setting up a Regency Council to carry out the Shah's constitutional functions while he was out of the country. He also declared that Khomeini was free to return.[134] Khomeini responded by announcing the establishment of the Council of the Islamic Revolution (CIR – the body, whose membership was initially kept secret, had in fact been set up the previous November to coordinate strikes and other actions against the Shah's government). The CIR caused unhappiness among the politicians of the Freedom Movement and the National Front, whose representatives in it felt outnumbered and marginalized by the clergy.

On 4 January General Robert E. Huyser arrived in Tehran, sent by President Carter to bolster as far as possible the support of the Iranian military for the Bakhtiar government and, as a secondary purpose, to keep open the possibility of a military coup if it proved necessary. Huyser was a natural choice because he had been in Iran in the spring and summer of 1978, drawing up a command and control system for the Iranian armed forces, liaising with the highest levels of the military and with the Shah personally. But on his arrival he was given a message from Washington by Ambassador Sullivan to the effect that his instructions were suspended. He soon realized that Sullivan regarded Bakhtiar as a dead duck, and the military as powerless to change the situation. Sullivan believed the only realistic option was to begin working with the opposition straight away. On 6 January Huyser was told to proceed with his contacts with the military as originally instructed, but the incident had given him a jolt. He convinced himself at the time that the Iranian military had the will and the cohesion to act decisively, and later, in retrospect, that, if they had, the military could have saved the Bakhtiar government. Given the fighting that took place later, before the final collapse of the Bakhtiar government on 11 February, the former conviction is at least tenable. But it seems implausible that military action could have saved Bakhtiar's government. By the end of January Huyser's presence had become generally known, and his name was appearing on placards at demonstrations. He left Iran on 3 February.[135]

By the beginning of January law and order had broken down over much of the country, and the authorities had wholly abandoned some towns, like Mashhad. People set up arrangements for their own localities, independent of government (in some areas with a separate or separatist tradition, notably Kurdestan and Khuzestan, these local arrangements took on the character of movements for autonomy). SAVAK offices were a special target for attacks.[136] Even in Tehran, the police were absent from the streets for the most part. Students were directing traffic, and food was being distributed from the mosques. There were occasional random clashes with the police and army:

> One of our neighbourhood boys, who lived on the other side of our road, always bothered my sister. He had light-brown hair and was a known troublemaker who was always bothering and teasing the girls. One day I was at home, and there was a lot of noise coming from our local petrol station, where a crowd of people were in a queue to fill up with fuel. At the same time two military vehicles were passing down the same street. This boy went on to the main road and blocked the two vehicles and started swearing at the military personnel. The soldiers in the vehicle shot him, in front of everyone, and continued down the street. But suddenly, there was a lot of noise and screaming from the crowd. I always remembered this boy – he was very brave and curious. Before the revolution this curiosity and bravery took the form of pestering and flirting with the women. But during the revolution he was one of the strongest supporters and was in favour of demonstrations for 'female protection'. He was martyred after his doings – God bless his soul, we saw a lot of such valiant people in the time of the revolution.[137]

Finally, the Shah ended the prevarication and took the decision to leave, delaying further only (as he thought) to see Bakhtiar established in office. But when Parsons made a final call on him on 8 January, the Shah was still bewildered by what had happened:

> Why, the Shah asked, had the people turned against him after all that he had done for them? I said ... the same forces which had humbled Nasruddin Shah in 1892 ... and had prevailed over Muzafferiddin Shah in 1906 over the constitution, had combined to bring down Mohammad Reza Shah – the mullahs, the bazaar and the intelligentsia. I had never admired the Iranian people as much as I had done in the past few months. Their courage, discipline and devotion to the cause of overthrowing the monarchy had been amazing ... The Shah agreed about the performance of his people but rejected my analogies with his Qajar predecessors. 'I have done more for Iran than any Shah for 2,000 years; you cannot compare me with those people.'[138]

Most of the Shah's household were still loyal, but from time to time messages, from whom no one seemed to know, had been appearing on his dining-table at lunchtime, bearing anti-Shah slogans. On 16 January he was flown from Niavaran palace to Mehrabad airport by helicopter. After a short delay while waiting for Bakhtiar to appear (he came straight from the ceremony in which the Majles confirmed him in office), he boarded an airliner with Queen Farah and a group of attendants. As the aircraft left Iranian airspace an hour or so later, heading for Egypt, the Shah asked for lunch. But there was none – catering staff at the airport had prevented the loading of any food, or crockery, cutlery or glassware. So the Shah and his wife ate some of the food his guards had brought for themselves – a pot of rice and beans – *baqali polo* – from paper plates, using some paper napkins and their fingers.[139]

Back in Tehran, as soon as the Shah's departure became known, there was a surge of rejoicing:

> We live in the south of Tehran which is the poor part of the city, but my family is not too poor. My father owns a grocer's shop. I will never forget the day the Shah left. It was January and everyone was out in the streets shouting 'Shah raft' (the Shah has gone), and my father took me out to march. He is not a religious man but he hated the Shah and was pleased that the 'Emam' (Khomeini) was coming home to become our president

[*sic*]. Almost every day we were in the street. Nobody worked or went to school. Guns fired in the air and it was like a holiday. Everyone was happy, strangers kissed and held hands, shouting 'Shah raft, Shah raft'.[140]

Ambassador Parsons reported by flash telegram the jubilation brought by the news that the Shah had left. (Flash telegrams were the highest-priority category of communications, before Immediate and Routine. The following is the full text.)

At 2p.m. local time the radio announced that the Shah had left the country. Within seconds there was a great burst of hooting of car horns and shouting of crowds. Looking from the chancery window, I can see people dancing in the streets, processions passing carrying Khomeini banners, all cars and buses with their lights on and horns blaring. The military guard outside our com-pound have removed their steel helmets and are waving pictures of Khomeini. People are rushing up to the soldiers and embracing them. A scene of wild jubilation which must be being enacted throughout Tehran.[141]

Up and down the country people went on to the streets to celebrate, and in many places they did so by pulling down statues of the Shah (where this had not been done already).[142] On 15 January, the British embassy had reported another large demonstration in Tehran, commenting that the Bakhtiar government was not exercising effective control (they had already commented on 10 January that prospects for a return to stability under Bakhtiar were 'bleak'), and that the army were widely thought to have passed up the opportunity of intervening. The marchers seemed to be deliberately wooing the military, 'putting flowers on their guns and vehicles'.[143] Another big march (to mark the forty days since Ashura) fol-lowed on 19 January.

It is not entirely clear why the Shah delayed his departure in the first half of January. It seems likely that he could not face the reality of it – the likelihood that, if he left, it would be for good and his reign would be over. He received contradictory advice. Perhaps he hoped something would just turn up, to give him another chance. The reason he gave for the delay was that he wanted to see Bakhtiar firmly established (in par-ticular, confirmed by the Majles) before he left.[144] But in fact, the delay achieved exactly the opposite: it fixed Bakhtiar in the minds of Iranians as the Shah's last prime minister and thereby discredited him.

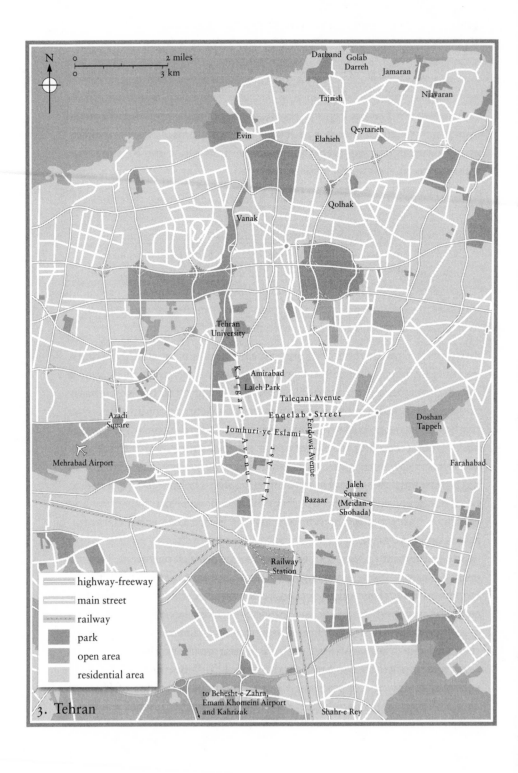

N

2 miles
3 km

Darband
Golab
Darreh
Jamaran
Niavaran
Tajrish
Qeytarieh
Evin
Elahieh
Qolhak
Vanak
Tehran
University
Amirabad
Laleh Park
Taleqani Avenue
Engelab · Street
Azadi
Square
Jomhuri-ye Eslami
Doshan
Tappeh
Mehrabad Airport
Farahabad
Karyar · Avenue
Valiasr Avenue
Ferdowsi Avenue
Jaleh
Square
(Meidan-e
Shohada)
Bazaar
Railway
Station

highway-freeway
main street
railway
park
open area
residential area

3. Tehran

to Behesht-e Zahra,
Emam Khomeini Airport
and Kahrizak
Shahr-e Rey

Bakhtiar's liberalizing announcements at the beginning of January had won over some to his support – notably Ayatollah Shariatmadari. Political prisoners were released, and the red light district in Tehran was closed down:

> one day I went to Tehran University for a demonstration. It was the day that Masud Rajavi (head of the MKO) was freed from prison, and he wanted to deliver a speech to the people. Many young people, like me, were influenced by the political prisoners and their courage. But we felt very intimidated by these people because of their knowledge of the Shah's regime – which was more than ours – and because of their record of resistance against the Shah. Mr Rajavi started speaking to the crowd, but his voice sounded like a woman's. I had expected a political prisoner would sound very masculine, but in this case I was surprised.
>
> On the same day a minibus arrived among the crowd of students, and I asked why this bus arrived here. I was told that a group of prostitutes, who lived in the houses in the Jamshidiyeh Street, were brought here to repent against their doings and to show their support and solidarity for the revolution and the revolutionaries. Apparently many of these women got married that day and changed their direction in life, but I don't know what they did after that.[145]

Ignoring as irrelevant Bakhtiar's efforts to present himself as the prime minister of a viable, liberalizing government, Khomeini condemned him from Paris, declaring that any government appointed by the Shah was illegal. Bakhtiar's former colleagues Sanjabi and Foruhar expelled him from the National Front, saying that there could be no settlement until the Shah abdicated. The demonstration on 19 January was again huge – over 1 million strong – and again it ended at Shahyad Square (which many were already calling Azadi Square – Freedom Square) with a political statement, declaimed again by Taleqani and Sanjabi. The statement announced that the Shah had been overthrown, that an Islamic republic must be established, that Khomeini should introduce an Islamic revolutionary council and a provisional government; and that Bakhtiar's government was illegal (because it had been appointed by an illegal Shah and an illegal Majles). The army should not move against the revolutionary movement; the strikes and demonstrations had to continue until the final aims of the revolution had been achieved.[146]

And continue they did, making the operation of Bakhtiar's government impossible. Some of his ministers and members of the Regency Council began to abandon him. On 20 January Khomeini announced that he would return to Iran within the next few days. Despite his earlier statement that Khomeini was free to return, Bakhtiari closed down Mehrabad airport. Between 26 and 28 January there were many deaths outside the airport as demonstrators were gunned down by troops enforcing the closure.[147] These deaths finally sealed Bakhtiar's fate. He appeared like just another of the Shah's prime ministers, presiding over the killing of demonstrators. The movement that backed the demonstrations and strikes, that regarded Khomeini as their leader, had no time for Bakhtiar. But he still had the support of the military, as was confirmed by General Qarabaghi to General Huyser on 31 January. The airport reopened the same day; Bakhtiar stipulated only that Khomeini should not be allowed to fly by Iran Air (the airline was all but shut down in any case, because of the strikes).[148]

When Khomeini finally returned on 1 February 1979 (in an Air France aircraft) he confirmed Mehdi Bazargan as his prime minister and initiated a tense period in which there were briefly two governments in Iran. But eventually, as described in the prologue, after the armed confrontation between air force personnel and Imperial Guard troops loyal to the Shah at Doshan Tappeh on 10–12 February, Bakhtiar and the military commanders saw the impossibility of the situation and gave in, leaving the field clear for Khomeini and his supporters.

Why Do Revolutions Happen?

It is a commonplace observation that it is the failures of governments that make revolutions, not the cunning or the commitment of revolutionaries.[149] The Shah's government failed in a variety of ways – there was the short-term economic difficulty but, more importantly, a deep-seated failure to recognize or nurture the political aspirations of the people. Beyond the failure of the government, a number of unusual things have to happen in order for a popular revolution like that in Iran to succeed. People have to see the government as the problem,[150] blame the government and want to remove it (there are plenty of other things they might blame for their problems – other individuals, groups or classes;

fate or even themselves). The government has to fail to mollify them. People have to be prepared to defy the government, perhaps to the point of risking their lives. They have to avoid the divisions within the burgeoning revolutionary movement widening to split their effort. And this has to be sustained for long enough for the government to give in, or collapse. It is quite a tall order. Like a series of mirrors facing each other, the revolution depended for its success on a series of perceptions of perceptions. It was necessary, through the confusion of the times, for people to perceive that others, in sufficient numbers, had already perceived that resistance to the regime could succeed and would act upon it, and, in addition, perhaps, that the morale of the armed forces had been sapped by the perception that they might lose the confrontation, or by sympathy with the revolutionaries. Through the summer and autumn, those perceptions became established – but it could have gone the other way. Several commentators have emphasized the collective psychology of the revolution, the absence of any simple, single cause, and the importance of the dynamic by which the confidence of the opposition in its own viability grew from spring to summer to autumn in 1978, as the confidence of the Shah and the regime faded. More even than is the normal case with historical study, the causes of the revolution are best explained not by heavy theory, but by placing the course of events in a narrative, within which the responses of individuals and groups to successive events and crises can be properly understood.[151] A series of events changed the position that the people were in, gradually removing deference to the government, increasing indignation and determination that Shah must go. Paradoxically, the growth of the revolutionary movement was helped in the early stages by the regime's own self-belief; by the government's complacency. Initially, revolution was indeed unthinkable. As more groups joined in, their different grievances and aspirations flowing into the broad oppositional stream, the sense of shared participation and commitment increased.

But one should not go from the judgement that there was no single, simple cause to the revolution, or from the judgement that a growing sense of collective solidarity was important, to thinking it was all aimless or contingent – some kind of mass psychosis.[152] Repeatedly, since the late nineteenth century, when secular government had got into trouble, ordinary, pious Iranians had turned to the other authoritative institution in Iranian society for leadership – the Shi'a clergy. Up to the

1960s and 70s, the Shi'a clergy, faced with the challenges of social change, economic change and Western influence, had as a body been divided and uncertain about how to respond; now siding with liberal intellectuals, now with the monarchy. But by the 1970s Khomeini had learned from previous episodes and could provide new answers and clear principles for the leadership of the clergy in its own right.[153] Allied to that was the popular enthusiasm for Islam, in opposition to Westernization and foreign interference in the country. That was one part of what happened. The other was, since 1906, the longstanding demand from a broad swathe of the Iranian people for a free society and representative government. The mechanism of the revolution was determined by the gradual gathering of confidence and solidarity among the Iranian people through 1978, but the form the revolution took was determined by the leadership of Khomeini and the clergy, and the demand for free institutions. In January and February 1979, it seemed possible that the two could be kept out of conflict with each other. But within a few months it became clear that such a conflict could not be avoided.[154]

3

Like the Person He Ought to Be:
Islamic Republic, 1979–80

Khomeini

One of the scurrilous allegations contained in the *Ettela'at* article of January 1978 that led to riots in Qom was that Khomeini was not Iranian, but an Indian (this allegation in turn lent force to another in the article, that Khomeini had been a British agent – an assertion the Shah himself seems to have believed).[1] The story about Khomeini's Indian origins derived from the fact that his grandfather had borne the name Seyyed Ahmad Musavi Hindi, and had lived in Kintur near Lucknow.[2] Lucknow, under the Shi'a rulers of Awadh (themselves a dynasty of Iranian origin), was one of the most Persianized cities in India and a centre for Iranian immigration, especially in the eighteenth century, when a series of disasters had prompted many who could to leave Iran. It seems that one of Khomeini's ancestors had gone to Lucknow at this time, or earlier (from Nishapur in Khorasan). But in the 1830s Ahmad went on pilgrimage to the shrine of the Emam Ali in Najaf in Ottoman Iraq, where he met another mullah who suggested he should move to Iran and settle in Khomein (a small town between Isfahan and Tehran).

Khomeini came from a family that descended from the Prophet, denoted by the title *seyyed* and the black turban they wore. They traced their lineage back to Mohammad's daughter Fatima, through the seventh Shi'a Emam, Musa al-Kazim. Heads of Khomeini's family had been mullahs for generations. When Khomeini's grandfather Ahmad came to Khomein he bought a large house there and was soon established as an important figure among the local Shi'a clergy. As time went on he acquired more property in the area. Ahmad's son Mostafa was born in 1856 and followed the usual family path into the clergy. He studied in Isfahan, Najaf and Samarra and married the daughter of another distinguished clerical family. His property, status and learning placed him in the upper levels of the *ulema*, well above more junior mullahs whose families could not afford the long training, who had to struggle for the patronage of more senior figures and make a living from fees as teachers, legal notaries or preachers. Mostafa's third son, Ruhollah, the future leader of the revolution, was born in September 1902.

Status brought responsibilities, but danger also; Mostafa was murdered the following year while travelling to get help for the people of Khomein from the government against some local bandits.[3] In the years that followed, conditions only got worse. Over the years of chaos following the Constitutional Revolution and during the First World War the economy broke down, the country became a playground for the soldiery of foreign powers, famine and epidemics of disease broke out, and law and order collapsed in many parts. In Ruhollah's early years Khomein was raided a number of times by Lori tribesmen. In 1918 his mother died in a cholera epidemic just as he was about to go into the seminary nearby in Soltanabad. His elder brother Pasandideh (later a distinguished cleric in his own right) became head of the family; it seems likely that being an orphan intensified Ruhollah's independence and ambition to succeed. Later he moved to the famous Faiziyeh *madreseh* in Qom as a student of Sheikh Abdolkarim Haeri, an apolitical but practical-minded scholar and *marja* (who was responsible for restoring Qom to pre-eminence as the centre for religious learning in Iran in the 1920s, drawing back many Iranian students from the shrine cities of Iraq).[4] In Qom Khomeini received the usual mullah's training in logic and religious law,[5] becoming a *mojtahed* in about 1936, which was young by comparison with others and a sign of his promise.

From the time that he became a *mojtahed*, Khomeini could teach and write in earnest. Early on he had an interest in poetry and mysticism (*erfan*) that was quite unconventional, these being objects of disdain for many conservative mullahs. Among other works, he studied Molla Sadra's *Four Journeys* and Davud al-Qeisari's commentary on the *Fusus al-Hikam* of Ibn Arabi (both classic texts for the tradition of mystical philosophy within Islam); he wrote a commentary on the latter in 1937.[6] In the 1930s he studied philosophy and *erfan* with Mirza Mohammad Ali Shahabadi, who as well as being an authority on mysticism was more interested in contemporary politics than many of the *ulema*, believing it was important to explain religious ideas to ordinary people in language they could understand. This combination of mysticism and political engagement might seem strange from a Western perspective, but not in the Shi'a Islamic tradition:

> The very heart of *erfan* is the destruction of the distinction between subject and object – an experience of the world in which seer and seen are one. And teachers of *erfan* seek to impart to their students a sense of the fearlessness toward everything external, including all the seemingly coercive political powers of the world, which true masters of *erfan* should have.[7]

Shahabadi opposed the rule of Reza Shah and also influenced the development of Khomeini's political thinking.[8]

Khomeini had a strong sense of his own personal dignity as a *mojtahed*, and the dignity of the *ulema* as a whole. He always dressed neatly and cleanly – not affecting an indifference to clothes or appearance as some young mullahs did. He struck many new acquaintances as aloof and reserved, and some as arrogant, but his small circle of students and friends knew him to be generous and lively in private. For his public persona as a teacher and mullah it was necessary for him to exemplify authority and quiet dignity. Through the 1940s and 50s, continuing to teach in Qom, it is perhaps correct to think of Khomeini taking a position between the activism of Ayatollah Kashani on the one hand – active in parliament, anti-colonial and anti-British – and that of Ayatollah Hosein Borujerdi on the other – more conservative, more withdrawn, tending to quietism and intervening only seldom in political matters (in the 1950s Khomeini was close to Borujerdi in Qom, did work for him and followed his example by staying out of politics).[9] But Khomeini's combination of intellectual strength, curiosity and unconventionality made him different from either; potentially more creative and innovative, though for the time being still politically quiescent, deferring to his superiors in the hierarchy of the *ulema* in the period of rapprochement between clergy and monarchy after the fall of Mossadeq. Khomeini became an ayatollah after the death of Borujerdi in March 1961, by which time he was already attracting large and increasing numbers of students to his lectures on ethics and was regarded by some as their *marja*.

The events of 1963–4 made Khomeini the leading figure opposed to the Shah, along with Mossadeq, who was still under house arrest and thus effectively neutralized (Mossadeq died in 1967). Khomeini, though he disapproved of constitutionalism in private, had been careful to speak positively about the constitution in public.[10] His attack on the new law governing the status of the US military was calculated to win over nationalists, some of whom might previously have been suspicious of a cleric. Intellectuals like Al-e Ahmad gave him their enthusiastic support. He was already applying the political method by which, through addressing popular grievances and avoiding pronouncements on issues that might divide his followers, he would later make himself the dominant national leader. He had learned from the lessons of twentieth-century Iranian history – from the period of constitutionalism, from the rule of Reza Shah, from the premiership of Mossadeq and from his own experiences in 1963–4, from the example of religious leaders like Fazlollah Nuri, Modarres and Kashani. The clergy might make alliances of convenience with the monarchy or with secular intellectuals or others, but they could not trust any of them. For Khomeini, the logic of the clergy's position and experience seemed to point just one way – to the rule of the clergy. And the mood of the times seemed to be shifting their way; young intellectuals like Shariati were turning away from Western models in favour of what they saw as the authenticity of Islam and Iranian Shi'ism.

From 1964 Khomeini was out of Iran, exiled after his involvement in the demonstrations and disturbances of 1963–4, and to all appearances out of Iranian politics. In a sense, Iranian politics was itself exiled, taking place among Iranian students and others living abroad. Khomeini went initially to Turkey, then to Najaf in Iraq, where he spent most of the next fourteen years. But although he was out of Iran, he continued to comment on matters within Iran, and his words were taken into the country by his supporters; including later on by means of cassette tapes that were copied and proliferated once they had been smuggled in. He was like an Old Testament prophet denouncing a sinful world from the wilderness; like John the Baptist denouncing the corrupt court of Herod from his underground prison.

Khomeini used his period of exile to develop a theory of Islamic rule that would supply the guiding principle that had been missing in 1906 – that would enable the *ulema* to govern in their own right without deferring to secular politicians. From 1970 he gave a series of lectures in Najaf about religious law and government, which later became a book (*Hokumat-e Eslami – Islamic Government*)[11] and, in turn, the theoretical foundation of the Islamic republic after the revolution of 1979 – the principle of *velayat-e faqih*.

One could see *velayat-e faqih* as the apotheosis of the deep-seated mistrust of secular authority that is grounded so deep in Shi'a Islam, and as the culmination of the Usuli position as it had evolved, creating its own hierarchical structure, since the seventeenth century. The term *velayat-e faqih* needs explaining. The word *vali* signifies a regent or deputy, someone standing in for the person with real authority. *Velayat* means guardianship or deputyship, or rather, by extension, the authority of the guardian, deputy or regent. The term *faqih* (plural *fuqaha*) signifies a jurist, an expert in Islamic law – *fiqh* (in Iranian Shi'a terms, a *mojtahed*; a member of the *ulema*). The logic of the concept was that the shari'a, derived from the word of God and the example of the Prophet and the Emams, was there to regulate human conduct and was the only legitimate law. In the early centuries after the death of the Prophet, the Emams had been the legitimate leaders to interpret and apply the shari'a. But in the absence of the Hidden Emam (since AD 874), the *mojtaheds* had, of necessity, taken over that responsibility (on a provisional basis – hence *velayat*). They were the right people to interpret the shari'a and to guide its application in practical everyday matters, high or low. So to whom other than they could sovereignty and the responsibility of government properly devolve?

The theory of *velayat-e faqih* meant that the secular authority of other governments, of whatever form, was illegitimate. In the absence of the Hidden Emam, the only rightful rulers were those selected by the *ulema* (Khomeini's thinking was not entirely new – the idea that the *ulema* should rule had been current, though never dominant, during the reigns of the last two Safavid Shahs in the period 1666–1722).[12]

The book *Hokumat-e Eslami*[13] began with an analysis of how Islam had been eclipsed in the modern world, saying baldly (and without further explanation) that pressure on Islam had begun with the Jews, joined later by 'other groups ... about three hundred years ago'. These groups were motivated by materialism and saw Islam and the belief of the people in Islam as the main obstacle to their ambitions. 'They therefore plotted and campaigned against Islam by various means', using 'agents' in educational institutions, in religious institutions, and in government. 'Orientalists' in the service of 'imperialistic states' were working at the same time to the same ends.[14] This analysis reflected the experience of the *ulema* in the 1930s; confronted with the Westernizing policies of Reza Shah and other contemporary Middle Eastern rulers and politicians in the foreground, and the influence of Western powers in the background.

Khomeini (sounding rather like Shariati) declared: 'Islam is the religion of militant individuals who are committed to truth and justice. It is the religion of those who desire freedom and independence.' But the Westernizing forces –'servants of imperialism' – created a false view of Islam in men's minds, according to which Islam had nothing to say about big questions of political principle and government, only concerning itself with pettifogging matters, such as 'ritual purity after menstruation and parturition'. The educated classes were particularly affected by these false, Western-inspired ideas. But it was not just the servants of imperialism that were to blame, because it was true that some *ulema* ('*akhund*'; a pejorative term) had really preoccupied themselves with these trivial matters, turning aside from the bigger questions. 'They too are at fault' – for the neglect that took over in seminaries and *madresehs*, unwittingly contributing to the success of the imperialists.

In a paragraph dealing with the Constitutional Revolution, Khomeini wrote that, despite some Islamic window-dressing, 'agents of Britain' had taken advantage of the constitutionalist movement to create the constitution of 1906 – 'the basis of the laws that were now thrust upon the people was alien and borrowed' – going on to say that the constitution was opposed to Islam, primarily because (adducing various proofs from the Koran and *hadith*) Islam was opposed to monarchy and the hereditary principle. Showing himself to be a spiritual descendant of Fazlollah Nuri,[15] Khomeini asserted the falsity of the constitution and the idea of Islam promulgated by the imperialists (but also, departing from Nuri's example, monarchy). What was necessary was Islamic government –'Know that it is your duty to establish an Islamic government' – based on the principles of Islam, and the authority of the Prophet Mohammad, passed down through the Shi'a Emams. Khomeini said that this would be just government, because the people would be governed not by people, but by law – the law derived from the Koran and the *hadith*.

But there was a conceptual gap. In the section entitled 'The Form of Islamic Government'[16] Khomeini did not really say what Islamic government was going to be. He wrote that it would not correspond to any existing form of government; it would be based on Islamic law: 'Islamic government may be defined as the rule of divine law over men'. In lieu of a legislative assembly, a 'simple planning body' would draw up programmes for different ministries 'in the light of the ordinances of Islam'. This would be facilitated by the fact that Islamic law, based on the Koran and the *hadith*, was recognized and accepted by Muslims already. With the monarchy gone, there would be no huge system of corruption and embezzlement; nor the 'superfluous bureaucracies and the system of file-keeping and paper-shuffling that is enforced in them, all of which are totally alien to Islam'.

But instead of elaborating further, Khomeini restated the reason why *velayat-e faqih* was the legitimate form of government. Legitimate government was the rule of God, as expressed through divine law. In the time of the Prophet, the Prophet himself governed. After him, the Emams were the legitimate governors – not for their spiritual qualities, but because they were pre-eminent in their knowledge of law and justice. What of the time after the occultation of the twelfth Emam? Should there be anarchy and chaos because the Emams were no longer active in the world? No – despite their disappearance, knowledge of law and justice were still present – in the *ulema*, the *fuqaha*, the scholars of *fiqh*, shari'a law. The fact that these men might be deficient in spirituality by comparison with the Emams did not matter in this context, because the important thing for government was not spirituality, but knowledge of law and justice. They were the ones entitled to govern:

> Now that this much has been demonstrated, it is necessary that the *fuqaha* proceed, collectively or individually, to establish a government in order to implement the laws of Islam and protect its territory. If this task falls within the capabilities of a single person, he has personally incumbent upon him the duty to fulfil it; otherwise, it is a duty that devolves upon the *fuqaha* as a whole.

So, government by the *faqih* or the *fuqaha*, a simple planning body, and ministries. But beyond this thin outline, nothing. *Hokumat-e Eslami* gave no constitution, no structure explaining how different elements of government would relate to each other and no mechanism for representation of the wishes of the people. Khomeini wrote that the law of Islam was comprehensive and covered every eventuality – therefore it was unnecessary to go into further detail. But this conceptual gap left it unclear what would happen if Khomeini or his followers eventually were to put their ideas into practice, and left plenty of room for reinterpretation. Why was there this gap? It may be that Khomeini intended deliberately to leave some flexibility for interpretation, in case he needed it later. But ultimately he was a religious thinker, not a constitutional expert. It seems likely that, like the clerics in 1906, *he simply did not know* (at least not in 1970) what form the constitution might or should take.

Khomeini's ideas in *Hokumat-e Eslami* did not gather much support among the *ulema*, and before 1978–9 were not widely circulated beyond religious circles. No senior figure endorsed them (except Ayatollah Montazeri, one of Khomeini's own former students), and the most senior ayatollah in Najaf at the time, Abol-Qasem Khoei, rejected Khomeini's arguments on the basis that he had exaggerated the significance in *fiqh* of the concept of *velayat*, which (according to Khoei) was properly confined to the guardianship of widows and orphans. Khoei and his successors (notably Ali Hosein Sistani) in Najaf have continued to reject Khomeini's principle of *velayat-e faqih* down to the time of writing.

From the time of the appearance of *Hokumat-e Eslami* onwards Khomeini demanded the removal of the Shah and the establishment of Islamic government: clear and consistent demands that the whole country could understand (at least, they thought they could – what exactly Islamic government might mean in practice remained less clear) and which, as discontent grew through the 1970s, increasingly made him the focal point for opposition to the Shah.

In 1978 Khomeini was forced to leave Iraq by Saddam Hussein, following the rapprochement between Iran and Iraq achieved through the Algiers Accords. Having been refused entry to Kuwait, Khomeini went to Paris in October, where he lived in the suburb of Neauphle-le-Château, attended by his son Ahmad, his son-in-law Eshraqi and members of the Freedom Movement including Abol Hassan Bani-Sadr, Sadegh Qotbzadeh and Ebrahim Yazdi. These supporters served as a buffer between him and the unfamiliar Western world.[17] Hundreds of journalists wanted to speak to him, but the interviews showed a serious mismatch of expectations. The idea of an interview in which inconsequential, polite chat set the parties at ease before the serious, sometimes blunt questioning began was quite alien to Khomeini, who was used to deferential petitions and respectful requests for advice from students and others in the hushed precincts of the seminary. He sometimes appeared to find the journalists irritating. The BBC journalist Stephen Jessell commented:

This tremendous presence from some remote century made no effort to welcome us, or at least me, and hardly gave us a glance. He sat on a pile of cushions in the corner of a small living room, eyes lowered, and harangued my colleague's tape recorder . . . It falls to a journalist, if he or she is lucky, to see at close quarters some of the people who leave their stamp on history. Of them all, I have never met anyone who made so great an impression as this man to whom the nuances and compromises of the twentieth century were, it seemed, of as little lasting significance as the snow that fell that winter.[18]

This goes some way to explain the notorious incident in the airliner as Khomeini flew back to Tehran, when he was asked by the ABC journalist Peter Jennings (through an interpreter) what his feelings were on returning to Iran. Khomeini replied, with a slight, even smug smile as if to dismiss the question as absurd: 'Hichi – Hich ehsasi nadaram' ('Nothing – I have no feelings').[19] The interpreter preferred to translate this as 'He doesn't make any comment,' but since that time Khomeini's opponents have presented his words as expressing his indifference to Iran and the Iranian people; or as pointing to his preference for Islam over any form of Iranian nationalism. It seems more likely that Khomeini regarded the question as trite and inappropriate – but at a deeper level, that he was beyond feelings of the kind meant by Jennings. This prompts an enquiry as to what Khomeini's attitude to himself and his role really was.

In addition to his public theory of *velayat-e faqih*, Khomeini also had a complementary private theory, of principles for the religious life, that informed his view of his own significance and his role. This drew upon his studies of mysticism; on his study of Ibn Arabi and Molla Sadra in particular, but also other authors. It is important to remember that his interest in mysticism was in itself a major departure from the normal orthodoxy of the *ulema*; for many years Khomeini concealed his philosophical and mystical inclinations.[20] Khomeini saw prayer as part of a process of development, of self-improvement, as a kind of ladder toward God.[21] This drew upon an idea found in the work of many Islamic mystics, but especially that of Ibn Arabi – the concept of *al-insan al-Kamil* – the Perfect Man. Ibn Arabi wrote that human experience was divided between the macrocosm – the experience of the external world – and the microcosm, the internal world. These two worlds reflect each other, albeit imperfectly; but through religious contemplation and self-development, Man can 'polish his soul' until the two worlds are congruent. He can improve and perfect himself until he takes on the form of the divine – becoming the Perfect Man.[22] Khomeini wrote as early as 1929:

> The Perfect Man ... is the holder of the chain of existence, with which the cycle is completed. It is the beginning and the end, it is the external and the internal, the totality of the Divine Book. He is God's great sign, created in God's image. Whoever knows the Perfect Man has known God.[23]

This was, in effect, the project of Khomeini's life. The Perfect Man is a copy of God, achieved by religious discipline, prayer and mystical devotion, and becomes a conduit for the will of God in the world. In Shi'a terms, this is what the Emams had been in their time. According to Khomeini's studies of Molla Sadra's *Four Journeys*, the fourth and final journey brings the traveller to the point of *velayat* (a term Khomeini used also in this context) or prophethood, at which he can guide the wider community toward God.[24] Khomeini believed that he reflected the spiritual reality of the world and was a vehicle for the mind of God[25] – hence the absence or irrelevance of personal feelings.

This account of Khomeini's internal life might seem of marginal relevance to the political events of 1979; but he himself would have seen it as central, and he would have had a point. After all, on the day of his return to Tehran from Paris and in the unique atmosphere of the early months of 1979 there was a congruence between the will of Khomeini and the will of the Iranian people – *ana al-haqq wa al-khalq* – 'I am the truth and the people'.[26] He did seem to be a conduit for both the mind of God and the will of the people. Microcosm and macrocosm really did seem, albeit briefly, to be as one.

Islamic Government – Theory and Practice

Many books, whether because they focus on the Shah or for other reasons, break off with the events of February 1979 and the success of the revolutionary movement. But an understanding of the struggle thereafter over the formation of the institutions that followed the revolution is at least as complex and problematic, and as intriguing, as what went before. How would the tension between religious and liberal democratic principles be resolved? What would fill the conceptual gap over the form of government that Khomeini himself had left in his book *Hokumat-e Eslami*? What were Khomeini's intentions in the first few weeks after his return to Iran? Did he expect from the beginning to establish a religious dictatorship with himself at the head of it? There is good reason to think not, and to believe instead that the eventual form of the Islamic republic came about as a result of a process of adjustment, action, reaction, struggle and consolidation over the first year or more after the revolutionary movement achieved supremacy on 11 February 1979 – and that Khomeini initially expected a more distant role for himself, relying on secular politicians that he felt he could trust to carry out the day-to-day business of government. Khomeini later emphasized the collegiate nature of decision-making at this stage, between himself and the other members of his close circle. He, or rather they, managed the early phases of the revolution with great skill. In the French and Russian revolutions, those who took power after the initial success of the revolutionary movement were displaced from power by other revolutionaries within a relatively short period. But Khomeini, against the expectations of many liberals and leftists in particular, took power and succeeded in holding it until his death. Initially, he did so partly by letting others take responsibility for government, and by allowing *them* to be displaced.

The theory of *velayat-e faqih* was, and is, open to different interpretations. Proponents of reform within the Iranian system have in recent years argued again for a more restricted role for the *vali*, which would mean that he would only intervene when he saw the principles of Islam threatened, or when he was asked for guidance by the elected representatives of the people (Morteza Mottahari was arguing for something like this early in 1979). The form that the *velayat-e faqih* took in practice after 1979 was not a foregone conclusion – a variety of other outcomes were possible.

In a little more than a week after Khomeini's return Bazargan was appointed prime minister, and Bakhtiar's government collapsed.[27] In the jubilation that followed the Shah's departure and the success of the revolutionary movement, there was another outpouring of political and journalistic activity, as in the period before the Constitutional Revolution, and again in 1941–53, and again briefly in 1963. New newspapers and political societies appeared. For example, within a few weeks there was a split in the National Front, with a younger-spirited, more leftist party appearing under Hedayatollah Matin Daftari, calling itself the National Democratic Front (NDF).[28] Another newcomer was the Muslim People's Republican Party (MPRP), with its strongest support in Iranian Azerbaijan. This party had a system of values and a social support base similar to that of the Freedom Movement but took its membership from (mainly middle-class) Iranians who regarded Ayatollah Shariatmadari as their *marja-e taqlid* (the party received his blessing in return).[29] The situation was fluid, and within a short time the unity that had held the different elements of the revolutionary movement together through the struggle to remove the Shah began to break down.

Despite the popular adulation around him, Khomeini acted with caution in this early phase. Initially, in keeping with the conservative instincts of the religious class, he was anxious that radicals on the streets should disarm and cease rioting and looting. The police, gendarmerie and army should not be attacked: 'They have returned to us, and are one [with] us.'[30] He did not make an immediate grab for power and full control but set himself and his followers to the task of consolidation and a more indirect extension of their power. Before his return, in their meetings in Paris, he had given liberal nationalists like Sanjabi and Bani-Sadr[31] the impression that he favoured democratic government with a supervisory role for the clergy – similar to the constitution of 1906 but with the Shah removed and the position of the clergy only moderately strengthened. Bazargan, Qotbzadeh and the other politicians of the Freedom Movement received the same impression, and thought that after the initial drama of his return, Khomeini would fade into the background, leaving politics to the secular politicians. Khomeini allowed them to continue thinking that way, and the initial form of government he set up, with Bazargan at the head of it, seemed to confirm the same thing. The more radical line he had taken in *Hokumat-e Eslami* was still not widely known.

Khomeini could rely on the Council of the Islamic Revolution (CIR), using it as a coordinating body for his most loyal supporters.[32] Through it, and through personal contacts, he could communicate with the local revolutionary committees (*komiteh*) and revolutionary courts that had been set up throughout the country, and with the Friday prayer leaders in the mosques, over whom he also gained control within a short time.

In addition, already in February 1979 he and his followers set up the Islamic Republican Party (IRP) to represent the political interests of his followers among the *ulema*. Ayatollah Beheshti was the leading figure in the IRP from the start, along with others who would become central later, including Hojjatoleslam Hashemi Rafsanjani, Mohammad Javad Bahonar and Ali Khamenei, and Mir Hosein Musavi (an associate of Beheshti and one of several non-clerics). The most senior members among the founders had all, or nearly all, been members of the Jame-ye Ruhaniyat-e Mobarez (Combatant Clergy Association) in 1977 and 1978 and were members of the CIR also. Membership of the IRP grew rapidly, and it brought out a new newspaper, *Jomhuri-ye Eslami* (*Islamic Republic*).[33]

Up and down the country the first months of 1979 were euphoric for many and exciting for the politically minded, but chaotic and terrifying for some. Daily necessities like staple foods and kerosene for cooking and heating were still in short supply because of the strikes that had gone before. Groups of young men, some of them armed, roamed the streets looking for SAVAK functionaries or anyone associated with the old regime. Some targeted foreigners; embassies were threatened, and on 14 February Fedayan radicals attacked and occupied the US embassy. Ambassador Sullivan and the other diplomats in the building were held for a while, but were released later after the Provisional Government intervened.[34] Over the following months the situation settled down in some ways, but remained disturbingly uncertain. Old patterns of authority were disrupted, and people did not know where to look for reassurance and security. When initiatives with public consequences were undertaken, ordinary people did not necessarily know who was responsible or why what was done had been done. There were too many independent or semi-independent poles of authority. This was the first phase of the Islamic republic, and in some respects it was the defining phase. To a reduced but still significant degree, that uncertainty, the multipolar political system and also the occasional application of extra-judicial violence, still persist in Iran today.

Central authority had broken down, and local *komiteh* had taken over in many places, like the Soviets in Russia in 1917–18. It was estimated that there were 1,500 *komiteh* in Tehran alone at this time.[35] For the most part the *komiteh* were sympathetic to Khomeini, but it took some effort for the CIR and IRP to purge them of leftist and liberal elements they found undesirable, and in areas with large ethnic or religious minorities like Kurdestan and Khuzestan (and the areas in the north-east where Turkmen tribes lived) the local feeling for autonomy was strong and resistant to the reimposition of central control (members of the Fedayan did their best to encourage and radicalize some of these regional movements). Khomeini was elderly, and came from a conservative social and intellectual background that distrusted anarchy and social disorder. He had held back from ordering mass violence against the Shah's government at a number of points between November and February, and even at the climactic moment on 11–12 February had sought to restrain violent elements on the side of the revolutionaries. Among these, the Fedayan and the MKO had been most significant on that occasion; they had been gathering strength rapidly from the point of near-extinction at the hands of SAVAK before 1978 (Tudeh also regained some of its former strength). Khomeini had spoken out against these violent, leftist groups even while he was still in Paris. After his return he was acutely aware that, when it came to armed force, his own supporters were weak; and aside from the militant leftists, the army, though it had declared itself neutral and was bruised after the events of January and February, was also still a potential threat (as would be demonstrated later).

To address this vulnerability, Khomeini and his supporters set out to strengthen their own faction and to neutralize the threats to it where they could. Three groups aligned with Khomeini and prepared for violent action crystallized out of the revolutionary mass of those who had gathered for demonstrations, and the *komiteh*. Of these, the Mojahedin-e Enqelab-e Eslami (Mojahedin of the Islamic Revolution) were set up on a basis rather like the Fedayan and the MKO. Similarly the Sepah (Sepah-e Pasdaran-e Enqelab-e Eslami – literally, Islamic Revolutionary Guards Corps),[36] though these from the beginning had a more disciplined character, as a militia intended as an ultra-loyal cadre to defend against the lingering possibility of a military coup. In the long run, the Sepah (set up initially by Khomeini's order on 5 May) became the most important of these new bodies. By September 1979 they were around 11,000 strong and were under the command of Hashemi Rafsanjani. Finally, the Hezbollah (Party of God) served as strongmen who could be sent in with clubs and fists to disrupt meetings, beat up opponents and intimidate any group Khomeini's people found it necessary to target.[37] All three were recruited largely from the poorest classes, on the calculation that they would be the most loyal to Khomeini and his programme and the least likely to be affected by leftist, liberal or Westernizing influences.

In addition, Khomeini's people sent *Namayandeh-ye Emam* (Emam's representatives) commissar-style into the regular army units to ensure their loyalty and purge them of royalists and other troublemakers. Similar agents were sent into most civilian offices and branches of government, with similar purposes.

Broadening out further the sector owing allegiance to Khomeini, his followers also took over the Pahlavi Foundation, with all its property and other assets, including factories, farmland and overseas investments; renaming it the Bonyad-e Mostazafan (Foundation for the Oppressed). The Bonyad, along with other, similar institutions, was used both to make payments to those the IRP deemed worthy recipients of charitable support and as a pool of patronage to give jobs to the right sort of people, strengthening Khomeini's cause.

As Khomeini's followers were boosted by the enthusiasm of young students and others from poor backgrounds, who were sent into recalcitrant sectors of the former regime to ensure proper revolutionary and Islamic attitudes and behaviour, so at the same time the supporters of the parties based in the middle class, the National Front and the Freedom Party (many of whom, at work, found themselves intimidated by Khomeini's earnest young agents), found their support eroded by emigration as large numbers of middling and prosperous Iranians left the country. In the heightened political excitement of the time, this emigration also tended to taint the political activities of those left behind. As the months passed, Bazargan, his provisional government and the political parties from which he and they drew support found themselves demoralized and rendered almost superfluous by the creation of new Khomeini-aligned bodies, and by the arrogation to themselves by Khomeini's party of control and influence in pre-existing institutions.

Middle-class emigration was stimulated and accelerated by the activities of the revolutionary courts. Headed by judges sympathetic to Khomeini, and supplied with victims by the *komiteh* and other groups, the revolutionary courts replaced previous civil codes with shari'a law and operated under a particularly harsh revolutionary version of it, condemning former functionaries of the Shah's regime and others like prostitutes and allegedly corrupt businessmen for crimes justified from shari'a text like being 'at war with God' and 'spreading corruption on earth'. Most prominent of the judges was Hojjatoleslam Sadegh Khalkhali, who gave the impression of enjoying his work. Beginning with the four executions on the roof of the Refah school on 14 February (Rahimi, Nasiri and two others), a series of further judicial killings followed, and continued despite protests from Bazargan and other moderates, and international indignation. Several leading clerics, including Shariatmadari, also protested (though the militant leftists of the MKO and Fedayan urged the courts on to execute even more of the previous regime's office-holders). The trials were quick and rudimentary, often held in secret, with little attempt at a defence, nor any detailed examination of evidence. The accused (most of whom were former members of SAVAK, army officers and police involved in the repression of the previous months) usually had no defence lawyer. Condemned men were often shot dead shortly after being sentenced. By 14 March the courts had executed seventy victims. Following the complaints, Khomeini ordered a halt later in March, but the trials resumed on 6 April after Ayatollah Montazeri and a committee drew up guidance for their operation. There are indications that Khomeini felt obliged to support further executions as retribution for the deaths of demonstrators the previous year in order to secure his support among young radicals – and to avoid them joining the growing ranks of the even more radical Fedayan and MKO.[38] By October several hundred had been executed.[39] Khalkhali defended the courts and their methods by saying that they were 'born out of the anger of the Iranian people'.[40]

Former Prime Minister Amir Abbas Hoveida was executed at Qasr prison at Khalkhali's orders on 7 April, despite many efforts both from outside Iran and from within to intercede on his behalf. Hoveida had been arrested the previous November, in a vain effort by the Shah to distance himself from the failures of the past. The arrest prevented Hoveida from following the Shah out of the country, but after the Shah's departure and the collapse of Bakhtiar's government he did not try to save himself when his SAVAK guards made themselves scarce. When he was rearrested by revolutionaries he did not resist. Like a spider with a specially juicy fly, Khalkhali took special care over Hoveida and ensured no last-minute intervention could save him by effectively cutting off the prison from communications from outside. He noted pruriently that

Hoveida slept naked and continued to do so despite the disapproval of his guards (pious Iranian men would always wear at least shorts and a T-shirt in bed).[41] When the Shah heard of Hoveida's fate, in exile, he showed grief. But he had done little enough to protect Hoveida, and it was not the only example of his ingratitude to loyal subordinates.[42]

Another victim of the new regime was General Hassan Pakravan, who had been head of SAVAK in the early 1960s, before Nasiri (he served also as deputy prime minister and later as ambassador to Pakistan and France). He had the reputation of having been more humane than Nasiri. When Khomeini was arrested in 1963, Pakravan had striven to save his life. He had eaten regularly with him while he was in prison and was alarmed when he heard that Khomeini had been condemned to death, believing that it would cause further serious unrest among ordinary Muslims. But Pakravan's previous efforts on Khomeini's behalf did not help him in 1979. He was arrested on 16 February:

> he took some friends to our house for lunch, and they had a wonderful time ... Then at 3.30 my husband told them, 'I want to rest, please ...' So they went.
>
> At five o'clock he got up to go to the kitchen to get a glass of water. There was lots of noise outside – shouting and all that. He said to our servant, 'What's the matter?' This young man came back pale and said, 'Timsar, they've come to take you away.'
>
> [The servant told the story later] 'He never took the trouble to put on shoes, and walked out with his slippers ... They were so respectful. They bowed to him. They opened the door ... I ran after the car, because it was the end of winter, very cold, and he had gone without a coat or anything ... they stopped the car and took his coat to him. And I was crying.'[43]

His son was told he had not been arrested, but was rather a guest of the Ayatollah (Khomeini). Pakravan was executed on 11 April.[44]

Through the trials and generally, new terms and phrases became commonplace, and with repetition established themselves as a new jargon of revolution. *Moharaba* ('waging war against God') and *mofsed fel-arz* ('spreading corruption on earth') have already been mentioned as anti-revolutionary crimes. A common term for partisans of the previous regime and other opponents of the regime was *taghuti* (literally, 'idol-worshippers'). The MKO (*monafeqin* – hypocrites) were guilty of *elteqat* (eclecticism) for their promiscuous combination of Marxist ideas with Islam. Another potential revolutionary crime was *enheraf* (deviation). By contrast, *maktabi* were politically correct, committed regime supporters. Imperialism was *jahan-khor* (world-devouring) – the United States was *shaytan-e bozorg* or *estekbar-e jahani* (the great Satan, or world arrogance). Many of these terms, like the duality of *mostakber* and *mostazafin* (oppressor and oppressed), were coined first by Khomeini in his speeches. Although he drew upon Koranic usages, Khomeini's introduction of this new revolutionary language was one of the ways in which he demonstrated the innovatory nature of his religious and political thinking.[45]

While Bazargan's Provisional Government earnestly set about the practical tasks of getting the country back to work and preparing the way for a new constitution, the IRP and Khomeini's followers in other bodies gradually extended their institutional grip and their political influence, inexorably undercutting Bazargan and his colleagues. In addition to the running dispute over the activities of the revolutionary courts, there were many other disagreements; for example over the lower-intensity intimidation, arrests and confiscation of property carried out by the *komiteh*. In each case, whenever Bazargan regarded the matter as serious enough, he appealed to Khomeini for redress. But such appeals only strengthened Khomeini and his supporters, even if he initially gave decisions that appeared to be a compromise. Each appeal reinforced still further Khomeini's position as the ultimate arbiter in the state – cementing his personal power and reconfirming the classical, traditional position of the *ulema* as a class. Indeed, in this respect the decade between Khomeini's return and his death in 1989 was really the ultimate apotheosis of the *ulema* – surpassing the previous high-water mark of their power and influence, in the last years of the Safavid dynasty, around 1700. This effect was strengthened by the fact that Bazargan's government was also under constant criticism from the leftist groups, who saw it as insufficiently radical, excessively middle-class, capitalist and bourgeois in its economic policies and dangerously, suspiciously moderate in its foreign policy (Bazargan and Sanjabi, his foreign minister, favoured discussion and reconciliation with the West and the US). Khomeini appeared to hold a middle position between the different factions. But Khomeini's decisions always served the interest of the IRP and his followers in the end. In each case he was, in effect, both a party to the dispute and the judge of it. Bazargan could not win. Nor could he make Khomeini commit himself on more practical, technical issues that would have forced him to take greater responsibility for the day-to-day operation of government. On such non-essential matters, Khomeini held aloof.

Women

In 1963–4 Khomeini had focused criticism on the Shah's measures to emancipate women, and particularly to give women the vote – partly to avoid more politically divisive subjects like land reform. Now the Shah was gone, the way was clear for restoration of more properly Islamic arrangements. But the Islamic republic's handling of these matters has been full of paradox. The status of women had an emblematic significance within the story of the revolution as well as a real significance for ordinary women in the conduct of their lives. The intrusion of revolutionary ideology into the lives of ordinary women caused much hardship.

Reza Shah's ultimately unsuccessful attempt to ban the veil in the 1930s, the inclusion of the right of women to vote in the White Revolution programme of 1963 and the introduction of the Family Protection Law in 1967 meant that the status of women was a significant part of the overall Pahlavi programme of development and Westernization. For the Shahs' traditional-minded religious opponents and for many of the clergy, these measures were an insult to the honour of Muslims and were bound up with other developments for which the government could not be held directly responsible – like the presence of prostitutes in parts of Tehran and the screening of mildly racy Western or Western-inspired films (advertised by racier billboards) in cinemas. Together, they touched on something deep and visceral about maleness, control and self-respect in Iranian society that is not easy to convey. Often, in the past, the honour of women had been conflated with national honour, such that whatever detracted from the honour of women was felt to detract from national self-respect also.[46] In traditional Iranian society, it was important for the self-respect of an Iranian man that he should be married, and that his wife should be demonstrably under control – spending most of her time in the family home, consorting only with close family members, and veiled and accompanied when out of the house. Any lapse exposed him to ridicule and loss of face. In fact, because it was expensive to maintain this situation, it is likely that only a small minority of men were ever able to subject their women to it – indeed part of the point of the phenomenon was that it was a sign of the social status of some and an aspiration (often a hopeless aspiration) for many more. That minority were predominantly (though not exclusively) the urban middle class of prosperous *bazaaris* and clerics. Outside the cities and larger villages, the lives of ordinary peasants and nomads (always the majority of the population) were very different, and most women had to work in the fields, or at any rate in public, in ways that could never be combined with seclusion or heavy veiling.[47]

This is still the case to some extent, as an internet blogger commented in March 2004:

> Why is it that women in villages are so much freer in comparison with our urban women (at least when it comes to choosing what to wear)? It's incredible but they are not only freer in how they dress, but also in their activities and movements. Why is it that they don't 'endanger Islam' by not wearing headscarves, as they freely mingle, laughing and chatting with the menfolk? Is it due to their heavy participation in work? Or is it that work will be stopped without women? God Forbid![48]

So when Khomeini and his supporters reimposed traditional values, reapplied shari'a law and annulled the Family Law of 1967 in the early part of 1979, the traditions they were reimposing were in fact rather less traditional than they seemed. It was done, nevertheless. But not without opposition – in particular, there were a series of large, peaceful demonstrations by women for several days from 8 March onwards in Tehran to protest at the reimposition of the veil and the removal of the Family Law. Khomeini appeared to relent for a time in the face of the protests, but in the end the changes went ahead, and women had to accept them. Perhaps the most important change entailed in the removal of the law of 1967 was that women lost custody rights in the event of divorce. But it also meant that a woman's word was worth less than that of a man in all law proceedings, and renewed emphasis on the man as the head of the household meant that a woman had to have the permission of husband or father in order to travel (the cruel humiliation of this is shown poignantly in Jafar Panahi's film *The Circle*).

Perversely, although rights were withdrawn, responsibility was extended. Because girls were thought to mature earlier than boys, the age of legal responsibility for girls was reduced to nine years, while for boys it was fifteen. As a result girls have been prosecuted for serious crimes, including murder, at very young ages. In theory polygamy and child marriage again became possible, but the social stigma against such practices meant that they rarely happened. Similarly with the reapplication of shari'a punishments like stoning and whipping – although they became possible again and have been used, the general mood of society has been against them, and many even of the religious leadership have come to regard them as an embarrassment. Nonetheless, Iran today has the highest rate of executions of any country except China, and the highest rate of executions for minors anywhere in the world.[49]

But even in this symbolically important area of women's rights and status, Khomeini was cautious. He did not repeal the right of women to vote, as his pronouncements from 1963 might have led some to expect. The early months of the Islamic republic were a bitter disappointment to many of the women who had demonstrated for the removal of the Shah in 1978,[50] but some of the losses were more superficial than real, and in the longer term social changes and changes in education meant that the status of women in the Islamic republic improved in a variety of important respects.[51]

Islamic or Democratic?

At an early stage in the political discussions of the first weeks after 11 February there was a dispute on a subject that Khomeini regarded as an essential matter of principle – the name by which the new state established by the revolution should be known. Khomeini insisted that it should be called the Islamic Republic; notably in a speech he made on his return to Qom on 1 March (he spent most of the next few months in Qom). The Freedom Movement and the moderates generally preferred the title Democratic Islamic Republic, and some leftist groups, including the Fedayan, wanted People's Democratic Republic. Khomeini stuck to his preference, arguing that inclusion of the word Democratic would imply that Islam was undemocratic, and that it was undignified for the term Islam to be partnered by any other qualifying word. As usual, he got his way.

This debate formed part of the early clashes over the form of the referendum on the new republic that was held at the end of March. Khomeini and the Provisional Government formulated the referendum simply as a ratification of the decision Khomeini believed the people to have taken in favour of an Islamic republic through their mass demonstrations the previous December. It would ask people whether they wanted an Islamic republic or a monarchy. Others disputed this – the NDF, Shariatmadari and many others said that voters should be given more of a choice about the nature of the future government. The NDF argued that the referendum should be held after the new constitution had been drafted, and the leftist MKO and Fedayan agreed. But the Provisional Government persevered, and when it came to the vote (held on 30 and 31 March) only the NDF, the Fedayan and the Kurdish groups boycotted it. Khomeini urged as many as possible to vote, and after the count the government announced that, of 15.7 million votes, 98.2 per cent had gone in favour of the Islamic republic. There may have been some irregularities in the referendum, but most balanced observers then and since have accepted that whatever the conditions, a referendum at that time with that question would always have given a massive majority for the same result.[52]

Kurds did not just boycott the referendum – by this time they were in open revolt. The prime political grouping among them was the Kurdish Democratic Party of Iran (KDP-I), whose armed wing were known as the Peshmerga, but a number of other, smaller groups like the Kumeleh were also involved. Although the Shah had used the Kurds in Iraq against the Iraqi regime when it suited him in the 1970s, he also practised discriminatory policies against the Iranian Kurds, who had made bids for autonomy earlier in the century, after 1918 and after 1945. By the time of the revolution there were around 4 million Kurds in Iran. Most of them lived in the north-west, but there was also a large group in the north-east, settled around Quchan in Khorasan. Levels of economic development and literacy were some of the lowest in the country. The KDP-I and others had been active in the movement against the Shah in 1978 and were hoping to win at least a measure of self-rule from the new revolutionary settlement. They called for internal autonomy for Kurdestan, while remaining under the wing of the Islamic republic for foreign relations and defence. Cultural, educational and political matters were to be regulated by a freely elected Kurdish parliament. The central government should allocate funds to help develop the region, which was backward due largely to the deliberate, repressive policy of the previous regime; and Kurdish representatives should have a say in the policy-making of the Iranian state. They also had demands for expansion of Kurdish territory. The Marxist Fedayan gave the Kurds political and armed support. Ayatollah Taleqani visited Kurdestan and spoke in favour of the Kurds' concerns. But after an initial phase of prevarication and some suggestions of compromise in negotiations the Provisional Government responded with force, claiming that other armed secessionists would be encouraged by any signs of weakness; and banned the KDP-I and Kumeleh. The armed Kurds had some successes, and the revolt spread to Sanandaj, Mahabad, Naghadeh and Marivan, but there were many casualties as the army recovered its cohesion and the Sepah joined in the fighting. In August the town of Paveh was bombed and shelled, with much loss of life. Villages were destroyed. Both sides took hostages in the fighting. Sadegh Khalkhali went to Kurdestan and executed hundreds of captured Kurds. Despite growing military pressure from the Islamic regime, the Kurds fought on for several years, pulling back to remote and inaccessible valleys when necessary.[53]

There were armed revolts also among the Turkmen in the north-east, who had taken advantage of the Shah's fall to occupy valuable agricultural land that had previously belonged to members of the royal family and the court. Here too the Fedayan supported the insurrection; here too Taleqani tried to mediate; but as in Kurdestan the talks failed, and the government applied force. Khalkhali and his executioners turned up and carried out similar summary executions. There was unrest also among the Arabs of Khuzestan (in the worst incident, a large number of demonstrators were shot dead in Khorramshahr at the end of May), and in Baluchestan. All these revolts and disturbances showed a degree of Iranian chauvinism among the politicians of the Provisional Government and the CIR. Their prime concern was to preserve the territorial integrity of Iran and to concentrate on the political struggle in Tehran. Aside from a few enlightened individuals, there was little serious interest in the demands of the minorities.[54]

Another unsettling event in the spring was the assassination of Morteza Motahhari, co-founder of the Hoseiniyeh Ershad and the Combatant Clergy Association before the revolution, and at the time of his death the chairman of the CIR. He was killed on 1 May by an obscure Islamic militant group, the Forqan, whom he had offended (along with the MKO) by attacking those who, according to him, used Islam as a screen while pursuing a Western-inspired agenda. Khomeini was deeply grieved by the loss, personally and emotionally as well as politically. Motahhari had been one of Khomeini's students and his firmest ally, but had his own intellectual hinterland as an independent thinker and had not been a mindless fellow traveller nor a yes-man by any means. Shortly before he died he wrote (somewhat in contradiction of Khomeini's *Hokumat-e Eslami*):

> *Velayat-e faqih* does not mean that the *faqih* himself heads the government. The *faqih*'s role in an Islamic country is one of being an ideologue, not a ruler. The ideologue's role is to supervise the implementation of the right ideology. The people's perception of the *velayat-e faqih* . . . was not, and is not, that the *fuqaha* should rule and manage the administration of the state.[55]

Motahhari's death was a blow to Khomeini and a shock – demonstrating the seriousness of the ideological struggle and the dangers of failure, showing that nothing could be taken for granted and that the supremacy of the clergy still had to be defended and fought for. It may have sharpened Khomeini's response to opposition in the following months. It is important to remember this. The actions of Khomeini, the IRP and its supporters, looking at it with comfortable hindsight, were sometimes extreme and brutal. But at least some of their competitors for power were prepared to be equally brutal and ruthless – perhaps worse (as emerged later). The essence of Khomeini's apparent ruthlessness was his determination not to lose (as had many of his political-clerical forerunners, like Nuri and Modarres). It is a perennial dilemma in politics, especially revolutionary politics[56] – the danger that the methods necessary to the game may discredit the principles the game was played for, and that the politician who justifies means by ends finds himself languishing in a moral limbo. A few months later, at a time when conflict between his supporters and the leftists on university campuses was growing, Khomeini told some of his people a story about the cleric and politician Hasan Modarres, and how Modarres had instructed Khomeini with the principle: 'You hit first and let others complain. Don't be the victim and don't complain.'[57]

The murder of Motahhari contributed, along with other deaths and departures later, to a narrowing of the movement of the revolutionary clergy and a greater emphasis on the thought and personality of Khomeini alone. With Taleqani, Motahhari had been the linking personality to Bazargan, the Freedom Movement and the secular intellectuals.[58] Had he lived, he might have exerted a moderating influence.

The Constitution

The drafting of the constitution had featured in the arguments around the referendum, and the question of the constitution was central in the political debates over the rest of the year. Initially, responsibility for drafting the constitution fell to the Provisional Government, and Bazargan gave the job to one of his ministers, Yadollah Sahabi (although it seems some of the early work on a draft had been done by his son Ezzatollah Sahabi and others while Khomeini was still in Paris).[59] Many of the moderates were still attached to the old constitution of 1906, and Sahabi used that text as one of his models, but the old constitution had been designed around a constitutional monarchy, and at the very least the new one had to cater for a new, republican principle. Some elements were taken from the French constitution – the Gaullist constitution of the Fifth Republic, in use since 1958, which meant a strong presidency. A range of politicians and others were consulted informally over the draft, including Ayatollah Shariatmadari (a consistent supporter of the constitution of 1906), before it was approved by the Provisional Government and the CIR. The Islamic element in this first draft was not so marked – there was to be a council for checking legislation to ensure its compatibility with Islam (the constitution of 1906 had also included a body of this kind), but its powers were limited, and the *velayat-e faqih* was present neither in terms nor in spirit.

Khomeini's handling of the first draft of the constitution was revealing. He made two small amendments, both concerning the position of women – the effect was to prevent women being judges or being appointed to the presidency.[60] Otherwise, he was content to see the constitution drafted by Sahabi enter into force with merely another referendum to approve it (when it was published on 14 June, he declared the draft 'correct'). If this had happened, the Islamic republic would have been set up on a moderate, democratic, almost secular footing. Khomeini's handling of the matter confirms his previous caution and suggests at least that he was prepared to play a long game in order to secure dominance for his own vision of the Islamic republic; alternatively that he expected cooperation in government with the liberal moderates to be a long-term arrangement. But Bazargan and Bani-Sadr objected to the idea of the constitution entering into effect with such minimal scope for democratic revision, and like them, a wide swathe of political opinion was unwilling to see that happen without it being debated and amended by an elected body – a constituent assembly of some kind. This proved to be a major mistake by the moderates and leftists. Rafsanjani apparently warned Bani-Sadr what would happen – that an elected assembly would be dominated by unmanageable radical clerics.[61] If they had gone for the original draft without further debate, the moderates would have secured a constitution much more aligned to their thinking than the eventual one. They became victims of their own principles.

Parties and journalists fell over themselves to bring forward theoretical arguments and to propose amendments and wholesale alternative versions. Some wanted a more Islamic constitution, others a more radically leftist one. Eventually it was agreed that the constitution would be reviewed by an Assembly of Experts (Majles-e Khubregan), composed of seventy-three elected members. The elections were arranged for 3 August,[62] and the Assembly first convened on 18 August.

In the run-up to the elections there were intensive informal discussions on the constitution in the media and generally, and a number of more formal discussions in seminars that were arranged for the purpose. But there was also a good deal of intimidation by the IRP and its subordinate organizations, and many groups and parties hostile to them protested at irregularities in the election. Only roughly half the numbers that voted in the March referendum (over 20 million) voted in the August elections for the Assembly of Experts.[63] The result was startling – fifty-five of the elected members of the Assembly were clerics (Bani-Sadr was one of the minority of secular members). The elected Kurdish delegate, Abdul Rahman Qasemlu (leader of the KDP-I) was not allowed to take part. Khomeini announced in an inaugural message (Rafsanjani read it out to the Assembly)[64] that the new constitution should be 100 per cent Islamic, and (in accordance with the principles of

Hokumat-e Eslami) that non-clerical delegates, lacking the qualifications to do so, should not meddle in discussions of the Islamic articles of the text.

Between the elections and the first meeting of the Assembly, the Provisional Government brought into effect a new press law, the result of which was to close many newspapers and journals. The newspaper closures began with ten papers accused of having been connected with the Shah's government (including the popular independent paper *Ayandegan*) and continued with more than twenty leftist or liberal papers accused of being un-Islamic or against the revolution. Several parties, including the NDF and the National Front, boycotted the Assembly of Experts elections in protest at the new law – the Kurds also boycotted them. The brief spring of the free press since the fall of the Shah came to an end – or at least entered a much frostier phase. Hezbollah broke into the offices of *Ayandegan* and sacked them and also attacked the head offices of the Fedayan, the MKO, Tudeh and the NDF. By the autumn a new, IRP-aligned paper was operating out of the old offices of *Ayandegan*, and two other long-established and popular publications, *Ettela'at* and *Kayhan*, were taken over by the IRP-controlled Bonyad-e Mostazafan.[65] These events brought in a new political atmosphere in Tehran and set the scene for the redrafting of the constitution. It had almost the character of a coup. More confident now (though feeling the pressure from the leftists and the Kurdish revolt), Khomeini and his followers were tightening their grip:

> Enqelab Street always was the busiest street, and all the political groups brought their books and pamphlets there to sell to the people and discuss them. Gradually the Hezbollah formed and they attacked the bookshops. Those who were Hezbollah were mainly from a poor family background, and because nobody could say anything against them, they flourished and eventually ruled the revolution, mainly because everyone supported the poor people. At the beginning of the revolution cleanliness, studying to have a better life and money and so on, were considered as values, but being poor was the greatest honour – people thought of them as the owners of the revolution.[66]

As the mood changed, the poet Ahmad Shamlu wrote the poem 'In this Dead End', from which the following is an extract:

They sniff your mouth
Lest you have said, 'I love you.'
They sniff your heart.
These are strange times, my beloved . . .
And they whip love
At the roadblock.
We must hide love in the back room.
They keep the fire burning
In this crooked dead end of the cold
With fuel of songs and poems.
Do not risk a thought.
These are strange times, my beloved . . .[67]

Montazeri and Beheshti were elected as chairman and deputy chairman of the Assembly of Experts respectively, and the Assembly set about a thoroughgoing revision of the draft constitution. Beheshti ran the debates and (despite protests) did so as a director of business pursuing a previously determined plan rather than an impartial chairman facilitating discussion. There could be no serious opposition. As the deliberations of the Assembly went on, the concept of *velayat-e faqih* gained ground. Beheshti did not force it initially, instead letting it emerge from the body of the clerics in the Assembly.[68] Although the leftist parties, Shariatmadari and many moderate and liberal politicians continued to voice their disapproval, there was little sign of strong popular opposition to the concept of *velayat-e faqih*. Given his previous caution, it seems likely that Khomeini was surprised by the ease with which he was able to achieve his principal aim. The moderate politicians, the heirs of Mossadeq and the constitutionalists of 1906, the people he had been accustomed to regarding as the main political opponents to himself, his aims and the clerical class as a whole, were conceding the central powers of the state to him almost without a fight. And this was happening primarily because of the continuing, enormous popular swell of support for him personally and for the idea of Islamic government.

Mohammad Beheshti was fifty-one years old in 1979. He was born in Isfahan and had studied at the University of Tehran as well as in Qom. Like Montazeri and Motahhari, he had been one of Khomeini's students in Qom. He learned English, and later taught it; he was a firm believer in the expansion of the seminary curriculum to include science subjects and modern languages. From 1965 to 1970 he was head of the Islamic Centre in Hamburg in Germany, organized around the Emam Ali Mosque established there a decade earlier (Mohammad Khatami followed him there later, in the 1970s), and learned German too. Beheshti was widely respected, a confident speaker and a practical organizer. He was a natural as a political mullah – an easy choice as leader of the IRP and for the most demanding tasks in the formation of the Islamic republic. Along with Motahhari and Montazeri, he was one of Khomeini's principal and most trusted lieutenants in this early phase; and of all of them he was the most competent in organizational and practical matters.

The debates in the Assembly addressed some fundamental questions of political philosophy, including the nature of sovereignty and the separation of powers. Under Beheshti's guidance the work proceeded in an orderly manner, with each article of the constitution discussed and amended in turn, and with a series of sub-committees discussing the articles separately in advance of plenary sessions of the whole Assembly. But many sessions grew heated (Khomeini's injunction that non-jurists should not speak on matters bearing upon Islam did not hold), and the debates were discussed energetically in the broadcast and print media. The proceedings had initially been planned to last one month, but when that time was up, the Assembly were only halfway through. So they voted themselves more time.

One should not exaggerate the dominance of Khomeini and the IRP at this stage. The Provisional Government's draft was still the basis of the constitution, and the principle of democratic sovereignty remained, albeit in uneasy tension with the principle of divine sovereignty, *velayat-e faqih*. At various points Khomeini's supporters asserted strongly that there was no conflict between the democratic principle and the religious principle, because the rule of Islam was itself, if properly applied, fully democratic. At any rate, the principle of popular elections to the Majles and the presidency survived.

Given the conceptual gap in Khomeini's thinking identified earlier, as manifested in *Hokumat-e Eslami*, it is legitimate to question what Beheshti and the other architects of the constitution were drawing on in their discussions in the Assembly of Experts. It appears they may have been drawing on a work by the Iraqi cleric Ayatollah Mohammad Baqr al-Sadr, his *Preliminary Legal Note on the Project of a Constitution for the Islamic Republic in Iran.* Mohammad Baqr al-Sadr came from a prominent family of Iraqi clerics and *seyyeds* (Moqtada al-Sadr, who came to prominence in Iraq after 2003, was his son-in-law). Comparison between Baqr al-Sadr's *Note* and the constitution in its final form shows a number of strong similarities, and, in particular, the role for popular suffrage is striking. By comparison with Khomeini, Baqr al-Sadr's thinking generally showed a greater awareness of Western ideas of political thought, and a greater attachment to the principle of popular participation in government. *Hokumat-e Eslami* contained little or no mention of popular consultation in government, whereas in Baqr al-Sadr's *Note* and in the eventual constitution it is much more prominent. The articulation of the role of the leader seems also to owe a lot to the *Note*. The strong impression is that those framing the constitution reached for al-Sadr's *Note* to supply an Islamically acceptable remedy for the deficiencies of *Hokumat-e Eslami*.[69]

The debates in the Assembly over the *velayat-e faqih* were the most heated, and the crucial article declaring the authority of the *faqih* (article 5) was debated and voted on in early September. Only eight members voted against; four abstained (including Bani-Sadr, who stayed away), and the remainder voted in favour. The article declared that, in the absence of the Hidden Emam, the *velayat* and the leadership of the people devolved to 'the just and pious *faqih* who is acquainted with the circumstances of his age; courageous, resourceful, and possessed of administrative ability . . .'.[70] In later articles (107 onwards, but mainly in article 110) he was given sweeping powers that gave effect to the principle laid down in article 5. He was to appoint the heads of each of the armed services, and the joint chief of staff of the armed services, and the head of the Revolutionary Guards. He had the responsibility for declaring war or peace and ordering mobilization. He was also to appoint the head of the national TV and radio organization. Before presidential elections, he had to approve the candidates before they could run for office and he could dismiss a president declared incompetent by the Majles or Supreme Court.

As in the first draft a twelve-man Guardian Council was provided for to approve legislation agreed by the Majles before it could become law (to ensure it complied with the principles of Islam and the constitution). The *faqih* was to appoint six of them directly, and the remaining six were to be selected by the Majles from a list of jurists compiled by the Supreme Judiciary Council, most of whose members, including the head, were also appointed by the *faqih* (the Guardian Council's notorious responsibility for vetting candidates before elections was not part of the original constitution of 1979, emerging only later). The question of the succession was addressed in article 107, which, after confirming Khomeini as *faqih* for life, stated that at his death a new Assembly of Experts would deliberate whether any of the jurists available was outstanding enough to be sole *faqih*. If not, they might select a three- or five-man leadership council of jurists instead.

Other articles in the constitution declared the primacy of Islam and the sovereignty of God: article 2/1 declared 'His exclusive sovereignty and the right to legislate, and the necessity of submission to His commands.' Freedoms of association and expression were protected (articles 26 and 24), but subject to Islam and the interests of the republic.

The constitution had a fairly standard governmental structure, with executive, legislature and judiciary, and separation of the powers between them, as clear as Montesquieu himself could have devised it. But above and beyond this stood the *faqih*, with the power and the responsibility to intervene directly in the name of Islam; indeed with powers greater than those given to most monarchs in constitutional monarchies. Below the *faqih*, the presidential and prime ministerial offices lingered as vestiges of the superseded constitution originally drafted by the Provisional Government (the prime minister was to be appointed by the president and approved by the Majles).

Other significant provisions included a mention in the preamble to the constitution to the effect that the Sepah would be responsible inter alia for 'fulfilling the ideological mission of jihad in God's path; that is, extending the sovereignty of God's law throughout the world', and again in article 10:

> In accordance with the verse: 'This your nation is a single nation, and I am your Lord, so worship Me,' all Muslims form a single nation, and the government of the Islamic Republic of Iran has the duty of formulating its general policies with a view to the merging and union of all Muslim peoples, and it must constantly strive to bring about the political, economic and cultural unity of the Islamic world.

This was taken to signify a mission to spread the revolution to other Islamic countries.[71]

In article 1 the constitution declared the importance of the referendum held at the end of March for establishing the Islamic republic, and article 6 established the principle of government according to public opinion as expressed through elections for the Majles and the office of president; but neither of those articles mentioned sovereignty – sovereignty belonged to God (article 2/1, already quoted), in whose name and in the fulfilment of whose law the *faqih* was to operate. Although the constitution gave primacy to the sovereignty of God, it effectively froze into itself an unresolved rivalry between popular sovereignty and the sovereignty of Islam. At the centre of this tension was the question of submission. Were the people the masters, or were they subjects? The constitution, through the many elections it provided for various bodies and offices, appeared to embrace a democratic principle. But it also committed the Iranian people, in the orthodox manner of the Islamic faith, to submission to Islam[72] and the will of God; and to the guardianship of the *faqih*, according to that principle. Underlying this was a deep-seated attitude among at least some of the *ulema* – a traditional, conservative, paternalistic attitude – that the people were children to be guided and disciplined, that they could not be trusted with power (an attitude not unlike that of the Shah): 'Several members appeared uncertain whether the mass of the people, "illiterate, poor and envious", as one delegate put it, would be able to resist the blandishments of rival religions and ideologies.'[73]

A few dissenting members of the Assembly, including three clerics, warned of the dangers of giving the *faqih* such power in the state. Bani-Sadr spoke up, warning: 'We are drafting these articles in a manner that, step by step, we introduce a kind of absolutism in the constitution ... Tomorrow, a military man might come and use these articles against you.'[74] Some pointed to the contradiction with the principle of popular sovereignty, arguing that the powers of the *faqih* were just too broad: critics would say that the clergy had made a power grab in their own interest, and eventually the people would set aside these provisions of the constitution. Others warned that, although the office of the *faqih* might function while Khomeini was the incumbent, it was unlikely that such an exceptional candidate could possibly be found again when Khomeini died. One member, Ezzatollah Sahabi, made a speech outside the Assembly warning that these powers would bring upon the clergy the kind of criticism normally levelled at politicians and would bring about the beginning of the decline of Islam.[75]

Years later, he would himself echo just those arguments, but in the autumn of 1979 Ayatollah Hosein-Ali Montazeri took the other side in the debate, saying that the government could not be considered Islamic if the *faqih* did not have power to confirm in office and to supervise the president and the other prime office-holders of the state. Other clerics could not see any danger from an over-mighty *faqih* – they believed rather the contrary, that the office of *faqih* would *protect* the country from encroachment by an over-ambitious president or other politician. Like the Prophet himself in his time, the *faqih* would bring mercy, kindness and justice to the people, not tyranny or absolutism.[76] In a sense, Iran has remained stuck ever since in the debate between Islam and democracy that swung back and forth in the Assembly of Experts that autumn.

As the debates of September moved into October and the final form of the constitution took shape, some concerned politicians tried to act to head off what was happening. One member of the Assembly, Mohammad-Javad Hojjati-Kermani (one of the clerics, but a dissenter from the majority line) suggested that a skeleton version of the constitution, stripped of the more controversial articles, be passed to Khomeini himself for revision. Then, with the guidance of expert advisers, Khomeini could complete it before referring it back to the Assembly for final approval. But few other members of the Assembly supported his suggestion, and it faded. Then in mid-October Bazargan was associated with another attempt, which seems to have taken the form of a memorandum to Khomeini from most of the ministers of the Provisional Government, calling for the Assembly to be dissolved, on the basis that in altering the original draft constitution so radically it had exceeded both its remit and the time allocated for its task. The instigator of the memorandum was Abbas Amir-Entezam, who served as Bazargan's aide, spokesman and deputy. Khomeini rejected the initiative in apocalyptic terms, declaring that the *velayat-e faqih* would not lead to dictatorship; nor was it the creation of the Assembly of Experts: it had been ordained by God. Opposition to it was equivalent to a declaration of war on Islam.[77]

But opposition outside the Assembly was growing. Ayatollah Mahmud Taleqani, who had played such a prominent part in the demonstrations against the Shah the previous year, and who had warned against a return to despotism earlier in 1979, expressed unhappiness about the way the constitution was going before his death on 9 September 1979, suggesting that it looked worse than the constitution of 1906 – 'may God forbid autocracy under the name of religion'.[78] Some have been suspicious about the circumstances of his death. His departure was another blow for the advocates of moderation (to honour his memory the old Takht-e Jamshid Avenue in Tehran was renamed Taleqani Avenue). But others too disliked the constitution. The MKO, the Fedayan, the Kurds and other regional groups were unhappy as the draft neared completion that the constitution did not address their demands. In October, two years on from the events that had helped to start up the revolutionary movement, the Writers' Association announced a new series of poetry evenings, to be held from 24 October to 3 November, with the aim of defending free speech and opposing censorship. But the organizers said it would only go ahead if the safety of participants could be guaranteed. The poetry evenings never happened.[79] Most seriously, Ayatollah Shariatmadari, with his power base in Azerbaijan and the support of the MPRP, continued to oppose the excesses of the IRP and Khomeini's followers, and specifically the principle of *velayat-e faqih* as it appeared in the constitution. In December he warned: 'We seem to be moving from one monarchy to another.'[80]

So as the work of the Assembly neared completion (it brought its deliberations to a close on 15 November), opposition to the constitution it had created was building from a number of different angles. But before that opposition could develop further or unite its strength, a new crisis erupted, which would change the political scene in Iran permanently and dramatically. On 1 November, Bazargan met Zbigniew Brzezinski in Algiers, with Khomeini's knowledge, in an attempt to restore something like normal relations between Iran and the US (and to secure resumption of the supply of military spare parts). He was accompanied by Ebrahim Yazdi, as foreign minister. Over previous days Khomeini had been building up anti-American rhetoric after the Carter government allowed the Shah into the US for medical treatment on 22 October (since his departure from Iran he had shuffled, his health deteriorating all the time, from Egypt to Morocco, the Bahamas and Mexico). Although initially the Shah's arrival in the US won little attention in Iran, Khomeini and his followers used it successfully to create a furore, linking the news about the Shah with allegations that friends of the Shah and the US were still active in the government and among Khomeini's opponents.

On the streets of Tehran at this time, the situation was chaotic and uncertain. No one knew what to expect or who was in control. Two accounts of this time illustrate this, from different perspectives – firstly from Bill Belk in the US embassy:

> the government had absolutely no control over what was happening . . . Armed bands of revolutionary zealots were roaming the streets and taking the law into their own hands. The police were powerless to stop them, because the worst thing you could possibly be in Iran was a policeman . . . Most of the people who had been policemen were in hiding. The streets were literally turned over to these armed *komitehs*. Khomeini had appointed a Provisional Government, but they didn't have any real authority. The traditional institutions through which a government administers and functions were the very same institutions that were being attacked by the revolutionaries and the vigilante groups . . . So dealing with the Provisional Government was like trying to deal with a shadow — you could see it, but talking to it was pointless. In reality, there was no substance there.[81]

Secondly from a student radical, Massoumeh Ebtekar:

> We students couldn't prove it at the time, of course, but we were sure that foreign elements were actively involved in attempts to weaken and undermine the young republic. Like weeds, thousands of tiny political groups had sprouted during less than six months, each one attempting to convince the people to adopt its views. Every day their newspapers circulated the wildest rumors. It was as if they were determined to create an atmosphere of endless uncertainty. Ethnic and tribal uprisings, which they rushed to support, broke out in all regions of the country. And through it all the Provisional Government dithered and wavered, with the result that security had almost collapsed.[82]

To student radicals, the Shah's presence in the US looked like part of a plot. The timing was unfortunate for Bazargan's mission, to say the least. Many believed that the US, with the connivance of members of the Provisional Government, was plotting a coup like that of 1953, to crush the revolution. A confederation of students loyal to Khomeini from the university-level institutions in Tehran, calling themselves 'students following the line of the Emam' conferred rapidly, taking care to exclude MKO activists or others they feared might try to sabotage their intentions.[83] On 4 November they broke into the US embassy, occupying the building and detaining the diplomatic staff and marines they found there. Several hundred unarmed students took part in the action. The marines brandished their weapons, but did not shoot (though some tear gas grenades were let off in the confrontation). As one of the students brushed past on the stairs, he whispered to a jittery marine: 'Don't worry, you're safe. We won't hurt anyone.'[84] In fact several of the hostages were beaten and threatened over the next few hours as the intruders interrogated them, trying to identify the CIA officers among the staff and trying to get them to open safes. Six US diplomats who were out of the embassy at the time were able to avoid detention, taking refuge in the Canadian and Swiss embassies.

Bruce Laingen, who in the absence of an ambassador was chargé d'affaires and head of mission, along with two others, was away on a call at the Ministry of Foreign Affairs when the embassy takeover began. He went back to the Foreign Ministry to protest and demand redress and ended up being held there instead of at the embassy. Once the students were in control of the embassy compound, they issued a press communiqué demanding that the 'criminal, deposed Shah' be returned to Iran. Photos and TV images of the hostages, handcuffed and blindfolded, made a deep impression in the US and the world generally.

The Hostage Crisis

Although some of the students believed on the day of the takeover that their spiritual guide, Ayatollah Musavi-Khoeniha (a member of the IRP central committee, another former student of Khomeini and a friend of his son Ahmad), was attempting to inform Khomeini of the plan, there is no direct evidence that Khomeini ordered the action or that any other group or organization beyond that of the students themselves was involved in the planning, such as it was. And it seems that the intention of the students initially was just to stage a temporary protest of a few hours or days. There are some indications[85] that Khomeini himself (still in Qom), when first told of the embassy occupation, saw the incident as an unimportant act of unruliness and, as with the incident in February, was inclined to see the students leave again quickly (this could have happened; the following day there was a similar intrusion at the British embassy which ended when Khomeini's son Ahmad called it off).[86] But the occupation was very much in line with the trend of Khomeini's agitation against the US over the preceding hours and days. Perhaps having been reassured that the students involved were solidly loyal to him personally, perhaps only when it became clear that the US and the West would not threaten military action,[87] he decided that the occupation should be supported, and should continue, at least in the short term. Early on 5 November he made a statement saying that there had been plots organized from the embassy, that it was a lair of espionage (also translated as 'den' or 'nest' of spies) and hailing the students' act as a second revolution.[88] Later he told the students themselves 'the Americans can't do a damn thing', leading Iran into a twilight zone of diplomatic breakdown and international isolation from which the country has never really re-emerged.

Bazargan tried to defend his meeting with Brzezinski and demanded the immediate release of the US diplomats, condemning the students' action as an unacceptable violation of international law and the civilized practices of diplomacy. But the atmosphere was febrile, and his reasonable words disappeared in a welter of renewed demonstrations and shrill anti-imperialist rhetoric, not just from the IRP but also from the MKO, the Fedayan and the other leftists, who strongly supported the occupation of the embassy (playing into Khomeini's hands and destroying any chance of a united front against the constitution). On 5 November Beheshti, Montazeri and a selection of other figures and bodies aligned with Khomeini issued statements supporting the students. Outflanked and finally seeing the impossibility of his moderate position, Bazargan resigned on 6 November. In a speech addressed to visitors from Isfahan University Khomeini commented: 'Mr Bazargan is respected by everyone . . . He was a little tired and preferred to stay on the sidelines for a while.'[89]

Within Iran, the taking of the hostages produced an atmosphere of radicalism and crisis that renewed the revolutionary fervour of the previous year. Khomeini succeeded in making his moderate opponents look like allies of the US, and a threat to the revolution. This was helped along by the release of documents captured in the US embassy that showed contacts between liberal figures and the US government (documents that might have shown contact with IRP clerics did not surface). The first victim of the changed mood was Abbas Amir-Entezam, the originator of the memorandum to Khomeini against the constitution. He was arrested in mid-December, released, sent to Sweden as ambassador, recalled and eventually, in 1981, sentenced to life imprisonment (at the time of writing he is still in prison, at the age of eighty).

In this atmosphere, the referendum on the constitution that was held on 2 and 3 December could have only one result. It was boycotted by the MPRP and the National Front, and participation was much lower than in the referendum of March, but the figures announced gave only 30,866 votes against the constitution out of 15 million voters.[90]

Shariatmadari continued to attack the constitution and the principle of *velayat-e faqih* throughout the referendum campaign. There were demonstrations by Khomeini supporters outside his house in Qom, and demonstrations by his supporters against Khomeini in Tabriz, and later in Qom also. For a time, Shariatmadari appeared to be growing into a serious rival to Khomeini, at least in the important province of Azerbaijan (Tabriz had long prided itself as the cornerstone of the Constitutional Revolution, and as the most advanced city in Iran, where new developments always appeared first). The rivalry grew more heated. At one point Khomeini apologized for the excesses of his supporters in Qom and went to Shariatmadari in person to try to resolve the conflict. But the temperature in Tabriz rose still further, with demonstrations of several hundred thousand, and finally some MPRP demonstrators took over the TV and radio stations in Tabriz. Shariatmadari's supporters demanded the annulment of the constitution, the lifting of censorship and the formation of a united front against the IRP. The CIR responded by sending in the Sepah to take back the broadcasting stations, and mediators to try to calm the situation. The IRP also staged pro-Khomeini demonstrations in Tabriz. The huge pro-Shariatmadari demonstrations continued, but Shariatmadari himself was unwilling to push further confrontation into serious violence, and backed down. The student hostage-takers and other pro-Khomeini groups were alleging that Shariatmadari was in alliance with former SAVAK agents and the United States – some MPRP supporters were arrested, tried by revolutionary courts and executed for rioting. The IRP demanded that the MPRP dissolve itself. Shariatmadari replied bitterly that there was no need, since the government would gradually dissolve all political parties, labelling them anti-Islamic, Zionist or American, so there was no need to worry about it. Eventually, recognizing defeat, the MPRP complied, before the new elections for the presidency, which took place on 25 January 1980.[91]

Shariatmadari's bid to oppose the new constitution was the most serious confrontation yet to threaten Khomeini's supremacy. His timing was bad, and his resolution in the struggle proved weak. He was a gentle man, a spiritual leader and not really a politician – certainly not the sort of ruthless politician Khomeini was proving himself to be. But his effort emphasized that the instincts of the *ulema* as a class were still far from uniformly in favour of the *velayat-e faqih*. There was still a deep well of feeling for constitutional democracy among the Iranian people, and to some extent even among the *ulema*; albeit eclipsed for a time by revolutionary fervour.

In the meantime the hostages were still being held in the embassy building. As weeks lengthened into months the confinement settled into a routine. The hostages were blindfolded and handcuffed when they were moved about or when they broke the rules. Senior Iranian figures visited them, including Khalkhali ('a short, fat little guy. He was trying to be jovial'),[92] Montazeri and Khamenei. Those that had been identified as CIA officers, along with senior diplomats like John Limbert and Bruce Laingen, were still subject to interrogation, held in isolation and sometimes threatened, but for the most part the beatings stopped. One of the CIA men, Bill Daugherty, realized that the interrogators were disappointed with their investigations. They had discovered that there were only four CIA men in the embassy and were incredulous that none of them could speak Persian. Reports they had found indicated that the CIA station was somewhat at sea in post-revolutionary Iran, finding it difficult to make contact with useful informants and making ill-founded assessments of the political situation.[93]

An exception to the general routine of treatment was Michael Metrinko, who had been a young political officer in the embassy. Unlike most of the other members of the embassy, Metrinko had been tasked with going out and meeting Iranians, but this was also his inclination. Many of the other embassy staff, tending to be compound-bound like most expatriates in Iran at the time, had regarded him as something of an eccentric. He met a wide variety of people, improved his Persian and developed an appreciation of Iran and its culture. But this did not make him well disposed toward the hostage-takers. Aside from the violation of standards of international diplomacy, he regarded the students' action as a violation of Iranian cultural norms, morality and decency, and was able to tell the students so in their own language. In blunt terms. For this he was treated worse than any of the other hostages, all through the period of their detention. He spent much of his time in solitary confinement. He insulted Khomeini, was beaten for it and on one occasion was kept handcuffed for over three weeks. At Christmas 1979, when other hostages were together, eating a Christmas dinner provided by their captors, Metrinko was in solitary. His guards brought him the same dinner. Metrinko took it and, in their sight, flushed it down the toilet, further enraging them.[94] Because he spoke Persian and because of his attitude, the students were convinced that Metrinko belonged to the CIA. Massoumeh Ebtekar, one of the students who later wrote an account of the hostage-taking, said of Metrinko that he 'hated everyone and was hated in return. He preferred to stay alone and bounce a ball against the wall of his room from morning until night.'[95]

The discussions between the hostages and the students were in a sense the front line in the confrontation between the US and Iran. On this front line, there was a near-total mutual failure of understanding. The American hostages were naturally indignant and angry at their detention and their treatment and could see no circumstances in which it might be understandable (though there was a range of reactions to the detention: some of the hostages were friendlier toward their captors and one or two tried to ingratiate themselves). The Iranian students believed what they had been told by Khomeini and the IRP leadership; that the US embassy staff were mainly spies, plotting a coup, as in 1953, to reverse the success of the revolution. They knew the history of foreign and US interference in Iran; the embassy officials were largely ignorant of it. Some of the students had been prisoners themselves – prisoners of SAVAK, who they believed (correctly) to have been trained and assisted by the CIA. As time went on a few of the students doubted the wisdom of the continuation of the hostage crisis, but most were firm supporters to the end. A group of thirteen hostages, women and African Americans, were released on 19 and 20 November 1979 as a goodwill gesture.

Another one was released in July 1980 because he was showing the symptoms of serious illness (he was later diagnosed with multiple sclerosis). The other fifty-two hostages stayed in captivity.

Presidential Elections

The campaign for the Islamic republic's first presidential elections was an untidy affair, and it took place for the most part against the background of the continuing unrest in Azerbaijan. Khomeini realized the significance of the success he had achieved with the new constitution and again was careful not to overreach. He ordered that clerics should not run for the presidency, which was a disappointment for Beheshti, who otherwise would have been a prime candidate. Bazargan might have run, but was intimidated by the damaging flow of documents emerging from the occupied US embassy. The MKO leader Masud Rajavi was vetoed by Khomeini because his party had boycotted the referendum on the constitution, and the IRP candidate Jalal od-Din Farsi had to drop out at a late stage because it was realized that, with an Afghan father, his candidacy breached the constitution's requirement that the president must be an Iranian national of Iranian origin. Out of the candidates that eventually went to the vote, Abol Hassan Bani-Sadr won by a comfortable margin, helped both by his known close relationship with Khomeini and his reputation as a liberal, acceptable to the educated middle classes. He received 10.7 million of the 14 million votes cast.[96]

Bani-Sadr was born in Hamadan in 1933 and came from a clerical family like many other secular politicians, intellectuals and writers of his generation. As a young man he had persuaded his father to let him study at Tehran University rather than the Faiziyeh seminary in Qom, and had studied law as well as theology. But he always kept a strongly Islamic cast to his politics, even when he went to Paris to study in the 1960s. He was inspired by Khomeini's outspoken opposition to the Shah in 1963–4 and by the radical politics in Europe of the later 1960s, and became a devoted opponent of the Shah. He also opposed the growing American influence in Iran and the dominance of the US and Western capitalism in the world and was an enthusiast for popular politics and political freedom (some have suggested that his ideas came close to anarchism in their enthusiasm for individual liberty and their opposition to most forms of authority). In the 1970s he met Khomeini in Iraq, and the two developed a close relationship, almost like father and son. Bani-Sadr was associated early on with Mossadeq and the National Front, and later with the Freedom Movement, but was independent-minded and not a little vain, regarding himself as a thinker and a force in politics in his own right. He wrote extensively, notably a book on Islamic economics, and developed his own theory of Islamic government in which, somewhat different to that of Khomeini (but more like that of Mohammad Baqr al-Sadr, the dominant *marja* in Najaf), there was a much greater emphasis on popular sovereignty and the individual Muslim's right to interpret holy texts for himself, and to voice his own opinion within the Islamic polity.[97] He was close again to Khomeini in Paris in 1978, accompanied him to Tehran in February 1979 and became finance minister in Bazargan's Provisional Government. After Bazargan's fall he was briefly acting foreign minister under the authority of the CIR before being elected president at the end of January. Bani-Sadr's Islamic liberal ideological background was similar to that of Bazargan. But he was more individualistic, more self-assertive, more of a natural political populist; and at least initially, he enjoyed a better relationship with Khomeini.

Bani-Sadr came to the presidency with a confidence in the mandate the people had given him in the election, and a strong belief in himself. He believed that the vote for him showed that popular feeling was swinging against the IRP, which (given among other things the confused nature of the election and the IRP's clumsy handling of it) was probably wrong. But the beginning of his period of office looked like another chance for the moderates and liberals, for those who had hoped and believed that Khomeini and the clerics would pull back from a forward role in politics and leave the scene to secular politicians. It may be that Khomeini intended this too, at least with half his mind, but when conflicts arose he felt compelled to take greater control for himself and his supporters rather than risk a reverse. At any rate, this was for him, Beheshti and their followers a phase for consolidation after their success over the constitution.

Bani-Sadr frequently referred to himself as Iran's first freely elected president, and this reflected genuine enthusiasm about his election in the country, from many sectors of opinion. He wanted as a priority to rebuild the institutions of the state, disorientated by months of purges and intimidation, and to bring the new institutions aligned with the IRP under state control – including the student hostage-takers, who had become an institution in their own right. He and his supporters were further encouraged when Khomeini gave him the chairmanship of the CIR (7 February) and delegated to him his powers as commander-in-chief of the armed forces, including the Sepah (19 February). He was also given control of the broadcasting services. Khomeini's son Ahmad acted as a go-between, helping Bani-Sadr to keep Khomeini's trust, and Khomeini gave a New Year message on 20 March that echoed many of Bani-Sadr's ideas, including the aim of bringing the revolutionary courts back within the structure of the judicial system, the rebuilding of the armed forces, and a general call for a return to normality and order in state and society. But Khomeini also made Beheshti head of the judiciary, which meant that the most able IRP figure was in position to resist any attempt to slacken the grip he, Khomeini and his followers wanted shari'a law to have over the country.[98] And of course, the prime example of revolutionary disorder, the hostage crisis, continued.

Before he was elected president, Bani-Sadr had reacted to the occupation of the US embassy with disapproval. As president, he had to moderate his opposition to the students and their action, but he worked to resolve the crisis and get the hostages returned to the US. On the US side, there was frustration that the Carter administration could not find an authoritative interlocutor with whom to negotiate. Iranian demands that the Shah be returned to Iran, that his wealth be returned too and that the US should apologize for past crimes against the Iranian people were impossible to contemplate. US officials might feel they were making progress, only for their talks to be undercut by a new declaration from Khomeini. Toward the end of February Bani-Sadr and his foreign minister, Qotbzadeh, thought they had achieved the outlines of a deal through the mediation of Olof Palme, nominated for the purpose by the UN. The deal included a UN commission to visit Tehran to examine Iranian grievances against the US. But just before the UN commission arrived, on 23 February Khomeini made a statement announcing that a decision on the hostages would have to be made by the new parliament, which would not be elected until May, and the deal unravelled.

By March, Bani-Sadr was attempting to address the crisis indirectly by trying to get the Shah extradited from Panama (the Shah had moved there from the US in December – he moved on to Egypt on 23 March when he caught wind of the extradition attempt). In the Carter administration, the view was that negotiation had failed and other methods must now be attempted. On 25 March Carter sent Bani-Sadr a message in which he said that unless the hostages were transferred to the control of the Iranian government (as a necessary preliminary to their release) by 31 March, the US government would take 'additional non-belligerent measures',[99] which were generally taken to mean additional sanctions (the US had already, on 14 November, frozen 11 billion dollars of Iranian assets in the US and had banned the import of Iranian oil).[100]

Operation Eagle Claw

On the evening of 24 April, eight US Navy Sea Stallion helicopters took off from the USS *Nimitz* as it cruised in the Arabian Sea off the southern coast of Iranian Baluchestan. They flew northwards and westwards over the Iranian coast, at low level to avoid radar detection. Six C-130 Hercules transports flew the same route, but originating further south, from an air base on the island of Masirah, off the coast of Oman. They were flying toward a point in the Iranian desert between Yazd and the small town of Tabas, which was to be the base ('Desert One') in Iran for an attempt by US special forces to rescue the hostages. The operation was codenamed Eagle Claw. Preparations for it, on a contingency basis, had begun the previous November.

Unfortunately for the mission, the helicopters flew into two dust storms, which disorientated the pilots, seriously delayed their progress and may have contributed to mechanical faults in the aircraft. One helicopter (before encountering the dust) was forced to land with a suspected crack to a rotor blade; its crew were picked up by one of the other helicopters. Another turned back to the *Nimitz* when its instruments began to malfunction in the dust storm (allegedly, according to one version,[101] caused by overheating after someone had dumped a flak jacket and a duffel bag over a cooling vent). The remainder arrived safely at Desert One a little later than the C-130s, only to discover that the hydraulic system on another of the helicopters had developed an irreparable fault. It had been decided in the planning of the operation that a minimum of six helicopters were needed if the rescue was to have a chance of success. Because there were now only five left, the commander on the spot asked permission to abort the operation, and this was granted from Washington, after some hesitation (it has been suggested since that the commander could have improvised and carried out a slimmed-down version of the rescue plan).

But there was worse to come. As the aircraft manoeuvred in the dust and darkness to organize refuelling for their return flight, one of the helicopters crashed on to the top of one of the C-130 transports, and both aircraft began to burn. The thirty-nine soldiers inside the C-130 rushed to a rear door to escape, scrambling over the enormous fuel 'bladder' inside the fuselage. They bunched up at the door as men ahead of them jumped out, but kept their discipline and left smoothly and quickly, following the drill for parachute jumps they had learned in training (one of them, who had been asleep, thought in the confusion that it *was* a mid-air jump, and hit the dirt in full spread-eagle free-fall position after a descent of about six feet). In the heat of the fires ammunition started to explode. Some of the last men were badly burned as they made their way through the aircraft. Most of them got out before the bladder blew up, throwing a final man out of the door with great force and tossing a great column of flame up into the night sky. But five air force crew members who did not make it to the rear door died in the C-130, and three crew in the helicopter (the pilot and co-pilot of the helicopter crew managed to escape).[102] The remainder of the force, abandoning the other helicopters (which had been damaged by flying fragments in the fires and explosions), were able to fly safely back to Masirah. In obeying orders to leave as quickly as possible, the helicopter crews abandoned classified documents in the helicopters, including detailed plans of the rescue mission itself.

The first that the Iranian leadership knew of the failed mission came when they were told that it had been announced on American TV. In his role as the regime's aficionado of the macabre, Sadegh Khalkhali visited the crash site in the desert and brought the bodies back to Tehran. He gave a press conference in the occupied embassy and took a severed hand and a wristwatch out of one of the body bags for the cameras (there were nine bodies because an Iranian had also died at Desert

One – the driver of a fuel tanker lorry that turned up unexpectedly at the site. The US special forces had blown up the lorry to prevent it escaping, and the driver had died in the explosion).

The failure of Operation Eagle Claw was a disaster in a series of ways. In the immediate aftermath, most of the hostages were moved out of Tehran to dispersed locations, making any repeat attempt at a rescue effectively impossible. In Iranian politics, it appeared to confirm the assertions of the radicals – that the revolution was at risk from US interference and that the Americans were incorrigibly disposed to interfere in Iran's internal affairs, using covert methods and military force if necessary. The corollary was that it weakened yet further the position of the liberals and moderates and intensified fears about foreign agents at work within the country. It was used to legitimate new rounds of purges and arrests; over the following month there were a series of scares about invasion and *coups d'état* from within the armed forces.[103]

In the US, the debacle in the desert deepened the national humiliation of the hostage crisis. It intensified the bitter anger felt by Americans toward the Islamic republic and, among the less reflective, towards Iran and Iranians in general. Carter himself believed that the failure of the hostage rescue mission was a major contribution to his failure to secure re-election for a presidential second term later in the year.[104] Memory of the hostage crisis and the failed rescue has poisoned US–Iran relations ever since.

The rescue mission had been ambitious, to say the least of it. When the decision to go ahead with it had been considered by President Carter and the National Security Council on 22 March, the chairman of the Joint Chiefs of Staff, General David Jones, had noted as he briefed Carter that the plan was 'exceptionally complex' and said he felt better about the viability of its individual parts than about the plan in its entirety. When the decision to go ahead was made on 11 April its most trenchant critic, Secretary of State Cyrus Vance, was absent. It was decided because other options appeared to have been exhausted. When Vance returned to Washington a further meeting of the NSC was called to hear his objections, but no one supported him.[105]

The journey to Desert One should have been the easy part, in relative terms. Getting from there to Tehran, getting to the embassy, killing or disabling the student guards, finding, securing and removing the hostages, then extracting them and all the military personnel involved – all would have been tough tasks. Each stage, each task, had to be completed successfully for the next to be possible. But for the success of Israeli special forces in the rescue of hijacked passengers at Entebbe four years earlier, Eagle Claw would probably not have been attempted. Subsequent investigation by the Holloway Commission identified some of the flaws in the planning and conduct of the operation. These included an excessive emphasis on operational security which, for example, had prevented pilots and crew from seeing the operations plan, and especially the weather annex; it had also imposed strict radio silence, which prevented aircraft crews from alerting each other to dangers and problems as they arose. Given the remoteness of the regions over which they were flying, complete radio silence was perhaps unnecessary. The Commission also drew attention to the failure adequately to allow for or to assess weather conditions, to command and control problems, and the failure to remove classified material before evacuation from Desert One. After the failed mission, a Counter-Terrorism Joint Task Force was set up – a tacit recognition that rivalry between the services had contributed to the failure. Before Eagle Claw, each service had insisted that it should participate, with the result that the mission had used Navy helicopters, Marine helicopter pilots, Air Force C-130 aircraft and pilots, and troops from the Army's newly established Delta Force.[106]

Cultural Revolution and a Revolutionary Majles

The incursion of US special forces on Iranian territory added to the growing atmosphere of tension in Tehran. Another contributory factor to the tension, though relatively minor at first, was a deterioration of relations with Iraq, where Saddam Hussein had deposed Ahmad Hasan al-Bakr and made himself president in July 1979. Among other loose talk from the revolutionaries about exporting revolution, some Iranians had been saying that the new regime would no longer respect the Algiers Accords of 1975. Iran was believed to be backing various Shi'a opposition movements in the region, including in Iraq. In Iraq the main vehicle for the Shi'a opposition was the Da'wa Party. Whether the Iraqi government really felt threatened by such developments or used them as an excuse, in early 1980 they arrested one of the two most prominent Shi'a clerics in Iraq, Ayatollah Mohammad Baqr al-Sadr (he had been arrested several times before). In response, in April there were a series of bomb attacks against government targets in Iraq and assassination attempts against two senior officials – including Tariq Aziz, who was later to become Saddam Hussein's foreign minister and right-hand man. The Iraqi regime responded by murdering Mohammad Baqr al-Sadr and his sister in prison.[107] Saddam Hussein also expelled a large number of Iranians who had been living in Iraq (including some with merely remote Iranian forebears or Iranian-sounding names).

Mohammad Baqr al-Sadr had been an important figure not just in Iraq, but among Shi'a Muslims generally. He had been in regular contact with Khomeini and those around him, and Khomeini had been making statements for the Shi'a Muslims of Iraq in his support. We have already considered his likely influence on the Iranian Constitution. Baqr al-Sadr's ideas were at variance with those of Khomeini in important ways. In particular, he laid greater emphasis on popular sovereignty. Khomeini announced Baqr al-Sadr's death to Iranians in mid-April, prompting a wave of outrage. There were, inevitably, comparisons drawn with the martyrdom of Hosein at the hands of Yazid. Tension between Iran and Iraq intensified further.

Since February 1979, as before that date, the universities had been a focus for intense political and ideological debate. On his return, Khomeini had praised the students for their activism against the Shah. In the initial phase thereafter, the IRP was strong in the universities and came out well in the lead in student elections. But by the early part of 1980 leftist groups and parties, including the MKO, had supplanted the IRP in such elections. The IRP appeared to be losing ground: the leadership responded in April 1980 by closing the universities. Khomeini explained later: 'Universities were bastions of communists, and they were war rooms for communists.' Bani-Sadr, hoping to woo opinion in the IRP and like them, seeing a chance to do down the leftists, supported the closure. But predictably enough, his middle-class, liberal supporters took a dim view of the closure of the universities, whatever the rationale – the policy (along with other initiatives that came at the same time) was given the unhappy epithet Cultural Revolution (*enqelab-e farhangi*). Like other decisions Bani-Sadr made, it proved too clever by half, and self-destructive.[108]

To put in place the last blocks in the arch of government, elections for the Majles were held in two stages in March and May 1980. Candidates who won an absolute majority succeeded in the first round; the remainder went to the second round, in which the candidate with the highest number of votes was successful. But this procedure was criticized (by Bani-Sadr among others) for favouring the IRP and tending to exclude candidates from smaller parties, and there were other accusations of rigging, intimidation and manipulation. Turnout was again relatively low, comparable to that for the Assembly of Experts the previous year, at 10.8 million. The result yielded a strongly pro-IRP Majles, with 130 IRP and IRP-affiliated members out of 241, 40 liberals and the remainder independents, many of whom in practice followed the IRP lead. No MKO candidates were elected. Elections were not held in many parts of Kurdestan because of the continuing insurgency, and those Kurds who were elected did not take up their seats. Some elected members were rejected by a credentials committee, which was used by the IRP to exclude members they didn't approve of (one, Admiral Madani, who had previously run as a presidential candidate against Bani-Sadr, had been accused of anti-revolutionary activities in the press and left the country rather than face the committee). Karim Sanjabi, the leader of the National Front, was rejected in this way. Rafsanjani was elected speaker of the new Majles; a position he used cleverly over the coming years to build a powerful position for himself within the new system.[109]

Ahead of the second round of elections, Bani-Sadr had struggled to be allowed to elect his own choice of prime minister. He cast around desperately for people who might be approved by Khomeini – at one stage he even suggested Khomeini's own son, Ahmad. But like the Americans, he was told to wait until the new Majles convened. After it did, Bani-Sadr chose a member of the IRP central committee; but having approved the man as a possibility, the IRP then rejected him, and put forward Mohammad-Ali Rajai instead.

Rajai was born in Qazvin in 1933; his father died when he was only four years old. He had known Ayatollah Taleqani and was a close associate of Mohammad Javad Bahonar and of Beheshti. He was a small man, modest like many pious Iranians, with a quiet smile; a contrast to the flamboyant Bani-Sadr. He was a former schoolteacher, from a poor family background; had been a member of the movement against the

Shah and had been imprisoned before the revolution. He had little reputation as an independent figure, but was trusted by the IRP leadership for his loyalty. One could take him as typical of the new class of politicians and administrators brought forward by the revolution; people who, with few family connections and little wealth, would never have had much chance to advance themselves under the Pahlavi regime.

As Some Rise, Others Fall

For Rajai and many others like him, from humble backgrounds, who had inserted themselves into the new institutions, the revolution had opened up new opportunities. But for others, it had closed them down, and had turned their previous achievements to nothing. Parviz Natel Khanlari was born in 1914, the son of a government official in Mazanderan. He studied Persian literature at Tehran University, and taught in schools in Gilan after graduation, before taking his doctorate (entitled 'Critical Research into the Development of the Use of Rhyme and Metre in the Persian Ghazal') and doing his military service. He then started teaching at Tehran University. In the 1930s he published poems and prose works, as well as academic studies in the fields of literature and linguistics, and was associated with the innovatory Rab'eh circle of writers (named after the Arabic word for four) founded by Sadegh Hedayat. Khanlari was the editor of the important literary journal *Sokhan* from the 1940s until 1979. During the reign of Mohammad Reza Shah he was governor of Azerbaijan for a time, as well as keeping his professorship at the University of Tehran. He was later minister for education and the head of a variety of educational and cultural institutions – most notably the Iranian Cultural Foundation. His most lasting achievement was perhaps his work on the collected poems (*Divan*) of Hafez, which culminated in what is still the definitive scholarly edition of Hafez.

After the revolution *Sokhan* ceased publication, the Iranian Cultural Foundation was closed, its functions merged with other bodies, and Khanlari was imprisoned for a time by revolutionary courts as a functionary of the previous regime. His house was confiscated, and when he was released he was poor and ill. He died in September 1990.[110] For every Rajai who rose, there was a Khanlari who fell; executed, exiled, imprisoned or left in limbo to waste away.

After two months of impasse over Rajai's appointment, Khomeini intervened, and Bani-Sadr accepted Rajai as prime minister in August. The two men then disagreed over the appointment of ministers to the cabinet: most of Rajai's suggestions were again associates of Beheshti and Bahonar – most of them young, idealistic university graduates (Mir Hosein Musavi was one of them). The arguments rolled on for months: Bani-Sadr accepted fourteen of Rajai's ministers in September, a few more in December and another in March 1981; but some of the posts were not filled at all before Bani-Sadr fell from office. The dispute set a time-wasting precedent that has become a dismal tradition in Iranian politics. By insisting on his authority in the matter, Bani-Sadr helped to discredit his presidency.[111]

Over the first half of 1980 Bani-Sadr's attempts to curb the revolutionary courts and to bring them (and the *komiteh*) within the state-controlled justice system faltered and failed. Despite criticism of the abuses and injustices of the courts by important figures like Ayatollah Ali Qoddusi, and some apparently helpful support from Beheshti and Montazeri, they were able to resist assimilation and avoid abolition. Khomeini himself declared that the revolutionary courts should continue until the justice system as a whole was made compatible with the shari'a, and Beheshti set about a reform of the legal codes to bring this about. In some regions, revolutionary courts actually targeted officials of the state justice system. There were many allegations of corruption, especially over the confiscation of property. The Bonyad-e Mostazafan was a prime beneficiary of property confiscations.[112] In fact, in important respects, the duality in Iranian law has never been removed. Individual clerical judges, or even clerics outside the justice system altogether, may still make judgements that disregard the provisions of the legal code, but which nonetheless carry the force of law.

Another feature of the so-called Cultural Revolution was a ferocious anti-narcotics campaign, which Bani-Sadr also supported. He appointed Khalkhali to pursue it; given the reputation Khalkhali had already acquired, this was a sign of earnest intent. Hundreds of executions followed, and because of the devolved and disorganized arrangement of the revolutionary courts, it proved difficult to stop or abate them once the campaign had begun. The ease with which death sentences were passed habituated the courts to a mode of conduct in which other crimes or sins were punished similarly harshly, which again fed on the prevailing fevered atmosphere of exaggerated rhetoric and heightened emotions. Men and women were executed for sexual offences, political dissent and perceived anti-revolutionary activities. At least 580 people were executed between February 1980 and January 1981 – the most intense period being between May and September. As unease grew among the leadership over the scale of the killings, Khalkhali was forced to resign by Beheshti and Bani-Sadr in December; but as with Al Capone, the official reason given was financial irregularities rather than his homicidal activities.[113]

Plot, Purge and Conflict

The mood of crisis and paranoia came to a climax in high summer. A revolutionary tribunal had been set up under Hojjatoleslam Mohammad Reyshahri (who later became minister of intelligence) to try cases of old-regime allegiance and anti-revolutionary activity in the military. In June Reyshahri announced a coup attempt that had been organized around the Piranshahr base in West Azerbaijan, predominantly a Kurdish area. The plot, such as it was, seems to have been primarily related to the continuing Kurdish revolt. But Reyshahri did his best to inflate its significance. It was probably not directly related to a much more serious attempt that came to light in July. This involved several hundred military personnel, including air force, army and former Imperial Guard and SAVAK officers; acting in concert with Shapur Bakhtiar, who by this time was in Baghdad. Their plan included a devastating strike on Khomeini's residence at Jamaran in north Tehran by F-4 Phantom aircraft with anti-personnel bombs, to be carried out by aircraft from Nozheh air force base near Hamadan (this base was chosen because aircraft at other bases had been disarmed deliberately to prevent them taking part in a coup attempt). The aim of the coup was to kill Khomeini and arrest the other revolutionary leaders, put Bakhtiar back in power on a provisional basis and conduct a new, free referendum to select the form of government.

Recent investigation[114] has shown that the Nozheh coup plot was serious, that it was backed by Iraq and Iraqi money, and that Iraqi plans to invade Iran, which may have been ready as early as October 1979, were probably delayed to give the coup a chance. But the plot was prevented by a series of arrests outside the airbase just as it was about to take effect on the night of 9/10 July. Altogether 300 or more military personnel were arrested and put on trial, including two air force generals, Brigadier General Ayat Mohagheghi[115] and Brigadier General Saied Mehdiyoun. It is not clear by what means the revolutionary government were warned of the coup, but so many people were involved that it is not surprising that there were leaks. One version suggests that Israeli intelligence found out details of the plan earlier in the day on 9 July, and the Israeli government passed these on to the Iranian regime, making the arrests possible at the last minute. This might seem implausible, although it would fit with other Israeli behaviour at this time – Israeli leaders saw Iraq as a greater threat to their interests than Iran, and despite the revolutionary government's anti-Zionist rhetoric, were hoping to rebuild good relations with the Iranians. But for the tip-off to have been made in this way, the information would have had to have passed from an informant to the Israeli government, to the Iranian regime and onward to the Sepah in Hamadan, all within three hours, which seems too short a time.[116]

Rafsanjani, as speaker of the Majles, blamed the National Front for involvement in the plot (building on the connection with Bakhtiar). *Hezbollahis* duly sacked their offices and closed down their newspaper, effectively putting an end to the Front, the creation of Mossadeq, as an active political organization. Unlike some of the scares that had been put about since April, the July plot was genuine, with broad ramifications across the armed forces, but the response to it was nonetheless extreme, and damaging: 144 participants were executed, and investigations and purges in the armed forces went on for weeks. Just over a week later, Bakhtiar narrowly escaped an assassination attempt in Paris.[117] It has been estimated that the purges, in one form or another, affected as many as 4,500 military personnel, mainly air force, mainly officers. The effect within the armed forces was highly disruptive and demoralizing, at what turned out to be a crucial juncture. Bani-Sadr called for moderation and presented himself as a protector of the military;

but the IRP and the leftists pressed for more sweeping purges and began to associate Bani-Sadr with the doubtful loyalty of the military to the revolution.

Later the same month, on 27 July, the former Shah finally died, in Egypt. Just under two months after that, on 22 September, Iraq invaded Iran.

4

Jang-e Tahmili:
The Imposed War, 1980–88

In the time of the Achaemenid, Parthian and Sassanid Empires Iranian monarchs had ruled Mesopotamia, the territory of modern Iraq. The later dynasties had their capital near the site of modern Baghdad and fought interminable wars with the Romans and their successors the Byzantine Greeks to retain control of the rich land of the rivers Tigris and Euphrates. But with the rise of Islam in the early seventh century, the Sassanid Persians lost first Mesopotamia, then the Iranian plateau and eventually their throne altogether to the invading Arabs. When the Safavid dynasty took control of Iran in the early sixteenth century,[1] they too tried to extend their rule over Mesopotamia, and were successful for a time. But after long wars with the Ottoman Turks, embittered by the religious schism between Sunni and Shi'a, in which not only Baghdad but also Tabriz changed hands a number of times, the Treaty of Zohab settled the border between Iran and Ottoman Iraq in more or less its present-day position in 1639. The Ottomans invaded Iran across that border in the 1720s; there were further clashes in 1821 and 1840, and again during the First World War; but for the most part it proved stable, if somewhat fuzzy in places. In the north, Kurdish tribes moved across the border to find fresh pasture and to avoid over-zealous or oppressive governors, whether Persian or Ottoman; and Arab tribes near the border in the south had a similar quasi-independent attitude.

Some accounts of the Iran–Iraq War give the impression that the border had been fought over for centuries and had been the focus for deep mutual resentment, and that this was a significant contributory factor in bringing about the war.[2] But this is a doubtful judgement that needs to be qualified. Aside from the question of the line of the Shatt al-Arab, which became important mainly in consequence of the expansion of oil exports from both countries, and in essence concerned the *usage* of the waterway, there was no serious dispute over the possession of territory between Iran and Iraq. Iran's western border was its longest-established and most stable; in the eighteenth and nineteenth centuries Iran lost large slices of territory on every other frontier but that one. The older history of war with the Ottomans was hardly relevant in the 1980s, and as an independent Arab state, Iraq was young, having come into existence only in 1932. The Shatt al-Arab question had almost come to a head at the end of the 1960s, and the Shah had been backing Kurdish rebels in northern Iraq in the early 1970s,[3] but prior to that relations between Iran and Iraq had been cordial for the most part.

Peoples that have lived adjacent to each other for centuries tend to have prejudices about each other, and this is no less true of Iranians and Arabs than it is for the British and the French, the Russians and Poles, or Swedes and Finns. Or Swedes and Norwegians. The Arab conquest of Iran in the seventh century cast a long shadow in the thinking of Iranian nationalists;[4] there was a tendency among some to regard the Arabs not only as the originators of everything that had gone wrong in Iranian history, but also as culturally inferior. Some Sunni Arabs regard Shi'a Iranians as devious and unreliable. But those kinds of prejudices seldom start wars on their own.[5]

Again, some have suggested that the main cause of the war was Iranian propaganda about exporting revolution.[6] There is no doubt that this kind of political rhetoric was a feature of the revolutionary scene in Iran in 1979–80; nor that some Shi'a Iraqis were influenced and encouraged by it. Saddam made use of unrest among Shi'a Iraqis in the summer of 1979 to remove his predecessor, President Bakr. But to suggest that Saddam was somehow forced to invade Iran by the threat of destabilization distorts the reality of power in Iraq at the time. The dominance of Saddam and the Baath Party in Iraq was not seriously in question in the summer of 1980 and if it had been, invading Iran would not have been the solution.

Saddam still resented the Shah's bullying behaviour in the early 1970s and what he saw as the pro-Iranian nature of the Algiers Accords settlement (which he had signed for Iraq as vice-president). He saw an opportunity for some quick gains on the Shatt al-Arab and possibly the oilfields of Khuzestan while Iran was weakened by revolutionary turmoil and the debilitating effect of the military purges. It is likely that Shapur Bakhtiar was instrumental in convincing him that Iran would quickly fold after an invasion. The propaganda of the Iranian regime against the rule of the Baath Party in Iraq made him want to slap down the mullahs responsible (for whom he had contempt).[7] He also saw an opportunity to make himself look like a powerful national leader in the wider Arab world and a protector to the Arabs of Iranian Khuzestan; to appeal to the pan-Arabist sentiment that had been part of the original ideology of the Baath Party, from which he sprang. He was a political adventurer and opportunist who fancied himself as a warlord.[8] Those were, in a nutshell, the aims of the Iraqi invasion and the prime causes of the Iran–Iraq War.

Invasion

Between the murder of Ayatollah Mohammad Baqr al-Sadr in April and the outbreak of war there was sabre-rattling on both sides. After the murder, Khomeini called on the Iraqi people to rise up against the Baath regime and destroy it.[9] In Iran there was speculation about Iraqi involvement in the Nozheh coup plot. In July Saddam declared 'We do not want war . . . this is for Khomeini to decide'[10] – the sort of declaration that achieves the opposite effect to the intention indicated by the words used. Saddam continued to make aggressive announcements of his peaceful intentions. He did so again when between 6 and 13 September he sent Iraqi troops into two small areas along the border, at Zain al-Qaws and Saif Saad, which had been ceded to Iraq as part of the border delimitation carried out under the Algiers Accords, but never relinquished by Iran. There were a series of skirmishes, shellings and bombings along the border from 2 September onwards.

On 7 September an Iranian F-14 Tomcat fighter destroyed one of five Soviet-built Iraqi Mil Mi-25 attack helicopters near Zain al-Qaws.[11] This incident was significant in a number of ways. It was the first air-to-air combat kill achieved by the new Tomcat fighter in any theatre.[12] The F-14 was one of the most powerful and sophisticated air superiority fighters in the world at the time, if not *the* most powerful, and with its AWG-9 radar and AIM-54 Phoenix long-range air-to-air missiles, its Iranian pilots believed it to have significant advantages even over aircraft developed later, like the American F-18 and the Soviet MiG-29. It was designed for the US Navy; intended to defend American aircraft carrier groups against oncoming hordes of Soviet warplanes. Iran was the only other country ever to operate the F-14. The Iranians still fly it today,[13] after the US Navy retired the aircraft in 2006. The Shah ordered eighty of them, and seventy-nine were delivered before the revolution.[14]

Ever since the revolution, Western defence experts have been dismissive about the Iranians' ability to operate the F-14 effectively (and have been similarly sceptical about the Iranians' ability to use other sophisticated military technology bought by the Shah). They have emphasized the dependence of Iranian pilots and technicians on US advisers and trainers in the Shah's time, the downgrading of some of the avionics on the aircraft before export,[15] the sabotage carried out by some of the advisers before they left Iran in the weeks before the Shah's fall, the turmoil and the purges of pilots and trained maintenance personnel in the Iranian armed forces after the revolution, the progressive deterioration and inoperability of the aircraft due to lack of spare parts; and the overall ineffectiveness of the Iranian Air Force (IRIAF) as (supposedly) observed during the Iran–Iraq War.[16] But newly emerged evidence, especially from interviews carried out after the war with Iranian pilots, suggests that many of the analysts' doubts were based on little more than prejudice, exaggeration, chagrin that this powerful weaponry had fallen into the hands of the Islamic republic and a certain wooden-headed inability to comprehend a different kind of war fought in an unfamiliar context.[17] The F-14 and its workhorse companion, the F-4 Phantom, employed mainly in the ground-attack role, were used effectively by Iran against the Iraqis, and their highly sophisticated weapons systems were exploited to the full. But not always in the way their American trainers might have suggested. Partly to make this point, but also because it gives a vivid impression of this aspect of the war, I have included some of this evidence in what follows.

The Iraqi attack helicopter destroyed on 7 September was hit not by an air-to-air missile, but by the F-14's 20mm rotary cannon (configured like a nineteenth-century Gatling gun, firing from six rapidly rotating barrels, sounding from a distance like tearing corrugated cardboard). As an air superiority fighter, the F-14 should probably not, according to the standard doctrine, have been engaging the helicopters at all; and its crew should have used a Sidewinder air-to-air missile rather than the cannon (in fact the F-14 fired two Sidewinders that missed before resorting to the cannon). But the result was that a helicopter was destroyed, and the Iraqi attack was disrupted. A satisfactory result in practice, if not for theory, as the US Navy would have seen it.[18] This is a minor example, but significant – many aspects of the Iran–Iraq War have been misunderstood, for one reason or another; and since 1991 the war has been neglected as an area of study by comparison with the two later wars that took over the title Gulf War, originally applied to the conflict of 1980–88.

Having tested Iranian responses with his action against Zain al-Qaws and Saif Saad, on 17 September Saddam announced that Iraq would no longer be bound by the Algiers Accords. On 20 September Iran called up its reservists, and on 22 September about 45,000 Iraqi ground troops entered Iranian territory in four major thrusts, accompanied by a series of strikes against ten Iranian airbases by large numbers of Iraqi aircraft.[19] Neither the Iranians nor the rest of the world had expected an Iraqi attack on this scale, despite the tension and the border clashes over the preceding weeks. The Iraqis were able to make significant gains initially because of the surprise they achieved. In normal circumstances they should not have been able to take the Iranians by surprise, but as was apparent earlier (with the Kurdish revolt for example), the politicians in Tehran, clerical and secular, were absorbed with the problems and demands of politics in Tehran, taken up with revolutionary euphoria and 'a degree of hubris'.[20] This persisted: events were articulated in terms established by revolutionary politics – so in this case the Iraqi invasion was taken to be part of an American plot, in which Saddam Hussein was acting merely as a tool of the US.

The broad military balance between Iraq and Iran at the outbreak of war favoured the Iraqi land forces. The Iraqis had an army of 200,000 men in twelve divisions, well-equipped with tanks, armoured personnel carriers and artillery; the Iranian army had been reduced in strength to below 160,000 (from 285,000 before 1979), the disorder created by the purges and the other effects of revolution had not yet been rectified and a portion of the Iranian tanks and other equipment were inoperable due to breakdowns, undermanning and the prevailing disorganization. The effects of the revolution were probably less severe in the air force; the Iranians had 450 aircraft to the Iraqis' 340, and personnel numbers are thought to have fallen to about 70,000.[21]

Saddam employed his most powerful offensive forces in the south, sending an armoured corps against Mehran and two against the Iranians in Khuzestan. Against them the Iranians had only border guards of the gendarmerie, some scattered infantry units and one depleted armoured division based at Ahwaz. The Iraqis were able to advance quickly into Iranian territory. The majority of Iran's armed forces were deployed as in the time of the Shah, in regional centres and along the northern borders, facing the Soviets. They began rapidly to move south – some too precipitately. Some tank units moved south huge distances without tank transporters, causing excessive wear to tracks and running gear and contributing to later breakdowns. Across the country reservists headed for their depots, but volunteers also came forward, particularly for service with the Sepah.[22]

Khomeini's public reaction to the invasion and the first bombings (including against Mehrabad airport in Tehran) was calm, even contemptuous: 'A thief has come, thrown a pebble and fled back to his home.' But according to Bani-Sadr, the real reaction of the regime in Tehran to the invasion was near panic – 'Khomeini, Beheshti and Rafsanjani all believed that we would be defeated.' They knew how unprepared the Iranian military were, and how dependent the armed forces were on American weaponry, for which there was little prospect of new spare parts. Bani-Sadr said that Rajai and the Sepah leadership began to speculate about how the Sepah might conduct a guerrilla war against the Iraqis after an Iraqi victory.[23] Some of the US embassy hostages, still in captivity, assumed at first that the US had gone to war with Iran when they heard the first bombing raids.[24]

Saddam's air offensive on the first day involved nearly 200 aircraft, more than half of his air force. It was a massive strike, aimed at destroying Iran's air force on the ground and at rendering Iranian airbases inoperable by cratering their runways with bombs. This was what Göring had attempted against the RAF in the first phase of the Battle of Britain in 1940, and what Israel had achieved, devastatingly, against Egypt in 1967. But Saddam's air force was not up to the task and the strikes were a failure. Few Iranian aircraft were damaged or destroyed, and the scant damage to runways was easily repaired. The Iranian airbases were well prepared, with hardened shelters and tough ground defences. Iraqi bombs were thrown wide when pilots nervous about ground fire failed to make straight and level bomb runs, or did not explode because the pilots had not armed them. After bombing, many of the Iraqis headed straight for home, missing the opportunity to strafe parked aircraft (some parked invitingly in line abreast). Part of the reason for this was that many of the Iraqi aircraft were operating at extreme range, without air-to-air refuelling. There were exceptions – the base at Kermanshah (Bakhtaran) was badly hit, and the runway put out of action. But in general, the Iranian bases emerged from the attacks unscathed or with minimal damage. Foreign observers looking at intelligence reports reacted to the outcome with some surprise. A US State Department official speculated to a US analyst that the Iraqis had intended only to make a demonstration. The analyst said no – the Iraqi pilots were just that bad.[25]

What followed was an object lesson for Saddam about the need, if you hit first, to hit hard. Iranian ground crew worked through the night preparing F-4 Phantom and older F-5 Tiger aircraft for a counter-strike the next day. They were supported by Boeing 707 and 747 tanker aircraft for air-to-air refuelling, which in turn were protected by F-14s. The attacks were carried out according to plans made in the Shah's time. About 140 aircraft attacked altogether, early in the morning of 23 September, flying into Iraq at low level to avoid radar detection and hitting almost all of Iraq's airbases. The Iraqi bases were less well defended and prepared, and the Iranian strikes were more effective. Several installations were badly hit, with buildings destroyed and runways so badly cratered that they were rendered inoperable. One account suggests that the Iraqis lost twenty aircraft on the ground,[26] but it is difficult for anyone to assess these figures accurately. What is better evidence for the effect of the Iranian strikes is the Iraqi response. Large numbers of Iraqi aircraft – as many as a half or even two-thirds of the total – were evacuated to nearby Arab countries; especially Jordan, but also Kuwait, Saudi Arabia, North Yemen and Oman.[27]

The Iranian strikes continued for three more days, and when Iraqi artillery shelled Iranian oil installations at Abadan on 25 September, the Iranians responded later the same day with air strikes against Iraqi oil installations at Zubair, Basra, Mosul and Kirkuk. They also hit several Iraqi airbases again, and targets in Baghdad. Following the attacks on Baghdad, a flak-damaged F-4 Phantom was being escorted home by two more F-4s when they were attacked by Iraqi MiG-21s. In the ensuing fight one MiG was shot down, but the two escorting Phantoms were also damaged. The three F4s, now all damaged, then detected more

Iraqi MiGs heading toward them. At this point two Iranian F-14s, escorting a tanker aircraft that was waiting for the F-4s in Iranian airspace, decided to intervene (against orders – with few exceptions, the F-14 crews were under standing orders to stay within Iranian airspace). As the MiGs moved in to attack, one of the F-14s fired a Phoenix missile at long range, destroying the lead Iraqi aircraft, a MiG-23. More Iraqi MiGs were now moving in, and in the dogfight that followed the F-14s destroyed two of them with Sidewinder missiles, and then a third; but one of the Phantoms was hit by an Iraqi air-to-air missile and destroyed, with the crew ejecting into Iraqi captivity. Finally, one of the other F-4s shot down a damaged MiG-23 with its cannon before the two sides disengaged and the Iranians escaped back over the border.[28] According to the most recent research, the MiG-23 destroyed by the Phoenix missile was actually the fifth kill (at least) with that weapon achieved by the Iranian F-14s by that date – despite the belief at that time and since among Western analysts that the Iranians either were unwilling to (or more likely) incapable of using their Phoenix missiles, and that the F-14 Tomcats were nowhere to be seen in air fighting.[29]

Another feature of this action was the Iranians' use of the Combat Tree device, which made use of the signals hostile aircraft sent out automatically for identification purposes (IFF – Identification: Friend or Foe) to establish the range and heading of the enemy as well as the aircraft type; an invaluable supplement to the radars, computers and weapon guidance systems on board the F-4s and F-14s, especially in this sort of situation, when vulnerable aircraft, low on fuel, were outnumbered by enemies. It enabled the Iranians to track the most threatening hostile aircraft, and to select the most appropriate weapons to fire off at each one. The F-14 could track and select weapons to fire at up to six hostile aircraft at the same time. Again, Western analysts assumed the Iranians could not use this equipment.[30]

Once more, the Iranian attacks on 25 September were devastating, doing serious damage to many Iraqi oil installations and other targets. After this, both sides generally avoided attacks on oil production facilities, though oil export installations were still targeted and, later, tankers.

By 30 September, despite the trend of the war in the air, Iraqi ground forces were close to Dezful, Ahwaz, Khorramshahr and Abadan. Iranian resistance on the ground had been uncoordinated and weak, but resistance stiffened as more troops came up, including Sepah volunteers. The new Sepah troops were keen, but inexperienced, and suffered heavy casualties in the early months of the war as a result. Iranian air superiority gradually increased the efficacy of IRIAF attacks on Iraqi tanks and troops – particularly those carried out by army helicopter gunships. But ground attack missions were always hazardous, with a high risk of losses of pilots and aircraft. Ground troops on both sides would tend to fire small arms, anti-aircraft artillery and missiles at any aircraft they saw, assuming they were hostile: they were often unable to differentiate between friend and foe in any case.

An illustration of this (from a few months later, in mid-January 1981):

> We were near Dar-Balut [south of Pol-e Zohab in Bakhtaran province, west of Kermanshah]. Our major, who smoked opium, got us together and told us that if we saw Iraqi aircraft we should not fire on them, because that would give away our position. But when he had gone, I called the men together again and told them this was wrong – the aircraft were made of light alloy and flying at less than 100 metres height; small arms fire could hit a vulnerable part like munitions, a fuel tank or the pilot himself, causing a crash. They should shoot, but they needed to be sure they were not firing at our own aircraft. A few days later I was walking near the front line with corporal N— when suddenly we heard the sound of aircraft, and two planes appeared. We fired at one of them and saw smoke coming from it immediately – we were convinced that our bullets had hit. Later we heard that an Iraqi aircraft had crashed near Sumar. A few days after that incident, we saw another aircraft falling out of the sky in the distance. Two of us went to see if we could find it. On the way, we were told that a corporal from another unit had shot it down, and we were celebrating. But when we found the crashed aircraft, it was one of our own – an F-4 Phantom.[31]

Some important features of the war had already emerged by the end of September 1980. Iranian ground forces were initially weak at the war front, but increased in numbers later. The Iraqi ground forces were strong and well equipped with tanks and other armoured vehicles, but tended to halt and act defensively when they encountered stiff resistance, especially in built-up areas. Both sides often tended to use their tanks without adequate infantry support.

The Iranian air forces were better equipped and better trained than the Iraqis and quickly established their dominance. The Iranian pilots had been given a high standard of training before the revolution both in Iran by American instructors and in the US at US Navy and Air Force training bases. By comparison, the Iraqis had received less training, of a lower standard, by Soviet and Warsaw Pact training teams sent to Iraq for the purpose. They had not been sent out of Iraq for training, probably for political reasons. In addition – and this was a feature of Cold War military development generally – US military aviation technology (particularly avionics, including weapon targeting systems, radar detection and electronic countermeasures) outclassed the Soviet equivalents carried on Iraqi aircraft; often to a degree that was only fully appreciated after the Cold War ended. Many of the lessons of the Iran–Iraq War to this effect were ignored or overlooked, or obscured by other factors.

One reason the lessons were overlooked was that Iranian air superiority did not translate into a war-winning factor as Western analysts might have expected it to do. Saddam said publicly in November: 'Now, the Western media are asking why we have used only one-third of our air force ... We will not use our air force. We will keep it. Two years hence our air force will still be in a position to pound Bani-Sadr and his collaborators.'[32] But the Iranian regime had a similar attitude to its aircraft: they were too valuable to throw away in a full-on aggressive onslaught to acquire air superiority. The aircraft could not be replaced, given Iran's isolation internationally. So, after the desperate initial phase of the war, the Iranians also tended to use air power defensively and conservatively – especially the precious F-14s, which almost without exception were held back to defend Iranian airspace and avoid losses.

Although a perceived need to keep a reserve against the possibility of intervention from outside the region was perhaps also a factor, the key to this, for both Iran and Iraq, was probably the dependence of both countries on oil. Both countries needed to retain air power as a deterrent, and to defend against air attacks on its oil industry because, without oil, neither could expect to sustain its war effort for long. The Iran–Iraq War only lasted as long as it did because both countries could use their oil industry to fund it (and, especially in the case of Iraq, could seek loans using future oil production as collateral). Perhaps more importantly, neither the Iranian regime nor the Iraqi regime could expect to survive politically if its oil industry or oil revenue were destroyed. Because neither country could afford to lose its oil, neither could afford to lose its air force; as a result, neither could risk it by using it to full effect. The situation was a little like that between the British and German high seas fleets in the First World War, to which Churchill referred when he said of Admiral Jellicoe that he was the only man who could lose the war in an afternoon.

It is impossible to quantify, but the activity of Iranian Air Force pilots in these early days had a major effect in slowing the Iraqi advance. Ironically, some of the pilots fighting the Iraqis were newly released from prison – other pilots they had trained with were still there. Some had been tortured. The Shah's pilots, as they were called, were some of the elements in the military that were least trusted by the revolutionary regime, especially after the Nozheh coup attempt. Bazargan's government had actually attempted to sell back the F-14s to the Americans; they had appeared to be among the most excessive of the superfluous weapons Khomeini had criticized the Shah for wasting money on. The Shah himself had been a pilot, and his pilots had been some of those officers among his armed services that he had most favoured. Under Khomeini, they were some of those most despised by the revolutionaries; and many of their successes in destroying Iraqi aircraft were attributed, for public consumption, to the Sepah. As the fighting continued, more and more of the pilots were released from prison. In October, following pressure from Bani-Sadr and others, a batch were released who had actually been under sentence of death. The value of the training they had received in using the sophisticated weaponry of the F-14s and F-4s outweighed doubts about their political allegiance. A few pilots, having acquired their freedom, later defected with their aircraft; but surprisingly few in the circumstances. The large majority (the same applied for army and navy personnel) swallowed whatever antipathy they may have had for the revolutionary government and resolved to defend their country come what may.

There is reason to believe that Saddam intended the war to last only a few weeks, or even a few days – he believed that the Iranians would be so unprepared, and the invasion would be such a shock, that they would grab the chance of an early peace in order to avoid further defeat and further damage. That had, after all, been the experience of most recent wars in the Middle East – they had lasted a few weeks, or months at most. So when the UN Security Council, in Resolution 479 of 28 September 1980, called for a ceasefire, Saddam accepted it. But the Iranians did not. That, and the unexpectedly tough Iranian air response, and the Iranian preparedness to broaden the conflict to include targeting Iraqi oil assets, must have alarmed Saddam and made him realize he was in for a longer and bumpier ride than he had anticipated.[33] As the weeks went on, there was no sign of revolt among the Arabs of Iranian Khuzestan in support of the Iraqi invasion, as Saddam had hoped. There were, however, some indications of dissent among Shi'a troops in his own army.[34] An aid worker later asked an Iranian Arab who had fought for the Iranians and had been taken prisoner by the Iraqis why the Arabs of Khuzestan had not supported the Iraqi invaders:

> It's true that we're Arab and proud of it, but we're not Iraqi and that's what's important. It's not true that we weren't happy with the Emam. In the past we had had some trouble with the Persians, for they can be very arrogant and the Shah encouraged that attitude. So we were glad when Khomeini came back, but then things started to go wrong. We wanted Arabic to be the first language in our schools, and we wanted more of the money the government earned from the oil in the province. But they wouldn't agree with our demands, so we demonstrated. As a result, they sent a new governor called Madani to the province and he used violence against the people. We defended ourselves, but when the war started it was our duty to defend our country. We are Muslims and the Persians are Muslims and for me that's what's important. Anyway, I don't like Saddam. He's a Baathist and not a very good Muslim. Iraqis drink beer and whisky but we don't. We're better Arabs and better Muslims than them.[35]

Before the war began, the question of autonomy for Khuzestan had drawn some international attention when on 30 April 1980 a group of men from what they called the Democratic Revolutionary Front for the Liberation of Arabistan broke into the Iranian embassy at Prince's Gate in Kensington in London, took hostage the occupants of the building (one of them a Syrian journalist who had gone there for an interview about the occupation of the US embassy in Tehran) and demanded the release of Arab separatists being held in Iranian prisons. They had entered the UK on Iraqi passports. Six days later (after the hostage-takers shot one of their captives) soldiers from the SAS regiment assaulted the building, freeing most of the hostages and killing all but one of the hostage-takers. A second hostage died in the assault.[36] Initially the Iranian government accused Britain of having organized the occupation of the embassy; later they thanked the British government for ending the siege. But the Iranian embassy did not reoccupy the building until 1993 and arguments rumbled on for years between the two governments about payment for the damage done in the assault.

On the Iranian side, Bani-Sadr was energetic and highly visible in the early weeks of the war. He moved to Khuzestan, setting up an operations centre in Dezful to be closer to the front (though he shuttled back to Tehran for consultations each week). He did his best to lift morale in the armed forces, speaking up for air force officers in particular, as he recalled later:

> The demoralization of the army in this period came not from the enemy, but from our own ranks. The pilots, whom I considered the saviours of Iran, were the mullahs' favourite target. In a meeting on the Dezful air base, one of the pilots asked me to read the interview of a [Majles] deputy in the Islamic Republic Party newspaper who blasted specialists and technicians, all of whom were servants of the Americans. This pilot's anger was understandable. 'This is how we are repaid! You say we are Iran's saviours and parliament treats us like CIA agents!' How could these pilots, who were risking their lives every day, help but feel demoralized?[37]

Others, even in those desperate times, were still so distrustful of the Shah's armed forces that they wanted them disbanded altogether, to be replaced by the Sepah. Bani-Sadr believed Khomeini's own attitude was equivocal – one moment praising the troops, and at another saying they were treasonous (he is supposed to have said 'they have the Shah in their blood'):

> In fact, when he [Khomeini] sent [his representative] Ardebili to tell me that there were reports accusing the army of treason, it was an Iranian-style message, that is, coded. He wanted to let me know that I should not link my fate too closely to the military.[38]

There was bad feeling at the front between the army and the Sepah, which Bani-Sadr did his best to smooth over. Khomeini exhorted all

Iranians under arms to defend the towns and cities of Khuzestan to the last. In Khorramshahr they did so: the Iraqis fought their way into the city on 24 October but did not achieve full control of it until 10 November. By mid-October most of the buildings had been destroyed by heavy artillery bombardment over the previous weeks, and it has been estimated that about 7,000 were killed or seriously injured on each side in the fight for the city. The Iraqis had lost about 100 tanks and other armoured vehicles; the best part of an armoured division.[39] The Iraqi tactics of shelling civilian centres from entrenched positions excited the anger of ordinary people throughout Iran, as did reports of rape and killings of civilians by the Iraqis. Refugees from the front in Khuzestan were evacuated eastwards in tens and hundreds of thousands. Khorramshahr took on a significance in the war similar to that of Stalingrad on the Eastern Front in the Second World War – a strategic objective that also became important as a symbol and a focus for propaganda.

There are indications that, having agreed to the release of pilots from prison, and provoked by Iraqi missile attacks on Iranian cities (ex-Soviet FROG-7 missiles were fired at Dezful on 8 October), Khomeini personally ordered air attacks on targets deep in Iraq in response. This led to a daring and complex operation at the end of October, when Iranian aircraft attacked the al-Hurriyah airbase near Mosul, in northern Iraq, where French advisers were helping Iraqi pilots to convert on to the Mirage F1EQ. The plan was for a mixed group of aircraft, including six F-4 Phantoms armed with bombs, two 707 tanker aircraft and two F-14s to escort the tankers, to fly through Turkish airspace in order to arrive over their target near Mosul from the north, thereby avoiding surface-to-air missile batteries and patrols of Iraqi fighter aircraft that protected the eastern approaches. The raid was exceptional in a number of ways – normally the tankers and F-14s were not allowed beyond Iranian airspace.

The operation was a complete success, causing extensive damage on the ground. When a group of four Iraqi MiG-23 fighters tried to intervene, the Iranian F-14 Tomcats attacked and destroyed all of them, using Phoenix and Sidewinder missiles. All the Iranian aircraft returned safely to base; the French personnel were ordered home. The Iranian pilots had made full use of the training they had received from US Navy specialists:

At almost 520 mph, low on fuel and with an Iraqi MiG-23 on his tail, Sedghi performed what the Americans call a break turn – he pulled the control column all the way back, then kicked in full rudder to generate a large yaw and roll rate to slow the jet down, using the Tomcat as a foil in a high-pitch position ... the Tomcat's speed dropped down to 150 mph within seconds. The nose of the jet went through the vertical and then dropped down on the MiG-23 as it flashed by at high speed. Engaging afterburner, Sedghi closed on the Iraqi's tail and got a good tone from his last Sidewinder. The missile hit the MiG's lower tail section, causing the jet to roll over on its back, trailing flame and smoke. The Iraqi pilot ejected seconds later.[40]

Even before this attack, Saddam made a speech on 20 October attributing part of the reason why victory had eluded Iraq so far to the superior training and equipment of the Iranians, and what he called 'geographical injustice': 'Their aircraft can ... reach any spot in Iraq with full loads because their range is greater than that of many of our aircraft, and because Iraq has a smaller area than Iran.' To make up for these realities, and portraying Iraq as the victim and the underdog, he exhorted the Iraqi people by the example of the Arab victory at Qadesiyya in AD 637.[41]

The other city that the Iraqis were pushing hard for in October was Abadan. By mid-October the defenders in the city were virtually surrounded, but reinforcements and supplies could still reach them by water from the south. The Iraqis, after their experience in Khorramshahr, were reluctant to risk further heavy casualties in house-to-house fighting. Abadan continued to hold out, despite heavy bombardment from artillery and dug-in tanks. Sanandaj was also besieged. Finally, the Iraqis launched another offensive in the north, taking Marivan in Iranian Kurdestan. But further progress in the south was halted by the rains that began in the third week of November, and then there was a lull.[42] Although the Iran–Iraq War lasted nearly eight years, it was not eight years of constant high-intensity warfare at the pitch of those first few months. Periods of intense fighting were interspersed with periods of relative quiet, while both sides recuperated, took stock and prepared for new campaigns, and troops on the front line watched enemy positions for signs of suspicious activity. The following incident took place in January 1981:

One day at our base in Islamabad-e Gharb [west of Kermanshah] our colonel was talking with a young woman, who was crying. It turned out that her husband had been killed trying to take a position on the mountain of Choghalvand. I took some volunteers to try to find the body. I made a visit to reconnoitre and could see the bodies through binoculars near the Iraqi position. We went out the next night with ten to twelve men, a radio man and two mules. We told the Sepah who had positions on the next peak what we planned to do, and asked them to give covering fire if shooting started up. We got up close by using a gully on one side of a huge slab of rock, and managed to retrieve three bodies and some weapons, improvising with blankets as stretchers. We got back (even though the Sepah nearly shot me by mistake, despite our warning) and we got some leave. But none of the bodies was that of the woman's husband – some Kurdish paramilitary found him later.[43]

Conflict in Tehran

Bani-Sadr had put himself at the forefront of national resistance in the first months of the war, appearing on TV, giving interviews and publicizing his activities in a variety of innovatory ways (including through his own newspaper, *Enqelab-e Eslami – Islamic Revolution*), encouraging new efforts and discouraging defeatism. And Khomeini supported him, or appeared to – in mid-October 1980 Bani-Sadr was made chairman of the Supreme Defence Council, and at the beginning of November Khomeini directed clerics to refrain from commenting on or interfering in military matters (Khomeini had already delegated his powers as commander in chief to Bani-Sadr the previous February).[44] But Bani-Sadr and Prime Minister Rajai were still in disagreement, and as time went on Bani-Sadr's criticisms of the IRP grew more insistent. The antipathy at the war front between the armed forces and the Sepah was paralleled in Tehran by the hostility between Bani-Sadr and his supporters on the one hand, and the IRP on the other. He spoke out against the use of torture, and in January warned of a drift towards dictatorship. Others were protesting on this and related issues, including the use of political violence: in early February a group of thirty-eight writers, lawyers, academics and journalists wrote an open letter to Khomeini protesting against the regime's autocratic behaviour in a series of areas, comparing it with what had happened under the Shah.[45] At the same time, IRP members spoke up about the danger of Bani-Sadr's connection with the army, and the possibility that he might use the army for the pursuit of his own political ends, against the revolution, as a latter-day Bonaparte. They also criticized the apparent reluctance of the army (and therefore of Bani-Sadr) to go on the offensive. They were silenced for a time by an attack by Iranian armoured forces in the Susangerd area on 5 January, but by the end of the month this offensive was a failure, with the loss of many tanks. As time went on, other political elements rallied to Bani-Sadr in his struggle with the IRP.

Through the outbreak of war and the dramatic early campaigns the US embassy hostages were still being held by the students. As time went on, some of the students were called away to fight. One of the hostages commented:

> It was amazing what the war did to the guards ... The war was very close to them ... Not only were bombs falling on Tehran, but they had brothers and friends fighting at the front. Their friends and relatives were dying every day ... All their arrogance was gone, and they were very subdued in their treatment of us ... There were times when I actually felt sorry for them.[46]

Sympathy for the student guards was not a widespread feeling among the hostages. But already by the time war broke out, elements of a solution to the hostage crisis were beginning to come into place. The death of the Shah had removed one obstacle. Early in September one of Khomeini's aides, Sadegh Tabatabai, made contact with Carter's administration through the West German government, and the two sides met in Bonn on 16 and 18 September, with Tabatabai leading for the Iranians (Bani-Sadr was kept out of it) and Warren Christopher for the US. Shorn of the demand for an apology for past US crimes and with the demand for the Shah's return now defunct, the remaining Iranian conditions were amenable for discussion – consisting of a commitment from the US not to interfere in Iranian internal affairs, and the financial points about the unfreezing of assets. On the question of the $50 million worth of military spares paid for by the Shah but still undelivered, the US side told the Iranians that the material could be quietly passed on once 'the other aspects of the dispute were resolved'. But the financial points were capable of lengthy further debate. Carter believed later that the Iraqi invasion delayed the hostages' release; but towards the end it became fairly plain that the Iranians had waited deliberately until Carter himself left office in January, as one last low blow.

That much is known fact – but some have speculated and investigated further, to suggest that people close to Ronald Reagan's presidential election campaign negotiated secretly with the Iranians deliberately to delay the hostages' release until after Reagan had won the election and taken office (the speculation has usually been called the October Surprise theory). For Reagan's people, the key gain from such negotiations would have been the delay. Early release of the hostages would definitely have given Carter's re-election campaign a major boost (the US presidental election took place on 4 November 1980 – Reagan won a landslide victory). For the Iranians, the prize would have been to secure vital spares and war supplies. And the Iranians did get such supplies (perhaps not as many or for as long as they had hoped), from the Israelis – in rather a similar way to that in which war materials were passed to Iran at US instigation via Israel during the Iran-Contra episode a few years later. It is possible that they also obtained them directly, though covertly, from the US, in large quantities, from NATO stocks held in Belgium, after Reagan took office.[47] There is not space to go into the detail of it here, and the magnitude of the traitorous cynicism of the US negotiators would be appalling, if true: but the old political question applied to murky and uncertain dealings, *cui bono?* (who benefits?), applied in this case just to those known facts, points to the plausibility of something like the October Surprise theory.[48]

In fact, senior figures in the Iranian regime had realized early in the autumn of 1980 that there was little further benefit to the IRP from holding on to the hostages, and that the international isolation the hostage crisis had brought on Iran was much more damaging now Iran was at war.[49] The students' spiritual guide, now an IRP member of the Majles, Mohammad Musavi-Khoeniha, set it out frankly at the end of October, giving at the same time a succinct account of the hostage-takers' motivations:

> We have reaped all the fruits of our undertaking. We defeated the attempt by the 'liberals' to take control of the machinery of state. We forced Mr Bazargan's government to resign. The tree of revolution has grown and gained in strength. We have demonstrated both to our own people

and to international opinion that we have the weapons not only to resist but also to defeat the all-powerful United States, which believed it held Iran in the palm of its hand.[50]

The hostages finally flew out of Iran on 20 January 1981, after 444 days of captivity, a matter of minutes after the inauguration ceremony in Washington for President Reagan. They flew to Germany, where they rested and received medical attention before returning to the US, where they were reunited with their families. John Limbert's Iranian wife, Parvaneh, commented later:

> When I first saw John, I was very, very happy, but it was also hard for me. Talking to him on the phone was much easier than seeing him face to face. For me it was a bit hard at the beginning because I am an Iranian. Thinking that my own people had done this to him – had taken him hostage – that made it very hard. Throughout the entire ordeal, I always had feelings of guilt, and I was frightened, because I wasn't sure how John would feel. There were times when I would wonder, 'How can I face him?' But at the same time, I love him very much, and I was excited and happy. Fortunately, he understands me and what happened very well.[51]

In the end, after all the sums were done, Iran received only something over $4 billion of the $12 billion of assets that the Carter administration froze at the beginning of the hostage crisis. The amount was reduced by a sum set aside to cover loans made to the Shah's government, and an amount to be held in escrow to cover outstanding claims against the Iranian government. The US official Gary Sick commented later that 'it appeared that the longer Iran negotiated, the less it got'.[52] Money was not the reason for the detention of the hostages, nor for the length of their detention. But the settlement was criticized in Tehran, not least by Bani-Sadr, who called in aid protests from the governor of the Central Bank about the premature repayment of the loans, and the status of the legal claims.[53] Bani-Sadr also criticized the delay over the hostages' release. His position won him support in some quarters, but went down badly with the IRP, adding to the lengthening list of their grievances against him. It was another of his damaging political successes.

On 5 March Bani-Sadr enjoyed another one. He was heckled (including, according to his own account, with the words 'Bani-Sadr, Pinochet! Iran will not become another Chile!') at a public meeting held to mark the anniversary of Mossadeq's death. But his supporters in the audience arrested the hecklers, searched them and handed them over to the police. It was shown that they were all from IRP-aligned groups and committees: Bani-Sadr read out their identity cards to the audience. So far, so good. But the IRP responded by criticizing the arrests, and the people arrested took legal action against the president. Khomeini expressed his dismay (and perhaps his anger that this political infighting was taking place while ordinary Iranians were dying in the defence of their country) by retreating into silence for ten days. Beheshti and others spoke up in support of the hecklers; Khalkhali said the president could be tried for high treason. Bani-Sadr rapidly found that he was on the slide (he admitted later that he had overreached himself with his actions on 5 March). On 11 March the Majles passed a new law permitting the prime minister to appoint acting cabinet ministers, which meant Rajai could bypass Bani-Sadr and, finally, appoint his own choice of foreign minister.[54]

On 15 March Khomeini held a meeting to try to resolve the strife. Bani-Sadr was seriously outnumbered. Though Bazargan and Ahmad Khomeini were there effectively as neutrals, ranged against him were Rajai, Beheshti, Rafsanjani and, according to some accounts, Khamenei. The arguments rolled back and forth: Bani-Sadr declared that only he had legitimate authority in the state, and that his opponents were ignorant and unfit to take part in government; the others said it was impossible to work with him and implied that he had delusions of grandeur. In the end Khomeini ruled that both sides should stop their personal attacks on each other and banned speeches and inflammatory articles until the end of the war. He appointed a three-man commission to investigate the disputes and to monitor the media for infringements of his ban.[55] The choice of the three was intended to produce a commission that would be impartial. But the settlement did not endure; the IRP chiefs had no intention of backing down, and Bani-Sadr had no intention of dropping his confrontational line. It brought about a period of relative calm between the president and the IRP for which ordinary people and the fighting forces were thankful. But there were clashes between Hezbollah and the MKO in April, after Khomeini stepped up his criticisms of what he called their eclecticism – in other words, their promiscuous absorption of non-Islamic, Western and Marxist notions into their ideology.

Saddam's Attacks Falter

On 19–20 March Iraqi troops tried and failed to take Susangerd; there were further missile attacks on Dezful and Ahwaz using FROG missiles on 12 and 22 March. On 4 April eight Iranian F4s, supported by two F-14s and tanker aircraft, attacked the Al-Walid complex of airbases, near Iraq's border with Jordan, in an operation that followed the successful attack on Mosul on 29 October in many respects. The Iranians had intelligence, possibly from Israel, that the bases were being used to bring foreign aircraft and technicians (notably, again, French) into the country, via Jordan. The attacks were again devastating, destroying at least twenty-seven and possibly as many as thirty-eight aircraft on the ground, including two newly arrived French Mirage F1EQs. Some reports indicated that Saddam had six senior air officers and pilots executed after the attack for incompetence, and a number of others imprisoned.[56]

Over the summer, the Iraqis made a major effort to take Abadan, but the Iranians fed large numbers of fresh troops into the city and were able to outmanoeuvre the Iraqis, finally succeeding in pushing them back over the Karun river in September. Coming after the Iraqi failure at Susangerd in March, it looked as though the edge had come off Saddam's offensive drive. From then until September, both sides limited themselves mainly to exchanges of artillery fire at a distance.

In early June there was an incident that serves to highlight another aspect of the Iran–Iraq War that has been neglected or misunderstood – Israel's support for Iran in the conflict. On 7 June 1981, Israeli F-15 and F-16 aircraft bombed the Iraqi plutonium research reactor at Osirak/Tuwaitha south-east of Baghdad, flying through Jordanian and Saudi airspace to get there. The reactor (built with French assistance) was destroyed, and the Israeli aircraft all returned safely to their base at Etzion, near the Gulf of Aqaba. Although there was no overt Iranian involvement, there is evidence that Iran shared intelligence with the Israelis about the target following an unsuccessful Iranian attack on it on 30 September the previous year; and gave permission for Israeli aircraft involved in the operation to use the Iranian airbase at Tabriz in case of emergency.[57]

Just over a month later, an aircraft carrying Israeli arms to Iran crashed near the Soviet–Turkish border. Iraqi propaganda made the most of the Iranian connection with Israel – Iran has never avowed it. But it has been estimated that Israel supplied $500 million worth of weapons to Iran in the period 1980–83. The simple reason was that Israel regarded Iraq as a greater threat at that time – but there was more to it than that. In the time of the Shah, Israel had seen Iran as her natural ally in the Middle East. Many senior Israeli politicians and officials, including former (and subsequent) prime minister Yitzhak Rabin, continued to take that view, despite the revolution and Khomeini's rhetoric against Israel. Shortly after the Iraqi invasion, former defence and foreign minister Moshe Dayan held an impromptu press conference (while he was in Vienna on other business) to urge the US to settle its problems with Iran – notably the hostage crisis – and help Iran defend itself. The indications are that Begin's government started sending Iran arms and other assistance just after that. There may subsequently have been an interruption following an intervention by President Carter, but Israeli support resumed after the release of the hostages, if not before. Israeli technical assistance was also given – notably to help Iran manufacture spare parts for the Iranians' US-built weapons – for example, tyres and undercarriage brake components for the Iranian F-14 Tomcats. But the Israelis also helped with more high-tech adaptations. On at least one occasion (in 1985) Israeli technicians worked in Iran on such projects.[58] Given the hostility between Iran and Israel at the time of writing, it is ironic that Israel (apart from Syria) was probably Iran's most consistent supporter in the Iran–Iraq War.

Khomeini's attitude to Israel was longstanding and hostile, but there was some ambiguity in his attitude to Jews, and to the Jewish community in Iran, reflecting deep-seated ambiguities in Iranian and particularly clerical attitudes to Jews. There was anti-Semitism in Iran, as in almost every country in which Jews have lived. In the nineteenth and early twentieth centuries there had been attacks on Jews led by mullahs. But when the Jewish community looked for protection against such attacks, they turned to – other mullahs. The history of the Iranian Jewish community goes back to Cyrus and beyond, and over that long period there had been oscillations between long periods of tolerance and periodic outbreaks of persecution. Jews were entitled to respect and protection according to the shari'a as People of the Book, and the higher *ulema* tended to uphold those principles. But lower-level preachers trying to make a name for themselves were not above calling for attacks on the Jews and could draw upon prejudice based on ancient notions that Jews, like other non-Muslims, were unclean (*najes*). Khomeini himself, despite things he had written in *Hokumat-e Eslami* for example, seems to have made a clear stipulation early in 1979 that Jews were to be protected. This may or may not have been influenced by a story that the Jewish hospital (the Dr Sapir Hospital) in south-central Tehran had taken in wounded demonstrators after the Jaleh Square massacre when other hospitals had turned them away for fear of SAVAK reprisals.[59]

Since the revolution the unspoken deal has been that the Jews have to condemn Zionism, but otherwise for the most part are left in uneasy peace to run businesses and worship in synagogues. Large numbers of Jews have in fact left Iran since 1979, emigrating to the US, to Israel and to Europe, but Iran still has by far the largest Jewish community anywhere in the Middle East outside Israel (estimates vary between 25,000 and 35,000). In general, Christians and Jews have been discriminated against since the revolution and have suffered a steady, low-level intimidation by the regime, with occasional flare-ups of greater nastiness.

The Islamic regime has tended to treat Jews worse than Christians, but the Bahais have been treated worse than either (it is estimated that there are still something above 300,000 Bahais in Iran today). In August 1980, the Sepah arrested all nine members of the Bahai National Spiritual Assembly of Iran. None of them were ever seen again. The Bahais elected another nine to the Assembly – all but one were arrested and secretly executed. Killings continued, until (according to the Bahais) 177 had been killed by the end of 1984. Persecution has continued since then at a less intense pitch, but still with occasional killings and disappearances.[60]

Over the period of the Iran–Iraq War Iran maintained its rhetoric against Israel, but with quiet pragmatism accepted the help Israel gave.[61]

Bani-Sadr Falls

At some point in April Khomeini was shown evidence[62] taken by the students from the US embassy that Bani-Sadr had been contacted by the CIA in Paris in 1978, and later in Tehran. It seems the CIA had done so initially to get his views on the Iranian economy as a consultant. On 20 May the Majles passed a new law, enabling Rajai to appoint the heads of a further raft of organizations, including the Central Bank. On 27 May Khomeini made a speech that included what was taken as an attack on Bani-Sadr (who by now was disregarding the constraints on his political activities), saying that the nation was hostile to personality cults and that anyone trying to subvert the authority of the Majles could be prosecuted and could face the death penalty.[63] Rajai and Bani-Sadr exchanged barely veiled criticisms and threats. Some of Bani-Sadr's associates were arrested, and the IRP were talking about him being impeached. In early June Bani-Sadr's paper, *Enqelab-e Eslami*, was closed down, along with several others; but Bani-Sadr continued to put out his own views in a publication with a new name. From Hamadan, still defiant, he called on Iranians to resist tendencies toward dictatorship; Khomeini broadcasted on radio that Bani-Sadr had to obey the Islamic organs of the state – the parliament; the supreme court. Otherwise Khomeini would do to him what he had done to the Shah. Khomeini and Bani-Sadr exchanged letters in which the latter tried to demand he be allowed to exercise proper presidential authority; Khomeini reiterated that the president had to be subject to the law and the decisions of the Majles. Finally, having received declarations of loyalty from military chiefs, Khomeini stripped Bani-Sadr of his delegated powers as commander in chief on 10 June. Bani-Sadr returned to Tehran on 11 June, but many of his close followers had already gone into hiding, and he joined them two or three days later.

On 10 June there was a large MKO demonstration and serious clashes with Hezbollah, with several dead and hundreds injured. Shortly afterwards the National Front called a major protest demonstration for 15 June. The MKO and some other leftists declared their support for Bani-Sadr, but, alerted to the seriousness of the crisis by a dramatic last-minute speech from Khomeini (in which he said the call for the demonstration was an invitation to an uprising and poured scorn on the record of the National Front), Bazargan and the Freedom Movement dissociated themselves from the president. Large numbers of middle-class supporters of Bani-Sadr, the National Front and other groups turned out for the demonstration, but they were cowed by *hezbollahis* and the numbers of IRP supporters from south Tehran. The demonstration was a failure. As late as 12/13 June Khomeini and Rafsanjani were holding out for Bani-Sadr to stay on as president, if only he would fall into line. But his obduracy and the prospect of an alliance between him and the MKO seems finally to have changed their minds, and on 17 June Rafsanjani, as speaker of the Majles, allowed a debate on Bani-Sadr's competence for the following week. This was to bring about the president's impeachment.

The debate took place on 20 and 21 June. There had been many outbreaks of violence over the preceding days between *hezbollahis* and the MKO, and as the debates went ahead a huge crowd of IRP-aligned demonstrators surrounded the Majles building, calling 'death to Bani-Sadr' and 'death to the liberals'. The operation of the Majles under the pressure of bloodthirsty threats from a working-class crowd could have evoked a memory of some of the worst episodes of the French revolution. There was more violence as large numbers of MKO, Fedayan and other leftists demonstrated elsewhere in Tehran (the MKO leader, Masud Rajavi, had called for armed resistance). Rafsanjani made the opening speech in the debate; foremost among those attacking Bani-Sadr were Musavi-Khoeniha, Ali Khamenei and Ali Akbar Velayati. He was accused of spreading division and dissent, of failing in his conduct of the war, of opposing Emam Khomeini and lacking faith in the principle of *velayat-e faqih*, of shaming Iran through his campaign against torture, of 'haughtiness' and 'insincerity'. The radical Khalkhali, true to form, spoke up to say that it was not enough to remove Bani-Sadr alone; the opposition generally had to suffer too: the revolutionary tribunals 'must today execute fifty of them' to show that the IRP meant business.[64] Only three of the forty or more Majles delegates who had previously shown support for Bani-Sadr had the courage to speak up in his defence in the debate. Ali Akbar Moinfar deplored the political situation – he said it was not the constitution that was running the country, but the law of violence and the *hezbollahis*. Ezzatollah Sahabi (like Moinfar a member of the Freedom Movement) said that Bani-Sadr had made mistakes, but also criticized the way that demonstrations and incitement were being applied to decision-making. When it came to a vote, most of the previous critics of the IRP were not present; of those that were, thirteen abstained, and only one voted in favour of Bani-Sadr. The motion declaring him incompetent was supported by 177 delegates. Within a few hours the order went out for Bani-Sadr's arrest, and when Khomeini was formally notified of the vote, he removed Bani-Sadr from office.[65]

Both were severe blows to moderate, liberal, middle-class opinion in Iran, but there were important differences between the fall of Bani-Sadr and the fall of Bazargan nineteen months earlier. In particular, Khomeini's attitude to Bani-Sadr had been different. By the time Bani-Sadr came to office, Khomeini and the IRP had already secured their constitutional objectives. It seems that Khomeini had genuinely wanted to work with Bani-Sadr. But ultimately, this could only have happened if Bani-Sadr had capitulated to Khomeini's vision of Islamic government. Bani-Sadr's own description of the difference between them is quite vivid, if one allows for his angle:

> For the mullahs, unfortunately, public opinion did not exist. Khomeini explained his point of view to me quite clearly. 'You are always talking about the 11 million people who voted for you, but there is no such thing as public opinion, neither in Iran nor anywhere else. It is a fabrication ... It is plain to see that governments manufacture public opinion out of nothing and manipulate it at will.' This theory basically implies that the people understand nothing. It is taken directly from the philosophy of Aristotle, who said that some men are born to govern, others to be governed. A few are aware and the rest are sheep; Plato said the same thing ... This was yet another source of contention between the two sides in our revolution. The mullahs concluded that my election was a mistake since the people, by definition, know nothing.[66]

It may be that some among the leadership of the IRP were determined to get rid of Bani-Sadr from the start, and to win the full run of top governmental offices for the IRP. But that had not been Khomeini's view. If Bani-Sadr had been more cautious, a little more subtle, and a bit less confrontational, he might have had more success. The lack of support for him in the final Majles debate should not obscure the continuing level of support he had in the country as a whole – not least, perhaps surprisingly, among clerics. Sheikh Ali Tehrani (a student of Khomeini and brother-in-law of Ali Khamenei) supported Bani-Sadr at the time of the confrontation in March 1981; Ayatollah Mohammad Taqi Alemi supported him in June – both left Iran after Bani-Sadr fell from power. He had support from other clerics too – his newspaper reported a (somewhat exaggerated) statement from Khomeini's grandson Seyyed Hosein Khomeini in March 1981 that 90 per cent of clerics favoured

Bani-Sadr, but could not make their views felt because they were not part of the political sphere. Khomeini and Beheshti made dark threats over this period against dissenting clerics.[67]

It would have helped also if Bani-Sadr had built up or taken over some kind of party base for himself – as a lone warrior he was too vulnerable. Whether or not he would have agreed with Bani-Sadr's characterization of him as a kind of anti-democratic philosopher-prince along the lines of Plato, Khomeini was no fool. He was aware of the dangers for the clergy in being seen to govern alone – the risk that the clergy would be discredited by the dirtiness of politics. Bani-Sadr could have been useful to him; he was reluctant to see him thrown to the wolves, and there is good reason to believe that his effort to work in partnership with him (albeit with the president as very much the junior partner) was genuine.

In addition, the class dimension of the clash between the IRP and Bani-Sadr was apparent in his last days, and important. His jibes at the ignorance of the IRP leaders and their accusations of arrogance against him reflected this; and wider attitudes in society more generally. If Bani-Sadr had been a little more patient and measured, he could have developed and made more use of his support among the educated middle class. There was a division between his view of politics – the liberal view, albeit in an Islamic and highly individual Bani-Sadr form – and that of Khomeini. Khomeini's desire to govern in partnership with Bani-Sadr was also, in part, a recognition of the political importance of the liberal middle class. Politics is partly about the creation of coalitions to bridge such divisions – and wider ones have been bridged successfully. Bani-Sadr was about to enter into an alliance with the MKO: an association requiring at least as much compromise – or abandonment of principle – as that with Khomeini.

Internal Strife and Revolutionary Terror

Bani-Sadr went into hiding, latterly with the MKO leader Masud Rajavi, and in July left Iran with Rajavi to go into exile in Paris (flown out of the country by the same pilot who had performed that service for the Shah, Colonel Behzad Moezi). In Paris he struck up a formal alliance with the MKO under the umbrella of what was called the National Council of Resistance, but it did not last long. Bani-Sadr found he could not live with the inherently undemocratic, if not anti-democratic, values and modes of action of the MKO, and went his own way in 1984 (his daughter had married Rajavi in October 1982, but the marriage did not long survive her father's political divorce).[68] He still lives in Paris at the time of writing. The clashes on the streets of Tehran between the MKO and the supporters of the IRP had got worse through May and June 1981, but the IRP leadership had reason to think that they had, with the removal of Bani-Sadr, successfully crippled the opposition to them and reconfirmed their dominance.

That belief proved premature. On 28 June, only a week after the vote in the Majles to remove Bani-Sadr, a huge bomb blew up the IRP headquarters building, collapsing the roof of the main hall while almost the entire leadership were there to discuss the direction they should take after Bani-Sadr's departure. Over seventy died, including twenty-seven Majles deputies. Of those killed, Beheshti was the most prominent; he had been speaking as chairman when the bomb went off. Rafsanjani and Rajai had left the assembly hall just a few minutes before. Montazeri's son Mohammad was among the dead. The MKO never admitted responsibility directly, but the attack seemed to be part of an MKO campaign that included a bombing in Qom a few days before, the assassination of the governor of Evin prison three days later, the murder of IRP radical Hassan Ayat on 5 August and the wounding of Ali Khamenei at a press conference by a bomb concealed in a tape recorder on 27 June.[69] It fitted also with Masud Rajavi's earlier declaration of armed resistance.

Rajai was elected president to succeed Bani-Sadr and took office on 2 August. Rajai got 88 per cent of the poll, better than Bani-Sadr had achieved in January 1980 (at 69 per cent of voters, the turnout was about the same). This was a rebuke to Bani-Sadr, who had called on voters to abstain. Rajai appointed Mohammad Javad Bahonar as prime minister. But he was not to hold the post for long: on 30 August Rajai and Bahonar were killed by an incendiary bomb, along with the chief of national police, at a meeting of the National Security Council that had been called to discuss the threat from terrorism. This time Rajavi, in Paris, claimed responsibility on behalf of the MKO/NCRI. Khomeini declared four days of mourning.[70]

A week later, another bomb killed the revolutionary prosecutor-general, Ayatollah Ali Qoddusi. The regime called victims who survived attacks, like Khamenei and Rafsanjani, *shahid-e zendeh* – living martyrs; because the bomb that killed Qoddusi had blown him out of an upper-storey window, others with black humour called him *shahid-e parandeh* – the flying martyr.

The bombs and assassinations had achieved almost a clean sweep of the regime's senior office-holders and the IRP leadership. The loss of Beheshti, who had dominated discussion of the constitution and had been probably the most influential personality among Khomeini's followers, was particularly grave. It was another caesura in the history of the Islamic republic, and brought personalities into the front rank who might otherwise have stayed in the background.

Initially Khomeini called for restraint in the response to the MKO onslaught, but after another serious outbreak of street fighting on 2 September, a week later he called for stronger measures against them. He called them *monafeqin* (hypocrites – a Koranic term that had become the standard way for the regime to refer to the MKO; originally it had been applied to those Medinans who had secretly allied themselves with the Meccans against the Prophet).

The IRP response to the killings was harsh – the activity of the revolutionary courts, the number of arrests and executions was stepped up. The war with Iraq and the internal war with the MKO created an atmosphere of fear, uncertainty and paranoia which (as in the bloodiest phases of the French revolution) both fed and, for some, excused the severity of the reaction. There were more and more armed confrontations on the streets between Sepah and MKO fighters. Thousands were killed – Amnesty International afterwards counted 2,946 executions in the year after Bani-Sadr's removal from the presidency. The MKO themselves gave 7,746 deaths from executions, deaths under torture in prison and deaths in street battles between June 1981 and September 1983, 90 per cent of whom were connected with the MKO. It became a struggle to the death between the two movements – the greatest internal challenge Khomeini and his followers had faced since the fall of the Shah. The internal organization, discipline and ruthlessness of the MKO made them formidable – in some ways a mirror image of the IRP themselves. But again, it was an unequal struggle. The MKO, like the other groups opposed to Khomeini, fought their battle against him and his followers on their own (albeit with some support from the Fedayan, the Kurds and some other leftist groups smaller than themselves) and suffered from that isolation. Their ideology led them to believe that they would gain momentum and broaden their mass support to include all classes of society. But that never happened.

The MKO leadership's next objective was to disrupt the new elections for the presidency that took place on 2 October. After nearly a month of disorder, on 27 September there were another seven hours of bloodshed around the campus of Tehran University and central Tehran generally. The election went ahead anyway, yielding an even higher figure for turn-out – 80 per cent – than the one that had elected Rajai two months before. Hojjatoleslam Ali Khamenei won the vote overwhelmingly with about 95 per cent of the poll – over 16 million votes.[71]

Khamenei and Musavi

Khamenei was born in 1939. His family, another family of clerics, came originally from Azerbaijan, but he was brought up in Mashhad. He studied in Najaf, and then in Qom, with Khomeini. He was involved in the insurrection of 1963, and then returned to Mashhad when Khomeini went into exile. He was arrested and imprisoned several times in the 1960s and 70s. Khamenei was involved in literary societies, translated works from Arabic into Persian and wrote his own books on religious subjects, but he was never considered to be a distinguished religious scholar. He was active in 1978–9 and was a favourite with Khomeini, who called him 'Ali Agha' as a term of affection. After Beheshti was killed he was made general secretary of the IRP, despite having been injured himself by a bomb the day before. That wound left him with a permanent disability to his right arm.[72]

Initially Khamenei tried to appoint his close associate Ali Akbar Velayati as prime minister, but the Majles took the opportunity to remind the new president of their powers in the matter and vetoed the appointment. They accepted his second choice, Mir Hosein Musavi, on 28 October. Musavi was thirty-nine years old in 1981 – he too had been imprisoned in the time of the Shah and had lived outside Iran for a period in the 1970s thereafter, studying interior design in London. He was born and brought up in Khameneh in Azerbaijan – the same place that Khamenei's family came from (in fact the two were distantly related). He qualified as an architect at the National University of Tehran with a masters degree in 1969, where he met and married Zahra Rahnavard, who later became an important figure in the intellectual and political life of Iran in her own right (indeed somewhat more important than Musavi himself in his wilderness period between 1989 and 2009). He also attended Shariati's lectures at the Hoseiniyeh Ershad and was associated with Bazargan's Freedom Movement. After the revolution he was editor of the IRP newspaper *Jomhuri-ye Eslami* and gained a reputation as a radical. He had been a strong critic of Bani-Sadr through the period of his presidency. He wasted little time as prime minister before he began new, tough purges of the civil service, aimed at removing leftists, including members of Tudeh. In the economic questions that were rising up the political agenda at this time he was on the left of the IRP, favouring extensive nationalization, greater state control of the economy and redistribution of wealth.[73]

The new Iranian leadership faced a daunting series of critical problems. Not only were large slices of Iranian territory occupied by the Iraqis; the Sepah were still fighting the Kurds in the north-west, and the struggle with the MKO in Tehran and elsewhere had almost the character of a civil war. In addition, the country was in financial crisis because of a fall in oil revenue and the consequences of previous ill-advised fiscal and currency exchange decisions. To fight the war, Iran desperately needed to import weapons and spares for weapons, but was short of money and short of friends willing to supply war materials. In the crisis atmosphere of the autumn of 1981 it would have seemed foolhardy to predict it, but unlike their immediate predecessors, these new office-holders were going to last much longer – indeed the combination of Khomeini, Khamenei and Musavi would last nearly eight years, until the summer of 1989.

Human Wave

Until September, when the Iraqis were forced out of Abadan in some disorder after some clever manoeuvring by the Iranians that encouraged them to weaken their defences, the war fronts had been generally quiet, with occasional artillery shelling of each side's entrenched positions. But the Iraqi withdrawal from Abadan, as well as encouraging the Iranian military and people, meant that the roads around Abadan became free again for the movement of troops and supplies, creating possibilities for new Iranian offensives.[74]

Despite the onset of the rainy season, the Iranians launched a surprise offensive on 29 November from Susangerd, north-westward toward Bostan. About 13,000 Iranian troops took part; more than a third of them were Sepah, and this was the first time that what became known as 'human wave' attacks were used. Despite rain and mud, Sepah troops surged forward so enthusiastically that regular commanders had to abandon their plan for a preparatory artillery barrage for fear of hitting their own people. Bostan was recaptured and the Iraqis retreated several miles back towards the border. The Iranians carried out a further successful operation (al-Fajr – 'Dawn') in December near Qasr-e Shirin, recovering more territory.[75]

By mid-March the Iranians had built up the strength of their forces in the area around Dezful and Shush to somewhere around 100,000, including 40,000 Sepah and 30,000 Basij volunteers – the latter mainly young, with only rudimentary training and some unarmed, or carrying Kalashnikov assault rifles captured from the Iraqis. On 22 March they attacked in the first phase of what was called Operation Fatah or Fath ol-Mobin (Victory), initially with waves of Sepah and Basij armed with rocket-propelled grenades and rifles, following up with regular troops, targeting Iraqi conscript units first where possible, to try to force them back and expose the flanks of more experienced troop formations. Before the main ground forces went in, commando troops were carried behind the Iraqi lines by Chinook helicopters to destroy Iraqi artillery. The Iranians suffered heavy casualties but their tactics were successful, pushing the Iraqis back and beginning to encircle them. Iraqi air strikes had some success in stemming the Iranian advance in one area, around Chenaneh, but large numbers of Iranian F-4s and F-5s, plus helicopter gunships, were also in action against Iraqi tanks and troops. The Iranian offensive lasted a week, and by the time it ended more than 300 Iraqi tanks and other armoured vehicles had been destroyed, and a similar or larger number had been captured, along with more than 15,000 Iraqi prisoners. When the Iraqis managed to stabilize their front by bringing in reinforcements, their positions were back within 5–10 miles of the border.[76]

Some of the Basij volunteers that fought in the war were thirteen or even younger (though there were also older men, in their sixties and seventies) and some of them lied about their age to be allowed up to the front with their friends. One spoke to an aid worker in an Iraqi prisoner-of-war camp after he had been captured about his motive for joining up:

> I am not very religious so I don't know much about the subject. It's true that martyrdom is important to Shi'ites – we all learn about the Emams and how they died – but I didn't go to war to die for Islam. I went to defend Iran and I think most of my friends went for the same reason.[77]

Another boy, asked a similar question, gave a more conventional religious answer, talking about martyrdom and dying for Islam, but even he put that reason second, saying first: 'All Iranians came to war to defend their country from the Iraqi invasion. That is a normal thing to do. I think British people did the same in the Second World War against Germany.'[78]

This is another misunderstanding – or failure of understanding – about the Iran–Iraq War. A lot was written at the time about the so-called fanaticism of the Iranian human wave attacks, about the way the Iranians were whipped into a frenzy by the mullahs, about young men anxious to be martyrs, and so on. But most Iranian veterans speak in this same sober way about their experience and their motivation. We should not need to displace the fact of their bravery into categories like fanaticism and martyrdom in order to comprehend it. Newsreel images from the time show soldiers being harangued by mullahs, chanting religious slogans and beating their chests rhythmically (as in the Ashura rituals), but they also show scared young men preparing for the fighting with determination despite their fear.[79] They were rather like the young men of Kitchener's army preparing for similar infantry attacks against prepared defences on the Somme in 1916 or elsewhere; with much the same patriotism and commitment to their comrades, and encouraged to volunteer by much the same wish for adventure. They were exploited in much the same way by their governments and generals, because governments and generals need naive young men and boys to fight for them – older men tend to be more cautious. Another boy said:

> It was a game for us ... We didn't understand the words 'patriotism' or 'martyrdom', or at least I didn't. It was just an exciting game and a chance

to prove to your friends that you'd grown up and were no longer a child. But we were really only children.

He was asked by the same aid worker whether it was right for Iran to use such young boys in the war:

I am not sure, but it was difficult to stop them. And anyway, the boys who attacked the Iraqis were a very important weapon for the army, because they had no fear. We captured many positions from the Iraqis because they became afraid when they saw young boys running towards them shouting and screaming. Imagine how you would feel. Lots of boys were killed, but by that stage you were running and couldn't stop, so you just carried on until you were shot yourself or reached the lines.[80]

Another, interviewed separately, years later, recalled his time as a prisoner in Mosul in 1985–6:

When the war started I was sixteen years old. I gave up school and studying and went to the front, but I didn't last long and after less than six months I was captured. I was there in the camp without anything to do, so started studying. We didn't have any books – just an English dictionary which was passed around between at least twenty people, and this was the way all of us learned English. I remember that on any given day I could only use the dictionary for an hour – it was torn badly and the pages were in the wrong order. One day, I will never forget, the United Nations Red Cross staff came and asked me what I needed – I replied, a dictionary. But I realized I could only use this dictionary for an hour a day, so another idea occurred to me – to start chatting with the Iraqi guards and learn Arabic. Now, since my release, I can speak English, Arabic and some French.[81]

The commander in Operation Fatah was a young regular army officer who had been promoted recently to chief of staff – General Ali Sayad Shirazi. Shirazi had proved his revolutionary credentials by demonstrating against the Shah, and being demoted and imprisoned before the revolution, and so despite his youth was a natural choice for the revolutionary leadership at a time when they distrusted senior officers who had been promoted by the Shah. Sayad Shirazi was a talented commander and proved his abilities in several later battles also, bridging the gap between the regulars and the Sepah and coordinating their efforts to enable them to make effective attacks together.

The outcome of Operation Fatah was an important encouragement to the Iranians, and appeared to endorse their tactical innovations – particularly the human wave attacks favoured by the Sepah and Basij. A little more than a month later, on 30 April, a further offensive (codenamed Qods/Beit al-Moqaddas – Jerusalem) using similar tactics began, this time towards Shalamcheh. Despite Iraqi counter-attacks the Iranians were successful, and Saddam was again forced to withdraw troops rather than see them encircled and cut off. The Iranians reached Shalamcheh on 9 May – one effect was to put greater pressure on the Iraqi garrison of Khorramshahr, to the south. In the second phase, the Iranians attacked Khorramshahr itself on the night of 22–3 May and within a day had retaken the city, capturing 12,000 Iraqis.[82]

The recapture of Khorramshahr was a major morale victory for the Iranian military and the Iranian people, as its loss had been a humiliation. For Iraq, following on from the previous defeats, it was a moment of crisis – there was unrest and rioting in several Shi'a-dominated towns and cities in southern Iraq. Many observers, within and beyond the region, expected that Saddam would be replaced as Iraqi leader. Instead, Saddam intensified the repression of Shi'a dissidents, reshuffled the top leadership in the country under him (to include more Shi'as, among other changes), offered peace again to Iran, and on 20 June began a withdrawal to the pre-war borders. The withdrawal was completed by the end of the month, but despite Saddam's announcements the Iraqis stayed in occupation of some Iranian territory. Saddam may also, as a provocation, have ordered the assassination of the Israeli ambassador in London, Shlomo Argov. Argov was shot in the head and permanently paralysed on 3 June 1982; the assassins belonged to Abu Nidal's organization, which had split from Yasser Arafat's PLO in 1974 – but one of them was also a colonel in Iraqi intelligence.[83] Although the main, more deep-seated reasons for the invasion were a more important motivation (principally, the desire to remove the PLO from Lebanon), the assassination attempt was used by Israel to justify its invasion of Lebanon on 6 June. When Saddam offered peace again at the end of June, in parallel with the withdrawal to the pre-war borders, he also suggested that this be done so that both Iran and Iraq could use their forces against the Israeli invasion of Lebanon.

Iran and Lebanon

Because Lebanon had been home to a large Shi'a minority for centuries, there was a longstanding connection between Lebanon and Iran. In general the Shi'as of Lebanon were a downtrodden group, who had traditionally been pushed aside by more politically dominant Sunnis and Christians (the relative size of minorities in Lebanon is disputed and controversial, but the Shi'a are believed to make up around 28 per cent of the population).[84] This made them receptive to the revolutionary Shi'ism of the Iranians after the revolution of 1979. There had been contacts early on between Iranian revolutionaries and members of the Lebanese Shi'a community, and Ayatollah Montazeri, who at the time was one of the principal advocates for the establishment of Islamic governments elsewhere in the Islamic world, devoted special attention to Lebanon, coming into conflict with Bazargan's Provisional Government over it. It was in these early months that Montazeri's close associate Mehdi Hashemi, who was a violent radical and had been arrested by SAVAK for murder before the revolution (including for the murder of a cleric who had insulted Montazeri, as well as the killing of prostitutes and drug-dealers),[85] set up a group within the Sepah for the support of Islamic liberation movements outside Iran. Even before 1982, there was tension between Montazeri and others in the leadership over these activities, as Montazeri and Mehdi Hashemi tried to prevent others from making contacts in the countries involved, especially Lebanon. One of their prime opponents was Mostafa Chamran, who had longstanding connections with members of the Shi'a Amal organization in Lebanon, was appointed by Khomeini to a position in the Sepah and became defence minister before being killed in circumstances that have been called suspicious near the war front in June 1981.

The secrecy of the contacts compounds the factional conflicts in both countries in making it difficult to know what happened in detail. But it is known that only six days after the Israeli invasion in June 1982 a large number of Sepah fighters and regular troops (some of them fresh from the fighting in Khorramshahr) were flown into Lebanon. Many of them went home soon after, but more than a thousand stayed on in the Bekaa valley to train Lebanese fighters, who later became the original core of Lebanese Hezbollah. Ali Akbar Mohtashemi, who had been close to Khomeini in the period of his exile in Najaf, was particularly important in the earliest phases of the establishment of Lebanese Hezbollah (from his base in Damascus)[86] and continued to have an interest in Lebanese affairs for some years afterwards. Mohtashemi had visited Lebanon in the 1970s, when Beirut in its heyday had been called the Switzerland of the Middle East:

> One can see numerous centres of prostitution, cabarets, wine shops, dance halls, theatres and cinemas showing degenerate programmes and films, and sexy publications. It is a society totally alienated from Islamic and even Eastern culture and customs, and it wallows in the corrupt culture of the West.[87]

After the expulsion of the PLO from Lebanon by the Israelis, some Shi'as who had been active with the PLO gravitated toward the Sepah camp. One of them was Imad Mughniyyah, who later set up Islamic Jihad (always closely connected with Hezbollah – some have suggested that they were always effectively one and the same). Under Iranian influence and with advice from Khomeini and others in Tehran, a Council of Lebanon formed in the latter part of 1982 and early 1983, which went on to create Lebanese Hezbollah. Most of the early members were Lebanese Shi'as from the Bekaa valley.[88]

Islamic Jihad were responsible for two huge suicide bombings in Beirut in April and October 1983, wrecking the US embassy and two barracks near the airport respectively. Sixty-three died at the embassy and nearly 300 at the barracks, which had been occupied by US Marines and French paratroopers. The incidents followed a series of developments in which, after the foreign peacekeeping troops had been welcomed initially, feeling turned against them when US warships fired on positions inland in support of the Lebanese army. After the barracks bombings, the US and other international peacekeeping troops pulled out of Lebanon. In November, the Israeli military headquarters in Tyre was hit by a suicide bomb, killing twenty-eight Israelis. The Israelis hit the Iranian base in the Bekaa in retaliation, killing twenty-three Sepah.[89]

These are the main incidents of suicide attacks that have been seriously connected with Iran.[90] Despite the link that is frequently drawn between Iran and terrorism, even with these attacks the question of Iranian connection or direction is unclear, involving the ambiguity of the Iranian relationship with Hezbollah. The attacks seem to be related to an early phase of zeal around the formation of Hezbollah and Islamic Jihad, at a time when Iran was at war with Iraq (and blaming the US for it) and when the US appeared to be intervening beyond its original mandate in the increasingly bitter Lebanese civil war (the massacres in the Palestinian refugee camps of Sabra and Shatila took place in September 1982). Iranian clerics since that time have outlawed suicide attacks, and in more recent years it has been a characteristic tactic of Sunni terrorist groups. But Iran was blamed, at the time and since, and the incidents added to the bitterness between Iran and the US (and Iran and Israel). Imad Mughniyya's people were later implicated in the taking of Western hostages in Beirut.

Internal Strife, Another Plot

Although the struggle against the MKO continued into 1983, the most intense period of urban guerrilla activity and repressive terror by the regime in response was over by the spring of 1982. On 8 February a raid by the Sepah on a house in Tehran resulted in the deaths of Musa Khiabani (the top MKO leader in Iran after Rajavi's departure to Paris) and nine other members of the MKO central committee. The MKO regrouped after this blow, and there were further bombings and attacks in May and afterwards, but thereafter the regime and the IRP had the upper hand. By September Rafsanjani was claiming that they had taken enough MKO safe houses to make up a city, and enough weapons to arm several divisions. As time went on it became clear that the MKO would not win over mass support beyond that which it had achieved by 1980–81, and that most Iranians regarded their activity as a damaging distraction from the main threat, from Iraq.[91] The MKO survived, but many of its core supporters went into exile. Some joined the Kurdish revolt. Other leftist groups that had risen against the regime with the MKO in the summer of 1981 were effectively wiped out.

Some of the groups opposed to the IRP, notably those who were followers of Bazargan and Bani-Sadr, failed and were pushed out of power at least partly because they had scruples – they were not ruthless enough. With the MKO, this was not the case. They showed in 1981 that they were at least as ruthless as the IRP, but they lost because they did not have the organizational depth and the mass support that the IRP and

Khomeini could draw upon. Whereas liberal politicians like Bazargan represented the older members of the educated middle classes, the MKO and the Fedayan were the natural allegiance of their more radical sons and daughters. Of all the opposition groups, they perhaps came closest to dislodging the IRP. But if they had succeeded, would they have done any better? Their record in 1981, and since, suggests not. In fact, it is likely that they would have been rather worse. Like other ruthless revolutionary organizations, they were driven by the need to acquire power, and every other value, whether it be liberty, truth or anything else, was subordinated to that.

When it comes to propaganda, the MKO have proved themselves particularly egregious. Like some other leftists of their generation their political analysis told them that all politicians lie and that all politics (except their own) was false consciousness; they seem therefore to have made it a dictum that it was necessary to lie in order to persuade, to be cleverer than their enemies and to take power. But in exile they reached the point in their propaganda that lying was not just a necessity, but a virtue; deception was a sign of seriousness, and honesty or an attachment to the truth was foolishly naive. As with individuals, so with politicians and political groups – deception, concealment and manipulation only work for a limited period. In that period the liar may acquire a sense of power – even omnipotence – that makes the habit difficult to kick thereafter. But that sense of power is dangerous, leads the liars to overreach themselves, proves delusory and ultimately childish. Once the deceived notice the deception, the liars are no longer taken seriously, even when they try to tell the truth, and they might as well give up the game altogether. In exile, the MKO took this phenomenon off down a particularly extreme and deranged cul-de-sac.

Although the fortunes of the MKO faded, the regime was still jumpy about other internal threats. In April 1982 Sadegh Qotbzadeh, who had accompanied Khomeini during his time in Paris in 1978–9 and had served as foreign minister under Bani-Sadr in the first part of 1980, attempting to negotiate toward the release of the hostages, was arrested on a charge of plotting to assassinate Khomeini and to overthrow the Islamic republic. He denied intentions against Khomeini's life, but admitted attempting to change the government. Others were implicated in the conspiracy, including (once again) officers in the armed forces, but also clerics. A total of 170 people were arrested, including 70 officers, who were tried secretly. Qotbzadeh was executed on 15 September 1982 in Evin prison, after a trial that was partly televised.

But Qotbzadeh also implicated Ayatollah Shariatmadari, saying that he had known of the coup attempt and had given it his blessing. Evidence purporting to come from documents captured in the US embassy was brought forward to show that Shariatmadari had been equivocal in his support for the revolution in 1978; in fact he was to be punished for his resistance to the IRP and the new constitution at the end of 1979. He was put under house arrest and also had to make a televised confession. Later an announcement was made that his status as *marja-e taqlid* had been removed – an unprecedented act in Shi'a Islam, and in traditional terms, impossible. Other non-IRP clergy were scandalized, but kept quiet, as did Shariatmadari's former core supporters in Azerbaijan. The incident demonstrated the extent to which Shi'ism in Iran had been politicized – that is, the degree to which Shi'a traditions and precepts had already been subordinated to the interests of Khomeini and the IRP as a political movement.[92]

The Choice

The Iraqi withdrawal from Iranian territory at the end of June 1982 presented the Iranian leadership with a choice. Up to this point, Khomeini had rejected calls for peace, insisting reasonably that there could be no ceasefire until all Iraqi forces had left Iranian territory. But now he and the rest of the leadership had to choose whether to seek peace, or continue the war. Should they insist that Saddam be removed? Should they keep fighting and keep up the pressure on the Iraqis so that someone, by one means or another, would remove him? There was an attempt on Saddam's life, the latest in a long series, on 11 July – the would-be killers attacked his motorcade with machine-guns and rocket-propelled grenades, killing ten of his bodyguards; but Saddam was unhurt, and 150 people were killed in reprisals in the town where the attack took place. Or should the Iranians, as they had been saying in their propaganda for some time, push on to Najaf and Karbala, the holy places of Shi'a Islam, and liberate the Iraqi Shi'as? After all, the élan of the Sepah seemed to have carried all before them in the latest battles. The godless

Baathist regime and its army had been humiliated, and had retreated in some disarray. It might be about to collapse.

In these discussions, initially at least, it seems Khomeini himself did not want to pursue the war further into Iraq. Again rather contrary to the impression many have of him as an autocrat and a dominant personality, he did not always feel the need to assert his own line. Often, and especially on what he regarded as questions with a significant technical element, he was content to seek the opinion of others and reach a collective decision. At an earlier point he had urged clerics not to interfere in the conduct of the war: he seems to have been reluctant to direct military decisions on his own judgement alone.

After the end of the war in 1988, the question of responsibility for the continuation of the war became controversial, and a demonstration of the saying that although success has many fathers, failure is an orphan. In interviews, Rafsanjani indicated that he was against continuation of the war in 1982, and that Khomeini himself was against taking the war into Iraqi territory. Khomeini had apparently argued that offensives on to Iraqi territory would turn ordinary Iraqis, other Arab states and international opinion against Iran. Khomeini's son Ahmad suggested that his father had argued for ending the war, and Montazeri's memoirs supported the same view. But there is reason to be sceptical that Montazeri himself opposed continuing the war at the time, and Akbar Ganji later (in 2000) accused Rafsanjani of having supported continuation of the war. It seems fairly plain that the main advocates for offensives into Iraq were military commanders (in particular at a meeting held between them and Khomeini on 10 June 1982) – notably Sepah commanders and perhaps especially Mohsen Rezai, which may be a partial explanation for his contrition and Khomeini's anger toward him in 1988.[93]

From the account given in Rafsanjani's memoirs, it seems that at the crucial 10 June meeting of the Supreme Defence Council Khomeini was against an invasion of Iraqi territory, but in favour of continuing the war (discussion of these matters may have been coloured by reports earlier in the day, refuted by the end of it, that Saddam had been assassinated). When army commanders argued that it was not possible to do the latter without the former, Khomeini acquiesced in allowing troop movements on to Iraqi soil:

The Emam was emphatic about continuation of the war and he would not allow any kind of discussion that might lead to doubt among the people or the armed forces. War aims should be presented in such a way as to prepare the people for a long war. And in addition he could not accept that Iranian forces should occupy Iraqi territory. In the evening meeting, in the Emam's presence [and with Rafsanjani also present] the military commanders discussed the matter with the Emam from their professional viewpoint and convinced him that it was not possible to continue the war without entering Iraqi territory. The enemy was still present on Iranian soil in many places. If they were to realize that our forces would not enter even a small part of Iraqi territory, and if they never abandoned those key strongpoints and avoided giving us any advantage, then they could advance into our territory again whenever they wished. For these reasons, the Emam agreed that Iranian forces could enter Iraqi territory, but he ordered that they must aim to move into less populated areas where there would be less risk to the Iraqi population.[94]

A few days later, on 22 June, Rafsanjani was told that Montazeri had said 'the scent of dollars came to the nose of the authorities and they want to finish the war' – but Rafsanjani believed Montazeri knew Khomeini's mind on the matter and did not credit the report, speculating that one of Montazeri's associates had spoken out of turn.[95]

One could look at the decision to continue the war and see it as unduly aggressive, vengeful, and as evidence of Iranian intentions to export revolution. The last-mentioned is really a separate matter – we have seen that there is evidence in Iranian rhetoric and in the beliefs of some that the revolution should be expanded and spread to other Muslim countries. Aside from such considerations (and aside from the question of whether it was, with hindsight, the wise or overall correct decision), were there legitimate reasons for Iran to continue the war?

One reason to do so would have been a judgement that it was necessary for Iran's security to remove Saddam Hussein. The need to remove Saddam was, in fact, the reason most frequently given by Iranian leaders for continuing the war. Given Saddam's attack in 1980, the view that Iran would not be safe while he was still in power carried some weight. The judgement that Saddam was inherently untrustworthy, given to military adventures, unprincipled and disposed to using the most extreme measures in pursuit of his ends was, after all, effectively the same judgement that the US and the UK reached somewhat later, in 2002-3, when they finally decided to invade and remove him after nearly a decade of failed attempts to get him to abide by the commitments he made after their previous war with him in 1991.

With hindsight, it probably was a mistake for Iran to continue the war in 1982-3. But if so, that is because the Iranian leadership made a misjudgement about the difficulty of removing Saddam, and the cost in lives and material. In the circumstances, the objective of removing Saddam was justified.

At any rate, by about 20 June 1982 the choice was made, and a number of statements made plain over the next few weeks that the war would continue. On 12 July a statement from the Sepah announced that a 'Grand, historic battle' was imminent: 'Now is the time for Saddam to be toppled and his Baath regime to die, so that the warmonger may be destroyed and the war may be ended.'[96] Rafsanjani's memoirs say that the possibility of ending the war was discussed again in September and October, but although Khomeini was prepared to accept a ceasefire, Sepah and army commanders insisted on continuing the struggle. On the former occasion, at a meeting of the Supreme Defence Council, the commanders asked for more time to prepare the next offensive: 'But we said that if they needed so much time, it would be better to end the war. The country cannot bear such a prolonged war. Discussion became very heated.'[97] But in the end the decision to continue the war stood.

In accordance with the decision to carry the war into Iraq, the Iranians launched a major offensive – Operation Ramadan – across the border in the direction of Basra on 13 July 1982 (the fasting month of Ramadan ended that year on 16 July). Despite in-depth Iraqi defences incorporating barbed wire, minefields, bunkers and entrenchments, and despite a lack of tanks and artillery, the Iranians broke through and advanced ten miles; but then a counter-attack by Iraqi reserves against the Iranians' flanks threw them back. Casualties were high on both sides. Further assaults on 22 and 28 July were also frustrated, with more heavy losses – it was estimated that over the three weeks of the offensive the Iranians lost 1,000 killed, wounded or captured each day. The Iraqis used gas for the first time – albeit non-lethal tear gas – and it was effective in disrupting Iranian attacks, prompting the use of deadly mustard and nerve gas agents later in the war. Despite earlier unrest in Iraq, and despite the exhortations of the Iranian clerics, the Iranian move into Iraqi territory did not inspire Shi'a Iraqis to revolt against Saddam. Rather the contrary – defending their own soil, the resolve of the Iraqi troops, including the Shi'as, stiffened. At the same time, many volunteers on the Iranian side, who had taken up arms to expel the Iraqis from Iran, left military service once that goal had been substantially achieved.[98]

With Iran moving on to the offensive in the war and with pressure on the Da'wa Party within Iraq increasing, Da'wa followers and others who had sought refuge in Iran set up an umbrella body in Iran in November 1982 which was called the Supreme Council for the Islamic Revolution in Iraq – SCIRI. But whereas Da'wa, following the line of Baqr al-Sadr, had been more independent of Iran, SCIRI took a more openly pro-Iranian position, favouring the establishment within Iraq of an Iranian-style revolutionary Shi'a government.[99] Over time it evolved to become an Iraqi government in waiting, backed by the Iranian regime. After the fall of Saddam in 2003, SCIRI took a strong position in Iraq, establishing an armed wing, the Badr brigade. It also sought to distance itself somewhat from Iran, emphasizing its commitment to democratic politics and changing its name in 2007 to the Supreme Islamic Iraqi Council.

Operation Ramadan established a pattern for much of the rest of the war. Saddam favoured a defensive posture for the Iraqi forces, partly because he wanted to avoid heavy casualties that might have rekindled dissent among his Shi'a troops. He was no longer seeking to force the Iranians into surrender or peace through offensive operations – his aim was rather merely to survive, and to wear down the enemy by attrition. He relied on well-prepared defences, backed up by armoured formations to nip off any breakthroughs the Iranians might make. The Iranians relied on masses of enthusiastic infantry to make breakthroughs, which they often did – but lacking adequate artillery or tank support they suffered heavy casualties and were often unable to hold the ground taken against counter-attacks. The impasse, and the superiority of the defensive, again paralleled the First World War on the western front. Since 1918, military tactics and technology had evolved to break the grip of the defensive principle and re-establish offensive, mobile warfare – primarily through the use of massed tank formations and ground-attack strikes by aircraft. But both Iran and Iraq, for different reasons, were reluctant or unable to use those options, at least not to their full, decisive potential. The outcome was a dreadful, drawn-out war of terrible conditions, terrible waste of human life, and a terrible, crippled failure to win decisive results.

The Iranians launched further offensives in October, in the direction of Mandali, on the way to Baghdad; but again successes that the Iranians made were contained by Iraqi counter-attacks. The Iraqis responded also with Scud missiles fired at Iranian cities; another aspect of the war that was to repeat itself and become a recurrent feature. Khomeini repeated his requirement for peace – that Saddam must go: Saddam responded with massive demonstrations in his support in the streets of Baghdad, and claimed that Khomeini's real objective was to conquer and occupy Iraq.[100]

By the end of the year Khomeini was confident enough that the MKO had been beaten that he issued a decree (on 15 December) which aimed to bring revolutionary courts, *komiteh* and Sepah under control, restraining previous arbitrary and violent behaviour. Arrests and confiscations of property were in future only to be made on the basis of an order from a properly appointed judge. The decree also stated that homes and privately owned business should be safe from entry by others without the permission of the owner, and that eavesdropping and telephone tapping would not be permitted, except in very limited circumstances, and (again) by order of a judge. The decree also included a reference to what were called past mistakes, suggesting that the authorities would only consider present behaviour and would from now on disregard what might or might not have been done in the time of the Shah.

Some Iranians, both within Iran and in exile, were doubtful about the decree, suspecting that it might be a ruse to give dissidents a false sense of security, and to draw back exiles so that they could be arrested. But Khomeini followed up with measures to ensure that the decree was enforced. Former revolutionary prosecutors were dismissed on grounds of abuse of power. Committees were set up to hear grievances, and a new Headquarters for the Implementation of the Emam's Decree. Intrusive and aggressive vetting for government job applications was curtailed. The aim was to reassure middle-class Iranians, and to invite some of them who had left to return to Iran and help the war effort. It was successful in restoring a more relaxed, normal atmosphere, but relatively few of those who had emigrated did return.[101]

By this time Iraq was having more success than Iran in securing weapons imports. France was supplying Saddam with AMX-30 tanks as well as F-1 Mirage fighters and R-550 Matra Magic air-to-air missiles (the Iraqi air force was also able to use these with its existing stock of Soviet-built MiG aircraft). The R-550 was the French counterpart to the US Sidewinder and significantly improved the interceptor capability of the Iraqi fighters. After a hiatus, Iraq was again receiving Soviet equipment and spares, and the new, fast, high-flying MiG-25s. As the IRP's relationship with the Tudeh Party worsened, Soviet arms supplies to the Iranians dried up. But after a long period of frustrating delay, the Iranians succeeded in 1982 in mastering the Peace Log computer system that controlled the vast inventory of spares for US-built aircraft and other military equipment that had been purchased by the Shah, easing some of their repair and maintenance problems. They also managed to bring back into production an arms factory that had been set up in the time of the Shah to produce weapons to Soviet patterns, including surface-to-air missiles and AK-47 Kalashnikov assault rifles.[102] As the war went on, Iran's ability to produce weapons domestically developed and matured.

Iran's success in the campaigns of early 1982 and the subsequent incursions into Iraq had worried many neighbouring Arab states and had stimulated many of them to increase their support for Iraq. Egypt and Jordan had even discussed the possibility of sending units to fight at the front on the Iraqi side. But Syria went the other way, ending the transit of Iraqi oil, and taking in Iranian crude for refining in Syria instead. Syria had been more or less hostile to Iraq since the 1960s; despite the regimes' theoretical sharing of a Baathist ideology, suspicion of each other's motives, differences over Israel and competition for pre-eminence as rivals for leadership of the Arab world proved more important. In the 1980s Syria became, and has remained, one of Iran's few dependable allies.

False Dawn

On 6 February 1983 Iran began a new offensive, codenamed Fajr (Dawn). Its objective was to capture Amara, on the Baghdad–Basra road. Rafsanjani said: 'This Fajr offensive is the final move towards ending the war, and it should determine the final destiny of the region.'[103] But it wasn't, and it didn't. There were problems of coordination between the Sepah troops and the regulars who manned the tanks of the armoured formations. On 9–10 February an armoured division achieved a break-through, but lost contact with supporting infantry as it moved forward and was destroyed by counter-attacking Iraqi tanks. Sepah troops apparently held their positions and did not move up in support. Else-where the human wave tactics were used, sometimes as diversions to draw Iraqi forces away from the true intended point of greatest pres-sure. One boy who fought in the Basij, taken prisoner at thirteen, recalled:

> After only a month's training at a camp near Khorramshahr, I was sent to the front. When we arrived we all assembled in a field where there must have been thousands of us, young boys, some younger than me, and old men as well. The commander told us we were going to attack an Iraqi position north-east of Basra which guarded the road to Qurna, to try to capture the road.
>
> The following morning we set off at 4.00 a.m. in army trucks, and I had been given a gun and two hand grenades. At the camp we'd been taught to use a Kalashnikov . . . The sun was beginning to come up as we started walk-ing towards the Iraqi lines, and boy, was I scared! . . . When we got to the top of a hill, we started running down the other side towards the enemy position. I wasn't afraid any more. We all shouted 'Allah-u-Akbar' as we ran, and I could see the soldiers in front of us – a line of helmets – then they started firing. People dropped all around me, but I kept running and shout-ing, kept going while many were being killed.
>
> By the time I reached the trenches, I'd thrown my grenades and somehow had lost my gun, but I don't remember how. Then I was hit in the leg and fell over and lay for a long time right in front of the lines.[104]

The offensive was a failure, and many Iranian troops were killed and captured. Saddam displayed 1,000 captured Iranians in a parade in Baghdad. On 14 February Rafsanjani doggedly declared that Operation Fajr would continue. In fact, over the following years there would be Operations Fajr two, three, four, five, six, seven, eight and nine in various locations along the front – another echo of First World War battles, where the tactical stalemate persisted through the first to the fifth battles of Ypres and the first to the *twelfth* battles of the Isonzo (in northern

Italy). The naming of the battles with numbers differed in the Iran–Iraq War by not being named after places or geographical features as was done in 1914–18 – but it gave the same numbing sense of repeated efforts to achieve an impossible goal. Operations Fajr-2 and Fajr-3 followed in July and August; in the north around Haj Omran and further south around Mehran, respectively. In both the Iranians made some gains, but they did not recapture Mehran.[105]

Over the course of 1983 Khomeini's attitude to the regular armed forces changed. In 1982 a new, distinct ministry for the Sepah had been set up (with Mohsen Rafiqdust as minister), and most successes in the field had been attributed to them, even when the regulars were largely responsible. But morale in the regular armed services suffered, and relations between them and the Sepah got worse. The evidence showed that low morale and inter-service rancour was having an effect on the troops' performance in battle, and in 1983 Khomeini shifted his position to give more credit to the regulars, which had a beneficial effect.[106]

In the air, the new aircraft available to the Iraqis had taken the edge off the air superiority the Iranians had initially enjoyed, but the Iraqis still had nothing that could cope with the F-14 and tended to disappear speedily if they became aware that one of them was around. The Iraqi MiG-25s were faster than the F-14 at high altitude, but the latter's sophisticated radar and Phoenix missiles compensated for the deficiency.[107] The Iranians, lacking purpose-built airborne early-warning aircraft (the Shah had ordered these from the US, but as with other orders the revolution intervened and they were never delivered), were using the F-14s as a substitute. The F-14's powerful AWG-9 radars made them suitable for this purpose, at least as an improvised stop-gap. To perform this function the F-14s would patrol for many hours – sometimes as long as twelve hours – refuelling in mid-air from tanker aircraft several times.

Historical Inevitability Has a Hiccup

By the end of 1982 the IRP had turned its attention to the Tudeh Party. Tudeh had supported the revolution and had supported the IRP against Bazargan, Bani-Sadr and the MKO. The rationale for this was that

Khomeini's revolution was, according to Marxist theory, a bourgeois revolution – and would inevitably be followed by a socialist revolution. Inevitable – well, perhaps; but it hasn't happened yet. While they were waiting, in mid-1982 a Soviet defector, Vladimir Kuzichkin, passed details of the Soviet relationship with Tudeh, and of 400 Soviet agents in Iran, to the British government. The British, happy to inflict damage on the Soviet intelligence effort, passed this information on to the Iranians. Along with the deteriorating weapons sales relationship, the evidence of spying activity and the traditional antipathy of the clerics toward the communists, this was enough to push the IRP into action against Tudeh in February 1983. There were a series of arrests and televised confessions, including by the party secretary-general, Nureddin Kianuri. The party was proscribed and in April, eighteen Soviet diplomats were declared *persona non grata* and removed from the country. The fundamental reason that the IRP turned on Tudeh was perhaps that the regime no longer needed to tolerate them; they were no longer much of a threat, but the IRP didn't need to put up with them any more, either. This was effectively the end of Tudeh; more a whimper than a bang, in keeping with their ineffectual record since 1953. Never able to emerge from under the burden of ideological theory and Soviet direction, they had lost out at every stage to political movements that were more flexible, more charismatic, more in tune with Iranian realities and less hidebound.[108]

With Tudeh gone the neutered Freedom Movement was the only remaining political grouping still permitted to operate, apart from the ruling IRP. Khomeini and the IRP had successfully used the conflict with the Kurds, the hostage crisis and the war with Iraq to destroy all political opposition.

The War in Kurdestan

The situation in Kurdestan at this time was complex. The KDP-I, led by Abdul Rahman Qasemlu, were still fighting the Sepah along with the Kumeleh and were strong in the southern part of Iranian Kurdestan. They made some gains in 1981, helped by elements from the MKO and the Fedayan, and invited Bani-Sadr to join them, but Bani-Sadr held aloof. Saddam Hussein was helping the KDP-I against the Iranians. At the same time a group of Iraqi Kurds calling themselves the Patriotic Union of Kurdestan (PUK) under Jalal Talabani were fighting Saddam's regime within Iraq – but the PUK were also fighting the Iranians alongside the KDP-I in Iran. As a counter, the Iranian regime encouraged the sons of Mulla Mostafa Barzani, Masud and Idris, to fight the KDP-I and the PUK alongside the Sepah. Mulla Mostafa Barzani was the Kurdish leader that the Shah had supported before 1975 – he had retreated to Iran when the Shah's support dried up after the Algiers Accords and had died there in 1979. So both the Iranian and the Iraqi regimes were funding Kurdish insurrections and paying Kurds to fight other Kurds. And some Kurds (the PUK) were fighting both Baghdad and Tehran, and the Barzani Kurds too. As the war continued many Kurds, unsurprisingly, grew disillusioned with their Iraqi and Iranian paymasters.

In 1982–3, sustained offensives coordinated and led by General Sayad Shirazi beat back the gains made by Qasemlu and the KDP-I. In the fighting in the Fajr-2 offensive in the summer of 1983, Barzani's followers fought the Iraqis alongside the Sepah, and some of them were resettled into villages captured from Qasemlu's supporters afterwards. In a further offensive around Penjwin in October – named Fajr-4 – the Iranians made more gains, but their troops were also targeted by the Iraqis with lethal mustard gas. By 1984 Kurds of all factions had been somewhat cowed by the full-scale offensives across their territory. The KDP-I had retreated, but Barzani and his followers were reluctant to follow up into Iraq, as the Iranian regime were urging them to do. At the same time, Talabani and the PUK had fixed up a ceasefire with Saddam Hussein.[109]

As the war went on, troops suffered terrible conditions in the ice and snow of the mountains in the northern sector of the front. This account comes from a member of the army serving near Saghez in 1985:

> In the mountains of Kurdestan in the middle of the cold weather and heavy snow, with the snow a metre and a half deep, we were patrolling to prevent any Iraqis from breaking through there. But we were sure that apart from the seven or eight of us, no one else would want to set foot in this frozen place. Snow and frost had closed all the communication routes, lack of food and fuel put us in a critical situation, and we were losing all hope, until we heard the sound of a helicopter – we thought someone must have

sent us help. We came out from under our plastic tent. Two packages were dropped – we searched through the snow and found these two parcels and brought them into our tent. We expected it would be food for us but to our surprise and disappointment it was clothes – clean underwear.[110]

The Islands of Madness

In the second part of February 1984 the Iranians launched their biggest offensive so far, in three phases – Operations Fajr-5 and -6, and Khaibar. All were aimed at cutting the highway between Baghdad and Basra – the first two aimed broadly towards the town of Kut al-Amara, and the last into the marshland further south. All told, the offensives are thought to have involved as many as 300,000 men on the Iranian side. The initial attacks achieved some gains in ground, but their main purpose was to draw Iraqi reserves away from the Howeizeh marshes, toward which the main attack began on 22 February. The Iraqis had regarded the marshes as an impassable obstacle for troop movements, but the Iranians used small boats, large numbers of helicopters and temporary bridges to swarm into them. Once there, they could fight on a more equal basis because Iraqi armour could only operate in restricted parts of the marsh region, and the Iranians could make the most of the experience they had gained with infantry assault tactics. The Iranians succeeded in taking the Majnun Islands ('Majnun' means mad or crazy) on 27 February – artificial islands in the marshes created by oil industry development – and held them despite repeated Iraqi counterattacks in the early part of March, including air attacks with mustard gas bombs, and possibly Tabun or Sarin nerve gas. They nearly took Qurna on the vital Baghdad–Basra road on 29 February. Although possession of the islands did not enable the Iranians to cut the Baghdad–Basra road as they had intended, it did bring them tantalizingly close. But the cost was heavy – one estimate suggests that 20,000 Iranians died, and 7,000 Iraqis. [111] The following accounts come from two young Basijis who were captured:

About a thousand of us came across in small rubber dinghies to attack twenty Iraqi positions in the lakes area which were easy to take. We captured the enemy troops who gave up without fighting and looked very frightened when we landed and attacked them. I think the sight of so many young boys scared them. It's true, you know, that they're afraid when they see hundreds of boys running at them. We have no fear because a ten-year-old boy doesn't understand what he's doing when he runs toward enemy soldiers. We finished the mission and were about to return to Iran when Iraqi soldiers surrounded us . . . We tried to defend ourselves to let as many of our side get away as possible. As the Iraqis closed in, I was hit in the stomach – the bullet went in one side and came out the other. I thought I was going to die. I dug with my hands into the sand bank where I was and crawled into the hole and waited. After a while I heard voices speaking Arabic coming closer and closer and then they were in front of me and one of them dropped a rock on my helmet. They pulled me out of the sand and I surrendered.

The second, from a different sector:

There were four units involved of about 300 men each. We came across in helicopters, landed and established our position. Then some Iraqi fighter planes came over and saw us, but they turned round and went back. After a while, a whole lot of Iraqi tanks drew up to within firing range and began to bombard us – for three days and nights. Out of 1,200 men, I think only thirty-four survived. A few of us got away, but not many. I was one of the unlucky ones to be captured because I wish I had died.[112]

Although the Iranians made extensive use of transport and gunship helicopters in the Khaibar offensive, stocks of other Iranian aircraft were depleted by wear and tear and losses. Nonetheless, F-4s and F-5s were making ground attack sorties, and F-14s were providing effective air cover over the Howeizeh marshes area. On 26 February, further away, a single F-14 shot down three MiG-23s. But the F-14s were spread thin: they could not provide cover continuously, and when the Iraqis found a gap the consequences could be dire. In one incident on 27 February a group of fifty Iranian transport helicopters lost eight of their number, their crews and the Sepah troops they were carrying to attacking Iraqi fighters in the Howeizeh area in just a few minutes.[113]

Warfare is of course always a dirty, shocking, miserable and disgusting business, but the use of chemical weapons makes it worse. Of the various poison gases that have been used in warfare, mustard gas is one of the most unpleasant. It penetrates clothing and is particularly active against the naturally moist parts of the body: armpits, crotch, eyes – and bronchial passages and lungs if inhaled. It is a vesicant, which means it causes blistering burns on the skin – but it takes effect only gradually, so in the initial phase, when counter-measures might be effective, the victim will probably not realize he or she has been affected. By the time the victim's skin starts to itch and form yellowish blisters it is too late to take preventive measures. The burns can be serious – as serious as conventional second- or third-degree burns – they take a long time to heal, are painful and are liable to secondary infection. If extensive over the body, they can cause death. If the lungs are affected, damage can be permanent or, again, fatal. In fatal cases the victims often take several weeks to die (by comparison nerve gases are normally faster-acting and more likely to be fatal). The chemical is carcinogenic, so even if he or she survives initially, the victim is more likely to be liable to cancer in later years – and the victims are more liable to other diseases also.[114]

The following is an account of a gas attack from Ahmad Dehqan's autobiographical novel about his war experiences, *Journey to Heading 270 Degrees*:

More bombs fall from the plane further back but do not explode. We know this because the earth doesn't shake as it did before and there are no sounds . . . There is a white cloud covering the earth up ahead and everyone has his own opinion about it.

'Chemicals.'

'No way – phosphorus. They drop it as a signal to the next planes to bomb here.'

'Wait a minute. Isn't phosphorus lighter than air? It rises, but this is spreading out over the ground.'

Men emerge from the white cloud and run away . . . all of a sudden there is a smell of garlic. Everyone shouts 'Chemicals!'

We drop frantically to the ground. Holding my breath, I put my mask over my face, tightening the straps. My heart is pounding furiously. I glance around. With their masks on, the boys look alien. Someone standing in front of me, his voice choking, says, 'Can't breathe.'

I remove the filter cover from the front of his mask. He takes a long breath . . . The cloud approaches us, then passes . . .

It feels warm inside the mask. In fact, I'm roasting; sweat is pouring from the metal snout down into my collar. The eyepieces of my mask are fogged, making everything outside look dark. I sit down and lean against the embankment.

Vehicles drive past. The drivers are not wearing masks. Masood takes his off. We wait to see what happens to him. He breathes deeply and exclaims 'No more smell!'

We rip off our masks and fill our lungs with cool fresh air. I breathe freely, but my face is soaked, and my matted hair smells of rubber.[115]

By the time of that incident (in 1987), Iranian troops at the front were equipped with gas masks and other counter-measures as standard issue, but that was not the case in 1983 and 1984, when many Iranian troops had no protection at all against gas attack. Mustard gas was first used by the Germans in the First World War, and later by the British and other combatants. Saddam manufactured it at Samawa, south of Baghdad, and used it against the Iranians in 1983, but again more intensively in 1984 on 25 and 26 February, and again on 2, 3, 7 and 9 March.[116] The Iraqis tended to use gas to halt Iranian breakthroughs, or in counter-attacks, so the strategic effect of its use was again to reinforce the defensive and the tendency to stalemate. The Iranians never retaliated with gas weapons, though they did have the capability (Prime Minister Musavi announced that Iran had developed her own chemical weapon capability in December 1986):[117] the regime declared them to be un-Islamic. Many Iranian veterans, with scarred lungs, still suffer the after-effects of gas thirty years later.

Factions and Elections – Rast va Chap (Right and Left)

After the banning of Tudeh in 1983, with the IRP in undisputed control, splits and factions within the IRP itself became more prominent. In September Khamenei alluded to this in a speech:

> There are differences of opinion among the members of the central committee but both [camps] follow the [doctrine] of the Emam and agree on most issues ... it is OK for the two camps to think differently on issues related to *fiqh* or the economy ... No one should speak badly about Mr Musavi or Mr Asghar-Owladi [a prominent conservative], as they are both distinguished revolutionaries.[118]

These differences of opinion mainly concerned economic policy, but had other ramifications. In the latter part of 1981, while the regime had been locked in its struggle with the MKO, it had also been faced with a serious economic crisis as its oil revenue slumped – oil exports went below 700,000 barrels a day, but Iran needed to export three times that amount to earn the foreign exchange it needed. Imports were at a high level, due partly to the war and the import of war materials – also as a result of consumer demand. But Iran was having trouble paying for the imports: it had followed a policy of supporting high oil prices, but this meant keeping production levels low. The financial clauses of the hostage crisis settlement had been unfavourable for Iran's fiscal position, and foreign exchange management had been incompetent. The new government, with Musavi as prime minister and like-minded men including Behzad Nabavi and Mohsen Nurbaksh as labour minister and governor of the Central Bank respectively, had to take firm measures to get the situation under control. In general (as tends to happen in wartime) this meant greater state control over the economy, and a greater emphasis on pragmatism rather than revolutionary zeal in the running of government offices and businesses alike. Imports were cut, oil prices were cut, and deals were made with foreign oil buyers that included concealed discounts.[119]

Greater state control of the economy also offered opportunities to those on the political left of the IRP, like Musavi and his associates, who favoured state intervention in order to redistribute wealth and improve living standards for the poorest in society. These aspirations had been there in the public pronouncements of Khomeini and the IRP since the beginnings of the revolutionary movement. But the *bazaari* class, who along with the peasants and the urban poor were the staunchest social group supporting the IRP, were unhappy at statist economic measures that tended to act against their interests. Conservative members of the clergy favoured the same line as the *bazaaris*, and their dominance in the Guardian Council gave them a position from which they could impede or block leftist initiatives. Conservative and leftist factions in the IRP and in the Majles formed around these differences of interest, and the removal of authoritative figures like Motahhari and Beheshti had probably exacerbated the bickering between the factions. But it was also a natural consequence of the fact that the IRP had eliminated the previous opposition; once their opponents had been excluded from power, they began to fight for dominance among themselves.

The emerging left/right division reflected another paradox about the revolution itself, and about Khomeini's own views. The revolution was a fusion of conservative and radical ideas, intimately mixed. Its commitment to the *mostazafin*, to raising up the lower classes, to improving their living conditions and access to education and health services, was not mere propaganda – it was genuine, and served to initiate real changes and improvements. Genuine too was the sense that the underprivileged somehow represented the real Iran – an element of social chauvinism was also involved – that the poor were more Iranian, more Islamic and more virtuous than the pampered, westward-looking middle classes and intellectuals. The revolution was not just a political revolution, a reshuffling of political personalities – it was (like the French and the Russian before it) a real social revolution also, raising up large numbers of members of the lower social classes and bringing down or marginalizing many members of previously privileged elites.[120] Notwithstanding that, many of the *mostazafin* stayed stuck in poverty.

But the revolution was also a conservative revolution, serving the conservative instincts of the clergy and their *bazaari* confederates. This was reflected in Khomeini's rulings to protect the sanctity of the home and to protect private property, as well as to enforce traditional limits on the status of women. In some areas, notably in the emphasis on resistance to Western culture and Western political innovations, conservative resistance to alien novelties was in harmony with a leftist hostility to Western imperialism and so-called American global arrogance. But in other areas, like land reform and redistributive economic policies, leftism and conservatism clashed and continued to clash.

Significant on the right was the shadowy grouping known as the Hojjatieh. This had first formed in the 1930s under the influence of Mirza Mahdi Isfahani, whose writings laid emphasis on the importance of the twelfth Emam, and the unacceptability of any usurpation of his authority. The Hojjatieh was in favour of radical measures to cleanse Muslim society of the influence of communism, and of the Bahais – like many if not most orthodox clergy they regarded the Bahais as heretics because they had accepted Baha'ullah as a prophet, contradicting the doctrine that there could be no more prophets after Mohammad, the Seal of the Prophets. The Hojjatieh were significant in the persecution of the Bahais in the 1950s, and again after the revolution, when their leader was Shaikh Mahmud Halabi. Several of their people became

1. Reza Shah established a new, reforming monarchy in Iran, but by the time the allies deposed him in 1941 he had lost most of the popular support that had helped him take power in the 1920s.

2. Mohammad Mossadeq. Mossadeq's removal from power in 1953 reinforced Iranians' bitter mistrust of foreign interference in their country.

3. Mohammad Reza Shah. The Shah's emphasis on magnificence and the heritage of monarchy served only to distance him from his people.

4. A crowd listens to a speech by Ayatollah Taleqani at Tehran University in January 1979 (one of David Burnett's photographs from Revolutionary Tehran – some of the most evocative images of the revolution).

5. A typical confrontation on the streets of Tehran, at the end of December 1978. Note the British-built Chieftain tanks.

6. At the beginning of January 1979 there was chaos at Mehrabad
airport as thousands of foreigners tried to get flights out of Iran.

7. The newspaper headline says *Shah raft* – Shah gone – 'A scene of wild
jubilation which must be being enacted throughout Tehran'.

8. A famous image of Khomeini's return to Tehran on 1 February 1979.
Behind him on the aircraft steps are Morteza Motahhari, who was murdered
just three months later, and Hasan Lahuti.

9. Khomeini waves to the crowd from a window at the Refah school; an over-enthusiastic woman grabs his elbow. Rafsanjani is behind Khomeini's right shoulder. On the far right is Ayatollah Rabbani-Shirazi; next to him is the elder Seyyed Hadi Khosrashahi.

10. Khomeini is served tea at the Refah school by Sadegh Khalkhali. On the left is Hasan Lahuti; close to Khomeini in early 1979, he later fell from favour, was put in prison, and died there. Between them is Hasan Sanei, who later headed the 15 Khordad Foundation that put a bounty on the life of Salman Rushdie.

11. Early in 1979 Taleqani, Beheshti, Rafsanjani and Bani-Sadr pose for a photograph in front of a toppled statue of the Shah.

12. At the time, many Iranians saw the taking of the embassy hostages as legitimate preemptive action to prevent a coup like that of 1953. In the US, it created a popular hostility toward the Islamic republic and Iranians that still persists.

13. High-water mark: A knocked-out Iraqi tank lies abandoned near Susangerd, August 1981.

14. Iran was the only country to operate F-14 aircraft apart from the US; complex and difficult to maintain, but the Iraqis had no answer to them. This one carries AIM-54 Phoenix missiles under the fuselage and AIM-9 Sidewinders under the wings.

15. The Shah's pilots: a group of F-4 Phantom pilots photographed before the revolution. Under the Islamic Republic the pilots were not trusted and the authorities only reluctantly released some from prison to fly against the Iraqis.

16. In the Howeizeh Marshes and on the Shatt al-Arab, the Iranians became expert in infantry infiltration tactics, often using specially trained frogmen.

17. Mohammad Beheshti, a central figure in the politics of the Islamic Republic until he was murdered by the MKO in June 1981.

18. Abol-Hasan Bani-Sadr, who was close to Khomeini and had a reputation as an expert in economics. Elected President in February 1980, he was impeached and removed only sixteen months later.

19. Ayatollah Montazeri, Khomeini's chosen successor until 1989. Later he acquired a reputation as a reformist, but in the early years of the revolution he was regarded as a militant radical.

20. A key figure in the war effort against Iraq as commander of the Sepah, Mohsen Rezai later ran against Ahmadinejad in the disputed elections of 2009.

21. An oil tanker burns in the Straits of Hormuz. Saddam Hussein's attacks on shipping succeeded in escalating the tanker war in the Persian Gulf, and eventually in bringing greater international pressure to bear on Iran.

22. 290 Iranians were killed when the USS *Vincennes* shot down a civilian airliner in July 1988 – an event that contributed to the end of the Iran–Iraq war.

23. Ali Khamenei. After Khomeini died in 1989, Khamenei succeeded him as *rahbar* (Leader) but has never been able to match his predecessor's unique political and religious authority.

24. Hashemi Rafsanjani was probably the most powerful President in the history of the Islamic republic after his election in 1989, but lost ground politically thereafter.

25. Ali Larijani and his brothers became indispensable to Khamenei from the late 1990s onwards.

26. As President (2005–2013), Ahmadinejad created outrage internationally with his populist rhetoric, but eventually alienated the conservative establishment within Iran.

27. Mohammad Reyshahri, who ran the Special Court of the Clergy in the 1980s and was the first Minister of Intelligence and Security from 1984.

28. Mohammad Khatami's election as President with a huge majority in 1997 raised great hopes for reform in the Islamic republic, but by the time he left office in 2005 those hopes had faded.

29. Hardline clerical conservatives: (*left to right*) Ayatollahs Mesbah Yazdi, Vaez Tabassi and Ahmad Jannati, photographed at a meeting of the Assembly of Experts in September 2001.

30. Hope for change: in the last days before the June 2009 elections many thought a swell of support was growing behind Mir Hosein Musavi. The film actress Pegah Ahangarani, shown here voting on 12 June, was arrested a month later for alleged anti-regime activities (and again in 2011) and spent several weeks in Evin prison.

31. 'Where's my vote?' Hope turned to anger after the Presidential elections of June 2009. Note that this demonstrator has covered the lower part of her face to conceal her identity from the authorities – not for religious reasons.

ministers under Musavi in 1981, including Habibollah Asghar-Owladi and Ahmad Tavakoli, and although they were later edged out (they resigned after the government imposed rice rationing after food riots at the end of July 1983), others had positions in the Guardian Council and other important institutions.[121]

Hojjatieh members were prominent among the conservative faction, taking a firm pro-*bazaari* line against government control of the economy and in favour of free enterprise. But their traditional Shiʻa views and emphasis on the Hidden Emam meant that their adherence to the principle of *velayat-e faqih* was dubious at best. They swallowed their principles and voted for the constitution in 1979, but their criticisms resurfaced again later, and in July 1983 they dissolved themselves. This followed a critical speech by Khomeini, who at this time and later attacked economic conservatives like those of the Hojjatieh for favouring the kind of Islam that dominated Saudi Arabia, and Iran in the time of the Shah – what he sometimes called American Islam, which was indifferent to the well-being of the poor. Nonetheless, the grouping seems to have continued on an informal basis, and its former members have continued to hold important positions. Some believe that President Ahmadinejad's frequent references to the theme of the twelfth Emam and his return show the influence of the Hojjatieh.[122]

The earliest major point of dispute arose over land reform. In April 1980 the Revolutionary Council put into effect radical measures for land reform, which legitimized many ad hoc land grabs made by peasants who had exploited the turmoil immediately after the revolution. But implementation proved difficult and controversial, and was disputed both by members of the clergy (upholding the shariʻa principle of private property; in addition to their own interest as landowners in some cases) and landlords. Khomeini had to suspend the reform law. Successive land reform bills passed by the left-leaning Majles were blocked by the Guardian Council, leaving the ownership of more than 800,000 hectares of land in legal limbo until 1986, when a law finally went into force, legitimating the status quo so that those who were actually farming the land (including many of those who had taken possession in 1980 or earlier) were finally given property rights over it. There was a similar impasse over bills to nationalize foreign trade, passed in 1981 and 1984 only to be vetoed by the Guardian Council on both occasions. Nationalization of foreign trade had been stipulated in article 44 of the constitution; it was defended as a way to avoid the pernicious influence of foreign powers and to restrict the import of corrupting luxuries – beyond the more pragmatic motive of the Musavi government to control the movement of hard currency in wartime.[123] The division in the Majles stood for a social division between the two classes most important as supporters of the IRP – the urban poor and the *bazaaris*. The economic interests of the two tended to conflict, which meant in turn that the division in the Majles and in the IRP would persist.

In April and May 1984 elections were held for the second Majles to convene under the 1979 constitution. About 16 million voted, out of the 24.5 million that were eligible. Of the 270 seats, 130 were taken by members of the IRP, and the remaining 140 were independents (but as before, many of the independents were in fact IRP-aligned). The results tended to strengthen the leftist element in the Majles, but Musavi soon ran into trouble, with conservative members opposing him in a vote of confidence. He won the vote, but then was criticized by Khomeini for making difficulties for the private sector with his economic policies. Through all these disputes, Khomeini tried to keep a balance, as did Rafsanjani. Montazeri was generally perceived as favouring the left. Khamenei was more aligned with the conservatives, and after his re-election as president in 1985 he attempted to remove Musavi as prime minister, until Khomeini intervened again, this time in Musavi's favour. Musavi continued as prime minister, but the animosity between him and Khamenei lingered.[124]

Factionalism also affected the question of who should follow Khomeini as *rahbar* (leader) after Khomeini's death (the word *moazzam* was only added to the title, producing the term translated as 'supreme leader', after Khomeini's time, as an honorific: it does not appear in the 1979 constitution, nor in the amendments of 1989). In accordance with the constitution, another Assembly of Experts was elected at the end of 1982 to consider this question, but it did not meet until 1983 and announced no decisions at that time either (though Khomeini's will was shown to the Assembly, and that may have given them a hint). As time went on, it emerged that Khomeini was treating Montazeri as his successor-in-waiting, delegating some responsibilities to him (including responsibility for theological colleges and the prestigious position of Friday prayer leader in Qom) and allowing him to make statements on national issues of the day.

Montazeri

Hosein-Ali Montazeri was born in Najafabad near Isfahan in 1922. He studied initially in Isfahan and later in Qom, where he met Khomeini and became one of his followers in the 1950s. In the turbulent events of the early 1960s he was one of Khomeini's most prominent supporters and he continued his political activities after Khomeini's exile, leading to his arrest in 1966. After his release, he travelled to see Khomeini in Iraq and was rearrested on his return. When not in prison (where he was tortured), he was regarded informally as Khomeini's representative in Qom in the later 1960s and the 1970s, and wrote a series of books and other theological works aligned with Khomeini's teachings. He was arrested again in 1975 and stayed in jail until he was released with other political prisoners in 1978. In Evin prison, he took precedence over other clerics (Rafsanjani for example) and led prayer, despite his hesitant manner. Unlike some other religious prisoners, he would talk to anyone, including leftists, and was respected for his openness and honesty – but others mocked him for his awkwardness and unimpressive appearance. He kept his rural accent all his life. After the revolution he was Friday prayer leader in Tehran for a time, and then returned to Qom. Aside from Khomeini he was one of the few senior *marjas* to agree with the principle of *velayat-e faqih* and he wrote an important book on the underpinning theory of it. But in later years he tended to emphasize the need for the *vali-ye faqih* to be elected and supervised by the people.[125]

Montazeri generally favoured more radical and leftist positions than other clerics, in both domestic and foreign policy. This meant he favoured economic policies to improve the lot of the poor; and in turn that traditionalist clerics aligned with the *bazaaris* tended to disapprove of him. Like other radicals at the time, he strongly supported Khomeini's desire to export the revolution to other countries, a position somewhat at odds with the image he acquired in the West in later years. For example, after suicide bomb attacks in Kuwait in December 1983, Montazeri spoke up for them as acts 'in performance of Islamic duty'.[126]

From 1983 onwards, Montazeri's picture was displayed in public places with Khomeini's.[127] But Montazeri's identification with statist and leftist economic policies meant that opinion was divided over whether he was suitable as a future leader. Although he was the most distinguished cleric after Khomeini among the IRP leadership circle, some conservative clerics did not think his religious credentials were elevated enough; others thought him too scholarly and too lacking either in political sense or in charisma.

The Assembly of Experts met again in November 1985, and this time formally selected Montazeri as Khomeini's successor. But the decision was not announced officially, and only emerged when it was leaked at Friday prayers in Qazvin on 22 November.[128] Montazeri's position as successor was now more or less in the open, but his identification with the radical faction and the fact that Khomeini himself had to maintain some kind of balance or impartiality between the factions augmented what was perhaps a natural tendency for the heir to become a pole of attraction for dissenters and a kind of alternative court to the circle around Khomeini (a phenomenon with resonances earlier in Iranian history, back to the Qajars, to Nader Shah and beyond, to the *Shahnameh* of Ferdowsi). Ultimately this damaged Montazeri's prospects.

Cities and Tankers

In addition to Iraq's greater use of chemical weapons, over the course of 1984 the war escalated and diversified in other ways too. For some time the Iraqis had been responding to Iranian attacks on the ground by indiscriminate bombing or missile attacks on Iranian cities, killing Iranian civilians. Dezful in particular had suffered. The Iranians had also shelled Basra. At the beginning of 1984 the Iraqis let it be known that they now had Soviet SS-12 missiles, which, with a range of 500 miles or more, could hit almost all of Iran's major population centres. As the Iraqis realized that a major Iranian offensive was brewing in February, they threatened to hit named cities near the war zone with bombs and missiles and called for civilians in those cities to be evacuated. The Iraqis hit Dezful with SCUD-B missiles on 11 February; the Iranians bombed Mandali and Khanaqin in retaliation, and shelled Basra the day after. Strike and counter-strike continued over the following months, dwindled and then flared up again in June, interspersed with threats and counter-threats. It became known as the War of the Cities. In mid-June, with UN assistance, both sides agreed a moratorium on attacks against civilian targets, which was effective initially, but began to be breached again (by Iraq) after a few months, and full-out attacks on cities broke out again in 1985.[129]

Like others before him, Saddam and his generals hoped that attacks on civilians would demoralize the Iranians and induce them to rebel.[130] But the history of air campaigns against civilian targets shows fairly consistently (although there are exceptions) that they tend to have the opposite effect, reinforcing a sense of solidarity between civilians and troops, and a sense of national resistance, often independent of political feeling about the national leadership. It also strengthens a general feeling of bitter hostility against the perpetrators.[131] This happened in Iran too.

As with the attacks on Iranian cities, Iraqi attacks on targets connected with Iranian oil exports had been going on sporadically for some time, but intensified in 1984 as Iraq sought by any and all means available to increase pressure on the Iranians to desist from ground offensives and accept a ceasefire. The Iranian oil export terminal at Kharg Island (at the top of the Persian Gulf) had been a favourite target. But by early 1984 Iraq had received supplies of French Super Etendard aircraft and Exocet anti-ship missiles (which had recently received a great deal of free publicity for their manufacturers by sinking British ships in the 1982 Falklands conflict). The Iraqis began to use them to attack international shipping that was taking oil from the Kharg terminal and they also laid mines. It is difficult to destroy an oil tanker; they are big and because oil is lighter than water, they are not easy to sink. But the international oil trade is a delicately balanced business, and just raising the price of insurance on the ships trading in Iranian oil could potentially have a serious effect. The Iraqis hit ships on 28 and 29 March; the Iranians retaliated against Kuwaiti and Saudi vessels carrying Iraqi oil, and the attacks escalated. The Iraqis in effect put Kharg Island under siege, declaring an exclusion zone in the waters around it at the head of the Persian Gulf (another echo of the Falklands War). Saddam was successful, by initiating what came to be called the Tanker War, in drawing regional and global powers further into the conflict. Iraq made most of the attacks on shipping, but as time went on the Iranians got most of the international opprobrium, especially after they made unwise threats to close the Straits of Hormuz. The US began to intervene, sending warships into the Persian Gulf to protect the waterway and the right of international shipping to use it. The British also sent ships, to constitute what became known as the Armilla patrol.[132]

In October 1984 the Iranians attacked again near Mehran, in an offensive named Fajr-7. They threw the Iraqis off some of their positions around the town, but made no more significant gains. The Iraqis made two attacks at the end of January 1985 at the Majnun Islands, where they made a small dent in the Iranian defences, and at Qasr-e Shirin. But the next major attack came from the Iranians, again towards Qurna, from the Howeizeh marshes, in an offensive codenamed Operation Badr (named after one of the Prophet's most famous victories over the Quraish of Mecca). It began on 11 March 1985 and repeated the pattern of earlier offensives, but by this time the Sepah were better equipped and trained to fight more like conventional infantry, rather than using the human wave tactics. The Iranian attacks broke through the Iraqi defences and by 14 March reached the Tigris river north of Qurna. That night, a body of 3,000 Sepah got over the river using pontoon bridges, and finally reached the Baghdad–Basra road at Qurna on the other side. But on the 15th and 16th the Iraqi reserves counter-attacked with massive firepower on three sides against the narrow salient established by the Iranians, using nerve agents as well as the chemical weapons they had used before. A young survivor recalled:

> We came across at night and landed and I was in charge of the mortar. When we reached the town, we were firing at everything and I killed many Iraqis. They were mostly civilians I think because we didn't see any soldiers. On the road we set up our position and waited for reinforcements to arrive. But then Iraqi jets came across and started bombing and reinforcements never did arrive, so we were captured before we could retreat.[133]

By the 17th the surviving Iranians who managed to avoid capture were retreating back to their start lines and, despite a further attack in a nearby sector between 19 March and 23 March, Badr was another terrible failure. It has been estimated that the Iranians lost around 10,000 dead, and the Iraqis 2,000. Beyond the front itself, Saddam responded with renewed and heavy attacks on Iranian cities and Kharg Island. There was more sporadic fighting in the marshes over the following months, with commando-style units from both sides probing each other's defences using small boats in the maze of reed-beds and waterways, but there were no decisive results until January 1986, when the Iraqis regained part of the Majnun Islands in a surprise attack.[134]

But Operation Fajr-8, which began on 9 February 1986, did prove decisive. A hundred thousand men in total took part on the Iranian side, and the attack was designed to look initially like an attempt to take Basra. But that was only a feint (the Iranians made additional diversionary attacks at the same time towards Qurna again). The real objective was the Fao peninsula. The Iranians were able to get to the Shatt al-Arab, cross it with frogmen and Sepah assault troops and move reinforcements and materials over it quickly on the night of 10/11 February to establish a bridgehead in pouring rain, which prevented Iraqi attacks from the air. Having done so, the Iranians spread out over the peninsula and moved heavy weapons into it, securing the whole area by 14 February. Heavy Iraqi counter-attacks continued until mid-March and were unsuccessful, but they prevented a further Iranian move towards Umm Qasr. Nonetheless, the Iranian success at Fao meant they controlled the southernmost stretch of the Shatt al-Arab, and had almost sealed Iraq off from the sea. They could also base Silkworm anti-ship missiles on the peninsula.[135]

Having failed to retake Fao, Saddam attacked Mehran, capturing it by 17 May and offering to render it back to the Iranians in exchange. Instead, the Iranians attacked on 20 June with an offensive they named Karbala-1 and retook Mehran, causing heavy Iraqi casualties. The incident was also significant because in the brief period that the Iraqis controlled it Saddam Hussein offered Mehran to Masud Rajavi, the MKO leader, as a base. Rajavi had arrived in Iraq from Paris in May and turned Baghdad into the headquarters of the MKO once it became clear Mehran was no longer an option. Rajavi may have thought that siding with Saddam was a cunning move. But if he believed that siding with Iran's enemy in the middle of a war would enhance his prospects and the prospects of the MKO within Iran, he was mistaken. Perhaps no other decision showed so clearly his anti-democratic cast of thought. The effect of Rajavi's decision was to destroy the reputation of the MKO and to sink it as a political force within Iran.

At the same time the Iranians were fighting an offensive in the north, Fajr-9, toward Suleimaniyeh, supported by Barzani's Kurds. Like the other Iranian attacks north of Fao, this had been intended mainly as a diversion,

Iraq–Iran border demarcation
established by Algiers Concords

N

IRAQ

Fish Lake

Jasim Canal

IRAN

Bandar Mahshahr •

Basra •
Shuaiba •   Abu Khasib
Zubair •

• Duaiji
• Shalamcheh

Bandar Khomeini •

• Khorramshahr

Abadan
•

Shatt al-Arab

• Khosrowabad

Umm Qasr •

KUWAIT

Fao •

0   20 miles
0   30 km

4. The Shatt al-Arab

but it made significant progress toward Suleimaniyeh. One soldier of the
regular army recalled the following incident near Divandareh (north of
the road between Sanandaj and Suleimaniyeh) around that time in 1986:

> There was no news of fighting in the Divandareh mountains, which are
> located near the border between Iran and Iraq. The mountains and valleys
> were very hard work and made it too difficult for the Iraqis to attack the
> Iranians. If the Iraqis had wanted to attack they had first to drop down
> into the valley, then climb up the other side. But the army positioned the
> four of us as lookouts (spotters) in that area. One night for a joke we were
> looking over at the other side of the valley when suddenly we saw Iraqi
> soldiers there coming towards us – not just a few but more than 500. In a
> panic we went to our tent and told our officer, and he came out – he was
> concerned and made a report to the Sepah, who were a few kilometres

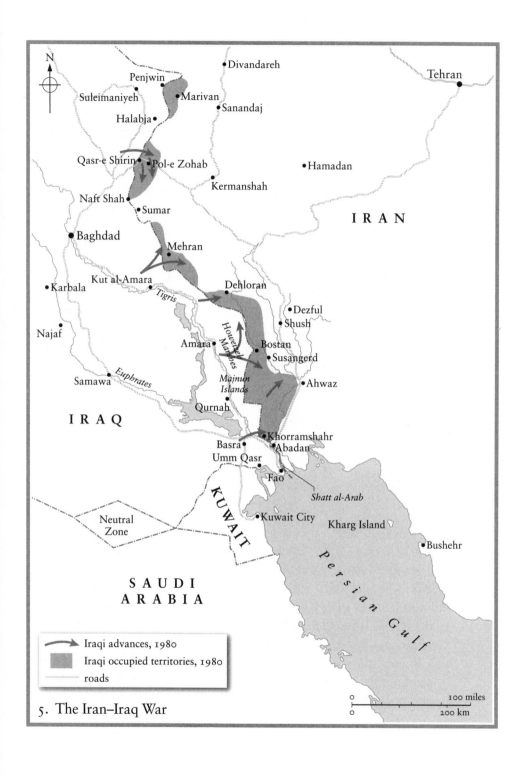

N

Divandareh

Tehran

Penjwin

Suleimaniyeh Marivan

Sanandaj

Halabja

Qasr-e Shirin Pol-e Zohab

Hamadan

Kermanshah

Naft Shah

Sumar

I R A N

Baghdad

Mehran

Karbala Kut al-Amara

Dehloran

Tigris

Dezful

Shush

Najaf

Houeizeh
Marshes

Amara

Bostan

Susangerd

Euphrates

Majnun
Islands

Ahwaz

Samawa

I R A Q

Qurnah

Khorramshahr

Basra

Abadan

Umm Qasr

Fao

Shatt al-Arab

K U W A I T

Neutral
Zone

Kuwait City

Kharg Island

Bushehr

S A U D I
A R A B I A

Persian Gulf

Iraqi advances, 1980
Iraqi occupied territories, 1980
roads

100 miles

200 km

5. The Iran–Iraq War

away. They told us they would come over by the following day. But we were sure that the Iraqi soldiers would get to the top of our hill before then so we were only thinking how to escape. We had lost confidence in our officer, who we knew had been taking opium previously. So we were getting ready to escape as soon as the Iraqis got close to us. Our officer went into his tent again, and to our surprise emerged half an hour later full of enthusiasm – and set about firing down into the valley at the Iraqis with a machine-gun. We never believed that our officer could be so brave – at any rate the Iraqi soldiers stopped advancing, and the next day the Sepah arrived. Despite our concerns [warnings], these Sepah, each armed with a gun, went down into the valley shouting 'Allahu Akbar.' I don't remember seeing so many martyrs in my whole life [in other words, many or most of them were killed].[136]

At the end of August and beginning of September the Iranians made further attacks (Karbala-2 and Karbala-3). The first secured high ground near Haj Omran in the north; the second was a commando-style attack on an Iraqi command post in the sea to the south of Fao. This too was a success and enabled the Iranians to set alight the Iraqis' al-Bakr oil platform nearby, reinforcing the sense that the Iranians now had the upper hand in the land conflict at least. But despite speculation, propaganda and ominous signs of a build-up of troops and war materials, no further major Iranian offensive was forthcoming before the end of the year.[137]

Iran-Contra

In the meantime, the Iran-Contra affair became public. The roots of the affair ran back to Israel's arms supplies to Iran at the beginning of the Iran–Iraq War, to Iran's involvement in Lebanon after the Israeli invasion in 1982 and perhaps back to the October Surprise. Put as simply as possible, the deal was for Israel to supply Iran with much-needed weapons and weapon spares, for Israel to be paid by Iran and be resupplied by the US, for Israel to feed the proceeds of the sales to the Contra rebels in Nicaragua (the US Congress had forbidden the Reagan administration to fund the Contras directly) and for Iran to use its influence to bring about the release of American hostages being held by pro-Iranian groups in Lebanon. It became public when Mehdi Hashemi, an Iranian associate of Ayatollah Montazeri (Montazeri's daughter had married Hashemi's brother Hadi), leaked information on secret meetings between US and Iranian negotiators to a Lebanese newspaper, *Al-Shiraa*, which published them on 3 November 1986.

The Iran-Contra deal broke all kinds of taboos. The US under Reagan had a forthright policy on hostages (stiffened by the memory of Carter's humiliating dealings with Iran, and perhaps by the congruent policy of the UK under Margaret Thatcher), that no ransom should be paid for hostages – indeed that the US government should not even negotiate with hostage-takers. In addition, the US at this stage had an equally firm policy that no arms should be sent to Iran, and had been successfully applying pressure to prevent other countries supplying Iran – this effort had been called Operation Staunch. The US had appeared to favour Iraq at this stage in the war, and inter alia had been helping Saddam with information derived from satellite intelligence of the war zone. This was aside from the constitutional impropriety of funding the Contra rebels by this dubious route, against the will of Congress.

But it is often forgotten in the West that the affair broke Iranian taboos at least as dramatically. Collusion with the US (let alone Israel) had been a damning accusation in Iranian revolutionary politics, enough on its own to sink some individuals, and contributing to the fall from grace of Bazargan, Bani-Sadr and Shariatmadari. When the news broke, the Iranian regime had to admit dealings with the US, but continued to deny any negotiations with Israel, and eventually Khomeini intervened to stop further investigation of the affair.

One could suggest that in subverting so many principles, the Iran-Contra affair demonstrated something even stronger: the continuing natural convergence of interests between Iran, the US and Israel. On the Israeli side, those involved were quite clear that they judged it was in their country's long-term best interests to re-establish a good strategic relationship with Iran; and at various stages the US side also avowed that one of the purposes of their involvement, along with the release of the hostages, was to improve relations with Iran. In particular, both the US and Israel hoped that they were positioning themselves to re-establish a working relationship with a more moderate Iranian regime once Khomeini had died. To that end, it seemed to make sense to woo those who appeared to be moderates within the Iranian system, and to try to strengthen them, insofar as that was possible.

The affair began with an effort by Manuchehr Ghorbanifar, an associate of Hashemi Rafsanjani, to circumvent Operation Staunch and obtain weapons and spares for Iran's war effort. Most prized, given Iran's existing inventory and history of arms imports, were US-made weapons and parts. The Saudi arms dealer Adnan Khashoggi apparently advised Ghorbanifar that the best way to get the attention of the US government was through Israel. Rafsanjani and his associates directed Ghorbanifar to pursue the idea – Khashoggi made contact with the Israelis, and the Israelis made contact with the US. The central figure on the US side was Robert McFarlane, the national security advisor. The policy wonk Michael Ledeen was also involved, as an adviser to McFarlane. Concern that if the US did not reach out to the Iranians then the Soviet Union might move into the vacuum helped to sway the Reagan administration in favour of the effort, but for Reagan personally the main objective was to secure the release of the hostages. After a meeting in Hamburg between Iranians and Israelis in July 1985, Reagan gave his approval, and the first delivery of weapons (100 TOW anti-tank missiles) went ahead on 6 August. After a second shipment on 15 September, the first American hostage (Benjamin Weir) was released. There were further meetings – McFarlane met Ghorbanifar in London in December – and more arms shipments (including powerful HAWK ground-to-air missiles).

By this time McFarlane was becoming disillusioned, feeling that the affair was turning into a straight arms-for-hostages deal that offered little prospect for improving wider relationships. The talks and shipments continued. McFarlane resigned (and others got involved, including Oliver North), but was persuaded to take part in a trip to Tehran in May 1986, for which there were great expectations. Despite taking with them a chocolate cake and a bible with a handwritten inscription from Reagan himself as presents (as well as more weapons and parts), the Americans did not get the high-level meeting with Rafsanjani or other senior figures that they had hoped for, and there was a delay after their arrival that suggested the Iranians did not quite know, once they were there, what to do with them. But the talks they eventually had with Mohammad Hadi Ali Najafabadi, who was chairman of the Majles Foreign Affairs Committee and an adviser to Rafsanjani, were cordial, and Najafabadi indicated that although the time was not right to take things further, Rafsanjani wanted to keep in contact. After that, there were further arms shipments; some more hostages were released too, but more were abducted also. After the affair became public in November there was one further meeting, in Germany in December, but the US side closed the contact down at that point. The revelations caused a furore in the US. Despite President Reagan's open avowal of the deal on TV on 25 November, including the statement that part of the motive had been 'to probe for a better relationship between our countries', investigations into the affair dragged on for months, damaging Reagan's presidency (and also the relationship between the US and Israel). In polls of US public opinion, Reagan's personal approval rating dropped from 67 to 46 per cent.[138]

One account suggests that, in addition to the TOW and HAWK missiles and parts for them, the Iranians also received parts for their precious F-14s in the autumn of 1986:

> By June 1986, only 18 to 20 F-14s were combat-ready, and only half had fully-operational AWG-9 [radars]. But from October large quantities of spare parts started arriving in Iran directly from the United States, allowing us to return between 30 and 35 F-14s to fully operational status once again. The fighting through the winter of 1986–7 was so intense, however, that by mid 1987 these spares had all been used up and the number of operational aircraft had declined once more.[139]

Iran-Contra demonstrated just how sore a wound the Iran–US relationship had become, and turned it septic for a further extended period. Having contributed to the fall of one American president (Carter), the Iran Problem had now damaged a second – with little in either experience to encourage any third to try to fix it. After Iran-Contra, as if in an attempt to regain its credentials for seriousness in the region, the Reagan administration turned much more firmly against Iran in the Iran–Iraq War.

Within Iran, none of those most closely involved in the negotiations suffered by Iran-Contra. Rafsanjani glossed the affair and the McFarlane visit in particular, saying that the Americans had been under arrest after they landed, and implying that Khomeini had sanctioned the contact. Senior Iranians covered themselves by denouncing the US. Attempts by leftists to use the affair to attack Rafsanjani and their other opponents in the Majles were scotched by Khomeini's intervention to halt further investigations. The main Iranian to suffer by the exposure of

Iran-Contra was the one who had leaked it – Mehdi Hashemi, who was arrested with forty others a few days before the news broke on another matter that also seemed to demonstrate an excess of zeal – some of his people kidnapped the Syrian chargé d'affaires. This kind of blatant extra-legal action was becoming less acceptable. Eventually Hashemi made a televised confession accusing himself of 'deviation' and was executed with some others after a trial in August 1987.[140] Reyshahri masterminded the interrogation, trial and execution, and later gave an account of the process in his memoirs which is intriguing for its chilling understatement, leaving aside whatever doubts one may have about what may have been omitted. Reyshahri wrote there that he had carried out three important interrogations or trials before – General Moghagheghi after the Nozheh coup attempt, Qotbzadeh, and Ayatollah Shariatmadari. But at first he and the other investigators had little success with Mehdi Hashemi. Reyshahri consulted the Koran, and then went back to the interrogation with a sense of renewed strength:

> Reyshahri: Are you not frightened of God?
> Hashemi: Yes, sure (*chera*).
> Reyshahri: (repeats) Are you frightened?
> Hashemi: Yes.
> Reyshahri: God knows what you are up to, and you know what you have done, so why don't you say what happened?
> Hashemi: I have said it already. Some details I may not have told.
> Reyshahri: Have you told all the points?
> Hashemi: No.
> Reyshahri: OK, tell.
> Hashemi: OK, I will tell.

In that way simple words were exchanged between us, but each word had a significance beyond what was normal. God put force into the simple words such that the accused was brought up short. After that, Mehdi Hashemi promised to tell the truth. I gave him a little advice and I frightened him with the thought of scandal and the expectation of the next world . . . 'Imagine that God is going to interrogate you, and answer to him' . . . His real interrogation started from that date. He admitted some of the murders he had committed before the revolution and his cooperation with the interrogators was remarkable. After a few days he asked for pen and paper and wrote a letter to me, and in that letter he swore he had told everything and had nothing left to tell. He gave the letter to my investigator colleague, but then took it back, and tore it up. Then he started crying, like a person suffering from mortal pain ... He said 'I wrote a lie when I said there was nothing more to tell.' He asked for pen and paper to write further. The main part of what he had not told was revealed after this incident. He made himself ready for the interview [*mosahebeh* – in other words, the video confession] ...

In fact, there were two confessions. One of these was for public use, was relatively short, and consisted mainly of Hashemi's admission of the crimes he had committed before the revolution – notably the strangling of Ayatollah Shamsabadi, the second-ranking cleric in Isfahan at that time ('nothing important', as Reyshahri put it). The other was seen only by Khomeini, Montazeri and the other main figures of the regime, but was longer and contained the admissions of guilt and error that Khomeini and Reyshahri needed. Reyshahri described it as 'acceptable'.[141]

As the process approached its inevitable end, there was a strange echo of the execution of Hoveida. Apparently, after an intervention by Montazeri on Hashemi's behalf, Khomeini's son Ahmad telephoned Reyshahri at the last minute to tell him the Emam wanted to halt the execution. But Reyshahri told Ahmad he needed to have this instruction in writing, and then quickly carried out the execution before the document could arrive.[142]

The Hashemi affair weakened Montazeri, deepening the divisions already opened up by left–right factionalism and creating new resentment between him and Khomeini. According to Reyshahri's memoirs, Khomeini had written to Montazeri already in the spring of 1986 ('at the beginning of the year 1365'), ordering him publicly to dissociate himself from Mehdi Hashemi and his actions, and to ban him from his office.[143]

The Last Major Iranian Offensives

In the long series of Iranian offensives, with their propagandistic titles and numbers, Karbala-4 was perhaps the most miserably wasteful. It was another offensive associated particularly with Hashemi Rafsanjani, but the Iraqis seem to have been warned of the troop build-up by US satellite intelligence. It began on Christmas Eve, 24 December 1986. The initial attack was made by Sepah frogmen, crossing the Shatt al-Arab in the darkness to establish a bridgehead at Umm Rasas. The attackers were lit up by searchlights and raked with machine-gun fire but managed nonetheless to overwhelm the defences on the far side of the Shatt before getting pinned down among the remains of date palm groves, minefields and barbed wire. At dawn they were shot up by everything the Iraqis could bring to bear – machine-guns, mortars, artillery and helicopter gunships. Reinforcements sent to help them suffered the same fate. The attacking troops gained no further ground, and those who were not killed or captured escaped back over the Shatt al-Arab by nightfall on the 25th. The Iranians had lost an estimated 10,000 men, and bodies were strewn everywhere over the small area of ground they had fought for.[144]

Karbala-4 was just the first act of a bigger drama. Since 1982 the Iraqis had excavated millions of tons of clay to create a huge artificial lake on the eastern bank of the Shatt al-Arab, at the point where the border between Iraq and Iran left the Shatt and ran north, to block an attack towards Basra (the works had reputedly cost the equivalent of a billion dollars). Below the surface of the lake, which served also as a fish hatchery, lurked a profusion of barbed wire, mines and even electrodes to electrocute intruders. It was called Fish Lake.

On 9 January 1987 the Iranians attacked across the lake and through the heavily fortified neck of land to the south, between the lake and the Shatt al-Arab. The Iranians broke through to the Shatt al-Arab and were able to advance along it toward Basra. Heavy bombardment killed the fish in the lake, which floated in it belly-up and started to rot, adding a new stink to the battlefield.

Ahmad Dehqan's novel *Journey to Heading 270 Degrees* gives a vivid, only lightly fictionalized account of his own experiences in the Karbala-5 offensive. The book begins with the narrator, Naser, pursuing his studies at home with his family, having already served at the front with the Basij. Aware that his former comrades are still there, he is already feeling that he should join them when his friend Ali appears on two days of leave and makes his mind up for him. They leave for the front, arriving as the troops are preparing for the offensive, and move forward to follow up on the initial attacks, occupying foxholes vacated by the Iraqis. Then Naser is ordered to lead forward a team armed with rocket-propelled grenades (RPGs) drawn from several platoons in a night attack to destroy some Iraqi tanks lying up between them and the Shalamcheh–Basra road. They move up in the darkness toward the tanks, crawling closer and closer until they are only thirty metres away. Naser orders Ali to fire at first one tank, then another. Both are hit and destroyed, but then the remaining tanks start to fire back and try to manoeuvre out of trouble:

> Ali separates from us and goes after the tank that has just started up and has us in its sights. I cry out, 'STOP RIGHT THERE! HIT IT NOW!'
>
> As I turn away I see Ali facing the tank as it speeds towards him. I shout 'ALI, FIRE! WHAT ARE YOU WAITING FOR?'
>
> I leap towards him . . . What is he waiting for? I am but a few steps from him when there is a wave of fire from his RPG that lifts me off my feet, but even as I am flying through the air my thoughts are with Ali. I see the rocket he has just fired hit the turret of the tank and ricochet off it. I land flat on my back, but before losing my breath I scream, 'ALI, GET OUT OF THE WAY!'
>
> After a few moments, I raise my head and see Ali jump to the left. The left tread of the tank stops and it pivots to confront him again. Unable to move, Ali remains helpless before it. I sit up, catch my breath and cupping my hands over my mouth, yell, 'ALI . . . ALI, OUT OF THE WAY! LET SOMEONE ELSE FIRE AT IT!'
>
> The tank charges Ali like a wild horse. As he staggers a few steps away, the fires from the tanks burning behind him cause his shadow to fall on the advancing tank. Ali emits a cry that does not sound human to me as he becomes woven into the treads and disappears under the carriage. When the tank passes me, I notice it is on fire and moving through the heart of the scorched field, it draws a fiery line that divides the field in half.
>
> I race madly toward Ali, but it seems like I am running on clouds and will never reach him . . . when I finally get to him, I stand over what is left of his body. He stares up at me with a look of horror and disbelief. I sit. The tread has crushed his midsection. His main artery is still spurting blood and his left eye is moving. He has been cut in half, exactly two pieces. I take his head and the upper part of his body into my arms; the lower part

is mashed into the tank tracks . . . I can't take my eyes off his face, which is etched with an immense agony. When I caress his face with my hand, his lips part and shards of teeth fall out of his mouth. I feel that if I don't scream I will suffocate.[145]

Naser has to leave the dying Ali and lead his comrades to rejoin their unit. They advance and, under fire from mortars, they dig foxholes for themselves in the side of another embankment. They are shelled and attacked by tanks and then move up to a position by a bridge over the Zowji canal, which the counter-attacking Iraqis are trying to cross with more tanks. They beat off one attack but are losing men all the time, and Naser himself is wounded by shrapnel from a mortar. He makes his way back down the trench. He is ordered to the rear with a group of other wounded, but they are still under fire from mortars and artillery, and several of them are killed or wounded again as they pick their way back to a crossroads where there are shelters for the wounded and field ambulance vehicles waiting. The most mobile wounded run straight for the nearest ambulance. Unfortunately the crossroads is a good target for the Iraqi artillery:

> The first ambulance had been trying to make a U-turn when someone cried 'THEY HIT IT!' I peeked out of the shelter to see it engulfed in a ball of flames. The young medic tells us to stay where we are while he stands there waiting for the next ambulance to come. It turns around and pulls up to the entrance. The medic rushes to open the rear door and then makes a dash for the shelter, yelling 'RUN! RUN! IT'S HERE!'
>
> With the exception of two men on stretchers all of us are ambulatory. The medic loads the stretcher cases first and we climb in after them . . .
>
> He slams the door . . . The ambulance driver turns his head and says to us, 'Hold on. We're going to try to outrun the shelling on the road.'
>
> He is in his late thirties with greying hair. The ambulance lurches forward . . .
>
> We have reached the causeway that cuts through Fish Lake. There is a firestorm raging everywhere, as all the enemy guns have homed in on this one spot. A line of Katyusha rockets explodes in the lake, catapulting fish of all sizes out of the water. For a moment they seem like flying fish playfully gambolling through the air. Waves of dead fish break along the sides of the road; the stench is everywhere . . .

The ambulance swerves to avoid a ditch in the middle of the road, which sends us flying. The ditch is filled with water. Beside the road is the overturned carcass of a vehicle and farther ahead, a burning truck. It was probably loaded with ammunition, as things keep bursting and popping inside it. The driver hunches over, saying, I think, 'Watch it!'

As we crouch down instinctively there is a large explosion in the truck that sends dust pouring through the cracks in the rear of the ambulance . . . The road bends and the enemy fire abates . . .

Naser is put aboard a bus camouflaged with mud that takes the wounded to an improvised hospital in Ahwaz. On the way there they get stuck in the city traffic:

The bus begins to move. Men and women walk up and down the sidewalk, paying no attention to us. Having just returned from the world of bombs and combat, we are avid spectators of ordinary life; but we ourselves have become an ordinary sight for the people, one of the dozens of mud-splattered buses loaded with wounded that pass by every day. They just go on with their daily lives as though we do not exist.[146]

Dehqan's book was controversial in Iran when it appeared in 1996 because it avoided the rhetoric of some Iranian writing associated with the war in favour of a direct, deadpan, pared-down approach. But those qualities helped it to become a bestseller and it won several prizes.

The Karbala-5 offensive involved 35,000 Sepah troops in the initial assault, with a further 65,000 following up shortly afterwards. They succeeded (as Dehqan's account shows) in breaking through the Iraqi defences around Fish Lake and moved forward to new positions beyond it. The Iraqis counter-attacked in force and again used chemical weapons, but their efforts were handicapped by a number of factors that had not affected earlier campaigns. Firstly, the effect of artillery and mortars was somewhat reduced by the wet and marshy conditions, which meant that rounds tended to plop below the surface and explode with lesser effect. Secondly, the Iranians used the new TOW anti-tank missiles and HAWK anti-aircraft missiles they had obtained from the Americans, along with some other new weaponry, to mitigate the effect of the Iraqis' general superiority in tanks and aircraft. Helicopter gun-ships armed with the TOW missiles were particularly effective. In addition, the Sepah used troops with experience from previous offensives to infiltrate enemy positions at weak points rather than to attack en masse as they had earlier in the war (Dehqan's account also indicates a continuing Iraqi failure to support their tanks with infantry, leaving them vulnerable to the anti-tank weapons of the Iranian infantry). So the Iranians were able to break through, move forward and hold the gains they made. By mid-January they had advanced about five miles of the twelve between their start lines and Basra. The offensive was renewed on 29 January and 22 February, and the Iranians made further gains, but they did not break through to Basra. Estimates of the number of Iranian dead have ranged as high as 20–25,000.[147] The Iranian commanders ended the offensive on 26 February and claimed a victory. Again, as in the First World War, the Big Push that had been aimed at the capture of a strategic city was acclaimed afterwards as a success because it achieved, at appalling cost, an advance of a few barren miles. The Iraqis tried to throw the Iranians out of the new positions at the beginning of March, but failed. They had suffered too – in addition to many thousands of men it has been suggested that the Iraqis lost as many as fifty aircraft during Karbala-5; by this time they could replace the aircraft but were seriously short of trained pilots.

In retaliation for the onset of Karbala-5 the Iraqis had renewed the War of the Cities in mid-January. The Iranians responded in kind but came off worse, with an estimated 3,000 civilians dead and 9,000 injured over the following month. Between February and April the Iranians also attacked in the central region of the front around Qasr-e Shirin, and in the north, making some ground in the Ruwandiz region of Iraqi Kurdestan and taking advantage of a rapprochement between Barzani's followers and the PUK. The Iranians also made a further push west of the Fish Lake on 6 April (Karbala-8) but only took a small amount of new ground, with more heavy casualties.

By 1986 the Iranians were evading the Iraqi attacks on Kharg Island by using installations on Sirri and Larak Islands – much further east, towards the Straits of Hormuz – to load tankers. Iraqi aircraft overflew and threatened Sirri on occasion but seemed not to have the long-range refuelling capability to do serious damage there. Arguing that he was fighting Iran on behalf of all the Arab states in the region, Saddam was using Kuwaiti ports to export oil and to import war materials and was receiving large loans from Kuwait, Saudi Arabia and the other Arab states of the Persian Gulf. In retaliation, Iran had been hitting Kuwaiti-flagged tankers that it suspected were carrying Iraqi oil. Early in 1987, US intelligence learned that the Iranians were setting up Chinese-made Silkworm anti-ship missiles in the Straits of Hormuz. The Silkworm was several times more powerful than the air-launched Exocet, and was capable of sinking a ship rather than just damaging or crippling it – in theory at least the weapon was capable of closing the mouth of the Persian Gulf to international shipping, as the Iranians had earlier threatened they might do. Faced with this threat, in the aftermath of the Iran-Contra debacle, the US began to take a more aggressive stance against Iranian action in the Persian Gulf. In the name of protecting international shipping, the US was effectively intervening in the Iran–Iraq War against Iran; pressuring Iran to accept a ceasefire. In May 1987 Kuwait reflagged eleven tankers as US vessels in order to get US navy escorts for its shipping. Kuwait also chartered Soviet tankers.

With mines lurking under water, anti-ship missiles in the air and the general atmosphere of tension, it was inevitable that there would be incidents that broke the fragile balance of peace between the various parties. The US strengthened its presence in the Persian Gulf in early 1987; so did the Soviet Union, and the British reinforced their Armilla patrol escort squadron also. On 14 May 1987 two Iraqi F1 Mirage aircraft approached the USS *Coontz* aggressively (a powerful escort vessel classified at that time as a guided missile destroyer); they sheered off when engaged by the *Coontz*'s fire control radar. But three days later a single Iraqi Mirage F1 armed with two Exocet missiles approached the USS *Stark* about 85 miles north-east of Bahrain and fired the missiles at it. The Exocets hit the *Stark* amidships; one failed to explode but the other detonated in crew quarters, killing thirty-seven and injuring several more. The *Stark* had sent a warning to the attacking Iraqi aircraft but received no response; the incoming missiles were not detected by any of the ship's defensive systems – the crew spotted them visually in the final seconds before they struck, but too late for any preventive action. Two Saudi F-15 fighters that were nearby and aware of the attack failed to pursue the Iraqi Mirage. The ship managed to contain the fires and sail to Bahrain with the help of other US Navy vessels. The captain of the vessel was later relieved of command and reprimanded. Bizarrely, President Reagan made a speech in which he blamed Iran as the party to the conflict that was really to blame for the incident; Iraq later apologized for the attack.[148]

The Iraqi pilot probably mistook the *Stark* for an Iranian vessel, but the interpretations and accusations continued to reverberate – in any case, the thrust of US policy in the Persian Gulf was not to be thrown off so easily. The Americans reaffirmed their commitment to protect Kuwaiti and other shipping and may have reinforced their intelligence cooperation effort with the Iraqis. In July 1987 one of the Kuwaiti tankers flying the US flag hit an Iranian mine near Farsi Island; on the 27th the UN Security Council passed Resolution 598, repeating a similar resolution from the year before, calling for a ceasefire in the war. The US had pushed hard for the new resolution: Iraq accepted it, but Iran did not. By September the US Navy had around forty vessels engaged in the task of protecting shipping in the Persian Gulf, and on 21 September US forces attacked an Iranian vessel, the *Iran Ajr*, which they suspected of laying mines not far from the position where the *Stark* had been attacked four months earlier. When they boarded, the US sailors found mines on the vessel. Iraqi and Iranian attacks on shipping intensified; the Iraqis using aircraft and missiles; the Iranians using mines and small, fast boats. After capturing the Fao peninsula they could launch Silkworm missiles at Kuwaiti-flagged ships in Kuwaiti waters, where they were not under US protection. Despite the Iranians' efforts to avoid getting drawn into a direct confrontation with the US, there were a series of further Iranian/US incidents.[149]

Massacre at Mecca

Another event that took place toward the end of 1987 seemed to emphasize again to Iranians their isolation and the strength of the forces arrayed against them. Since the revolution Iranian pilgrims on the Hajj to Mecca had been involved in confrontations with the Saudi authorities on several occasions, and several of them had turned violent. These clashes reflected deep-seated tensions and hostility between Iran and Saudi Arabia, as the pre-eminent states of Shi'a Islam and Sunni Islam respectively.

Iran is often labelled a fundamentalist Islamic state, but, as we have seen, that is largely a misnomer. By contrast, the Sunni Islam of Saudi

Arabia is genuinely fundamentalist. Saudi Arabia was founded after the First World War, in the aftermath of the Arab revolt and the failure of the project of a pan-Arab state. But the origin of Saudi Arabia goes back a further 150 years, to the alliance between the al-Saud family and the religious reformer Mohammad ibn Abd-al-Wahhab, from whose name the term Wahhabism derives. Abd-al-Wahhab's teaching from the 1740s onward urged a purification of Islam and a return to its original principles, as he saw it expressed in the Koran and the lives of the earliest predecessors, (*salaf* – hence the related term salafism), the companions of the Prophet Mohammad. Any religious practices that could not be justified in this way were to be condemned as innovation (*bid‘a*) or idolatry (*shirk*). The movement was also hostile to non-Muslims. The al-Saud family undertook to spread the practice of Wahhabism to all the territory they controlled, so all the ingredients necessary for an intolerant, aggressive, expansionist movement were combined. In its hostility to any religious practices that partook of what it regarded as idolatry or innovation, the movement naturally sought to eradicate Sufism and Shi‘ism wherever it could (the corollary is that Wahhabism was an extreme version of just the kind of intolerance, mindless attachment to empty rules and hypocritical Puritanism that Sufism, in its classical form, had always opposed).

By the end of the eighteenth century the al-Saud controlled much of the Arabian peninsula, and in 1801–4 their forces sacked Najaf, Karbala, Medina and Mecca, destroying tombs and shrines and killing those who resisted them. In 1812 one of the sons of Mehmet Ali Pasha, the ruler of Egypt, reconquered the holy places of Mecca and Medina, defeating the al-Saud, restoring the authority of the Ottoman Sultan and checking the hegemony of Wahhabism for over a century.

In the modern Saudi state Wahhabism has been dominant: the ruling family support it in schools and in the mosques as they always have, but have done their best to send inconvenient extremists (like Osama bin Laden) out of the country and to present a more acceptable face to their Western allies.

After the revolution of 1979 Iranian Shi‘a dislike of Wahhabism combined with revolutionary antipathy toward monarchy in principle and Saudi Arabia as one of the prime allies of the US in the Middle East to create a major rift between the two countries. The Saudis were also concerned about Iranian influence on the Shi'a minority in the eastern part of their country. Khomeini tried to minimize conflict with Sunnism in important respects[150] but regularly abused the Saudi monarchy in his speeches. On the Hajj, Iranian pilgrims made provocative demonstrations and often clashed with the Saudi police. On 31 July 1987, the first day of the annual Hajj, Iranian pilgrims, protesting against Israel and America as they went, found their way barred by police as they made their way toward the great mosque of Mecca. Scuffles turned into a riot and the police reacted harshly, although the degree of their response has been disputed. According to the Saudis, 402 pilgrims died when the crowd surged away and people were trampled. The Iranian version said that the Saudis used live ammunition, and many died of gunshot wounds.[151]

In a message to the surviving pilgrims on 1 August in response to the massacre, Khomeini blamed 'the mercenaries of the arch Satan – the criminal United States'. Accusing the Saudis of following the path of Yazid and those who had opposed the Prophet Mohammad, he went on, with savage irony:

> If we had wanted to prove to the world that the Saudi Government – these vile and ungodly Saudis, are like daggers which always pierce the heart of the Muslims from the back – we would not have been able to do it as well as demonstrated by these inept and spineless leaders of the Saudi Government . . . How opportune it was that immediately after the incident at a time when the bodies of our beloved ones were still lying on the ground, Saddam and the Jordanian Husayn and Moroccan Hassan, in support of Al Sa'ud's crime, announced their solidarity, as though Arabia had conquered a great fortress. How opportune it was that by massacring hundreds of defenceless Muslim men and women, using machine-guns on them, and walking over their pure bodies, it achieved a great military victory that they could congratulate one another about.[152]

The incident seemed to add to other evidence that Iran was at war not just with Iraq, but with almost the whole world.

Hashemi Rafsanjani made a number of statements in the last months of 1987 that seemed to threaten another major offensive. But by this point Iran was close to economic and psychological exhaustion, and despite their commitment to the war and their outward defiance, many of Iran's leaders were growing increasingly uneasy at the escalation of international pressure against them. It began to look as if the attrition that they had intended to wear down Saddam, could instead erode away the Islamic republic if the war were not brought to an end. In 1988 the balance tipped further against Iran.

5

The End of the War, the Death of the Emam, and Reconstruction: Khamenei and Rafsanjani, 1988–97

AMFORTAS: *What is the wound, its raging pain,*
Against the distress, the torments of hell,
Of this Office – to be accursed!
Wagner, *Parsifal*, Act I

Halabja

At the beginning of 1988 the Iranians made two new attacks in Iraqi Kurdestan, in January and March. As part of the latter, with PUK support, the Iranians captured the town of Halabja on 15 March. Halabja was a town of at least 70,000 people, mainly Kurds. The Iranians did not send many troops into the town itself, instead reinforcing strategic positions around it. On 16 March the Iraqis bombed Halabja with chemical weapons – nerve agents, but possibly cyanide also. Several thousand people died; perhaps 4,000, maybe more, and many more were injured, some permanently, with brain damage and other disorders of the nervous system:

> Dead bodies – human and animal – littered the streets, huddled in doorways, slumped over the steering wheels of their cars. Survivors stumbled around, laughing hysterically, before collapsing ... Those who had been directly exposed to the gas found that their symptoms worsened as the night wore on. Many children died along the way and were abandoned where they fell.[1]

Almost all of the victims were Kurdish civilians – Iraqi citizens. The Iranians rushed journalists to the town – both their own and foreign correspondents – but their eagerness to show the world the evidence proved counter-productive; it induced scepticism, and within a short time the US State Department, drawing on information prepared by the Pentagon and deriving ultimately from their Iraqi intelligence contacts, were briefing from their embassies around the world that both sides had used chemical weapons around Halabja. As a result the eventual UN resolution condemning the use of chemical weapons was expressed in general terms and did not blame Iraq as the culprit. Later it became evident that the Iraqis were solely responsible for Halabja and that Iraqi accusations against the Iranians at the time were no more than spoiling tactics and propaganda.[2] Halabja was an early taste of the genocidal retribution Saddam would take against the Iraqi Kurds in what became known as the Anfal. Sustained attacks on Kurdish civilians, particularly on villages and areas that had supported the PUK, went on until the autumn. Gas was used again many times, along with attacks on settlements, removal of villagers to holding camps and round-ups of young men, after which the men were taken away by Iraqi troops and shot. Somewhere between 150,000 and 200,000 Kurds were killed.[3]

Some within the US intelligence system may have genuinely believed that the Iranians used chemical weapons during the Iran–Iraq War, but their belief was based on little beyond an expectation that if bad things were being done, the Iranians were likely to be doing them. The Halabja incident showed (among other things) how far US and international opinion had swung against Iran – how isolated Iran had become.[4] But also, for the Iranians at least, it was another demonstration (like the empty declarations of neutrality and the flouted arms embargoes earlier in the war; not to mention Iran-Contra) of the way that the norms held up by the Western nations as standards of international behaviour seemed in fact to be flexible and mutable when it suited Western nations to change or overlook them – even when it involved genocide.

The Iranian F-14s were still flying in 1988 and still destroying Iraqi aircraft. On 9 February three F1 Mirages were shot down by Iranian Tomcats, and for once (because the aircraft went down in the Persian Gulf and the splashes were witnessed by Western navies) these kills were acknowledged by Western analysts.[5] The last Iraqi aircraft to be destroyed by a Phoenix missile fired from an F-14 was a MiG-25 that went down near Tabriz on 22 March, but by the summer the French had supplied the Iraqis with new equipment that made the Mirage F1s a tougher proposition for the Iranians. On 19 July 1988 two Iranian F-14s were shot down by four Mirage F1s using the new Matra Magic Super 530D air-to-air missile: the Iranians believed that the Iraqis had been able both to jam the F-14's AWG-9 radar and use its emissions as a homing signal for the missiles. But over the course of the war the Iranian F-14 pilots destroyed many more aircraft than they lost, apparently by a factor of around ten to one.[6]

Since Iraq's partial retreat from Iranian territory in 1982, its forces had stayed largely on the defensive in the land war. But in the spring and summer of 1988 they went on the offensive again, aiming at the recapture of Iraqi territory the Iranians had taken at Fao, in Kurdestan, the Howeizeh/Majnun Islands sector, and around the Fish Lake/Shalamcheh front east of Basra. From the end of February to 20 April the Iraqis also renewed their bombing and missile attacks on Iranian cities, at a new level of intensity. Tehran suffered particularly, with 133 missile attacks between mid-March and mid-April. Many people left the city: schools and some government offices closed. This renewal of the War of the Cities, coinciding with the Halabja incident, had the additional effect of a warning to the Iranian leadership that if Saddam were pressed to new extremes by some future Iranian success in the war, he could combine the gas weapon and the long-range missile weapon and use poison gas against civilians in Iranian cities.[7]

The first major blow of 1988 was the Iraqi attack on the Iranian positions on the Fao peninsula on 16 April. Most of the Iranian troops were deployed across the neck of the peninsula, facing north-west towards Basra. Because the Iraqis had stayed passively on the defensive for so long, the Iranians had grown complacent and were not prepared for them to go on the offensive. The Iranian troops were hit with a massive artillery barrage, in which chemical shells were mixed in with conventional explosive ones. While this was happening Iraqi assault troops (imitating previous Iranian tactics) landed from boats and helicopters on the south coast of the peninsula, which was only lightly defended. Once the Iraqis had established themselves there, the Iranians defending the peninsula were in an impossible position and by the morning of 18 April they had withdrawn back over the Shatt al-Arab.[8]

The effect of the loss of Fao was compounded by events in the Persian Gulf, where the US guided missile frigate *Samuel B Roberts* had hit an Iranian mine on 14 April. The warship nearly sank but managed to get into Dubai without loss of life. In what was called a measured response (with the codename Operation Praying Mantis) the US Navy attacked on 18 April, destroying two oil rigs, the Iranian frigate *Sahand* and a speedboat, crippling a second frigate, the *Sabalan*, and damaging another speedboat. There has been speculation since that time that the US told the Iraqis of their intentions in advance, and that the Iraqis timed their offensive at Fao to coincide with Praying Mantis.[9]

On 25 May, after making smaller attacks on preceding days in the central and northern sectors of the front, the Iraqis attacked in strength against the positions east of Basra around Fish Lake and Shalamcheh, which had cost the Iranians so many lives to occupy in the course of Karbala-5 the previous year. Again, in addition to the use of chemical shells as part of artillery barrages, and powerful new anti-personnel cluster munitions, the Iraqis employed tactics that indicated they had learned from Iranian practice in earlier offensives (it may also be that some changes were prompted by US advice);[10] instead of attacking with masses of tanks as they had earlier in the war, they sent in select groups of assault troops first, infiltrating and identifying weak points, then following up with tanks in support. They also hit Iranian rear areas with mustard gas, to disrupt reinforcements and troops that might be ordered forward for counter-attacks. The new effectiveness of the Iraqi forces may also reflect the fact that Iraqi generals had by this time forced Saddam Hussein to give them some freedom of action, and to stop interfering in the planning and conduct of operations. Saddam liked to pose in uniform, but (as was demonstrated at the strategic level by his decision to invade Iran in 1980, and again by his invasion of Kuwait in 1990) his military judgement was poor.

The Iraqis succeeded in driving all the way through to the line of the border; the Iranians lost all their previous gains. The losses were especially humiliating for the Sepah, who had been primarily responsible for the defence of Fao and Shalamcheh. Their commander, Mohsen Rezai, made a public apology for recent mistakes.[11] On 19 June the Iraqis attacked at Mehran, again using chemical weapons, took it briefly and then withdrew.

The next blow came on 25 June, when the Iraqis attacked again, using similar tactics and several of the same units, against the Iranian positions around the Majnun Islands. They succeeded in taking them within a day. The rhetoric of defiance from Rafsanjani, Khomeini himself and the other Iranian leaders continued much as normal, but already

Iran began to put out diplomatic signals that suggested they had a new interest in finding a way out of the war. Earlier, in March, economic planners had told the leadership that with oil revenue slumped (partly due to Iraqi attacks on oil installations and shipping) there would have to be reductions in subsidies on staple commodities to continue the war, which would damage the (already low) living standards of the poorest in society. They said the country had reached, or had perhaps already overshot, a financial red light.[12] Iranian oil revenue was running at about three-fifths of that of Iraq in the early part of 1988; among other factors, US purchases of Iraqi oil had greatly expanded.[13]

Already, in 1986, Bazargan had sent Khomeini an open letter criticizing the war and Khomeini's conduct of it. After the defeats of the spring of 1988 he did so again, in strong terms:

> Since 1986 you have not stopped proclaiming victory and now you are calling on the people to resist until victory. Isn't that an admission of failure on your part? . . . You have spoken of the failure of Iraq and the crumbling of its regime, but thanks to your misguided policies Iraq has fortified itself, its economy has not collapsed, and it is we that are on the verge of bankruptcy. You say that you have a responsibility to those whose blood has been spilt. To this, I say, 'When will you stop the commerce with the blood of our martyrs?'[14]

Bazargan was, of course, no longer anywhere near the centre of power in Iran, but he had the courage to write and publish what many thought in private. In fact, he was at least partly wrong in his comparison between the economic and fiscal state of Iran and Iraq at this time – Iran's isolation had prevented the country from taking major loans from foreign lenders, but Iraq had borrowed heavily, notably from Saudi Arabia and Kuwait.

Absolute Guardianship

By mid-1987 the factionalism and infighting within the IRP, among other problems, had led to a widespread disillusionment with the party as an institution. Khamenei and Rafsanjani both wrote reports for Khomeini on the matter; both were critical. Acting on their advice, Khomeini decided to dissolve the IRP, and this took effect on 2 June 1987. It seems that Khomeini intended this as just the first step in a series of reforms designed to tidy up the system, to adjust it to changed conditions and get it in good order for the future – a future that before long might not include him.

In December 1987 a leftist minister asked Khomeini what should be the proper relation between the state and the private sector in the provision by the state of utilities like water, telephones and electricity. Earlier, in July, Khomeini had delegated some of his powers in this area to the government. In reply, Khomeini stated that it was legitimate for the government to impose conditions on the operation of private businesses. A conservative member of the Guardian Council then queried what seemed to him to be a dangerous extension of state power (little suspecting what was to come). In his response Khomeini restated his commitment to the institution of the Guardian Council, but confirmed that the state was entitled to make demands on the private sector in return for services it provided – and he added that this was one instance of a more general principle. The leftist faction were jubilant. A few weeks later (on 1 January 1988) Khamenei, with some temerity, attempted to gloss Khomeini's statements from a conservative position by saying in a Friday prayer sermon that what the Emam had really meant was that, although the state had considerable powers, its actions were limited by Islamic laws (*ahkam*). This intervention by Khamenei has been interpreted as a quasi-liberal one, attempting to limit the power of the Islamic state, but that is misleading. It is important to see it in the context of the factional struggle between left and right, and Khamenei's position on the right of that tussle.[15]

Khomeini's response was abrupt: he declared the next day that the president 'clearly did not understand the ruling'. He went further – much further:

> The government that is part of the absolute vice-regency [*velayat-e motlaq*] of the Prophet of God is one of the primary injunctions of Islam and has priority over all other secondary injunctions, even prayer, fasting and hajj . . . The government is empowered unilaterally to revoke any shari'a agreement that it has conducted with people when those agreements are contrary to the interests of the country or of Islam.[16]

After this snub, Khamenei tried to regain favour by restating the new ruling in terms that showed he really had understood this time:

The commandments of the ruling jurist are primary commandments and are like the commandments of God ... obedience to them is incumbent ... The Mandate of the Jurist [*velayat-e faqih*] is like the soul in the body of the regime. I will go further and say that the validity of the Constitution, which is the basis, standard and framework of all laws, is due to its acceptance and confirmation by the ruling jurist. Otherwise, what right do fifty or sixty or a hundred experts have ... ? What right do the majority of people have to ratify a Constitution and make it binding on all the people?[17]

Other dignitaries within the regime hurried forward to praise and endorse Khomeini's new ruling, but Ayatollah Lotfallah Safi, one of the most authoritative *fuqaha* on the Guardian Council, objected to it and resigned his position. In fact, the ruling exceeded even the previous radical position of the *velayat-e faqih* within Shi'a legal thinking and took the Islamic republic into uncharted waters. Uncharted that is, for theorists of Islamic law: the notion that *maslahat* – expediency, or the interests of the revolutionary state – should trump religion, political ideology or moral law, was not new. Robespierre and Stalin, for example, had been there before. It may have begun with a mundane discussion of public utilities, but before long the effect of Khomeini's new ruling of *velayat-e motlaq* (absolute guardianship) would be felt in an altogether more frightening context.

In February 1988, emerging out of these events, a new body was established, the Majma-e Tashkhis-e Maslahat-e Nezam (literally, the Council for Discerning the Expediency of the Regime) or Expediency Council. The purpose of the new body was to resolve disputes between the Majles and the Guardian Council, which up to that time had been so disruptive, but in practice, further changes to the constitution within a few months made the Expediency Council largely redundant. Nonetheless, at the time the effect of this innovation was to emphasize the new doctrine of *velayat-e motlaq*, the strengthening of the state and those running it, the upper hand of the statist, leftist faction and the relative weakness of the right.

Discussion of the *velayat-e faqih* and the basis of the constitution was specially sensitive and relevant because all those involved were aware that, on the usual four-year cycle, new Majles elections were looming. These were held on 8 April; once again the leftists were stronger in the new Majles, with around 160 deputies against eighty representing the right. Just before the elections, again building on the recent successes of the leftist faction, another association formed – the Majma-e Ruhaniyun-e Mobarez (MRM – Association of Combatant Clergy). With explicit permission from Khomeini, it formed out of a split away from the Jame-ye Ruhaniyat-e Mobarez (JRM – usually translated as the Combatant Clergy Association or Combatant Clerics Association). The MRM was intended explicitly as a group for the leftist faction. The radical nature of the group was shown in its membership, which included Mohammad Musavi-Khoeniha (sometime guide to the embassy hostage-takers) and the hanging judge Sadegh Khalkhali. But its members also included future reformists Mehdi Karrubi and Mohammad Khatami. All were united against what Khatami, using Khomeini's language, called the 'American brand of Islam' – in other words, the Islam of profiteers and capitalists who preferred to ignore the suffering of the *mostazafin*.[18]

The USS Vincennes

As part of the continuing operations to protect shipping carrying Iraqi oil in the Persian Gulf, on 3 July 1988 a US warship (the USS *Vincennes*), commanded by Captain William C. Rogers III, sailed into Iranian waters in pursuit of some Iranian fast boats (Swedish-supplied Boghammer launches, 40 feet long) after some of them were thought to have fired on a US Navy helicopter.[19] The *Vincennes* was a guided missile cruiser; a powerful and expensive vessel for the kind of duties involved in Persian Gulf operations – some have suggested that its duties would have been better performed by frigates or other smaller vessels, and that what followed may have happened at least partly because Rogers (mindful of what had happened to the USS *Stark* and its commander)[20] was jumpy about the possibility of air attack on his valuable ship – 'the "supership" of the Persian Gulf'.[21] Rogers seems to have been regarded as an aggressively minded officer by some of his colleagues in the Persian Gulf. Some of them gave the *Vincennes* the nickname Robocruiser.[22]

When the *Vincennes'* crew saw an aircraft approaching on their radar, the concern that it could be a hostile Iranian warplane quickly turned into an assumption that it was an F-14 on an attack run. They read their radar plots as showing the aircraft descending toward the *Vincennes*; it was in fact climbing away from take-off at Bandar Abbas airport, as was clear to crew monitoring the same data on another US Navy vessel nearby, the USS *Sides*.[23] Subsequent investigations suggested that the crew in the Combat Information Centre (CIC) on board the *Vincennes* ('three platforms below the bridge, in a space bathed with soft, pale blue light surrounded by the hum of air-conditioning and electronics')[24] were subject to a psychological phenomenon that was called scenario fulfilment syndrome, in which information that did not conform to the current interpretation of events was simply ignored. They sent multiple warnings on military frequencies to the Iranian plane, but warnings on the civilian emergency frequency were inaccurate in detail, and no signal was sent on the civilian air traffic control frequencies. There was a lot of noise in the CIC from crew making reports or other remarks, and they were being thrown around by the ship heeling over as it made sudden changes in direction. When the aircraft held its course despite the warnings, the *Vincennes* launched two missiles (after *twenty-three*[25] failed attempts to enter the correct launch codes), destroying it shortly afterwards. Seeing the flash in the sky as the missiles detonated, the crew of the *Vincennes* cheered at the destruction of a hostile aircraft.

But it wasn't an F-14 (an attack on the *Vincennes* by an Iranian F-14 was in itself unlikely),[26] it was an Iran Air Airbus A300 on a regular scheduled civilian flight (Iran Air 655) from Bandar Abbas to Dubai, in the United Arab Emirates. It was blown apart by the missile strikes; bodies and debris fell into the sea over a wide area, and 290 passengers and crew were killed. As part of the investigation that followed, it was discovered that the new AEGIS computer system on board the *Vincennes* had received and recorded the automatic IFF (Identification: Friend or Foe) transmissions from the Airbus announcing itself as a civilian aircraft, but they were disregarded at the time because the ship had also received (somehow) signals that on some occasion previously had been associated with Iranian F-14 aircraft.

In the international furore that followed, the Reagan administration gave explanations that contained more misleading inaccuracies and self-justifications than contrition and blamed Iran for failing to accept the previous year's UN ceasefire resolution. As with Halabja, other Western nations took their cue from the US – a leader article in the UK

Times speculated that the Airbus might have been flown by a suicide pilot.[27] In the prevailing atmosphere in the US in 1988, with the memory of the hostage crisis and hostile acts attributed to the groups aligned with the Iranians in Lebanon still fresh, it would have taken political courage to discipline American servicemen for the Iran Air 655 incident or to apologize to the Iranians (in a poll by the *Washington Post*, 75 per cent blamed Iran more than the US and 61 per cent opposed compensation to the families of the victims).[28] Instead, in 1990 President George Bush awarded Captain Rogers the Legion of Merit medal for the period of his command of the *Vincennes*. The Iranian regime refused to accept that the destruction of the airliner was an accident.[29]

Something that is often overlooked about autocratic regimes is that censorship, propaganda and the control of the flow of information, even in regimes that have not attained the extremes of full-blown totalitarianism, as in the former Soviet Union, though it may be intended to shape and contain the opinions and judgements of the general population, also has the effect of moulding and limiting the opinions and judgements of the leading elite themselves.[30] The imperfect information and imperfect understanding deriving from this have contributed to major policy miscalculations in the Middle East and elsewhere. This was probably a significant factor in Saddam's decision to go to war with Iran in 1980; and his decision to invade Kuwait a decade later; and in the Iranian decision to continue the Iran–Iraq War into Iraqi territory in 1982. It also played a part in the Iranian response to the *Vincennes* incident – but in this case the misunderstanding contributed to a broader judgement that was probably correct. The conviction that the destruction of the airliner was deliberate helped to persuade the Iranian leadership that the United States would go to any lengths to prevent Iran winning the war. This in turn, coming on top of other factors that pointed to the same conclusion, helped to force the realization that they should finally accept the ceasefire.

Ceasefire and Massacre

The crucial figure in this was Hashemi Rafsanjani, who since 1982 had been prominent in the aggressive prosecution of offensives against Iraq – both in the public presentation (as spokesman for the Supreme Defence Council) and in the backroom coordination between the Sepah and the regulars. By mid-1988 the mixed results of the most recent Iranian offensives, and the grave losses of veteran troops in them, plus the success of renewed Iraqi offensives, and the escalating pressure against Iran in the Persian Gulf, had already had its effect on Rafsanjani's assessment of Iran's chances in the conflict. However bold and uncompromising his public statements, the Iran-Contra episode showed already that Rafsanjani had a less ideological and more pragmatic, realistic attitude to the war than some others among the leading group. But by this time they too (including Musavi-Ardebili, Ahmad Khomeini, Mir Hosein Musavi and Khamenei) had come to the conclusion 'they [i.e. the US] will not allow us to win the war'.[31] At the beginning of June Khomeini delegated to Rafsanjani the responsibility of commander-in-chief, ordering him to make a general reappraisal of the war situation and to take further steps to coordinate the operations of the Sepah and the other armed services. It seems that this move was already intended to prepare the ground for a ceasefire, should it prove necessary, by bringing Rafsanjani into a position to neutralize or face down opposition from gung-ho elements in the Sepah. Rafsanjani had already been making a series of visits to the front, which he continued; and he asked the Sepah commander Mohsen Rezai for a summary of what Rezai believed it would take for Iran to be able to win the war:

> After the fall of Faw [Fao] and the astonishing retreat of our forces . . . I went to the south and had comprehensive negotiations with the commanders, experts and the combatants. They explained that the main reason for the retreat was the lack of troops and the enemy's extensive use of chemical bombs. Following the retreat of the forces from the Karbala V zone and Majnoun Islands, I repeated my trips: the realities of the front became more apparent and the blunt statements of the best commanders gave more information . . . Following the unacceptable retreat from Mehran, I went to the west, where I had more to do with the Army, where lack of forces and materiel and lack of volunteer forces were mentioned as the reason for the weakness . . . In conclusion, in frank discussions with the commanders who were in favour of continuing the war, they defined their requests, ideas and deadlines and timings for the preparation of vast, rapid attacks. The frankest opinions came from [Admiral of the Sepah] [Ali] Shamkhani and Shahid Ahmad Kazemi [of the Sepah].

... After a lot of discussion with the commanders of the Sepah and the Army and clarifying the preconditions for continuing the war, Mr Mohsen Rezai wrote all the necessities of the front, and the conditions for success (these kinds of requests had been raised orally before), and the probable timings for renewing active operations on the front line ... I discussed his letter with the heads of the branches [of the government] and after investigation and calculation, it was agreed that the country was not capable of providing for such needs.[32]

Rezai's response showed how far morale had slumped; especially when one bears in mind the Sepah's previous reputation for enthusiasm:

No victories are in sight for the next five years ... If we become able to organize 350 infantry brigades, purchase 2,500 tanks, 3,000 [artillery pieces], and 300 warplanes, and be able to manufacture laser and nuclear weapons which are nowadays among the necessities of modern warfare, then, God willing, we can think of offensive war activities ... [If we are to defeat the Iraqis] we need to double the military and increase the [Sepah] seven fold, and even evict the Americans from the Persian Gulf (which we cannot); nonetheless, we have to continue the war.[33]

Rafsanjani showed Rezai's letter to Khomeini, and went to discuss it with him at a meeting on 14 July 1988:

After a lot of discussion over all the details of the letter Emam Khomeini believed we could not provide the requirements set out there. Before this, the Prime Minister and the Minister of Finance had written in a report to Emam Khomeini that even at current levels of spending the country could not sustain the cost of the war. This goes beyond the economic red line. But what made Emam Khomeini accept this was the chemical bombing of Halabja and Sardasht. It was predicted that in the future we would see the use of Weapons of Mass Destruction by Saddam (with a green light from the superpowers) against cities like Tabriz, Isfahan, Qom and Tehran, with the launch of chemical missiles.[34]

Khomeini accepted the main point of the Rezai letter, and the need to end the war. His only adverse comment was that given the thrust of Rezai's other comments, the pious coda that the war must continue was mere 'sloganeering' (Khomeini's resentment in early 1988 toward Sepah commanders may reflect blame he attached to them for persuading the leadership to continue the war into Iraq in 1982). According to his own account Rafsanjani undertook to take the blame if the outcome of the decision to accept the ceasefire turned out badly, but Khomeini would not agree to that. He told Rafsanjani that he should gather the key authorities and decision-makers in the country, and persuade them to cooperate with the decision to accept the ceasefire.[35] After further discussions that same day, a gathering of leaders at Khamenei's presidential residence voted in favour of accepting Resolution 598 without conditions. The next day senior Majles figures conferred with Rafsanjani and agreed the same, and that evening Rafsanjani conveyed these views to Khomeini. On 16 July the Assembly of Experts, after further liaison by Rafsanjani, formally gave their opinion to the same effect – but the account of the meeting broadcast by the state media gave little hint of a change in policy, quoting Rafsanjani as saying: 'We will continue the sacred defense until we achieve our just rights.'[36] Khomeini gave his assent in writing, and Khamenei drafted a letter to the UN announcing the decision. The letter referred to the way the war had expanded to draw in other countries, and to the 290 civilians killed in the *Vincennes* incident. It was delivered to Perez de Cuellar, the UN secretary-general, at midnight on 17 July 1988.[37]

The collegiate nature of this decision is significant. In some states, the top man would have made the decision, perhaps after some consultation with advisers, and simply ordered his subordinates to carry it out. But despite the centralized character of revolutionary Iran, and the political dominance of Khomeini, Khomeini did not rule like a classic dictator. It was still important to persuade and to carry the main figures of the political elite along with major decisions. It was still the case that the business of government was carried out by these people, and then referred to Khomeini for guidance and approval. But it is also noteworthy that Montazeri seems not to have played any significant role in these discussions.

Most Iranians, having been given no hint of a change, and with the rhetoric of struggle and resistance still fresh in their ears, were bewildered when news of the decision was announced. Khomeini made a statement on 20 July, broadcast by radio, that began as a speech to mark the anniversary of the deaths of Iranians killed by the Saudis while on pilgrimage to Mecca the year before, but veered away from that subject to deal with Iran's acceptance of the ceasefire resolution. He said that accepting the ceasefire was in the interests of the system and the revolution, but that it had been 'a very bitter and tragic issue for everyone and particularly for me ... more deadly to me than poison, but I am [content] to submit to God's will'. He said that no other country had influenced the decision, but that he had heard the views of all senior political and military figures before making it. No one should criticize the officials for the decision they had taken, because it had been hard for them too. He warned that Iranians must stay vigilant because the problem of the war had not been resolved – 'we must be ready and prepared to repulse the enemy's possible aggression and our nation should not think the issue is over yet'. He added that people might debate the wisdom of the decision in the future, and that would be a valuable subject for discussion, but that it should be postponed until a later time. He reiterated that he would never have accepted it, but that it had been in the interests of Islam and Muslims – 'the acceptance of this issue is more bitter than poison for me, but I drink this chalice of poison for the Almighty and for his satisfaction'.[38]

Over eight years Khomeini had for public consumption consistently maintained a strong pitch of determination to prosecute the war, to remove Saddam, to march to Karbala and even to Jerusalem, but it may be that in private he all along kept the reservations that he expressed in 1982 when Iran took the offensive into Iraqi territory. At any rate, the acceptance of the ceasefire was a great blow for him personally, as his son Ahmad later recorded:

> When, on balance, he felt he should accept the ceasefire, when he drank the poisonous chalice, I was with him. The television was showing our soldiers and he kept hitting himself with his fists saying 'ah'. No one dared to see him. After accepting the ceasefire he could no longer walk. He kept saying 'My Lord, I submit to your will.' He never again spoke in public. He never again went to speak at the Jamaran mosque and [eventually] he fell ill and was taken to the hospital.[39]

This was not just a political or a moral crisis for Khomeini, it was a spiritual and psychological crisis too. He believed that God had inspired and guided him, and the Islamic republic. But now God had decided to withhold from Iran the victory for which her leaders had sacrificed so many lives. Why? It is sometimes said that Khomeini and the leadership of the Islamic republic regarded the war as a blessing – in that it united the country behind the leadership, enabled them to overcome political opponents and to consolidate revolutionary institutions. There is truth in all that, but it would be wrong to suggest that was the prime motive behind the war or the continuation of the war. Khomeini believed, and the others like him, that it was a just war, and that Iran's pursuit of it was justified. As we have seen, any attempt to be objective should conclude that, for the most part, they were right in that (even if wrong in the practical assessment of the possibility of victory). The political advantages to the regime were real, and more than incidental, but they were collateral effects of a war that appeared to them to be just and necessary.

Nonetheless, the outcome of this just war fought in God's name had not turned out as its proponents had hoped or expected. It is a bold voice that declares it speaks for God. Khomeini believed he had polished his soul to such a point that his mind had become an instrument for the performance of God's will in the world.[40] Had he not polished enough? That could not be true. Instead, he seems to have concluded that submission and acceptance was the only course. Despite disillusion and anger, in whatever degree (and whatever the direction of his blame), and weakness and illness, his determination to persist with the principles of Islamic government he had established did not diminish.

Unfortunately, Iranian acceptance of Resolution 598 did not end the fighting. Showing his accustomed determination to be clever at all costs, it seems Saddam now decided that just to acquiesce in a cessation of hostilities, despite having advocated it for so long, would be somehow beneath his dignity. He wanted to assert Iraq's military superiority, to surprise everyone who thought it was all over with a new masterstroke and perhaps make some gains that could be useful in the bargaining of an eventual settlement.

To give himself cover for what was coming, Saddam made conditions for a ceasefire agreement, which were delivered to the UN through a letter from his foreign minister, Tariq Aziz, on 20 July. These included an insistence on direct talks about the ceasefire between Iraq and Iran. The purpose of this stipulation was that if Iran were to participate in direct talks, it would mean a de facto recognition of the legitimacy of the Iraqi regime and an effective abandonment of one of Iran's prime war aims – the removal of Saddam. Iraq's other conditions included UN intervention to ensure free passage along the Shatt al-Arab and through the Straits of Hormuz. Making these conditions had the effect of stalling progress towards an actual ceasefire.

Then, on 22 July, Iraqi offensives began up and down the front line from north to south. Up to this point, the response from Iranian volunteers had been sluggish by comparison with previous years but now, urged on by TV and radio broadcasts stressing the gravity of the situation, renewed waves of volunteers came forward. The new attacks reminded Iranians, and the world, of the way the war had begun eight years earlier.

In most of the areas attacked by the Iraqis, they were held. The Iranians evacuated Qasr-e Shirin and some other places when the attacks included chemical weapons. The southernmost offensive advanced forty miles into Iranian territory, towards Ahwaz, before it could be stopped; having done so, the Iranians then were able to push the Iraqis back to their start lines (by 25 July). But another attack began in the central sector on 26 July, pushing into Iranian territory towards Kermanshah (Bakhtaran). This offensive was carried out mainly by the 7,000-strong armed wing of the MKO; Iranian exiles who called themselves the National Liberation Army (NLA). They declared that they were marching on Tehran – many of them were women fighters, and for the most part they were not experienced troops. After its breakthrough (achieved with the help of substantial Iraqi air support) the Iranians allowed the attacking column to penetrate 100 miles into Iranian territory, almost to Kermanshah, before they were stopped by ground troops and air attacks. Then, as the column fell back, the Iranians hit it with F-4 Phantom aircraft and Cobra helicopter gunships at the Pattaq pass near Pol-e Zohab. By this time Iraqi air support had faded, and the battle became a massacre, with scenes that since have been compared with those along the Basra road when the Iraqis pulled out of Kuwait three years later. The shocked survivors fled on foot for the border. On 29 July the Iranians announced that 200 enemy tanks and 700 other vehicles had been destroyed. Thousands of MKO fighters, including some senior commanders, were killed, and many who were captured were executed on the spot. A few days later Khomeini sent a letter of congratulation to the commander of the air base from which the strikes had been made.[41] Saddam's last punt had lost him his stake – but the troops were not Iraqis, and it was not a loss he regretted too much.

This was just the prelude to another massacre. There was a heightened sense of crisis at the time, and some may have really believed that there was a danger of the MKO reaching Tehran, to be met by an uprising of

MKO sympathizers. But what followed was an overreaction by any measure.

Several thousand MKO prisoners had been in jail in Iran since 1981, and there were several thousand more Kurds, Fedayan, Tudeh and other political prisoners. Conditions were grim. Many of these people were, of course, motivated revolutionaries who had supported the revolution against the Shah, whose groups had fallen out with the IRP later (though some were youngsters and others with only tenuous connections to the MKO or other opposition groups). The prisons of Evin and Gohar Dasht were the mouths of the revolution as it ate its children. Although most of the MKO prisoners were young, in their twenties or early thirties (typically from middle-class backgrounds; the radical children of liberal parents), others were older, and some of them had been prisoners also under the regime of the Shah and SAVAK (as had some of their jailers, including Asadollah Lajevardi, who was warden of Evin in the first half of the 1980s).

As the confrontation with the MKO and the other violent extremists had grown more serious in the 1970s, and as the Shah's government had shifted away from its earlier democratic aspiration towards Rasta-khiz and one-party government, conditions in the prisons had got worse, and torture became commonplace (the change may have come directly as a consequence of the Siahkal incident in 1971 – the attack in which leftist guerrillas attacked a gendarmerie post in Gilan). SAVAK had used a variety of methods, including sleep deprivation, extended periods of solitary confinement, beating, mock executions, pulling-out of fingernails, electric shocks from cattle prods, rape and the electric chair. Snakes were found to be effective in breaking women prisoners. But the most effective was apparently the traditional *falak* – the bastinado or beating on the feet.[42]

In the time of SAVAK the torture had been directed at getting information – typically, the names and whereabouts of other dissidents. Under the Islamic republic there were changes, which overall, according to the unlucky ones who experienced both, made the new prison regime even worse.[43] Now the torture was normally directed at getting a confession, or interview (*mosahebeh*), usually recorded with a video camera. The push to recant from the authorities, from other prisoners who had recanted already, from loudhailers and all sorts of propaganda was unrelenting, and this psychological pressure was what made the new conditions so unbearable. Lajevardi boasted that 95 per cent of his prisoners recanted eventually. Because torture (*shekanjeh*) was formally outlawed under the 1979 constitution, what happened in prison was redefined as *ta'zir* (corporal punishment) because that was permitted in the shari'a. Sexual organs were not targeted any more, and the victims were always blindfolded. Electricity was not used, but there was an innovation, the Coffin – a 50 × 80 × 140 cm box in which a prisoner might be kept for months. Some went mad in it. The prisons were also much more overcrowded than in the time of the Shah, and several had to be rebuilt to accommodate new wings for extra prisoners. Evin, which had been designed for 1,200, held 15,000 by 1983. The overcrowding resulted in conditions that were effectively torture anyway – insanitary and unhealthy. Some cells held so many prisoners that sleeping time had to be rationed to three hours in twenty-four for want of enough floor space for more to lie down. Many inmates acquired serious illnesses.[44]

By 1988 several thousand prisoners had been executed already – the majority of them MKO. A reasonable estimate suggests a total of just under 8,000 between June 1981 and June 1985, of whom just under 6,500 were MKO. So those still in prison in July 1988 were the survivors. After Khamenei's letter to the UN accepting the ceasefire resolution and the announcements that followed it, many of the prisoners were optimistic, thinking that the end of the war was coming and they might be released. Others, when they heard of the MKO offensive toward Kermanshah, were also encouraged and hopeful, albeit for different reasons.

Angered by the MKO offensive; perhaps advised that there was a danger of prison breaks, or even that the overcrowding in the prisons had to be reduced, possibly influenced by others who had been meditating the idea for some time, Khomeini issued the following *hokm* (decree or order) on or about 28 July:

> Since the treacherous Monafeqin do not believe in Islam and whatever they say stems from their deception and hypocrisy, and since according to the claims of their leaders they have become renegades, and since they wage war on God ... it is decreed that those who are in prisons throughout the country who remain steadfast in their support for the Monafeqin are considered to be Mohareb [waging war on God] and are condemned to execution. The

task of implementing this decree in Tehran is entrusted to Mr Hojjatoleslam Nayyeri [the Religious Judge] and his Excellency Mr Eshraqi [Prosecutor of Tehran] and a Representative of the Intelligence Ministry. Even though unanimity is preferable, the view of a majority must prevail. Likewise, in prisons and provincial capitals, the majority views of the Religious Judge, the Revolutionary Prosecutor or the Assistant Prosecutor, and the Representative of the Intelligence Ministry, must be obeyed. It is naïve to show mercy to Moharebs . . . The decisiveness of Islam before the enemies of God is among the unquestionable tenets of the Islamic regime. I hope that you satisfy almighty God with your revolutionary rage and rancour against the enemies of Islam. The gentlemen who are responsible for making the decisions must not hesitate, nor show any doubt or concerns with detail. They must try to be 'most ferocious against infidels'. To hesitate in the judicial process of revolutionary Islam is to ignore the pure and holy blood of the martyrs.[45]

In accordance with the order, on 29 July the prisons were closed to visits. Radios and TV sets were taken away from the prisoners, letters were not accepted for them and telephone calls were not permitted. In addition, the regular law courts were closed (to prevent the families of prisoners from applying to them). The hearings began – to call them trials would be an exaggeration.

The head of the judiciary, Musavi-Ardebili, seems to have queried the order, asking whether it was meant to be applied only to those who had already been condemned to death or whether it was really to be applied to those who had been tried and given lesser sentences. Khomeini replied curtly, saying that it must be applied to all those who maintained their support for the MKO and ordering: 'Annihilate the enemies of Islam immediately.' In Tehran, Nayyeri, Eshraqi and Mostafa Purmohammadi (for the MOIS) set about their interrogations, and similar commissions went to work in provincial prisons. The prisoners had no inkling initially that their answers meant life or death – they were told that the commission was preparing materials for an amnesty settlement and that the purpose was to distinguish Muslims from non-Muslims. Those who declared themselves openly still to support the MKO were sent straight for execution. Those who responded to questioning by saying they had changed their views and recanted were asked tougher questions to test their sincerity. Would they denounce other MKO supporters, for example.

Some were even asked whether they would be prepared to pull on the rope to hoist up their former colleagues to hang them and, if they demurred, were sent off for execution themselves, on the basis that they seemed still to hold to their old allegiance. Very few of the MKO prisoners escaped death. In an echo of the prison massacres of the French revolution in 1792 and other mass killings in previous decades and centuries, Nayyeri in Tehran indicated the verdict in each case by saying 'take them to the left' (those fortunate few whose recantation was accepted were sent out of a door to the right). The condemned were allowed to write a will, and then they were hanged in batches of six. There was no drop, so they strangled slowly; some taking fifteen minutes to die.[46]

As July wore on into August and September the scope of the commission expanded to include other prisoners – mainly Tudeh members, Fedayan and other leftists. It is possible that Khomeini issued another decree in early September to this effect. Once again, many of the prisoners did not at first appreciate the significance of the questioning. For example, it was important when asked 'Were you brought up and educated as a Muslim?' to answer 'No' – because to answer 'Yes' would mean that a later avowal of Marxism was apostasy from Islam, to be punished by death. If prisoners could sustain the impression that they had been brought up in ignorance of Islam, they might be spared and could persuade the jailers they had recanted from their atheistic beliefs by praying, but lapses from the rituals of a pious Muslim were punished by brutal whippings.

As the interrogations and executions went forward in secret, the families of the prisoners were frantically worried, having had their normal channels of communication cut off. Several of them appealed to Montazeri in Qom, including a cleric who wanted to know what was happening to his thirteen-year-old daughter (the girl was executed).[47] Clergy tasked with carrying out the interrogations also appealed to him. When Montazeri found out what was happening (having had responsibility for the prisons a few years earlier, he was familiar with the system), he wrote to Khomeini:

> Three days ago, a religious judge from one of the provinces, who is a trustworthy man, visited me in Qom to express concern about the way your recent orders have been carried out. He said that an intelligence officer, or a prosecutor – I don't know which – was interrogating a prisoner to

determine whether he still maintained his [old] position. Was he prepared to condemn the hypocrite organisation [the Mojahedin]? The prisoner said 'Yes'. Was he prepared to take part in a [television] interview? 'Yes,' said the prisoner. Was he prepared to go to the front to fight the Iraqis? 'Yes,' he said. Was he prepared to walk into a minefield? The inmate replied that not everyone was prepared to walk over mines and, furthermore, the newly converted could not be expected to do so. The inmate was told that it was clear that he still maintained his [old] position, and he was duly dealt with. The religious judge's insistence that a decision should be based on a unanimous, not a majority, vote fell on deaf ears. He said that intelligence officials have the largest say everywhere and in practice influence others. Your Holiness might take note of how your orders, that concern the lives of thousands of people, are carried out.[48]

Khomeini did not waver, however. Far from turning Khomeini's resolve, Montazeri's intervention on the killings seems to have been one of the decisive factors in deciding Khomeini that Montazeri would not succeed him, after all.[49] Montazeri did not let up – on 3 August, as part of a longer speech, he said that it was important to preserve the values of the revolution and the execution of justice: those who committed crimes should be punished, but 'revenge should not override everything ... and lead us to exceed the bounds of justice'.[50] On 13 August he spoke to Eshraqi, Nayyeri and Purmohammadi in person, upbraided them and told them they should at least stop the killings for the month of Moharram, which was about to begin. They responded that they had already executed 750 of the MKO prisoners in Tehran and only had a further 200 to go – when that was over Montazeri could issue orders as he wished.[51] Overall numbers for those killed are hard to establish. By 15 August Montazeri believed that between 2,800 and 3,800 MKO prisoners had been executed,[52] but that was before the second wave of killings of leftists and other prisoners began. Part of the difficulty of establishing the truth about the killings has been the need to examine evidence presented by the MKO themselves, which has to be treated as unreliable. The MKO claimed that 30,000 died in total: the reality is probably nearer 4–5,000. In Tehran the bodies were disposed of in unmarked mass graves in cemeteries at Behesht-e Zahra and Khavaran/Khavarestan. Relatives were discouraged from going there to mourn; indeed discouraged from marking the passing of the victims in any way at all. Many of them only found out what had happened to their sons and daughters when the authorities forwarded small parcels containing the personal belongings the victims had taken into prison with them.

The regime never admitted the full extent of the killings, and although Amnesty International alerted opinion to them early on with an Urgent Action, awareness and concern about them outside Iran developed only slowly. But senior figures made statements at the time or afterwards that indicated, in more or less coded terms, that they knew what had happened. Musavi-Ardebili said at Friday prayers on 5 August:

> The judiciary is under very strong pressure from public opinion asking why we even put them [the MKO] on trial. Why are some of them jailed and why are all of them not executed? . . . the people say they should be executed without exception.[53]

In December, in an interview with Austrian TV, Mir Hosein Musavi said as prime minister that the MKO had been planning killings and massacres, and that it had been necessary to crush the conspiracy. In February 1989 Rafsanjani admitted there had been executions of political prisoners, but said that the number had been less than a thousand.[54] In February 1989, Khomeini himself wrote of having 'issued the decree of God on the Monafeqin . . . and the counter-revolutionaries' – linking that act with the occupation of the US embassy (the 'nest of spies') and the conduct of the war as things that could not be questioned.[55]

Some have suggested that the prison massacres were planned further in advance and were not a direct reaction to the MKO offensive of July. Whatever the truth of that, what happened does seem to bear the interpretation that Khomeini used the massacres, as he had used the hostage crisis, to create a complicity among the leadership of the country, to enforce a renewed radicalism and to weed out those whose commitment was lacking. Again, it has been suggested that he aimed deliberately to provoke and thereby to remove Montazeri from the succession by means of the massacre. That was certainly the outcome – but to see those sorts of outcomes as the result of deliberate plans is to over-interpret somewhat. Montazeri might not have reacted as he did. The point is that the action worked either way – it made clear who was to be trusted and who was not.

This kind of situation was addressed by the philosopher and social theorist Ernest Gellner when he wrote in 1995:

A collectivity united in a belief is a culture. That is what the term means. More particularly, a collectivity united in a false belief is a culture. Truths, especially demonstrable truths, are available to all and sundry, and do not define any continuity of faith. But errors, especially dramatic errors, are culture-specific. They do tend to be the badges of community and loyalty. Assent to an absurdity is an intellectual *rite de passage*, a gateway to the community defined by that commitment to that conviction.[56]

If Montazeri had gone along with the killings, he would have committed himself, as Khamenei and Rafsanjani and Musavi did. If not, then not, and he could be cast out.[57] One should also say that Montazeri's own motives may have been mixed. He had not, at an earlier stage, balked at strong measures against the enemies of the regime. He could, after earlier disputes, have been looking for a cause to justify a split with the ruling group. But that is ungenerous – one should not look too deeply into motives. In the circumstances, Montazeri's actions were brave and principled. They demonstrate a continuing truth of Iranian Shi'ism – that the *ulema* were never a monolithic bloc, but a loose assembly of thinking individuals; and that (unlike many secular ideologies in similar cases) the deep religious principles of Shi'ism provided a moral rock on which to base resistance to political expediency and abuse of power – and thus a source of hope.

There was, as part of the resurgence of war spirit after the Iraqi attacks of July, a strong feeling of revulsion and hatred toward the MKO among many ordinary Iranians. The Iranian leadership were certainly aware of this (leaving aside personal motives some of them may have had of revenge for the MKO's assassinations in 1981). One could see the killing of the MKO prisoners as an expression, even a legitimate expression, of that strong public mood. After all, the number killed were a tiny fraction of those killed in the preceding eight years of war. But that cannot be any kind of justification for what happened in the prisons, and the concealment is an indication that the leadership themselves knew that. Most of those who were killed had already been tried and sentenced for their political activities – some (who were called *mellikesh*) had actually completed their sentences and were still in prison only because they had continued to refuse to recant.[58] Some young prisoners had been sentenced to short terms for distributing MKO literature in school, and then were executed along with unrepentant, diehard

MKO activists. Whatever the views of the prisoners, no law could punish them for the actions of others (for the MKO offensive towards Kermanshah, for example) – to do so was just as much a violation of the normal standards of shari'a law as of any other kind of law, as Montazeri pointed out at the time. The questions put to the MKO prisoners were not designed to establish guilt or even traitorous intent; they were designed to entrap and to sweep away as many of the prisoners with a connection to the MKO (however weak) as possible – as was shown by Khomeini's clarification to Musavi-Ardebili of his initial order, and the deadly injunction in the original order to take a majority verdict and to disregard what it called detail. Such was the early fruit of the new doctrine of *velayat-e motlaq*. Did Khomeini really believe that God had inspired him to order such atrocities, so absurd in terms of Islamic or any other moral law? It was the blackest episode in the record of the Islamic republic.[59] And it may have served, for some of those who came after, as a precedent for ruthlessness and cynicism in the pursuit of what they perceived to be the interests of the republic.

As the executions were going on, the war was finally, really coming to an end. The Iranians had rejected Saddam's demand for direct talks, and Khomeini had authorized the government's foreign minister, Ali Akbar Velayati, to negotiate the ceasefire on Iran's behalf. The renewed Iraqi offensives after Iran's acceptance of Resolution 598 had made an impression on international opinion, denting the previous received wisdom that Iraq was the one looking for peace and Iran the warmonger. Opinion shifted to favour Iran. When Iran took the position that the Iraqi demand for direct talks was a unilateral, additional condition beyond the provisions of Resolution 598, the majority of UN Security Council members agreed, and Iraq came under heavy pressure to drop its demand for direct talks. Saddam backed down ahead of a ceasefire on 6 August. The UN Security Council agreed the implementation arrangements for the ceasefire on 8 August; on 9 August Rafsanjani ordered Iranian forces not to initiate any further attacks.[60] The ceasefire entered formally into effect on 20 August and was monitored by UN-mandated observers from twenty-five countries.

On 12 August President Khamenei made a speech that attempted to sum up Iran's experience of the war. He said that Iran had won a victory and had defended itself successfully despite the 'arrogant powers' of East and West joining hands and hatching plots against the Islamic republic. This was a lesson to others in the Third World who were struggling against oppression. Iraq had been given weapons and the finance to pay for them, but Iran's armed forces, Sepah-e Pasdaran and 'popular forces' had emerged from the war stronger than ever. Khamenei said that 'the war and the revolution proved that one can live without dependence on others and defend his country's honor and prestige'.[61]

Both the Iranians and the Iraqis claimed victory in the conflict. To the extent that both had claimed that the other was the aggressor, and both could say they had beaten off the attacks of the other and survived, both were correct. But Iran had been the victim at the beginning of the war and could claim with some justice that in its final year Iran had been fighting not only Iraq but also an informal alliance of other states, including the US and most of the countries of the southern shore of the Persian Gulf; notably Saudi Arabia, of course.

Over the period of the war various Western and other governments had supplied Iran or Iraq with weapons and had given other forms of help despite UN bans and embargoes. Several had given help to both sides: Britain had helped Iran with spare parts for Chieftain tanks in the earlier part of the war, only to help Iraq (notably through the murky Matrix Churchill/Supergun dealings) towards the end. The US and Israel had sent weapons to Iran; the US helped Iraq with satellite imagery towards the end of the war. The Soviets had sent weaponry to both Iran and Iraq at different times, but had given more help to Iraq. German companies had helped Iraq manufacture chemical weapons; France had sent powerful weaponry, especially aircraft; Kuwait, Saudi Arabia and other Arab states had assisted Iraq in a variety of ways, but especially with large loans. China, North Korea and Singapore also supplied weapons to one side or the other or both. Often the motives behind the various deals were mixed, not necessarily expressing a desire for one side to prosper more than the other. The arms deals were lucrative, provided hard currency to make balance of payments statistics look healthier, and were used to support defence industries that were in danger of becoming unviable. Towards the end of the war the overall balance of arms supply favoured Iraq, reflecting a degree of consensus among the international community, led by the US, that Iran was primarily responsible for the prolongation of the war. As a display of cynicism, of irresponsibility and of the failure of the international system to resolve conflict, the war set a depressing precedent. For many Iranians, the experience reinforced the belief that Iran could depend only on her own resources, and that fine words in international institutions counted for little.

Since the end of the war, various figures have been given for the number of dead: estimates vary wildly. It is often said that a million died on both sides; that Iran suffered a million casualties, 500,000 of them killed – but people have also said that 1 million Iranians died. In 2001, the then commander of the Sepah, General Rahim Safavi, said at Friday prayer in Mashhad that 213,000 had died, with 320,000 disabled. These figures were probably a sober assessment, but imply a larger number of wounded that had made a fuller recovery than those classified as disabled.[62]

Since 1988 the war has had an important place in the Iranian psyche. In those eight years almost everyone in the country was touched by it – it was not a distant war fought by career professional soldiers, but a war of volunteers, conscripts and reservists. Men spent time at the front, then came home. Some came home injured, some permanently disabled. Some went back again, several times; some were taken prisoner and returned only years later (because a proper peace settlement was never agreed with Saddam, some prisoners on both sides languished in camps until the late 1990s).[63] And many never came home. Their families worried about them when they were gone and tended to them when they came back. They watched television, listened to radio and read newspapers for news of the fighting. The war dominated the media – whether news or propaganda or a mingling of the two. Shortages and rationing also touched everyone – and then there were the bomb and missile attacks on the cities, touching the lives even of those remote from the front, creating fear and anxiety as well as yet more death and destruction.[64] Millions of people were displaced by the fighting, forced out of the war zone and ending up in the cities as refugees, looking for work, along with refugees from Iraq and from the war in Afghanistan (to be joined before long, after 1991, by a new wave of Shi'a refugees from southern Iraq).

It was a long war of intense experiences for many, many people – in general the sorts of experiences (comradeship at the front, shared fear in the bomb shelters) that drew people together, and it left a mark. Opinions on the war differed, but for many the successful defence of the country was a matter for pride. Before the revolution and the war, Iran's history for decades and centuries had been a history of humiliation, powerlessness, foreign invasion, occupation; of foreign interference and foreign domination, and Iranian politicians and governments that had connived at foreign interference. It is difficult for non-Iranians fully to grasp the deep frustration and resentment at that. Now, for once, the country had set up its own government by its own efforts, had rejected foreign meddling and foreign threats, had defended itself for eight years despite great suffering against tough odds and had come through. Iran was now a *real country*, with *real* independence, not looking to any other country for support, advice, help or guidance. The confidence and pride in that achievement, and the anxiety lest the country slip back into dependency, go a long way to explain what for many foreigners seems inexplicable about contemporary Iran and the behaviour of Iran's leaders since 1988. And it does not just apply to supporters of the Islamic regime, but also to many opponents of the regime and even some of those most bitterly opposed among the Iranians in exile.

This emerges in many different ways, but a good example is the following passage in Hooman Majd's book *The Ayatollahs' Democracy* (2010) in which he talks about his father's attitudes (his father had served as a diplomat under the Shah, but lived in the United States after the revolution):

> When I talk to my father today, and tell him stories about my meetings with current Iranian ambassadors and other officials, I see in him an envy, not for their positions or jobs, but for the way they behave and for their ability to act completely in the interests of their country, without regard for whether a greater power might object. And he, like so many of the old guard who detest the rule of the mullahs, expresses an (often reluctant) admiration for a government that has been able to accomplish so much in terms of its influence and power on the world stage. To the astonishment of those like my father though, it took what they considered the un- or under-educated, the provincial and unsophisticated, those who never succumbed to the temptations or the conventions of Western society, to turn Iranian dreams of past glory into realistic ones for the future. And sometimes even those most opposed to the likes of Ahmadinejad can reluctantly admire him for his in-your-face *por-roo'ee*, cheekiness or impudence, in the face of foreign attempts to control Iran or its development.[65]

The war had many bitter and painful consequences, but this new confidence also emerged from it – many Iranians prized it highly, and still do.

Whatever the overall consequences of the war on the nation as a whole, individual memories may be more about the intense emotions thrown up by random events and may often have a more ambiguous, ironic or bitter import, haunting people years later. The following are recollections from two different people; the first formerly an officer in the Sepah:

> We were going along a road when we heard some noises from people in a trench. We lay down immediately and took positions and started firing at them – they fired back. We were exchanging fire and launching RPG-7s at each other; it intensified, and some of our people were injured. As a result we had to get them away from the fighting area, and the firing slackened. But as it did we could hear the others, opposite us, who were attacking us, shouting 'Allahu Akbar'. We were astonished by this and said to ourselves, what strange Iraqis – they have become like us Iranians and call out 'Allahu Akbar' when they are fighting! But as we listened to them a bit longer we realized that they were speaking Persian, and then we realized that we had been fighting with another group of own Iranian forces.[66]

The second was an ordinary Sepah fighter:

> I can never forget the faces of my comrades – these faces are always in my mind. In one military operation we had been defeated, we were escaping. Everyone was trying to save his own life. I was fleeing too, when someone grabbed my leg – I looked at him and saw one of our comrades from our group – he aimed his gun at me [he was wounded] and said 'If you don't take me with you I will kill you.'[67]

The Economy

Even before the ceasefire came properly into effect, members of the leadership were talking about the need for economic reconstruction and the magnitude of the task facing Iran once the war was over. Montazeri commented to this effect in a speech on 3 August, pointing up as ever the sufferings of the *mostazafin*, and the need to alleviate the effects on them of the prevailing high rate of price inflation. As the ceasefire was about to come into effect and as it became clearer that it would prove effective and could hold, Rafsanjani spoke on 19 August, admitting that the economy had been damaged by the war ('If the aim of the enemies was to deliver an economic blow to us, they succeeded to some extent'), but saying that Iran had emerged much stronger than formerly, with its own effective war industries and large numbers of trained reservists. He added that, if peace held, reconstruction would become the prime concern – rebuilding cities and infrastructure, 'reactivation of industries ... and providing for the needs of the people'. He also referred to 'different views which exist on this matter' and said that the planning and budget committee of the Majles were already studying the country's post-war priorities.[68] In fact, the question of reconstruction was to prove highly divisive, following on from the arguments that had rolled back and forth in the war years, and Rafsanjani would be at the centre of the controversy over most of the next decade.

Although Iran came out of the war without the massive debt burden under which the Iraqis were labouring (and which would in turn prompt Saddam's invasion of Kuwait two years later) the Iranian economy was in a serious mess. It has been estimated that the war itself, by the end, had cost Iran around $200 billion. The combination of low oil prices since 1986 and war damage to the oil infrastructure meant that Iran's oil revenue was low by 1988, with the effect of depressing further the already low level of Gross Domestic Product (GDP). It has been suggested that GDP had fallen by 1988 to 54 per cent of its peak level in 1976.[69] The conditions of war had made the import of raw materials difficult, and the demands of war had diverted investment away from productive industry.

The policies of subsidizing consumer staples and controlling prices pursued by the government during the war had the effect of exacerbating the factors that always had the effect of weakening the non-oil sector in Iran's quasi-rentier economy. The economy was heavily dependent on oil (90 per cent of foreign exchange receipts), and nearly a third of those in employment had jobs in the public sector. Iran still had a high birth rate: the population went from 38 million in 1979 to 60 million in 1990 and 65 million later in the decade. Through the war the regime had encouraged a high birth rate as part of its patriotic propaganda – the census of 1986 revealed an annual population growth rate of 3.9 per cent, which was among the highest in the world at the time.[70] This meant a predominantly young population – more than half under twenty years of age in the early 1990s and nearly a third under ten. It also contributed to high unemployment; the official figure was 14 per cent, but private estimates suggested around 26 per cent. Rafsanjani's government shifted policy rapidly after the war in favour of contraception and family planning.

Consumer price inflation is believed to have risen from 18.9 per cent in 1986 to 24 per cent in 1987 and 25.4 per cent in 1988 (possibly higher, and to rise further; one should also bear in mind that the figures were artificially *low*, because of the dampening effect of price controls).[71] Many factories, Rafsanjani admitted in the summer of 1989, were operating at only 20, 30 or 40 per cent of their potential capacity. Over the period since 1979 large numbers of skilled people from a range of economic sectors had left the country. Much capital had been sent out of the country also – the *Tehran Times* estimated around $120 billion. Massive investment was needed in the war zone (and in cities away from the front that had been hit by long-range rocket attacks and bombing) to replace and repair destroyed and damaged infrastructure and housing. It was a daunting prospect.[72]

A New Republic

Khomeini was already ill in the summer of 1988, but the next few months were not going to spare him. It is hardly an exaggeration to say that the political landscape of Iran was transformed between the summer of 1988 and the summer of 1989; building on earlier developments like the dissolution of the IRP, the promulgation of the doctrine of *velayat-e motlaq*, the creation of the Expediency Council and arguably, the prison massacres. Some have called it an Iranian Thermidor; others have gone so far as to say that what emerged was a second republic.[73]

In September 1988 Salman Rushdie published his novel *The Satanic Verses*. Initially, the controversial dream sequences in the book, which included prostitutes who took on the names of the Prophet's wives, an apocryphal story that the devil had tried to insert subversive verses into the revelation of the Koran, and a fanatical religious leader called the Emam, seemed to create little concern in Iran. The passages that offended some Muslims were not central to the main themes of the book, which was about the ambiguities and the unease experienced by emigrants, and the cold hostility of Western culture, as perceived by them. Much as with the occupation of the US embassy in 1979, Khomeini seems to have reacted initially with indifference, only to reconsider somewhat later. It seems that when the question of the book was first put to him, he dismissed Rushdie as a lunatic and said the book was not worth taking seriously. The novel was imported into Iran and reviewed. But early in 1989 excitement was building over it – there were demonstrations against it by British Muslims, and in Pakistan, Bangladesh and Kashmir, where some turned violent, and people were killed. At this point Khomeini and his advisers decided that they should take a leading role in the international Muslim reaction against the book, and on 14 February Khomeini issued what is conventionally called the *fatwa* (though technically a *hokm* – a religious judgement or order):

> In the name of God Almighty. There is only one God, to whom we shall all return. I would like to inform all the intrepid Muslims in the world, that the author of the book entitled 'Satanic Verses' – which has been compiled, printed and published in opposition to Islam, to the Prophet and to the Koran – as well as those publishers who were aware of its contents are sentenced to death.
>
> I call on all the zealous Muslims to execute them quickly, wherever they find them, so that no one will dare to insult the Islamic sanctities.
>
> Whoever is killed on this path will be regarded as a martyr, God willing. In addition, if anyone has access to the author of the book, but does not possess the power to execute him, he should point him out to the people, so that he may be punished for his actions.[74]

Like the hostage crisis, perhaps like the prison massacres in 1988, the order against Rushdie reasserted revolutionary radicalism, and opened up a new gulf between the regime and those it had designated as its enemies. It demanded new commitment from regime supporters. It made a huge splash internationally and was widely condemned. In the immediate aftermath, a new body called the 15 Khordad Foundation sprang up (named after the date of the uprising in 1963), offering a reward of $1 million to anyone who killed Rushdie; they later doubled the amount. Khamenei criticized the foundation and suggested that Rushdie might be forgiven if he repented (Rushdie tried to respond to this and made a limited apology; something he later regretted). But

Khomeini slapped the president down again, saying that it was important for the Islamic republic to stick to its principles, in order to keep the confidence of the people and maintain the stability of the regime. On 28 February the Majles passed a bill breaking off diplomatic relations with Britain.[75]

No attempt against Rushdie's life ever came off, but his Japanese translator was murdered and his Italian and Norwegian translators seriously injured in separate attacks between 1991 and 1993. The EU collectively withdrew their ambassadors from Iran, and for a time Britain was represented within Iran by an interests section that operated out of the Swedish embassy. Diplomatic relations between Iran and Britain were restored in 1990, but they only exchanged ambassadors again in 1998, after a settlement between the two governments that included a commitment from the Iranian side that their government would not take any action to threaten Rushdie's life or encourage or assist anyone else to do so.[76]

There were many ironies about the Rushdie affair. Rushdie's underlying values of anti-colonialism and scepticism about Western politics were in some ways aligned with those of the Iranian revolution, and he had been awarded a literary prize by the Iranian government for one of his previous novels. After the Iranian death threat and some deliberation, the British government of Margaret Thatcher felt compelled to give him the most intensive category of close police protection but did not disguise a degree of distaste in doing so – Rushdie had long taken a firmly leftist political position and in *The Satanic Verses* had satirized the prime minister as 'Mrs Torture'.[77] Rushdie's relations with the police who became his daily companions and the other agents of the state assigned to look after him were often troubled – they were not natural bedfellows, and it was a relief to him when he was able to move from the UK to New York and a more open lifestyle at the end of the 1990s. One of the consequences of the affair that hit him hardest was the banning of the book in India and the Indian government's refusal to give him a visa, on the basis that his presence in India could encourage religious strife there.[78]

Khomeini's pronouncement on Rushdie was one of a series of interrelated events that blew up together in February 1989. 11 February was the anniversary of the revolution of 1979, and several Iranian figures had been asked for their reflections on the occasion. Interestingly,

Rafsanjani said that, if he could have changed anything over the last ten years, he would have prevented the outbreak of war, and suggested that it had lasted too long – 'some of us were opposed to the continuation of the war after 1982'.[79]

But Montazeri's statement was the most controversial. He urged officials of the Islamic republic to 'make up for past mistakes' and create an open society. He asked what had happened to the unity and devotion the country had enjoyed at the beginning of the revolution. Had the government lived up to the ideals of the revolution? Had it fulfilled its promises to the people? Had the regime done 'a good job during the war'? Or had Iran's enemies, who imposed the war on Iran, emerged victorious? It was necessary to count the losses, and the destruction, and then to repent the mistakes that were made. Montazeri questioned whether the slogans of the last ten years had isolated Iran in the world and turned the people against the regime. 'On many occasions we showed obstinacy, shouted slogans and frightened the world. The people of the world thought our only task here in Iran was to kill.' He praised Khomeini's recent decision to allow an amnesty for (surviving) political prisoners, and urged honest self-criticism and openness. There were two ways to celebrate the anniversary: one would be to keep the people in ignorance; the other would be to acknowledge mistakes and to invite everyone, whether within or outside Iran (alluding to the 'nearly four million' Iranians abroad who wanted to return but were scared to do so) to help with reconstruction.[80]

This statement was a direct challenge to Khomeini's conduct of government since 1979. Montazeri was still deputy leader, and still carried out the functions of deputy leader, and even if those in control knew that he had been isolated from the centre of power for some time, his views still carried weight (this presentation of them was a restatement and amplification of things he had been saying in lectures in Qom over the previous year, which had been serialized in the newspaper *Kayhan*). Some commentators took up his criticisms and agreed with them.[81] It seems possible that Khomeini's *hokm* against Rushdie two days later was a response to Montazeri – particularly to the line 'The people of the world thought our only task here in Iran was to kill.'[82] It would have been characteristic of Khomeini to counter-attack in such a way as to confirm the thrust of his previous actions with something even more dramatic and radical, that would make Montazeri's protests irrelevant – with something that would deepen and entrench Iran's confrontation with the West and with Western values for years to come. When the war ended in frustration, Khomeini laid a vicious blow on the MKO – even on naive children who had ended up in prison for showing a passing interest in the MKO. Betrayed by his chosen successor, who had dared to show some concern at the way foreigners regarded Iran, in his wrath he delivered an unprecedented and crushing sentence on Rushdie, reinforcing Iran's international isolation (and went on to lay waste Montazeri's political future too). Others were tasting the bitterness of Khomeini's poisoned cup.

Montazeri's statement was not the only thing to irritate Khomeini at this time. In a peculiar episode the previous month, Khomeini had sent a letter to President Gorbachev, suggesting that now the Soviet bloc was dissolving (Gorbachev had announced an end to the Brezhnev doctrine and Soviet domination in Eastern Europe a few months earlier) Gorbachev should turn against communism and embrace Islam. Khomeini sent three scholars to Moscow with the letter; Gorbachev heard them politely and told them he was honoured to have received a personal letter from Khomeini. But the letter to Gorbachev was controversial among the clergy in Qom because, in suggesting that Gorbachev should convert, Khomeini had sought not to persuade him with the writings of conventional Islamic authorities, but had recommended mystics and philosophers like Sohravardi, Ibn Arabi, Molla Sadra and Avicenna. This infuriated a selection of clerics in Qom, who sent him a letter remonstrating with him over his unorthodox choice of religious thinkers. This annoyed Khomeini in turn, reinvigorating his old animus (expressed in *Hokumat-e Eslami* and elsewhere) against the old-fashioned, narrow-minded mullahs of his youth who had disapproved of any form of study outside their own blinkered pursuit of arcane points of religious law. He replied to the Qom clerics on 22 February with a letter that made his views plain:

> This old father of yours has suffered more from stupid reactionary mullahs than anyone else. When theology meant no interference in politics, stupidity became a virtue. If a clergyman was able, and aware of what was going on [in the world around him], they searched for a plot behind it. You were considered more pious if you walked in a clumsy way. Learning foreign

languages was blasphemy, philosophy and mysticism were considered to be sin and infidelity.[83]

Khomeini was in combative mood. His blast at the clergy may have been motivated primarily by irritation at their attitude to his mysticism, but it also served as another blow to conservative elements among the clergy. He used the letter also to answer Montazeri's criticisms, particularly about the conduct of the war, denying that Iran had been defeated, and going further: 'Each day of the war brought a blessing which we used to the full.' He declared that, through the war, Iran had revealed the deceitful face of her enemies, the 'world-devourers' (i.e. the US and other Western nations), had realized the need to 'stand on her own two feet' and had consolidated the roots of the Islamic revolution. The war had been a religious duty – Iran had fulfilled that duty and could not therefore have anything to regret. He also took a side-swipe at 'sell-out liberals' and stressed the need to avoid compromising in order to please them.

His anger was not spent. He may already have decided that Montazeri would not follow him as leader, but when at the beginning of March Montazeri's letters from the previous summer about the prison massacres were published in the West and rebroadcast to Iran on the BBC Persian Service, Khomeini decided enough was enough (the presumption was that Montazeri's followers organized the publication of the letters). After discussion with Rafsanjani, Khamenei and two others, and after consultation with a gathering of the Assembly of Experts on 26 March,[84] Khomeini sent Montazeri an angry letter, telling him that he was 'no longer eligible' to succeed Khomeini as the legitimate leader of the state. Khomeini wrote that he had never really regarded Montazeri as suitable, but as had been the case also with Bazargan and Bani-Sadr, he had allowed himself to be persuaded by friends. He said he was heartbroken, and his breast was full of agonizing pain that Montazeri, 'the fruit of my life's labour', was so ungrateful. He had not thought that Montazeri could prove so gullible. He accused Montazeri of being in league with the liberals and the MKO; he alluded to Montazeri's patronage of Mehdi Hashemi, and the latter's trial and execution for 'deviance'. He ordered Montazeri to stop taking money in religious donations, and to refrain from interfering any further in political matters – otherwise 'I will definitely be obliged to do something about you. And you know me, I never neglect my obligation.' Looking forward to a time when the letter would be published, he finished with a peroration addressed to the Iranian people: 'I beseech God to forgive me and to take me away from this world so that I no longer have to experience the bitter taste of my friends' treachery.'[85]

Faced with this letter (Khomeini was only with difficulty persuaded against making it public immediately), Montazeri had no choice but to accept and make the best of it. He did so on 27 March with a reply in which he said he was not ready to take the job, that he had disagreed with the idea from the start (he pointed out that he had told the Assembly of Experts so at the time), asked that he be allowed to return to the seminary as a student and teacher and urged that no one should speak up on his behalf (there were some demonstrations in his support nonetheless).[86] Khomeini acknowledged Montazeri's letter on 28 March – by now somewhat calmer, he confirmed his affection for Montazeri and thanked him for his resignation. He wrote, 'the leadership of the Islamic republic is a difficult, heavy ... responsibility which requires strength beyond your capacity', and made reference again to the doctrine of *velayat-e motlaq* and *maslahat*/expediency: 'In Islam the interests of the system take priority over all other issues, and all of us should abide by that.'[87]

As with the acceptance of the ceasefire resolution, the general public were unprepared for Montazeri's fall from grace (within a short time his portraits disappeared from public places and his status as grand ayatollah was removed). Articles appeared in the papers to discredit Montazeri, saying that he had been taken in by evil-minded people, and alluding to the Mehdi Hashemi episode. Some alluded to his 'distancing from executive tasks and lack of firmness in dealing with opportunist elements'.[88]

Death of the Emam

Montazeri's removal meant that another successor for Khomeini had to be found. That question widened further the pending questions about the constitution, about factionalism and the strife and stasis it produced, and the uncertainties around the roles of the leader, the president and the prime minister – the ship of state had an overcrowded captain's cabin. Resolution of these questions was all the more pressing because Khomeini was seriously ill with cancer and heart disease, and his condition was worsening. On 24 April 1989, after petitions from the Majles and the judiciary, Khomeini appointed an Assembly for Revision of the Constitution, which set to work immediately. He also let it be known privately that Khamenei was his choice for his successor as leader. But because Khamenei was too junior and was not a *marja*, as the constitution required, the constitution had to be altered to fit him. The Assembly applied themselves to make these changes, but its members had not completed their work when Khomeini died on 3 June.[89]

Khomeini had been in hospital for several days and had come through a serious operation for stomach cancer. But then he had a heart attack. Khamenei, Rafsanjani and others visited him and there were emotional scenes around his bed as his health faded. On the final day he spoke to his family at 1 p.m. and asked them to put the light out because he wanted to sleep. After that he did not speak again and he had a further heart attack at 10 p.m., shortly after which he was pronounced dead.

The mass emotion that followed, especially at his funeral on 6 June, was comparable only with that on the day of Khomeini's return from exile ten years earlier. Several million people (estimates ranged between 2 and 5 million) came out for the funeral, and Shi‘a mourning traditions combined with the unique devotion Khomeini had inspired to produce extraordinary scenes. In the savage heat of high summer, the physical temperature exacerbated the emotional. Several people were killed and hundreds were injured in the crush as they tried to get close to the Emam's body. Firemen sprayed water on the crowds to try to cool them down and avoid heatstroke. Arrangements for a funeral procession and for the participation of VIP mourners had to be abandoned because the crowds could not be controlled. Instead, the body was taken by helicopter to the Behesht-e Zahra cemetery, but once there the crowds burst forward again, and mourners swarmed over the body, tearing up the shroud to take pieces away as relics:

> When the Huey carrying Khomeini's body touched down, the dam broke and the multitude began flooding into the empty square. Mourners converged on the open coffin as it was lifted from the helicopter. Revolutionary Guards hoisted it onto the roof of an ambulance in an attempt to carry it through the crowd to the grave only fifty yards away.

Frenzied men clambered onto the ambulance, straining to touch the shrouded body. Arms reached into the coffin. Hands caressed the bearded face of the Ayatollah. His body was pulled partly out of the shroud.[90]

Television cameras stopped filming. The body was retrieved, and the Sepah tried again later, using larger numbers and moving quickly. Eventually they got the body into the ground.[91]

Such was the grip on power of the ruling group, that the fact that Khomeini had died before the constitution could be amended made little difference. Despite the fact he was not a *marja*, the hastily convened Assembly of Experts elected Khamenei *rahbar* (leader) on 4 June 1989, less than a day after Khomeini's death, and before the funeral. The decision was controversial, and Khamenei himself at least affected some reluctance, as a video recording of the event shows (it also demonstrates the leading role Rafsanjani took in the proceedings).[92]

The Assembly for Revision of the Constitution completed its work of revision on 8 July. The main provisions were the abolition of the office of prime minister, and the stipulation that the leader need not be a *marja*. But some powers were moved from the president to the leader, and the power of the Majles was also reduced to some extent. In addition, the Council of Guardians was given greater powers to vet the religious qualifications of candidates for the Assembly of Experts[93] – a provision that was used later to remove radicals like Mehdi Karrubi and Sadegh Khalkhali. A Supreme National Security Council (SNSC), to be chaired by the president, was set up to coordinate and take decisions on key questions of foreign policy and national security (its decisions were to take effect once ratified by the leader). On 28 July the Iranian people voted both to approve the revised constitution in a referendum, and to choose Rafsanjani as the new president (Khomeini had apparently let it be known that this also was his wish before he died). Rafsanjani received 15.5 million votes out of 16.5 million cast.[94]

Thermidor?

So less than two months after Khomeini's death Iran had a new, conservative-aligned leader and a skilful centre-right/pragmatist president, along with the previous, leftist Majles. Some have called this convulsion in

Iranian politics the Thermidor of the Iranian revolution,[95] thereby comparing it with the coup in July 1794 that ended the radical rule of Robespierre and St-Just, bringing in a period of reaction and moderation that led to the rule of the Directory in 1795. But this comparison is misleading and to characterize the changes in this way, simply as a replacement of radicalism by reaction and consolidation, is to miss at least some of the point.

Over the preceding months Khomeini had intervened consistently to *reinforce* radicalism in the revolutionary system and to entrench it. Such was the effect of the *hokm* against Rushdie, and the intended effect of the new Expediency Council. So also was the intention of the ruling in favour of *velayat-e motlaq*, and Khomeini's general drift over this period to favour *fiqh-e puya* (interpretation of religious law to favour flexibility) over *fiqh-e sonnati* (interpretation that favoured tradition).[96] He kept a balance; he did not seek to crush the influence of the right within the system. But his recent actions had definitely favoured the left, and their statist, centralizing agenda.

At least, in terms of the previous left/right factionalism, they had appeared to do so. His actions had unforeseen effects after his death. As it turned out, the Majles was weakened by the imposition of the Rafsanjani/Khamenei duumvirate, and weakened further as the Guardian Council exercised more aggressively its responsibility of vetting candidates for election to the Majles, the presidency and other offices. But the traditional right did not benefit especially from the changes either; at least not initially. Rather than right or left, the state and those in control of the state were the immediate beneficiaries. In particular, Rafsanjani and those that supported him benefited. Faced with his own demise, Khomeini knew no one within the system would have his authority after his death. There was a danger that the previous factionalism, in his absence, would be even more crippling – even destabilizing. His overall purpose appears to have been to enhance the powers of the two men he had chosen to succeed him, so that they would be strong enough to maintain the revolutionary course he had chosen. Effectively, by means of the doctrine of *velayat-e motlaq*, he transferred to Rafsanjani and Khamenei the authority that his personal charisma had given him in his lifetime. In addition, he gave them one or two added nudges to remind them what that revolutionary course was, to uphold its radicalism and to ensure (as far as he could) that they would adhere to it. As it turned out, he was remarkably successful. It was not really a Thermidor (for all that some in the West hoped it would prove so, seeing the new prominence of the pragmatist Rafsanjani, the interlocutor McFarlane had hoped for in 1986). The state was strengthened, but what went before was not a reign of untrammelled radicalism and terror as in revolutionary France; and what followed was not a victory for the conservatives either – at least not for the main conservative faction.

In doing what he did, and by the combination of the *velayat-e motlaq* and the removal of the qualification that the leader must be a *marja*, Khomeini had moved justification for the Islamic republic on to very different ground. In the name of maintaining an Islamic state, principles of religion had been wholly subordinated to the requirements of power. To say that power corrupts is a commonplace – but perhaps misleading if taken too literally. There is corruption in the Islamic republic, as there was in the time of the Shah, and as there is in many other countries. But corruption in its narrow sense is not the worst that power has done. As in other revolutionary states, power has eaten up almost everything else; subjected every other principle to its own purposes. Rather than saying that power has corrupted, one might say that it has purified, by destroying or coopting everything that has stood in its way, in order more nearly to approach a point of perverse perfection at which power alone is worshipped, power only is enhanced, supported, facilitated and upheld.

Rafsanjani

Akbar Hashemi Rafsanjani was born in 1934 into a landowning family based near Rafsanjan in Kerman province, in south-eastern Iran. They were pistachio farmers, and it is often said that his large extended family today has since gained effective control over Iran's lucrative pistachio trade (Iran is the main world producer, with California a poor second in both quantity and quality). Like Montazeri and Khamenei, Rafsanjani had studied under Khomeini in the 1950s and early 60s. He was less scholarly, but all along showed a greater organizational and political flair. He was known to SAVAK as a close associate of Khomeini and was imprisoned repeatedly – in 1963-4, 1967, 1972 and again 1975-7.[97] After the revolution he was always close to the centre of the crucial political discussions and moved into position as one of Khomeini's main advisers, if not the main one, after the MKO assassinations of 1981 and the deaths of more senior figures (having survived an earlier attempt on his own life). In doing so, he acquired the nickname *Kuseh* (the shark) – though this was as much for his inability to grow a beard as for his predatory nature. He was an admirer of the nineteenth-century reforming minister Amir Kabir, about whom he wrote a book.

Rafsanjani used his office as speaker of the Majles and spokesman of the Supreme Defence Council during the war to reach a position of near-dominance under Khomeini, in which he became the decisive figure in balancing political factions and conducting the war. His support for Khamenei's elevation to the position of leader looked initially like a classic Machiavellian move (reminiscent of other skilled politicians in Iranian history, like Nader Shah).[98] He placed Khamenei in the top position, in circumstances in which Khamenei's weak religious credentials kept him effectively crippled, as a figurehead, while retaining most of the real decision-making power for himself as president. Khamenei's feeble position was emphasized by an embarrassing debacle toward the end of 1989, when Nicolae Ceaus̡escu of Romania was permitted to make a state visit (18–20 December) by Khamenei's close associate and foreign minister Velayati on Khamenei's invitation, just a few days before Ceaus̡escu returned to Romania, where he was deposed and executed (on 25 December). The visit was widely criticized at the time and afterwards, and Rafsanjani did not speak up to support Khamenei – some have taken this as the point at which their relationship began to sour. Khamenei also came under attack in the same month from Montazeri, whose followers put out *shabnameh* ('night letters' – circulated secretly) from Qom, criticizing Khamenei and disputing his suitability for the leadership on the basis that his religious credentials were inadequate.[99]

The transfer of power after Khomeini's death was carefully managed, and depended quite heavily on the recollections of Rafsanjani and a few others about what Khomeini's wishes had been. It is fair to say that no Iranian president has been as powerful as Rafsanjani was at the beginning of his first term.

Rafsanjani's presidency began well in the summer of 1989. Despite some radical opposition, he succeeded in getting the Majles to approve his choice of cabinet ministers quickly. Some succeeded more narrowly than others, but all passed their vote of confidence. A particularly significant case was that of the post of interior minister. Radicals petitioned Rafsan-jani to retain the previous incumbent, Ali Akbar Mohtashemi; and Rafsanjani himself made positive noises about him. But perhaps mindful of the role of the Interior Ministry in the conduct of elections, at the end of August Rafsanjani removed him and proposed Abdollah Nuri in his place. Despite the radicals' previous stance, the Majles confirmed Nuri's appointment with 224 votes to 20, with 15 abstentions.[100]

Similarly, a number of radicals expressed reservations about the five-year economic plan for reconstruction that Rafsanjani brought forward, but it was eventually approved by the Majles on 9 January 1990. It was helped in this by the fact that it was based on a draft brought forward initially by Musavi's government; but Rafsanjani and his colleagues made numerous modifications. Their basic judgement was that the economy was too much under central government control, and that government running of the economy was inefficient. Rafsanjani's followers called him the commander of reconstruction – *sardar-e sazandegi*. Central to the reconstruction plan were arrangements for the privatization of 800 or more factories and businesses that the state had taken over since the revolution – many of them administered by the Bonyad-e Mostazafan. Because many of them were in no condition to be successful as private businesses, investment was necessary to make them fit for privatization. At the same time, massive investment was needed in the oil sector and in the petrochemicals industry to bring production back to something nearer to full capacity (it was estimated that the installations at Abadan, for example, were operating at only around a tenth of their potential in 1989/90, as a result of war damage and lack of investment over the war period). Agricultural productivity was to be boosted by putting state-owned land into the private sector, and again, through investment. More investment was needed to repair war damage to roads and other infra-structure, and to housing. In later years there were many complaints about the patchy and partial way this was carried out. Another dreadful problem was landmines. After the war the UN estimated that there were 16 million of them scattered over the war zone in Iranian territory. By 2002 only 12 per cent had been cleared; it has been estimated that two decades after the end of the war three million hectares of land were still infested with mines, and people were being killed or injured by them at a rate of two *every day*.[101]

Investment on the necessary scale would only be possible on the basis of large-scale borrowing. The level of borrowing that would be required was disguised in the plan by optimistic forecasts for the value of future exports, including non-oil exports. The requirement for foreign credits was assessed at $112 billion (up from $97 billion under the Musavi plan); later revised to $116 billion. Majles deputies expressed concern about this at the time (on religious, ideological and practical grounds) but eventually acquiesced. Iran had come through the war and emerged solvent, but was now to embrace debt in order to facilitate reconstruction. The question of what economic policy the Islamic state should follow had never really been resolved, and had been shelved of necessity in wartime. Now the statist policies of the left were being set aside in favour of a more free-market approach, albeit one that retained major *dirigiste* elements in its preparedness to determine developments in key sectors like agriculture, oil, defence industries and motor vehicles and to stimulate economic recovery more generally.[102] The episode shows a number of similarities with the way that the Soviet leadership, rather against its instincts, resuscitated the Soviet economy with more liberal policies (called state capitalism at the time, or the New Economic Policy, NEP) in the period 1921–8, after the destruction of the civil war.

A greater emphasis on economic freedom under Rafsanjani was complemented to an extent by an opening-up of Iranian international trade, of foreign policy and, to some extent, of cultural policy at home. It was often called the Open Door policy. Rafsanjani's conduct of government succeeded, at least for a time, in teasing and tantalizing those within Iran and outside who hoped for change in a more liberal direction. But despite some positive developments, it never quite happened.

Saddam Goes to War Again

Iraq's invasion of Kuwait in August 1990 and the crisis that followed were a challenge to Rafsanjani's new policies of pragmatism and reconstruction. Iran had already been engaged in a policy of reconciliation and improved relations with the countries of the Gulf Cooperation Council (GCC – Saudi Arabia and the other states of the southern littoral of the Persian Gulf), and Rafsanjani was unwilling to abandon the progress he had made. Iran condemned Iraq's invasion of Kuwait, but as it became clear that the US would intervene, and coalition troops began to build up in Saudi Arabia for the campaign to liberate Kuwait, the left in the Majles (and some others) began to see the increased American presence as a greater evil. Mindful above all of the damage done by Iran's war with Iraq and the huge task of recovery after it, Rafsanjani was determined to keep Iran out of any new conflict. He resisted calls for a firmer stand against the growing US presence in the Persian Gulf – he had prevaricated also when Saddam had made new offers of talks before the invasion, in what became clear with hindsight had been an effort to secure Iraq's flank before the attack.

Rafsanjani continued to refuse urgings for Iran to intervene when the coalition offensive to liberate Kuwait began in January and February 1991, and when Saddam Hussein flew most of his air force out of Iraq to Iranian airfields to avoid their destruction (by this action also Saddam was attempting to draw Iran into the conflict). The Iranians took the aircraft into their own air force, in lieu of war reparations.[103] Some on the left went so far as to advocate support for Iraq against the coalition, but Rafsanjani was obdurate, and his ally Hassan Ruhani countered their arguments in the Majles. Nor was Rafsanjani persuaded to intervene against Saddam when the Shi'as of southern Iraq revolted (having been exhorted to do so by the US and UK) and asked for Iranian help.[104] The revolt became a massacre when Saddam turned his forces on the Shi'as, including helicopter gunships. An estimated 2 million refugees fled over the border into Iran, where many of them stayed until 2003. Much criticism, with good cause, has been made of the US and UK governments for encouraging the Shi'a revolt and then abandoning the insurgents to be massacred by Saddam. But it has often escaped notice that Iran had encouraged and then abandoned them too (though perhaps with more justification, given her recent experience of war).

After Saddam's rapid defeat the left looked foolish, and Rafsanjani's position was strengthened, which helped his supporters in the Majles elections that followed, in April 1992. Although the Council of Guardians had previously asserted their authority over the electoral process by vetting candidates in other elections (notably, in excluding former members of the Assembly of Experts from re-election to that body in the summer of 1990 – major figures on the left like Mehdi Karrubi, Sadegh

Khalkhali and Mohammad Musavi-Khoeniha),[105] this was the first time they used their powers to exclude large numbers of candidates in an election to the Majles. The formal powers of the Council of Guardians to supervise all aspects of the electoral process (including supervision of the Interior Ministry's handling of elections), in accordance with article 99 of the constitution, had been enhanced by amendments to the election law in August 1986,[106] but while Khomeini was still alive the powers had not been exploited to their full potential. Now Rafsanjani, Khamenei and their allies in the Guardian Council used the vetting of candidates to exclude from the election a large number of their opponents on the left, and to change the character of the new Majles in their favour. The Guardian Council rejected 1,060 candidates out of 3,150; including prominent previous members of the Majles like the deputy speaker Asadollah Bayat, and Sadegh Khalkhali. Other well-known members of the left faction like Mohtashemi, Musavi-Khoeniha and Karrubi were allowed to run, but did not get elected – the mood of the country had in any case shifted against the radicals. The main leftist grouping, the MRM, suspended its operations in chagrin after the defeat. The outcome of the election was a rout for the left, and a younger Majles dominated by new members and by the right – itself a turning point in the history of the Islamic republic.

Ali Akbar Nateq-Nuri was elected speaker in the new parliament, having previously been interior minister. Given the significance of the position previously, his appointment as speaker was a sign from the leadership circle that they had marked him for higher office in future. Hassan Ruhani was appointed deputy speaker. Within a few months, the new right-aligned Majles took a further scalp – after weeks of heavy criticism of his liberal-minded running of the Ministry of Islamic Guidance (known as the Ershad – responsible for censorship and the licensing of newspapers, among other matters), Mohammad Khatami resigned his job as minister. The left faction retired hurt, to regroup and rethink.[107]

Rafsanjani's economic reform and reconstruction achieved a number of successes. Economic growth accelerated – Rafsanjani claimed 12.1 per cent growth in 1990/91 and 9.9 per cent in 1991/2 – 8 per cent on average over the five years of the plan. This was one of the highest rates of growth in the world at the time. The government also made progress in balancing the books – bringing state expenditure closer to the level of state income. More state expenditure was devoted to development rather than current spending as a proportion of the total. Agricultural production rose, as did non-oil exports, and unemployment fell (to 11.4 per cent in 1993 and 10 percent in 1994 according to official figures). The government's new, more pragmatic birth-control programme brought the birth rate down from its previous frenetic levels to something more sedate and manageable (from 3.9 per cent 1976–86 to 1.2 per cent in the early years of the new millennium).[108]

Education

Whereas much effort in the first decade after the revolution had been dedicated to ensuring ideological correctness in education, in the period of Rafsanjani's presidency this shifted toward quality, making the education system more efficient, comprehensive and technically useful – and less centralized. After the Cultural Revolution, the universities reopened in 1981 (about half the academic staff had been purged), and in addition to the previous institutions, new, privately funded universities appeared – the *daneshgah-e azad-e eslami* or free universities (usually referred to as the Azad universities). If they could pay the fees, students could attend these universities even if they had failed the tough university entrance exam (*konkur*) that controlled access to the state universities. By 2011 about half of Iran's 3.5 million students were attending the Azad universities. Much of the teaching in them is done by academics whose main job is at the more prestigious state universities, but who take on the extra teaching to augment their salaries. Rafsanjani has been a strong supporter of the Azad universities and their expansion – another reflection of his orientation away from statist solutions and institutions.

Education policy in Iran has been one of the prime achievements of the revolutionary regime, in that primary education was finally extended to all, even in rural areas, and to girls; thereby achieving a high literacy rate (80 per cent). Because education at secondary level was segregated under the Islamic republic, and veiling was enforced, many traditional-minded fathers who previously would have kept their daughters at home, allowed them to go to school. Education in Iran is highly competitive, and in addition to the Azad universities there are also private schools at secondary level, for which parents pay fees in order to bypass some of the problems in the state sector and give their children a better chance in examinations (not unlike the situation in the UK). The emphasis on education reflects Iran's long history as a literate, civilized culture, and the respect for learning of ordinary Iranians; but the policy commitment to it, sustained even in wartime, also reflects the intellectual values of the clergy as the dominant political class. As in the time of Reza Shah however, the irony is that despite efforts to inculcate ideology through textbooks and so on, many of the newly educated youth of Iran have used their education to question the values of the regime that gave them their education.

One respect in which education policy has been less successful is in the schools in minority areas. The regime has insisted that teaching be carried out in Persian, but often the standard of teaching Persian to those who do not have it as their mother tongue has been deficient, producing lower literacy rates and standards of achievement among Azeris, Kurds and Baluchis and contributing to those groups' general sense of ill-treatment and of losing out.[109]

What Went Wrong for Rafsanjani?

In August 1979 Khomeini had said 'Economics is a matter for donkeys [i.e. idiots]. Our people made the revolution for Islam, not to eat melon.'[110] But Rafsanjani had presented himself and his purposes in a different way – as a statesman who would bring development and improve living standards after a long period of deprivation for many Iranians. He had put himself forward as a competent, practical man who could be trusted to achieve these things – in contrast to other, more ideological or less practical-minded politicians. But before long under his management the economy was running into new trouble. Initially the reconstruction plan was helped by relatively high oil prices, but after the success of the US-led Desert Storm campaign in Kuwait in early 1991 the oil price began to fall. Economic planning had been calculated on the assumption of an oil price around $30 a barrel, but by the end of 1993 it had fallen to around $14 a barrel. As a result, with imports booming and foreign exchange receipts falling, foreign debt ballooned (to an estimated $30 billion), and a large proportion of government foreign exchange revenue had to be devoted to servicing interest payments. In the midst of these developments, the rial fell heavily against the dollar in currency markets, especially in the latter part of 1993, when official devaluation failed to halt the slide in the value of the rial. Devaluation made imports and the servicing of foreign debt more expensive and boosted domestic inflation, which reached 35 per cent in 1993 – some say as high as 50 per cent.[111]

Dissatisfaction with the government's handling of the economy was growing, and there were demonstrations and riots in some parts of the country in 1992. When Rafsanjani put himself up for re-election as president in June 1993 he succeeded, but with a lower turnout than first time (just over 50 per cent as compared with 70 per cent) and a higher proportion of the vote going to his opponents than formerly (35 per cent). And when Rafsanjani submitted his cabinet for approval to the new, supposedly tamed Majles, the incumbent economics minister, Mohsen Nurbaksh, failed to be confirmed.[112]

Although Rafsanjani's second term had another three and a half years to run, the currency crisis at the end of 1993 damaged his reputation severely – given his previous emphasis on technocratic, practical policy-making aimed at restoring a thriving economy through greater liberalization, to fail in the area of economic management was especially humiliating. The gap between Rafsanjani and Khamenei opened a little further when Khamenei sent an open letter to the president urging him to pay more attention to the plight of the underprivileged, and to reduce the country's dependence on imports and foreign sources of funding, whether through loans or oil sales.[113] In the Majles, the government was criticized for failing to bring any reconstruction to many of the regions devastated by the war, which still lacked basic infrastructure.

Rafsanjani's proposals to retrieve the situation included big increases in prices for fuel oil, utilities, telephones and petrol; the Majles reduced the size of the increases and the size of the overall budget. Rafsanjani also tried to bring forward new legislation to facilitate foreign investment, which would have permitted companies to be up to 45 per cent foreign-owned. But this proposal ran into strong opposition from many sectors of opinion, and when the US government brought in the Iran/Libya Sanctions Act (ILSA) in 1996 (the Clinton administration had already applied executive orders to restrict US investment in Iran the previous year) it looked as though Rafsanjani's plans to bring foreign money into the country would be blocked at both ends.

Prime among the US government's reasons for bringing in ILSA were concerns over the Iranian government's support for groups like Lebanese Hezbollah, Islamic Jihad and Hamas, who were committed to the destruction of Israel, including through the use of violence. There were concerns also that Iran was pursuing a nuclear weapon programme, and in addition a series of terrorist incidents through the 1990s pointed, with a greater or lesser degree of certainty, to Iranian involvement.

In August 1991 Shapur Bakhtiar (who had been prime minister briefly at the beginning of 1979 as the Shah left Iran) was assassinated at his home in Paris. He had been active in exile politics against the Islamic regime and had survived an earlier attempt on his life in July 1980, after the Nozheh coup plot. One of the perpetrators was arrested and convicted; when he was released later (in 2010) he returned to Tehran.

In March 1992 a suicide bomb in a truck destroyed the Israeli embassy in Buenos Aires, along with a number of other nearby buildings (including a school). Nearly thirty people were killed, and hundreds were injured, most of them Argentine citizens with no connection to the embassy, some of them children. Islamic Jihad claimed responsibility, saying that the bombing was retribution for Israel's killing of a Lebanese Hezbollah chief; but the US claimed they had evidence of Iranian state involvement also.

In September 1992 three Iranian Kurdish leaders, including Sadegh Sharafkandi, were murdered with their translator at the Mykonos restaurant in Berlin. Sharafkandi had been Abdul Rahman Qasemlu's successor as head of the KDP-I after Qasemlu himself had been assassinated in Vienna in July 1989. An Iranian and a Lebanese were arrested and eventually convicted for the killings; when the convictions came through (in April 1997) the Berlin judge issued international arrest warrants for Iranian intelligence minister Ali Fallahian, as well as for Rafsanjani and Khamenei.

At one time the US blamed Iran for involvement in the Khobar Towers bombing of June 1996 in Saudi Arabia (which killed nineteen US servicemen and one Saudi), but more recently that attack has been attributed to Al-Qaeda (notably, by the Saudi government).

In addition to the various assassinations and bombings, the threat to Salman Rushdie was still current through most of the 1990s, contributing to Iran's image in the West as a rogue state and impeding Rafsanjani's efforts to normalize Iran's relations with the rest of the world. These actions may reflect continuing militant bitterness within the regime over the unsatisfactory outcome of the Iran–Iraq War, and the indifference of the international community to Iran's sufferings in it. But if the Khobar Towers bombing was not connected to Iran, it looks rather as though Rafsanjani's government halted these kinds of actions from the latter part of 1992 onwards, as part of his wider effort towards reconstruction and normalization.

The last Western hostages held in Lebanon had also been released by mid-1992, largely through the intervention of Rafsanjani's government – something for which the Iranians felt they did not get enough credit from the US. In particular, Brian Keenan was released in August 1990, John McCarthy a year later, and Terry Waite in November 1991 (Waite had been taken hostage in January 1987, after having travelled to Lebanon in a series of attempts to secure the release of hostages taken earlier). The US view was that the Iranians had at least partly instigated the hostage-taking in the first place and should not therefore be rewarded for belatedly doing the right thing – a view that was not wholly justified. Hezbollah were not under the thumb of the Iranians to the degree that some in the US believed.[114] The Iranian foreign ministry under Velayati made tentative attempts to move towards a deal with the British government to overcome the Rushdie problem over the same period.[115]

No Peace Dividend for Iran

A number of different factors conspired to prevent Rafsanjani from achieving the reconciliation with the West in general, and the US in particular, which some had hoped for and expected. The collapse of the Soviet Union should have created opportunities geopolitically, but Iran's uniquely bad relationship with the US, now the US was left as the only superpower, proved to have the opposite effect. There may also have been personal factors involved. Rafsanjani made largely successful efforts to end the more aggressive *ultra vires* activities of the regime that had burgeoned from the last years of the war and made a speech in December 1991 that was widely interpreted as a signal of a change in policy (drawing a line under previous activities in Lebanon, most obviously):

> The Islamic Republic now needs a prudent policy more than it needs anything else ... we need a prudent policy, both for inside the country, in order to strengthen our base, and for our foreign policy, so that we can have a presence and help people without being accused of engaging in terrorism, without anyone being able to call us fanatics. We have no need to speak fanatically. We have no need to chant impractical slogans. We do not need to say things which are not acted upon, needlessly frightening people and blocking our own path.[116]

But to no avail. President George H. W. Bush had said of relations with Iran at his inauguration in 1989 that 'goodwill begets goodwill'. But he was sensitive to suggestions that he personally had been involved in Iran-Contra (and/or the notorious October Surprise at an earlier stage) and even once the Lebanon hostage problem was resolved, and despite contacts with Rafsanjani's people that for a time looked promising, his officials were discouraged by the violent incidents associated with Iran, and the continuation of the Rushdie affair. Bush was unwilling to take risks with foreign policy as his campaign for re-election came closer. The Clinton administration that followed in 1993 was initially more focused on domestic matters and, in the Middle East, on the Israel/Palestine question; and it has been suggested that Clinton's first secretary of state, Warren Christopher, was especially hostile to Iran because of his memories of negotiations over the embassy hostages under President Carter. There was a further factor also – after the fall of the Soviet Union there was an unemployment problem within the US state system: former Kremlinologists were looking for a job. Some found it in Iran policy; but unfortunately they carried over too much of their previous thinking too uncritically, slotting Iran into the role of the former Soviet Union and labelling the Islamic republic therefore as totalitarian, expansionist and of course, doomed; none of which was ever necessarily the case.

This line of thinking had a number of effects. Over the years, it contributed to an attitude among some in the intelligence agencies (already seen at work during the period of the Iran–Iraq War) – an attitude that has proved dangerous in other contexts – whereby the expectation that Iran was up to no good, over time, helped to produce the evidence that demonstrated it. Intelligence contacts tend to tell their controllers what they think they want to hear. The Soviet model helped also to produce the policy that was called Dual Containment (drawing on ideas advanced originally by George F. Kennan for the handling of the Soviet Union in the late 1940s) – the idea that Iran and Iraq should be regarded as inherently hostile, to be contained and sanctioned rather than negotiated with. The fundamental fact was that Iran had such a bad image in the West, and memory of violent rhetoric and violent acts associated with Iran was still so fresh, that an alternative policy of rapprochement looked unappealing, risky – and also unnecessary. With the Soviet Union gone, with (as some were saying) history at an end, and no apparent major external threats to the US, there appeared to be no pressing need to look for problems to solve. Tentative attempts under both Bush and Clinton had been met with what seemed to the Americans to be indifference from the Iranian side. Awkward Iran could be left to lie fallow.[117]

Squabbles in the Seminaries

Over these years there were some changes and shifts of influence among the senior clergy, in which Ali Khamenei tried but ultimately failed to augment his spiritual authority.

Back in the time when Khomeini was in exile in Najaf, the dominant personality among the clergy there was Grand Ayatollah Abol Qasem Khoei, whose family came from Khoy in Iranian Azerbaijan. Not just in Najaf – Khoei was probably the most important and widely respected Shi'a *marja* of his generation. His opposition to Khomeini's doctrine of *velayat-e faqih* was a major obstacle for Khomeini. Khoei strongly favoured the quietist tradition in Shi'ism, which up to the time of Khomeini had always tended to be the prevailing view, opposing involvement of the clergy in politics.

So when Khoei died in 1992 (at the age of ninety-two), it looked for a time as though there could be an opportunity to assert the hegemony of the Khomeini tradition and *velayat-e faqih* over Shi'ism as a whole, by making Khamenei the sole *marja*. All the more because two other elderly *marjas* died over the next two years – Ayatollah Golpaygani in 1993 and Ayatollah Araki in 1994.

But despite great efforts on Khamenei's behalf by his supporters in Qom, this did not happen. Other clerics could not stomach the subversion of tradition and the permanent loss of authority that granting sole status of *marja* to Khamenei would have signified – in addition, they still could not accept his scholarly credentials as adequate. Rather like a student who is so daunted by the prospect of the *viva voce* examination that he cannot present his thesis, Khamenei still had not produced a *resala* – the treatise on religious matters, comprising guidance to followers on points of religion and law, which has to be approved by other clerics before an aspiring *mojtahed* can become a *marja*. The clerics in Qom put forward seven names for new *marjas*, one of which was Khamenei. But he had to accept that he could only be a *marja* for Shi'as outside Iran, a move intended largely to maintain his continuing authority over Shi'as in Lebanon.[118]

This was an extraordinary outcome, removing the practice of the clerical regime and of *velayat-e faqih* yet further from the traditions of Shi'ism. The influence of the quietist tradition was not broken – Khoei's followers (in Iraq, but also within Iran) largely swung behind his former pupil, Ali Sistani, who continued with much the same line. It was another humiliation for Khamenei, emphasizing further the weakness of his position, and the glaring contrast between his authority and that which Khomeini had enjoyed. Even in Lebanon Khamenei did not gain the full support he had hoped for – Mohammad Husein Fadlallah declared himself *marja* and gained a significant following among Lebanese Shi'as.[119]

The End of Rafsanjani's Presidency

The economic reforms of the Rafsanjani government had mixed fortunes in his second term, and by the end of it, despite some successes, they were generally perceived to have failed. To try to address the problem of inflation and high prices for consumer staples, which were attributed partly to failures in distribution, the government opened a series of Rifah stores – state-funded supermarkets, the first of which opened in February 1995. Naturally, the *bazaaris* and their political allies disliked this competition, which was hardly in line with the original policy of liberalization and decentralization – nor, perhaps, with the analysis of those who claim that Rafsanjani was in power primarily to further *bazaari* interests. It is probably fair to say that his most solid support was among the technocrats and bureaucrats in the public sector and the managerial class, rather than the *bazaaris*. To deflect criticism, the umbrella companies owning the new shops were eventually configured so that the government holding was reduced to 35 per cent.

Meanwhile, on the other flank of the government's reform programme, the Majles passed a bill in the summer of 1994 that crippled the privatization initiative, by stipulating that beneficiaries of privatization should be war veterans (*janbazan* – literally, those who risk their souls) and Basijis only. In practice, this meant that most of the businesses targeted for privatization remained under the control of the Bonyad-e Mostazafan ('Foundation for the Oppressed', renamed around this time as the Bonyad-e Mostazafan va Janbazan). Not only were future privatizations blocked, previous ones were annulled, and many became subject to actions in the courts. In addition, there were further clashes over the Ministry of Islamic Guidance, where the right in the Majles succeeded in installing a new minister whom Rafsanjani criticized for narrow-mindedness and intolerance.

By the end of the term of the fourth Majles in the spring of 1996, for all Rafsanjani's cleverness, the divide between the elected assembly and his government was wider than that between his government and the supposedly leftist third Majles, its predecessor. His conduct of government was widely regarded as having benefited a few at the expense of the many (producing, allegedly, a new thousand families of wealthy *bazaaris* and regime hangers-on, to compare with the old elite of a thousand families that were the great landowners before the 1960s), and as having produced only a mediocre advance in development and reconstruction. In fact, much of the renewal of economic activity after the war had spent itself in a construction boom and in property speculation. Some referred to his presidency as the Imperial Presidency, and even compared him with the Shah. People drew attention to the way that his wealth and the wealth of his family had grown:

> Last night a few friends were round our house. One of them told a joke that I have to share with you.
>
> When Rafsanjani is asked about his financial standing before and after the Revolution, he replies that 'Before the Revolution I had a piece of land in the centre of Rafsanjan . . . Now the town of Rafsanjan is [a piece of land] in the middle of the land I own.'[120]

A group of Rafsanjani's supporters responded to his critics in the Majles in January 1996 with a statement that suggested the Majles as an institution had been at its best when he had been speaker (and by implication, had declined since), a position that seemed to many to emphasize Rafsanjani's grand sense of himself, however much his own supporters might agree with it.[121] The statement was a precursor to another, more formal innovation. With elections for the fifth Majles coming up, in January 1996 Rafsanjani's supporters brought forward a new grouping to try to combat the over-mighty right faction in the outgoing Majles. They were called the Servants of Reconstruction – Kargozaran-e Sazandegi (sometimes called instead – without irony – Kargozaran-e Nezam, or Servants of the System).

Prominent among adherents of this new grouping was Gholam-hosein Karbaschi, who had made a name for himself and had achieved some popularity as mayor of Tehran, at a time when the reputation of politicians generally had retreated to a low ebb. In addition to steps he took to attempt to beautify the city with extensive tree planting, Karbaschi had a flair for populist actions that nonetheless had a political edge and won him the approval of many, even of the poorest. One example was his handling of wealthy *bazaaris* suspected of evading taxes – they found their shops walled up overnight. When they asked for the shops to be opened up again, they found that the bill for doing so matched the original tax demand.[122]

The right faction, still led by Nateq-Nuri in the Majles as speaker, reacted with great hostility to the appearance of Kargozaran, unsuccessfully disputing the loyalty of the new group to Khamenei. When the elections were held in March and April 1996, Kargozaran did well, winning around seventy seats and, together with a few left-faction members and other independents, creating a voting bloc substantial enough to resist the right faction organized around the JRM. This was despite some attempts to readjust the results after the fact – Nateq-Nuri managed to boost his vote by claiming that some of his supporters had been confused by the similarity between his name and that of Abdollah Nuri. The authorities obligingly gave Nateq-Nuri half of Abdollah Nuri's votes.[123]

It was in this tetchy atmosphere of political point-scoring, disunity and disillusionment that Iran slipped into the run-up to the 1997 presidential elections, the outcome of which was to prove a shock for everyone.

6

Bim-e Mowj (Fear of the Wave): Khatami and Reform, 1997–2005

As the presidential elections of 1997 approached, there were rumours a year or more ahead of the date that Rafsanjani might somehow amend or avoid the provision of article 114 of the constitution that a president could only be re-elected once and not run for a third term. This was plausible – more plausible than that a big fish like Rafsanjani would have no plan for the continuation of his prominent role in Iranian politics. But a message from Khamenei was read at the opening of the fifth Majles on 1 June 1996 in which he said that 'with divine succour and guidance' the president's responsibilities for government would pass to a new 'prominent and elected personality'. This was interpreted to mean that Khamenei would not allow Rafsanjani a third term (though speculation continued thereafter). Whether Rafsanjani himself decided not to pursue a third term of office or whether Khamenei blocked the move, in the end nothing came of it, leaving hanging the question of what Rafsanjani would do with himself once his presidency ended.[1]

It was assumed from an early stage that the candidate of the right, supported by Khamenei and the JRM, would be Nateq-Nuri, the speaker of the Majles since 1992. How and by whom he might be opposed remained unclear for rather longer – but most presidential elections had in effect been coronations rather than real contests up to that time. Many would have assumed that, with the support of the state media and the *nezam* (the system – i.e. the revolutionary state) as a whole, Nateq-Nuri would become the next president without any serious opposition. That certainly seemed to be Nateq-Nuri's own assumption – he was not a lovable or impressive character,[2] and his conduct in the run-up to the elections suggested that he saw himself as president already. People joked that whereas in Western countries results of elections might be known within twenty-four hours, in Iran they were known three months in advance. By letting it be known that he was the preferred candidate so far ahead of the election, Nateq-Nuri's own arrogance, and the arrogance of the right in pushing him forward, which seemed to show that they thought they owned the system itself, gave the opposition to him both impetus and time to build, consolidate and organize.

As part of this process, Mehdi Karrubi announced in October 1996 that the MRM would be resuming their political activities, and at the same time called upon Mir Hosein Musavi to stand for president. But a month later, perhaps prompted by the memory of his clashes with Khamenei when the two were prime minister and president respectively in the 1980s, Musavi declared he would not run for the presidency. For a time, it looked as though Rafsanjani's supporters and the MRM would not be able to agree on a candidate. Nateq-Nuri and former intelligence minister Mohammad Reyshahri announced themselves formally as candidates in November.

Then at the end of January 1997, backed by the MRM, Mohammad Khatami announced that he would stand for the presidency. Kargozaran gave him their support too, within a few weeks; as did other groups aligned against the right.[3] At this time, having resigned as minister of Islamic guidance in 1992, Khatami was serving as the head of the National Library. There is a story that at the time his candidacy was announced, Khatami was attending an international conference of librarians, and was due to speak, but when his time came the chairman of the conference went to the podium and announced that unfortunately there had to be a change in the programme because Mohammad Khatami had been called away to be president of Iran.

Khatami

Khatami was born in Ardakan in Yazd province in 1943, the son of Ayatollah Ruhollah Khatami, a distinguished cleric, *seyyed* and friend of Khomeini. Khomeini appointed Ruhollah Khatami as Friday prayer leader in Yazd in 1982; one of Mohammad Khatami's brothers, Mohammad Reza, married Khomeini's granddaughter Zahra Eshraqi.

Mohammad Khatami studied in Qom under Montazeri and Mottahari and was especially close to the latter, but also studied philosophy (including Western thinkers like Kant, Hegel and Rousseau) on courses at secular universities in Tehran and Isfahan. In the 1970s he became a member of the circle of Khomeini's supporters and, in particular, a close friend of Khomeini's son Ahmad. At the time of the revolution he was director of the Islamic Centre in Hamburg, following on from Beheshti. He was first appointed as minister of Islamic guidance in 1982 by Musavi, but was confirmed in that office later when Rafsanjani became president. So although he presented himself as a rather bookish, modest, academic character (when speaking to student audiences he often called himself 'little student') Khatami was well connected politically, and from his time at the Ershad he had strong and friendly contacts in film, TV, journalism and literary spheres also. Having been a founding member of the MRM he came from the left, but had served also under Rafsanjani, and had represented a strand of Rafsanjani's tentative liberalization. His clash with the right in the Majles over cultural policy had given him credibility both with the left and with Rafsanjani's supporters, and had shown his principled commitment to greater intellectual freedom in Iran's public life. But he also had strong religious credentials, and was a *seyyed*, which gave him some protection from attacks by traditionalists.[4]

Although state media favoured Nateq-Nuri both editorially and with the amount of airtime they gave him (Ayatollah Mahdavi-Kani was quoted in a newspaper article as saying that Khamenei favoured Nateq-Nuri), the support given by many journalists and media people for Khatami's platform of greater cultural freedom and what he called civil society more than outweighed Nateq-Nuri's initial advantage. Civil society meant respect for the rule of law and the constitution, human rights, the rights of minorities and women, social justice and a greater role for real democracy – it had deep historical resonances back to the Constitutional Revolution and beyond. Khatami was fully conscious of the historical significance of what he was trying to do and discussed these aspects openly. Nateq-Nuri appeared on TV and in public to be a complacent supporter of the status quo, and personally boring and uninspiring. Most Iranians were unhappy with the status quo, and Khatami and his advisers (notably, former deputy intelligence minister Said Hajjarian) set out deliberately to appeal to them. He travelled around the country, talking to young people, students, Kurds, Arabs and other groups to whom regime politicians had not bothered to talk for years. Women liked Khatami and many of them had been irritated by a decision of the Guardian Council to rule out female candidates for the presidency (the Guardian Council approved four candidates on 8 May 1997 – Nateq-Nuri, Khatami, Reyshahri and Reza Zavarei, a former member of the Guardian Council).

Khatami's media support was innovative and intelligent; Nateq-Nuri's campaign came across by contrast as clunky, patronizing and dull. Khatami's educated, modest, quietly smiling personality appealed to Iranians partly because he reflected the way they wanted to think about themselves and their country – Nateq-Nuri by contrast reminded them of what had gone wrong since 1979. Unwisely, he made a trip to Russia, where he was welcomed in person by President Yeltsin and treated as if he had already won the election. Another *faux pas* emerged when it was revealed that Nateq-Nuri's close associate Mohammad Javad Larijani (the eldest of the five influential Larijani brothers) had made a trip to London, had allegedly held secret talks with British Foreign Office officials, and in the course of them had spoken negatively about the competence of the supreme leader and dismissively about Khomeini's decree against Rushdie. Nateq-Nuri and his supporters seemed to be hobnobbing with Iran's old enemies and to be subverting the institutions and values they had professed to uphold.[5]

The Larijani brothers were the sons of the prominent cleric Ayatollah Mirza Hashem Amoli and derived their influence largely from their close relations with Ali Khamenei. After Mohammad Javad's *faux pas* in 1997 his career waned somewhat, but his brother Ali, who had been a deputy commander of the Sepah, had held ministerial positions in the 1980s and under Rafsanjani in the 90s, and was then head of the state broadcasting corporation IRIB, later went on to be speaker of the Majles, secretary (and Khamenei's representative) on the Supreme National Security Council and (briefly) Iran's chief negotiator on the nuclear question. A third brother, Sadegh Larijani, was appointed head of the judiciary in June 2009, having served on the Guardian Council since 2001.[6] Having pinned their fortunes to those of Khamenei, the brothers have become perhaps the ultimate regime insiders.

As the 1997 election campaign progressed, it seemed Nateq-Nuri and his supporters could do nothing right. When *hezbollahis* targeted

Khatami's meetings with students (some of his earliest and most enthusiastic supporters were students) and heckled, their boorishness contrasted badly with his dignity, and their violence served to reinforce the point of his civil society message (Ansar-e Hezbollah also attacked some of Khatami's campaign offices, and law enforcement authorities stood aside to let them do so). Khatami's supporters alluded to the growing power of religious extremists in Afghanistan and called Nateq-Nuri and his people the Taleban of Iran.

No one predicted the overwhelming nature of the eventual result, but in the weeks before election day on 23 May there were signs that support for Khatami was building, and that in three short months his message and his campaign had caught the nation's imagination. In the last few days before the poll, as excitement grew, concern also grew that the authorities might interfere with the election, and Rafsanjani made an important speech on 19 May warning against any such action: 'The worst crime I know of is manipulating the will of the electorate; it is an unpardonable sin.' Attacks on Khatami's reputation from the hardline right intensified, alleging incompetence for office and lack of hard experience. There was speculation that the Sepah or the Basij might intervene to prevent Nateq-Nuri being defeated. But it seems Khamenei held back from the sin of which Rafsanjani had spoken – this time. On the day, with a high turnout of 80 per cent, Khatami won 70 percent of the vote, and a huge mandate for his reform agenda.[7]

The election success of what came to be called the 2 Khordad Movement (after the date of the election in the Iranian calendar) was important in a number of ways. It seemed to show that the Iranian system was capable of change from within; that even if democracy in Iran was far from perfect, it was nonetheless a form of democracy that could deliver nasty surprises for those who sought to contain it, and provide a new government based on the wishes of the people. It gave reason for renewed faith in the system set up by the revolution, and hope for further changes for the better in the future. It was a time for enthusiasm and euphoria, and a feeling of national near-unity and optimism that had not existed since 1979. Only in Mazanderan (Nateq-Nuri's home province) and Lorestan did Khatami not win a majority. Even in Qom, dominated by the religious seminaries, he got over 58 per cent of the vote. In Tehran he got over 75 percent; in Khuzestan over 82 per cent.

It was rumoured (though verification has been elusive) that even within the Sepah 70 per cent voted for him.[8]

Reformists and Hardliners

Behind the euphoria, there were some strange features to Khatami's reform movement. Khatami was a man of principle, but some supporters followed the banner of reform primarily because the movement was the best opportunity for defeating their enemies on the right. Part of the bitterness of the election battle had derived from the fact that some on both sides felt that some personalities (notably the Larijani brothers, but figures on the reformist side too) could have jumped either way. Despite its popularity with the young and its strong emphasis on the need for change and renewal, the movement included many figures who had been heavily involved in the politics and government of the Islamic republic for a long time – including Mehdi Karrubi, Said Hajjarian, Ataollah Mohajerani, Behzad Nabavi, Abdollah Nuri, Hadi Khamenei (brother of the supreme leader) and Gholamhosein Karbaschi. Some reformists had a radical past – including Mohammad Musavi-Khoeniha, the prime mover behind the embassy hostage crisis (and Ali Akbar Mohtashemi, the early enthusiast for export of the revolution and a major figure in the establishment of Lebanese Hezbollah). Several other prominent reformists had been among the hostage-takers, including Hajjarian, but also Abbas Abdi (one of the first student leaders into the compound) and Massoumeh Ebtekar (whom the hostages had called Screaming Mary), who later became Iran's first female vice-president under Khatami. Most notoriously of all, Sadegh Khalkhali became a reformist (he died in 2003).

A blogger commented in January 2003:

> The funny thing is ... this new lot of reformists we have in the Government ... try to claim anyone these days who stands up to the regime as one of their own ... and give interviews saying that we support free speech and reform ... They think we have forgotten that some of these people who are now 'reformists' called Montazeri a naïve fool when he resigned![9]

Iranian politics was, and is, often more about personalities and the relationships between them than about political groups or parties, which have tended to have an ambiguous or ephemeral significance. The ban on most political parties under Khomeini had the effect of reinforcing this tendency. Groups have tended to be loose, with little internal discipline or coordination of policy lines, which in turn has made it difficult for them to sustain a consistent identity over time or create lasting loyalty toward them among the general population.[10] Powerful, successful figures have supporters, relatives and hangers-on of varying degrees of usefulness, who receive jobs and patronage in return.

Typical for many of the reformists was a process of growing up – for many of them the experience of revolution had turned them away from previous sloganeering rhetoric (deriving partly from the foolish language of 1960s student radicalism in the West) of extremism, direct action and violence towards more mature, liberal positions of non-violence and con-stitutionalism. Politicians, like anyone else, are entitled to change their minds in the light of experience – indeed, one might say it is a duty to do so. Nonetheless, people like Ebrahim Yazdi, Dariush Foruhar and Ezzat-ollah Sahabi, who had stuck to their Islamic liberal principles all along, and had suffered for them, were entitled to be sceptical about some of the apparent conversions (Mehdi Bazargan, the grand old man of Islamic liberalism in Iran, had died in 1995). Some Western observers whose seri-ous interest in Iran began with Khatami's surprise election victory in 1997 missed out on the ambiguous hinterland of some in the reform movement.

The gap between appearance and reality, and the difficulty (some would say, the impossibility) of perceiving the latter truly, are central to the business of politics. Both reformists and hardliners traded on a vir-tuous self-image and suffered abuse for a negative portrayal by others. Both the positive and negative pictures usually contained an element of truth; otherwise they would not have gained currency. The hardliners were often portrayed as hidebound, unimaginative; often corrupt, vindictive or ignorant. But even some of their enemies respected the integrity, modesty, trustworthiness and adherence to principle of many on the right. In a political culture where much depends on personal relationships and commitments, this kind of personal integrity is impor-tant. The reformists followed attractive principles of openness, freedom and the rule of law; they had the aura of youth and freshness; many of them were well educated, articulate and charismatic. But some at least (not Khatami himself) were tainted with a suspicion of opportunism or unreliability; as a whole, the movement had a fissiparous streak.

There was, again, a class element involved. The reformist leadership tended to be educated and middle-class; they wore suits and sported what in the West would have been called designer stubble. The hardliners were more likely to be bearded, less sharply dressed, coming from lower-middle-class, *bazaari* or rural backgrounds. But at least in this phase, the reformists were able to reach out and win mass support across class divisions.

Theories of Reform

By 1997 a new intellectual movement had sprung up to complement and underpin the political movement for reform. It is striking that this movement was strongly religious in character – not seeking to remove religion from politics as such, but looking critically at the way religion and politics operated within the existing system and trying to find ways to make it work better. Important within this movement were Abdolkarim Sorush, Mohammad Shabestari, Hasan Yusefi Eshkevari and Mohsen Kadivar, but also active politicians like Said Hajjarian, Abdollah Nuri and Khatami himself.

Of these, Sorush was one of the first to make a name for himself. After the revolution, he served for a time with the body responsible for purging the universities at the time of the so-called Cultural Revolution, but later left it because he was unhappy with the extremism of some of the other members and their decisions, and avoided other official appointments, teaching instead at Tehran University. He wrote prolifically in the 1980s and 90s; his works were widely read and debated, especially in the universities, and from 1996 onwards he spent an increasing part of his time outside Iran because of the adverse reaction of hardline elements of the regime to his criticisms of the system. Developing from the positions of Shariati, Bazargan and others, he again urged the need for Islam to adapt to new conditions. He suggested that there was, and should be, a dialogue between different kinds of knowledge, from whatever source – whether religion, reason or science. Each responded to the others – 'the shari'a is not independent of our understanding of nature and science, and changes to it'. But the clergy were too traditional-minded and not open enough to other sources of knowledge. What was necessary, argued Sorush, was not the ideological form of Islam advocated by Shariati, but openness and debate on the basis of reason, within the forum for equal debate provided by democratic institutions. Sorush also argued for a greater separation of religion and politics, on the basis that secularization of politics was not done in a spirit hostile to religion, but rather the reverse – religion had to be kept out of politics in order to prevent it becoming contaminated by politics, as had happened under the Islamic republic.[11]

These thoughts were held in common by the reformist thinkers, and many other ordinary Iranians, one of whom commented in May 2003:

> The call to prayer, the Allahu Akbar, still makes me feel like a stronger person ... but I rarely enter a mosque ... all that awaits you there are the hypocrites, thugs and oppressors.
>
> We replaced one corrupt monarch with thousands of corrupt clergy ... yet the only thing they did was destroy our belief in the religion they said they were safeguarding ... We were already Muslims and did not have a revolution to become Muslims ... our dreams were of equality, independence and justice ... but I hope that when they leave we will still be Muslims ... and my God can be Great again.[12]

There was general agreement among the reformist thinkers that the traditional concept of *ijtihad* (the interpretation and application of holy texts to practical problems through the use of reason) needed to be radically expanded and made more flexible to cope with modern conditions. Shabestari advocated 'continuous *ijtihad*' (*ijtihad-e mostamar*) – given the rapidly changing world, Islam needed new *ijtihad* on all fronts, and again, this could only be done in a free, democratic society:

> I endorse democracy because it is the only system in contemporary times that allows mankind to reach the twin ideals of freedom and justice, without which humanity cannot fulfil its true potential and adequately perform its responsibilities before the Almighty. Only through free choice can mankind meet the full range of his responsibilities before God.[13]

Mohsen Kadivar's writings, though they trod carefully, presented a firm advocacy of human rights as developed in the West in philosophy and law, and given in the UN charter. He distinguished between Koranic and what he called Historical Islam: the latter gradually incorporated, for reasons of political and social convenience or necessity, notions that were either not contained in the Koran, or which in some cases were in direct contradiction of it. Freedom of belief and religion were entirely in accordance with the Koran, and equality between the sexes; it was not acceptable to punish apostasy with death. There was no incompatibility between Islam and democracy – Eshkevari has also put much emphasis on this aspect, and the centrality in Koranic Islam of the idea that secular authority should flow from the people.[14] Kadivar also examined at length the theory of *velayat-e faqih*, distinguishing between the version of *velayat-e motlaq* that Khomeini was bringing forward towards the end of his life, and what Kadivar called *velayat-e entekhabi-e moqayyadeh*, conditional and elected guardianship, as advocated by Montazeri (similar also to the ideas advocated by Baqr al-Sadr in Iraq). The latter emphasized the elected element of the concept of guardianship and the need for the *vali* to be actively supervised by other elected figures and bodies. But in any case, Kadivar stated that *velayat-e faqih* was not a necessary feature of Islam, or a logical development from it. Islam could be consistent with a wide variety of political arrangements or systems, and *velayat-e faqih* was 'based on an incorrect understanding of *fiqh* and jurisprudence'.[15]

In addition Shabestari, Kadivar and Eshkevari gave serious attention to women's rights, again bringing out fully the way that Islam as it had been traditionally interpreted by the *ulema* actually innovated from or subverted Koranic positions to constrain and subject women in ways that were simply not legitimate. As earlier, except perhaps even more so, debates on the status of women have been central to the most important political thought of the decades since 1990. In this as in other ways, one can see this reformist intellectual movement as exploiting the opening that previous thinkers like Shariati and Khomeini himself had opened up, by attacking the foolish, encrusted Safavid Shi'ism of the traditional *ulema*, in order to reinterpret Islam in ways that discarded socially expedient and conventional mores and to examine whether Islam could be made compatible with ideas of liberty, representative government and human rights. They succeeded in making a convincing case for Islam as a religion that is not only compatible with notions of democracy, political freedom, equality of the sexes and equality before the law, but which, properly considered, has an innate bias in those directions and away from unfair, harsh, violent or oppressive practices often associated with Islam – both by Islamic extremists and by Westerners who think themselves hostile to Islam as a religion. Their writings often have as much of value to say to such Westerners as to Iranians and Muslims.

All these thinkers have suffered to a greater or lesser extent for their views under the Islamic republic. While figures with weak intellectual or religious credentials but with good political connections have been made ayatollah (there has been a new wave of inflation of religious titles – ayatollahs have become much more commonplace since the revolution; where previously they might be numbered in a few hundreds, there are now thousands), these thinkers have not been allowed to progress, whether as academics or clerics. Eshkevari has had his religious credentials removed altogether and has gone into exile, as have Soroush and Kadivar. But their thinking has become an important and often dominant part of the contemporary intellectual debate in Iran. Reformism had a solid intellectual base.

Khatami in Government

Immediately after the election, both sides appeared anxious to conciliate and consolidate, to show respect both for the people's will and for the system. Khatami included a number of previous, right-aligned ministers in his new cabinet, and the right-oriented Majles did not reject any of his proposed ministers. But Khatami removed two notable right-wing ministers, Velayati and Fallahian (Foreign Ministry and Ministry of Intelligence and Security respectively) – a sign of his intention to shift Iran's foreign policy. And some of his appointments were more contentious, receiving higher adverse votes in their votes of confidence than others – Abdollah Nuri, for example, as interior minister, and Ataollah Mohajerani. This was a warning of trouble in the future.[16]

On 14 November, Ayatollah Montazeri spoke up in Qom to support Khatami and the reform movement, and to attack Khamenei in forthright terms. He warned Khatami's opponents not to try to block his reform programme, and recommended to the president that if he were not given a free hand by Khamenei, he should resign. He also suggested that it was time that political parties were allowed to develop, the better to represent the views and wishes of the people; and (echoing Sorush) that there should be a greater separation between the clergy and the state. But he went much further in criticizing Khamenei himself, urging him not to interfere in the business of the senior clergy (*marjaiyat*) or to try to turn the seminaries of Qom into 'a ministry of government officials'. He said bluntly: 'You are not a *marja-e taqlid* and you bear no resemblance to a *marja-e taqlid.*' The speech prompted anti-Montazeri demonstrations, in the course of one of which Montazeri's own offices in Qom were attacked. Montazeri's movements had already been restricted for some years; from this point on he was kept under house arrest. But he continued periodically to speak out against the hardliners and in favour of reform.[17]

Prime among Khatami's successes in his first term as president was his policy of opening up freedom of speech, presided over by Mohajerani as minister of Islamic guidance, who stated early on that he saw himself more as a minister of culture than as a minister with responsibility for censorship.[18] It was not only a success in itself; it also created a vigorous new wave of publications and media activity that, while varied, also served as a weapon for the reformists against their opponents. By mid-1998, 740 newspapers and journals were being published in Iran, many of them strongly critical of the previous conduct of government.

Film

A related phenomenon was the burgeoning development of Iranian cinema. This development was not limited to the Khatami years, but many of the film-makers were aligned with the reform movement (and later, with the Green movement). Where literature in Iran since the revolution has been of mixed quality, Iranian cinema has flourished. The restrictions of state censorship, which have tended to gag or stultify literary effort, making independent-minded writers and poets reluctant to risk committing their real thoughts to paper, seem only to have made Iranian film more subtle and refined, delivering artistic and often social and political messages all the more effectively. Iranian film producers have profited from the fact that only a trickle of Western films have been allowed to be shown in Iranian cinemas every year. Prevented by cultural distaste as well as by the censors from exploiting sex and violence in the way regarded as indispensable by Hollywood, Iranian directors like Abbas Kiarostami, Jafar Panahi (*The Circle*), Mohsen Makhmalbaf, Samira Makhmalbaf (*The Apple*), Majid Majidi (*Colour of God*), Tahmineh Milani, Kamal Tabrizi, Marziyeh Meshkini, Davud Mir-Bagheri, Bahman Ghobadi and Asghar Farhadi have created films of unique poetic artistry and universal appeal, demonstrating afresh the full scope and potential of the medium itself. Many of their films have dealt with subjects like the mistreatment of women, the vulnerability of children, the effects of war, the distortions of Iranian politics and society and other themes critical or tending to be critical of the Islamic regime. There is a divide in Iranian cinema between sometimes inaccessible high-art films like Makhmalbaf's *Taste of Cherry* and Kiarostami's *Gabbeh*, many of them successful in Western film festivals but with limited appeal in ordinary Iranian cinemas, and the thrillers and romantic comedies that such cinemas show as their everyday norm (which seldom get seen outside Iran). War films, drawing on the experience of the Iran–Iraq War, have also been a popular genre. But others have bridged the gap between high art and popular cinema; sometimes achieving a degree of political notoriety along the way.

One such was Mir-Bagheri's *Adam Barfi* (*The Snowman*), which became something of a craze in the mid-1990s for its indirectly subversive message about an Iranian man marooned in Turkey who dresses as a woman in order to get a visa to go to the United States. Another was Kamal Tabrizi's *Marmoulak* (*The Lizard*), from 2004, in which a criminal impersonates a mullah in order to escape from prison, but has to continue the pretence to stay free. He finds it surprisingly difficult to hitch a lift, because no one wants to give a ride to a mullah, but surprisingly easy to officiate at prayer, because he can just mumble and get away with it.[19] Both films got into trouble with the authorities and were eventually banned.

In Jafar Panahi's films, social criticism has been more direct. *The Circle* (2000) showed episodes in the lives of several women who had been in prison, mostly for prostitution. It depicted a series of experiences in which their lives were limited and crippled by petty acts of constraint, repression or cruelty. It was banned. More recently, his film *Crimson Gold* showed a war veteran, struggling to make a living as a pizza-delivery man and hoping to get married, being pushed inexorably towards criminality by the indifference and inequality he experienced in a Tehran sharply divided between idle rich and hopeless poor. The resolutely understated quality of both films (it is easy for non-Iranians to miss entirely the theme of prostitution in *The Circle*, for example), which use amateur actors extensively, serves only to make them more moving.

Initially after the revolution, censorship was so restrictive as to make film production almost impossible, but within a few years (ironically, under the aegis of an official of the Ministry for Culture and Islamic Guidance, Mehdi Argani, who was blind) rules were relaxed somewhat, and some films were given help with funding. Under Khatami's presidency films produced by or about Iran's ethnic minorities were approved for the first time, permitting Bahman Ghobadi for example, to make a series of films, including *A Time for Drunken Horses* and *Turtles Can Fly*, set in Iranian and Iraqi Kurdestan respectively.

If some were inclined, following Montazeri's words to the effect that foreigners would think Iranians only wanted to kill people, to have a depressing, bleak, negative image of Iran, Iranian cinema helped to show a more rounded picture of the country, and to remind the world that Iran's deeper cultural instincts were lighter, more positive, humane, critical and life-affirming.

Another story illustrates the way that censorship might affect book publishing. One of the most prolific translators of Western literature into Persian in the twentieth century was Mohammad Ghazi, a Kurd from Mahabad who died in 1998 at the age of eighty-five. One story says that a few years after the revolution, he was steering his translation of Ignazio Silone's great novel *Vino e Pane* (*Bread and Wine*) towards publication when he encountered some difficulty with the censor over the title, which in Persian should have been *Nan va Shorab*. The censor, disliking the word wine (*shorab*), suggested using the word for vinegar instead, giving the title *Nan va Serkeh*. He argued that people might misunderstand the significance of a book that appeared to advertise illegal alcohol in the title – and after all, vinegar was made from wine. Mohammad Ghazi responded that he would agree to the amended title

337

if the censor would allow the following couplet to appear at the front of the book:

> Mardom-e Iran, fekre enqelab konid
> Shorab serkeh shod, serkeh-ra shorab konid.

> (People of Iran, think about the revolution:
> They turned wine into vinegar; make the vinegar into wine.)[20]

Khatami's Foreign Policy

From the start, a more open foreign policy that sought to end Iran's isolation and bring better relationships with other countries, whether in the Middle East region, the West or more generally in the world, was an important part of Khatami's programme. Typically for him, it began on a philosophical level with the idea of a Dialogue of Civilizations – a notion Khatami was bringing forward from the beginning of his presidency onwards, plainly designed in opposition to Samuel Huntingdon's theory of a Clash of Civilizations. The idea of a year dedicated to a Dialogue of Civilizations was eventually taken up by the UN, and the symbolism was important; for once, instead of being a world leader in the language of confrontation, recrimination and conflict, Iran was taking a leading role in advocating contact between opposing world views, discussion and greater understanding. Unfortunately the year chosen by the UN, 2001, was dominated for many by the 9/11 attacks – hardly what Khatami had intended. In December 1997 Iran hosted a large and well-attended session of the Islamic Conference Organization in Tehran which Khatami addressed, saying that it was necessary, if Islamic civilization was to progress, for it to understand Western civilization as it really was, and address it properly, good and bad. Lying stuck in an idea of Islamic culture as it had been in the past was not an option – but neither was it correct to imitate the other and lose one's own identity. Khatami said that Iran was now secure and confident enough in her identity to pursue this aim of mutual understanding.[21]

Khatami reiterated many of these themes in an interview he gave to Christiane Amanpour of CNN a month later in January 1998, in which he seemed to hint at the possibility of some kind of reconciliation with the United States. The interview was important because he addressed directly the gap of hostility between the US and Iran, and the ideological element to it, which many before and since have claimed to be unbridgeable – the alleged incompatibility of liberalism and democracy, on the one hand, with religion, particularly Islam, on the other: 'In my opinion, one of the biggest tragedies in human history is this confrontation between religion and liberty, which is to the detriment of religion, liberty and the human beings who deserve to have both.'

Taking the interview to an intellectual level that few Western politicians would have attempted, Khatami drew upon de Toqueville's *Democracy in America* to point out the religious foundations of democracy and liberty in the United States, and their origin in the quest by seventeenth-century puritans and nonconformists for a space in which to live and worship freely. Religion had provided the social glue that had permitted liberty and democracy to flourish without becoming self-destructive. The United States was still a more firmly religious country than many other Western states:

> Therefore the approach to religion, which was the foundation of Anglo-American civilisation, relies on the principle that religion and liberty are consistent and compatible. I believe that if humanity is looking for happiness, it should combine religious spirituality with the virtues of liberty.[22]

Khatami was, of course, addressing a domestic audience as well as the American one. He was telling the Americans that Iran and its system were not as strange as they might think, and that the religious state in Iran was also capable of liberty; but he was also telling the Iranian audience that the religious state needed to allow liberty back in.

Khatami's foreign policy was not all theory and fine speeches – it achieved some real results. Although some in the West could not cope with the idea of a liberal Iranian in a turban, and were sceptical of his message, others had noted the size of his electoral success and the changed atmosphere it had brought in Iran, and were prepared to give him a chance. In September 1998 his new foreign minister, Kamal Kharrazi, made an agreement in New York with the British foreign secretary, Robin Cook, that appeared to overcome the Rushdie problem between the two governments. Despite hostile noises from hardliners in Iran thereafter, the deal held and the two countries exchanged ambassadors the following May. This was significant because it could not have happened without the approval of Khamenei too – it indicated that, albeit for motives that probably had more to do with inward investment, the supreme leader supported Khatami's effort to improve relations with EU countries, at least. The deal on Rushdie, combined with the advent of the Khatami government and its new, more congenial policies, enabled EU countries collectively to enter into a friendlier phase in their relations with Iran. Khatami and Kharrazi also made progress in improving relations with the GCC states. These developments combined to reassure all those who were gingerly responding to the new language of the Khatami government that the change was real and sincere. Some, notably in intelligence circles and in the US, remained sceptical, but the Clinton administration also began to take Khatami seriously.[23]

Back in Iran the blossoming of the free press and the success of Khatami's first steps in foreign policy only deepened the distaste of the hardliners in the Majles, the Guardian Council, the circle around Khamenei, the Sepah leadership and the Ministry of Intelligence and Security, and sharpened their determination to oppose and overturn his reform programme. Rather than attack Khatami directly, they targeted his popular associates and ministers. First to be attacked were Karbaschi, who had given Khatami and his supporters substantial help during the presidential election campaign, and Nuri, who as interior minister had quickly set about reforming regional governorships in such a way as to threaten the hardliners' grip in the provinces. Several of Karbaschi's colleagues and associates were arrested and interrogated in the summer and autumn of 1997 on charges of having misappropriated civic funds for use in both the Khatami election campaign and the Majles elections of 1996 (the underlying message being, of course, that the anti-right side had in each case only succeeded because of corrupt practices). Some of them were tortured. Karbaschi himself was then arrested on similar charges in April 1998. In July 1998 he was convicted and sentenced to five years in prison. He was also fined the equivalent of $6 million and banned from involvement in politics for twenty years.

After Karbaschi's trial, Rafsanjani and Kargozaran distanced themselves somewhat from the reform project. It may be that Rafsanjani had decided already at this point that Khatami did not have the grit to face down the hardliners and that he and Kargozaran had to look to their own interests. It has been speculated that Rafsanjani did some kind of deal with Khamenei, another element of which was an agreement to reduce or commute Karbaschi's prison sentence. In the end, his sentence was reduced to two years by the appeal court. Another part of the alleged deal was apparently a fix to arrange the Assembly of Experts elections and permit Rafsanjani to be the new chair of that body. In the event, the candidate list for the election was heavily vetted by the Guardian Council, turnout was low (less than 50 per cent) and although Rafsanjani topped the poll, the new Assembly voted to keep the incumbent chairman, Ayatollah Ali Meshkini. Rafsanjani may have wanted to position himself as the arbitrator and kingmaker between the reformists and the hardliners, but he never quite managed it. Speculation about Rafsanjani around this time was heightened by rumours about Khamenei's ill health, attributed variously to cancer or to the after-effects of the injuries he had suffered in the assassination attempt of 1981. He was rumoured in addition to be taking opium for pain relief.[24]

Abdollah Nuri, after months of accusations from hardliners in the Majles, was finally impeached in June 1998 and forced to resign. His successor as interior minister, Abdolvahed Musavi-Lari, like Nuri, was unable to take proper control of the police and other law enforcement authorities (for example, to prevent *hezbollahi* attacks on reformist student gatherings) because those authorities ignored their formal subordination to the Interior Ministry and instead took their direction from Khamenei's leadership circle. This was the kind of thing Khatami meant when he spoke of the need to assert the rule of law and the application of the constitution.[25]

The attacks on Karbaschi and Nuri were calculated for a double effect. They removed or crippled active and capable reformist politicians and prevented them from making changes that would have damaged the hardline right and their hold on power. But Khatami's inability to protect his close associates tended also to make him look weak and to shake the confidence of his supporters. Time and again, Khatami went to Khamenei in an attempt to get redress or to resolve conflicts. Khatami believed in dialogue to resolve conflict. Sometimes he got some redress – but more often not. He was seeking redress from someone who appeared formally to be in the position of an impartial arbiter, but in reality was one of his opponents in the dispute, and at bottom was keen to see Khatami's project fail (as with Bazargan and Khomeini in 1979, only more so, because Khomeini had always been in a stronger position than Khamenei, and therefore had the freedom, if he chose, genuinely to decide on an impartial basis). Initially, the hardline group had been dismayed and disarrayed by the success of the reformists. But Khatami's apparent weakness encouraged them to find new ways to reassert themselves.

The Ministry of Intelligence and Security

The early origins of the intelligence organization that became the Ministry of Intelligence and Security (MOIS) are disputed, but there are a number of indications of continuity from pre-revolution days, including eyewitness accounts of interrogation methods and other procedures. One version suggests that Hosein Fardust, the schoolday friend of the Shah and later head of his Special Intelligence Bureau, was kept on in Iran by the new regime after the revolution (having been of service in helping to block effective military action against the revolution in February 1979) and supervised the transition of SAVAK to SAVAMA (Sazeman-e Ettela'at va Amniat-e Melli-ye Iran). According to this version, senior SAVAK figures were purged, and some bureaux were largely purged, but many lower-level operatives were retained and reindoctrinated. This story is supported by the account of the KGB defector Vladimir Kuzichkin, who noted inter alia the way that surveillance of the Soviet embassy in Tehran resumed as normal with the same procedures and personnel in May 1979, after a hiatus February to April. Fardust's own memoirs, published in 1990, unconvincingly deny this version without offering any alternative, or any alternative explanation of why the Islamic regime allowed Fardust to survive until his death in 1987 when so many other adherents of the previous regime, including many more junior than he, were executed. Fardust's memoirs, which were serialized in government newspapers at the time of publication, contain a large amount of rhetoric against the Shah's regime and it seems, were amended and released by MOIS for their own purposes after Fardust's death.[26]

At any rate, it is clear that many changes were made from the summer of 1984, when Mohammad Reyshahri was appointed by Mir Hosein Musavi as the first minister of the new Ministry of Intelligence and Security (Vezarat-e Ettela'at va Amniat-e Keshvar, or VEVAK, but normally referred to by Iranians as the Vezarat or Ettela'at, or in

English language publications as the MOIS). As well as subsuming the previous SAVAMA, the MOIS took over a number of other intelligence operations that had sprung up since the revolution (but did not take over the separate intelligence office of the Sepah). The new ministry was largely the creation of Reyshahri, who had been head of the revolutionary tribunal responsible for trying members of the military in the early years of the revolution, and had supervised the investigations into the Nozheh coup plot, and thus had experience in this line of work. From 1987 Reyshahri supervised the Special Court of the Clergy, which was used to discipline mullahs who deviated from the line of the regime, and in 1989 he handed on responsibility for the MOIS to Ali Fallahian.[27]

Having been associated with the left faction in the 1980s, and after the debacle of the left in the Majles elections of 1992 and the rethink that followed, Reyshahri became associated with a phenomenon known as the New Left, which continued to favour egalitarian and redistributive social and economic policies but supported a more totalitarian ideological line including harsh repression of dissent and a strong commitment to the supreme leader. In other words, as Khatami, Musavi, Hajjarian and other former leftists turned reformist and became in effect more liberal, Reyshahri and his associates, of whom there were many in the MOIS, sided with the right. Alternatively, one could see Reyshahri, his associates and MOIS as preserving the rhetoric and the commitment to direct, violent action that had typified those engaged in the struggle against military coups and the MKO in the first years of the revolution. The so-called New Left appeared first with the creation of a group called the Association for the Defence of the Values of the Islamic Revolution (Jame-ye defa az arzeshha-ye enqelab-e eslami) early in 1996, but achieved little political traction, and Reyshahri's candidacy for the presidency in 1997 won little electoral support (the group dissolved itself in November 1998). Some have suggested that the movement was merely a creation of the MOIS for reasons of its own; it came to cooperate with some among the most hardline members of the JRM, including the chairman of the Guardian Council, Ayatollah Jannati, and Ayatollah Mesbah-Yazdi. In 1971 Mesbah-Yazdi had been the founder, with Beheshti, of the Haqqani seminary in Qom, with which (although it also has a high intellectual reputation) a variety of MOIS and other figures have been associated as either students or teachers, including Reyshahri, Fallahian, Mostafa Purmohammadi, Ali Yunesi and Jannati.[28]

Some experts have suggested that one of the main roles of an intelligence service in an authoritarian state is to reinforce the regime's misperceptions of the outside world.[29] That seems to have become one of the MOIS's core functions. The ideology of some within the organization was a witches' brew of wilful ignorance, religious extremism, embittered revolutionary zeal, casual brutality and self-serving deference to power. At some point after Khatami's election, someone decided to turn loose some of the most hard-bitten MOIS operators on writers, intellectuals and other supporters of Khatami's reform movement.

On 21 November 1998 Dariush Foruhar and his wife, Parvaneh Eskandari, were murdered in their flat in Tehran. They died of multiple stab wounds and their bodies were found mutilated. Foruhar had been a nationalist politician within the National Front in Mossadeq's time, had been imprisoned for a total of fifteen years under the Shah, had been active with Sanjabi and others in agitating against the Shah in 1978 and had been labour minister in Bazargan's provisional government in 1979. In 1980 he had been a candidate for the presidency in the first presidential elections, running against Bani-Sadr. In the weeks after the murder of Foruhar and Eskandari, more bodies were found, including those of two writers, Mohammad Mokhtari and Jafar Puyandeh, on waste ground in the south of Tehran. The killings became known as the Serial Murders, and a number of other suspicious deaths in the period 1995–9 were added to the list. People recalled a bizarre incident from 1995, when a busload of writers on their way to a poetry conference in Armenia nearly died when their driver aimed their bus at a precipice and jumped out; the bus hit a rock at the edge, deflecting it, and they survived – only to be told by the authorities to keep quiet about the incident. In particular, the death of Majid Sharif, who died just a few days before the Foruhar killings, was regarded as suspicious. He had been a journalist and translator, critical of the regime, and his body was found at the side of the road. The authorities gave out the cause of death as heart failure. Others have suggested that the death of Khomeini's son Ahmad in March 1995 could also have been connected to the perpetrators of the Serial Murders. The death had also been attributed to a heart attack at the time; but he was still quite young, and the circumstances were suspicious. Ahmad had been associated with figures on the left in his father's time (like Musavi-Khoeniha and Ali Akbar Mohtashemi) and he had recently been making critical speeches.[30]

The killings shocked the country; everyone was asking what had happened and who lay behind it. Khamenei made a speech blaming foreign enemies, but a statement from a group calling itself the Fedayan-e Eslam appeared (there is no evidence of a connection back to the Fedayan-e Eslam of Navvab Safavi), taking responsibility for the killings and attacking Khatami's policies. It said that the deaths should serve as a warning to all writers working for foreign countries.

Then, at the beginning of January 1999, the MOIS issued an astonishing statement in which it admitted that a group of its own people (which they called a rogue element) had committed the killings, though even then the statement added the suggestion that no doubt the killers had been acting in cooperation with foreigners.

It seems that the prime aim of the killings (at least those committed in 1998) was again, like the actions against Karbaschi and Nuri, to weaken and discredit President Khatami. But this time it backfired. Said Hajjarian, who had been instrumental in the establishment of MOIS in the early 1980s, was appointed by Khatami as part of a committee to investigate the killings, and was significant in exposing the MOIS operators as the killers. It seems that after the killings of Foruhar and his wife, Hajjarian brought Khatami a tape of a telephone call in which the killers – with Parvaneh audible in the background – had asked their bosses at the ministry what they should do about her, because her husband was already dead. They were told to kill her too.[31] Apparently Khatami had wept as he listened to the tape. He had gone to Khamenei, had refused to go along with a cover-up and had insisted that unless the MOIS admitted what had happened, he himself would announce it. He also insisted on the removal of the minister and head of the MOIS, Dorri-Najafabadi.

After several months, it emerged that a MOIS officer by the name of Said Emami had led the group responsible for the murders, but that in the interim he had committed suicide in prison by drinking hair-remover liquid. Some of his associates were tried and sentenced to death, but the trials were conducted in secret, and the sentences were later commuted to life imprisonment. There was speculation (particularly in articles by the journalist Akbar Ganji) that Ayatollahs Jannati and Mesbah-Yazdi among others had authorized the murders, and that others in the MOIS or associated with it (notably former minister Ali Fallahian and deputy minister Mostafa Purmohammadi) had confirmed authorization for the action. In fact, it seems that Hajjarian and his colleagues exposed a well-developed structure of committees organized for the destruction of the regime's opponents, but that Ali Fallahian, who was near the centre of the structure, threatened to make the involvement of the highest levels of the regime public (including Khamenei and Rafsanjani) if his own position was endangered, using material he had stored as security for himself outside the country. Khatami was able to use the evidence Hajjarian brought him to win concessions from Khamenei, but only up to a point, and he held back rather than bring down the whole system.[32] These revelations were a further inducement encouraging Rafsanjani to draw away from the reformists and back toward Khamenei.

The exposure of MOIS involvement was damaging to the ministry and to the hardline camp. But they did not give up. The arrests of Said Emami and his colleagues were followed by the detention of thirteen Jews in Shiraz on espionage charges, and it became plain (not least from the transparent ordinariness of the victims) that disgruntled MOIS officials had arrested innocent people in order to attempt to rehabilitate their organization with the public by portraying it as bravely resisting some kind of Zionist plot. It was perhaps also a scornful side-swipe at Khatami's attention to the rights of minorities during his election campaign. MOIS claimed at the time that a number of Muslims (nine, eight, three or two according to different statements) had been arrested in connection with the same case, but details were hazy and it seems this was a screen to disguise the anti-Semitic aspect of the action. Eventually all the Jews were released, but some had been convicted of spying for Israel in the interim (for which the normal penalty, if proved, would be death), and some of the releases were only on a provisional basis, so the men might be liable to rearrest should the MOIS find that convenient.

The detention of the Shirazi Jews succeeded in throwing an obstacle in the way of Khatami's rapprochement with Western countries. The action was widely criticized outside Iran; particularly after an announcement from Ayatollah Jannati that the detainees could be put to death. The EU slowed down some of its plans for improving relations with Iran. In the UK, Robin Cook, jumpy after awkward moments in his early months in the job and unwilling to risk his personal political future, suspended plans to make the first visit by a British foreign secretary to Iran since the revolution[33] (Jack Straw, when he became foreign secretary, took up the initiative again after the Al-Qaeda attacks of 9/11). Khatami was in a difficult position: he could not condemn the detentions – all he could do was insist ineffectually that the detainees would be tried fairly.

In parallel, there was also an intensification of persecution against the Bahais. Young Bahais had been prevented from attending university; when they set up their own study groups some of those involved were arrested for alleged conspiracy, and there were more deaths.[34]

A number of other incidents helped to exacerbate further the febrile atmosphere in this period. In April 1999 Sayad Shirazi, who had been such a prominent figure as a general during the Iran–Iraq War, was assassinated outside his house in Tehran as he set off for work. The MKO claimed responsibility; one of a series of bombings and killings carried out by them around this time. In August the previous year the MKO had murdered Asadollah Lajevardi, who had been notorious for his running of Evin prison in the early 1980s. Mohsen Rafiqdust, who had driven Khomeini away from Mehrabad airport on his arrival in Tehran on 1 February 1979, and who later served as minister for the Sepah, was the victim of another assassination attempt in the summer of 1998. A sniper tried to shoot him through the window of his office but missed, and he survived. This attempt was not connected to the MKO however – it turned out that the perpetrator was an aggrieved war veteran. By this time Mohsen was head of the Bonyad-e Mostazafan va Janbazan; in 1995 his brother Mortaza had been convicted for embezzlement, and there was a general air of sleaze around their financial dealings. In 1999 Mohsen was removed as the head of the *bonyad* (he was later given another, smaller one). He was widely believed to have been protected by Khamenei.[35]

Since that time, people have suggested that the EU and the US should have done more to support Khatami. More could have been done. At the time, there were various conflicting counter-indications. Western intelligence services, taking their lead from the CIA, and shaping up to depict Iran as the bogey to slot into the space vacated by the Soviet Union, were broadly in agreement with each other that nothing good could be expected from Iran under the Islamic Republic. Their view (ignoring the mass support he enjoyed from ordinary Iranians) was that if Khatami was genuine, he was powerless, and he was probably not

genuine anyway. Others within Western governments were more positive about Khatami, but the politicians were uncertain whose advice to
take, and given the doubts and uncertainties about Iranian politics,
tended understandably to play safe. In reality, there was probably little
that anyone in the West could have done to help Khatami. If he was
going to succeed, he had to succeed on his own, and clumsy attempts
from outside to help him would have been counter-productive. But if
Clinton had anticipated Obama's open hand and had welcomed Khatami
to the US in 1998 or 1999 (on one of his trips to the UN General Assembly in New York), who knows?

Khatami's opponents were shaken by the revelations that followed the
Serial Murders case, but they did not retire from the game. Said Emami's
funeral was attended by several hundred mourners, many of them personnel still working within MOIS. Several of those who left MOIS
because of the scandal were taken into a new intelligence unit based in the
supreme leader's office. In January and February 1999 *hezbollahis* armed
with iron bars attacked Friday prayers in Isfahan as they were being led
by the reformist Ayatollah Jalaloddin Taheri, and also attacked Hadi
Khamenei, the supreme leader's reform-minded brother, in Qom.[36] The
reformist cleric and thinker Mohsen Kadivar was arrested in February.
Reformists did well in the local council elections held in February (the
first held since the revolution – provision for them in the constitution had
previously been ignored), but hardline criticisms of Ataollah Mohajerani
and his open policy toward the media intensified. This culminated with
the closure of the paper *Salam* in July (MOIS had complained after the
paper, published by Mohammad Musavi-Khoeniha, had published a letter in which Said Emami had argued that freedom of speech had to be
limited). The Majles had recently pushed through legislation to make the
press law more restrictive (it was later tightened further).

On 8 July a small number of students demonstrated in Tehran against
the closure of *Salam*. In response, *hezbollahis* and police broke into a
university dormitory and savagely beat up the students they found there.
Some were thrown from windows, and several died – the number has
never been established. Hundreds were arrested. After this, more
students went out on the streets in much bigger numbers, and the demonstrations spread to Mashhad, Isfahan, Shiraz and Tabriz. Students
chanted slogans in favour of liberal politicians of the past, like

Mossadeq and Bazargan.[37] Initially Khamenei condemned the attacks on the students in the dormitory, but as the protests spread and turned violent he and other regime figures turned against them, claiming that they were counter-revolutionary and acting in the interests of foreign forces, and so on. At the same time, twenty Sepah commanders sent Khatami a letter threatening that they would have to take action if the unrest continued. It was published in the right-wing paper *Kayhan* a week later.

On 13 July Khatami distanced himself from the demonstrations and blamed the violence on so-called rabble rousers. He may have been influenced by the Sepah letter, but the situation presented him with an impossible choice. All along he had argued for non-violence and engagement in dialogue as the way to resolve conflicts. He could not now back the students and the street violence against the system. At the same time, Khamenei seemed to recognize that things had gone too far. The Sepah letter was widely condemned – Khatami pointed out that Khomeini had made very plain that the armed forces should stay out of politics. As the unrest died down, some police were arrested and suspended for the attack on the dormitory, but large numbers of students stayed in jail. Some went on trial, were forced to make the familiar, revolting televised confessions admitting collusion with foreign powers, and received death sentences (which were not carried out, leaving them in limbo and serving effectively as political hostages).

One student, Ahmad Batebi, became a symbol of the protests and their repression. When the dormitory was attacked, another student was shot next to him: 'The bullet hit the wall and ricocheted back into my friend's shoulder. I heard the bullet go by my face ... It sounded like a bumblebee going by my ear.'[38] Batebi used a shirt to put pressure on the wound. Later he took the bloodstained shirt to demonstrations and held it up to show the brutality of the attacks. He was photographed; one of the photos appeared on the front cover of *The Economist*, and Batebi was arrested for having defamed the Islamic republic. He was sentenced to death; the sentence was later reduced, but while in Evin prison he was repeatedly tortured and beaten until he developed serious health problems. Eventually, in 2008, he escaped from Iran (with the help of Kurdish groups) after being temporarily released from Evin prison for medical treatment, and now lives in the US.

The outcome of the unrest and Khatami's siding with the system against the students disillusioned many of his supporters, especially among the young. He was probably right that escalating the conflict at that juncture would have led to a brutal crackdown and that the reformists would have lost the struggle anyway. But however many small successes he won through his conciliatory methods, and despite the mistakes made by his opponents, the reformists' defeats were always more damaging.

The months after the student demonstrations of July were dominated by the run-up to the elections for the sixth Majles, which were held on 18 February and 5 May 2000. Over this period the national debate opened up as never before; the surge of journalistic activity, political book publishing and the breaking down of taboos (for example, on relations with the US, in favour of renewal, on which Montazeri had spoken up; and Israel) has been compared with earlier episodes when censorship retreated; before 1906, and after 1941. The reformists were determined to secure a strongly reformist Majles and fielded a huge number of candidates. In an interview with foreign journalists Montazeri, despite his house arrest, urged people to vote in large numbers and to support the reformists. Overwhelmed by the number of candidates the reformists fielded, perhaps somewhat chastened by the unrest of the previous summer, the Guardian Council disqualified only 10 per cent of the 6,851 who offered themselves. Another major feature of the campaign was the candidacy of Rafsanjani, who became a target for the reformist press as the day of the vote came nearer. The hardliners continued to target other reformist politicians, however. In the autumn of 1999 Abdollah Nuri was arrested, seemingly to prevent him from running in the elections and becoming speaker, the job Rafsanjani was aiming for. Nuri was accused among other things of statements in support of Ayatollah Montazeri, whom he had openly avowed as his *marja*. The trial became a *cause célèbre*, which boosted both Nuri's own personal popularity and that of the reformists, as he made a spirited defence based largely on the sayings of Khomeini, but in the end (in November 1999) he was convicted for insulting Islam and questioning the authority of the supreme leader, and was sentenced to five years in prison (he was released in 2002).[39] Mohajerani was finally forced to resign in December 2000[40] after criticism from Khamenei among others (having survived months of abuse, and an impeachment attempt that only narrowly failed).

The outcome of the Majles elections was an overwhelming victory for the reformists, but it proved to be another Pyrrhic one. Because it was clear immediately, after the first round of voting, that the hardliners had suffered a serious defeat, the Guardian Council took months to ratify the results, and did their best to manipulate them where they could. Reformist candidates eventually secured around 189 seats out of 290. Initially, it did not look as though Rafsanjani would be elected; humiliatingly, he came in bottom of the list of thirty candidates elected in Tehran. An attempt to rear-range the votes to lift him further up the list only drew more scorn from the reformist press, and eventually he withdrew. In between the two rounds of the elections, Said Hajjarian was shot by assassins on 12 March. The cir-cumstances of the shooting strongly suggested MOIS involvement; it was motivated probably as much by his role in unmasking the background to the Serial Murders as for his tactical masterminding of the reformist elec-tion campaign. He survived the attack despite being shot through the head but has been severely disabled since and is confined to a wheelchair.

The hardliners blamed the reformist press for their failure in the first round of the elections, and in order, from their perspective, to redress the balance, the judiciary proceeded in the long gap between the two rounds to ban newspapers. Papers had been banned before – *Salam* and *Neshat*, for example – but several of them had quickly reopened after the bans, from the same offices and with the same staff, but with new titles. This time the courts were more aggressive – on 23 April, twelve publications were banned, and a further twelve were closed down before early August. In addition, the judiciary ordered the arrest of a series of journalists, editors and other public figures aligned with the reformists, including Akbar Ganji, Hasan Yusefi Eshkevari, Mashallah Shamsolvaezin, Ezzatollah Sahabi and Shirin Ebadi. Several of these were arrested after their participation at a conference organized by the Heinrich Böll Stiftung in Berlin in early April, designed as a forum for debate on the Majles elections and the prospects for reform, which degenerated after exile opposition groups (notably the Workers' Communist Party and the MKO) staged disruptive actions. These included one woman doing an impromptu erotic dance to protest against the Islamic republic's rules on *hejab*, and others removing *chadors* to reveal bikinis and anti-regime slogans. There were television cameras present and the reports (carefully edited for full effect by the state TV corpora-tion) caused outrage when broadcast in Tehran. Eshkevari's return to

Iran was delayed and he was arrested later – he had used the conference to deliver some of his most thoughtful ideas on the position of women in Islam.[41]

Despite the continuing press crackdown, the reformists did well in the second round of elections also, winning two-thirds of the sixty-six seats that were left open after the first round. After further delays, particularly over the voting from Tehran, and only following an intervention from Khamenei, the Guardian Council at last approved the results on 20 May.[42]

The struggles over the Majles elections of 2000 were messy and protracted and were a dispute not just between two factions, but between the two principles that had lain uneasily together in the constitution since 1979: the principle of democracy and the principle of religious authority – of guardianship. Both sides in the dispute respected both principles (for some, the respect may only have been lip-service, but all recognized the necessity at least for that). The hardliners did not, ultimately, overturn the results; they tried to hobble the reformists by banning newspapers in the hope and belief that if the misleading propaganda of the reformist press were crippled, the people would return to what they regarded as the correct Islamic, revolutionary principles. It did not happen. Even if often expressed clumsily, their fears were real: that if freedom and democracy were given full rein, the institutions and achievements of the Islamic revolution would be swept away in a flood of Western cultural influence.

The Majles finally convened for its first session on 27 May, but when it attempted to act against the newspaper closures by bringing forward a new press law, Khamenei prevented it. On 6 August (in some uproar) the Majles heard a letter from him banning the assembly from discussing or amending the press law passed by the previous Majles – an unprecedented use of his position as supreme leader. Montazeri spoke out again against Khamenei's action, warning that the people's wishes should be respected and that the supreme leader's overruling of the Majles was the way to despotism. But the episode showed that the other institutions of the state were powerful enough to limit and contain the actions of the Majles if they were determined to do so, as had been demonstrated already in the period of the leftist third Majles, 1988–92. In the long run, the press crackdown proved more damaging to the reformists than the hard-won success in the Majles elections was a benefit. The free press had been an achievement and a weapon for the reformists, and a challenge to their enemies; but by the end of August their activities had been harshly curtailed, and one of the last reformist papers – *Bahar* – had been closed down (though others started up again later). Between March 2000 and March 2001, total circulation of newspapers in Iran slumped by 45 per cent, from 3.12 million to 1.75 million.[43] Reformist editors and journalists did not give up, but over time the attrition of closures, moving premises and arrests wore them down:

> Our chairs were completely wrecked because of repeatedly being moved. The newspaper's staff had a right to feel discontented and uncomfortable, but there was nothing we could do to rectify the situation, as we did not have enough money. We didn't even have enough of the broken chairs. Whenever anyone came to a meeting of the headline council or the editorial council, they had to sit on a bookshelf, a windowsill or a filing cabinet because there were no chairs left.
>
> My colleagues referred to this kind of journalism in Iran, which was associated with difficult conditions, repeatedly moving, and the constant danger of arrest, as 'guerrilla' journalism . . .
>
> The lifespan of our publications had decreased from eighteen months to a year, from a year to six months, and from six months to four months. They refused to give us a license. Even if we found someone who already held a license, he was no longer willing to collaborate with us due to the existing dangers. We no longer had an investor or sufficient funds. As a result, it was clear that [we] could no longer have a newspaper.[44]

By the time of the second poll on 5 May, the reformist press had been weakened by closures, and even the pro-reform papers and journals that were still operating had calmed down somewhat, realizing the danger of overreaching themselves. But the damage had already been done. In particular, the press attacks on Rafsanjani had been extreme, and probably unwise. Akbar Ganji and others had suggested that he had at least known of the machinery that had produced the Serial Murders, that he had been at least partially responsible for prolonging the war, and that his family had benefited from his position to amass large personal fortunes. They ridiculed Rafsanjani's use of the title of ayatollah, and Ganji called him the 'Red Eminence' – both an allusion to the sinister behind-the-scenes manipulation of events of a modern Richelieu, and a suggestion that he had bloody hands. Rafsanjani responded with attacks on the reformists that compared the situation in 2000 with the conflicts of 1979–81, and suggested that then as now the opponents of the clergy were in fact agents of foreign powers. This was remarkable language, given that Rafsanjani had supported the reformist project at the outset; it backed up the rhetoric of more extreme figures like Mesbah-Yazdi and was effectively a threat to individual reformists that they could be regarded as traitors to the state. His failure in the election damaged Rafsanjani's standing, but he was still a force in Iranian politics, and few could match his ability to manipulate the political system. After May 2000 he was not only aligned against the reformists; he was embittered against them too. The success of the hardliners in containing and reversing the reformist wave owed a lot to Rafsanjani's support.[45]

From this point on, the hardline elements in the system were able to block the efforts of the reformist Majles, and to use the state-run TV and radio to depict it as an ineffectual talking-shop. Many of the newly elected members were inexperienced newcomers, and the original reformist leadership around Khatami had been largely stripped away by the arrests, trials and imprisonments. The loss of Hajjarian, who had been the master-tactician of the reform movement, was particularly damaging. Legislation passed by the Majles was blocked by the Guardian Council, and Majles committees found themselves unable to carry out the investigations into administrative malpractice and corruption that had been promised during the election campaign.[46] Another development in the summer of 2000 began a new phase of pressure on Iran over longstanding suspicions (supported by the assessments of Western intelligence agencies) that the regime, despite international treaty commitments not to do so, was developing a nuclear weapon. In July Iran successfully tested a new missile, the Shahab 3, which had the range easily to reach Israel, and even the territory of countries on the eastern edge of the European Union.[47]

Despite the frustrations and disappointments, public support for Khatami and reform was still strong, as was demonstrated when Khatami was re-elected as president in June 2001. With a lower turnout than 1997 (68 per cent) he won nearly 80 per cent of the vote, with an even higher total number of votes than the first time. Ali Fallahian, who presumably ran against him with a surge of optimism, got 0.2 per cent of the vote. The most successful conservative candidate was Ahmad Tavakoli (a cousin and close associate of the Larijani brothers), who was supported by just under 16 per cent of the voters.

Afghanistan, and 9/11

The Iranian reaction to the attacks on the World Trade Center and the Pentagon on 11 September 2001 was striking and seemed to many to create an opportunity to bypass the continuing stalemate in US–Iranian relations. For once, at least initially, reformists and hardliners were united – both Khamenei and Khatami condemned the attacks in the strongest terms, and ordinary Iranians went on to the streets and lit candles in spontaneous demonstrations of support. This contrasted with other parts of the Middle East, where in places people celebrated the blow against America. When it emerged that the Al-Qaeda perpetrators of the suicide attacks were Saudi Arabians and Egyptians, and Sunnis rather than Shi'a Muslims, initial suspicions in some quarters in the US that Iran might have been involved, evaporated. As minds turned to the necessity for action against the Taleban in Afghanistan, who had sheltered Al-Qaeda, it became clear even to some of the most ignorant and prejudiced that for once there could be a major coincidence of interests between Iran and the US.

For many years, Iran had been supporting the Northern Alliance, led by Ahmad Shah Masud, against the Taleban in the civil war that had followed the Soviet withdrawal from Afghanistan. The Northern Alliance included a variety of ethnic and religious groups; some of them were Shi'a (notably the Hazaras), though Ahmad Shah Masud was himself a Sufi-inclined Sunni. The Taleban were fundamentalist Sunni. By August 1998 the Taleban had driven into the area around Mazar-e Sharif in northern Afghanistan and began massacring Hazara Shi'as. Later they took the town itself and the massacre continued there, in the course of which the Iranian consulate was also attacked, and eleven Iranians were killed (as the Taleban eventually admitted). Ten of them were Sepah personnel, but may have had diplomatic status; the eleventh was a journalist. The Iranians responded robustly and in mid-September massed 200,000 troops along the Afghan border. War was only narrowly averted.

In addition to the Taleban, Iran blamed Pakistan for the killings of its people and the general massacres of Shi'as in Mazar-e Sharif. Pakistani military intelligence, the ISI, had for many years been supporting the Taleban and their Al-Qaeda allies in the fighting in Afghanistan. So had Saudi Arabia and the CIA; after the Russians left Afghanistan and after the communist government of Najibullah fell in 1992, the US, Saudis and Pakistan had been effectively fighting a proxy war with Iran in Afghanistan. As in Iraq, where the US had supported Saddam Hussein in the latter part of the Iran–Iraq War, so in Afghanistan: the US, in seeking to contain Iranian influence, ended up helping to create monsters that proved much more damaging to US interests in the long run. The civil war in Afghanistan was a brutal business and there were many massacres on both sides, but part of the motivation of the Taleban and Al-Qaeda fighters in Afghanistan was sectarian hatred of Shi'as; a motivation at least as strong among them (shared by many in Saudi Arabia, and by many extremists in Pakistan) as hatred of the US or the West. Many Saudis and Sunni Muslims from elsewhere, including Pakistan, went to Afghanistan and joined Al-Qaeda in order to kill Shi'as.

It is widely accepted that Al-Qaeda's assassination of Ahmad Shah Masud on 9 September 2001 was intended as a payment to the Taleban in advance, in return for Taleban protection in the aftermath of the planned attacks in the US. The Taleban honoured the deal, but it was to have a high cost for them. By that time, the Northern Alliance had been pushed back into a small area in the north-east corner of Afghanistan (the majority of the forces fighting them were non-Afghan Al-Qaeda fighters). When the Taleban refused to render up Al-Qaeda operators connected to the 11 September attacks, a US-led coalition began military operations on 7 October 2001 against the Taleban, in cooperation with the Northern Alliance. That cooperation was facilitated by the Iranians, and the Iranians assisted in the campaign that followed, without contributing actual military forces (they gave permission for overflights by US aircraft, for example; a significant if not startling concession, if one recalls Operation Desert Claw). Most of the actual fighting was done by the Northern Alliance, with the help of US, British and other special forces, and coalition air strikes. With this help, the Northern Alliance quickly overcame the Taleban and reconquered the country, taking Kabul on 13 November. Remaining Taleban and Al-Qaeda forces were destroyed or fled the country within a few weeks after that, notably after intensive bombing drove them out of the Tora Bora caves near the border with Pakistan. But neither Osama bin Laden nor the Taleban leader, Mullah Omar, was killed or captured, and Taleban resistance resurfaced two years later.

Talks for the arrangement of democratic institutions in post-war Afghanistan followed the fall of Kabul, and were held at an international conference at the Petersberg near Bonn in December 2001. Before, during and after the conference the Iranians gave significant help in persuading Afghan politicians and warlords to accept the democratic structures that the US and her allies were also pushing for. Senior US officials who had taken part in the negotiations later acknowledged this publicly. It seems that Iranian and US diplomats were meeting at hotels in Geneva and Paris all through this period to discuss these and other matters – including what to do with Al-Qaeda fugitives who had escaped into Iran. According to one account, two such fugitives were deported from Iran back into US hands in Afghanistan (more were deported later), and the Iranians provided copies of the passports of 200 more.[48]

President Khatami, despite his other troubles, had maintained a relatively strong position in directing Iran's foreign policy (through his foreign minister, Kamal Kharrazi) and had secured the support of Khamenei and the hardliners for his Afghan policy through the SNSC. So after the success of the US-led coalition and the Northern Alliance in Afghanistan, this policy seemed to be a success, and it seemed reasonable to suppose that Iranian help in Afghanistan might yield some benefits; perhaps in trade relations, perhaps even in some development of US–Iranian diplomatic relations, which would please Khatami's domestic political supporters and show some progress for the reform project.

Instead, in the State of the Union speech made by George Bush on 29 January 2002 Khatami was rewarded by the inclusion of Iran (with Iraq and North Korea) in what Bush called the Axis of Evil – a phrase that seems to have been added to the speech rather at the last minute and without much discussion or thought.[49] Critics pointed out at the time that unlike other notable geopolitical Axes (notably, that of Germany, Italy and Japan during the Second World War), there was little cooperation or coordination between the three named states. In fact, of course, rather the contrary: Iran had fought an eight-year war with Saddam's Iraq, in the latter phases of which the US had given Iraq substantial support. The immediate background to the speech was that Israel had announced at the beginning of January that it had intercepted in the Red Sea a shipment of 50 tons of weapons including powerful Katyusha-type rockets on board a vessel called the *Karine-A*, which had loaded the weapons on or near the Iranian island of Qeshm in the Persian Gulf and was destined for Gaza. The boat was apparently owned by the Palestinian Authority and captained by a former member of Fatah.[50] Khatami questioned other branches of the Iranian regime at a meeting of the SNSC about the shipment, but was told that no one had knowledge of it – Khatami told the US government so in a formal communication sent through the Swiss, but this was discounted. Some have noted that the timing of the discovery of the vessel was convenient for Israeli purposes, and questioned why Iran would send weapons by this route when it already had a known and much safer air route operating through Syria to Lebanese Hezbollah (with tacit Turkish consent). Iran had never denied its support for Lebanese Hezbollah, Hamas and Islamic Jihad.

It is possible that the Sepah Qods force (the body through which most contact with Lebanese Hezbollah has been coordinated) or some other body made the *Karine-A* shipment without the knowledge of Khatami or his government; others have speculated that the Israelis made up the whole story.[51] It damaged relations between the US and Iran at a delicate point. But such was the attitude of most members of the Bush administration to Iran that one could see the *Karine-A* and Axis of Evil merely as the occasion for a restoration of the norm of mutual hostility that would have happened, then or at some other point, in any case. There was a hiatus in the monthly sessions of bilateral talks, but they continued (despite new complaints from the US that the Iranians were sheltering members of Al-Qaeda) until May 2003, when they came to an end after their existence was revealed in the newspaper *USA Today*.[52] Meanwhile, the question of relations with the US had surfaced again in Iran too – in September 2002 Abbas Abdi, a reformist journalist and former member of the student group that had held the US embassy hostages, helped to carry out an opinion poll to establish the attitude of the Iranian public to a possible restoration of US–Iranian relations. The poll appeared to show over 70 per cent in favour and was publicized by IRNA, the state press agency. But on 4 November (the anniversary of the embassy occupation in 1979) Abdi was arrested and prosecuted for collusion with the US polling organization Gallup, among other charges (more serious espionage charges were eventually dropped). He was sentenced to five years, but was released in 2005.[53]

Within Iran, the Axis of Evil speech was seen as a slap in the face for Khatami, whose foreign policy had previously been regarded as one of his more successful achievements. It reinforced the hardliners' position on the US and the West – that they could not be trusted and that Iran should not make any new efforts in their direction.

Throwing Away the Roadmap

Already, before the Axis of Evil speech, irregular US–Iran contacts had included discussion of the situation in Iraq. Before the US–UK invasion in March, the Iranians had not expressed support directly, but had urged that the US position in Iraq thereafter should not used for an attack on Iran, and had given the US side to understand that they would be helpful if US pilots were forced to eject and land in Iranian territory. Other observers believe the Iranians encouraged the groups it was in contact with in Iraq to assist reconstruction after the invasion rather than resist the occupation. According to the most detailed and authoritative account of what followed,[54] the Iranian leadership were impressed and disturbed by the rapidity of the coalition victory in Iraq. The goal of defeating Saddam and taking the major cities of Iraq, which had proved impossible for the Iranians over eight long years of war, had been achieved in under two months with minimal casualties for the invading forces. But the success of the US and British forces meant that Iran was almost encircled by them to the west, south (the US navy in the Persian Gulf, with bases in Qatar) and east (Afghanistan, with US forces stationed to the north-east also, in Uzbekistan). Some in the US were talking boldly of a new era of democracy and freedom in the Middle East, spreading out from a democratic Iraq. Some were saying that Iran should be next on the list for military action and regime change.

According to this interpretation some on the Iranian side wanted if possible to forestall action against Iran, and put together an offer of rapprochement with the US that would cover and seek to resolve all the outstanding subjects of dispute between them, including Iran's support for Lebanese Hezbollah, Hamas and Islamic Jihad, recognition (in effect) of Israel itself,[55] the question of Iran's nuclear programme and older, hoarier matters like the question of Iran's frozen assets in the US. (There was an informal contact around the same time or a little earlier that may or may not have been related, but which at any rate gives another indication of the way senior Iranians were thinking: at a conference in Athens, former Sepah commander Mohsen Rezai told a group including Americans, Israelis, and Palestinians that he could envisage a situation in which, if the US ended its policy of isolating Iran, Iran could in return bring an end to its policy of active opposition to the existence of Israel, changing instead to what he called a Malaysian or Pakistani position of passive non-recognition and ending its action against Israel through proxies.)[56] In return for the Iranian concessions, the US would end any aspiration to regime change in Iran and drop sanctions.

The draft of the proposals for negotiation was framed in the form of a balanced set of Iranian aims and US aims, and was apparently drawn up between Iran's ambassador to France, Sadegh Kharrazi, nephew of the Iranian foreign minister Kamal Kharrazi, and the Swiss ambassador in Tehran, Tim Guldimann, on 21 April 2003. In the absence of direct diplomatic relations between the US and Iran, Switzerland was acting as Protecting Power for US interests in Iran; so as Swiss ambassador, Guldimann had a formal position as an intermediary between the two estranged governments. Kharrazi and Guldimann called their draft a Roadmap.[57] Sadegh Kharrazi took it to Kamal Kharrazi, Khatami and Khamenei for their perusal. It was not circulated more widely within the system (to have done so would have been to increase the likelihood of leaks). Khamenei had two meetings with Sadegh Kharrazi to discuss it, and amendments were made. Sadegh Kharrazi then passed the amended version of the Roadmap back to Tim Guldimann, for him to deliver on to Washington, which he did with a message to the State Department on 4 May. He appended a letter to the State Department, explaining how the proposal had come about, and went in person to Washington a few days later to talk it through.

Suddenly, after so many years of mistrust, the prisoner of Iran–US relations seemed to be on the point of springing free from her chains. It may be that there was an element of creative ambiguity in the early stages (the Iranians themselves said all along that they did not initiate the proposal 'but rather responded to an American proposal'),[58] but such is the stuff of the best kind of diplomacy. The accusation made since by some (made to exculpate the Bush administration for its subsequent mishandling of the proposal), that the Roadmap was invented by Guldimann and its alleged approval from the Iranian regime was unreliable, is unfounded.[59]

Whatever the manner of its conception, what happened from this point on is not in dispute, nor can it really be in dispute that it represented the best chance for a settlement of the outstanding problems of US–Iranian relations – and indeed of Iran's international position altogether – since the revolution. Except unfortunately, it didn't work.

What happened from this point on was, more or less, nothing. The Roadmap proposal, which came to be called the Grand Bargain offer, was welcomed in the State Department. Whatever other doubts they may have had, they were certain that what lay before them had 'the approval of the highest level of authority in Iran'.[60] Secretary of State Colin Powell and his advisers, with support from Condoleeza Rice, then national security advisor,[61] took the proposal to President Bush and argued for a positive response to the Iranians, with the aim of moving toward serious negotiations. But especially just after the spectacular US victory in Iraq, the State Department had relatively little sway. The Pentagon was dominant (as was to become dismally plain in the disastrous aftermath of the military victory in Iraq).[62] Secretary for Defense Donald Rumsfeld and Vice President Dick Cheney vetoed the proposal, on the grounds that 'We don't speak to Evil' (a bold but questionable declaration, given Rumsfeld's infamous handshake with Saddam Hussein in December 1983). There was no further discussion of the proposal at inter-agency level. It was later alleged that Washington rebuked the Swiss for passing it on,[63] though that may not in fact have been the case.

Within three years Khatami was out of office, the Iranian presidency and Foreign Ministry were again in the hands of the right, the question of Iran's nuclear ambitions was more and more pressing, the US was in serious trouble in both Iraq and Afghanistan, people were talking about a new era of Iranian hegemony in the region and Iran's foreign policy had become much more confrontational. By that time the mood of hubris in Washington had passed and the rejection of the Grand Bargain offer came to be seen for what it was – a terrible mistake (recognized as such, it seems, even by senior figures in Israel).[64]

Disappointment, Unemployment, Drugs and Sex for Money

By 2003, many previous supporters of reform in Iran were seriously disillusioned. In order to make progress with political reform, Khatami and his government had held back from major moves for economic reform, which would have been painful and divisive. But many ordinary Iranians had supported Khatami's promises for a shake-up of the system largely because they hoped that the ruling elite's grip on the economy would be broken and opportunities for all would be freed up. They were encouraged by the fact that the reform movement originated on the left, and many leading figures within it had been, long before the slogan of Reform was thought of, strong advocates of measures to help the poor and unemployed. But they were disappointed. Similarly with minority groups like the Kurds, Baluchis and Arabs. Any geographical mapping of Khatami's electoral support in the regions of Iran shows areas where those minorities were strongest as among those where Khatami was most successful. But again, for fear of raising further divisive and emotive problems, no plans for improving the situation of the minorities were brought forward – in particular, nothing was done to give them progress toward a degree of regional autonomy and self-government, their longstanding request.

Young people, having been some of Khatami's staunchest supporters, were particularly disillusioned. School leavers take a tough exam (the *konkur*) to get a university place – in 2001 1.5 million sat the exam, and only 150,000 were accepted (through this decade around 60–65 per cent of them were women). But when they graduated, only one in twenty-three could get a job. Because they cannot get a job, they have no money to marry or pay rent for a flat, so most have to stay living with parents, year after year. They cannot drink openly, or go out with a boyfriend or girlfriend. They are in limbo, infantilized. In this context, the fall in the birth rate in Iran since the beginning of the 1990s can be seen not as a success, but rather as a by-product of a continuing disaster. The response of the hardline clerics to what they saw as dissolute behaviour arising out of the frustrations of young people was – more flogging. In August–September 2001 there was a wave of more than 400 public beatings, mainly of youths convicted for drinking alcohol or illicit sex. There were a number of riots by young people in 2001–2, some of which began with excitement on the streets as crowds emerged after football matches, but which turned to criticism of the regime and particularly Khamenei.

Unemployment has exacerbated widespread poverty and desperation (it has been estimated that, partly thanks to the birth-rate overhang, 85 per cent of Iranians under twenty-five were unemployed in the first decade of the twenty-first century), producing a surge in the inevitable attendant phenomena of prostitution and drug addiction. Given the reputation of the Islamic republic, the prevalence of prostitution may come as a surprise, but the following may help to illustrate the reality of it:

Parisa had been arrested and flogged after a brothel raid ... Ironically, I found that her costume of choice was the all-enveloping conventional black chador, concealing an outfit that would not look out of place in any red-light district in the world, yet it was practical, as a prospective client could get a flash of what was on offer.

'You were married before?' I asked.

'You could call it that,' she said. 'When I was 14 my father gave me away to Dariush. Every time we had an argument, Dariush would tell me to shut it as he had paid 50,000 tomans for me ...'

'What was Dariush like?'

'He was a pimp. He would bring a friend round, then pop out for cigarettes and return three hours later, by which time his friend would have left. He didn't like to turn up and see them straight after ...'

'When did you get divorced?'

'Our marriage was never registered anyway. One day Dariush just disappeared back to Afghanistan. After he left, his friends kept coming round so much that the landlord threw me out ...' [65]

Sometimes the arrangement was more improvised (it is normal in Tehran to share taxis with strangers, and to get on and off them rather like buses):

About a year ago, a few weeks after my arrival in Tehran, I got on a taxi heading to Takht-e Tavous Street [Motahhari Avenue]. When I got in the taxi there was no-one in it except the driver and me. After being there for a few minutes, a young girl who seemed to be in her early twenties got in. After just two minutes, she started to talk. It went like this.

Girl: Can you give me 45,000 tomans [about $45 in 2005]? I desperately
need that sum.

Driver: I don't have that sort of money, Ma'am.

Me: No, Ma'am. I don't carry such an amount of money . . .

Girl: I would offer myself or anything you wish to have!

Driver: No, Ma'am. I am not the type you think!

Me: (my mouth was open big time and I was looking at her with a surprised
expression on my face – I could not say a word!) –!

Girl: Believe me, I am not who you think I am! I am doing this because I go
to school (grabbing her bag and taking out her university card) and I live
with four roommates. Our rent is due and I owe them 45,000 tomans. So,
that is why I am offering myself.

We all remained silent for a few minutes then the driver said, 'Ma'am, I
can't do anything for you. Would you like to stay in the taxi?'

Girl: No, thanks I'll get off here.

I was so frustrated and sad that for the next two days I could not think
properly![66]

Prostitution often arises, as elsewhere, out of drug abuse, or marriage
or family breakdown. But unlike elsewhere, in Iran there is a traditional
phenomenon of so-called temporary marriage (*sigheh* or *mut'a*), sanctioned by Shi'a Islam (it is not acceptable under Sunnism), which permits
something very like prostitution. Temporary marriage is not unknown
among Shi'as in some other countries and it is not common in Iran by any
means, but despite general opprobrium it has never quite died out, because
it can be convenient (traditionally, one context in which it has been more
common is in shrine cities and around *madresehs*, where widows have
looked after the sexual needs of religious students who cannot yet marry
properly). At various points the Islamic regime has tried to make use of the
institution to address social problems, but these initiatives have always
died away amid general disapproval and ridicule.

Iran, being the first stop on the heroin highway from Afghanistan to
Europe, is said to be the country with the highest level of drug addiction
in the world, with 5 per cent of the total population users of heroin,
opium, crack, hash, ecstasy or other drugs:[67]

He lay in an alleyway near Tajrish town hall. People are walking past
throwing money (a traditional practice, to ward off evil or to contribute

toward burial). A couple of policemen are standing by, waiting for the 'death wagon'. I ask what happened . . . And they tell me 'He was an addict' . . .

He was alive this morning and now it's only noon . . . the shopkeepers and street pedlars carry on with their business . . . colourful women and girls pass by, inspecting the cheap make-up that they sell on the streets . . .

I ask another man: 'Had you seen this guy before? Did he always hang around here?' 'He was an addict,' he says and doesn't say any more. Puzzled, he looks at this inquisitive woman and screws up his face: 'A heroin addict.'[68]

In July 2002, the reformist Friday prayer leader of Isfahan, Ayatollah Taheri, resigned in protest at the corruption and greed of the ruling clique and their blocking of reforms, and his resignation was followed by two days of riots. The judiciary intervened to ban any reporting of the riots, or of the letter in which Taheri had explained his resignation. The newspaper *Nowruz* printed the letter and was closed down. Other commentators noted sadly Khatami's silence through the episode.[69] Khatami attempted a renewal of his message and his programme in the summer of 2002 with a speech on 28 August committing himself again to what he called Religious Democracy. This he followed up in September and later with two draft laws in the Majles: one to limit the powers of the Guardian Council, and the second to enhance the powers of the president as guardian of the constitution (as already set out in article 113 of the constitution). But both laws were rejected, predictably, by the Guardian Council, and Khatami eventually withdrew them in April 2004, effectively admitting defeat.[70]

Jubilation, Bad Grace and Tragedy

Amid the growing gloom, another event gave reformists cause for rejoicing in the autumn of 2003 – Shirin Ebadi was awarded the Nobel Peace Prize. The award was made in recognition of her courageous work as a lawyer and human rights activist, defending in particular the rights of women, children and critics of the Iranian regime.

Ebadi trained as a lawyer in the time of the Shah and served as a judge before the 1979 revolution (the first female judge ever appointed in Iran). But after the Islamic revolution she was stopped by a ruling that women could not be judges. For many years she was unable to practise as a lawyer at all but began to do so again in 1992. In the later 1990s she represented several victims of injustice, including the families of Dariush Foruhar and Parvaneh Eskandari.

The award of the Nobel Prize in October 2003 produced a burst of spontaneous enthusiasm, and large crowds greeted her at the airport on her return. Some outward flights had to be cancelled because passengers could not get through the flocks of well-wishers. Two among them wrote afterwards:

> When I heard the roaring crowd chanting in one voice 'Free all political prisoners!' . . . I burst into tears . . . This morning our office caretaker wanted to know when she [Ebadi] was coming . . . 'Why do you want to know?' I asked . . . he replied that he and his wife were going to the airport to welcome Shirin back to Iran . . . I knew then that I would not be alone [there] . . .
>
> Mrs Ebadi spoke to us briefly: 'This prize belongs to all of the people' . . . She could not contain her tears either and wept too.

And:

> We had all come to see our lady of peace . . . old men and women, students, human rights and women groups . . . Jafar Panahi [the film director] was there, as was Ali Daei [captain of the Iranian football team] . . .
>
> Balloons, accordions, drums, music, songs and slogans. On the way back I saw so many abandoned cars on the motorway that it looked like a huge car park . . . The main slogan was 'Free political prisoners!'[71]

By contrast, the response of the regime was awkward and grudging. A brief announcement on state TV suggested she had won the prize for her work for a children's charity. Later, hardline papers predictably alleged that the prize was part of an anti-Islamic American conspiracy, and sneered: 'Don't think that by getting that $1.1 million prize, like the pro-democracy spinster of Burma, you are now invulnerable.'[72]

Even Khatami contributed to the effort to run down the significance of the event: he commented that the Nobel Peace Prize was comparatively unimportant – only the Prize for Literature mattered.

Shirin Ebadi continued her work after 2003, defending victims of regime oppression, including Bahais. Pressure on her and her family increased: in 2008 her offices were attacked and eventually closed down, and threats were made against her daughter, Nargess. But in the time of the Bush administration in the US she also spoke out against talk of forcing regime change on Iran and defended Iran's right to a civil nuclear programme. At the time of the disputed elections of 2009 Dr Ebadi was outside Iran, and was advised not to return, after which she lived abroad, 'in airports', as she put it.[73]

Two months after Shirin Ebadi won the Nobel Prize, the city of Bam in south-eastern Iran was hit by a devastating earthquake that killed over 26,000 people and left a larger number injured.[74] A wave of sympathy for the suffering of the citizens of Bam led to offers of help from around the world, including from the US. Initially the American offer was refused, but eventually the Iranian government relented, and US military aircraft flew in to assist (for the first time since the debacle of the hostage rescue mission twenty-three years earlier).

After the disaster, there was general agreement that building standards and emergency reaction measures had been inadequate. Many ordinary Iranians left homes and jobs and went to Bam to help with the relief effort, joining foreigners who had flown in from over forty countries. Their concern and drive to help was contrasted by some with the apparent incompetence or complacency of at least some in government and the state-controlled media:

> I wanted to put my hand into the TV and force the man talking about the Grace of God to tell people instead how to make stronger buildings – and what precautions to take before, during and after a natural disaster.[75]

Disillusion

Toward the end of Khatami's presidency, Iranians blamed the hardline right for blocking reform, but they also blamed Khatami for not being tough enough. His non-confrontational style was part of his charm and part of his appeal, but such was the determination of the right to resist, and to hold on to the good things that the revolution had given them, that reform could never have been achieved without confrontation. Had he, reluctantly, confronted the right over the arrest of Karbaschi or Nuri, or over Khamenei's intervention to prevent the overturning of the press law in August 2000; had he threatened to resign then, as Montazeri had suggested earlier, threatening, effectively, the collapse of the system, he would have had 70–80 per cent of the country behind him. It need not have meant violence – civil disobedience in various forms could conceivably have been effective. Ultimately, Khatami wanted to uphold and reform the system established by the revolution; he warned that his reforms represented the last chance for the Islamic republic, but he was not the man to risk overturning it.

Despite the disappointments, the Khatami years achieved some successes. The victories of the reformists in elections and the brief surge in free journalism raised hopes, and developed the political consciousness of young people particularly, boosting a sense of what could be possible, even if the immediate outcome was negative. Despite the press crackdown, journalists continued to push the boundaries of what is acceptable when they could. The loosening of *hejab* that took place in the Khatami years, though localized and subject to periodic bouts of regime repression, has proved irrepressible. The everyday defiance of women pushing the limits of officially respectable *hejab* by showing a few more millimetres of hair or a little more make-up might be thought superficial or trivial by someone who has never lived under an authoritarian government, but it is a real and visible act of passive resistance that carries potentially serious risks with it. The seriousness is belied by the following assessment from 2002, which is nonetheless a good illustration of the range of options:

From My Personal Street Research
If you wear a short jacket, lots of make-up and a shawl hanging loosely over your head, all men in Tehran will come on to you.

If you wear a tight short jean manteau, lots of make-up, have strands of hair strategically showing, 80 per cent of men in Tehran will come on to you.

If you wear a tight black manteau above the knee, use your dark glasses as an Alice-band, with a thin black scarf, 70 per cent of men in Tehran will come on to you.

If you wear a baggy cream long robe, lots of make-up, and have a few strands of hair showing, 60 per cent of men in Tehran will come on to you.

If you wear long black robes, no make-up, and no hair showing, 30 per cent of men in Tehran will come on to you ...

A chador and no make-up ... will not get you a man.[76]

Disillusion with the reformist experiment and with politics in general manifested itself in a low turnout for the local council elections of 2003 – in Tehran unprecedentedly low (12 per cent). As later, in the presidential elections of 2005, out of frustration at the vetting of candidates some reformists had called for a boycott of the elections. The outcome was that all seats on the Tehran council went to conservatives, who in turn elected \ a new mayor – Mahmud Ahmadinejad.

7

Everything Must Change, So That Everything Can Stay the Same:[1] Ahmadinejad and Khamenei, 2005–12

Ahmadinejad

Mahmud Ahmadinejad was born in the small town of Aradan, near Garmsar, south-east of Tehran, in October 1956. His father ran a grocery shop there, but was devout and also gave classes teaching the Koran. His mother came from a *seyyed* family. Only one or two years after little Mahmud was born, his father moved the family to Tehran in search of better work, changing his name to Ahmadinejad from his previous family name, Sabaghian – which signified a dye-worker – in order to conceal his humble rural origins. The name Ahmadinejad means 'of the tribe or family of Ahmad', Ahmad being another name connected with the Prophet Mohammad. Suggestions that he changed the family name because the original one indicated a Jewish origin seem to have no basis. Once in Tehran, Mahmud's father set up a small workshop making metal window-frames and doors with two others in Narmak, on the eastern edge of the city. As time went on Narmak became more prosperous and so did the Ahmadinejad family, in a modest way. Mahmud's father made enough money to pay the fees for a private school, but he also made his sons get up early to study the Koran with him (Mahmud had two brothers and four sisters). Photographs of Mahmud from his schooldays and youth in the 1960s and 70s show a short, rather cocky boy. At the end of his school years, in 1975, he did well in the university entrance exams and went on to the Elm-o-Sanat – the University of Science and Technology, which was based nearby.[2]

At the university Ahmadinejad studied development engineering, remained devout and followed the trend of student politics of the time, reading the work of Shariati and possibly developing an association with the Hojjatieh, though this was trumped by his devotion to Khomeini when Khomeini returned from exile in 1979. It was suggested after he became president that Ahmadinejad was one of the students involved in the hostage crisis (and some former hostages even identified him from photographs), but in fact, although he was one of the most forthright student activists at his university at that time, and had dealings with wider student organizations involved in revolutionary activities, Elm-o-Sanat was the only one of the five Tehran universities that did not participate in the hostage-taking. Being more inclined to the religious right than the left-inclined students at the other universities, the students of Elm-o-Sanat, like Ahmadinejad, tended to come from humbler backgrounds. Some have suggested that Ahmadinejad was more in favour of occupying the Soviet embassy, seeing the communist Russians as a greater threat than America; alternatively that he took seriously an injunction from Khomeini not to take part in provocative actions. It seems quite likely that once the occupation of the embassy began, he regretted that he had not got involved, but the students in the embassy were quite jealous of their prize at the time and wary of outside involvement in any case.[3]

A few months after the beginning of the hostage crisis, when the universities were closed down as part of what was called the Cultural Revolution, Ahmadinejad was apparently instrumental first in ensuring that Elm-o-Sanat was one of the first to close, and then in the activities of one of the committees set up to purge leftist students and university teachers. But the friendships and contacts he made at Elm-o-Sanat remained important to him. From there he went to West Azerbaijan, where he worked with Mojtaba Hashemi Samareh (another Elm-o-Sanat graduate), who had been appointed as the deputy to the provincial governor responsible for political affairs. Ahmadinejad was responsible for helping to combat the Kurdish separatists in the region. He spent the next few years on similar work in different parts of Azerbaijan; work that became only more pressing for the regime after the beginning of the war in September 1980. He kept up his studies and passed his first degree while in Sanandaj in 1986 before going on to serve with the Sepah for two years, allegedly taking part in a daring raid on Iraqi oil installations at Kirkuk at one point (in September 1987). But details of this period in his life are hazy. Some have suggested that he served with the Basij rather than the Sepah as such, and that his role as an engineer was technical rather than as an active combatant. After the war, he continued his administrative and political career, and was sent in 1993 to be governor of Ardebil province, where he stayed until 1997, when Khatami and Nuri replaced previous provincial governors with reformists of their own choosing.[4]

While he had been serving as governor in Ardebil, Ahmadinejad had also been working on a doctoral thesis in transport engineering and planning through Elm-o-Sanat, on a distance basis. In 1997 he took his doctorate and returned to his old university to teach; he continued to do so even after he became mayor of Tehran in 2003. All through this period he was still involved in politics, and particularly in the reaction of the hardline right to the Reform phenomenon. He stood in the local elections of February 1999 without success, and was selected again as a candidate for the Majles elections of 2000, but again saw his hopes swept away by the success of the reformists. Through all this period, Ahmadinejad had close connections to the Ansar-e Hezbollah street fighters who periodically broke into offices or disrupted meetings of the reformists, shouting slogans, wielding fists, clubs, knives and chains. They were also on the streets to enforce *hejab* (with less and less effect, at least in affluent areas like north Tehran) and to reprimand couples holding hands in parks. Many of them were present or former members of the Basij. Because of the support given them by clergy like Ayatollah Jannati, and especially Mesbah-Yazdi (and more or less openly, by Khamenei himself), and through the complicity of the judiciary, the police and the law-enforcement authorities, for the most part the *hezbollahis* could act with impunity.[5]

In Kerman at this time (2002), there were a series of murders carried out by *hezbollahis*; murders of people they regarded as morally reprehensible, mainly for sexual reasons. One couple were abducted and drowned in a ditch while on an outing to look for accommodation – they were about to get married. Their bodies were dumped in the desert outside the city. When taken to trial, the six perpetrators confessed to five killings out of a total of eighteen suspicious deaths, but claimed they had received personal guidance from Mesbah-Yazdi authorizing them to kill people who were acting immorally (Mesbah-Yazdi had apparently made the humane reservation that the victims should be given at least two warnings to desist from their immorality first). When asked about this alleged guidance, Mesbah-Yazdi was evasive and attempted to get Khamenei to make a judgement on the matter – an attempt that the supreme leader also seems to have evaded. The six (all Basijis) were convicted, but appealed to the supreme court in Tehran. The supreme court returned the case to a different court in Kerman province for retrial. This happened three times, and each time the regional court convicted the six over again (feeling in Kerman was strongly against them, naturally enough). The police chief who had made the arrests and prepared the evidence was sacked from his job. Encouraged by what had happened in Kerman, religious vigilantes carried out similar killings in Tehran and Mashhad. The supreme court could not bring themselves to uphold the local verdicts, nor to condemn the defendants, whom they saw as 'pious individuals', nor to say that the (dubious) shari'a justification for the killings, as set out by Mesbah-Yazdi, was incorrect. Eventually, in April 2007 a fourth court in Kerman acquitted the killers.[6]

Abadgaran and Usulgarayan

In Tehran, Ahmadinejad was near the centre of debate and discussion among people of his generation and political background. They were frustrated by the lack of political success of the right over the past few years, and to a certain extent at the way that the paternalist-minded hardline leadership failed to engage with or listen to younger grass-roots activists like themselves. But as Khatami's second term wore on, and as the shine went off the reformist movement, they also sensed an opportunity. In the run-up to the local council elections of February 2003, Ahmadinejad and some like-minded colleagues formed a new political grouping, calling themselves the Abadgaran, which means 'developers' – an awkward choice that always sounded as though it was selected because the terms for reform and reconstruction were already taken. Eventually the term was dropped in favour of Usulgarayan, which means 'followers of principle' – sometimes translated awkwardly as 'principle-ists' or 'principlists'. The term Usulgarayan had first appeared earlier, in the 1990s; it derived a certain dignity through its association with Usulism, the school of Shi'ism that overcame the Akhbaris in the eighteenth and nineteenth centuries. Ahmadinejad became their election campaign manager. He focused on getting Basijis and their families to come out to vote for candidates of the right – many of whom in Tehran, like him, identified with Abadgaran. Because reform-oriented voters stayed away (disappointed particularly by the childish behaviour of some of the reformist councillors elected in 1999) the right swept the board, winning all but one of the seats. Elsewhere in the country the right did similarly well, on a low turnout, for similar reasons.[7]

The new councillors selected Ahmadinejad for mayor of Tehran – a natural choice given his position among them up to that point. Initially Khatami's Interior Ministry refused to accept him, but eventually they relented. Where his predecessor Karbaschi had planted trees in Tehran, Ahmadinejad planted martyrs. In the battlefields of the war with Iraq, bodies were still being found. Rather than put them in the usual cemeteries, Ahmadinejad proposed putting them in busy squares, parks and other open spaces, to remind people of the soldiers' sacrifice in the war. But the policy had provocative generational and class overtones, seemingly formulated as a reproach to younger and richer Iranians less affected by the war. It seemed that he was targeting north Tehran particularly, and parks where young couples tried to spend a few illicit minutes together. When some bodies were buried in an open space at Tehran University, students rioted. The initiative became a national scandal, and Ahmadinejad retreated from some of the more provocative plans (the episode became a part of a wider debate about the instrumental use – *estefade-ye abzari* – of those who had suffered or died in the war for political purposes).[8] Most of his other initiatives as mayor had a similarly pointed political significance. In council spending he did his best to favour Basijis, the Sepah and other groups of the right. He used the Sepah's considerable resources to help him carry out major construction projects, and gave them easy terms for schemes of their own within the capital.

On 20 February 2004 elections were held for the seventh Majles since the revolution. The reformists attempted to repeat their tactic from 2000, swamping the Guardian Council with reformist candidates, but in the run-up to the elections the Expediency Council (chaired by Rafsanjani and sending also a signal about its attitude to Khatami's ill-fated constitutional reform legislation) had agreed to quadruple the Guardian Council's budget, so it could cope with its task of vetting large numbers of candidates. Accordingly, in January 2004 the Guardian Council rejected 3,600 out of the 8,200 candidates who had put themselves forward, including eighty who were sitting members of the reformist-dominated sixth Majles. There were protests; the reformists were outraged, but little could be done:

> What moron out there dares to think our elections are not free? When for each constituency, on average, there are 19 candidates . . . and then you have the nerve to say we do not have free elections? For instance in our village! We don't need more than one elected candidate, do we?
>
> You can vote for Hajji Aghah. God forbid you don't think he is suitable. His daughter is also standing in the elections! Well, there is no difference between men and women? Is there?
>
> Now listen, you dog eaters! You don't like her? His son is also a candidate. All the more his uncle and his sister-in-law and . . . all are candidates! How could an election be more free than this?[9]

For some time, reformist figures like Akbar Ganji (from prison, in his case) had been saying that Khatami should resign and the reformist movement should boycott elections to show their disgust for the machinations of the hardliners and their manipulation of the institutions of the state (though Khatami and others urged people to vote). Some reformist candidates who had been approved withdrew in protest. The reformist interior minister threatened to postpone the elections, but on 11 February Khatami again put the system before reform and said they should go ahead. The reformist movement began to go into a sulk. As they did so, many ordinary Iranians who were already half-disposed to see them as spoilt rich kids and fickle windbags turned away.[10]

The immediate consequence was that, as with the local elections of 2003, the hardliners won a major victory. Khamenei was able to say as he made his vote on election day that the boycott showed how the enemies of the revolution and the country 'are trying to prevent the people from going to the polling booths'. Turnout was lower than for any previous Majles election – around 51 per cent. Conservatives won over 150 seats in the first round. The right could now see, through manipulation of the system, through the reformists' abdication from the process and through populist politics, their way forward. In Tehran, Ahmadinejad was massaging and building up his connections with a support base that could help him on his next move – as candidate for the elections to the presidency in 2005.

As with previous Iranian presidential elections, there was a script for the elections of 2005. They were supposed to go to Rafsanjani – apparently. By now, after his humiliation in 2000, most hardliners seemed to have forgiven him for siding with the reformists in 1997. Some regime media supported him – even the strongly hardline newspaper *Jomhuri-ye-Eslami* supported him. The Guardian Council again excluded reformist candidates – Khamenei intervened to allow one of the least charismatic, Mostafa Moin, to run for form's sake, in addition to Mehdi Karrubi. Once again, many leading reformists demanded that their supporters boycott the elections in protest at the behaviour of the Guardian Council. In pre-election polls, Rafsanjani was well ahead – one poll gave him 19.1 per cent of the vote, with his nearest competitor (Qalibaf, the leading hardliner) with 9 per cent and Ahmadinejad coming next to last with 2.8 per cent. Despite his efforts in Tehran, Ahmadinejad was still little known and not taken particularly seriously. But Khamenei and his advisers may have intended an unpleasant surprise for Rafsanjani – hence (if so) the decision to allow eight candidates to run, reducing the likelihood that any would win an outright victory in the first round of voting by getting over 50 per cent of the votes.

In the election campaigning, there were some contrasts. Somewhat unnoticed, Ahmadinejad was already more active outside the capital than any of the other candidates – emphasizing his humble, man-of-the-people image. Repeatedly he had to deny reports that he would drop out of the race to give other candidates of the right a better chance. By contrast, Rafsanjani was already presenting himself in a presidential style, leaving most of the actual electioneering to his supporters. Qalibaf, striving to portray himself as a man of action (he had previously been head of law enforcement) was sometimes coming across as an eccentric, making his supporters doubt their wisdom in backing him. At one point he even made the gaffe of suggesting that he would be the Reza Khan of the Islamic republic. It has been suggested that this contributed to a decision at a meeting held by Khamenei just a few days before the poll that the hardline circle should withdraw their support from Qalibaf (who was also suspected of financial irregularities) and back Ahmadinejad instead. An instruction was issued via the supreme leader's representative to the Sepah that indicated that they should allocate their votes and their support according to the simple lifestyle and modest campaign funds of their chosen candidate – which was taken as a clear directive to swing behind Ahmadinejad.[11]

On the day (17 June 2005), there were seven candidates, because Mohsen Rezai had withdrawn to try to reduce the split in the hardline vote. When the results came through, Rafsanjani topped the poll with 21 per cent, but Ahmadinejad surprised everyone by coming second with 19 per cent. Karrubi came third with 17 per cent, followed by Moin and Qalibaf. The turnout was about 62 per cent; again low by Iranian standards, thanks to the reformist boycott. Several of the candidates (including Rafsanjani) protested about irregularities in the poll; protests that were taken rather more seriously after the elections of 2009. The Guardian Council had taken some time to produce the results, and there were rumours of ballot-boxes being stuffed, particularly in out-of-the-way constituencies where Ahmadinejad did well. In a twist reminiscent of Gogol or Hogarth, members of the Sepah were alleged to have voted several times by using the identities of people who had died, but whose birth certificates had not expired.

Rafsanjani, probably thinking he was sitting pretty and that the reformist votes would swing to him, dropped his objections, but Karrubi continued to protest vigorously (at the time, he was also accused of having bribed voters). He would have needed only a few more votes to have beaten Ahmadinejad to second place and to have gone ahead against Rafsanjani in the run-off. But his complaints achieved nothing, and in the event the runoff was between Ahmadinejad and Rafsanjani. The second round of voting was held just a week later – enough time for the contrast between the aloof, establishment mullah with the palatial lifestyle and the proletarian, populist newcomer to become much more apparent. The right swung their support fully behind Ahmadinejad; Rafsanjani attempted but failed to draw the reformist vote out to support him. Ahmadinejad was invited to speak to the Majles, and told them that there had been a smear campaign against him, orchestrated by foreign powers. He benefited from the fact that he was not a member of the post-revolution political elite, was not a mullah and obviously was not wealthy or from a well-to-do, educated background. When the count was finished (the turnout was 3 per cent or so lower than in the first round), Ahmadinejad had won with just over 60 per cent of the vote; Rafsanjani about 36 per cent. Again, there were questions. Rafsanjani, defeated and humiliated yet again, cried foul. Comparing voting from the two rounds, it looked as though reformist voters had switched over to vote for Ahmadinejad, which was improbable (alternatively, that people who had voted reformist in the first round had not voted at all in the second, and a roughly equal number who had not voted in the first round came into the poll for the second, and all voted for Ahmadinejad – equally implausible). But again, those who disputed the results got nowhere, and against all the expectations of just a few weeks earlier, Ahmadinejad was president.[12]

A central point about Ahmadinejad was that, unlike almost all the prominent politicians of the Islamic republic who preceded him, he was an outsider. This was true even where he had most support, within the Basij and the Sepah – Ahmadinejad had never been a part of the upper circle of Sepah commanders, like Qalibaf, Ali Larijani or Rezai. The reformists had tried to bring in a new form of politics, but their well-known main politicians had all been familiar figures from the 1980s and 90s. Reformism had been new wine in old bottles. By contrast, no one had really known anything about Ahmadinejad before 2003; the people he brought with him into office (many of them associates from his time at Elm-o-Sanat) were equally unknown. Ahmadinejad's outsider status and his lower-class origins doubtless had something to do with the cheeky, provocative streak in his character – he was happy to upset people. This just reinforced the scorn with which he and his followers were regarded by many middle-class Iranians. They also scoffed (more or less openly) at his obscure background, his doctorate in traffic studies, and his uneducated, uncultured hangers-on:

> 'Mongoloid,' said one leading member of the old guard, himself the son of an Ayatollah and a noted reformist, for every name I mentioned in the Ahmadinejad clique. 'Mongoloids, all of them.' Sitting there in his home in North Tehran, sumptuously decorated with Persian antiques, he wasn't aware of the offensiveness of that term in the West ... he meant that they were grossly unqualified for their jobs.[13]

While many in Iran were sneering and running him down, others outside Iran were dramatizing him and the threat he represented – Niall Ferguson hailed him in the summer of 2005 as the Stalin of the Iranian revolution; whether this signified a greater misunderstanding of Stalin, of Ahmadinejad or of the Iranian revolution is not easy to say.[14] Neither the sneering nor the scaremongering seems to have bothered Ahmadinejad much – in fact both benefited him in his relationship with the only constituency he cared about – the Basijis, the poor, the uneducated and traditional-minded Iranians from the provinces. They liked his simple language, his cheap clothes and his nationalist rhetoric – they felt he was like them. They liked it that he offended privileged, rich people and foreigners. His occasional wackiness and apparent ignorance either did not trouble them, or went over their heads.

Ahmadinejad made the most of his humble origins, but he knew the system and was not in awe of it. He was keen in his first months to show his allegiance to Khamenei as the supreme leader, but he saw no reason to defer to the rest of the political establishment. When it came to nominating his cabinet, his choices were his own, and many of them were disliked by the Majles. After ten days of wrangling, most of his choices were approved, but four were not, including his selection for the important Petroleum Ministry. All of the four rejects had worked with him as mayor of Tehran. His second choice for the Petroleum Ministry was rejected too, and only his third suggestion (Kazem Vaziri Hameneh) was accepted. In general, Ahmadinejad's cabinet reflected his conservative and hardline views, and his desire to reassert them after the reformist episode; many of his ministers had been members of the Sepah or were war veterans. Two of them, Gholamhosein Mohseni Ejei and Mostafa Purmohammadi, were restored to high office after having been removed from the Intelligence Ministry or demoted after the Serial Murders scandal. Ahmadinejad made them minister of intelligence and minister of the interior respectively.[15]

Ahmadinejad was keen from the start to mark a dividing line between his conduct of government and the way his predecessors had operated. He held his first cabinet meeting in Mashhad and a succession of the following meetings in other provincial towns and cities. Within a few months he recalled Iranian ambassadors from a variety of overseas posts, including all ambassadors to EU countries, and replaced them with new men closer to his own outlook (this was perhaps a sly retaliation for the Khatami government's sacking of provincial governors in 1997, in which Ahmadinejad had lost his own job). But his conduct of government was soon also showing a departure from the image he himself had presented during the election campaigns. Then he had made economic policy and the plight of the poor his main concern; declaring he would bring the oil money to the table of the underprivileged and questioning how wealthy people had prospered at the expense of the *mostazafin*. He had made no secret of his piety, but had expressed himself mainly in secular terms. Now in office, he began to emphasize Iran's foreign policy and international position, the nuclear issue and his religious beliefs much more.

The Nuclear Question

In the 1970s the Shah, with the full support of the US and several other Western countries, had embarked on a plan for the generation of civil nuclear power that would eventually have resulted in the building of twenty-three nuclear power stations around the country, securing Iran's energy needs well into the future, independently of her huge oil and gas reserves, and making possible the export of electricity to neighbouring states. Using oil profits in this way seemed then a sensible way of investing a finite resource in order to create an infinite one. Two nuclear reactors were begun at Bushehr with the help of German contractors Kraftwerk Union (KWU), and work had reached an advanced stage by 1979. But as in other ways, the Shah's policy anticipated that of the Islamic republic in the twenty-first century by covertly pursuing a nuclear weapon capability in addition to the civil nuclear programme; despite having already signed up to the Nuclear Non-Proliferation Treaty as a non-nuclear-weapon state (in 1968). The idea of a nuclear-armed Iran seems to have been acceptable to the US at the time – it fitted with Iran's geostrategic 'policeman' role and US sales to Iran of other high-specification weaponry. In June 1974 the Shah told a Western journalist that Iran would have nuclear weapons 'without a doubt and sooner than one would think' – later he retracted the statement.[16]

Immediately after February 1979 the leadership of the Islamic republic took a similar attitude to both the civil nuclear programme and the possibility of nuclear weapons to that it held towards the expensive conventional weapons that the Shah had bought – they were signs of extravagance and excess, and were not needed. Khomeini disapproved of nuclear technology in general. Beheshti was in favour of a nuclear programme, but he was an isolated voice in the leadership in the early 1980s, and Bazargan's government stopped work on the plants at Bushehr.

From 1984 there was renewed activity after Khomeini apparently reversed his previous decision to abandon the nuclear programmes. But potential international partners were wary of making new commitments to Iran, especially while the war continued, and KWU eventually refused to resume work at Bushehr. Despite talks and rumours of talks with a variety of countries including China, Argentina, North Korea and Pakistan, serious work on nuclear technology seems not to have begun again until the presidency of Hashemi Rafsanjani, whose government finally agreed a deal with Russia in January 1995 to renew work on the reactor in Bushehr that was nearest completion. The reactor was supposed to be finished within four years, but was subject to extended delays due to technical problems, sanctions and other international interference. There was a launch for the reactor in August 2010, and the first fuel was loaded, but then there were further delays because of damage to a cooling pump. The reactor began low-level operation in May 2011,[17] and on 4 September 2011 Iran announced the plant had finally begun producing electricity.

But in addition to the civil nuclear programme, there were persistent rumours about Iranian plans to build a nuclear weapon, supported by statements from Western countries that their intelligence services believed Iran was engaged in such activities.[18] Iran consistently denied this, but after the testing of the Shahab 3 missile in 2000, concern intensified. On 14 December 2001 Rafsanjani made a statement at Friday prayers that addressed the regional nuclear balance and speculated about the possibility that 'the world of Islam' might acquire nuclear weapons to balance those of Israel. He suggested disturbingly that if that were to happen, a nuclear exchange could destroy Israel but 'only cause damage' to Islamic countries.[19] This gave some in the West the impression that, despite the pacific position of the Khatami presidency, there was an underlying commitment by the *nezam* – the system – to the acquisition of a nuclear weapon capability. This would have contravened not only Iran's continuing obligations under the NPT and her repeated declarations of adherence to it, but also religious statements by the supreme leader and others that possession or use of nuclear weapons was un-Islamic. Others suggested that Iran could still be consistent with all these statements and commitments, and still pursue a weapon capability, if she did so on the basis that the programme worked all the way through the development of a weapon, but stopped just short of the final stage of actually assembling it. This would give Iran a deterrent, without the opprobrium of breaching either treaty or religious commitments (there are other so-called threshold states that do not possess nuclear weapons but could quickly produce them if necessary – notably Germany and Japan).

The Nuclear Non-Proliferation Treaty, which entered into force in 1970, is something of an oddity in the world of diplomacy and international law.[20] Most multilateral treaties have, for hundreds of years, been drawn up on the principle of parity between the states that sign; that all the signatories are committed to honour the same commitments. The NPT is unusual in that it discriminates between the five nuclear-weapon states (NWS – the US, Russia, Britain, France and China) and the rest, designated as non-nuclear-weapon states (NNWS). The basic structure of the treaty is that the NNWS commit themselves not to acquire nuclear weapons in return for a commitment from the NWS to help them with civil nuclear energy and (in article VI – often overlooked) to negotiate 'in good faith' toward an eventual treaty on general and complete disarmament. Some have criticized this structure for fixing an unjust inequality between nations. Israel, India, Pakistan and North Korea have acquired nuclear weapons independently of the treaty (either having never signed up to it, or having withdrawn from it). Those who defend the treaty do so on pragmatic grounds, saying that whatever its defects and inequities, it has helped to preserve a degree of geostrategic stability and has prevented a nuclear free-for-all in which a diversity of states that could ill afford it might have acquired nuclear weapons for fear that their neighbours would do so first. Its detractors question it on a variety of grounds. From an Iranian perspective, some find it hard to understand why, if a state like Britain for example (in the middle of peaceful Europe, and protected by EU and NATO alliances) continues to value nuclear weapons for self-defence, the same should not apply for a state like Iran, which suffered attacks from Iraqi weapons of mass destruction in the 1980s, and whose neighbours include some that are unstable (Iraq, Afghanistan), several near-neighbours that are nuclear-armed (Russia, Israel, China) and one neighbour that is both unstable and nuclear-armed (Pakistan). But Iran is a party to the NPT, and the international community expects Iran to abide by its provisions.

Iran was already under serious pressure to sign up to the Additional Protocol to the NPT (which provided for a more rigorous inspection regime to ensure compliance) when in August 2002 the MKO announced that the Iranian regime was building two secret nuclear installations, including one at Natanz between Isfahan and Kashan in central Iran designed for enriching uranium. Many commentators believed that the MKO had been used as a front for release of the information, probably by Mossad, but the information itself was accurate and was later confirmed by the Khatami government. The Iranians claimed with some justice that they were not under an obligation to notify the installations to the International Atomic Energy Authority (IAEA – the UN body responsible for monitoring compliance with the NPT) because they were not yet operational, but from this point on international pressure on Iran was stepped up further.

Uranium enrichment is achieved by spinning uranium hexafluoride gas in a centrifuge to separate out the more fissile uranium 235 isotope from the less fissile uranium 238 isotope. Uranium 235 is the isotope needed for nuclear reactions. Uranium enriched to 2–3 per cent Uranium 235 is satisfactory for a civil nuclear reactor, but needs to be further enriched to 90 per cent or more for a nuclear weapon. This is the problem: civil uranium enrichment is a legitimate activity under the NPT (as a non-nuclear-weapon state Iran is entitled to develop civil nuclear power, *and* to receive help from other treaty signatories toward that end) but the difference between enrichment to levels consistent with civil use and the levels necessary for weapons may be difficult to verify from outside once the enrichment process has begun. Iran has been enriching uranium since at least February 2006, and estimates for the time needed to gather enough highly enriched uranium for a bomb have ranged from two to eight years (depending on the number of centrifuges and the efficiency of their operation).

Under Khatami's presidency Iran's chief nuclear negotiator was Hasan Ruhani, who also served as secretary to the SNSC. In 2003 he was discussing Iran's nuclear policy with representatives from the UK, France and Germany (the EU Three), and in October he accepted that Iran would sign the Additional Protocol, which authorized the IAEA to make short-notice inspections. This was, of course, also the epoch of the US/coalition conquest of Iraq and the Guldimann Grand Bargain offer. If, in that context, Iran could have secured a wider settlement, it is possible that the regime would have abandoned Iran's nuclear weapons plans permanently – the US National Intelligence Estimate judged later (at the end of 2007) that Iran had halted work toward a nuclear weapon in the autumn of 2003.[21] In October 2004 Iran agreed to suspend nuclear enrichment activities temporarily, pending proposals from the EU Three for a more permanent settlement.

This was a delicate juncture, but the two sides' interpretations of it were very different. The Iranians had emphasized that the suspension of work towards enrichment was temporary, but for the EU Three suspension was the main objective. Behind the EU Three, as the Iranians knew, was the US, and the US was unwilling to allow the Iranians an enrichment capability or any kind of nuclear programme. This made any attempt by the Three to negotiate possibilities for uranium enrichment outside Iran, or for some kind of supervised nuclear programme, almost impossible. The Bush administration would neither negotiate with the Iranians, nor allow the EU Three the negotiating freedom to do so meaningfully. The ultimate failure of the negotiations is unsurprising in the circumstances.

When Ahmadinejad came to power in June 2005 it was clear that there would be a hardening of Iranian attitudes. Iran no longer felt as vulnerable as it had in 2003; the occupation of Iraq was not going well for the US, and Iran was already in an influential position there. Even before becoming president, Ahmadinejad, taking his lead from the hardline Majles elected in 2004, was critical of the Iranian team that had agreed to suspend enrichment. On 5 August, after the EU Three finally presented their 'Framework for a Long-Term Agreement', Ahmadinejad's government rejected the proposals derisively, calling them an insult. Ruhani resigned as the chief nuclear negotiator and was replaced by Ali Larijani. In his first visit to the UN General Assembly in New York the following month, Ahmadinejad was defiant, saying that the stance of the 'hegemonic' Western powers on Iran's alleged nuclear weapon programme was just a ploy to prevent Iran from developing civil nuclear power (later, back in Iran, he claimed that while speaking to the General Assembly he had been surrounded by a protective halo of light, and that the assembled world leaders had not blinked for several minutes, as if a hand was holding them there, and had 'opened their eyes and ears for the message of the Islamic Republic').[22] At a separate meeting with representatives of the EU Three, he accused them of being

lackeys of the US. This was not the kind of language to which the diplomats were accustomed. In February 2006 the plant at Natanz began
enrichment, and within a short time Ahmadinejad was announcing that
Iran had enriched uranium successfully, could now do so on an industrial
scale, had mastered the uranium fuel cycle from its own resources and had
joined the nuclear club.[23]

The IAEA continued to make their assessments of the Iranians' nuclear
activities. After the revelations of 2002 they had said that the Iranians
had repeatedly failed to meet safeguards obligations and that they could
not be confident that there were no further undeclared nuclear activities
or materials in Iran. The IAEA chairman, Mohamed El Baradei, called
for greater cooperation and openness from the Iranians to dispel legitimate suspicions about an Iranian nuclear weapon programme. In the
autumn of 2005 the IAEA declared that Iran was not in compliance with
the NPT Safeguards agreement. The UN Security Council called upon
Iran to suspend uranium enrichment, and eventually, with resolution
1737 on 23 December 2006, imposed the first of a series of sanctions
measures.[24]

Ahmadinejad's confrontational, declamatory stance on the nuclear
issue shocked and worried many among the international community,
and worried some within Iran itself. In October 2007 Ali Larijani resigned
as nuclear negotiator, because like Ruhani before him he had been constantly undercut by Ahmadinejad's statements. He was replaced by Said
Jalili, but along with his other brothers, continued to be influential in the
circle around Khamenei. He became speaker of the Majles in 2008 and
his brother Sadegh was made head of the judiciary in 2009.

Within Iran the nuclear dispute produced an upsurge of nationalist
feeling in favour of Iran's right to nuclear power, and it was difficult
(not just because of regime censorship, but because of the general strong
feeling on the subject) for anyone to express dissent. Ahmadinejad may
not have invoked the ghost of Mossadeq or memories of 1953 specifically, but the parallel (with foreigners again interfering in Iranians' right
to exploit their own natural resources) was too obvious to miss. The
enthusiasm for nuclear power shaded ambiguously into support in some
quarters for Iran to be a nuclear power – i.e. a power with nuclear
weapons like Pakistan, India, Israel, France, the UK and the US. Since
2006, with the centrifuges spinning, Israel has warned that it may take

military action to destroy the Iranian nuclear (weapon) programme if the programme is not halted by other means. At times the Bush adminis-tration, with Cheney and Rumsfeld leading the way, appeared to be considering the options for military action against Iran, but pulled back after senior military commanders rebelled against the idea.[25] Some inter-preted the National Intelligence Estimate (NIE) of November 2007, which had the effect of dampening speculation about an attack on Iran, as a similar rebellion, this time by intelligence experts within the US system (the main operational conclusion of the NIE was that Iran had halted progress toward a nuclear weapon by the end of 2003).[26] Again, Iraq was in the background: the experts were embarrassed that their assertions about Saddam Hussein's weapons of mass destruction had proved exaggerated or unfounded once Saddam's regime fell, and part of their caution on Iran may have expressed a reluctance to repeat the error.

At the beginning of 2008, after further talks with the IAEA had bro-ken down, Iran announced it would be enriching uranium to 20 per cent for use in a medical research reactor. Following a similar Western pro-posal the previous year, in May 2010, Brazil, Turkey and Iran announced a deal whereby 1,200 kg of Iranian uranium enriched to a low level could be exported and swapped for 120 kg of uranium enriched to the 20 per cent level, which would have meant the Iranians would no longer have needed to enrich the uranium themselves. But despite having encouraged the initiative earlier, the US would not endorse it when it neared reality. The deal was not implemented, and in November the IAEA announced that Iran had enriched 25.1 kg of uranium to the 20 per cent level at Natanz.[27]

In the summer of 2010 it emerged that a computer virus or worm called Stuxnet had been used to target Siemens industrial software used on computers that the Iranians had been using to control uranium enrich-ment and other processes related to the nuclear programme. Centrifuges were damaged, and the enrichment process was delayed. The origin of Stuxnet was never directly avowed, but it has been assumed that the Israeli and possibly the US governments were behind it.

Despite everything, Iran continued to enrich uranium. It is hard to know how far his nuclear policy has benefited Ahmadinejad politically within Iran, but many Iranians who would be critical of him in other respects have supported his defence of Iran's nuclear interests.

Sanctions

Iran has been subject to trade sanctions imposed by the US for over thirty years, since the embassy hostage crisis. The severity and efficacy of them has risen and fallen over the years, and the US has tried more or less hard to pressurize other countries to match their sanctions against Iran. In applying that pressure the US government has gone beyond usual measures, to threaten varying degrees of extraterritoriality – seeking to punish foreign firms that have had dealings with Iran by action against their interests within the US, or even by threatening to apply US law against them as if they were US firms.

The Iranian economy has adapted to sanctions. For example, most computers in Iran, as elsewhere, use American software, and a high proportion use hardware manufactured by US companies also. Much of this has been imported via Dubai, where many wealthy Iranians have apartments and bank accounts. Smuggling has become a major activity, and, as in other authoritarian states, organs of the Islamic regime (especially the Sepah) have used their privileged position to take over a major role in smuggling operations. In this way, measures that were intended to pressurize and weaken the Iranian regime have often had the perverse effect of feeding extra revenue to parts of it. Like Mafia-type organizations in other places and times, the Sepah have profited by the increase in prices caused by restricted supply of some commodities in the economy generally, by controlling the flow of goods through a bottleneck. By contrast, many among the classes in society most closely identified with reform and opposition in Iran, the liberal middle classes, have seen their businesses punished by sanctions and the inflation caused by sanctions.

Since 2005, the UN Security Council has approved six resolutions demanding that Iran suspend uranium enrichment, four of which have applied sanctions against Iran, freezing assets, imposing an arms embargo and banning the supply of nuclear-related goods. Many countries have set up their own bilateral sanctions in addition, with varying degrees of severity, often focusing on dual-use goods and financial contacts. In the case of the UK, those measures have been tightened to the point that almost all goods may be subject to dual-use restrictions. Israel treats Iran as an enemy state by law and bans any trade or contact. US sanctions are scarcely less tough; almost all economic activity involving Iran is banned, requiring a licence from the US Treasury; the US Treasury has allegedly been active outside the US also, pressurizing foreign firms with Iranian contacts to curtail them or face adverse consequences in their dealings with the US.[28]

Another effect of sanctions has been to force Iran into closer trade relations with countries like China and Russia; so-called Black Knights who are prepared to supply goods sanctioned by others – for a healthy profit of course. But sanctions have had a damaging effect on the Iranian economy, causing shortages, inflation and a run on the rial in international exchange markets (in January 2012 the rate had fallen to around 17,000 or 18,000 rials to the dollar; about half its value two months earlier), and contributing to continuing high levels of unemployment. The rial suffered a further slide in value in the autumn of 2012; the rate fell to 40,000 to the dollar by the beginning of October. As Rafsanjani discovered in the 1990s, few things damage a government more than a currency crisis.

A new phase of even stronger sanctions pressure began in the autumn of 2011, after the (seemingly deliberately timed) announcement of an alleged plot against the life of the Saudi ambassador to the United States.

Ahmadinejad, Israel and the Holocaust

Ahmadinejad's position on the nuclear programme could, from a sympathetic perspective, at a stretch, be regarded as statesmanlike, if confrontational and populist. The nuclear issue involved serious Iranian national interests. But at the same time Ahmadinejad was pursuing a gratuitous campaign of provocation over Israel and the Holocaust that had little to do with Iran's national interests nor any other conventional policy objective. Again, he began with his new, radical line within a few months of taking office. In October 2005, quoting Khomeini, he included in a speech the words 'in rejimeh eshghalgareh Qods bayad az safeyeh ruzegar mahv shavad', which in a more or less literal translation means 'this Jerusalem-occupying regime must disappear from the page of time'. But many Western media reports used a pithier translation that had been used by the Iranian regime to translate the same phrase before – 'Israel must be wiped from the map'. As part of the same speech Ahmadinejad urged a single-state solution in Palestine, the return of

Palestinian refugees and a vote to decide the nature of the state (among Palestinians only). Later on Ahmadinejad used stronger language that came closer to the 'wiped from the map' translation, and the original phrase appeared on banners draped over missiles in televised military parades; a combination that delivered its own message, seeming to confirm the connection many had already made, with Iran's nuclear ambitions.

It may be that, when Ahmadinejad first made these remarks, he had no intention to be especially provocative, or to make provocation on this point a major part of his presidency. The October 2005 speech was made at a relatively minor venue (a conference of secondary-school students). Harsh words about Israel had been commonplace since the revolution; initially from the left, later from the right. In the immediate aftermath, Iranian diplomats claimed to be baffled, saying that Ahmadinejad had said nothing new – this had long been the position of the Islamic republic. The attitudes behind the things Ahmadinejad said were shocking in the West, but were nothing unusual in Iran, still less in Arab countries in the Middle East. Iranian politicians routinely described Israel as a 'tumour' or a 'cancerous tumour' in the region. In 2001 Khamenei had made a speech in which he had said that Zionists had collaborated with the Nazis in order to produce 'exaggerated statistics on Jewish killings' and thus facilitate the establishment of a Zionist state in Palestine. That speech had made little impact in the West.[29] But by October 2005 Western observers were looking for radical statements from Ahmadinejad: he was rapidly becoming their favourite bogeyman. And he was not averse to being elevated in that way. When he saw the worldwide reaction of outrage his words had created, he was not dismayed, still less ashamed – it seems he was encouraged.[30]

On a trip to Mecca in December 2005 Ahmadinejad elaborated further on his views of Israel. Ignoring the fact that in the first decade of Israel's existence roughly equal numbers of Jews had arrived there from European and from Islamic countries, he asked why the Palestinians should have had to pay for the Holocaust. If Germans and Austrians had mistreated Jews, then (he suggested) find a place for Jews to live in Germany or Austria. In another speech a day later he said that some European countries insisted on saying that 6 million Jews had been killed, and that people who denied it might be put in prison. With egregious equivocation, he went on: 'Although we don't believe this claim ... let's suppose it is true,' before suggesting again his notion of resettlement to Germany or Austria. In another speech later in the month, he referred to the 'myth' of the Holocaust, saying that in Europe it had been elevated above everything else, so that the deity and the prophets could be abused with impunity, but Holocaust denial was punished severely.[31]

Again, these comments were widely condemned outside Iran, and taken collectively, contributed among other things to a shift in position by Russia and China to take a stronger line against Iran in the UN. Within Iran too, some began to question what Ahmadinejad was up to. Some conservative and hardline politicians spoke out against Ahmadinejad's provocative statements, as well as reformists and moderates, questioning what effect they were likely to have on Iran's position internationally. It is rare for the Iranian Jewish community to assert itself in political controversies, but community leaders did so on this occasion, condemning Ahmadinejad's questioning of the Holocaust and warning that it could encourage an upsurge in anti-Semitism.[32]

But the regime continued to back Ahmadinejad. Khamenei stayed silent. Foreign Ministry spokesmen endorsed Ahmadinejad's declarations, saying that they reflected the views of the government. Then, in December 2006, a conference of Holocaust deniers was held in Tehran, under the aegis of the Foreign Ministry. This was a truly bizarre event, such as could only have been put together by someone who combined ignorance and *chutzpah* on Ahmadinejad's comic-heroic scale. Perhaps not since the release of Mel Brooks's *The Producers* can something simultaneously so appalling, so inadvertently hilarious and so bogglingly tasteless have burst upon the scene. Participants included a former head of the Ku Klux Klan, who rubbed shoulders with members of Neturei Karta, an ultra-orthodox Jewish Hasidic sect who opposed the establishment of the state of Israel, various assorted white supremacists, loony fringe wannabe historians and others whose views had won them prison sentences in free countries.[33] Ahmadinejad addressed the assembled delegates and made his now-familiar points on the Palestinians and Zionism. Forgetting past denunciations of racism by the regime the foreign minister, Manuchehr Mottaki, said the purpose of the conference was not to confirm or deny the Holocaust, but to 'create an opportunity for thinkers [sic] who cannot express their view freely in Europe about the Holocaust'.[34]

The conference deepened the baffled distaste with which many in the West viewed Ahmadinejad and the Iranian government. Ahmadinejad

believed he was renewing the revolutionary vigour of the regime; returning to the religious zeal of the revolution's early days. There were some
ironies to this – the most zealous and outspoken of the revolutionaries in
the early days, especially in foreign policy matters, had of course been on
the left: people like Montazeri and Musavi-Khoeniha. Since those days
many of those people had moderated and become reformists; only now
to find their old rhetoric being given new life by their political enemy. But
at a deeper level, to have such an intellectually bankrupt event run by the
Iranian state, given Iran's ancient history as a place of learning and tolerance, and given the ancient status of the country as a home and refuge for
Jews (dating back even beyond the beginnings of the Achaemenids in the
sixth century BC), was a national disgrace.

In the aftermath, a closed session of the Majles rebuked Mottaki for
his own involvement and for involving his ministry in the conference.
Other conservative voices denounced it, and Ahmadinejad's whole position on the Holocaust – notably the Baztab internet website, which
had connections to Mohsen Rezai and the Sepah. Dissatisfaction with
Ahmadinejad among veteran hardliners was spreading and deepening.
But there was no word of criticism from Khamenei, for whom the presidency of Ahmadinejad, whatever its wilder moments, was still in general
a welcome return to regime orthodoxy, and a relief from the challenges
and the turbulence of the Khatami years.

Iraq, Lebanon and the So-called Shi'a Crescent

Another result of Ahmadinejad's provocation and posturing was that,
once again, it became the norm to lay crimes at the Iranians' door for
which others were responsible. This was particularly noticeable as the
United States got into greater difficulties in Iraq in 2006. The Bush
administration (backed up as usual by Tony Blair) attempted to portray
Iran as a major cause of their difficulties in Iraq, if not the major cause.
But the evidence for this was thin, and it seemed inherently implausible
that the Iranians would seriously be trying to destabilize a government
in Iraq that represented the grouping in Iraq with which Iran was most
closely aligned. By contrast, there was good evidence that there was
a lot of support from individuals and groups within Saudi Arabia for

Al-Qaeda and the Sunni insurgency in Iraq, which was the more serious problem for the coalition (most notably, few incidents were more desta- bilizing, in creating serious inter-communal violence in Iraq, than the Sunni suicide bombing of the shrine of the Emam Ali in Najaf in August 2003). At one point, half of the foreign insurgents captured by coalition forces in Iraq were Saudis – many of them having trained as suicide bombers.[35] But because Saudi Arabia was supposedly the West's great ally in the region, these awkward facts have in general been ignored by Western media and politicians alike.

It is nonetheless likely that elements in Iran inspired by the perennial anti-Western rhetoric of the regime were giving some help to groups fight- ing Western forces. For example, in June 2003 the editor of the regime-aligned paper *Kayhan*, Hosein Shariatmadary, wrote:

> The American and British military are now within easy reach of Islamic and revolutionary countries. The revenge of the blood of innocent civilians mas- sacred by these savage militaries is easier than ever before. Today there is no need for revolutionary Muslims to go to the effort of carrying bombs and explosive materials to faraway bases, when the punishment of the Ameri- can and British military is possible with the use of grenades, Molotov cocktails or even sticks and stones. This is a blessing from God: Islamic countries have been given a golden opportunity for revenge against these aggressors.[36]

But despite much speculation in the Western media (particularly about the alleged supply of components for Improvised Explosive Devices – IEDs), the level of actual support from Iran has never been established with any clarity. As the Taleban insurgency in Afghanistan grew in severity in the period 2008–11, there was speculation about Iranian actions, but again, a huge question mark over Saudi involvement, whether directly or through Pakistan. Overall, by comparison, the adverse effects of Iranian involvement in Iraq and Afghanistan must have been relatively minor, though it may for example have been significant in contributing to the British withdrawal from Basra in 2007. The deaths of coalition troops in IED attacks were nonetheless tragic and Iranian involvement in them, whatever its true extent, particularly perverse and misguided. An example may help to illustrate the kind of incident involved. On 5 April 2007 a device exploded under a Brit- ish Warrior armoured vehicle on patrol west of Basra, killing five of the occupants. One of those killed was Second Lieutenant Joanna Yorke Dyer, an Oxford graduate who had only left Sandhurst a few months earlier. One of her colleagues said of her that her smile could light up a room; she was just twenty-four years old.[37]

Another theatre, where Iranian involvement was more plain, was Lebanon. On 12 July 2006 two Israeli soldiers were abducted by Hezbollah fighters after a clash at the border between Israel and south Lebanon. Israeli forces tried and failed to rescue the two men, after which a full-scale invasion ensued, with airstrikes and artillery bombardment. In the process, their forces took heavier casualties than expected from Hezbollah fighters, who proved to be well trained and equipped, using night-vision equipment, anti-tank guided missiles, bunkers and tunnels to good effect. They were also using unmanned aerial vehicles (drones) and computerized communications interception devices.[38] Most observers agreed that both training and equipment reflected the help given to Hezbollah by the Iranians via the Sepah (derived ultimately, of course, from the infantry tactics developed during the Iran–Iraq War). As with other actions beyond Iran's borders, most have assumed that military aid was extended to Hezbollah primarily through the Qods force of the Sepah; the longstanding unit tasked with the extraterritorial activities sanctioned by the constitution. Iran was vocal in its support for Hezbollah during the invasion. The conflict confirmed the deepening hostility between Iran and Israel, and the awareness in Israel of the multilayered threat from Iran. The fighting cost thousands of lives (mainly Lebanese civilians) and caused extensive damage to housing, and transport and power infrastructure. But some regarded it as a defensive success for Hezbollah. Among ordinary Iranians there was general sympathy for the Lebanese, but less enthusiasm for the money spent after the war by the Iranian regime to help Hezbollah rebuild war damage.

With the renewed prominence given to Hezbollah by the fighting in south Lebanon, and the Shi'a resurgence in Iraq following the defeat of Saddam Hussein, some began to warn of the danger of an Iranian-backed Shi'a wave that could damage existing regimes in the region and Western interests that depended on them. This was the so-called Shi'a Crescent theory, aired initially by King Abdullah of Jordan, and taken up by Hosni Mubarak of Egypt, the government of the UAE, Tony Blair and others.[39] It suggested that Iran was actively seeking to destabilize the region via radical Shi'a groups in countries with substantial Shi'a populations like Bahrain, Kuwait and Saudi Arabia. In fact, the theory originated at least as much in traditional Sunni sectarian disdain for Shi'as and the existential unease of regimes like that of Mubarak and the al-Saud family, which offered little in the way of representative institutions to their populations (in this sense one could see the paranoia of the Shi'a Crescent theory as heralding the Arab Spring of 2011). For privileged Sunni elites in the region, the theory served also perhaps as a smokescreen to divert Western attention away from the awkward fact that the most vicious anti-Western extremism and terrorism of the previous decade had been Sunni in origin, and had been connived at to a significant degree by some among those same elites (especially in Saudi Arabia). The Shi'a Crescent theory ignored the way that Shi'a confessional politics had developed in the Middle East since 1979. Many of the Shi'a communities and political groups on the southern shore of the Persian Gulf and elsewhere had connections with Iranian clerics. But the connections were not a simple case of Iran controlling such groups as a kind of puppet-master. In each state the Shi'as had their own preoccupations and concerns, and were not open to Iranian manipulation, as Laurence Louër has shown in an important book.[40] But the threadbare theory helped to raise the temperature of anti-Iranian sentiment by a few more degrees, contributing to the picture of Iran as a malevolent, manipulative influence in the region, whose real power was mysteriously greater than was immediately apparent.

In reality, Iran's enhanced influence in the region by 2005–6 was not the consequence of Machiavellian strategic manoeuvring by Ahmadinejad or other members of the Iranian leadership, but was a direct product of *American* military action in the region, which had destroyed Iran's two main enemies – Saddam and the Taleban. Iran's military spending was relatively low by comparison with her neighbours', and as a proportion of GDP at around 2.85 per cent on average between 2002 and 2007 (though the standard figures are questionable, and do not include spending on the Sepah, which should probably lift the figure by around another half of a percentage point).[41] For comparison, the equivalent figure for 2011 for Saudi Arabia was 11.2 per cent, for Israel 6.3 per cent, and for UAE 7.3 per cent. Arguably, these figures are misleading because those states have small populations relative to their strategic commitments, but other comparators (same year) include Iraq with 5.4 per cent and the US with 4.7 per cent. Another instructive figure (especially given the parallel sometimes drawn between Iran and the former Soviet Union) is that for Soviet defence spending – an estimated 15 to 17 per cent in the mid-1980s. By no measure is Iran among the leaders in regional or world defence spending.[42] If defence spending is any measure of militarism or a sign of expansionist intent, then Iran is not a militaristic or expansionist state.

The impression of irrationality and dangerous unpredictability in Ahmadinejad's conduct was strengthened by a number of other statements and incidents. Although when appointed by Khamenei as president Ahmadinejad kissed the supreme leader's hand as a sign of deference, Khamenei was allegedly surprised and amused to be told by Ahmadinejad that he did not expect to be in office for long, because the return of the Hidden Emam was imminent. Ahmadinejad repeated this view several times thereafter, more or less publicly, contributing to an upsurge in popular belief about the return of the Hidden Emam, and a belief in parts of the West in turn, as the phenomenon was reported, that Iran would use a nuclear weapon in order to bring about the apocalypse and the return of the Hidden Emam – the so-called Martyr State myth.[43] There can be few better examples of the way that bizarre irrationality on one side of the Iran–US divide has encouraged bizarre irrationality on the other. Ahmadinejad later told an audience in Kerman that the US was desperately trying to find the Hidden Emam in order to prevent his return – 'they are looking for his address so that they can go there and finish him off'. Would the CIA get to the right telephone book in time?[44] On later occasions Ahmadinejad wrote to President Bush in the US, attempting inter alia to convert him to Islam, and to Angela Merkel in Germany. In the latter case he explained that the victors of the Second World War had invented the Holocaust in order to humiliate Germany, just as the same powers had humiliated Iran. Iran and Germany should join forces to put those powers in their place and restore justice and order in the world. Ahmadinejad had unwittingly found the line of argument best fitted to reduce even the most self-satisfied modern German politician to squirming embarrassment.

Another incident that exacerbated tensions was Iran's detention of a group of British naval and marine personnel in March/April 2007. They were captured at sea by Sepah-manned launches on 23 March in an area adjacent to the mouth of the Shatt al-Arab. American and British coalition forces had come to an understanding among themselves about where boundaries between territorial waters were in this sector, but no one had thought to notify, still less consult the Iranians, and in reality the boundary between Iranian and Iraqi waters never had been conclusively defined. In the end the sailors and marines were released on 5 April by Ahmadinejad as an act of magnanimity in the full glare of world media coverage. British embarrassment was deepened by a succession of revelations based on paid interviews with the former captives, which revealed their conduct as less than Nelsonian.

Talk of war with Iran intensified through 2006 and 2007, feeding on these various stimuli, but faded after the NIE in November 2007.

Economy and Society

Failure to reform the economy, an overblown public sector, over-dependence on the oil sector and the effect of sanctions (notably the effect of sanctions in preventing inward investment in the oil sector, and especially petroleum refining) had all contributed to the continuing weakness of the Iranian economy, to inflation and unemployment. This had been much the same picture since the time of Rafsanjani's presidency. Inflation and unemployment were high – 10.1 per cent and 14.6 per cent respectively in 2010 – and probably higher than those official figures suggest.[45] And yet growth in years up to 2009 averaged around 5 per cent per annum, which compared rather well with many other countries, in difficult economic times; and although this growth rate was the result of rising oil prices to a substantial extent, there were other optimistic indicators; notably in education and engagement with new technologies.[46] The IMF estimated growth at 3.5 per cent for 2009/10, with good development in the non-oil sector.[47] The economy – or at any rate some parts of it – had adapted to sanctions. In particular, this was the case for the Sepah, whose economic interests had become broad and substantial, and which profited by controlling the limited flow of commodities through bottlenecks. It was widely believed that this included involvement in the illegal drugs trade on Iran's eastern border. This meant that, rather as with the classic Mafia mode of operation, the Sepah and the ruling clique actually benefited from sanctions, while the rest of the country suffered. Recent rounds of sanctions against Iran had been announced with the assertion that they would be smart sanctions that would target the elites, but in the past the Sepah had consistently proved themselves smarter than the sanctions.

Another surprise in 2011, in more than one sense, was the qualified success of a drive by Ahmadinejad to reduce state spending on subsidies. This began in 2007 with a deep cut in the subsidy to petrol prices, which was greeted with anguish at the time but was gradually, quietly accepted (many cars in Iran now run on liquid gas). More measures to cut subsidies on other staple commodities and services (including bread and public transport) were pushed through in 2008 and 2009, and in 2011 the IMF praised Ahmadinejad's government for making them work.[48] It was characteristic of Ahmadinejad that these should be the sort of essentially anti-statist, free-market measures favoured by the right; but also that he announced that the savings would be used to give handouts to the poor.

Women and Social Change

Over the thirty years since 1979, Iran has changed in many important ways. Many of these changes were in train already, in the Shah's time, but reached fruition only under the Islamic republic. Iran is now predominantly urban, and literate. The success of women's education, and the consequent expansion of the importance of women in the workplace and in the economy is a huge social and cultural change in Iran, and one that, in time, and combined with other factors, is likely to have profound consequences for Iranian society as a whole. It also contributes to the different atmosphere Iran has by comparison with other countries in the Middle East. Women are particularly prominent in skilled roles in the public sector – a third of doctors, 60 per cent of civil servants and 80 per cent of school teachers are women. But women also work in a wide variety of other jobs – including as taxi drivers. The following is an account taken from an internet blog of an interview with a formidable sixty-year-old taxi driver, Mrs Elahi:

> the journalist wanted to find out about our motivations for doing what we do, but it was as if she had already written up her article and wanted our answers to fit in with her preconceptions . . . 'Ladies,' she said 'what would you say is your main motivation for choosing this career?'

Mrs Elahi immediately answered, 'Money, obviously.'

The reporter looked at her ... as if she had not given the appropriate answer and said, 'I really need more elaborate answers for my report. I have to ...'

Mrs Elahi said, 'What do you want us to say? To lie?'

The reporter got closer to Mrs Elahi. The camera was now focused on her face and she said: 'You live in a country where you are denied many of the basic rights awarded to women. Yet you have taken up a profession that is generally considered a masculine occupation.'

'Well you really fail to appreciate who we are,' said Mrs Elahi, 'and clearly you don't think much of us ... You come from a country where women are astronauts and pilots and you still think it's amazing that we merely drive cars for a living!!' And then she added: 'Listen lady. You can ask as much as you like but my motivation is still money. Anyway, you know best.'

The reporter looked very serious, impatiently waiting for Mrs Elahi's words to be translated.

We all knew that Mrs Elahi was toying with the reporter.

When the reporter left, Mrs Elahi scornfully said, 'May she rest in peace! My grandmother could shoot an apple in half while galloping on horseback. Yet after all these years they think it's amazing that we drive cars!'[49]

It is remarkable that the changes in the position of women should have happened under the aegis of a socially conservative regime that acted initially, directly after the revolution, to constrain women and their rights in ways that appeared to reverse the progress made under the Pahlavis. One explanation is the war – women were able, quietly and without any kind of concerted plan, to take advantage of the war and the absence of men to aggrandize their position in society (as has happened in wartime in other countries). But the phenomenon also reflects the commitment of the clerical regime to education as a good in itself and a good for all, irrespective of its social or political effects. Surveys have indicated that the great change in the education and social position of women is already emerging in changed attitudes, more liberal attitudes, to education, the family, and work;[50] and is paralleled by other changes in attitude, away from religion toward more secular, liberal and nationalistic positions.[51] Some among the *ulema* (notably Shabestari, Kadivar and Eshkevari) have challenged the religious judgements on the status of women that were pushed through into law at the time of the revolution. Women were prominent in the reform movement, and again (especially) in the Green movement of 2009, even in the face of regime violence against street demonstrations. The social change to a more urbanized, highly educated society in which women play a much more assertive role is of huge significance, and is bound to change politics in Iran too in the medium to long term.

(As this book went to press in the autumn of 2012, in line with the general hardening of regime attitudes after 2009, the Iranian government announced that women would be prevented from attending a variety of courses at different universities, including engineering, computer science, English literature and business studies. They did not give reasons for their action, but the regime made statements around the same time calling for a return to traditional family values and a higher birth rate. It was also unclear whether the policy would be maintained, and how significant an effect it would have.)[52]

Even Ahmadinejad had seemed to acknowledge the new status and political power of women when in 2006 he attempted to organize a change to the rules by which women had been prevented from watching football matches. Strange though it may seem, this had been forbidden by religious experts previously because they believed viewing the naked limbs of the strapping lads would excite desire among the female fans. Ahmadinejad's attempt to allow women to watch football from segregated sections in the stands failed – the clerics overruled him and forced him to abandon the measure, not without some acrimony. The episode indicated that like any populist politician, Ahmadinejad was prepared even to take what might appear to be liberal positions if he saw a potential advantage for him in it. It was not forgotten by the conservative clerics, who already distrusted him and disliked his tendency to meddle in religious matters that were not his proper business.[53] But like the continuing struggles over *hejab*, it showed again the gap between the traditional clergy and the aspirations of ordinary Iranian women.

In 2009 another indicator of the shift in social attitudes emerged when the regime tried to humiliate a reformist prisoner, Majid Tavakoli, who had tried to evade arrest by dressing as a woman, by publishing photographs of him wearing a woman's *hejab*. Male friends and sympathizers in the Green movement showed their support for him and their disdain for the authorities by putting out on Facebook and other internet sites images of themselves, also wearing *hejab*, with the caption 'We are all Majid'. In this way, as Ziba Mir-Hosseini put it, Majid Tavakoli was multiplied, not humiliated.[54]

Another symbolic event was Women's Day, on 8 March 2009. In advance of the event, activists had drawn attention to it as an opportunity to bring forward the one million signatures campaign, an initiative across the Islamic world for women to have equal rights before the law. But in Tehran on the day the women demonstrators had their event broken up, and many of them were beaten harshly by the police and arrested. With hindsight, some have pointed up the incident and the authorities' treatment of it as a precursor to the larger demonstrations that followed the disputed presidential elections in June.[55]

Elections 2009

The election of President Obama at the end of 2008 created a new predicament for the ruling group in Iran. His early declarations of openness to direct talks with the Iranians, his preparedness to speak of the Islamic Republic as such rather than in circumlocutory terms that avoided appearing to recognize the nature of the regime, as previous administrations had done, and his cleverly crafted Noruz message in March 2009 (in which, among other things, he spoke of 'the true greatness of the Iranian people and civilization' and 'your demonstrated ability to build and create')[56] challenged the stale rhetoric of the Iranian regime and forced them to contemplate a change in their own policies of intransigence. But both sides knew that little could be expected to shift in the US–Iran relationship in advance of the Iranian presidential elections scheduled for June 2009. Many people, both outside Iran and within, hoped the elections would produce an Iranian leader with a new, positive outlook to complement Obama's, permitting some real progress at long last.

It was not to be. Once again, the Iranian presidential elections produced a surprise – all the more so because this time the surprise was of a different order altogether from the surprises of past elections. In 1997 and in 2005, surprise outsiders had won the elections. This time the surprise was in the conduct of the elections themselves, which led to weeks of demonstrations and unrest of an intensity not seen since the revolution of 1978–9.

In the last weeks before election day on 12 June 2009, many observers discerned a growing wave of enthusiasm for the movement behind the leading opposition candidate, Mir Hosein Musavi. A journalist wrote afterwards:

The run-up to the elections was unlike anything that the generations that grew up after the 1979 revolution had ever experienced. On these nights the police left the campaigners alone. It was as if a breeze of liberty was blowing through the streets. The cries and slogans that resounded were voicing demands which did not conflict with the Constitution.

However, the previous year's message from the Leader of the Islamic Republic, addressed to Ahmadinejad's cabinet, was not forgotten by the people. It had stated that they must consider planning for the years ahead. It was brought to attention by people like Mostafa Tajzadeh, who said in a campaign meeting that on the eve of the elections news had arrived that the personnel in the Ministry of the Interior had been changed. Alongside the fraction-by-fraction steps towards liberty, he seemed certain that we were on the verge of witnessing some serious events take place.

For the first time in the Islamic Republic's election history, candidates debated with each other in the American style; publicly before the people. Heated words were exchanged about the country's current policies on a platform provided by the media whose head is selected by the Leader. Prior to this, no one had dared to utter a word about the corruption of the sons of Hashemi-Rafsanjani and Nateq-Nouri in front of the Iranian government's cameras. But now Ahmadinejad, in order to escape from being cornered, referred openly to these affairs, though, of course, he was not pushed by the Leader or any judicial institution to answer for this.

The televised debates caused an immediate reaction. The slumber that had characterised these years was left behind and people exploded out into the streets. The enthusiasm over the elections was at its peak.[57]

Another commented on the televised debates (each candidate faced each other one-to-one in a series of programmes broadcast between 2 and 8 June):

The debaters' bold and public criticisms of one another seemed to have lifted the dam of political censorship which usually prevented the people from saying what was truly on their minds. Society's public atmosphere also became freer for the greater criticism and the expression of people's true feelings. As a result, during the final month before the elections, everyone living in Iran, particularly in the bigger cities, witnessed a public enthusiasm, energy and excitement. The people were constantly speaking of a change of circumstances. Even in the days leading up to Mohammad Khatami's victory in 1997, when he was elected president with an unprecedented 20 million votes, society's public atmosphere was not as critical of the current conditions as it was at this time.[58]

Having served as prime minister in the 1980s, Musavi had been out of politics since 1989 and like Khatami before him, he appeared to have neither the track record nor the charisma of someone likely to shake the foundations of the state. The perception of a developing movement behind Musavi was reinforced by early indications of a high turnout on the day of the vote, suggesting that pro-reform voters who had boycotted the elections in 2005 had changed their minds and turned out this time. There were long queues outside polling stations in Tehran; in some, the voting hours were extended and in others they ran out of ballot cards. All of this augmented the expectation of those on the opposition side that they were about to win a major victory, and this seemed to be confirmed when Ali Larijani telephoned Musavi at 5 p.m. on 12 June (in advance of the polls closing) to congratulate him.[59]

But although the final results, when they emerged, certainly showed a high turnout – 85 per cent – they gave not Musavi but *Ahmadinejad* a whopping 63 per cent of the vote: well over the 50 per cent threshold needed to win the poll outright (less than 50 per cent would have meant a second round of voting, with a run-off between the two candidates who had won most votes in the first round).

No one has yet produced conclusive proof that the results of the presidential elections of June 2009 were falsified,[60] but there have been a number of suspicious indications and pieces of partial evidence that, taken together, produce a consistent picture to that effect. One sign was that previous precedents for release of the results were abandoned – normally results emerged by region, but this time successive announcements were made on the basis of a larger number of votes counted each time, for the country as a whole. The distribution of votes for each candidate, when the final results were out, showed a suspicious consistency across rural and urban voting districts, and in those dominated by religious and ethnic minorities – as if someone had picked figures for the final result and had then applied that formula to each part of the country in arbitrary fashion, with the help of a computer programme. Against all previous experience in Iranian elections, there was no significant sign of a swing towards candidates in their home districts: the proportional formula held up even there.

A defector from the Basij told a Channel 4 journalist later that they had received instructions through their chain of command that the supreme leader had decided that Ahmadinejad should win the election, and they should do all that was necessary to ensure he did. On the day, blank ballots and the ballots of illiterates and others were filled in for Ahmadinejad, irrespective of the actual wishes of voters; some ballot boxes were counted, but then all were sent back to 'the centre' with most still uncounted.[61]

The regime's handling of the results deepened suspicions to the point at which the election looked increasingly like a coup carried out by the ruling group to keep Ahmadinejad in office. Several months before the elections, Khamenei had made statements supportive of Ahmadinejad that already marked a departure from previous practice. After the election results came out, Khamenei spoke forcefully in support of Ahmadinejad's re-election within a few hours, acclaiming it as a divine judgement – previously the supreme leader had waited until the Guardian Council ratified the result, which usually took three days. Even before the final results were known, in the small hours of the morning, police and troops were on the streets to forestall demonstrations. They surrounded the Interior Ministry (from which the results were being announced) and Musavi's campaign headquarters, severely hampering the opposition movement's communications and their ability to respond to events. All these actions were unprecedented.

Over the following weeks a number of rumours emerged that, taken together, may go some way to explain how the election turned out as it did. It seems that the ruling clique became increasingly concerned in the spring of 2009 that the elections might develop a bandwagon effect comparable to that which resulted with the election of President Khatami in 1997 – an outcome they were determined to avoid. One version says that the government conducted a secret poll that showed an outright win for Musavi. Several reports purporting to come from dissidents in the Interior Ministry alleged that reformist-oriented staff were purged and swiftly replaced by Ahmadinejad's supporters, who set about a plan to falsify the results. There were a number of suggestions that the cleric most closely associated with Ahmadinejad – Ayatollah Mesbah-Yazdi – had issued a ruling that all means were legitimate to ensure the continuation of the prevailing form of Islamic government – 'everything is permitted'.[62]

There is little doubt that many voters did turn out for Ahmadinejad on 12 June. The usual judgement is that his support was strongest in the countryside and in the more remote parts of Iran. Voters who distrusted both the regime and the perceived urban sophistication of the opposition candidates may still have voted for Ahmadinejad because unlike other politicians, he looked and sounded like them – they understood him and felt they could trust him in spite of his failure to reverse worsening economic conditions and standards of living in his first term. Many Iranians supported his strong stance against the West and in favour of Iran's right to a civil nuclear programme. In the smaller towns and cities outside Tehran and in the countryside it was also easier for the regime to coerce voters – whether by increases in salaries just before the election, or by threats. But one should not go too far (as some have) in characterizing the elections as a confrontation between an urbanized, Westernized, vocal minority versus a relatively silent, rural majority. The population of Iran in 2009 was more than sixty per cent urban. It seems unlikely that more voted for Ahmadinejad in 2009 than did in 2005, when his opponent was Rafsanjani. One Western reporter, who went out of her way to speak to working-class Ahmadinejad supporters, found some that would be vocal in his support, only to whisper 'Musavi' to her afterwards, when they could be more confident that no one was listening.[63] But the suspicious behaviour of the regime, the furore over the election and the demonstrations that followed may have obscured the real level of support for Ahmadinejad, especially for observers outside Iran. Significant numbers of lower- and lower-middle-class voters, including urban voters from those sections of society, whose support had always been crucial since 1979, had shifted their allegiance toward him after the failure of the reform movement in Khatami's time. Whether those numbers amount to 20, 30 or even 40 per cent of the population is hard to assess. But part of the story of 2009 was that Iran had become a divided country. The actions of the regime could be ascribed either to panic in the face of the growing opposition movement or to the desire to avoid the unpredictability of a second round of elections, or both.

Whatever the truth of what happened, the immediate and strong reaction told its own story. Thousands of Iranians turned out on the streets of Tehran and other cities to protest, wearing scarves or bandanas in green, the colour of the Musavi campaign. No previous Iranian election had produced such demonstrations. Within a few days, the number of protestors had grown to hundreds of thousands, with estimates suggesting a million or more on Monday 15 June. Their numbers and their diverse origins belied the thought that this was merely sour grapes from an isolated group, disappointed that the result had gone against them. European and US news media reported excitedly that these were the biggest demonstrations in Iran since the revolution. In the evenings, Iranians gathered on rooftops to shout 'Allahu Akbar!' as they had in 1978–9.

Over the first weekend of demonstrations, Ahmadinejad referred to the demonstrators as 'Khas o Khashak' – dust and trash, or flotsam and jetsam, that would be swept away. But the demonstrations did not go away. Despite beatings and arrests, and despite efforts by the regime to prevent any reporting of the protests, they continued, and Iranians found ways to get reporting out of Iran, including through new internet channels like Facebook and Twitter. Several reports indicated that the hardliners themselves were unnerved by the demonstrations. One (derived from a US diplomatic telegram via Wikileaks) suggested that at a high-level meeting Ahmadinejad himself said that the people felt suffocated, and there should be greater personal and social freedoms, including freedom of the press. Angered by this, the Sepah commander Mohammad Ali Jafari responded: 'You are wrong! It is YOU who created this mess! And now you say give more freedom to the press!' According to the source, Jafari then slapped Ahmadinejad in the face, causing an uproar in the meeting.[64] Others suggested later in the year that Khamenei had an aircraft overhauled to ensure it was in good readiness to fly him out of the country at short notice, though the reliability of this story was doubtful.[65]

The ruling clique responded to the outcry, the demonstrations and the accusations of an electoral coup by alleging an attempted coup by the other side – saying that the regime had foiled a Western-backed attempt to overthrow the Islamic republic, along the lines of the Velvet Revolution of 1989 in Czechoslovakia, the Rose Revolution of 2003 in Georgia or the Orange Revolution of 2004/5 in Ukraine. They declared that the instigators of this new Velvet Revolution were, of course, the US and Britain.[66] To support the story, the MOIS arrested several Iranians working at the British embassy, all of whom were eventually released.

On the evening of 20 June, a young woman called Neda Agha-Soltan got out of her car, which was obstructed by the protesting crowds around Kargar Avenue in Amirabad in north-central Tehran, to escape the heat. She was accompanied by her middle-aged music teacher. Soon afterwards, she was shot in the chest and despite the efforts of those around her, including a doctor, to staunch the flow of blood, she was dead within a few minutes. Bystanders filmed the event on mobile telephones, and the images went around the world on YouTube. Neda became a symbol of the protests and of the brutality of the regime's conduct (their spokesmen later tried to claim that she had been shot by the CIA or other foreigners). Despite the dwindling of the street protests in later weeks, under pressure from the police and the Basij militia, demonstrators turned out again in large numbers on 30 July, the fortieth day after her death, to protest against the shooting.[67] There were demonstrations again on 18 September, when the regime attempted to hold its usual event (Qods day – Jerusalem day) to show support for the Palestinians against Israel. Opposition demonstrators, making use of the fact that the colour used to symbolize the Palestinian cause, like that of the Musavi campaign, was green, appeared again en masse, took over the event and shouted down the official slogans.

The demonstrators pulled off a similar trick on 4 November, when they took over the official event to mark thirty years since the occupation of the US embassy in 1979. Thousands of protestors appeared in Tehran, defying arrest by the police and the Basij, and there were similar manifestations in Isfahan, Rasht, Shiraz and Tabriz. Instead of the weary regime mantra of 'marg bar Amrika' ('death to America') some called instead 'marg bar hichkas' – 'death to nobody'.

Through the summer and autumn ugly stories spread of the torture and death of protestors in custody. Estimates of the number of deaths mounted to several hundred. At the end of July the supreme leader ordered the closure of the Kahrizak detention centre after protests about torture, and the death of Mohsen Ruholamini, the son of a prominent conservative politician. In November a young doctor, Ramin

Pourandarzjani, who had seen Ruholamini shortly before his death and had been pressurized to say that he had died of meningitis, himself died in suspicious circumstances at Tehran police headquarters.

Some Western commentators said or wrote that the outcome of the elections was immaterial because there was little to choose between the policy intentions of the two main protagonists, Musavi and Ahmadinejad. That missed the point. Musavi and his reformist supporters were not looking to overturn the Islamic republic, but what had happened was no less important for the fact that they were not following a Western-inspired agenda. By falsifying the election results (as was widely believed to have happened), the regime had gone much further than ever before in subverting the representative element in the Iranian constitution and had precipitated a crisis over the very nature of the Islamic republic. Important figures like former presidents Rafsanjani and Khatami were openly critical of what had happened. Opposition candidates Musavi and Karrubi refused to be silenced. Khamenei was forced to take a more partisan position than ever before, abandoning the notion that his office put him above day-to-day politics. The demonstrators rewarded him with the chant 'marg bar diktatur' ('death to the dictator'). His position was weakened.

Ever since the revolution, the Islamic principle and the constitutional, republican, democratic principle had worked uneasily together, and from early on the democratic element had been eroded. But after 12 June those who had cherished the representative strand, who had believed that had been one of the achievements of the revolution, and that its survival gave some hope for renewal and peaceful change, were faced with the bald fact that it had been snatched away. They were now being ruled under the threat of naked force, by a ruling group who had abandoned Khomeini's principle of balancing opposing forces under a regime umbrella, and whose claim to Islamic legitimacy had worn very thin. Several leading clerics were critical of the conduct of the elections, and others stayed pointedly silent. The crisis was not just a confrontation between the regime and a section of the populace; it was also a crisis within the regime itself, and it is still not resolved.

In the meantime, the regime continued to blame Western governments for instigating the demonstrations, presenting the Obama administration with a sharpened dilemma: should America pursue its policy of détente with a regime that had just, in the judgement of many of its own citizens, stolen an election in such a bare-faced manner? The logic of engagement with Iran had not depended upon the virtue or otherwise of the Iranian regime, and cautious attempts to engage with the Iranians continued. But revelations in the autumn that showed that the Iranian government had been constructing a further uranium-enrichment facility near Qom and was conducting new missile tests increased the pressure for new sanctions. The Obama administration seem to have concluded that their attempt at a reconciliation with Iran had been a failure, whereas in fact it had put the Iranian regime under greater pressure, more effectively, than thirty years of sanctions regimes, and had helped to precipitate the biggest challenge to those controlling the regime since the revolution. But Obama was subject to his own political pressures. From the autumn of 2009 Hillary Clinton became more prominent in the presentation of US policy toward Iran, which returned to the usual barren pattern of admonitions and exhortations familiar from earlier US administrations, and the grinding process of cranking out ever more restrictive sanctions measures.[68]

The elections and their aftermath further strengthened the position of the Sepah. Ahmadinejad's debt to them was well known, and there were many reports (as in 2005) of their engagement in the election campaign in his interest – though the firmness of their commitment to him was less clear. The regime's dependence on them to face down opposition and keep the ruling group in power was only intensified by the outcome of 12 June. The role of the Revolutionary Guards in every aspect of Iranian life, and especially in the economy, had been increasing and strengthening for many years. It was emphasized further in October 2009, when a company linked to the Sepah paid the equivalent of $8 billion for a controlling share in the state telecommunications monopoly. The country was looking more and more like a military dictatorship – a tighter and more effective version of what the revolution had brought down in 1979. After the 12 June elections, Ayatollah Montazeri commented, 'What we have is not Islamic republic, but military republic.'[69] The prominence of Montazeri and some other clerics in the opposition was another significant phenomenon in the aftermath of 12 June. One of them, Yusef Sanei, a reform-inclined moderate and a *marja* for many religious Iranians, had denounced the elections as illegitimate. Regime-oriented clerics attempted to begin proceedings to remove his status as *marja-e taqlid* (recalling the way Shariatmadari had been treated in 1982) but others resisted them on his behalf.[70]

Montazeri died in his sleep at the age of eighty-seven on 19 December 2009. There were further demonstrations associated with his funeral in Qom on 21 December, and pro-regime thugs attacked Musavi and Karrubi there in the street. There were further demonstrations on 27 December, the day of Ashura, in Kermanshah, Isfahan, Najafabad and Shiraz as well as in Tehran;[71] opposition demonstrators were again attacked, and Musavi's nephew was shot and killed:

> By noon, Tehran was practically ablaze with clashes. There were unprecedented numbers in the huge crowds of opposition supporters and people were confronting the regime's forces with more intensity than ever before. The clashes reached their peak in Vali Asr Square when the crowd seized a police kiosk and were met with extreme ferocity when the police drove a car straight into the throngs, running people over in front of everyone.[72]

The opposition's practice of using familiar dates in the calendar to take over official events was countered by the regime on 11 February 2010 (the anniversary of the final triumph of the revolution in 1979) by closing down internet servers and mobile phone networks, and by closing off access to Azadi Square by all but pro-regime supporters bussed in from outside. That attempt was the last for some time by the opposition to express their continuing disapproval of the regime on the streets. They tried again on 14 February 2011 – again the regime's tactics of flooding the streets with police and Basij, preventing small groups from coalescing into larger ones, and closing down telephone and internet communications, proved effective. But the hardline leadership were apparently scared enough this time to take Musavi and Karrubi into house arrest, where at the time of writing they remain. Large numbers of reformists, politicians, journalists and others have left the country and gone into exile since June 2009 (including Mohsen Makhmalbaf, Shirin Ebadi and Ataollah Mohajerani), and an unknown further number are still in prison (including the film maker Jafar Panahi, director of *The Circle* and *Crimson Gold*). A new low point was reached in the summer of 2011, when, after the death of the veteran liberal-nationalist Ezzatollah Sahabi, his daughter Haleh was assaulted by Basijis at his funeral and died shortly afterwards of a heart attack.

Totalitarian or Democratic? Or Neither?

Since 1979, despite much speculation and many predictions at different times of the imminent demise of the Islamic republic, despite the vicious eight-year war and various other attempts at regime change along the way, the Islamic republic has survived and has proved more stable than expected. It is not fanciful to make a connection between this stability and the fact that the republic is an Islamic republic, unlike the anti-clerical or secular regimes set up by the French and Russian revolutions, for example. Islam has given the regime deeper ideological roots in Iranian society than the innovative ideologies of the Jacobins and Bolsheviks achieved (ideologies that most of the mass of the French and Russian populations probably never understood). Islam could have sustained a more liberal, democratic regime; instead it has been used to sustain a less liberal, more autocratic form of government (albeit with democratic elements that are still significant, though in retreat). Islam is a more serious idea than Jacobinism or Marxism: it is more embedded in people's lives than those political ideas ever became; in the cultural/intellectual race, it has longer legs.

But those at the top of the regime run a risk – a known risk that people have been pointing out ever since 1979. Shi'ism more than any other form of Islam is traditionally, acutely, almost obsessively sensitive to the abuse of political power. Islam still works as a support to the regime because a significant portion of the population still accept its Islamic credentials. But when innocents are beaten up, tortured and shot for asking what has happened to their vote, and when peaceful funerals are broken up by club-wielding thugs, the risk run by the regime intensifies. An example of this is a statement by the young Basiji who witnessed abuse and rape of prisoners arrested after 12 June, who told a Western reporter: 'now I am ashamed in front of people ... and I am ashamed in front of my religion'.[73]

Islam is not susceptible to the control of the regime in the way that Jacobinism and Marxism were – it is an independent standard, which is ultimately beyond the reach of the regime. *No one owns the church.*[74] If a critical mass of believers among the Iranian people ever decide that the Islamic regime has become un-Islamic; if they begin to call it the rule of Yazid, as they did the government of the Shah, then Iran's rulers will be gone as if they had never been more substantial than a puff of smoke.

What do we in the West want to happen in Iran? Broadly, we want the Iranians to have a free democracy, for Iran to normalize her external relations with the US and other Western countries, to end whatever plans she may have for developing a nuclear weapon, to recognize Israel and stop funding Hamas and Hezbollah – to become what we would regard as a normal country. To come back into the international fold, to stop being a problem. The events of June 2009, when large numbers of Iranians demonstrated for their Green movement and against the re-election of President Ahmadinejad in what they believed to be an electoral fraud, indicated that many Iranians, perhaps a majority, think more or less the same way, on many of those points at least. But they did not get their way, and there is no sign that they will get their way in the immediate future. Why did they not succeed?

Some of the complexities, paradoxes and incomprehensibilities of Iranian behaviour are hard to grasp, even for those with an understanding of the events covered in this book. Some of the complexities are intractable, and it is a feature of contemporary comment on Iran that subjectivity tends to reassert itself over objectivity. Our response to Iran says as much about ourselves as about Iran. When struggling to assess what may happen, we tend to betray what we want to happen. And our problems with Iran to some extent reflect problems with our own, Western model of development.

Comparisons are sometimes made between contemporary Iran and the former Soviet Union.[75] Is Iran the Soviet Union of the twenty-first century? No ... and yes. Taken strategically, the comparison is dangerously misleading (and unfortunately, for various reasons, there are some who are ready to mislead, and to be misled). Iran is not a threat to the West in any remotely comparable way. Iran may be on the point of acquiring a nuclear weapon, but it does not have, and will never have the global strategic reach of the former Soviet Union, nor the offensive military power in conventional forces to back it up, nor the defence spending (as noted already above), nor the military-industrial complex, nor the military occupation of half a continent, nor the totalizing grip on the thought of its own population. Neither Stalin nor Brezhnev would have tolerated Musavi, nor demonstrations on the scale achieved by the Green movement. They would have sent in the tanks, as in 1956 in Budapest and 1968 in Prague.

The Iranian regime has been reluctant to use the full force available to it against demonstrators. The events of the Arab Spring of 2011 and since have provided a comparison for this (some Iranians have claimed that the demonstrations of the Green movement, and their innovative use of new technologies, were the precursors of and the inspiration for what happened in Tunisia and Egypt). The Iranian regime has used brutality, but it has not gone to war with its own people like Gaddafi in Libya or the Assad regime in Syria. For a long time, Musavi and Karrubi were allowed to stay at large, speaking out against what had happened. The regime still wanted to maintain its own myth of democracy. When he came under pressure, Khamenei closed down Kahrizak. The origins of the regime in popular struggle against tyranny still act as a restraining factor, albeit ever more feebly. Despite the regime's success in putting down the opposition, its response still looks more like Egypt in 2011 than Syria in 2011–12 (at the time this book went to print in the latter part of 2012, the Iranian regime was maintaining its firm support for the increasingly embattled and increasingly vicious Assad regime). So there is still uncertainty about how far the regime will go in its repression, and whether its security instruments will obey it if it goes too far. Some have questioned why overthrow of the regime in Iran did not follow on from the overthrow of other regimes in the Middle East in 2011 – that may yet happen, but the crushing effect of the repression, imprisonments and exiles that followed the events of 2009 is for now a sufficient answer.

The nuclear weapon programme is a concern, but Iran would never use a nuclear weapon against Israel or anyone else in a first strike. Like the states that have nuclear weapons already, it wants a nuclear weapon as a deterrent; its geographical position and history would be argument enough to justify that, if it were not for the treaty commitments Iran has made *not* to acquire nuclear weapons. In addition, where the Soviet Union represented an ideology that was persuasive to some within Western societies, and stood for one side of a debate or conflict within Western democracy itself, Iran's Islamic ideology has no such purchase within Western society. Some might argue that Islamists are indeed active in Western society; but they are active only within communities of Muslims, mainly immigrants. The general appeal of their views is limited and small; their views do not form one end of a continuum of political debate as Soviet-aligned communism in Western society used to do. Iran's attachment to the minority, Shi'a side of the Muslim schism further limits her ideological reach.

Does Iran, like the former Soviet Union, interfere in neighbouring countries and attempt to spread its revolution? Yes . . . and no. The present regimes in Afghanistan and Iraq, perhaps best called proto-democratic and supported by the US and the West, are pro-Iranian and were set up with Iranian help. As we have seen, Iranian involvement in the insurgency in Iraq became something of a chestnut between 2003 and 2009 as some tried to blame Iran for the Western coalition's difficulties, but there was much more evidence for the destabilizing effect of support for insurgency originating in Saudi Arabia, which tended to be ignored. Similarly now in Afghanistan. For the most part, Iranian rhetoric about exporting revolution did not survive the earlier phases of the Iran–Iraq War, and the Shi'a Crescent theory, of a threat of Iranian-backed revolt by the Shi'a underclasses of the Persian Gulf region, is bunk (despite its enthusiastic espousal by Tony Blair, in his unconvincing role as Middle East peace envoy). Iran has interests and associates in both Iraq and Afghanistan, and the interests, like the borders, are permanent (unlike, perhaps, those of the US and her allies). Iran does not like the heavy US and allied military presence so close to its borders. Though largely unproven, there probably has been covert Iranian involvement in both Iraq and Afghanistan.[76] But the closer to Iran's borders, the more pragmatic Iran's foreign and security policy has been. The stated Iranian policy towards both Iraq and Afghanistan has been to foster stability in both, and it is a serious failure of Western (and Iranian) diplomacy that we have been unable to make better use of the strong alignment of interests between ourselves and the Iranians.

On a minor scale, the comparison between Iran and the Soviet Union is more apt. Opposition to the US is a fundamental ideological tenet of the Iranian regime, and the enmity and supposed interference of the US is used to justify internal repression. As in the former Soviet Union, the ideology has become fatigued and the ruling clique increasingly uses its security apparatus to uphold its dwindling authority.[77] There are other similarities. In his book *Living in Truth* Vaclav Havel described the debilitating effect of living in a society like that of Czechoslovakia under communism, in which dishonesty and lies were necessary for survival and essential for preferment, entering the soul and creating a kind of moral anomie. Azar Nafisi (author of *Reading Lolita in Tehran*) and others have described a similar effect in the Islamic republic, where the dishonest nature of the regime and compromise with it is made more dismal by the unemployment that keeps many Iranians, especially young Iranians, in a limbo of desperate inactivity and disappointed ambitions, and induces others to do a deal with the regime.

And yet ... Sartre once wrote that the French were never so free as they were under Nazi occupation, in the sense that moral choice and the pressing seriousness of consequences were never so sharp as they were at that time. That too is true in Iran. In many Western countries, for many of us, we have it easy and have become morally lazy, relativistic and cynical. In Iran, the essentials of right and wrong, freedom and repression have been everyday matters of discussion and choice. This moral earnestness emerges in some Iranian cinema. One outcome of the furore over the 2009 elections was that the authority of the supreme leader, once taboo, now came openly into question. The field of debate, under repression, actually widened – at least in that area.

Is Iran a democracy?[78] We are probably too ready to dismiss democracies for not being perfect – for example some said Britain was no longer a democracy after the invasion of Iraq in 2003 because large numbers had demonstrated against the invasion, and opinion polls suggested a majority opposed it. Democracy has some categorical attributes. Firstly, it needs a democratic constitution. Iran has that, at least potentially; it is flouted and manipulated by the regime in many respects, but elections have been held regularly, politicians have accepted loss of office and government has proceeded without *coups d'état* (albeit with a question mark over the events of June 2009). More importantly, it needs a democratic people, in other words, a people who believe in or aspire to democracy. Iran has that too, as the Green movement has demonstrated, and Khatami's reform movement before that. If democracy is most alive where people are most willing to struggle, suffer and even die for it, then the events of 2009 showed democracy alive and vigorous in Iran. Some have suggested that this is the most important aspect of the events of 2009 – that they marked the renewal of the Iranian people's commitment to the principles of democracy and freedom.[79] But a functioning democracy, in which the will of the people is expressed through elections and determines the nature of the ruling government – no, Iran does not yet have that.

Crisis of Legitimacy?

The crisis of 2009 threw into high relief a number of important questions about a subject dear to the hearts of academics – the legitimacy of government.

It is plain that the legitimacy of the Islamic regime in Iran, and especially that of its supreme leader, Ali Khamenei, was damaged by the events of 2009. But when the regime still commands the loyalty of the security apparatus, the Basij and the Sepah, how much does that matter? Any attempt at an answer involves a number of intangibles. The stolen election of June 2009 may have taken Iranians closer to totalitarianism, but they are still not there yet. Someone once said that if communism could not succeed in Germany, it could not succeed anywhere. If not in Germany, how much less easy it will be to maintain a police state in Iran. It is as if you squeeze politics in Iran in one area, it bulges out irrepressibly in another.

This was demonstrated afresh by the public row between Khamenei and Ahmadinejad in the spring and summer of 2011. Beginning with a dispute over Ahmadinejad's attempt to dismiss his minister of intelligence, Heydar Moslehi, it developed into a major rift, with the dangerous accusation of 'deviance' being levelled at Ahmadinejad and the arrest of some of his associates (some of the latter, bizarrely, were also accused of sorcery). There was even talk of Ahmadinejad being impeached, like Bani-Sadr in 1981.[80] Given the lengths to which Khamenei went to defend Ahmadinejad's election result in 2009, few would then have predicted that within two years they would be so estranged from each other. It is not democracy, but it is not the frozen, moribund stability of the Soviet Kremlin either.

If there are limits to the degree to which the state will use its coercive power, there are limits also to the lengths Iranians are prepared to go against the regime. Since June 2009 there have been many reiterations of the opposition's commitment to non-violence, and it is a commonplace to hear Iranians say that they have experienced one revolution and they do not want another. In Iranian politics, the principle of non-violence may yet prove a strength rather than a weakness, but the reform movement generally, since the 1990s, has proved frustratingly weak at using its support to achieve real political results.

Revolutionary Iran

Many observers have stressed that the crisis of 2009 was as much a crisis within the regime itself as a confrontation between regime and citizens. The way that Rafsanjani has been (apparently) marginalized since 2009 is a measure of that. One element in the success of the Iranian regime in surviving since the revolution has been the way that its institutions have adapted to absorb faction and dissent. Khomeini himself organized and reorganized the system and shifted his interventions to favour now one faction, now another, to achieve that effect and to keep a diversity of elements and factions in play. But now, the hardline right have made themselves dominant, have excluded the left and the reformists, including a large number of prominent former regime adherents and supporters, have subverted revolutionary institutions, have become ever more reliant on naked force, and have fallen to squabbling among themselves.

It has been a phenomenon of revolutions that they develop towards extremes. The French revolution marched to the left, removing moderates and Brissotins, then removing dissident Jacobins like Danton, ending up with an impossible extreme under Robespierre and St-Just – not because those men had been incorrigibly evil from the start, but because of a combination of instability, ruthlessness and paranoia, and the pressure of events. In Iran the progression followed a different pattern, but with some family resemblances. In particular, the powerful charisma of Khomeini acted as a stabilizing factor up until 1989. In the early years, the IRP under Khomeini removed liberals, leftists and Tudeh from the scene, and further movement towards extremes was prevented because Khomeini's unique authority held factions within the IRP in balance, and in check.

But after Khomeini's death, the *nezam* began to march to the right. Khomeini had intended that the duumvirate of Khamenei and Rafsanjani would provide stability, but they fell out with each other and their visions diverged. Rather against expectations in 1989, Rafsanjani lost credibility and Khamenei emerged as the stronger. Unlike a Robespierre or a Stalin however, Khamenei may regard his office as a crushing duty rather than an opportunity for megalomanic ambition – he is more like the crippled King Amfortas in Wagner's *Parsifal* (or indeed, the former Shah), suffering physically and burdened intolerably by the example of his predecessor, whose shoes he can never fill. *Shahid-e zendeh* (living martyr) indeed.

Khamenei and the circle around him were taken aback by the success of Khatami in 1997, but ultimately they judged that they had to break the reformists, or see the right broken by them. After that experience in the Khatami years, he and the leading clique could not face repeating it in 2009. But the outcome of 2009 was a loss of credibility, a further loss of balance, greater dependence on naked force, a deeper entrenchment of the right and in particular the Sepah in the system, and a greater dependence of Khamenei personally on them. In the name of the revolution, and with Ahmadinejad capering on top of the regime barrel-organ, the country lurched ever further to the right, confirming the most conservative forces and classes in power, and excluding large swathes of Iranians from influence – especially young, educated and middle-class Iranians.

The outcome of thirty years of a revolutionary Islam since 1979 has been a conservative government that employs the rhetoric of revolution but represses dissent, and a potentially revolutionary opposition that holds back from violence.[81] For the hardliners, to paraphrase Lampedusa, everything had changed with the revolution, so that everything could stay the same. In particular, the revolution enabled the bazaar and the clergy (or rather, a self-selected element from among them) to preserve their values and what they regarded as their traditional position of power in Iranian society. In fact, that position has itself been distorted in the process; the political clergy have narrowed ideologically, have distorted the tenets of traditional Shi'ism, have pushed to the margin many clerics who dissent from the regime line, and have made themselves dependent on the Sepah, Basij and law-enforcement forces. Meanwhile, urbanization, universal education and the war have changed Iranian society enormously, in ways that will in the long run prove hard to govern; and a large proportion of the population languishes impoverished and marginalized by inflation and unemployment.

The *nezam* may endure under Khamenei, but with change sweeping through other countries of the Middle East, prompted by similar conditions of social, political and economic exclusion that persist in Iran, one has to question for how long that will be possible. The next event to watch will be the presidential elections of 2013; Ahmadinejad cannot stand for a third term, and there is no obvious *nezam* candidate who can also be expected to galvanize the large turnout that Khamenei and his circle will be hoping for.

It would be tempting to conclude that all that was at stake in 2009 was the survival in power of a cynical, self-interested ruling clique, that controls restive Iranian society through the Sepah and through its patronage system – notably the *bonyads*. The clique itself, plus its dependants, plus a further number that could be bribed or cajoled – perhaps the support for Ahmadinejad extended no further than that? But that would be too black and white a picture. If that had been the case, the Green movement might have swept them away. Just as Musavi and his people still upheld the Islamic identity of Iran's political structure, so democracy is also in the DNA of the ruling clique (albeit perhaps with a flawed gene). Otherwise, they would not have backed the democratic constitution for Afghanistan in 2002, and they might have made a more naked grab for absolute power in 2009, claiming an emergency and suspending the constitution for example, as has been done in other countries. The ruling clique *want to believe they are demo-cratic*, and they would have liked to have persuaded a clear majority to vote for them in a free election. But having failed to persuade a danger-ously large proportion of the people, they can't permit unfettered freedom, or let the strong role of the Islamic element in the constitution lapse.

Why not? This is the crux of the matter. It is because Iran's rulers fear that if they were to allow greater freedom in Iranian society, Western influence, Western culture and the forces of globalization would gather an unstoppable momentum (such is the yearning of many ordinary Iran-ians for them) and would bury them. They fear that they would lose Iran's hard-won independence and self-determination, and Shi'a Islamic character; the fruits of the revolution (and the war). And that is a real concern – no abstruse clerical obsession. They are right to be worried. That is why they stole the election (although of course they also enjoy and want to retain their positions of power). There are genuine reasons to dislike some of the consequences of the Western model – some of the outcomes of the Western idea of modernity. Drug abuse, family break-down, the collapse of traditional moral values, the homogenization and stultification of international culture through consumerism: they are concerns with which religious conservatives and others in the US and elsewhere might sympathize – from any other quarter. In the minds of the ruling clique in Iran, their clerical rule is the barrier that the revolution of 1979 erected against those things (notwithstanding that drug abuse and prostitution, for example, impelled by unemployment and deprivation, have become sadly rife in Iran since then). The crisis of 2009 was not just an Iranian crisis – it reflected global questions and tensions, and a problem with liberalism and the idea of political freedom generally, that affects us all: that free people may end up choosing things they really ought not to choose, to the detriment of society. Through the phenomena of cultural communication and globalization, freedom may destroy and homogenize traditions and cultural particularities that people value and which give them their identity. Once again, a phenomenon that looks peculiarly Iranian, proves on closer examination to be all-too-human, all-too-familiar; so far away, so close.

Since the revolution of 1979, religious conservatism and left-leaning republicanism, or if you prefer, Islam and democracy, have been continually in tension, in everyday politics as in the constitution, struggling for dominance in Iran. The events of 2009 may in the future be seen as the final, crushing victory of the hardline conservatives; or possibly as the consciousness-raising epoch of a new republican generation who will proceed inexorably from defeat to eventual triumph. But in 2012 it would be bold and probably foolhardy for a historian to predict either outcome.

The Iranian predicament is a particular and individual version of this common human predicament. The ruling clique, we might say, should have enough confidence in the Iranian people to let them choose, and to let the people work out for themselves, in the long run, the need to choose aright. Yes – but the same applies to us in the West, in a shifted sense. We and our governments need to set aside what *we* want for a time and to let Iranians resolve their predicament their way. To have enough confidence in the principles of freedom we believe in, to trust that they will eventually win through in Iran too.

Postscript

A series of events over the autumn of 2011 and the winter of 2011/12 again increased tension between Iran and the West, seemingly bringing closer the threat of war, as had happened four years earlier, under the Bush administration. In October 2011 it was alleged on the basis of an FBI investigation that Iran had inspired a plot to murder the

Saudi ambassador to the US in Washington (the same ambassador who had, according to Wikileaks, earlier urged US military action against Iran – to 'cut the head off the snake'). Although some of those involved in the alleged plot seemed unlikely characters, and despite the fact that the director of the FBI commented at a press conference that the allegations sounded like a Hollywood film script, the Obama administration seemed to take the story as already proven, blamed the highest levels of the Iranian regime, and announced that new sanctions would be applied. A few weeks later, on 8 November, the IAEA issued a new report on Iran's nuclear programme, which went into greater detail than ever before about suspicions that Iran was pursuing a nuclear weapon (drawing on information from Western intelligence agencies), but had little or no evidence to suggest that significant weapon development had gone forward since 2003 (seeming therefore to confirm the NIE of November 2007 on that point). But the report was much trumpeted before release, by Israeli and hawkish US commentators, as conclusive proof of Iranian misdoings. It looked rather as though the timing of these events had been coordinated as a new initiative to increase pressure on the Iranian regime. Certainly, the US and the West had the initiative in these months, where previously Ahmadinejad had been the one setting the agenda. There was renewed talk of military action against Iran, and of further rounds of sanctions. In mid-November the UK announced that (following the IAEA report) Iran would no longer be allowed access to British banking institutions, as part of what was hoped to be concerted international action. On 29 November police stood by while a mob of Basijis and alleged students broke into the British embassy compound in Tehran, ransacking staff accommodation and looting and destroying property. In the aftermath the UK withdrew her diplomats from Iran and expelled all the Iranian diplomats in London. Other Western countries also withdrew their ambassadors from Iran. In January 2012 the EU announced an oil embargo, to take effect from July. Over this period, there were several assassinations in Iran of people associated with the nuclear programme; the assassinations were widely believed to have been instigated by Mossad. A US unmanned aircraft crashed on Iranian territory in the east, near the border with Afghanistan; the Iranians refused to return it.

There was much discussion and comment at this time in the Western media about more sanctions and the threat of military action – but also a growing number of voices questioning Western policy and the apparent drift toward war.[82] There was a sense that greater pressure was being applied to Iran partly because policy-makers no longer knew what else to do, and because the process of securing international agreement to new sanctions measures in the UN Security Council had acquired its own momentum. New sanctions measures had become a way to deflect pressure from Israel, as figures within the Israeli government spoke more insistently about the likelihood of Israel taking military action against the Iranian nuclear programme. As the tension escalated, so too did the risk of miscalculation and war by accident.

Despite the new sanctions measures and increasing financial pressure, the Iranian regime remained defiant, resting on the conviction among the Iranian people, discussed in earlier chapters, hardened in the fires of the revolution and the Iran–Iraq War, that Iran would never again be bullied or humiliated by foreign powers. It would be a mistake to underestimate that determination to uphold national independence. Some doubted the wisdom of applying pressure to Iranian oil supplies. Whatever the other effects, an oil embargo would raise oil prices, at a time when the world economy, and especially the European economy, was vulnerable and weak. Two of the countries in Europe that were financially and economically most vulnerable, Italy and Greece, were also among those most dependent on Iranian oil, with refining infrastructure least capable of switching to other suppliers.

In this developing crisis, some of the essential elements of the problem remained somewhat vague and unfocused in the debates that went on. In Israel, the government of Benjamin Netanyahu maintained its account of the situation at a high pitch, accusing the Iranian regime of being aggressive, expansionist and irrational. It claimed that the possibility of an Iranian nuclear weapon was an existential threat to the state of Israel. Notwithstanding that some irresponsible voices from within Iran had made statements that played into this interpretation,[83] this line was exaggerated and irresponsible in itself. Most knowledgeable observers accepted that, even if Iran acquired a nuclear weapon, it would never be used against Israel in a first strike, or at all unless Iran itself were attacked, because the retaliation from the US and Israel would be so overwhelming. This view was reinforced by statements from within Israel – from Meir Dagan, former Mossad chief,[84] and from Yuval Diskin, a former head of the Israeli Shin Bet[85] (internal intelligence – counterpart to MI5), in March and April 2012 respectively. The statements came shortly after a visit to Washington by Benjamin Netanyahu, in the course of which Netanyahu failed to persuade President Obama to accept a position on Iran that said that an Iranian threshold capability was in itself an unacceptable red line[86] (Diskin accused Netanyahu of having misled the Israeli public with his dramatization of the threat from Iran). The threat to Israeli security interests was real and genuine, but what was threatened was the loss of the Israeli nuclear monopoly in the Middle East and the weakening of the Israelis' own (undeclared) nuclear deterrent – a serious matter, but not immediately apocalyptic. The supposed and oft-mentioned threat of an arms race in the Middle East was something of a chimera – Israel's possession of a nuclear weapon had not prompted Saudi Arabia, for example, to acquire one.[87] Another peculiarity was that the sanctions were all primarily directed at getting the Iranians to suspend their uranium enrichment activity – but that activity had by 2012 been running long enough and had developed to a point at which continuing enrichment seemed rather immaterial. More important than the actual uranium was the understanding of the enrichment process and the confident know-how the Iranians had acquired. Essentially, what the US and the EU were trying to do was to reverse the Iranian *intention* to develop a nuclear weapon. But the Iranians themselves continued to deny any such intention, and the evidence seemed still to indicate that substantial progress toward their nuclear weapon had halted in 2003. How would we know, beyond what we already knew, if we were to succeed in reversing this Iranian intention?

Some suggested that these and other ambiguities in the Western position indicated that the real Western objective was not resolution of the nuclear problem, but regime change in Iran – a situation reminiscent of a similar dangerous ambiguity before the US-led invasion of Iraq in 2003. An ambiguity that went some way to legitimate the resistance of the Iranian regime, and which objectively might be regarded – for example in the context of the clause in the NPT permitting a state to withdraw from the treaty if it considered itself to be under a serious security threat – as just cause for the Iranian regime to want a nuclear weapon after all.

It became apparent over the first half of 2012, as new negotiations on the nuclear problem unfolded in successive rounds in Istanbul, Baghdad and Moscow, that the Iranian side was negotiating with a greater degree of seriousness and application than in previous talks. In particular, the Iranian negotiators had a clearer and more direct mandate to speak with the full backing of the supreme leader than had been the case previously. Spoiling statements by Ahmadinejad, a feature of earlier talks, were conspicuous by their absence. The greater seriousness from the Iranian side may have reflected a perception on their part that these talks, with a more prominent and more serious level of US participation than ever before, in turn merited more concentrated attention from them too. Alternatively, they may have judged that they had secured most if not all of what they had intended in the way of progress with enrichment, and it was time to make a settlement and bank those achievements. Or (as many assumed) it may be that they were keen to see the new, tougher sanctions measures removed. Insistence that this should happen was certainly a prominent feature of the Iranian negotiating position in Istanbul, Baghdad and Moscow. In fact, it was most likely a combination of all these factors.

Strangely however, the US side at the Moscow talks seemed at one point to say that whatever concessions the Iranian side made in the talks, the sanctions could not be lifted (reflecting the institutional inertia of the sanctions process in the US Congress, the UN and the EU). It appeared that the US and the West expected not to negotiate, to make concessions in exchange for concessions (as is normal in diplomacy and negotiations of any kind), but to deliver an ultimatum and dictate a settlement. It is hard to imagine any government, except under the most extreme duress, capitulating to such a demand, and it was no surprise that the talks did not prosper. But they did continue – neither side wanted to break off. In fact, however Western governments presented the state of the talks, the real question was when and how the US (with Israel muttering dark threats in the background) would be prepared to come off their previous position of no enrichment, and accept the fait accompli of the Iranian enrichment capability – albeit at a low level (3–5 per cent) and with tougher inspection safeguards. The parameters of the deal that was in the offing were fairly plain – but it was plain too that the Obama administration, in the run-up to a presidential election in November 2012, was not in a position to seal that deal.

In the meantime, the assassinations of Iranian scientists, assumed to have been perpetrated by the Israelis, appeared to receive a response in incidents in Georgia and Delhi. In the latter case a car belonging to the Israeli embassy was targeted on 13 February 2012 with a magnetic bomb delivered by an assailant on a motorbike (the method resembling that used in the attacks in Iran), and four people were injured. The Delhi police said they believed there was a connection with the Sepah,[88] though doubts were raised about this later. Then on 18 July, a bomb exploded next to a tourist bus carrying an Israeli tour group at Burgas airport in Bulgaria, killing five Israelis, a Bulgarian bus driver and the man carrying the bomb. Initially the local authorities assumed it had been a suicide attack, but later it emerged that the bomb had probably been detonated remotely. There appeared to be a connection with Lebanese Hezbollah.[89] Responsibility for all these incidents remained unclear, but they contributed to the general air of tension, and together threatened to escalate, and to displace what fragile grounds for optimism remained in the continuing talks.

Amid this uncertainty and complexity, some firm realities stand out. The question of an Iranian nuclear weapon is an unwelcome extra problem in the Middle East, and potentially a dangerous one. But it is inextricably tied in with the long-running hostility between the US and Iran, and between Iran and Israel.[90] The nuclear weapon's only purpose is deterrence – in this case as an instrument to bolster Iran's hard-won independence and the survival of the Iranian regime. If there were no hostility, or if the level of hostility could be reduced and made safe, the threat and the need for deterrence would also be reduced. The fundamental problem is that hostility and the need to resolve it – easier said than done, of course. But it is perhaps relatively easy, notwithstanding the history, the harshness of the rhetoric, the intransigence, the failures of understanding and imagination on both sides, and the vested interests some have on both sides in the continuation of the hostility. Relatively easy because this dispute lacks many of the features that make other longstanding international crises and problems intractable. The three states most deeply involved, Iran, the US and Israel, share no mutual borders. There are no border disputes or territorial claims. There are no refugees demanding the right to return. There is no intercommunal violence. Within quite recent memory the peoples involved have been allies, and even today there is no deep-seated hatred between them – for the most part, indeed, rather the reverse.[91] When Obama made a serious attempt at reconciliation in the first six months of his administration, the response from ordinary Iranians was such that it helped to produce the Iranian regime's most serious crisis since 1979. Far from failing, the reconciliation effort worked more dramatically than anyone could have imagined. But then it was abandoned. It needs to be resumed, reinforced, and maintained with determination until it succeeds.

Glossary

Abadgaran: Developers

Achaemenid: dynasty that ruled the Persian Empire 549 to 331 BC

adalatkhaneh: House of Justice

AIOC: Anglo-Iranian Oil Company (formerly the Anglo-Persian Oil Company CAPOC)

Akhbari: Shi'a school favouring tradition; opposed to the *Usuli*

akhund: originally, teacher or preacher; later became pejorative term for a cleric

Allahu Akbar: 'God is Great'

anjoman: political or other kind of society

Anfal: genocidal campaign by Saddam's forces against the Kurds of Iraq in 1988

arba'in: Arabic term for the fortieth day after Ashura, or a bereavement, commemorated as day of mourning (see also *chelom*)

Arvand Rud: Persian term for Shatt-al-Arab waterway

Aryamehr: 'Light of the Aryans' – title for himself chosen by Mohammad Reza Shah

Ashura: anniversary of the martyrdom of the Emam Hosein

ayatollah: 'sign of God'

Baath Party: Arab nationalist/socialist party that achieved political dominance in both Syria and Iraq in the 1950s

Babi: religious movement of the mid-nineteenth century in Iran

Badr brigade: armed wing of SCIRI, backed by Iran

Bahai: new faith that emerged out of Babism in the later nineteenth century

baqali polo: traditional dish of rice and broad beans

barbari: one kind of Iranian bread

bast: sanctuary

Basij: revolutionary militia, paramilitary volunteers (mainly young men)

bazaari: merchant or artisan who works in the bazaar

bid'a: innovation (i.e. an illegitimate or heretical religious innovation)

bonyad: charitable foundation

Bonyad-e Mostazafan (va Janbazan): foundation for the oppressed (and war veterans – added in the 1990s)

chador: literally, tent; a common term for enveloping form of *hejab chap*: left (literally and in political sense)

chelom: Persian term for the fortieth day after Ashura, or a bereavement, commemorated as a day of mourning (see also *arba'in*)

CIR: Council of the Islamic Revolution

Daheh-ye Fajr: ten days of dawn

daneshgah-e azad-e eslami: free Islamic university (also known as Azad university)

Da'wa Party: political party supported by Iraqi Shi'as

din-e dowlat: state religion

Eid-e Fetr: celebration at the end of the Ramadan fast

Elm-o-Sanat: University of Science and Technology, in Tehran

elteqat: eclecticism

Emam: literally, leader, prayer leader; the term used in twelver Shi'ism to signify the twelve descendants of the Prophet believed by Shi'as to have been his legitimate successors; also used exceptionally for Khomeini

enheraf: deviation

Enqelab-e Eslami: *Islamic Revolution* (newspaper title)

enqelab-e farhangi: cultural revolution

erfan: literally, gnosis; a form of Islamic mysticism

Ershad: literally, guidance; a short term for the Ministry for Culture and Islamic Guidance, also known as Ministry of Islamic Guidance

estefade-ye abzari: exploitation or instrumental use of something

estekbar-e jahani: world arrogance

Ettela'at: literally, information or intelligence; the title of a major newspaper (but also used as a short term for the MOIS)

fajr: dawn

falak: term used for punishment or torture administered by beating the soles of the feet (bastinado)

faqih: a cleric qualified in *fiqh* (plural *fuqaha*)

Farmandeh: commander

farr: aura of rightful kingship, associated with just rule and military success.

fatah/fath: victory

fatwa: opinion or decision on a point of religious law

Fedayan-e Eslam: extremist Islamic organization (literally, the devotees of Islam)

Fedayan-e Khalq: (Sazeman-e Cherikha-ye Fedayan-e Khalq-e Iran), Militant Marxist organization

ferman: order or decree issued by the Shah

15 Khordad Foundation: body established to pay bounty for the killing of Salman Rushdie

fiqh: religious law/jurisprudence

fiqh-e puya: interpretation of religious law to favour flexibility

fiqh-e sonnati: interpretation of religious law to favour tradition

Forqan: militant Islamic group

gharbzadegi: West-sickness; also translated as 'Westoxication' or 'West-strickenness'

GCC: Gulf Cooperation Council

hadith: traditions of the Prophet and the Emams

Hajj: pilgrimage to Mecca

hejab: term for various forms of covering worn by women to comply with modesty rules

Hezbollah: Party of God

Hojjatieh: shadowy, highly conservative clerical group

hojjatoleslam: religious title below ayatollah; literally, 'proof of Islam'

hokm: religious decree

Hokumat-e Eslami: *Islamic Government*, a book by Ayatollah Khomenei

Homafaran: air force technicians

ijtihad: interpretation of religious law

ijtihad-e mostamar: continuous *ijtihad*

Iran Novin: New Iran, a party in the time of the Shah

IRP: Islamic Republican Party

janbazan: war veterans; literally, those who risk their souls

Jangali: rebel movement based in the forests of Gilan

Jang-e Tahmili: Imposed War (the Iran–Iraq War)

jahan-khor: world-devouring

Jomhuri-ye Eslami: *Islamic Republic* (newspaper title)

JRM (Jame-ye Ruhaniyat-e Mobarez): Combatant Clergy Association

jub: water channel running at the sides of streets

Kargozaran-e Sazandegi: Servants of Reconstruction (political grouping supporting Rafsanjani)

kar kar-e Ingliseh: work of the British

KDP-I: Kurdish Democratic Party of Iran

khalifa: caliph; literally, successor

khas o khashak: dust and trash or flotsam and jetsam

khoms: religious tax paid by pious Muslims

komiteh: committee – revolutionary committee

konkur: university entrance exam

Kumeleh: militant Kurdish separatist group

kuseh: shark (nickname for Rafsanjani)

madreseh: school

Majles: literally, assembly – the Iranian parliament

Majles-e Khubregan: Assembly of Experts

Majma-e Tashkhis-e Maslahat-e Nezam: literally, the Council for Discerning the Interests of the System, or Expediency Council

maktabi: fervent ideological supporter of the Islamic regime

Mardom: literally, 'people' – title of a party in the time of the Shah *marg bar . . .*: death to . . .

marja-e taqlid: source of emulation; traditionally, one of a handful of pre-eminent Shi'a religious scholars

mashruteh: constitutional movement

maslahat: expediency; the interest of the state

mellikesh: prison slang for prisoners who have served their sentence but remain in prison because they refuse to recant

Melliyun: title of a party in the time of the Shah

MKO: Mojahedin-e Khalq Organization (Sazeman-e Mojahedin-e Khalq), originally a Marxist/Islamist organization, also known as the MEK, PMOI

mofsed fel-arz: spreading corruption on earth

moharaba: waging war against God

Moharram: month of mourning for the Emam Hosein – the first month of the Islamic calendar

MOIS: Ministry of Intelligence and Security; see *Vezarat-e Ettela'at va Amniat-e Keshvar*

Mojahedin-e Khalq Organization: see *MKO*

mojtahed: cleric qualified to perform *ijtihad*

monafeqin: hypocrites (the Islamic regime's term for the MKO)

montazh: from the French *montage*: a loose assembly of possibly incompatible elements thrown together

mosahebeh: interview (televised confession)

mostakber: oppressor

mostazafin: the oppressed, the disinherited

MPRP: Muslim People's Republican Party

MRM (Majma-e Ruhaniyun-e Mobarez): Association of Combatant Clergy, a leftist offshoot of the JRM, later reformist

najes: ritually unclean

Namayandeh-ye Emam: Emam's representatives

National Front (Jebhe Melli): coalition of liberal and social-democratic parties established in the late 1940s

NCRI: National Council of Resistance of Iran (front for the *MKO*)

NDF: National Democratic Front

Nehzat-e Azadi-ye Iran: Freedom Movement of Iran

nezam: the system; the Islamic regime

NIE: National Intelligence Estimate (US)

NLA: National Liberation Army – armed wing of the *MKO*

NPT: Nuclear Non-Proliferation Treaty

Pahlavan: hero figure in Ferdowsi's *Shahnameh* and in the *zur-khaneh*

Pahlavi: term used for the Middle Persian language spoken in the time of the Parthians and Sassanids; appropriated by Reza Shah to denote his family and dynasty

Paykan: family car assembled under licence in Iran, based on the design of the British Hillman Hunter

Peshmerga: armed wing of the KDP-I

PUK (Patriotic Union of Kurdestan): Kurdish group fighting Saddam Hussein within Iraq under Jalal Talabani

Qajar: the dynasty that ruled Iran 1796–1925

Qods: Jerusalem

Quraish: ruling family of Mecca in the time of the Prophet (to which the Prophet also belonged, by a junior branch)

rahbar: leader

rahbar-e moazzam: supreme leader

rast: right (literally and in politics)

Rastakhiz: party established by the Shah in the 1970s as the single party in the state

resala: treatise qualifying a *mojtahed* to become a *marja-e taqlid*

rowzeh-khans: itinerant preachers who used to recite verse accounts of the martyrdom of Hosein

Safavid: dynasty that ruled Iran 1501–1722, turning the country into a Shi'a state

salaf: literally, predecessor (following the path of the venerable predecessors); *salafi* is a term applied to Sunni fundamentalists and activists following the same sort of line as the Wahhabis

sardar-e sazandegi: commander of reconstruction (title given Rafsanjani by his supporters)

Sassanid: dynasty that ruled Iran from AD 224 to 641

SAVAK (Sazeman-e Ettela'at va Amniyat-e Keshvar): National Intelligence and Security Organization

sazandegi: reconstruction

SCIRI: Supreme Council for the Islamic Revolution in Iraq

Sepah-e Pasdaran-e Enqelab-e Eslami: Islamic Revolutionary Guards Corps (Sepah for short)

seyyed: descendant of the Prophet

shabnameh: night letters (clandestine letters – samizdat)

shahid: martyr

shahid-e zendeh: living martyr

Shahnameh: Ferdowsi's epic poem telling the stories of the ancient kings of Iran

shari'a: religious law, derived from the Koran and *hadith*

shaytan-e bozorg: great Satan

shekanjeh: torture

Shi'a (Ali): 'the party of Ali', the dominant sect of Islam in Iran

shirk: idolatry

SNSC: Supreme National Security Council

Sunni: majority sect of the Muslims; literally, followers of tradition (*sunna*)

taghuti: idol-worshippers

Tasu'a: 9 Moharram; the day before Ashura and part of the Ashura commemoration *ta'zieh*: traditional street theatre re-enacting the martyrdom of Hosein

ta'zir: corporal punishment

Tudeh: literally 'the Masses', the Soviet-aligned socialist/communist party

2 Khordad Movement: reformist movement supporting President Khatami, named after the date of his election victory in 1997

ulema: the clergy

umma: the community of Muslims

Usulgarayan: followers of principle

Usuli: Shi'a school favouring *ijtihad*; opposed to the *Akhbari*

vali: deputy

velayat: guardianship; or the authority of a guardian or deputy

velayat-e faqih: guardianship of the jurist (see p.137)

velayat-e motlaq: absolute guardianship

VEVAK (Vezarat-e Ettela'at va Amniat-e Keshvar): Ministry of Intelligence and Security (MOIS) – often referred to by Iranians as Ettela'at or Vezarat

Wahhabism: fundamentalist religious movement founded by Mohammad ibn Abd-al-Wahhab and aggrandized by the al-Saud family of Saudi Arabia

waqf: religious endowment (plural *awqaf*)

White Revolution (Enqelab-e Sefid): reform programme imposed by the Shah in the 1970s

zur-khaneh: house of strength; traditional gymnasium

Select Bibliography

Abrahamian, Ervand, 'The Causes of the Constitutional Revolution in Iran' in *International Journal of Middle East Studies*, vol. 10, no. 3 August 1979, pp. 381–414.

Abrahamian, Ervand *Iran Between Two Revolutions*, Princeton 1982.

Abrahamian, Ervand *Radical Islam: The Iranian Mojahedin*, London 1989.

Abrahamian, Ervand *Khomeinism: Essays on the Islamic Republic*, Berkeley 1993.

Abrahamian, Ervand *Tortured Confessions: Prisons and Public Recantations in Modern Iran*, Berkeley 1999.

Abrahamian, Ervand *A History of Modern Iran*, Cambridge 2009.

Afkhami, Gholam Reza *The Life and Times of the Shah*, Berkeley 2009.

Afshari, Reza 'The Discourse and Practice of Human Rights Violations of Iranian Baha'is in the Islamic Republic of Iran' in Dominic Parviz Brookshaw and Seena B. Fazel (eds.), *The Baha'is of Iran: Socio-historical Studies*, Abingdon 2008, pp. 232–77.

Aghaie, Kamran Scot *The Martyrs of Karbala: Shi'i Symbols and Rituals in Modern Iran*, Seattle 2004.

Alam, Asadollah *The Shah and I: The Confidential Diary of Iran's Royal Court*, ed. Alinaghi Alikhani, 1968–1977, London 2008.

Alavi, Nasrin *We Are Iran*, London 2005.

Algar, Hamid (ed. and trans.) *Constitution of the Islamic Republic of Iran*, Berkeley 1980.

Alvandi, Roham 'Nixon, Kissinger and the Shah: The Origin of Iranian Primacy in the Persian Gulf' in *Diplomatic History*, vol. 36, issue 2, 2012, pp. 337–72.

Amirsadeghi, Hossein and Ferrier, R. W. (eds.) *Twentieth-Century Iran*, London 1977.

Andrew, Christopher and Mitrokhin, Vasili *The KGB in Europe and the West: The Mitrokhin Archive*, London 2000.

Andrew, Christopher and Mitrokhin, Vasili *The KGB and the World: The Mitrokhin Archive II*, London 2006.

Ansari, Ali *Iran, Islam and Democracy: The Politics of Managing Change*, London 2000.

Ansari, Ali *Modern Iran Since 1921*, Harlow 2003.

Ansari, Ali *Confronting Iran: The Failure of American Foreign Policy and the Roots of Mistrust*, London 2006.

Ansari, Ali *Iran Under Ahmadinejad: The Politics of Confrontation*, London 2007.

Ansari, Ali *Crisis of Authority: Iran's 2009 Presidential Election*, London 2010.

Arjomand, Saïd Amir *The Turban for the Crown: The Islamic Revolution in Iran*, Oxford 1988.

Arjomand, Saïd Amir *After Khomeini: Iran Under His Successors*, Oxford 2009.

Axworthy, Michael *The Sword of Persia*, London 2006.

Axworthy, Michael *Iran: Empire of the Mind*, London 2008a.

Axworthy, Michael 'Diplomatic Relations Between Iran and the United Kingdom in the Early Reform Period, 1997–2000' in Anoushiravan Ehteshami and Mahjoob Zweiri (eds.) *Iran's Foreign Policy from Khatami to Ahmadinejad*, Reading 2008b, pp. 105–13.

Azari, Farah *Women of Iran: The Conflict with Fundamentalist Islam*, London 1983.

al-Azm, Sadik 'Is the Fatwa a Fatwa?' in *Middle East Report*, no. 183, July/August 1993, p. 27.

Bakhash, Shaul *The Reign of the Ayatollahs*, London 1986.

Bakhash, Shaul 'The Troubled Relationship: Iran and Iraq, 1930–80' in Lawrence Potter and Gary Sick (eds.) *Iran, Iraq and the Legacies of War*, New York 2004, pp. 11–27.

Baktiari, Bahman *Parliamentary Politics in Revolutionary Iran: The Institutionalisation of Factional Politics*, Gainesville 1996.

Baktiari, Bahman 'Dilemmas of Reform and Democracy in the Islamic Republic of Iran' in Robert W. Hefner (ed.) *Remaking Muslim Politics: Pluralism, Contestation, Democratization*, Princeton 2005, pp. 112–32.

Bani-Sadr, Abol Hasan *My Turn to Speak*, Washington 1991.

Basmenji, Kaveh *Tehran Blues: Youth Culture in Iran*, London 2005.

Bayandor, Darioush *Iran and the CIA: The Fall of Mossadeq Revisited*, London 2010.

Behrooz, Maziar *Rebels with a Cause: The Failure of the Left in Iran*, London 2000.

Bergquist, Ronald E. *The Role of Airpower in the Iran–Iraq War*, Honolulu 2002.

Bill, James A. *The Eagle and the Lion: The Tragedy of American-Iranian Relations*, Yale 1988.

Bishop, Farzad and Cooper, Tom *Iranian F-4 Phantom II Units in Combat*, Botley 2003.

Bjerre Christensen, Janne *Drugs, Deviancy and Democracy in Iran: The Interaction of State and Civil Society*, London 2011.

Bowden, Mark *Guests of the Ayatollah: The Iran Hostage Crisis: The First Battle in America's War With Militant Islam*, New York 2006.

Brookshaw, Dominic Parviz and Rahimieh, Nasrin (eds.) *Forugh Farrokhzad: Poet of Modern Iran*, London 2010.

Brown, Ian *Khomeini's Forgotten Sons: The Story of Iran's Boy Soldiers: Child Victims of Saddam's Iraq*, London 1990.

Browne, E. G. *The Persian Revolution of 1905–1909*, London 1966.

Buchta, Wilfried *Who Rules Iran?* Washington 2000.

Buchta, Wilfried 'Mehdi Hashemi's Fall: An Episode of the Iranian Intra-Elite Struggle for Power under Khomeini' in M. Hamid Ansari (ed.) *Iran Today: Twenty-five Years after the Islamic Revolution*, New Delhi 2005, pp. 197–226.

Cambridge History of Iran (7 vols.), Cambridge 1961–91.

Carter, Jimmy *White House Diary*, New York 2010.

Chehabi, H. E., *Iranian Politics and Religious Modernism: The Liberation Movement of Iran Under the Shah and Khomeini*, London 1990.

Chehabi, H. E. 'The Banning of the Veil and Its Consequences' in Stephanie Cronin (ed.) *The Making of Modern Iran: State and Society under Reza Shah, 1921–1941*, London 2003, pp. 203–21.

Chehabi, H. E. 'Iran and Lebanon in the Revolutionary Decade' in H. E. Chehabi (ed.) *Distant Relations: Iran and Lebanon in the Last 500 Years*, London 2006a, pp. 201–230.

Chehabi, H. E. 'Iran and Lebanon after Khomeini' in *Distant Relations: Iran and Lebanon in the Last 500 Years*, London 2006b, pp. 287–308.

Chehabi, H. E. and Mneimneh, Hassan I. 'Five Centuries of Lebanese–Iranian Encounters' in H. E Chehabi (ed.) *Distant Relations: Iran and Lebanon in the Last 500 Years*, London 2006, pp. 1–47.

Choudhari, Huria 'Beating the Reporting Ban in Iran' [BBC] *World Agenda*, September 2009.

Chubin, Shahram and Tripp, Charles *Iran and Iraq at War*, London 1988.

Cole, Juan *Sacred Space and Holy War: The Politics, Culture and History of Shi'ite Islam*, London 2002.

Cooper, Tom and Bishop, Farzad *Iran–Iraq War in the Air, 1980–88*, Atglen 2000.

Cooper, Tom and Bishop, Farzad *Iranian F-14 Tomcat Units in Combat*, Botley 2004.

Coulson, Merope 'Revolution in Iran' in *Carousel: Diplomatic Service Families Association Magazine*, Autumn 2008, p. 30.

Dehqan, Ahmad *Journey to Heading 270 Degrees: A Novel*, trans. and ed. Paul Sprachman, Costa Mesa 2006.

Ebtekar, Massoumeh *Takeover in Tehran: The Inside Story of the 1979 US Embassy Capture*, ed. Fred A. Reed, Vancouver 2000.

Ehteshami, Anoushiravan *After Khomeini: The Iranian Second Republic*, London 1995.

Ehteshami, Anoushiravan *Iran and the Rise of Its Neoconservatives: The Politics of Iran's Silent Revolution*, London 2007.

Esfahani, Hadi Salehi and Pesaran, M. Hashem 'The Iranian Economy in the Twentieth Century: A Global Perspective' in *Iranian Studies*, vol. 42, issue 2, 2009, pp. 177–211.

Esfandiary, Soraya *The Autobiography of HIH Princess Soraya*, London 1963.

Fardust, Hussein and Dareini, Ali Akbar *The Rise and Fall of the Pahlavi Dynasty: Memoirs of Former General Hussein Fardust*, Delhi 1999.

Farhadpour, Morad and Mehrgan, Omid 'The People Reloaded' in Nader Hahemi and Danny Postel (eds.) *The People Reloaded: The Green Movement and the Struggle for Iran's Future*, Brooklyn 2010, pp. 130–36.

Farhi, Farideh 'The Antimonies of Iran's War Generation' in Lawrence Potter and Gary Sick (eds.) *Iran, Iraq and the Legacies of War*, New York 2004, pp. 101–20.

Fenton, Tom 'The Day They Buried the Ayatollah' in *Iranian Studies*, vol. 41, no. 2, April 2008, pp. 241–6.

Firmin, Rusty and Pearson, Will *Go! Go! Go!: The Definitive Inside Story of the Iranian Embassy Siege*, London 2010.

Firoozi, Ferydoon 'Iranian Censuses 1956 and 1966: A Comparative Analysis' in *Middle East Journal*, vol. 24, no. 2, spring 1970, pp. 220–28.

Fisk, Robert *The Great War for Civilisation*, London 2006.

Floor, Willem 'The Revolutionary Character of the Iranian Ulama: Wishful Thinking or Reality?' in *International Journal of Middle East Studies*, vol. 12, no. 4, December 1980, pp. 501–24.

Floor, Willem *Sexual Relations in Iran*, Costa Mesa 2008.

Gasiorowski, Mark 'The Nuzhih Plot and Iranian Politics' in *International Journal of Middle East Studies*, vol. 34, no. 4, November 2002, pp. 645–66.

Gasiorowski, Mark and Byrne, Malcolm (eds.) *Mohammad Mosaddeq and the 1953 Coup in Iran*, Syracuse 2004.

Gheissari, Ali *Iranian Intellectuals in the 20th Century*, Austin 1998.

Graham, Robert *Iran: The Illusion of Power*, London 1978.

Halliday, Fred '"Orientalism" and Its Critics' in *The British Journal of Middle Eastern Studies*, vol. 20, no. 2, 1993, pp. 145–163.

Harney, Desmond *The Priest and King: An Eyewitness Account of the Iranian Revolution* London 1998.

Hashemi-Rafsanjani, Ali Akbar *Karnameh va Khaterat* [*Report and Memoir*]: 1360–1363 (1981–5) (4 vols.) and 1367 (1988/9), Tehran 1999–2011.

Hiltermann, Joost R. *A Poisonous Affair: America, Iraq and the Gassing of Halabja*, Cambridge 2007.

Hiro, Dilip *Iran Under the Ayatollahs*, London 1987.

Hiro, Dilip *The Longest War: The Iran–Iraq Military Conflict*, London 1990.

Hoffmann, Birgitt (ed. and trans.) *Persische Geschichte 1694–1835 erlebt, erinnert und erfunden – das Rustam at-Tawarikh in deutscher Bearbeitung*, Bamberg 1986.

Hooglund, Eric J. *Land and Revolution in Iran 1960–1980*, Austin 1982.

Huyser, Robert E. *Mission to Tehran*, London 1986.

Issawi, Charles *The Economic History of Iran, 1800–1914*, Chicago 1971.

Johnson, Rob *The Iran–Iraq War*, Basingstoke 2011.

Kamrava, Mehran *Iran's Intellectual Revolution*, Cambridge 2008.

Kapuscinski, Ryszard *Shah of Shahs*, London 2006.

Karsh, Efraim *The Iran–Iraq War 1980–1988*, Botley 2002.

Kasravi, Ahmad (trans. Evan Siegel) *History of the Iranian Constitutional Revolution*, Costa Mesa 2006.

Katouzian, Homa *Sadeq Hedayat: The Life and Legend of an Iranian Writer*, London 2002.

Kaussler, Bernd 'British-Iranian Relations, *The Satanic Verses* and the Fatwa: A Case of Two-level Game Diplomacy' in *The British Journal of Middle Eastern Studies*, vol. 38, no. 2, August 2011, pp. 203–25.

Keddie, Nikki 'The Iranian Power Structure and Social Change 1800–1969: An Overview' in *International Journal of Middle East Studies*, vol. 2, no. 1, January 1971, pp. 3–20.

Keddie, Nikki *Modern Iran: Roots and Results of Revolution*, Yale 2006.

Khajehpour, Bijan 'Iran's Economy: Twenty Years after the Islamic Revolution' in John L. Esposito and R. K. Ramazani (eds.), *Iran at the Crossroads*, New York 2001.

Kian-Thiébaut, Azadeh 'From Motherhood to Equal Rights Advocates: The Weakening of the Patriarchal Order' in *Iranian Studies*, vol. 38, no. 1, March 2005a, pp. 45–66.

Kian-Thiébaut, Azadeh 'Women's Movement in Post-Revolutionary Iran' in M. Hamid Ansari (ed.), *Iran Today: Twenty-five Years after the Islamic Revolution*, New Delhi 2005b, pp. 314–29.

Kurzman, Charles *The Unthinkable Revolution in Iran*, Harvard 2005.

Kurzman, Charles 'A Feminist Generation in Iran?' *Iranian Studies*, vol. 41, no. 3, June 2008, pp. 297–321.

Kuzichkin, Vladimir *Inside the KGB: My Life in Soviet Espionage*, New York 1990.

Ladjevardi, Habib (ed.) *Memoirs of Fatemeh Pakravan* (Iranian Oral History Series, no. VI), Harvard 1998.

Laing, Margaret *The Shah*, London 1977.

Lambton, Ann K. S. 'The Tribal Resurgence and the Decline of the Bureaucracy in the Eighteenth Century' in Thomas Naff and Roger Owen (eds.) *Studies in 18th Century Islamic History*, Carbondale and Edwardsville 1977, pp. 108–29.

Leslie, Ian *Born Liars: Why We Can't Live Without Deceit*, London 2011.

Louër, Laurence *Transnational Shi'a Politics: Religious and Political Networks in the Gulf*, London 2008.

McDowall, David *A Modern History of the Kurds* (revised edition), London 2010.

Majd, Hooman *The Ayatollah Begs to Differ: The Paradox of Modern Iran*, London 2009.

Majd, Hooman *The Ayatollahs' Democracy*, New York 2010.

Mallat, Chibli *The Renewal of Islamic Law: Muhammad Baqer as-Sadr, Najaf and the Shi'i International*, Cambridge 1993.

Matthee, Rudi 'Transforming Dangerous Nomads Into Useful Artisans, Technicians, Agriculturalists: Education in the Reza Shah Period' in S. Cronin (ed.), *The Making of Modern Iran*, London 2003, pp. 128–51.

Menashri, David *Post-Revolutionary Politics in Iran: Religion, Society and Power*, London 2001.

Michaelsen, Marcus *Election Fallout: Iran's Exiled Journalists and Their Struggle for Democratic Change*, Berlin 2011.

Milani, Abbas *The Persian Sphinx: Amir Abbas Hoveyda and the Riddle of the Iranian Revolution*, London 2009.

Milani, Abbas *The Shah*, New York 2011.

Milani, Mohsen *The Making of Iran's Islamic Revolution*, Boulder 1988.

Mir-Hosseini, Ziba 'Women, Marriage and the Law in Post-Revolutionary Iran' in Haleh Afshar (ed.) *Women in the Middle East: Perceptions, Realities and Struggles for Liberation*, Basingstoke 1993, pp. 59–84.

Mir-Hosseini, Ziba '"Multiplied, Not Humiliated": Broken Taboos in Post-Election Iran' in Nader Hahemi and Danny Postel (eds.), *The People Reloaded: The Green Movement and the Struggle for Iran's Future*, Brooklyn 2010a, pp. 140–47.

Mir-Hosseini, Ziba, 'Mut'a Marriage in Iran: Law and Social Practice' in *Informal Marriages Register Amsterdam*, Amsterdam 2010b, pp. 1–17.

Mir-Hosseini, Ziba and Tapper, Richard *Islam and Democracy in Iran: Eshkevari and the Quest for Reform*, London 2008.

Mohammad Reza Shah Pahlavi, *Mission for My Country*, London 1974 (first published 1961).

Moin, Baqer *Khomeini: Life of the Ayatollah*, London 1999.

Momen, Moojan *An Introduction to Shi'i Islam*, Yale 1985.

Montazeri, Hosein Ali *Khaterat-e Ayatollah Montazeri*, Sweden, France and Germany 2001.

Morrison, George (ed.) *History of Persian Literature from the Beginnings of the Islamic Period to the Present Day*, Leiden 1981.

Moslem, Mehdi *Factional Politics in Post-Khomeini Iran*, Syracuse 2002.

Mottahedeh, Roy *The Mantle of the Prophet*, Harmondsworth 1987.

Naficy, Hamid *A Social History of Iranian Cinema* (4 vols.), Durham (NC) 2011.

Nafisi, Azar *Reading Lolita in Tehran*, London 2008.

Nafisi, Azar *Things I've Been Silent About*, London 2009.

Naji, Kasra *Ahmadinejad: The Secret History of Iran's Radical Leader*, London 2008.

Najmabadi, Afsaneh *The Story of the Daughters of Quchan: Gender and National Memory in Iranian History*, Syracuse 1998.

Najmabadi, Afsaneh *Women with Mustaches and Men without Beards*, Berkeley 2005.

O'Ballance, Edgar *The Gulf War*, London 1988.

Owen, Lord David *In Sickness and in Power*, London 2009.

Pahlavi, Farah *An Enduring Love: My Life With the Shah – A Memoir*, New York 2004.

Parsa, Misagh *Social Origins of the Iranian Revolution*, New Brunswick and London 1989.

Parsi, Trita *Treacherous Alliance: The Secret Dealings of Israel, Iran and the US*, Yale 2007 (large print paperback edition).

Parsi, Trita *A Single Roll of the Dice: Obama's Diplomacy with Iran*, Yale 2012 (Kindle version).

Parsons, Anthony *The Pride and the Fall: Iran 1974–1979*, London 1984.

Pesaran, M. Hashem 'The Iranian Foreign Exchange Policy and the Black Market for Dollars' in *International Journal of Middle East Studies*, vol. 24, no. 1, February 1992, pp. 101–25.

Peterson, Scott *Let the Swords Encircle Me: Iran – a Journey Behind the Headlines*, New York 2010.

Pezeshkzad, Iraj *My Uncle Napoleon* (trans. Dick Davis), New York 2006.

Potter, Lawrence and Sick, Gary (eds.) *Iran, Iraq and the Legacies of War*, New York 2004.

Poudeh, Reza J. and Shirvani, M. Reza 'Issues and Paradoxes in the Development of Iranian National Cinema: An Overview' in *Iranian Studies*, vol. 41, no. 3, June 2008, pp. 323–41.

Rahnema, Ali *An Islamic Utopian: A Political Biography of Ali Shari'ati*, London 2000.

Rahnema, Ali (ed.) *Pioneers of Islamic Revival: Studies in Islamic Society*, London 2005.

Rahnema, Ali *Superstition as Ideology in Iranian Politics: From Majlesi to Ahmadinejad*, Cambridge 2011.

Ramazani, R. K., *Revolutionary Iran: Challenge and Response in the Middle East*, Baltimore 1988.

Ranjbar-Daemi, Siavush *The Presidential Institution in Post-Khomeini Iran* (provisional title), forthcoming.

Reyshahri, Mohammad *Khaterat-e Reyshahri (Reyshahri's Memoirs)*, Tehran 1369 (1990).

Robertson, Geoffrey *The Massacre of Political Prisoners in Iran, 1988: Report of an Inquiry Conducted by Geoffrey Robertson, QC*, Abdorrahman Boroumand Foundation, 2009 (available online at http://www.iranrights.org/english/attachments/doc_1115.pdf) (accessed 28 May 2011).

Rogers, W. C. and Rogers, S. *Storm Center: The USS Vincennes and Iran Air Flight 655*, Annapolis 1992.

Rundle, Christopher 'Iran: Continuity and Change Since the Revolution' in M. Jane Davis (ed.) *Politics and International Relations in the Middle East: Continuity and Change*, Aldershot 1995, pp. 105–11.

Rundle, Christopher *From Colwyn Bay to Kabul*, Stanhope 2004.

Rushdie, Salman *Joseph Anton: A Memoir*, London 2012.

Ryan, Paul B. *The Iranian Rescue Mission: Why It Failed*, Annapolis 1988.

Sanasarian, Eliz *Religious Minorities in Iran*, Cambridge 2002.

Satrapi, Marjane *Persepolis: The Story of a Childhood*, London 2003.

Schirazi, Asghar *The Constitution of Iran: Politics and the State in the Islamic Republic*, London 1997.

Schuster, Morgan *The Strangling of Persia*, London 1912.

Schwarzkopf, H. Norman *It Doesn't Take a Hero*, New York 1992.

Shah, Mohammad Reza Pahlavi *Mission For My Country*, London 1974.

Sick, Gary *All Fall Down: America's Fateful Encounter with Iran*, London 1985.

Sick, Gary 'Trial by Error: Reflections on the Iran–Iraq War' in *Middle East Journal*, vol. 43, no. 2, Spring 1989, pp. 230–45

Sick, Gary *October Surprise: America's Hostages in Iran and the Election of Ronald Reagan*, London 1991.

Simpson, John and Schubart, Tira *Lifting the Veil: Life in Revolutionary Iran*, London 1995.

Slavin, Barbara *Bitter Friends, Bosom Enemies: Iran, the US and the Twisted Path to Confrontation*, New York 2007.

Souresrafil, Behrouz *The Iran–Iraq War*, US and UK (no further details) 1989.

Sullivan, William H. *Mission to Iran*, New York 1981.

Talattof, kamran *The Politics of Writing in Iran*, Syracuse 2000.

Tapper, Richard (ed.) *The New Iranian Cinema: Politics, Representation and Identity*, London 2002.

Wehrey, Frederic, Green, Jerrold D., Nichiporuk, Brian, Nader, Alireza, Hansell, Lydia, Nafisi, Rasool and Bohandy, S. R. *The Rise of the Pasdaran: Assessing the Domestic Roles of Iran's Islamic Revolutionary Guards Corps*, Santa Monica 2009.

Wells, Tim *444 Days: The Hostages Remember*, San Diego 1985.

Wilson, Sir Arnold *SW Persia: Letters and Diary of a Young Political Officer 1907–1914*, London 1942.

Zaccara, Luciano 'The 2009 Iranian Presidential Elections in Comparative Perspective' in A. Ehteshami and R. Molavi, *Iran and the International System*, Abingdon 2012, pp. 192–206.

Zibakalam, Sadegh *Ma Chegoneh Ma Shodim*, Tehran 1999.

Zibakalam, Sadegh 'Islam, Religious Fundamentalism and Reform: A Look at the Islamic Revolution after a Quarter of a Century' in M. Hamid Ansari (ed.) *Iran Today: Twenty-five Years after the Islamic Revolution*, New Delhi 2005, pp. 182–94.

Notes

INTRODUCTION: THE HIDDEN CONTINENT OF IRAN

1. For a full, short history of Iran from the earliest times, see my earlier book, *Iran: Empire of the Mind* (Axworthy 2008a).
2. Ervand Abrahamian devoted a large part of his classic book *Khomeinism* (Abrahamian 1993) to a convincing demonstration of this point.
3. Laurence Louër's book *Transnational Shi'a Politics* develops this point (Louër 2008, p. 300).

PROLOGUE: 'TEN DAYS OF DAWN' (*DAHEH-YE FAJR*)

1. Simpson and Schubart 1995, pp. 30–31.
2. Arjomand 1988, pp. 121–2.
3. http://revver.com/video/509944 (accessed 27 August 2009).
4. Moin 1999, p. 201; http://www.youtube.com/watch?v=ojAe8IMny2U (accessed 1 September 2009).
5. Extract from the BBC Persian Service series *The Story of the Revolution*, transcribed and available online at http://www.bbc.co.uk/persian/revolution/khomeini.shtml#01 (accessed 21 January 2012).
6. Huyser 1986, pp. 270–71.
7. Mohsen Milani 1988, pp. 225–6.
8. Simpson and Schubart 1995, pp. 33–4.
9. Moin 1999, p. 204.
10. Abrahamian 1982, p. 436.
11. Arjomand 1988, pp. 124–5; see also Huyser 1986, pp. 7–8 for the Shah's fear of a military coup against him.
12. Arjomand 1988, p. 126.
13. General Huyser wrote in his book about this episode that there had been around 100 desertions a day before the Shah's departure (Huyser 1986, p. 105), and 100–200 per day thereafter (ibid., p. 160). But Brzezinski and Sick both hold that Huyser himself had reported at the time, while he was still in

Tehran, desertions at the level of 500–1,000 per day. General Qarabaghi, the army chief of staff, is the source for the 1,200 figure (Arjomand 1988, pp. 121 and 122).

14. Arjomand 1988, p. 122.

15. Arjomand 1988, pp. 197, 201–2 has persuasive analysis on lower-middle-class frustration with the Pahlavi regime and consequent involvement in the revolutionary movement; as in other radical movements in other times and places.

16. Fardust and Dareini 1999, p. 419. Fardust's memoirs were published under the aegis of the Islamic regime and read in large measure like regime propaganda, with broad denunciation of corruption, freemasonry and attachment to Israel under the Pahlavi monarchy. See also Arjomand 1988, p. 123, and below, chapter 7.

17. Simpson and Schubart 1995, p. 37.

18. The following extracts are taken from episode 4 of the BBC Persian Service series *The Story of the Revolution*, transcribed and available online at http://www.bbc.co.uk/persian/revolution/rev_04.shtml (accessed 23 January 2012); see also Fardust and Dareini 1999, pp. 420–21 – Fardust presents his role in the discussions as prominent. Qarabaghi's account is more authoritative, but Fardust may have played a part in wider activity toward the same ends in the days preceding, at least as much in as what happened on 11 February itself.

19. Parsa 1989, p. 245.

20. Sullivan 1981, p. 253; Huyser 1986, pp. 283–4.

21. From Amin Farzanefar, 'Days of Dawn', trans. Mark Rossman, www.qantara.de/webcom/show_article.php/_c–310/_nr–168/i.html (accessed 24 August 2009).

22. Simpson and Schubart 1995, p. 41.

23. *Ettela'at*, 15 February 1979; Moin 1999, p. 207; the others were Manuchehr Khosrodad, former air force commander, and General Naji, who had been responsible for enforcing martial law in Isfahan. See also Khalkhali's memoirs, quoted on the Omid website: http://www.iranrights.org/english/memorial-case-3306.php (accessed 14 September 2009). There has been some confusion about the date of this event, but the *Ettela'at* report is quite clear. There is some doubt also about Khalkhali's role in it, given that it seems Khomeini appointed him prosecutor somewhat later.

CHAPTER 1: THE BACKGROUND: *MA CHEGONEH MA SHODIM?* ('HOW DID WE BECOME WHAT WE ARE?')

1. The title of Sadegh Zibakalam's book of 1999, which made an impact in Iran for its iconoclastic message that the country's past traumas and present problems had at least as much to do with internal politics and the actions of Iranians as with interference by foreigners.

2. There have been many other political revolutions in world history (the Chinese revolution of 1911 is perhaps the next most important example) but it is still correct to say that the French and the Russian are the two most present in the minds of Europeans and North Americans when they consider what revolution means, and that is what I am considering here.

3. Some diehard Marxists do claim the revolution of 1979 as a bourgeois revolution, but this serves to show rather their Procrustean devotion to the defunct theory than anything else.

4. For the rest of this book, 'Shi'a' normally signifies twelver Shi'a, the sect to which the overwhelming majority of Shi'as today belong.

5. See Hoffmann 1986, vol. 1, pp. 220–23, and Lambton 1977.

6. Kamran Scot Aghaie's book *The Martyrs of Karbala* (Aghaie 2004) gives a vivid account of the processions and rituals.

7. 'Zur-Khaneh', *Encyclopedia Iranica* (Houchang Chehabi).

8. Keddie 1971, pp. 3–4.

9. Abrahamian 1982, p. 83.

10. For an exploration of British actions in Iran over this period in greater depth, see Axworthy 2008a, chapters 6 and 7.

11. Browne 1966, p. 133.

12. Abrahamian 1979, pp. 408–9.

13. Today around 90 per cent of Iranians are Shi'a, about 9 per cent Sunni and the remainder other minority religions – Armenian, other Christian, Jewish and Zoroastrian. There may have been some differences in the balance 100 years ago, but the essential picture would not have been much different.

14. *Cambridge History of Iran*, vol. 7, pp. 206–7; Arjomand 1988, p. 46.

15. Wilson 1942, p. 9; Wilson went on to serve as the head of the British administration in Iraq after the First World War, then ran the Middle East operations of the Anglo-Persian Oil Company, later became a Conservative MP and died in action in 1940, having volunteered for the RAF as a rear gunner in a Wellington bomber.

16. Schuster 1912, p. 219.

17. Kasravi/Siegel 2006, p. 297.

18. Abrahamian 1982, p. 111.

19. Though initially they still were not very good at it, and provincial governors continued to rely upon locally raised tribal troops.

20. Matthee 2003, p. 140 and passim.

21. For a short introduction (only!) to this subject, see Axworthy 2008a, pp. 88–121.

22. Mottahedeh 1987, pp. 98–105; Abrahamian 1982, pp. 125–6.

23. Katouzian 2002, p. 163.

24. 'Jamalzadeh, Mohammad-Ali', *Encyclopedia Iranica*.

25. Axworthy 2008a, pp. 1–2.

26. Abrahamian 1982, p. 164.

27. Schwarzkopf 1992, pp. 3, 30–45.
28. Abrahamian 1982, pp. 304–5.
29. Abrahamian 1982, p. 305.
30. Arjomand 1988, pp. 84–5.
31. Abrahamian 1982, p. 234.
32. http://www.youtube.com/watch?v=zVVYi9Y5u_k (accessed 15 April 2010).
33. Parsa 1989, p. 193; quoting Khomeini.
34. It seems that Tudeh members may have been involved in the assassination attempt, without the leadership having sanctioned it. See Behrooz 2000, pp. 4–5 and 186–7.
35. Esfahani and Pesaran 2009, p. 181.
36. Abrahamian 1982, pp. 275–6.
37. Gasiorowski and Byrne 2004, pp. 247–8.
38. Afkhami 2009, pp. 116–17; Laing 1977, pp. 98–9; Laing's weak prose style contrives to give the incident an unintended comic character.
39. Abbas Milani 2011, p. 135.
40. Esfandiary 1963, pp. 105–6.
41. Gasiorowski and Byrne 2004, p. 249.
42. Esfandiary 1963, pp. 94–5; Abbas Milani 2011, pp. 188–9.
43. Darioush Bayandor's carefully researched book *Iran and the CIA* (Bayandor 2010, which I was fortunate enough to see in manuscript, and mentioned in my earlier book *Iran: Empire of the Mind* (2008a), p. 308 n 24) makes the case for revising the standard view of the CIA-run coup against Mossadeq, as set out most notably by Mark Gasiorowski. Gasiorowski points up some weaknesses of Bayandor's argument in a (forthcoming) review in *Iranian Studies*, but in my view Bayandor's preference for arguments that stress the role of Iranian politics in Mossadeq's overthrow, rather than external interference, still carries some weight.
44. Afkhami 2009, p. 172.
45. Bayandor 2010, pp. 131–4.
46. Gasiorowski and Byrne 2004, p. 256.
47. Afkhami 2009, pp. 175–6.
48. Gasiorowski and Byrne 2004, p. 257.
49. Bayandor 2010, pp. 131–2.
50. Bayandor's book is important for redressing this imbalance.
51. Behrooz 2000, p. 10.
52. Behrooz 2000, pp. 161–2.
53. Abrahamian 1982, p. 382.
54. Behrooz 2000, pp. 15–16; Tudeh revived later, but never reached the level of power and influence it enjoyed in the 1940s and early 1950s.
55. Gasiorowski and Byrne 2004, p. 177.
56. Gasiorowski and Byrne 2004, p. 257.
57. Abrahamian 1982, p. 420.

58. At least – see Abrahamian 1982, p. 421.

59. Mottahedeh 1987, p. 299.

60. Mottahedeh 1987, pp. 287–323; Morrison 1981, pp. 201–2 (Kadkani); for Simin Daneshvar's revelations see Talattof 2000, p. 160.

61. Esfahani and Pesaran 2009, p. 186. It is important to note (not in connection with this excellent article, but generally) that statistics for the Iranian economy, both before and after the revolution of 1979, may always be rather unreliable.

62. Issawi 1971, pp. 381–2.

63. Esfahani and Pesaran 2009, p. 189.

64. Moin 1999, p. 75.

65. Montazeri 2001, pp. 103–4.

66. Abrahamian 1982, pp. 423–5; Moin 1999, p. 74 and passim; ibid., p. 80 for the Coalition of Islamic Societies.

67. Moin 1999, p. 96, quoting Ruhani, *Nehzat*.

68. Moin 1999, p. 104.

69. Alam 2008, pp. 279–80.

70. Moin 1999, p. 123.

71. His grandfather's family lived nearby at Mazinan; Rahnema 2005, p. 35.

72. Rahnema 2005, pp. 215–16.

73. Rahnema 2000, p. 275.

74. Rahnema 2000, p. 191.

75. Rahnema 2000, p. 234.

76. Rahnema 2005, p. 236.

77. Rahnema 2000, p. 368.

78. Rahnema 2005, p. 244.

79. Rahnema 2005, pp. 208–45; Abrahamian 1982, pp. 464–73.

80. Ebtekar 2000, p. 45.

81. http://www.spiegel.de/international/germany/0,1518,627342-4,00.html (accessed 20 June 2010).

82. This atmosphere is also apparent from the account of Asadollah Alam; see Alam 2008.

83. His youth, his bringing forward of a new generation of politicians as ministers and his assassination have led some to compare Mansur with J. F. Kennedy; but the Nafisi story puts him in a different light (as have, of course, revisionist accounts of Kennedy too).

84. Nafisi 2008, p. 132 and passim.

85. Abbas Milani 2009.

86. Abrahamian 1982, p. 427; Esfahani and Pesaran 2009, p. 200.

87. Abrahamian 1982, pp. 430–31.

88. Esfahani and Pesaran 2009, p. 179.

89. Esfahani and Pesaran 2009, p. 189.

90. Shah 1974, pp. 199–205.

91. Abrahamian 1982, p. 429.
92. Abrahamian 1982, p. 430.
93. Abrahamian 1982, p. 447; Amirsadeghi and Ferrier 1977, pp. 185–6.
94. Keddie 2006, p. 152; Graham 1978, p. 27.
95. Hooglund 1982, pp. 133–7.
96. Keddie 2006, pp. 152–3.
97. Kurzman 2005, p. 82.
98. Hooglund 1982, pp. 59 and 148–9; Amirsadeghi and Ferrier 1977, pp. 184–6.
99. Abrahamian 1982, pp. 535–6.

CHAPTER 2: THE 1970S AND THE SLIDE TO REVOLUTION

1. Richard Strauss used a translation of Wilde's play *Salome* as the basis for the libretto for his opera of the same title. The opera is punctuated by interruptions from John the Baptist, in a deep bass, condemning the excesses and immoralities of Herod, his wife and his court from the cistern to which he had been exiled.
2. Ansari 2003, p. 143, quoting FCO sources.
3. Cf Ansari 2006, p. 59.
4. Bill 1988, pp. 183–4; Afkhami 2009, p. 413.
5. Humorists found plenty to snigger about in the event's pomposity and grandiloquence: 'A joke of the period claimed that an Iranian office worker was so enraptured by reading these words of the Shah in his newspaper that he went home unexpectedly early to tell his wife; there he found his wife and his neighbour, Cyrus, asleep together in his bed. Overcome by the drama of the moment he raised his hand and said, "Sleep easily, Cyrus, for we are awake"' (Mottahedeh 1987, p. 327).
6. Afkhami 2009, p. 412.
7. Afkhami 2009, p. 413.
8. Mottahedeh 1987, p. 328.
9. Rahnema 2005, p. 237.
10. Alam 2008, p. 114; see also http://www.iranian.com/main/2010/jun/asadollah–alams–memoir (accessed 11 October 2010). Alam was an Anglophile (though not slavishly so) and came from an ancient family from Khorasan/Sistan that traced their ancestry back to the Taherids, and the Sassanids and Parthians beyond that. Parsons wrote in his book of Alam: 'In his slightly old-fashioned, feudal way, he had a feel for the people, which was conspicuously lacking throughout the rest of the Pahlavi establishment' (Parsons 1984, p. 27).
11. Bill 1988, pp. 379–82.
12. Mottahedeh 1987, p. 273.

13. Azari 1983 (pp. 130–32 and passim) and Mottahedeh echo each other on this point.

14. None of this is unusual in our new, globalized world, except perhaps in degree: someone has said that we are all (except Americans) citizens of two countries – our own, and the United States. But observers at the time (including myself, as a teenager) found the US influence in Iran particularly marked and intrusive.

15. Ebtekar 2000, p. 61.

16. Mottahedeh 1987, pp. 270–72.

17. Ardavan Davaran left Iran in 1980 and taught for many years in California as a professor of comparative literature before his death in January 2009.

18. Brookshaw and Rahimieh 2010, p. 3.

19. 'Farrokhzad, Forough-Zaman', *Encyclopedia Iranica* (online edition), 15 December 1999, available at www.iranica.com/articles/farrokzad–forug –zaman (Farzaneh Milani).

20. Translation by Farhang Jahanpour.

21. Amirsadeghi and Ferrier 1977, pp. 120–26.

22. For British anxiety over Blindfire, see FCO 8/3377 of 1979, fol. 8a.

23. Parsons later admitted in his book *The Pride and the Fall* (as he had in the papers he contributed to British government assessments after the fall of the Shah) that the Callaghan government's economically traumatized insistence on the need to secure lucrative contracts and export agreements with Iran was a direct cause of his own embassy's failure to anticipate the revolution of 1979.

24. http://www.youtube.com/watch?v=FidkfaAbwHk (accessed 31 August 2010).

25. Parsons 1984, pp. 21–3.

26. English translation *My Uncle Napoleon*, trans. Dick Davis, New York 2006 (originally published in Persian in Tehran in 1973).

27. Alam 2008, p. 122.

28. Parsons 1984, p. 146. Parsons was one of the most accomplished diplomats of his generation, and it is plain that, notwithstanding his awareness of the Shah's faults, he liked him personally and had much sympathy with his predicament in 1978/9. His statements immediately following the one quoted, to the effect that the advice he gave the Shah was his own and was not directed from London, are borne out by my researches in the recently released diplomatic archives for 1978 and 1979. For confirmation of the Shah's attitude from the US side, see Sick 1985, p. 33.

29. FCO 8/3377 of 1979; Sir Anthony Parsons' valedictory despatch, dated 18 January 1979, para 12.

30. See Huyser 1986, p. 27.

31. Alam 2008, pp. 309, 522, 539; also, pp. 317, 415 for cliques and rivalry; Abbas Milani 2009, pp. 202–3.

32. Alam 2008, pp. 104, 429. Alam's adventures were curtailed by illness in the latter part of 1976, when among other unpleasant symptoms he confided in his diary that his genitals had swollen to several times their normal size (the Shah had his own health worries by this time, and they compared notes). Medical treatment in France gave Alam some relief, but he sadly recorded that things had not returned to normal: 'Invited an attractive young German girl to stay. We've known each other some time, and if nothing else I can still play backgammon with her' (p. 519). He died of leukaemia in April 1978.

33. Alam 2008, pp. 217, 267–8 and 299.

34. Alam 2008, pp. 207, 214.

35. Abbas Milani 2009, p. 105.

36. Alam 2008, pp. 137, 191, 217, 286.

37. Alam 2008, pp. 150, 548.

38. Laing 1977, pp. 231, quoted in Abrahamian 1982, p. 419; Alam mentioned Laing's difficult questioning in his memoirs, but recorded that he answered that the Shah's only real error was 'to assume that those around him are just as honest and well-intentioned towards Iran as he is himself' (Alam 2008, p. 448).

39. Alam 2008, pp. 152–3, 159.

40. Alam 2008, pp. 286–7; see also Kurzman 2005, pp. 88–90.

41. Cf. Parsons 1984, pp. 28–9. In the light of what the British official documents newly released say about the Shah's involvement, this section of Parsons' book dealing with corruption appears to have been a masterpiece of careful drafting.

42. Sir Shapur Reporter came from an Indian Parsee family. He had been active with the Rashidian brothers, Asadollah Alam and SIS/MI6 in 1953, and later was busy with a variety of commercial deals with Iran. See Alam 2008, pp. 55–6 and 356.

43. FCO 8/3377 of 1979, fol 26.

44. Alam 2008, pp. 109–10, 112, 210–11.

45. Shah 1974, pp. 172–4.

46. Quoted in Ansari 2003, pp. 178–9.

47. Abrahamian 1982, p. 439.

48. To all but diehard devotees of either ideology, the political methods of Bolshevism and Nazism had of course much more in common than they had to distinguish them one from the other.

49. Ansari 2003, p. 186.

50. Abrahamian 1982, p. 441; for the removal of the Shah's book, see Abrahamian 2009, p. 150.

51. Abrahamian 1982, pp. 498–9.

52. Alam 2008, p. 549.

53. Abrahamian 1982, pp. 443–4.

54. Momen 1985, pp. 256–7.

55. Abrahamian 1982, pp. 444–5; Ansari 2003, p. 189.

56. See the State Department report at http://www.iran–interlink.org/files/child%20 pages/USstatedept.htm (accessed 2 February 2011).

57. Abrahamian 1982, pp. 480–95.

58. Esfahani and Pesaran 2009, p. 190.

59. Esfahani and Pesaran 2009, pp. 189–90.

60. Kurzman 2005, pp. 87–8 illustrates these points particularly well.

61. These being the census years – see Firoozi 1970, p. 220.

62. Abrahamian 1982, pp. 446–7.

63. Esfahani and Pesaran 2009, pp. 202–3.

64. McDowall 2010, pp. 335–40.

65. Khomeini's innovative theory of *velayat-e faqih* is explained in greater detail in the following chapter.

66. Esfahani and Pesaran 2009, pp. 186 (figure 5) and 191.

67. Abrahamian 1982, pp. 497–8.

68. Alam 2008, pp. 535–7.

69. Mohsen Milani 1988, pp. 181–3 – but Cyrus Vance for example has denied that any direct pressure was applied by the US administration on human rights matters.

70. Abrahamian 1982, pp. 500–504.

71. Momen 1985, pp. 259–60; Abrahamian 1982, pp. 458–64.

72. Behrangi was an Azeri, a collector of folklore, author of short stories and especially stories for children. He drowned in 1967, and it was widely believed that SAVAK were implicated in his death.

73. Rahnema 2005, pp. 244–5.

74. Parsa 1989, pp. 177–80; Rahnema 2005, pp. 244–5; Moin 1999, pp. 183–4; Abrahamian 1982, p. 505. There is some confusion about these evenings: most sources suggest there were ten, but Parsa says sixteen and suggests (like Abrahamian) that the later ones took place at Aryamehr University. Esmail Khoie, who was a member of the executive committee of the Writers' Association at the time, was clear in a telephone interview with me (on 9 August 2011) that there were only ten evenings, that they were held at the Goethe Institut and that there was no violence or any deaths. I am grateful to him for the other details of the circumstances that he gave me. The role of the poetry evenings competes with the demonstrations around the death of Mostafa Khomeini for prominence in the early history of the revolutionary movement; a secular, leftist root to balance the Islamic, Khomeinist one.

75. Moin 1999, p. 185.

76. Moin 1999, p. 184.

77. Kurzman 2005, pp. 28–9.

78. Sick 1985, p. 28; Afkhami 2009, pp. 448–51.

79. Afkhami 2009, p. 449, quoting an interview with Queen Farah; Sullivan 1981, pp. 126–7.

80. Sick 1985, pp. 28–9.
81. Afkhami 2009, p. 452.
82. FCO8/3191 of 1978; letter dated 24 February 1978. The reply was signed off by M. S. Weir, but it appears that a more junior official left his more moderate original draft on file, to dissociate himself from Weir's comments. Parsons's own book, and the internal Foreign Office post mortem, have emphasized his failure to anticipate the Shah's fall. It seems that, as 1978 wore on, Parsons was more optimistic about the Shah's chances than some of his colleagues in London (notably Ivor Lucas, who was head of Middle East Department at the time, with whom I have discussed these matters). But the despatch to which Weir was replying demonstrates that Parsons was aware, earlier than many, and despite the scepticism of others, of the Shah's vulnerabilities.
83. Afkhami 2009, p. 453; Moin 1999, p. 186; Homayun apparently said later that the author was Ali Shabani – http://www.youtube.com/watch?v= PfBeHNeqfJ8 (accessed 23 February 2012).
84. Kurzman 2005, pp. 36–7.
85. Kurzman 2005, p. 46.
86. Kurzman 2005, pp. 47–9.
87. Kurzman 2005, p. 47.
88. Abrahamian 1982, p. 508; Kurzman 2005, p. 51.
89. Some have interpreted the pause as a mistake by Khomeini's followers, following which they had to crank up the pace of the demonstrations again – see Kurzman 2005, pp. 52–3 – but this may be incorrect.
90. Parsa 1989, p. 206.
91. Abrahamian 1982, p. 508.
92. Afkhami 2009, p. 457.
93. Abrahamian 1982, p. 509; Kurzman 2005, p. 62.
94. Afkhami 2009, p. 457.
95. See Satrapi 2003, pp. 14–15 for the view of Iranians at the time on the Rex Cinema fire.
96. Kurzman 2005, pp. 61–2.
97. Kurzman 2005, pp. 62–3; Parsa 1989, pp. 211–2; Abrahamian 1982, p. 514. I heard the demonstrations of 4 September from my parents' rented house on the Elahieh ridge. The stamp in my passport shows that I flew back to England from Tehran the following day (for the beginning of the school autumn term). I did not return to Iran until 1999, to find the house demolished and the pool filled with its rubble.
98. Afkhami 2009, p. 462.
99. Kapuscinski 2006, p. 117.
100. See, for example, Owen 2009, pp. 191–219, though, to be fair, his argument is more that, if Western governments (the US and UK in particular) had known the Shah was ill, they would have persuaded him to step down earlier,

in favour of his son. But there is good reason to think the Shah would have suspected the motives of those governments, and would have wanted to secure the succession to his son under his own hand. A greater role for the US and UK in events at that time would only have stoked support for Khomeini.

101. Pahlavi 2004, pp. 241–8, 252–8, 263–8, 294–5 (including the transcripts of the letters from Georges Flandrin, the main doctor).

102. Kurzman 2005, pp. 64–5.

103. Kurzman 2005, pp. 73–5; Abrahamian 1982, pp. 515–16; Harney 1998, pp. 17–19; the estimate for the number of dead on 8 September has been revised downwards since the revolution to about eighty. At the time the official figure was 87 dead and 205 wounded, which, though disbelieved then, was probably not far wrong.

104. Kurzman 2005, p. 125 and passim.

105. Sick 1985, p. 53.

106. Kurzman 2005, pp. 77–8; Abrahamian 1982, p. 517; Keddie 2006, p. 233; Parsa 1989, pp. 307–8.

107. Parsa 1989, p. 5; Kurzman 2005, pp. 100–101; Harney 1998, p. 121.

108. Arjomand 1988, pp. 200–202; Parsa 1989, pp. 304–9 and passim.

109. There were reports and some verified incidents of intimidation by opposition supporters in this period too, notably intimidation of strikebreakers; but relatively few, given the size and disparate nature of the movement – see Kurzman 2005, pp. 152–4.

110. Parsa 1989, pp. 115–16 and 226–33.

111. Kurzman 2005, p. 105; Parsa 1989, p. 230; Abrahamian 1982, p. 518.

112. Coulson 2008, p. 30. The third secretary who spoke to the demonstrators was David Reddaway, who twenty-four years later (in 2002) was rejected by the Iranian authorities as ambassador to Tehran and was refused a visa. The hardline newspaper *Jomhuri-ye Eslami* alleged incorrectly at the time that he was a Jew and a member of MI6. See also Harney 1998, p. 59.

113. Kurzman 2005, pp. 106–7.

114. Abrahamian 1982, p. 519.

115. Kurzman 2005, p. 108.

116. Owen 2009, p. 207.

117. Sick 1985, pp. 114–17.

118. Email correspondence with Lord Owen – to stand steadfast for the Shah was perceived to be important not least as a demonstration of support for the *Saudi* monarchy. The following statement is based on conversations with Ivor Lucas, who was head of Middle East Department in the Foreign and Commonwealth Office at the time.

119. FCO 8/3190 of 1978, fol. 563; see also Parsons 1984, p. 122.

120. FCO telno 72 of 9 January (1979) to Tehran, fol. 47 in FCO 8/3351 of 1979.

121. Kurzman 2005, pp. 112–13; Abrahamian 1982, pp. 521 and 523.

122. Abrahamian 1982, p. 520. Sanjabi's commitment to Khomeini was improvised on the spot – he did not have prior approval from his National Front colleagues, and the decision caused some of them (notably Shapur Bakhtiar) to distance themselves from him

123. Parsa 1989, pp. 230–35.

124. Abrahamian 1982, p. 522.

125. Abrahamian 1982, pp. 521–2; Kurzman 2005, pp. 117–24.

126. See also Parsons 1984, pp. 110–12.

127. Harney 1998, p. 115.

128. Abrahamian 1982, p. 522; Parsons 1984, p. 112.

129. Kurzman 2005, p. 123.

130. Interview with journalist from Tehran, October 2011.

131. Interview with former student from Tehran, October 2011.

132. Abrahamian 1982, p. 524; Parsons 1984, pp. 113–19 – Sadighi's efforts broke down because other National Front politicians would not support him.

133. Harney 1998, pp. 120–21, 126, 127; Parsa 1989, p. 235.

134. Abrahamian 1982, p. 525; Parsons 1984, pp. 121–3; Mohsen Milani 1988, pp. 225–6.

135. Huyser 1986, pp. 23–5, 244, 288, 297 and passim.

136. Parsa 1989, pp. 238–40.

137. Interview with teacher from Tehran, October 2011.

138. Parsons 1984, p. 126; in his telegram to London no. 85 of 9 January, Parsons commented on this same meeting that the Shah had 'obviously relinquished all power' (FCO 8/3351 of 1979).

139. Afkhami 2009, pp. 526–8.

140. These recollections came from a boy soldier captured in the war with Iraq (Brown 1990, p. 23).

141. FCO 8/3351 of 1979, fol. 58 (Tehran telno 142 of 16 January). I have corrected two minor spelling errors in the text that were no doubt made in the general excitement of the moment.

142. Parsa 1989, p. 238.

143. FCO 8/3351 of 1979 (Tehran telno 136 of 15 January; and telno 96 of 10 January).

144. Parsons 1984, p. 125.

145. Interview with journalist from Tehran, October 2011.

146. Parsons 1984, p. 127.

147. Abrahamian 1982, p. 528; Harney 1998, p. 169.

148. Huyser 1986, pp. 238 and 243.

149. Ali Ansari quotes Goethe to this effect (Ansari 2003, p. 192).

150. Parsa 1989, pp. 17–19.

151. Kurzman 2005, p. 166 – 'recognizing and reconstructing the lived experience of the moment' – Kurzman calls this anti-explanation, but it could be called an historical explanation.

152. Gholam Reza Afkhami's book of 1985, *The Iranian Revolution: Thanatos on a National Scale*, attributed the revolution to a national death wish.

153. As we have seen, the leadership position of the clergy was also helped by the swing towards them of many intellectuals in the 1960s and 70s, and, as Tudeh and other leftist groups largely collapsed, their greater ability to resist SAVAK repression and intimidation.

154. For discussion of these matters, see in particular Zibakalam 2005, Parsa 1989, pp. 1–30 and 219–315, and Kurzman 2005, pp. 163–72 and 184–5. Kurzman gives evidence for the judgement that, whereas the educated middle class were more motivated by the desire for liberal democracy, lower social classes were more motivated by what he calls Islamic themes.

CHAPTER 3: LIKE THE PERSON HE OUGHT TO BE: ISLAMIC REPUBLIC, 1979–80

1. The Shah believed Khomeini to be a British agent at least partly because the BBC Persian service reported the speeches Khomeini made while he was in exile. At the same time, Khomeini was listening to BBC reports on what was happening inside Iran (Moin 1999, p. 192).

2. Moin 1999, p. 2. Another version of the family's origins suggests that Khomeini's ancestors lived in Kashmir – see Abrahamian 1993, p. 5.

3. Moin 1999, pp. 1–8.

4. Mottahedeh 1987, pp. 228–9.

5. Mottahedeh's *Mantle of the Prophet* gives the best description in English of the traditional training undergone by the clergy.

6. Moin 1999, p. 43.

7. Mottahedeh 1987, p. 183.

8. Moin 1999, pp. 42–4.

9. Moin 1999, p. 64; Abrahamian 1993, p. 9.

10. Keddie 2006, p. 147.

11. Khomeini, *Hokumat-e Eslami*, trans. Hamid Algar, available at http://www.al-islam.org/islamicgovernment/ (accessed 13 February 2011) (the online text has no page numbers).

12. Cole 2002, p. 59.

13. Khomeini, *Hokumat-e Eslami*, Introduction.

14. It is worth noting at this point that Khomeini was writing several years ahead of Edward Said's *Orientalism*, published in 1978.

15. Abrahamian 1993 suggests that Khomeini was distantly related by family to Nuri, on his mother's side (p. 5).

16. Khomeini, *Hokumat-e Eslami*, section 3: 'The Form of Islamic Government'.
17. Moin 1999, p. 193.
18. Moin 1999, pp. 190–91.
19. http://www.youtube.com/watch?v=ZPpB–r5mMCI (accessed 13 August 2010).
20. Moin 1999, p. 51.
21. Moin 1999, p. 50.
22. Moin 1999, p. 47. My account here (profiting from conversations with Baqer Moin as well as from his book) is of necessity an over-simplification of a highly complex range of mystical ideas that draw upon Plato and neo-Platonism and the writings of Sohravardi as well as Ibn Arabi and Molla Sadra. See also my earlier book *Iran: Empire of the Mind* (2008a), pp. 109–10 and 265–6.
23. Khomeini, *Shahr-e Do'a al-Sahar*; quoted in Moin 1999, p. 48; see also ibid., p. 44.
24. Moin 1999, p. 49.
25. Khomeini never said openly that he had completed Molla Sadra's fourth journey – but it would have been impolitic vis-à-vis the rest of the *ulema*, and a departure for mystical tradition, as well as immodest, for him to have done so – Moin 1999, p. 51.
26. Moin 1999, p. 51.
27. As described in the Prologue.
28. Bakhash 1986, p. 68.
29. Bakhash 1986, pp. 67–8; Mohsen Milani 1988, pp. 241–3.
30. FBIS, 13 February 1979, 'Khomeini Addresses Nation'.
31. Interview with Bani-Sadr, 14 February 2011; http://www.euronews.net/2011/02/14/iran-s-ex-president-banisadr-talks-to-euronews/ (accessed 16 February 2011).
32. See Prologue, p. 3.
33. Bakhash 1986, p. 64; Mohsen Milani 1988, pp. 243–4.
34. FBIS, 14 February 1979, 'Tehran Cites Reports on US Embassy "Surrender"'; FBIS, 14 February 1979, 'AFP Reports Ambassador Sullivan Released'.
35. Bakhash 1986, p. 57.
36. In English, the term used to denote this body is usually Revolutionary Guards (or IRGC), but sometimes *Pasdaran* (Guards) is used instead. In this book I have chosen to use the word *Sepah* (Corps), which is the word Iranians mostly use.
37. Bakhash 1986, p. 63; Mohsen Milani 1988, pp. 244 and 257–8.
38. Moin 1999, p. 207.
39. Bakhash 1986, pp. 59–63; Mohsen Milani 1988, pp. 256–7.
40. Mohsen Milani 1988, p. 257.
41. Abbas Milani 2009, p. 324.
42. Abbas Milani 2009, pp. 304–5; Ladjevardi 1998, pp. 128–9.
43. Ladjevardi 1998, pp. 130–31.

44. Ladjevardi 1998, pp. 39–41; Pakravan's widow claimed that he had passed word to Ayatollah Shariatmadari, who had found a way to have Khomeini made an ayatollah, and that had saved him, because the Shah could not execute an ayatollah. There are other versions of the same story, but it seems that Khomeini was recognized as a *marja* at an earlier stage, in 1961, soon after Borujerdi's death.
45. See Halliday 1993, pp. 157–8; and Abrahamian 1999, p. 144.
46. See Najmabadi 1998 and 2005, passim.
47. For a more extended exploration of the history of the status of women in Iran, see Axworthy 2008a, especially pp. 193–4; also Chehabi 2003, pp. 203–4.
48. Alavi 2005, p. 168.
49. Interview with Shirin Ebadi, 10 January 2012.
50. This anger is reflected in Azari 1983, an important, thought-provoking and sometimes provocative collection of essays, for the most part published under pseudonyms.
51. Important explorations of this subject that take this view include Mir-Hosseini 1993 (p. 59 and passim) and Kian-Thiébaut 2005b (p. 315 and passim).
52. Bakhash 1986, p. 73; Mohsen Milani 1988, p. 261.
53. Parsa 1989, pp. 258–60.
54. Parsa 1989, pp. 261–2; Hiro 1987, pp. 112–13.
55. Mohsen Milani 1988, p. 267.
56. Explored among others by Sartre in *Les Mains sales* and Arthur Koestler in *Darkness at Noon*.
57. Moin 1999, p. 214.
58. Moin 1999, p. 216.
59. Moin 1999, p. 216.
60. Bakhash 1986, p. 74.
61. Bakhash 1986, p. 75; Mohsen Milani 1988, p. 262.
62. Bakhash 1986, p. 75; Moin 1999, p. 217.
63. Parsa 1989, p. 257.
64. Chris Rundle was there – email correspondence; see also his book (Rundle 2004), p. 109.
65. Bakhash 1986, pp. 88–9; Mohsen Milani 1988, p. 263; Parsa 1989, p. 285.
66. Interview with journalist, Tehran, October 2011.
67. Translated by Farhang Jahanpour. Shamlu's work was banned. He died in 2000, and thousands joined his funeral procession.
68. Bakhash 1986, pp. 81–3.
69. Mallat 1993, pp. 69–78 and passim.
70. Algar 1980, p. 29.
71. Algar 1980, pp. 22 and 31.
72. The word *islam* means literally 'submission'.
73. Bakhash 1986, p. 86.

74. Bakhash 1986, p. 87.

75. *Ettela'at*, 28 Shahrivar 1358 (19 September 1979) – see Bakhash 1986, pp. 85 and 268n.

76. Bakhash 1986, p. 85.

77. Mohsen Milani 1988, p. 268; Bakhash 1986, p. 86; Sick 1985, p. 203.

78. Parsa 1989, pp. 254 and 294.

79. Parsa 1989, p. 286.

80. Hiro 1987, p. 139 (taken from an interview with Shariatmadari in Qom on 12 December).

81. Wells 1985, p. 24.

82. Ebtekar 2000, p. 76.

83. Ebtekar 2000, pp. 47–55; Sick 1985, p. 204.

84. Ebtekar 2000, p. 67.

85. Bowden 2006, pp. 93–4.

86. FCO 8/3378 of 1979; full report on the intrusion at fol. 75a.

87. Moin 1999, pp. 226–7; Ansari 2003, p. 227. Moin believes (and Ansari agrees) that Khomeini took advantage of a more or less spontaneous action by the students; Sick suggests (1985, pp. 204–5) that the action was coordinated from Khomeini's inner circle, but that Khomeini himself stayed aloof from open involvement in case something went wrong. Kuzichkin suggests that the hostage-takers were not really students and that the Soviet embassy had evidence that their action was planned at the highest level (Kuzichkin 1990, p. 293).

88. FBIS, 5 November 1979, 'Khomeyni on Occupation'.

89. Mohsen Milani 1988, pp. 276–7; Moin 1999, p. 222. Bazargan once famously described his office as 'like a knife without a blade'.

90. Mohsen Milani 1988, p. 279.

91. Bakhash 1986, pp. 89–90; Moin 1999, pp. 230–32; Mohsen Milani 1988, pp. 279–80. For the date of the election (5 Bahman 1358), see http://web .archive.org/web/20040626100548/www.irisn.com/amar/amar_entekhabat .htm (accessed 22 March 2011).

92. Hostage Cort Barnes, quoted in Wells 1985.

93. Bowden 2006, p. 301.

94. Bowden 2006, pp. 22–7, 281–5 and 543–7.

95. Ebtekar 2000, p. 164.

96. Moin 1999, pp. 232–3; Bakhash 1986, pp. 90–91; Mohsen Milani 1988, pp. 280–81.

97. Bakhash 1986, pp. 94–5.

98. Bakhash 1986, pp. 100–101; Moin 1999, p. 234.

99. Sick 1985, pp. 273–4.

100. Bakhash 1986, p. 114.

101. Ryan 1988, p. 73.

102. Bowden 2006, pp. 459–64.

103. Bakhash 1986, p. 118.
104. Carter 2010, pp. 529–30.
105. Sick 1985, pp. 284–93.
106. The Holloway report in 1980 examined the conduct of the hostage rescue mission and made recommendations for future special forces operations. But it considered the question of damaging rivalry between the services only somewhat obliquely, as part of 'command and control issues': http://www .gwu.edu/~nsarchiv/NSAEBB/NSAEBB63/doc8.pdf (accessed 4 April 2011). See also Ryan 1988, pp. 72–6.
107. Sick 1985, p. 107.
108. Parsa 1989, pp. 265–7; Bakhash 1986, p. 110.
109. Parsa 1989, pp. 255–8; Bakhash 1986, p. 105.
110. http://www.angelfire.com/rnb/bashiri/Poets/Eagle.html (accessed 12 August 2011).
111. Bakhash 1986, pp. 107–9; Moin 1999, pp. 234–5.
112. Bakhash 1986, pp. 101–3; Moin 1999, p. 234.
113. Bakhash 1986, pp. 110–12.
114. Gasiorowski 2002.
115. http://www.youtube.com/watch?v=AM–x8nsSWTw (accessed 25 September 2011).
116. Gasiorowski 2002, p. 657 (and email correspondence with Mark Gasiorowski). This aspect of the events around the coup is nonetheless intriguing – the Sepah intervention had the air of something hurried and ad hoc, indicating that time *was* tight. For Israeli attitudes to Iran and Iraq at this time, see chapter 5 below, and Parsi 2007.
117. Gasiorowski 2002, p. 657; Cooper and Bishop 2000, p. 49; Bakhash 1986, pp. 118–19.

CHAPTER 4: JANG-E TAHMILI: *THE IMPOSED WAR*, 1980–88

1. See chapter 2.
2. See, for example, Hiro 1990, pp. xxii and 7–8.
3. For the Shatt al-Arab dispute, the Shah's dealings with the Iraqi Kurds and the Algiers Accords, see chapter 3; see also Alvandi 2012.
4. See chapter 3.
5. Souresrafil 1989 makes the same point.
6. For an extreme example, see Karsh 2002, pp. 12–14.
7. Ramazani 1988, p. 74.
8. Bakhash 2004, p. 25.
9. FBIS, 18 April 1980; Hiro 1990, p. 35.
10. Chubin and Tripp 1988, p. 29.

11. Cooper and Bishop 2004, pp. 22–3.

12. Eleven months before US Navy Tomcats destroyed Libyan aircraft in the Gulf of Sidra.

13. See, for example, http://www.youtube.com/watch?v=l_3jLuWo3Lo&NR=1 (accessed 5 May 2011).

14. Cooper and Bishop 2004, pp. 6–19.

15. This was done, as explained in Cooper and Bishop 2004, pp. 11–12; but the effect was minimal; one of the interviewees quoted commented that the capability of the AWG–9 radar supplied to Iran for jumping frequencies to avoid jamming was 'barely one hundredth of a second slower' than those used in US Navy F-14s.

16. Even before the revolution, there was doubt about whether the Iranians would be able to operate the F-14. It was a highly complex aircraft to maintain – requiring eighteen to twenty highly trained technicians, where the F-4 Phantom needed seven or eight (Cooper and Bishop 2004, p. 70). A US Senate report noted in 1976: 'Iran has purchased large quantities of some of the most sophisticated equipment in the US inventory including the F-14 Tomcat fighter ... The F-14 system is so complicated that the United States Navy is having major difficulty keeping it operational ... Most informed observers feel that Iran will not be able to absorb and operate within the next five to ten years a large proportion of the sophisticated military systems purchased from the US' (Ansari 2006, pp. 65–6).

17. See Bergquist 2002 (first published 1988). Bergquist's book shows an awareness of some of the Western military analysts' shortcomings, but seems to have a blind spot for some others. I am grateful to former US intelligence analyst Wayne White for his comments on the judgements made here.

18. Cooper and Bishop 2004, pp. 22–3. One of the oldest lessons of war is that theory is usually an early casualty.

19. Hiro 1990, pp. 39–40; O'Ballance 1988, pp. 30–37; the air strikes, *pace* Hiro, did not happen over the night of 21/2 September, but in the early afternoon of 22 September. The Iraqi aircraft took off from noon onwards (Cooper and Bishop 2000, pp. 72–5).

20. Chubin and Tripp 1988, p. 34.

21. Hiro 1990, p. 47; O'Ballance 1988, p. 20; Karsh 2002, pp. 18–19.

22. Hiro 1990, pp. 40–43; O'Ballance 1988, pp. 32–5; Bani-Sadr mentions the shortage of suitable tank transporters – Bani-Sadr 1991, p. 101.

23. Moin 1999, p. 236; Bani-Sadr 1991, p. 74.

24. Wells 1985, pp. 385–9.

25. Wayne White, by email. Bergquist's book agrees the Iraqi attacks were 'a total failure' (2002, p. 58), but some of his other judgements seem questionable.

26. Cooper and Bishop 2000, p. 80.

27. Hiro 1990, p. 41; Chubin and Tripp 1988, p. 55; Cooper and Bishop 2000, pp. 81 and 83. O'Ballance 1988 suggests that the aircraft were moved earlier, on the 21st (p. 42); some of the aircraft may have been moved then, but it is plain that the 200 or more engaged in the Iraqi strikes of 22 September, at least, could not have been.
28. Cooper and Bishop 2000, pp. 83–4.
29. For the Phoenix kills, see Cooper and Bishop 2004, p. 85; for the analysts' scepticism, O'Ballance 1988, p. 44. O'Ballance suggests that the Phoenix missiles should have been used against ground targets: the AIM-54 Phoenix was a dedicated air-to-air missile. The Iranian F-4s had and used plenty of Maverick air-to-ground missiles, which were the appropriate weapon for ground attack, along with laser-guided bombs. Whatever their nationality, it is sensible to treat the claims of pilots for air victories (kills) with some scepticism; it is a historical fact that they have always tended to exaggeration (for good reason – there is much scope for confusion in the hurly-burly of air combat). But the claims of Iranian pilots should not be treated with added scepticism (or discounted entirely as 'unconfirmed') just because they are Iranian.
30. O'Ballance 1988, p. 44.
31. Interview with former gendarmerie lieutenant, August 2011.
32. BBC/SWB, 6 November 1980 (ME/6568/A/9) – quoted in Chubin and Tripp 1988, p. 55.
33. Chubin and Tripp 1988, p. 54.
34. Hiro 1990, p. 45.
35. Brown 1990, p. 27.
36. Firmin and Pearson 2010, pp. 135–219.
37. Bani-Sadr 1991, p. 87.
38. Bani-Sadr 1991, p. 88.
39. Hiro 1990, pp. 42–5; O'Ballance 1988, p. 38. The figures for casualties come from O'Ballance – Hiro says the Iraqis lost 1,500 dead and 4,000 wounded.
40. Cooper and Bishop 2004, pp. 27–34.
41. Hiro 1990, p. 44.
42. Hiro 1990, p. 45; O'Ballance 1988, pp. 41–2.
43. Interview with former gendarmerie lieutenant, August 2011.
44. Bakhash 1986, p. 129; Hiro 1990, p. 45.
45. Hiro 1987, p. 173.
46. Former hostage Bill Belk, quoted in Wells 1985, p. 402.
47. Sick 1991, pp. 197–205.
48. Ansari 2006, p. 108; Sick 1991 passim.
49. Bakhash 1986, pp. 149–50; Carter 2010, pp. 464–7; Sick 1985, pp. 308–12.
50. Quoted in Bakhash 1986, p. 150.
51. Wells 1985, p. 447.

52. Sick 1985, p. 337.

53. Bakhash 1986, pp. 150–51.

54. Bakhash 1986, p. 151; Bani-Sadr 1991, pp. 138–9; Hiro 1987, pp. 175–6.

55. Bakhash 1986, pp. 154–5.

56. Bishop and Cooper 2003, p. 51; Cooper and Bishop 2000, pp. 118–20; earlier accounts like Hiro 1990 suggest as many as forty-six aircraft were destroyed (p. 50).

57. Cooper and Bishop 2000, pp. 91–2, 124–6; Parsi 2007, p. 191.

58. Parsi 2007, pp. 185–93; Cooper and Bishop 2004, pp. 37 and 68. See also below for Israeli involvement in the Iran-Contra affair.

59. I have been unable to trace an authoritative source for the hospital story, but my second book, *Empire of the Mind* (2008a), dealt with the history of Iran's Jews at some length (e.g., pp. 190–91, 202–3 208, 212–13, 233, 283–5). See also Parsi 2007, p. 15.

60. Sanasarian 2002, p. 116; thanks also to Dominic Brookshaw.

61. Parsi 2007, pp. 183–4.

62. Part of one of the documents, reassembled after a US official had put it through a shredder, is reproduced in Bani-Sadr 1991, pp. 171–2.

63. Bakhash 1986, pp. 155–6; Hiro 1987, pp. 179–80.

64. Baktiari 1996, p. 76.

65. Bakhash 1986, pp. 157–62; Moin 1999, pp. 239–40; Hiro 1987, pp. 181–2.

66. Bani-Sadr 1991, pp. 57–8.

67. Parsa 1989, pp. 294–5.

68. Abrahamian 1989, p. 247.

69. Bakhash 1986, p. 219; Hiro 1987, pp. 189–92 and 198. Bani-Sadr 1991 claimed that Rajavi later did accept responsibility for the 28 June bombing (p. 167). Sometimes it is suggested that Khamenei was wounded by the bomb that killed Beheshti, but that appears not to be the case.

70. Hiro 1987, pp. 193–4.

71. Hiro 1987, p. 197.

72. Moin 1999, p. 246; Hiro 1987, p. 197.

73. Hiro 1987, p. 199.

74. O'Ballance 1988, pp. 66–8.

75. O'Ballance 1988, pp. 68–9.

76. O'Ballance 1988, pp. 79–81; Hiro 1990, pp. 55–57; Cooper and Bishop 2000, pp. 130–31; Karsh 2002, pp. 35–6.

77. Brown 1990, p. 88.

78. Brown 1990, p. 86.

79. Again, Satrapi 2003, pp. 94–102 gives a strong impression of the methods used by the regime to motivate the young Basijis, and the general population – but also the scepticism many youngsters felt about those methods.

80. Brown 1990, p. 90.

81. Anonymous interview with a former Basiji, now a medical consultant, May/June 2011.
82. O'Ballance 1988, pp. 82–5; Hiro 1990, pp. 59–60.
83. Chehabi 2006a, pp. 213–14.
84. http://www.state.gov/g/drl/rls/irf/2008/108487.htm.
85. Buchta 2005, pp. 204–6.
86. Chehabi 2006a, pp. 216–19.
87. Chehabi and Mneimneh 2006, p. 31.
88. Chehabi 2006a, pp. 203–18.
89. Ramazani 1988, pp. 155–8.
90. See chapter 6 for the attack on the Israeli embassy in Buenos Aires in March 1992; the attack on the Khobar Towers in Saudi Arabia in 1996 was blamed on groups with connections to Iran at one time but is now generally attributed to Al-Qaeda. To my knowledge there is no indication of Iranian involvement in any suicide attack since 1992.
91. Bakhash 1986, p. 222 ; Hiro 1987, pp. 208–9.
92. Bakhash 1986, p. 223; Hiro 1987, pp. 219–20; Moin 1999, pp. 252–3.
93. For a discussion of the evidence on these matters, see the article by Ali Alfoneh for the American Enterprise Institute at http://www.aei.org/article/102603 (accessed 14 August 2011).
94. Hashemi-Rafsanjani Memoirs for 1361/1982–3; 20 Khordad 1361/10 June 1982, pp. 136–7.
95. Ibid., 1 Tir 1361/22 June 1982, p. 155.
96. FBIS, 12 July 1982, 'Tehran: Time for Grand, Historic Battle'.
97. Hashemi-Rafsanjani Memoirs for 1361/1982–3, pp. 155–7; the discussions in October appear on p. 289. Rafsanjani's account of these discussions has been disputed; notably by Akbar Ganji.
98. Hiro 1990, pp. 87–8; O'Ballance 1988, pp. 93–5.
99. Ramazani 1988, pp. 35–9.
100. Hiro 1990, pp. 91–3.
101. Hiro 1987, pp. 222–6.
102. O'Ballance 1988, p. 103.
103. O'Ballance 1988, p. 114.
104. Brown 1990, pp. 31–2.
105. O'Ballance 1988, pp. 114–20.
106. O'Ballance 1988, p. 120.
107. Cooper and Bishop 2004, pp. 46–7.
108. Bakhash 1986, pp. 238–9; Abrahamian 1999, pp. 179–84 and Behrooz 2000, pp. 128–30 and 160–65.
109. O'Ballance 1988, pp. 132–41.
110. Anonymous interview with former member of the regular army, May/June 2011.
111. Hiro 1990, pp. 103–4; O'Ballance 1988, pp. 142–8.

112. Brown 1990, pp. 32–3. Brown seems to have got the timing of the attacks in the marshes confused at one or two points.

113. Cooper and Bishop 2000, pp. 166–8.

114. Chris Rundle saw mustard gas victims suffering in this way in hospital in Tehran in 1984, while serving in the British embassy (email correspondence).

115. Dehqan 2006, pp. 91–2.

116. Hiro 1990, p. 105.

117. Hiro 1990, p. 201.

118. Quoted in Moslem 2002, p. 68.

119. Bakhash 1986, p. 230.

120. Arjomand has emphasized this phenomenon – see Arjomand 1988, pp. 197–206.

121. However, many members alleged to have had connections to the Hojjatieh have never openly acknowledged it, and the whole question has been made more ambiguous by accusations from the left against people who probably had no such connections – there was a phase in the early 1980s when these accusations were common.

122. Moin 1999, pp. 255–6; Hiro 1987, pp. 243–7.

123. Bakhash 1986, pp. 206–16; 'Economy X: Under the Islamic Republic', *Encyclopedia Iranica* (Vahid Nowshirvani); Schirazi 1997, pp. 194–7.

124. Moslem 2002, pp. 64–5.

125. Moini/Iran Research Group 1990 (*Who's Who in Iran*), pp. 29–31; http:// www.foreignpolicy.com/articles/2010/02/22/the_good_ayatollah?page=0,1 (article 'The Good Ayatollah' by Abbas Milani – accessed 22 September 2011).

126. Ramazani 1988, p. 26; as noted elsewhere, suicide attacks have in general been condemned by Shi'a clerics.

127. Hiro 1987, p. 265.

128. Hiro 1987, p. 380.

129. O'Ballance 1988, pp. 153–4.

130. Hiro 1990, p. 135.

131. The effect of the US/Allied atom bomb attacks on Hiroshima and Nagasaki in August 1945 might appear to be an exception, but if so, it really is the exception that proves the rule. The atom bomb was an exceptional weapon, with an exceptionally devastating effect, and Japan was already beaten in the war in any case. Plus, the war only ended then because of a personal intervention by the emperor: many if not most of the country's military leadership *still* wanted to fight on, even after the atom bombs.

132. O'Ballance 1988, pp. 154–7.

133. Brown 1990, pp. 33–4 (Brown mistakenly dates the attack to the previous spring).

134. O'Ballance 1988, pp. 160–66 and 172; Karsh 2002, p. 47.

135. O'Ballance 1988, pp. 173–9; Karsh 2002, p. 48.
136. Anonymous interview, May/June 2011; the point of the story is that the officer's courage revived after he took opium in his tent.
137. O'Ballance 1988, p. 189.
138. Parsi 2007, pp. 196–226; Ansari 2006, pp. 108–12; Ramazani 1988, pp. 253–69; Hiro 1990, p. 219.
139. Cooper and Bishop 2004, pp. 70–71: statement attributed there to an Iranian Air Force pilot, Major Ali (a pseudonym).
140. Abrahamian 1999, p. 166.
141. Reyshahri 1369/1990, pp. 71–5.
142. Buchta 2005, p. 200.
143. Reyshahri 1369/1990, p. 284.
144. O'Ballance 1988, pp. 190–91; Hiro 1990, p. 180.
145. Dehqan 2006, pp. 123–5.
146. Dehqan 2006, pp. 164–71.
147. Hiro 1990, p. 184; O'Ballance suggests around half that (O'Ballance 1988, p. 196).
148. Hiro 1990, p. 186; Cooper and Bishop 2000, pp. 244–5; Bill 1988, p. 307.
149. Hiro 1990, pp. 189–90.
150. Extreme Shi'a practices like the cursing of the first three caliphs have been discouraged under the Islamic republic; another example is the closure of the shrine of Abu Lolo in Kashan. Abu Lolo was the Persian-born assassin who murdered the Caliph Omar in the mid-seventh century AD.
151. Hiro 1990, pp. 224–5.
152. FBIS, 3 August 1987, 'Khomeyni Sends Message to Hajj Pilgrims'.

CHAPTER 5: THE END OF THE WAR, THE DEATH OF THE EMAM, AND RECONSTRUCTION: KHAMENEI AND RAFSANJANI, 1988–97

1. Quoted in McDowall 2010, p. 358.
2. Hiltermann 2007, pp. 2–3, 157–8 and passim.
3. McDowall 2010, pp. 357–9. The term al-Anfal derives from the eighth Sura of the Koran, in which Muslims were given permission to take spoils of war after the Battle of Badr.
4. Ansari 2006, p. 112: 'blaming Iran was now a bipartisan affair to which all Americans could subscribe … Iran had transcended regular politics and become a myth, part of political folklore … even Vietnam had not generated such a uniformity of dislike.'
5. Hiro 1990, p. 200; Cooper and Bishop 2000, p. 261.
6. Cooper and Bishop 2004 (pp. 84 and 85) suggest that the Iranians had lost only about 16 F-14s: three in air combat, four to Iranian surface-to-air

missiles in friendly-fire incidents, two more in unknown circumstances and seven in air accidents (mainly due to engine failure – a problem to which the TF-30 engines in the F-14s were particularly prone – in US Navy service also). Set against that, the same source suggests 159 confirmed kills by F-14s over the course of the war, with a further 34 probable or unconfirmed.

7. Hashemi-Rafsanjani Memoirs for 1367/1988/9, p. 18 (and below); Baktiari 1996, p. 148.

8. Hiro 1990, p. 203.

9. Hiro 1990, pp. 203–4.

10. See Ansari 2003, p. 238 for the Iranians discovering Western 'doctors' behind the Iraqi lines.

11. Hiro 1990, pp. 203–7.

12. Rundle 1995, p. 110; Hiro 1990, p. 243.

13. Hiro 1990, pp. 244, 284n.

14. Moin 1999, p. 268; Chehabi 1990, p. 301.

15. FBIS, 1 January 1988, 'Khamene'i Delivers Friday Prayers Sermons'; Moslem 2002, pp. 73–4.

16. Moslem 2002, p. 74; FBIS, 7 January 1988, 'Khomeyni Answers Khamene'i Letter on Authority'.

17. Arjomand 2009, p. 34; FBIS, 22 January 1988, 'Khamene'i Gives Friday Prayers Sermon in Tehran'.

18. Moslem 2002, pp. 69–70.

19. According to Rogers, after the helicopter was fired on, the crew of the *Vincennes* heard a radio signal from the Iranians: 'Over bridge-to-bridge radio an Arab voice exulted "We have destroyed the great Satan Blackhawk!" The voice was wrong on two counts. The helicopter was not a Blackhawk, nor was it destroyed' (Rogers and Rogers 1992, p. 5). Rogers was wrong on another count – Iranians are not Arabs.

20. Rogers and Rogers 1992, p. 90.

21. Rogers and Rogers 1992, p. 6.

22. BBC documentary *The Other Lockerbie* (broadcast 4 March 2000); Rogers and Rogers 1992, p. 133. To be fair to Rogers, his book is balanced, and includes material that is critical of his conduct. At other points he shows himself to be judicious and humane – notably later, when his ship is sailing out of the Persian Gulf, and he rescues a group of Iranian fishermen whose boat had sunk eight days earlier (p. 162).

23. Rogers and Rogers 1992, p. 133.

24. Rogers and Rogers 1992, p. 8.

25. As reported by *Newsweek* (Peterson 2010, p. 67); the BBC documentary *The Other Lockerbie* (broadcast 4 March 2000) said twenty-seven failed attempts.

26. As we have seen, the F-14 is an air superiority fighter, and although it could in theory carry bombs or other air-to-surface weapons, the Iranian F-14s hardly

ever did this, and never to my knowledge against targets at sea. The Iraqis, with their Super Etendards and Exocets, were much better equipped to attack ships from the air. But Cooper and Bishop 2000 gives evidence of an internal US Navy report dated 6 July 1988 to the effect that the Iranian F-14s could have the capability to attack ships (p. 277). Cooper and Bishop speculate that Captain Rogers might have heard about this report before it actually appeared. They do not consider the possibility that the report could have been produced quickly after the destruction of the Airbus in an attempt to reduce the opprobrium of the incident.

27. Fisk 2006, p. 333.

28. Hiro 1990, p. 240.

29. *The Other Lockerbie*, BBC documentary, broadcast 4 March 2000. Before Libyan responsibility for the December 1988 Lockerbie bombing was established, it was thought likely that the Iranians had commissioned that atrocity in revenge for Iran Air 655. Although Libyan responsibility has been established, that need not wholly preclude the possibility of Iranian involvement in some form.

30. This is not to say that elites in Western societies with free media are never deceived or never deceive themselves; but free media should at least make it more difficult.

31. Ali Alfoneh, 'The War over the War' (online article, American Enterprise Institute, http://www.aei.org/article/102603, accessed 24 May 2011). Alfoneh is quoting Rafsanjani.

32. Hashemi-Rafsanjani Memoirs for 1367/1988/9, pp. 14–15.

33. Rezai–Khomeini correspondence: http://www.eurasianet.org/departments/insight/articles/eav101606.shtml. When the Rezai letter first appeared, some Western commentators pounced on the implication that the Sepah commander appeared to be suggesting that Iran should acquire nuclear weapons. But, seen in the round, it is plain that the true meaning of the letter is almost the opposite: in order to demonstrate that the war had to be brought to an end, Rezai was presenting a string of conditions for success in the war that were manifestly impracticable or impossible (at least in the short term), one of which was possession of nuclear weapons. The point has been repeated nonetheless.

34. Hashemi-Rafsanjani Memoirs for 1367/1988/9, p. 18. Mohsen Rezai has disputed Rafsanjani's account since the memoirs were published.

35. Hashemi-Rafsanjani Memoirs for 1367/1988/9, p. 18.

36. FBIS, 17 July 1988, 'Khamenei, Hashemi-Rafsanjani address meeting'.

37. Hiro 1990, p. 242.

38. BBC monitoring, 20 July 1888; FBIS, same date; Moin 1999, p. 269; Hiro 1990, p. 243.

39. Moin 1999, p. 270, quoting Ahmad Khomeini.

40. Moin 1999, p. 297.

41. For Khomeini's message, see FBIS, 8 August 1988, 'Khomeyni Letter of Praise Presented to Air Base'; for the rest, FBIS, 29 July 1988, '900 vehicles destroyed'; also Hiro 1990, pp. 246–7; Moin 1999, p. 278; Cooper and Bishop 2000, p. 278.

42. Abrahamian 1999, pp. 106–7.

43. Abrahamian 1999, p. 167.

44. Abrahamian 1999, pp. 135–40 (the estimate of numbers of executions that follows is also taken from Abrahamian).

45. Robertson 2009, p. 42; although in the report the text is referred to as a *fatwa*, the correct technical term for this kind of document is *hokm* (with thanks to Sajjad Rizvi).

46. Abrahamian 1999, pp. 209–11; Moin 1999, pp. 278–9; Robertson 2009, p. 43 (Abrahamian has Hojjatoleslam Mobasheri as the third member of the commission in place of Purmohammadi).

47. Interview by BBC reporter Sadeq Saba with Montazeri: http://news.bbc .co.uk/1/hi/world/middle_east/7458709.stm (accessed 30 May 2011).

48. Moin 1999, p. 279.

49. Moin 1999, p. 290.

50. FBIS, 3 August 1988, 'Montazeri Remarks on 'Id al-Ghadir Reported'.

51. Robertson 2009, p. 62.

52. Robertson 2009, p. 49.

53. Robertson 2009, p. 44.

54. Robertson 2009, p. 2.

55. Moin 1999, p. 286.

56. Ernest Gellner, 'Anything goes – the carnival of cheap relativism which threatens to swamp the coming *fin de millénaire*', *Times Literary Supplement*, 16 June 1995, p. 6.

57. Abrahamian 1999, pp. 218–20.

58. Abrahamian 1999, pp. 109, 172.

59. Some Iranians will not believe that Khomeini gave the order, believing that others around him carried out the act without his permission, but the evidence to the contrary is quite clear.

60. FBIS, 9 August 1988, 'Hashemi-Rafsanjani Message'; see also Hiro 1990, pp. 248–9.

61. FBIS, 12 August 1988, 'Khamenei Delivers Friday Prayers Sermons'.

62. Potter and Sick 2004, p. 8.

63. See http://www.icrc.org/eng/resources/documents/misc/57jqbn.htm.

64. For a vivid sense of what it was like to be living in a city under missile attack, see Satrapi 2003, pp. 135–42.

65. Majd 2010, p. 138.

66. Anonymous interview, May/June 2011. Some veterans suggest that as many as a quarter of the casualties in the fighting may have been due to accidents and so-called friendly-fire incidents like that one.

67. Anonymous interview with a former member of the Sepah, May/June 2011.
68. FBIS, 3 August 1988, 'Montazeri Remarks on 'Id al-Ghadir Reported', and FBIS, 19 August 1988, 'Hashemi-Rafsanjani Gives Friday Prayers Sermons'.
69. Esfahani and Pesaran 2009, p. 192.
70. Kian-Thiébaut 2005a, p. 47.
71. Pesaran 1992, p. 110.
72. 'Economy X: Under the Islamic Republic', *Encyclopedia Iranica* (Vahid Nowshirvani); Esfahani and Pesaran 2009, pp. 192–3; Menashri 2001, pp. 107–8; Baktiari 1996, pp. 193–4; Khajehpour 2001, p. 99; Ranjbar-Daemi (forthcoming).
73. Ehteshami 1995, pp. 27–44 and passim.
74. FBIS, 14 February 1988, 'Khomeyni Exhorts Muslims to "Execute" Rushdie'; on the *fatwa/hokm* question, see al-Azm 1993.
75. Baktiari 1996, pp. 168–70; Rundle 2004, p. 147.
76. Rundle 2004, pp. 148–9; despite the 1998 settlement, bodies within Iran like the Sepah and the 15 Khordad Foundation continued periodically to restate the validity of Khomeini's sentence on Rushdie. I wrote the section in the main text on the Rushdie affair before the publication of Rushdie's book *Joseph Anton: A Memoir* in September 2012. That book mentioned me by name in connection with the events around the joint statements by Cook and Kharrazi in New York on 24 September 1998; and described, in particular, a meeting between Rushdie, the intelligence services and the police the following week, at which I represented the Foreign Office (Rushdie 2012, pp. 551 and 226). It was, in fact, my first day as sole head of the Iran Section in Middle East Department, having just taken over from Neil Crompton. At this meeting, Rushdie was told that despite the New York statements, the services' assessment of the threat to his life was unchanged, and that therefore the arrangements to protect him would remain in place. This did not entirely accord with what he had been led to expect in the run-up to the events in New York, and he was, understandably, disappointed. At the climax of the meeting, he pointed at me across the table and shouted 'If I am killed, you will be f****** responsible.' Doing my best to preserve professional sangfroid, I said I accepted that responsibility; and that I shared it with the others present. As I recall, I added that we were all, as ever, committed to preventing that happening. The New York agreement was the best prospect for preventing it and for improving his security position. As his book says, I then arranged a telephone call between him and Robin Cook. Over the following two years I met Rushdie again and spoke to him on the telephone many times, and our exchanges were cordial. Subsequent events have shown that the New York agreement produced a lasting improvement for Rushdie's security; the improvement in UK–Iran relations it produced was also real, but proved more ephemeral.
77. To be fair, the name 'Mrs Torture' is put into the mouth of one of Rushdie's characters, but the book also includes an episode in which the prime minister is

burned in effigy while a crowd chants 'Maggie Maggie Maggie – burn burn burn . . .'

78. Moin 1999, pp. 282–3; Rundle 2004, pp. 146–50; Axworthy 2008b; Kaussler 2011.

79. Moslem 2002, pp. 71–2.

80. FBIS, 12 February 1989, 'Montazeri on Revolution's Past Mistakes, Future'.

81. Notably in a piece in the *Tehran Times* on 13 February – FBIS, 13 February 1989, '*Tehran Times* Lauds Montazeri's Criticism'.

82. If so, it would be a further irony that Montazeri and Mehdi Hashemi had, at an earlier stage, been among the prime instruments for attempts to export the revolution, and the Iranian involvement with Lebanese Hezbollah in particular. Some have taken Montazeri's statement about killing as a criticism of the so-called *fatwa*, but it is clear from the record that it was made *before* Khomeini's sentence on Rushdie.

83. Quoted in Moin 1999, pp. 275–6 and 285–6; I am grateful to Baqer Moin again for his thoughts on this letter.

84. FBIS, 27 March 1989, 'Khomeyni Attends Meeting on Future Leadership'.

85. Moin 1999, pp. 287–9.

86. FBIS, 28 March 1989, 'Text of Resignation Letter'.

87. FBIS, 28 March 1989, 'Text of Khomeyni Reply'.

88. FBIS, 29 March 1989, 'Press on Montazeri resignation, State Interests'.

89. Moin 1999, p. 293; Arjomand 2009, p. 35.

90. Fenton 2008, p. 243.

91. Moin 1999, pp. 310–13; Hiro 1990, p. 268; Fenton 2008.

92. The clip is shown within a Swedish TV documentary at http://www.youtube.com/watch?v=xq2-_eGlshI (accessed 21 June 2011). At one point Khamenei leaves the podium with the words 'Anyway, I am against this . . .' When it comes to the vote, the overwhelming majority stand to approve the proposal, calling out 'Allahu Akbar' ('God is Great').

93. Baktiari 1996, pp. 185–6.

94. Baktiari 1996, p. 188.

95. Abrahamian 2009, pp. 182–3.

96. Moslem 2002, p. 77.

97. Abrahamian 1982, p. 475; Hiro 1987, p. 212.

98. Nader Shah defeated the Afghans in battle and restored the Safavid Tahmasp II to the throne of Persia in 1729, but retained real power in the state for himself. He deposed Tahmasp in 1732, ruled for a further four years as regent and only made himself Shah in 1736 (see Axworthy 2006). The clip of Khamenei's accession to the office of leader mentioned at note 92 above gives an insight into the relationship between him and Rafsanjani at this time: Khamenei rather lacking in confidence; Rafsanjani assured, controlled, cool and master of the proceedings.

99. Baktiari 1996, pp. 199–203.

100. Baktiari 1996, pp. 190–91.

101. Potter and Sick 2004, p. 9 (note 18); interview with Shirin Ebadi, 10 January 2012.

102. Baktiari 1996, pp. 194–6; Randjbar-Daemi (forthcoming).

103. Potter and Sick 2004, p. 9 (note 17).

104. Baktiari 1996, pp. 204–13.

105. Moslem 2002, pp. 158–9.

106. Baktiari 1996, p. 145.

107. Baktiari 1996, pp. 218–19; Randjbar-Daemi (forthcoming).

108. Kian-Thiébaut 2005a, p. 47.

109. 'Education XXIV: Education in Postrevolutionary Persia, 1979–1995', *Encyclopedia Iranica* (Golnar Mehran); and 'Education VII: General Survey of Modern Education', *Encyclopedia Iranica* (Ahmad Ashraf).

110. Quoted in Arjomand 2009, p. 56: I have altered the translation slightly. Khomeini made a number of statements to similar effect around this time.

111. Ehteshami 1995, pp. 115–17; Esfahani and Pesaran 2009, pp. 193–5; Baktiari 1996, p. 228; Randjbar-Daemi (forthcoming) has the higher figures for inflation: 50 per cent and 46.6 per cent for 1991/2 and 1992/3 respectively.

112. Baktiari 1996, pp. 228–9; Ehteshami 1995, pp. 63–9.

113. Randjbar-Daemi (forthcoming).

114. Chehabi 2006b, pp. 289–92.

115. Axworthy 2008b, p. 106.

116. FBIS, 23 December 1991, 'President Urges "Prudent Policy" Above All'.

117. The preceding section draws upon Ansari 2006, pp. 128–37, and Slavin 2007, pp. 178–83.

118. Arjomand 2009, pp. 174–6; Buchta 2000, p. 90.

119. Chehabi 2006b, p. 300.

120. Alavi 2005, p. 149.

121. Ansari 2000, pp. 59 and 82–3; Randjbar-Daemi (forthcoming).

122. Ansari 2000, pp. 84–5; Buchta 2000, pp. 16–17.

123. Randjbar-Daemi (forthcoming); Ansari 2000, p. 86.

CHAPTER 6: *BIM-E MOWJ* (FEAR OF THE WAVE): KHATAMI AND REFORM, 1997–2005

1. FBIS, 1 June 1996, 'Khamenei Hints at Change in Future Government Leadership'; Buchta 2000, p. 27; Ansari 2000, pp. 88–9.

2. 'His personality and political acumen excepted, Nateq-Nuri seemed to have much going for him' (Ansari 2000, p. 90); for the general situation, see Moslem 2002, p. 241.

3. Buchta 2000, p. 28; in the absence of formal political parties in the Iranian system, political societies and groups express their support for candidates in both

presidential and Majles elections. So a candidate may be the preferred choice of a number of different political groups. In Majles elections this can get complicated; societies publish lists of their preferred candidates. It has happened that a candidate may find himself on the list of a group or society of which he is not a member, and to which he may even be opposed, without being consulted.

4. Buchta 2000, p. 30.

5. Ansari 2000, pp. 96–103.

6. http://www.washingtoninstitute.org/templateC05.php?CID=3105 and http://news.bbc.co.uk/1/hi/world/middle_east/3625019.stm (both accessed 25 April 2012).

7. Ansari 2000, pp. 106–8; Buchta 2000, pp. 31–3.

8. Buchta 2000, p. 34.

9. Alavi 2005, p. 107.

10. This is one reason why, for example, I have avoided labelling Rafsanjani and his followers as 'pragmatists' or 'moderates' or 'the modern right' as have some others. Any neat definition like that raises awkward (and ultimately irrelevant) questions when the group concerned does something unexpected – as Rafsanjani has done several times.

11. Ansari 2000, pp. 74–6; Kamrava 2008, pp. 157–61.

12. Alavi 2005, pp. 118–19.

13. Kamrava 2008, pp. 168–70.

14. Mir-Hosseini and Tapper 2008, pp. 89–90.

15. Kamrava 2008, pp. 162–7.

16. Buchta 2000, p. 40.

17. Buchta 2000, pp. 125–7; Mir-Hosseini and Tapper 2008, p. 35. Anyone familiar with Wagner's opera *Parsifal* may see a parallel with the way that Titurel rebukes his wounded successor Amfortas from the grave. Some might take the parallel further, with Ahmadinejad as Parsifal; but, as time goes on, it is plainer that he was miscast for that role.

18. Buchta 2000, p. 124.

19. Kamal Tabrizi, many years before, had been among the US embassy hostage-takers and had filmed some of what happened at the embassy.

20. The story was given to me by Hashem Ahmadzadeh. Like the film *Marmulak*, *Vino e Pane* is organized around the idea of a man disguising himself as a cleric and develops some similar themes (there are similarities also with the whisky priest in Graham Greene's *The Power and the Glory*).

21. Ansari 2000, pp. 132–3.

22. Ansari 2000, pp. 133–7.

23. Axworthy 2008b, pp. 106–8.

24. Buchta 2000, pp. 150–53.

25. Buchta 2000, pp. 140–43.

26. Abrahamian 1999, pp. 159–60; Kuzichkin 1990, pp. 264–6; Fardust and Darieni 1999, pp. 429–32.

27. Buchta 2000, p. 19.

28. Buchta 2000, pp. 18–20 and 166.

29. I was alerted to this view by a passage in Leslie 2011 (p. 231), where he attributes it to Christopher Andrew. I have corresponded with Professor Andrew about it – he concurs with it, and explores the theme in his book *The Mitrokhin Archive*, notably in the Introduction to part II, p. 21.

30. See also Buchta 2005, pp. 213–15. Since the late 1990s it has been alleged that Said Emami confessed to the murder of Ahmad Khomeini, but that the confession was suppressed – http://www.netnative.com/news/00/sep/1113.html (accessed 18 August 2011).

31. Buchta 2000, p. 167; in my book *Empire of the Mind* (2008a) I gave the same story on the basis of information from other sources. According to Buchta, the tape also implicated the Intelligence Minister, Dorri-Najafabadi.

32. See Buchta 2000, pp. 161–2 and 166–8 (the latter for the revelations in *al-Mujaz 'an Iran*).

33. This was before Robin Cook became the darling of the British left for his opposition to the invasion of Iraq in 2003. His opposition was at its most animated in the brief period in the spring of 2003, when some people were talking about a brief hiatus in the campaign against Saddam as the prelude to a potential Stalingrad or Grozny, and speculating about the possibility of Blair falling from power, should the invasion fail. Over the period of the Iraq invasion Cook's star rose, with the left, as Clare Short's fell. Having met them both as a middle-level official, I thought Short was a woman of principle. Cook came across as an intelligent politician, with an acute sense of his career interests.

34. Afshari 2008, p. 265.

35. Ansari 2000, pp. 164, 195; Buchta 2000, p. 74.

36. Buchta 2000, pp. 177–8.

37. Alavi 2005, p. 53.

38. http://www.cbsnews.com/stories/2009/04/03/60minutes/main4917310.shtml (accessed 23 December 2011); Alavi 2005, pp. 141–2.

39. Ansari 2000, pp. 204–7; Buchta 2000, p. 194.

40. Arjomand 2009, p. 180.

41. Mir-Hosseini and Tapper 2008, pp. 36–8, 148–9, 173–4.

42. Menashri 2001, pp. 309–14.

43. Baktiari 2005, p. 124.

44. Michaelsen 2011, pp. 184–5 (reporting by Reza (Morad) Veisi, referring to this period and to the later period, up to 2005).

45. Menashri 2001, pp. 309 and 311; Slavin 2007, p. 111.

46. Ansari 2007, p. 27; Mir-Hosseini and Tapper 2008, p. 175.

47. The prototype for the Shahab-3 was the North Korean Nodong-1, the latter an apt name for a large weapon wielded by an otherwise miserably

unsuccessful state, perhaps. A test firing of the Shahab-3 can be seen at http://www.youtube.com/watch?v=hsMlwyOs3qY (accessed 27 July 2011).

48. Slavin 2007, pp. 197–9; see also the report from James Dobbins (leader of the US delegation to the talks in Bonn) in the *Washington Post*, 22 July 2007.

49. Slavin 2007, pp. 199–200.

50. Israeli Ministry of Foreign Affairs website: http://www.mfa.gov.il/MFA/Government/Communiques/2002/Seizing%20of%20the%20Palestinian%20weapons%20ship%20Karine%20A%20- (accessed 26 July 2011).

51. For some of the speculation, see Parsi 2007, pp. 419–22; Slavin 2007, pp. 91 and 199–200.

52. Slavin 2007, pp. 203–4.

53. Abdi later met former hostage Barry Rosen in Paris in an attempt at reconciliation, but seemed, twenty-five years on, still to believe that the hostage crisis did some good – see http://www.nytimes.com/2006/04/29/world/middleeast/29abdi.html (accessed 27 July 2011).

54. Parsi 2007, p. 435 and passim.

55. De facto Iranian recognition of Israel was implied by a provision within the 'US Aims' section of the proposal that Iran would recognize the 2002 Beirut Declaration of the Arab League, which was a Saudi initiative incorporating measures for a two-state solution to the Israeli–Palestinian conflict.

56. Parsi 2007, pp. 449–50 and an associated article by Guy Dinmore in the *Financial Times*: http://guydinmore.wordpress.com/2003/07/14/us-rejects-irans-offer-for-talks-on–nuclear-programme/#more-459 (accessed 19 January 2012).

57. Parsi 2007, p. 612.

58. Parsi 2007, p. 609.

59. See, for example, Michael Rubin's piece in the *Weekly Standard* of 22 October 2007, entitled 'The Guldimann Memorandum: The Iranian "Roadmap" wasn't a roadmap and wasn't Iranian': http://www.meforum.org/1764/the-guldimann-memorandum (accessed 19 January 2012); but John Bolton has suggested the same.

60. Parsi 2007, p. 445.

61. Though Rice claimed later, after the proposal had been rejected, that she did not remember having seen it (Slavin 2007, p. 205).

62. Cheney and Rumsfeld at the time claimed that their plans for Iraq would work to democratize the country much as Allied plans for Germany and Japan in 1945 had turned those countries into liberal democracies. But, as in other respects, Cheney and Rumsfeld failed to read the script. In both Germany and Japan, despite denazification and similar policies, previous elites, technocrats, administrators and managers were back running the country in their old positions within two or three years. In Iraq, the US (against the advice of experts in the region whose views were ignored) sacked the entire

officer corps of the Iraqi army and banned any former members of the Baath Party from responsible positions. As a result, the process of reconstruction was crippled, and many of those personnel (mainly Sunni Muslims) joined the insurgency against the coalition instead.

63. Parsi 2007, p. 447, drawing on the account of Lawrence Wilkerson, Colin Powell's chief of staff, who called the rebuke 'shameful'.

64. Parsi 2007, p. 427.

65. Alavi 2005, pp. 153–4.

66. Alavi 2005, pp. 157–8 (from 2004) (I have adjusted some punctuation). Pre-revolution street names are still used in everyday talk; it can be a low-level sign of political resistance, also perhaps a sign that someone does not want to be mistaken for a visitor or non-Tehrani.

67. Bjerre Christensen 2011, p. 3.

68. Alavi 2005, p. 150.

69. Baktiari 2005, pp. 125–8; interviews, November 2007.

70. Arjomand 2009, pp. 102–3.

71. Alavi 2005, pp. 283–4.

72. Alavi 2005, p. 289.

73. Interview with Dr Ebadi, 10 January 2012.

74. http://news.bbc.co.uk/1/hi/world/middle_east/3579173.stm (accessed 12 January 2012).

75. Alavi 2005, p. 256.

76. Alavi 2005, p. 171.

CHAPTER 7: EVERYTHING MUST CHANGE, SO THAT EVERYTHING CAN STAY THE SAME: AHMADINEJAD AND KHAMENEI, 2005–12

1. A loose translation of the words from Giuseppe Tomasi di Lampedusa's *Il Gattopardo* (*The Leopard*): 'Se vogliamo che tutto rimanga come è, bisogna che tutto cambi.'

2. Naji 2008, pp. 3–11

3. Naji 2008, pp. 18–25; Ebtekar 2000, p. 59.

4. Naji 2008, pp. 25–40.

5. Naji 2008, pp. 45–7.

6. Naji 2008, pp. 102–6.

7. Naji 2008, pp. 47–8.

8. Farhi 2004, p. 103.

9. Alavi 2005, p. 302 (some punctuation has been amended).

10. Arjomand 2009, pp. 106–8.

11. Ansari 2007, p. 35; Naji 2008, pp. 75–7.

12. Naji 2008, pp. 81–90.

13. See Majd 2010, p. 81; there were many jokes about Ahmadinejad, often reflecting a class prejudice, implying for example that he was stupid and didn't wash. See Naji 2008, p. xi; according to my *Parsifal* analogy, Ahmadinejad might have looked in 2005 like the innocent destined to rejuvenate the wasteland, but he proved a disappointment.

14. 'Iran's revolution is in its infancy – but it may have just found its Stalin' –*Sunday Telegraph*, 14 August 2005 – http://www.telegraph.co.uk/comment/3619032/Irans-revolution-is-in-its-infancy-but-it-may-have-just-found-its-Stalin.html (accessed 29 July 2011).

15. Ehteshami 2007, pp. 66–9.

16. Naji 2008; pp. 114–15; http://www.nti.org/e_research/profiles/Iran/Nuclear/chronology_1957_1985.html (accessed 28 August 2011).

17. http://www.nti.org/e_research/profiles/Iran/Nuclear/chronology.html (accessed 30 August 2011).

18. Some, rightly, have been sceptical (especially after the episode of the phantom Iraqi weapons of mass destruction in 2003) about intelligence evidence for an Iranian nuclear weapon programme which, because it derived from intelligence sources, cannot be opened to critical scrutiny. I too (I hope) have a healthy scepticism about information derived from secret intelligence; but, having worked in government, I broadly accept the view that Iran has (or at least has had) a nuclear weapons programme.

19. http://www.nti.org/e_research/profiles/Iran/Nuclear/chronology_2001.html (accessed 30 August 2011).

20. http://www.iaea.org/Publications/Documents/Infcircs/Others/infcirc140.pdf (accessed 4 September 2011).

21. http://www.dni.gov/press_releases/20071203_release.pdf (accessed 31 August 2011).

22. Naji 2008, pp. 94–5.

23. Naji 2008, pp. 123–7 and 134–5; http://www.nti.org/e_research/profiles/Iran/Nuclear/chronology_2006.html (accessed 31 August 2011).

24. http://www.iaea.org/newscenter/focus/iaeairan/unsc_res1737–2006.pdf (accessed 31 August 2011).

25. See, for example, the articles by Seymour Hersh in the *New Yorker*: http://www.newyorker.com/archive/2006/04/17/060417fa_fact (17 April 2006) and http://www.newyorker.com/archive/2006/07/10/060710fa_fact (10 July 2006) (both accessed 31 August 2011). Some of the comparisons between neoconservatism in the US and the right in Iran have been facile, but in one respect there is a similarity: in the US there has been a longstanding *idée fixe* on the right that people who knew a lot about other countries were somehow unreliable and un-American. This view has often been blamed, for example, for the failure of the US system to train enough diplomats and CIA operatives in foreign languages (as was noted in the novel *The Ugly American* as early as the 1950s). Similarly in Iran, ignorance

of the world outside Iran, for people like Ahmadinejad, has served to entrench suspicion of foreigners, ideas of foreign plots and so on. It is striking how often this kind of wilful ignorance is accompanied by political arrogance.

26. http://www.dni.gov/press_releases/20071203_release.pdf (accessed 31 August 2011).

27. http://www.nti.org/e_research/profiles/Iran/Nuclear/index.html (accessed 31 August 2011).

28. Allegations to this effect were made in the BBC Radio 4 Programme *File on 4: Iranian Sanctions*, first broadcast on 14 February 2012: http://www.bbc.co.uk/iplayer/episode/b01bwp6n/File_on_4_Iranian_Sanctions/ (accessed 26 February 2012).

29. Naji 2008, p. 144.

30. Naji 2008, pp. 139–40 and 145–8.

31. Naji 2008, pp. 153–7; Axworthy 2008a, pp. 293–4.

32. http://jewssansfrontieres.blogspot.com/2006/02/iranian–jews–condemn–ahmadinejad.html (accessed 1 September 2011); Naji 2008, pp. 156–60.

33. Some, like the author, may take the view that the conference was a good argument for *not* making Holocaust denial illegal.

34. http://news.bbc.co.uk/1/hi/6167695.stm (accessed 3 September 2011); Naji 2008, pp. 164–74; Ansari 2007, pp. 52–3.

35. On 15 July 2007 the *Los Angeles Times* reported, on the strength of comments by (anonymous) senior US military officers and others, that, although the finger had been pointed at Iran and Syria, the largest number (45 per cent) of foreign suicide bombers and insurgents in Iraq were from Saudi Arabia (plus 15 per cent from Syria and Lebanon, and 10 per cent from North Africa – figures for Iran were not given, presumably because they are off the bottom end of the scale). Suicide attacks have systematically killed larger numbers of civilians and soldiers in Iraq than other kinds of attack, and they were predominantly (if not entirely) carried out by Sunni insurgents. The same source claimed that 50 per cent of all Saudi fighters in Iraq came there as suicide bombers, and the article commented: 'The situation has left the U.S. military in the awkward position of battling an enemy whose top source of foreign fighters is a key ally that at best has not been able to prevent its citizens from undertaking bloody attacks in Iraq, and at worst shares complicity in sending extremists to commit attacks against U.S. forces, Iraqi civilians and the Shiite-led government in Baghdad.' See also Axworthy 2008a, p. 292.

36. Quoted in Alavi 2005, p. 75.

37. http://www.mod.uk/defenceinternet/defencenews/militaryoperations/second lieutenantjoannayorkedyercorporalkrisoneillprivateeleanordlugoszandking smanadamjamessmithkille.htm (accessed 22 October 2012).

38. http://www.guardian.co.uk/world/2006/aug/11/syria.israel (accessed 4 September 2011).

39. http://www.project-syndicate.org/commentary/broening1/English (accessed 4 September 2011).

40. Louër 2008, passim.

41. http://milexdata.sipri.org/result.php4 (accessed 5 September 2011).

42. http://www.rickety.us/2011/06/2010-defense-spending-by-country/ (accessed 5 September 2011). For the Soviet figure, see http://www.globalsecurity.org/military/world/russia/mo–budget.htm (accessed 6 September 2011).

43. See, for example, http://mideast.foreignpolicy.com/posts/2011/08/23/the_martyr_state_myth (accessed 7 September 2011).

44. Naji 2008, pp. 92–4.

45. http://www.indexmundi.com/iran/economy_profile.html (accessed 6 September 2011); the statistics are rather unreliable, as ever.

46. Esfahani and Pesaran 2009, pp. 195–6.

47. IMF Press Release no. 11/228 of 13 June 2011, following inspection by Dominique Guillaume of the IMF.

48. IMF Press Release no. 11/228 of 13 June 2011.

49. Alavi 2005, p. 205.

50. Kian-Thiébaut 2005a; Kurzman 2008, passim.

51. Brought out most clearly in the comparative surveys carried out by Mansour Moaddel, which also back up Kian-Thiébaut – for example, 73 per cent of Iranians surveyed believed a working mother could establish as warm and secure a relationship with her child as a mother who does not work, by comparison with 70 per cent in Turkey, 59 per cent in Saudi Arabia, 46 per cent in Egypt and 45 per cent in Jordan (78 per cent in the US). Survey at: http://www.psc.isr.umich.edu/research/tmp/moaddel_capitol –hill–may04.pdf (accessed 7 September 2011).

52. www.bbc.co.uk/news/world-middle-east-19665615.

53. Naji 2008, pp. 250–52.

54. Mir-Hosseini 2010a, pp. 140–41.

55. See the report by Frances Harrison of the BBC: http://www.youtube.com/watch?v=ui4pD2MhgoY (accessed 7 September 2011).

56. http://www.whitehouse.gov/Nowruz/ (accessed 22 September 2009).

57. Michaelsen 2011, pp. 39–40 (reporting by Ali Kheradpir).

58. Michaelsen 2011, p. 79 (reporting by Asieh Amini).

59. Majd 2010, pp. 3–5.

60. For two detailed analyses of what happened, see Zaccara 2012 and Ansari 2010, in addition to Majd 2010.

61. http://www.channel4.com/news/iran-militia-man-i-hope-god-forgives-me (accessed 7 September 2011).

62. Majd 2010, p. 11.

63. Choudhari 2009, p. 11.

64. http://blogs.telegraph.co.uk/news/davidhughes/100070584/a-slap-in-the-face-literally-for-irans-president-ahmadinejad/ (accessed 7 September

2011) – it is possible, perhaps likely, that the source or his interlocutor mistook a metaphorical slap for a real one. In Persian the phrase *sili be dahan* is often used in this metaphorical sense – Khomeini in particular used it many times. Whether or not the report is fully accurate, it gives an intriguing impression of the relationship between Ahmadinejad and the Sepah leadership.

65. http://hotair.com/archives/2009/12/29/too-good-to-check-khameneis-plane-being-overhauled-in-case-he-has-to-leave-iran/ (accessed 7 September 2011).

66. Majd 2010, pp. 263–4.

67. http://www.latimes.com/news/nationworld/world/la–fg–iran–protests31–2009jul31,0,7400028.story (accessed 10 September 2009).

68. Parsi 2012, passim.

69. Borzou Daraghi, 'Ayatollah Calls Government a Military Regime,' *Los Angeles Times*, 14 September 2009.

70. http://edition.presstv.ir/detail/115179.html (accessed 7 September 2011).

71. www.guardian.co.uk/world/2009/dec/27/iran-protests-riot-police-shots (accessed 16 February 2010).

72. Michaelsen 2011, p. 108 (reporting by Babak Ghafouri Azar).

73. Report by and interview with Lindsey Hilsum of Channel 4, http://www.channel4.com/news/iran-militia-man-i-hope-god-forgives-me (accessed 7 September 2011) as described in Peterson 2010, pp. 571, 687–8n and 696n.

74. A quotation from the Disney film *Pollyanna* – an unexpected authority perhaps, but one which illustrates the point well.

75. This comparison was the subject of a detailed and thoughtful contribution to *Foreign Policy* by Karim Sadjadpour: http://www.foreignpolicy.com/articles/2010/10/11/the_sources_of_ssoviets_iranian_conduct?page=0,0 (accessed 15 September 2011).

76. An appeal from Jalal Talabani to General Qasem Soleimani of the Sepah in March 2008 may have been instrumental in restraining Mahdi army violence in Basra (Majd 2010, p. 268).

77. Majd 2010, p. 268.

78. Majd 2010, pp. 60–66, 86–91 and passim.

79. See Majd 2010, and (for example) Farhadpour and Mehrgan 2010.

80. http://iwpr.net/report–news/ahmadinejad-way-out (accessed 6 September 2011).

81. The idea of a conservative revolution might at first seem odd, but the revolution of 1906–11 also had a strongly conservative element from the outset, and eventually swung to the right also.

82. See, for example, Zbigniew Brzezinski in the following interview: http://www.youtube.com/watch?v=Xat–C4SpBl4.

83. From Ahmadinejad himself at an earlier stage, of course, but there was an extraordinary call from within Iran in February 2012 by an Iranian Majles deputy for pre-emptive military strikes against Israel: http://www.al-monitor.

com/cms/contents/articles/opinion/2012/shaul-bakhash/exclusive-iranian-web-site-urges.html (accessed 26 February 2012).

84. http://www.cbsnews.com/8301-18560_162-57394904/the-spymaster-meir-dagan-on-irans-threat/.

85. http://www.bbc.co.uk/news/world-middle-east-17879744.

86. Netanyahu also made a gaffe in a speech to AIPAC while in Washington with an allusion to Iran as a 'nuclear duck': http://www.youtube.com/watch?v=3fyTGfoft68. An occasion when the duck really did seem to be out of the question.

87. Former British foreign secretary Jack Straw said in parliament on 20 February 2012: 'I hope that we hear less of the suggestion that were Iran to get a nuclear weapons capability, there would automatically be an arms race in the middle east. I do not believe that. A senior Saudi diplomat said to me, "I know what we're saying publicly, but do you really think that having told people that there is no need for us to make any direct response to Israel holding nuclear weapons, we could seriously make a case for developing a nuclear weapons capability to deal with another Muslim country?"' (taken from Hansard: http://www.publications.parliament.uk/pa/cm201212/cmhansrd/cm120220/debtext/120220-0002.htm#12022015000001 (accessed 26 February 2012)).

88. http://articles.timesofindia.indiatimes.com/2012-07-30/delhi/32941054_1_israeli-diplomat-houshang-afshar-irani-mohammad-reza-abolghasemi.

89. http://www.novinite.com/view_news.php?id=142259.

90. Linked in turn perhaps to the earlier question mark over the genuineness of the tolerance of our globalizing liberalism.

91. For a vivid illustration of this (notwithstanding that the presentation is at times sentimental) see the report by Rick Steves at http://www.youtube.com/watch?v=D61uriEGsIM&feature=share (accessed 27 February 2012).

Index

Qashqai (tribe) 35
Qasr-e Shirin 218, 248, 251, 262, 283
Qasr prison 148
Qatar xvii, 359
Qazvin 114, 181, 246
al-Qeisari, Davud 134
Qeytarieh 109, 128
Qoddusi, Ayatollah Ali 183, 215
Qods, operation 221
Qods force 358, 393
Qolhak 26, 128
Qom 16, 26, 62, 63, 101, 104–7,
    133–5, 153, 160, 168, 170, 173,
    214, 216, 244, 245, 279, 287,
    300, 301, 308, 320, 326, 328,
    334–5, 343, 348, 408, 409, 454
Qotbzadeh, Sadegh 99, 140, 144,
    175, 225–6
Quchan 154, 436
Quraish 17–18, 248, 429
Qurna 233, 237, 248–9, 251

Rabbani Shirazi, Ayatollah 92
Rab'eh circle 182
Rabin, Yitzhak 208
Rafiqdust, Mohsen 2, 234, 347
Rafiqdust, Mortaza 347
Rahimi, General Mehdi 14, 293,
    432, 445
Rahnavard, Zahra 217
Rajai, Mohammad-Ali 181–3, 192,
    202, 206, 210, 214, 216
Rajavi, Masud 129, 213–14, 224,
    249, 458
Ramadan operation (1982) 229–30
Rapier/Blindfire (anti-aircraft missile
    system) 84
Rasht 13, 406
Rastakhiz 82, 89–92, 95, 98, 105, 429
Reagan, Ronald 204–5, 252–5, 263,
    276, 438
Refah School 3, 7, 8, 14, 148

refugees 200, 293, 311, 389
Reyshahri, Mohammad 184, 256–7,
    325, 327, 342–4, 437, 461
Reuter, Baron Paul de 25
revolution, French (1789–91) 15, 32,
    57, 64, 143, 211, 215, 242, 287,
    410, 416, 441
revolution, Russian (1917) 6, 15, 32,
    35, 36, 57, 64, 143, 242,
    410, 441
Revolutionary Guards Corps see Sepah
Rex Cinema 108, 448
Rezai, Mohsen 227, 271, 278–9, 360,
    377–8, 391, 463
Riahi, General 53
Rice, Condoleeza 361
Rifah stores 321
Rogers, Captain William C. 275, 277,
    462, 462, 463
Roman Empire 18, 187
Roosevelt, Kermit 50, 53–5, 58
Roozbeh, Khosrow 57
Rousseau, Jean-Jacques 5, 326
rowzeh-khan (preacher) 23, 429
Ruhani, Hassan 311–12, 384–5
Ruholamini, Mohsen 406–7
Rumi (Molana) 60
Rumsfeld, Donald 361, 386, 470
Rushdie, Salman 297–301, 306,
    317–18, 327, 339–40, 426, 438,
    465–6
Russia xvi, 6, 15, 24–5, 27–33,
    35–6, 39, 42, 45–6, 57, 64,
    85, 143, 145, 188, 242, 356,
    371, 381, 382, 388, 390, 410,
    441
Ruwandiz 262

Sabaghian 370
Sabra and Shatila, massacre (Lebanon)
    224
Sadighi, Dr Gholam-Hosein 123